Novels
for Students

National Advisory Board

Novels for Students

Presenting Analysis, Context, and Criticism on
Commonly Studied Novels

Volume 20

Ira Mark Milne and Timothy Sisler,
Project Editors

Foreword by Anne Devereaux Jordan

THOMSON

™

GALE

Detroit • New York • San Francisco • San Diego • New Haven, Conn. • Waterville, Maine • London • Munich

THOMSON

GALE

™

Novels for Students, Volume 20

Project Editors
Ira Mark Milne and Timothy Sisler

Editorial
Anne Marie Hacht, Maikue Vang

Rights Acquisition and Management
Edna Hedblad, Sheila Spencer, Ann Taylor

Manufacturing
Rhonda Williams

Imaging
Lezlie Light, Mike Logusz, Kelly A. Quin

Product Design
Pamela A. E. Galbreath

Product Manager
Meggin Condino

ISBN 0-7876-6943-1
ISSN 1094-3552

Printed in the United States of America
10 9 8 7 6 5 4 3 2 1

Table of Contents

The Informed Dialogue: Interacting with Literature

When we pick up a book, we usually do so with the anticipation of pleasure. We hope that by entering the time and place of the novel and sharing the thoughts and actions of the characters, we will find enjoyment. Unfortunately, this is often not the case; we are disappointed. But we should ask, has the author failed us, or have we failed the author?

We establish a dialogue with the author, the book, and with ourselves when we read. Consciously and unconsciously, we ask questions: "Why did the author write this book?" "Why did the author choose that time, place, or character?" "How did the author achieve that effect?" "Why did the character act that way?" "Would I act in the same way?" The answers we receive depend upon how much information about literature in general and about that book specifically we ourselves bring to our reading.

Young children have limited life and literary experiences. Being young, children frequently do not know how to go about exploring a book, nor sometimes, even know the questions to ask of a book. The books they read help them answer questions, the author often coming right out and *telling* young readers the things they are learning or are expected to learn. The perennial classic, *The Little Engine That Could, tells* its readers that, among other things, it is good to help others and brings happiness:

"Hurray, hurray," cried the funny little clown and all the dolls and toys. "The good little boys and girls in the city will be happy because you helped us, kind, Little Blue Engine."

In picture books, messages are often blatant and simple, the dialogue between the author and reader one-sided. Young children are concerned with the end result of a book—the enjoyment gained, the lesson learned—rather than with how that result was obtained. As we grow older and read further, however, we question more. We come to expect that the world within the book will closely mirror the concerns of our world, and that the author will *show* these through the events, descriptions, and conversations within the story, rather than *telling* of them. We are now expected to do the interpreting, carry on our share of the dialogue with the book and author, and glean not only the author's message, but comprehend how that message and the overall affect of the book were achieved. Sometimes, however, we need help to do these things. *Novels for Students* provides that help.

A novel is made up of many parts interacting to create a coherent whole. In reading a novel, the more obvious features can be easily spotted—theme, characters, plot—but we may overlook the more subtle elements that greatly influence how the novel is perceived by the reader: viewpoint, mood and tone, symbolism, or the use of humor. By focusing on both the obvious and more subtle literary elements within a novel, *Novels for Students* aids readers in both analyzing for message and in determining how and why that message is communicated. In the discussion on Harper Lee's *To*

Kill a Mockingbird (Vol. 2), for example, the mockingbird as a symbol of innocence is dealt with, among other things, as is the importance of Lee's use of humor which "enlivens a serious plot, adds depth to the characterization, and creates a sense of familiarity and universality." The reader comes to understand the internal elements of each novel discussed—as well as the external influences that help shape it.

"The desire to write greatly," Harold Bloom of Yale University says, "is the desire to be elsewhere, in a time and place of one's own, in an originality that must compound with inheritance, with an anxiety of influence." A writer seeks to create a unique world within a story, but although it is unique, it is not disconnected from our own world. It speaks to us *because* of what the writer brings to the writing from our world: how he or she was raised and educated; his or her likes and dislikes; the events occurring in the real world at the time of the writing, and while the author was growing up. When we know what an author has brought to his or her work, we gain a greater insight into both the "originality" (the world of the book), and the things that "compound" it. This insight enables us to question that created world and find answers more readily. By informing ourselves, we are able to establish a more effective dialogue with both book and author.

Novels for Students, in addition to providing a plot summary and descriptive list of characters—to remind readers of what they have read—also explores the external influences that shaped each book. Each entry includes a discussion of the author's background, and the historical context in which the novel was written. It is vital to know, for instance, that when Ray Bradbury was writing *Fahrenheit 451* (Vol. 1), the threat of Nazi domination had recently ended in Europe, and the McCarthy hearings were taking place in Washington, D.C. This information goes far in answering the question, "Why did he write a story of oppressive government control and book burning?" Similarly, it is important to know that Harper Lee, author of *To Kill a Mockingbird,* was born and raised in Monroeville, Alabama, and that her father was a lawyer.

Readers can now see why she chose the south as a setting for her novel—it is the place with which she was most familiar—and start to comprehend her characters and their actions.

Novels for Students helps readers find the answers they seek when they establish a dialogue with a particular novel. It also aids in the posing of questions by providing the opinions and interpretations of various critics and reviewers, broadening that dialogue. Some reviewers of *To Kill A Mockingbird,* for example, "faulted the novel's climax as melodramatic." This statement leads readers to ask, "Is it, indeed, melodramatic?" "If not, why did some reviewers see it as such?" "If it is, why did Lee choose to make it melodramatic?" "Is melodrama ever justified?" By being spurred to ask these questions, readers not only learn more about the book and its writer, but about the nature of writing itself.

The literature included for discussion in *Novels for Students* has been chosen because it has something vital to say to us. *Of Mice and Men, Catch-22, The Joy Luck Club, My Antonia, A Separate Peace* and the other novels here speak of life and modern sensibility. In addition to their individual, specific messages of prejudice, power, love or hate, living and dying, however, they and all great literature also share a common intent. They force us to *think*—about life, literature, and about others, not just about ourselves. They pry us from the narrow confines of our minds and thrust us outward to confront the world of books and the larger, real world we all share. *Novels for Students* helps us in this confrontation by providing the means of enriching our conversation with literature and the world, by creating an *informed* dialogue, one that brings true pleasure to the personal act of reading.

Sources

Harold Bloom, *The Western Canon, The Books and School of the Ages,* Riverhead Books, 1994.

Watty Piper, *The Little Engine That Could,* Platt & Munk, 1930.

Anne Devereaux Jordan
Senior Editor, TALL
(Teaching and Learning Literature)

Introduction

Purpose of the Book

The purpose of *Novels for Students (NfS)* is to provide readers with a guide to understanding, enjoying, and studying novels by giving them easy access to information about the work. Part of Gale's "For Students" Literature line, *NfS* is specifically designed to meet the curricular needs of high school and undergraduate college students and their teachers, as well as the interests of general readers and researchers considering specific novels. While each volume contains entries on "classic" novels frequently studied in classrooms, there are also entries containing hard-to-find information on contemporary novels, including works by multicultural, international, and women novelists.

The information covered in each entry includes an introduction to the novel and the novel's author; a plot summary, to help readers unravel and understand the events in a novel; descriptions of important characters, including explanation of a given character's role in the novel as well as discussion about that character's relationship to other characters in the novel; analysis of important themes in the novel; and an explanation of important literary techniques and movements as they are demonstrated in the novel.

In addition to this material, which helps the readers analyze the novel itself, students are also provided with important information on the literary and historical background informing each work. This includes a historical context essay, a box comparing the time or place the novel was written to modern Western culture, a critical essay, and excerpts from critical essays on the novel. A unique feature of *NfS* is a specially commissioned critical essay on each novel, targeted toward the student reader.

To further aid the student in studying and enjoying each novel, information on media adaptations is provided, as well as reading suggestions for works of fiction and nonfiction on similar themes and topics. Classroom aids include ideas for research papers and lists of critical sources that provide additional material on the novel.

Selection Criteria

The titles for each volume of *NfS* were selected by surveying numerous sources on teaching literature and analyzing course curricula for various school districts. Some of the sources surveyed included: literature anthologies; *Reading Lists for College-Bound Students: The Books Most Recommended by America's Top Colleges;* textbooks on teaching the novel; a College Board survey of novels commonly studied in high schools; a National Council of Teachers of English (NCTE) survey of novels commonly studied in high schools; the NCTE's *Teaching Literature in High School: The Novel;* and the Young Adult Library Services Association (YALSA) list of best books for young adults of the past twenty-five years.

Input was also solicited from our advisory board, as well as from educators from various areas.

From these discussions, it was determined that each volume should have a mix of "classic" novels (those works commonly taught in literature classes) and contemporary novels for which information is often hard to find. Because of the interest in expanding the canon of literature, an emphasis was also placed on including works by international, multicultural, and women authors. Our advisory board members—educational professionals—helped pare down the list for each volume. If a work was not selected for the present volume, it was often noted as a possibility for a future volume. As always, the editor welcomes suggestions for titles to be included in future volumes.

How Each Entry Is Organized

Each entry, or chapter, in *NfS* focuses on one novel. Each entry heading lists the full name of the novel, the author's name, and the date of the novel's publication. The following elements are contained in each entry:

- **Introduction:** a brief overview of the novel which provides information about its first appearance, its literary standing, any controversies surrounding the work, and major conflicts or themes within the work.

- **Author Biography:** this section includes basic facts about the author's life, and focuses on events and times in the author's life that inspired the novel in question.

- **Plot Summary:** a factual description of the major events in the novel. Lengthy summaries are broken down with subheads.

- **Characters:** an alphabetical listing of major characters in the novel. Each character name is followed by a brief to an extensive description of the character's role in the novel, as well as discussion of the character's actions, relationships, and possible motivation.

  Characters are listed alphabetically by last name. If a character is unnamed—for instance, the narrator in *Invisible Man*—the character is listed as "The Narrator" and alphabetized as "Narrator." If a character's first name is the only one given, the name will appear alphabetically by that name.

  Variant names are also included for each character. Thus, the full name "Jean Louise Finch" would head the listing for the narrator of *To Kill a Mockingbird,* but listed in a separate cross-reference would be the nickname "Scout Finch."

- **Themes:** a thorough overview of how the major topics, themes, and issues are addressed within the novel. Each theme discussed appears in a separate subhead and is easily accessed through the boldface entries in the Subject/Theme Index.

- **Style:** this section addresses important style elements of the novel, such as setting, point of view, and narration; important literary devices used, such as imagery, foreshadowing, symbolism; and, if applicable, genres to which the work might have belonged, such as Gothicism or Romanticism. Literary terms are explained within the entry but can also be found in the Glossary.

- **Historical Context:** This section outlines the social, political, and cultural climate *in which the author lived and the novel was created.* This section may include descriptions of related historical events, pertinent aspects of daily life in the culture, and the artistic and literary sensibilities of the time in which the work was written. If the novel is a historical work, information regarding the time in which the novel is set is also included. Each section is broken down with helpful subheads.

- **Critical Overview:** this section provides background on the critical reputation of the novel, including bannings or any other public controversies surrounding the work. For older works, this section includes a history of how the novel was first received and how perceptions of it may have changed over the years; for more recent novels, direct quotes from early reviews may also be included.

- **Criticism:** an essay commissioned by *NfS* which specifically deals with the novel and is written specifically for the student audience, as well as excerpts from previously published criticism on the work (if available).

- **Sources:** an alphabetical list of critical material used in compiling the entry, with full bibliographical information.

- **Further Reading:** an alphabetical list of other critical sources which may prove useful for the student. It includes full bibliographical information and a brief annotation.

In addition, each entry contains the following highlighted sections, set apart from the main text as sidebars:

- **Media Adaptations:** a list of important film and television adaptations of the novel, including source information. The list also includes stage adaptations, audio recordings, musical adaptations, etc.

- **Topics for Further Study:** a list of potential study questions or research topics dealing with the novel. This section includes questions related to other disciplines the student may be studying, such as American history, world history, science, math, government, business, geography, economics, psychology, etc.

- **Compare and Contrast Box:** an "at-a-glance" comparison of the cultural and historical differences between the author's time and culture and late twentieth century/early twenty-first century Western culture. This box includes pertinent parallels between the major scientific, political, and cultural movements of the time or place the novel was written, the time or place the novel was set (if a historical work), and modern Western culture. Works written after 1990 may not have this box.

- **What Do I Read Next?:** a list of works that might complement the featured novel or serve as a contrast to it. This includes works by the same author and others, works of fiction and nonfiction, and works from various genres, cultures, and eras.

Other Features

NfS includes "The Informed Dialogue: Interacting with Literature," a foreword by Anne Devereaux Jordan, Senior Editor for *Teaching and Learning Literature* (*TALL*), and a founder of the Children's Literature Association. This essay provides an enlightening look at how readers interact with literature and how *Novels for Students* can help teachers show students how to enrich their own reading experiences.

A Cumulative Author/Title Index lists the authors and titles covered in each volume of the *NfS* series.

A Cumulative Nationality/Ethnicity Index breaks down the authors and titles covered in each volume of the *NfS* series by nationality and ethnicity.

A Subject/Theme Index, specific to each volume, provides easy reference for users who may be studying a particular subject or theme rather than a single work. Significant subjects from events to broad themes are included, and the entries pointing to the specific theme discussions in each entry are indicated in **boldface**.

Each entry may have several illustrations, including photos of the author, stills from film adaptations, maps, and/or photos of key historical events, if available.

Citing Novels for Students

When writing papers, students who quote directly from any volume of *Novels for Students* may use the following general forms. These examples are based on MLA style; teachers may request that students adhere to a different style, so the following examples may be adapted as needed.

When citing text from *NfS* that is not attributed to a particular author (i.e., the Themes, Style, Historical Context sections, etc.), the following format should be used in the bibliography section:

"*Night.*" *Novels for Students.* Ed. Marie Rose Napierkowski. Vol. 4. Detroit: Gale, 1998. 234–35.

When quoting the specially commissioned essay from *NfS* (usually the first piece under the "Criticism" subhead), the following format should be used:

Miller, Tyrus. Critical Essay on *Winesburg, Ohio. Novels for Students.* Ed. Marie Rose Napierkowski. Vol. 4. Detroit: Gale, 1998. 335–39.

When quoting a journal or newspaper essay that is reprinted in a volume of *NfS,* the following form may be used:

Malak, Amin. "Margaret Atwood's *The Handmaid's Tale* and the Dystopian Tradition," *Canadian Literature* No. 112 (Spring, 1987), 9–16; excerpted and reprinted in *Novels for Students,* Vol. 4, ed. Marie Rose Napierkowski (Detroit: Gale, 1998), pp. 133–36.

When quoting material reprinted from a book that appears in a volume of *NfS,* the following form may be used:

Adams, Timothy Dow. "Richard Wright: Wearing the Mask," in *Telling Lies in Modern American Autobiography* (University of North Carolina Press, 1990), 69–83; excerpted and reprinted in *Novels for Students,* Vol. 1, ed. Diane Telgen (Detroit: Gale, 1997), pp. 59–61.

We Welcome Your Suggestions

The editor of *Novels for Students* welcomes your comments and ideas. Readers who wish to suggest novels to appear in future volumes, or who have other suggestions, are cordially invited to contact the editor. You may contact the editor via e-mail at: **ForStudentsEditors@thomson.com.** Or write to the editor at:

Editor, *Novels for Students*
Thomson Gale
27500 Drake Road
Farmington Hills, MI 48331-3535

Literary Chronology

1802: Victor Hugo is born on February 26 in Besançon, France.

1804: Nathaniel Hawthorne is born on July 4 in Salem, Massachusetts.

1812: Charles Dickens is born on February 7 in Landport, Hampshire, England.

1819: George Eliot is born (Mary Ann Evans) on November 22 in Chilvers Coton, in Warwickshire, England.

1831: Victor Hugo's *The Hunchback of Notre Dame* is published.

1835: Mark Twain is born (Samuel Langhorne Clemons) on November 30 in Florida, Missouri.

1850: Robert Louis Stevenson is born in Edinburgh.

1851: Nathaniel Hawthorne's *The House of the Seven Gables* is published.

1854: Charles Dickens's *Hard Times* is published.

1854: Oscar Wilde is born (Oscar Fingal O'Flahertie Wills Wilde) on October 16.

1859: Kenneth Grahame is born on March 8 in Edinburgh, Scotland.

1861: George Eliot's *Silas Marner* is published.

1862: Edith Wharton is born (Edith Newbold Jones) on January 24 in New York City.

1864: Nathaniel Hawthorne dies in his sleep on May 19 while visiting Franklin Pierce in Plymouth, New Hampshire.

1866: H. G. Wells is born (Herbert George Wells) on September 21 in Bromley, Kent, England.

1868: Gaston Leroux is born on May 6 in Paris, a month before his parents, Dominique Alfred Leroux and Marie Bidault, are married.

1870: Charles Dickens dies of a stroke on June 9 at Gadshill, near Rochester, Kent.

1871: Stephen Crane is born on November 1 in Newark, New Jersey.

1880: George Eliot dies on December 22, after marrying John Walter Cross, who is twenty years her junior.

1883: Robert Louis Stevenson's *Treasure Island* is published.

1885: Victor Hugo dies on May 22 after suffering a stroke in 1878.

1889: Mark Twain's *A Connecticut Yankee in King Arthur's Court* is published.

1891: Oscar Wilde's *The Picture of Dorian Gray* is published.

1893: Stephen Crane's *Maggie: A Girl of the Streets* is published.

1894: Robert Louis Stevenson dies of a brain hemorrhage on December 3, while helping his wife fix dinner.

1896: F. Scott Fitzgerald is born to an Irish Catholic family with connections to the American aristocracy.

1898: H. G. Wells's *The War of the Worlds* is published.

1900: Stephen Crane dies of tuberculosis when he is twenty-eight.

1900: Oscar Wilde dies of meningitis on November 30.

1908: Kenneth Grahame's *The Wind in the Willows* is published.

1910: Mark Twain dies of heart disease on April 21.

1910: Gaston Leroux's *The Phantom of the Opera* is published.

1917: Edith Wharton's *Summer* is published.

1920: F. Scott Fitzgerald's *This Side of Paradise* is published.

1927: Gaston Leroux dies.

1932: Kenneth Grahame dies of a cerebral hemorrhage on July 6 in his home in Pangbourne.

1937: Edith Wharton dies after a series of strokes and a heart attack on August 7 at Pavillon Colombe, her home in Saint Brice-sous-Forêt, France.

1940: F. Scott Fitzgerald dies of a heart attack on December 21, while working on his last, unfinished novel, *The Last Tycoon* (1941).

1946: H. G. Wells dies after a prolonged illness on August 13.

Acknowledgments

The editors wish to thank the copyright holders of the excerpted criticism included in this volume and the permissions managers of many book and magazine publishing companies for assisting us in securing reproduction rights. We are also grateful to the staffs of the Detroit Public Library, the Library of Congress, the University of Detroit Mercy Library, Wayne State University Purdy/Kresge Library Complex, and the University of Michigan Libraries for making their resources available to us. Following is a list of the copyright holders who have granted us permission to reproduce material in this volume of *Novels for Students (NfS)*. Every effort has been made to trace copyright, but if omissions have been made, please let us know.

COPYRIGHTED MATERIALS IN *NfS*, VOLUME 20, WERE REPRODUCED FROM THE FOLLOWING PERIODICALS:

American Literary Realism, 1870–1910, v. 29, 1996. Copyright © 1996 by the Department of English, The University of New Mexico. Reproduced by permission.—*The Atlantic Monthly*, v. 274, November, 1994 for "The Double Life of Robert Louis Stevenson," by Margot Livesey. Reproduced by permission of the author.—*Children's Literature*, v. 16, 1988. Copyright © 1988 by The Children's Literature Foundation, Box 370, Windham Center, Connecticut, 06280. All rights reserved. Reproduced by permission by Yale University Press.—*Children's Literature Review Association Quarterly*, v. 23, 1998–99. Repro-

duced by permission.—*Colby Library Quarterly*, v. 21, March, 1985. Reproduced by permission of the publisher.—*Dickens Quarterly*, v. 7, June, 1990. Copyright © 1990 by *Dickens Quarterly*. Reproduced by permission.—*Dickens Studies Annual*, v. 25, 1996. Copyright © 1996 by AMS Press, Inc. Reproduced by permission.—*Dickensian*, v. 75, autumn, 1979 for "Hope and Memory in *Hard Times*," by Lewis B. Horne. Reproduced by permission of the author.—*Essays in Literature*, v. 21, fall, 1994. Copyright © 1994 by Western Illinois University. Reproduced by permission.—*Mark Twain Journal*, v. 22, spring, 1984. Reproduced by permission.—*Studies in the Novel*, v. 1, spring, 1969. Copyright © 1969 by North Texas State University. Reproduced by permission.—*Twentieth Century Literature*, v. 41, winter, 1995. Copyright © 1995, Hofstra University Press. Reproduced by permission.

COPYRIGHTED MATERIALS IN *NfS*, VOLUME 20, WERE REPRODUCED FROM THE FOLLOWING BOOKS:

Boyle, Robert. From "Oscar Wilde," in *Dictionary of Literary Biography*, Vol. 34, *British Novelists, 1890–1929: Traditionalists.* Edited by Thomas F. Staley. Gale Research, 1984. Copyright © 1984 by Gale Research, Inc. All rights reserved. Reproduced by permission.—Cohen, Philip K. From *The Moral Vision of Oscar Wilde.* Fairleigh Dickinson University Press, 1978. Copyright © 1978 by Philip Kent Cohen. Reproduced by permission.—Contemporary Authors Online. From "Gaston Leroux," in *Contemporary Authors Online.* Copyright © 2003 by the Gale Group. Reproduced by permission.—Costa, Richard Hauer. From *H. G. Wells.* Twayne, 1967. Copyright © 1967 by Twayne Publishers, Inc. All rights reserved. Reproduced by permission of The Gale Group.—Idol, John, Jr. From "Nathaniel Hawthorne," in *Dictionary of Literary Biography,* Vol. 223, *The American Renaissance in New England, Second Series.* Edited by Wesley T. Mott. Gale, 2000. Copyright © 2000 by The Gale Group. All rights reserved. Reproduced by permission.—McCracken, Elizabeth. From an Introduction to *The Hunchback of Notre Dame*, by Victor Hugo. Translated by Catherine Liu. The Modern Library, 2002. Copyright © 2002 by Elizabeth McCracken. Used by permission of Modern Library, a division of Random House, Inc.—Parrinder, Patrick. From *H. G. Wells: The Critical Heritage.* Routledge and Kegan Paul, 1972. Copyright © by Patrick Parrinder 1972. Reproduced by permission of Taylor & Francis Books Ltd.—Raser, Timothy. From "Victor Hugo," in *Dictionary of Literary Biography,* Vol. 119, *Nineteenth-Century French Fiction Writers: Romanticism and Realism, 1800–1860.* Edited by Catharine Savage Brosman. Gale Research, 1992. Copyright © 1992 by Gale Research, Inc. All rights reserved. Reproduced by permission.—Riley, Philip J. From *The Making of The Phantom of the Opera.* MagicImage Filmbooks, 1999. Copyright © 1999, MagicImage Productions, Inc. All rights reserved. Reproduced by permission.—Speaight, Robert. From *George Eliot.* Lowe and Brydone Ltd., 1954. Copyright © 1954 by Robert Speaight. Reproduced by permission of the author.

PHOTOGRAPHS AND ILLUSTRATIONS APPEARING IN *NfS*, VOLUME 20, WERE RECEIVED FROM THE FOLLOWING SOURCES:

Crane, Stephen, photograph. © Corbis-Bettmann.—Edith Wharton's home in Lenox, the Berkshire, Massachusetts, photograph by Lee Snider. Lee Snider/Corbis.—Eliot, George, drawing. The Library of Congress.—Film poster for *The Phantom of the Opera* (Fantomas) in Paris. Leonard de Selva/Corbis.—Fitzgerald, Francis Scott, photograph. Historical Society/Corbis.—Grahame, Kenneth, photograph.—Hawthorne, Nathaniel, photograph.—Hugo, Victor, portrait. Bettmann/Corbis.—Illustration based upon a description from *The House of the Seven Gables,* by Nathaniel Hawthorne. Copyright © by Mary Evans Picture Library.—Illustration from *A Connecticut Yankee in King Arthur's Court,* by Mark Twain, 1889. Special Collections Library, University of Michigan. Reproduced by permission.—Illustration from the 1925 edition of *The Picture of Dorian Gray,* depicting the death of Dorian Gray, illustrated by Henry Keen. Copyright © Mary Evans Picture Library.—Illustration of the Cathedral of Notre Dame, located in Paris, France. The Library of Congress.—Map by Monro S. Orr from *Treasure Island,* by Robert Louis Stevenson, 1937. Copyright © by Mary Evans Picture Library.—Scene from *The Hunchback of Notre Dame,* by Victor Hugo, 1939. RKO/The Kobal Collection.—Scene from *The Phantom of the Opera,* by Gaston Leroux, 1925. Universal/The Kobal Collection.—Scene from *The Picture of Dorian Gray,* by Oscar Wilde, 1945. MGM/The Kobal Collection.—Scene from *Treasure Island,* by Robert Louis Stevenson, 1920. Paramount/The Kobal Collection.—Scene from *The War of the Worlds,* by H. G. Wells. Paramount/The Kobal Collection.—Scene from *The Wind in the Willows,* by Kenneth Grahame, 1996. Allied Film Makers/The Kobal Collection.—Slums of New York Bowery, 1895, photograph. Getty Images.—Stevenson, Robert Louis, King Kalakaua, photograph. AP/Wide World Photos.—Twain, Mark, photograph. The Library of Congress.—Weaver at his loom, engraving. Copyright © by Mary Evans Picture Library.—Wells, H. G., drawing.—Wharton, Edith, photograph. Bettmann/Corbis.—Wilde, Oscar, photograph.

Contributors

Bryan Aubrey: Aubrey holds a Ph.D. in English and has published many articles on nineteenth-century literature. Entries on *Hard Times*, *The Picture of Dorian Gray*, and *Silas Marner*. Original essays on *Hard Times*, *The Picture of Dorian Gray*, and *Silas Marner*.

Cynthia Bily: Bily is an instructor at Adrian College in Adrian, Michigan. Entry on *Summer*. Original essay on *Summer*.

Kate Covintree: Covintree is a graduate student and expository writing instructor in the Writing, Literature, and Publishing department at Emerson College. Original essay on *Summer*.

Douglas Dupler: Dupler is a writer, teacher, and independent scholar. Original essay on *Summer*.

Joyce Hart: Hart has degrees in English and creative writing and is the author of several books. Entries on *The Hunchback of Notre Dame* and *Treasure Island*. Original essays on *The House of the Seven Gables*, *The Hunchback of Notre Dame*, *Silas Marner*, and *Treasure Island*.

Catherine Dybiec Holm: Holm is a freelance writer as well as a genre novel and short story author. Original essay on *Treasure Island*.

David Kelly: Kelly is an instructor of literature and creative writing at two schools in Illinois. En-

tries on *A Connecticut Yankee in King Arthur's Court*, *The Phantom of the Opera*, and *The War of the Worlds*. Original essays on *A Connecticut Yankee in King Arthur's Court*, *The Phantom of the Opera*, and *The War of the Worlds*.

Wendy Perkins: Perkins is a professor of English at Prince George's Community College in Maryland and has published articles on several twentieth-century authors. Entry on *Maggie: A Girl of the Streets*. Original essay on *Maggie: A Girl of the Streets*.

Annette Petruso: Petruso has a bachelor's degree in history and a master's degree in screenwriting. Original essay on *Maggie: A Girl of the Streets*.

Dustie Robeson: Robeson is a freelance writer with a master's degree in English. Entry on *The House of the Seven Gables*. Original essay on *The House of the Seven Gables*.

Daniel Toronto: Toronto has a bachelor's degree in creative writing and literature and currently works as an editor. Entry on *The Wind in the Willows*. Original essay on *The Wind in the Willows*.

Scott Trudell: Trudell is a freelance writer with a bachelor's degree in English literature. Entry on *This Side of Paradise*. Original essay on *This Side of Paradise*.

A Connecticut Yankee in King Arthur's Court

Mark Twain

1889

Throughout the centuries, people have looked to the legends of King Arthur and his Knights of the Round Table as the standard for a harmonious society. In the stories that have been passed down, knights were bold and chivalrous, fighting real and supernatural foes for the honor of themselves and the ladies they pledged themselves to. The king wisely watched over his subjects with an eye toward justice. In 1889, Mark Twain published the novel *A Connecticut Yankee in King Arthur's Court* to debunk the myths. The book has a man of Twain's era magically transported back to Camelot, the court of King Arthur. What he encounters is not a mystical time of dragons and sorcery, but a time of ignorance and suffering, when anyone who claims to have witnessed a supernatural event is believed by all. The King's court is balanced atop an unjust social system that ignores the rights of the working people and confers divine rights upon nobles who, having been born to wealth and power, have no idea of justice. The book's protagonist makes himself more powerful than the legendary magician Merlin by performing tricks that are simple for a man with contemporary knowledge. In addition, the protagonist sets about making wide-reaching social reforms, only to find that enlightenment ultimately does not work with superstitious, naïve people.

A Connecticut Yankee in King Arthur's Court continues to be as relevant today as it was in Twain's time. As a social satire by one of America's great humor writers, it remains one of the funniest books in our nation's literary history.

Mark Twain

Author Biography

Mark Twain (the most well-known pen name of Samuel Langhorne Clemons) was born in Florida, Missouri, on November 30, 1835, and grew up in Hannibal, a Missouri town along the Mississippi river. Hannibal was to play a significant role in some of Twain's most popular books and stories. When Twain was twelve, his father died. Twain then helped support his family by going to work as a printer's apprentice. After several failed business partnerships with his brother Orion, he took off across the American west, selling travel pieces to newspapers.

In 1857, Twain left on a trip to South America, with a contract to write about his adventures. While traveling down the Mississippi to the Gulf of Mexico, Twain struck up a friendship with a riverboat captain named Horace Bixby. Twain abandoned his plan and instead became Bixby's apprentice, earning his own license to pilot steamboats in 1859. It was around this time that he adopted the name Mark Twain.

During the Civil War, Twain served for a short time in the Confederate army and then went out west, first to Nevada and then to San Francisco. In both places, he ran into trouble with the local governments for his sarcastic writings and had to leave each city in a hurry. It was at this time that Twain published his short story "The Celebrated Jumping Frog of Calaveras County," which was printed in newspapers across America, making him famous. Twain's humor sketches and travel pieces provided him with a comfortable living. He married Olivia Langdon, who came from a wealthy, established family, and they eventually settled into Hartford, Connecticut, where they lived for the next twenty years.

Twain's first novel, *The Gilded Age*, was co-written with his friend and neighbor Charles Dudley Warner and published in 1873. Soon after that, he wrote the two books for which he is best remembered today: *The Adventures of Tom Sawyer* (1876) and *The Adventures of Huckleberry Finn* (1884). *A Connecticut Yankee in King Arthur's Court* followed in 1889.

Twain was as famous during his lifetime as a lecturer as he was as a writer, traveling extensively across the United States and Europe, telling his humorous anecdotes before crowds of thousands. He received an honorary master's degree from Yale in 1888 and an honorary doctorate from the same institution in 1901. In addition, Twain received honorary doctorates from the University of Missouri in 1904 and from Oxford University in 1907.

In his later years, Twain became increasingly angry with the moral weaknesses of the human race. This anger only solidified after the deaths of his oldest daughter in 1896 and then his wife in 1904. Twain's later writings and lectures were marked by the dark bleakness of his vision of humanity's future. When he died of heart disease on April 21, 1910, Twain was recognized as one of the greatest authors that America had ever produced.

Plot Summary

Preface

In the first chapter of *A Connecticut Yankee in King Arthur's Court*, Twain addresses readers as himself, telling of a trip he made to England when he made the acquaintance of a stranger at Warwick Castle. This stranger tells him that he was in England at the time of King Arthur. That night, the narrator reads a story about Sir Launcelot fighting giants, and the stranger comes to his room.

The stranger, Hank Morgan (his name is never actually revealed until Chapter XXXIX), explains that he was a gunsmith in Hartford, Connecticut, when, during a fight, he was hit on the head with a crowbar. When he came to, he did not recognize his surroundings and was told that he was in

Media Adaptations

- *A Connecticut Yankee in King Arthur's Court* was adapted as a light-hearted musical in 1949, starring Bing Crosby, Rhonda Fleming, Cedric Hardwicke, and William Bendix. The music is by Jimmy Van Heusen and Johnny Burke. It was released by Universal on VHS in 1993.

- Iconic American humorist Will Rogers had the starring role in the 1931 adaptation of Twain's story, called simply *A Connecticut Yankee*. Directed by David Butler, it was released by Twentieth Century Fox and is available on VHS.

- In 2001, comedian Martin Lawrence starred in *Black Knight*, a movie that was an adaptation of Twain's basic premise. In this version, Lawrence plays a contemporary amusement park operator who is transported back to medieval times. It is available on DVD from Twentieth Century Fox Home Video.

- A two CD recording of an abridged version of *A Connecticut Yankee in King Arthur's Court* is available from Naxos, published in 2001. It is read by Kenneth Jay.

- Comedian Carl Reiner recorded an abridged version of the novel for Dove Audio's Ultimate Classics series in 1993. It is available on three CDs.

- Blackstone Audio has an 8-cassette version of the book that is unabridged. It is read by Chris Walker and was released in 1999.

- The entire text of this novel is available on the Internet at http://www.literature.org/authors/twain-mark/connecticut/index.html in a searchable format.

- Almost anything that a student would want to find out about Arthurian legend is cross-referenced at the University of Rochester's web page at *The Camelot Project: Arthurian Texts, Images, Bibliographies and Basic Information.* This web page can be found at http://www.lib.rochester.edu/camelot/cphome.stm

---

Camelot. He gives the narrator a manuscript of his journal from that time, and the rest of the novel is told as if he (Hank) wrote it.

Chapter I–VII

Soon after arriving, Hank meets a young man he calls Clarence, who tells him that the year is 513. Hank is taken prisoner by Sir Kay the Seneschal and taken into the palace, where he observes the familiar characters of legend. However, Hank finds them to be exaggerators, liars, and naively superstitious. Sir Kay tells exaggerated tales about how he conquered giants; Sir Dinadan tells jokes that Hank knows from his own childhood. Merlin tells how King Arthur gained his enchanted sword, Excalibur. Hank explains that he himself is a magician and has been familiar with Merlin, in different guises, over the course of centuries. Because Hank knows that the date of a solar eclipse is eminent, he threatens to block out the sun if not released from custody. Just as Hank is being led to his execution, the eclipse occurs, and everyone marvels at Hank's powerful magic. Hank follows this trick by destroying Merlin's tower, which he manages by inventing gun powder, hiding it in the tower walls, and attaching a lighting rod as a detonator.

Chapter VIII–X

Hank is then accepted as the most powerful magician in the country. He is made an advisor to King Arthur and given a title: "The Boss." Over the next four years, Hank undertakes social reforms, such as starting a school system, reforming the mining system and the currency, and developing a telegraph and telephone system. Hank's employees in these adventures are kept separate from the rest of the population.

Chapter XI–XXVI

A woman, Demoiselle Alisande la Carteloise, comes to Camelot and tells the tale of forty-four maidens being held prisoner for twenty-six years by three one-eyed, four-armed brothers. Hank is skeptical, but King Arthur believes her tale and sends Hank out in armor with the girl to rescue her friends.

Traveling the countryside with Demoiselle Alisande la Carteloise, whom Hank nicknames Sandy, Hank sees the political situation as it really is. He finds that free men are not free at all because they have to pay large portions of their crops to the king and the church. Hank stops at the castle of Morgan Le Fey, Arthur's sister, and sees how a really cruel despot treats her subjects. He tours Le Fey's dungeons and meets a man imprisoned on the testimony of a masked, anonymous stranger: the man accepts cruel punishment because his wife would lose all that she owns if he were to confess. Hank sends the man and his wife to the Man Factory, a brain trust of the smartest and bravest citizens. Hank finds dozens of prisoners in the castle's dungeons who were put there so long ago that no one knows what they were convicted of. Hank frees them.

When Hank and Sandy eventually reach the castle that Sandy has described, it turns out to be a common pigsty, and the maidens that she said were being held prisoner are the pigs. She tells Hank that it just seems that way to him because of a magic spell, and he admits that it might be his view and not hers that is wrong.

On the way home, they join a group of pilgrims going to the Valley of Holiness, where they find that the sacred spring has stopped flowing. Hank examines it and finds a way to fix the well that feeds the spring. This act increases Hank's reputation.

Chapter XXVII–XXXIX

After returning to Camelot and establishing more improvements in law and journalism, Hank decides to travel the country disguised as a peasant. King Arthur decides to join him. They run across all sorts of social injustices while traveling, such as the fate of a family unable to maintain their farm because the adult sons are in prison for a crime they did not commit.

Presenting themselves as a farmer and his bailiff, Hank and King Arthur lunch in one town with the local tradesmen and argue about politics. Offended, one of the men manages to have King Arthur and Hank arrested and put into slavery. In London, Hank eventually manages to escape and goes to a shop that has one of the telephones on the network he has devised. Hank calls Clarence to send help from Camelot. Just as Hank and King Arthur are on the gallows ready to be hanged, Sir Launcelot and five hundred knights, riding bicycles, arrive and save them.

Back in Camelot, Hank is forced to face up to a challenge to duel that was made years earlier by Sir Sagramor, who has been off seeking the Holy Grail. Hank, without wearing armor and without carrying a lance, faces Sir Sagramor. Hank wears Sir Sagramor down with deft horse riding and then pulls him off his mount with a lasso. Other knights rise to challenge Hank. He uses the lasso seven more times before Merlin steals it. Hank then starts shooting the other knights with his pistol before the knights give up.

Chapter XL–Afterword

Three years pass. Hank is married to Sandy, and they have a daughter. When the baby becomes sick, Sandy and the baby go to France for a warmer climate. Hank returns to England to find the country practically deserted. Clarence informs him that King Arthur found out about the romance between Guenever and Sir Launcelot and ordered her burned at the stake. Clarence also tells Hank that Launcelot, in trying to rescue Guenever, killed several knights, leading to a massive Civil War. When all of the knights were dead, including King Arthur, the Catholic Church invaded the country.

Hank and Clarence organize fifty-two young men at Merlin's Cave to defend the free political system that has grown over recent years; however, the people side with the church. Practically the entire country rises against Hank and his men. A clever system of explosives and electrical fences traps the invaders, killing around 25,000 soldiers. Once their bodies start decomposing, the air becomes thick with pestilence. Clarence writes the last chapter of the journal, explaining how Merlin came to them in the cave and put a spell on the injured Hank to sleep for 1,300 years.

In the final chapter of the book, Mark Twain describes finishing the manuscript and going to the room of the stranger who gave it to him. The man is in the room, muttering to Sandy (his long ago wife), and then he dies.

Characters

King Arthur

Hank's general impression of King Arthur is that he is too sure of himself and too unaware of the realities of his country. From this assessment, Hank feels that King Arthur is therefore destined to rule poorly. While traveling on his quest to free the damsels, Hank becomes outraged at the inequities of the English economic system and disgusted at the way that peasants are refused any say in their fate. When King Arthur offers to go traveling with Hank (with the king and Hank traveling in disguise), Hank sees his opportunity to show the king what life is like for the large segment of the population. Hank finds King Arthur's regal bearing pitiful because he knows that the king understands only one set of behaviors. Hank also finds the king's actions annoying because he (King Arthur) expresses his own thoughts when he should be listening. Ultimately, King Arthur's behavior proves dangerous because his proclamations while dressed in common clothes are taken to be signs that he is insane, which makes it easy for Dowley to arrange to have Arthur and Hank sold into slavery.

While traveling together, however, Hank sees the admirable side of King Arthur. Entering a house infected with smallpox, King Arthur does not hesitate or think of his own health when bringing an infected child to his mother, who is too weak to stand. King Arthur's belief in the rights of royalty extends to his power over illness, which Hank finds ridiculous when peasants line up to have the king's hands laid on them. But, Hank is impressed that King Arthur thinks nothing of facing death to bring mother and child together.

While Hank thinks King Arthur is a fool for believing that he has powers beyond those of ordinary men, the rest of the population admires him, except in one thing: everyone in the kingdom except King Arthur knows of the affair between King Arthur's wife, Guenever, and Sir Launcelot. For that, the king is silently laughed at by his subjects.

The Boss

See Hank Morgan

Clarence

Clarence is a nickname that Hank gives to a young page that talks to him when he first arrives in the sixth century. At first, Clarence seems as slow-witted as all of the peasants around Camelot, but Hank sees potential in him. Clarence turns out to be a useful surrogate for Hank as the he travels around the country. Hank sends people in need to Clarence, and he telephones Clarence to give him instructions. Hank teaches Clarence how to be a good newspaper reporter, which he says is necessary in molding a civilized country. During the

final war, when Hank returns to England, Clarence tells him all that he has missed while traveling with his wife and child, and Clarence writes the final chapter of the ancient manuscript, describing how Hank was injured and then put under a spell by Merlin, which enabled him to live until his own time.

Sir Dinadan

Sir Dinadan is the Round Table's humorist. Sir Dinadan is more amused by his jokes than anyone else in the court. Sir Dinadan writes the very first book, which is a collection of jokes. Sir Dinadan includes a joke about a lecturer that Hank hates, and so Hank has Sir Dinadan hanged.

Dowley

Dowley is the blacksmith in a small village the king and Hank stop in while traveling. Dowley has a big mouth and is unintelligent. He cannot understand that the wages in his town buy less than the wages where his guests come from, and so his wages are valued less overall. Hank humiliates Dowley with a stunning argument, and as a result, Dowley has the two strangers arrested and put into slavery.

Puss Flanagan

Puss is Hank Morgan's girlfriend back in his own time. She lives in East Hartford, Connecticut, and is only mentioned once in the novel when Hank is considering how improper it would be for him to go traveling unchaperoned with Demoiselle Alisande la Carteloise.

Guenever

Guenever is the wife of King Arthur and the lover of Sir Launcelot. In most sources, her name is given as "Guinevere," but Twain gives it as "Guenever."

Hercules

Hercules is a strong man who works at the blacksmith shop with Hank in the nineteenth century. Hank explains that, during a fight, Hercules hit him on the head with a crowbar, which is what causes him to go back to the sixth century.

Hugo

Hugo is the man Hank finds imprisoned in Morgan Le Fey's castle. Hugo is charged with killing a deer. Hugo is tortured, but he will not confess to the crime. Hugo eventually tells Hank that he did kill the deer but does not dare confess because his wife will lose all that she owns. Hank has Hugo and his wife sent to join his Man Factory.

Sir Kay

Sir Kay is the knight who takes Hank into captivity soon after he arrives in the sixth century and brings him to Camelot, telling the knights there is a fantastic story about how he conquered Hank. Sir Kay refers to Hank with exaggerations like "giant," even though his listeners are standing right in front of him and can see that Hank is an ordinary man.

Demoiselle Alisande la Carteloise

See Sandy

Sir Launcelot

In the legend that Hank reads in the book's introduction, Sir Launcelot presents prisoners to the ladies of the court on behalf of Sir Kay. Later, Sir Launcelot leads the army of five hundred knights who storm London by bicycle to save Hank and the king from being hanged. As in the traditional stories, Sir Launcelot is in love with King Arthur's wife, Guenever, and she is in love with him.

The book explains that it is Sir Launcelot's affair with Guenever that destroys the kingdom. Sir Launcelot makes a shrewd investment that financially ruins King Arthur's nephew, Mordred, who, in retaliation, tells King Arthur about the affair. The war that ensues between Sir Launcelot's knights and King Arthur's knights decimates the social order, making it easy for the church to come in and take control.

Morgan Le Fey

Morgan Le Fey is King Arthur's sister and a familiar villain from the Arthurian legends. Hank Morgan stops at her castle while he is on his quest with Demoiselle Alisande la Carteloise. Le Fey is a cruel dictator, but she gives in to Hank when she realizes that he is the sorcerer that everyone has heard about. She grudgingly allows him to free prisoners in her dungeon and to show mercy to the mother of a page whom she (Le Fey) killed.

Amyas le Poulet

See Clarence

Marco

Marco is a charcoal manufacturer. When the king and Hank are traveling incognito as a farmer and his bailiff, Marco and his wife, Phyllis, have them over for dinner. Marco worries when Hank invites a number of other tradesmen, thinking that he cannot afford such a party, but Hank pays for a sumptuous meal and furnishings to accommodate all.

Merlin

Unlike the way Merlin the magician is presented in legends, the Merlin here is a braggart and a fool. His reputation is based on the way that he takes tales of ordinary events and adds details that make it look as if his supernatural powers were involved. When, in the third chapter, Merlin tells the story of how Arthur came to be king (with Merlin's help), Hank Morgan is charmed, but everyone in court, who has heard the story numerous times before, falls asleep. Merlin soon gets on Hank's bad side by insisting that he (Hank) be executed. When Hank has a chance to impress people with his own brand of sorcery, he does it by first bettering Merlin and then destroying his tower. Later, when Hank is facing one knight after another in a duel and besting them with his lasso, Merlin steals it from him and then tells King Arthur a lie about the lasso being good for only a set number of uses before it would vanish back to where it came from.

At the end of the book, Merlin proves to be a true magician and a wise politician. When Hank and Clarence and their supporters are fighting to establish a republic, Merlin is present, disguised as an old woman. When Hank is injured, Merlin puts a spell on him so that he will sleep for thirteen centuries, waking up in the time that he came from, thereby sparing him defeat in the war. Merlin dies laughing.

Hank Morgan

Most of the novel is presented as Hank's journal about his time in the sixth century, which he presents to Twain in the nineteenth century. In it, he tells of how he was transported by a blow to the head back to the court of King Arthur and the changes that he (Hank) made to their backward time. Hank brings them technological advances, such as railroads, telephones, telegraphs, sewing machines, and firearms. Hank promotes political reform, convincing King Arthur to abolish slavery and equalize the tax system so that it does not unfairly burden the poor.

Hank's one personal flaw is that he does not suffer fools well. When dining with Marco and the other tradesmen, for instance, Hank explains that he should not argue with Dowley to the point of humiliating the man, but he cannot help himself. The end result is that Hank and the king are perceived as a threat and sold into slavery. Hank makes a big show of pointing out the fraudulence of Merlin and the rival magician from the East who claims to know things that others are doing far away. Given that most of his attempts to bring nineteenth-century technology to the sixth century are kept in private, it is counter-productive for Hank to take such pride in unmasking the phoniness of the established world. While traveling with King Arthur, Hank actively struggles to suppress his opinion that the king is no better than any other man, knowing that no good can come of insulting the king.

After the kingdom has been torn apart by internal war and then taken over by the Catholic church's interdiction, Hank is the leader of a band of young men who try to keep the country free. When the battle is lost, Merlin, whose power Hank has previously unmasked as fraudulent, places a spell on him so that he will sleep for thirteen hundred years. This explains why, having been transported to the past at the beginning of the narrative, he is able to interact with Mark Twain in the nineteenth century.

Sir Sagramor

Early in the novel, Hank Morgan offends Sir Sagramor when he comments unfavorably about the stale jokes of Sir Dinadan. Sir Sagramor thinks Hank is talking about him. A duel is arranged, but Sir Sagramor has to leave almost immediately on the quest for the Holy Grail, so the duel is postponed. Years later, after Hank returns from slavery, the duel is called on again. Sir Sagramor, dressed in heavy armor, is unable to maneuver himself. Hank beats Sir Sagramor by throwing a cowboy lasso over him and pulling him to the ground.

Sandy

Sandy is the nickname Hank gives Demoiselle Alisande la Carteloise. She comes to the court in chapter XI with a story about a castle where maidens are being held prisoner by four-armed, one-eyed giants. When Hank is sent out to free the maidens, Sandy travels the countryside with him, boring him with long-winded discussions about her backward views. At the end of the quest, the maidens turn out to be a herd of pigs and the castle they are held in is a sty, which Sandy says just looks that way to Hank because of a magical spell. Their travels end with Hank leaving Sandy at a convent to rest.

Much later, Sandy is reintroduced into the book as Hank's wife. They have a very loving relationship and have a daughter together. When Hank has to leave Sandy and the child, he writes to her every day. Hank's final words on his death bed, hundreds of years later, are to her.

Themes

Science and Technology

With his modern technological knowledge, Hank Morgan is able to quickly make himself one of the most powerful personages in King Arthur's realm. Hank commands respect by appealing to the superstitions that the common people usually follow. Hank presents himself as a sorcerer more powerful than Merlin, who Hank sees as holding great political influence simply because he knows how to make himself sound important in his stories. When Hank displays knowledge of astronomy in predicting the solar eclipse and knowledge of pyrotechnics by blowing up Merlin's castle, he is doing things on a large and conspicuous scale so that the common people can marvel at what they perceive to be his powers.

Having earned the sobriquet "The Boss" by fairly simple applications of scientific principles, Hank develops more complex technological advances in private, so that the superstitious population will not revolt in fear. He has telephone and electrical lines run, but close to the ground or underground. When railroad lines are run and newspapers are sold on the street corners, Hank takes care to introduce them gradually so as to not overwhelm the population. The result of this gradualism is that he relies on a secret network of intellectuals to understand his concepts, develop them, and maintain them. When war ravages the country, the forces of ignorance rise up, and all of the scientific and technological advances that he brought from the future are destroyed before they can be misused by the wrong people.

Divine Right

By putting Hank into the royal court, Twain directly addresses the question of the rights and responsibilities of King Arthur. Hank Morgan is quite outspoken about his opinions of royalty. He calls it a delusion, a comfortable myth that the people believed in because it had been taught to them all their lives and had been taught to their parents and grandparents, too. At one point, Hank says that the concept of the divine rights of royalty was developed by the church in order to keep the masses meek and self-sacrificing.

Topics For Further Study

- Think of a period in history that you would like to visit. Write a short story detailing what it would be like if you went there and how you would influence the citizenry with your twenty-first century knowledge.

- The late nineteenth century was a time of great industrial progress; the late twentieth century was considered the Information Age. Research what people think the coming trends are and write an essay about what you guess will be the important social movement of the twenty-second century.

- The year that most of this novel takes place, 528 A.D., is also the year that the roots of Buddhism were established, when Siddhartha Gautama, who was to be called the Buddha, found enlightenment. Explain what would have happened if Twain's protagonist, Hank Morgan, had ended up in the presence of the Buddha instead of in the presence of King Arthur.

- In one chapter of this novel, Twain explains that there were actually two "Reigns of Terror." Research the French Revolution and explain what he means by this. Also, explain whether you think the French Revolution was more important to the world's history than the American Revolution. Provide facts from your research to support your claim.

- Twain explains newspapers as being essential to any civilized society. In what ways is he right? Are newspapers still important now that we have the Internet, or has their day come and gone? Pick a position and try to defend it an essay or debate this topic with another classmate.

In the book, King Arthur's abuses of his royal power are presented as a result of his being kept separate from the main population and being ignorant about the realities of their lives. After King Arthur has traveled among the common people and been sold into slavery, he abolishes the practice of slavery. King Arthur is shown to be an overall noble person who does the best that can be done with the monarchical tradition. The malicious abuse of the concept of divine right is presented through Twain's characterization of Morgan Le Fey, who thinks nothing of taking the lives and property of peasants on a whim. She is so careless about the lives of her subjects that, when she does not understand what the narrator means when he says that he would like to "photograph" the peasants, she is prepared to casually take a sword and kill them, rather than admit that she does not understand the meaning of the word.

Religion

In just one of the many places in the novel where he rails against the Roman Catholic Church's corrosive influence on society, Twain's narrator notes that, "In two or three little centuries it had converted a nation of men to a nation of worms. Before the day of the Church's supremacy in the world, men were men, and held their heads up, and had a man's pride and spirit and independence." Twain's rage is not confined to just the Catholic Church but also applies to any established church, which he sees as an instrument for suppressing the rights of people by taking their inherent power away from them, making them slaves to the whims of the powerful people who claim to speak for God.

Though Hank mentions the church frequently throughout the course of the novel, it does not play a very prominent role in the plot. In part, this is by design. Hank explains that he designs his political reforms specifically so that they will not attract the attention of the church and bring out its opposition. At the end, when Guenever's infidelity is pointed out to King Arthur, the battle between the Knights of the Round Table creates such an obvious rend in the social fabric that it would be impossible for the church to not notice it. As a result, they send troops to take over the country. All of the technological and social advances that Hank brought from the nineteenth century are destroyed, and English culture is reverted back to the primitive, enslaving mindset that it had when he arrived. The church is held responsible for opposing progress, and, therefore, for causing widespread suffering.

Style

Loose Structure

Twain has been faulted for the structure, or lack of structure, of *A Connecticut Yankee in King Arthur's Court*. In the broadest term, the story has a clear structure, beginning and ending with the speaker, Twain, visiting England, then introducing the character of the Yankee, and then settling into the story that the Yankee has written out, which takes up most of the book. The book returns to Twain at the end, at which point the Yankee dies.

Within the Yankee's story, however, there is little consistency. Plot elements begin and end haphazardly, characters enter and leave with little notice, and long episodes conveniently arise just as others end. The most egregious of these inconsistencies is the way that the character of Sandy disappears from the story some time around the Restoration of the Fountain, and then reappears, surprisingly, more than a hundred pages later, as Hank Morgan's wife and the mother of his child.

The plot's inconsistencies, and its segmented format, are attributed to the fact that Twain wrote this novel in sections, over the course of three years. Instead of having an organic unity that it would have if it were edited after the final section was written, the story was put together one piece at a time. The final product reflects a growing understanding of the implications of what started out as a light fantasy.

Setting

In some novels, setting is unimportant, but the setting is the whole reason for this book's existence. As an examination of Middle Age customs through modern sensibilities, it seems at first to be an indictment of the naïve notions that people had in the past. Because Twain is a careful and humane writer, though, the people of that time prove to be worthy of sympathy, despite their strange notions. King Arthur turns out to be a truly kind and stately person, and Merlin turns out to have supernatural power after all. Twain uses the bare outline of Arthurian legends, which often wax nostalgic for the loss of such chivalric customs as loyalty to the court, bravery among knights, and devotion to one's lady, and he infuses them with real-life problems, such as the court existing by exploiting peasant labor. Cutting through the haze of sentimentality that has surrounded these stories throughout the years allows Twain to create a setting that is at once familiar and new.

Historical Context

The Gilded Age

During the last one-third of the nineteenth century, after the end of the Civil War, America experienced a boom in manufacturing that catapulted it into position as one of the world's economic leaders. From 1870 to 1900, the country's consumption of bituminous coal, which was the leading source of energy of the time, multiplied tenfold; production of rolled steel was twelve times greater; and, the overall economy grew to approximately six times its former size. The number of people employed in manufacturing tripled during the same time, to 7.6 million.

At that time of expansion, fortunes were made. The railroads, which were stretched across the continent, and the telephone, invented in 1876, made the growth of nation-wide corporations possible. With these distribution and communication networks, corporations were able to reach markets anywhere in the land. Millions were made in such areas as steel, shipping, retail stores with catalog sales, and oil. The luxurious lifestyles of society's upper crust caused the era to be termed the Gilded Age, an expression coined by Mark Twain himself in the title of an 1871 book.

Unfortunately, only a small portion of the population was enjoying such wealth. Much of society was suffering in poverty during the Gilded Age. A flood of immigrants drove wages down, and rural Americans flocked to the cities, which could not provide jobs for all. With the boom in manufacturing, tenements arose, and with them the unsanitary conditions that spread diseases. Taking advantage of the largess of the wealthy and the ignorance of the masses of new voters, politicians earned a reputation for corruption that would last until reforms of the early twentieth century. It was out of this period in which the abuse of cheap, expendable labor enabled only a few individuals to become unbelievably wealthy that America's labor movement arose.

Compare
&
Contrast

- **528:** The vast majority of the population is uneducated. Only a few men associated with the church are educated in the ancient languages of Greek and Latin.

  1889: The King James Bible, an English edition that was finished in 1611, is in many homes and is a primary text for teaching children to read. School is not mandatory and is only attended regularly by a minority of children.

  Today: School attendance has been required in the United States for nearly a cent0ury, up to the age of 16 in most states.

- **528:** During the Middle Ages, little machinery exists, which means that all physical work has to be done by hand.

  1889: The past hundred years have brought an industrial revolution, with machines making it possible to create things on a grander scale than was ever imaginable before.

  Today: America is in a post-industrial age: most jobs that require physical labor are consigned to poorer countries, leaving the country with a service economy.

- **528:** Peasants followed the aristocracy unquestioningly, having been assured by the church that blind obedience is what the church required.

  1889: American political discourse thrives on diversity, to such an extent that a war has actually separated different factions of the nation.

  Today: America is solidly but informally a two-party political system, with power control held at any given time by either the Democrats or the Republicans.

- **528:** There are no news media: news travels by word-of-mouth, making it difficult to verify the truth.

  1889: The only real news source is the newspapers, leaving the truth at the mercy of the newspaper owners.

  Today: Although the ownership of newspapers, television, and radio is falling into fewer and fewer hands through corporate consolidation, the Internet has made it possible for individuals to tell their stories directly to strangers.

- **528:** Medical treatment is mostly unheard of. Magic is considered as effective as science.

  1889: When faced with a sick relative, as Hank is when his daughter comes down with the croup, a smart individual knows what steps to take.

  Today: Science has identified the cellular and molecular causes of many diseases, and there are high-tech medicines and treatment centers that were unimaginable just a few decades ago.

Arthurian Legend

There is much debate about whether the King Arthur as mentioned in the legends ever truly existed. Most scholars agree that there was an Arthur who lived in the sixth century and ruled Britain, but records from the time are incomplete, so there is no conclusive evidence to show whether this Arthur and the King Arthur of the stories are one and the same.

The first legends of King Arthur have been traced to Welsh sources in the seventh century. These sources linked King Arthur to Celtic mythology, which explains the story's legendary, supernatural elements, such as Arthur earning his throne when the Lady in the Lake gives him the enchanted sword Excalibur. For hundreds of years after that, the stories about the king and his court expanded, and the characters and locations that are currently associated with the story, including Camelot, the Round Table, Sir Lancelot, Guinevere, Merlin, and the rest, were added. At the same time, a romantic tradition grew up around the characters in the

Illustration from an 1889 publication of Mark Twain's A Connecticut Yankee in King Arthur's Court

legends, particularly in the French versions of the stories. Like modern soap operas, these stories concentrated on the loves and betrayals and moral decisions that the knights and ladies faced.

The first person to write a continuous narrative of the accounts of King Arthur and his knights was Geoffrey of Monmouth, a Welsh writer who told the story that is most familiar today. This narrative was called the *History of Kings of Britain* (1137). After that, there are frequent references to the story. The first major literary treatment of the tales in English was Sir Thomas Malory's *L'Morte d'Arthur* (or, *The Death of Arthur*), published in 1485. Twain refers to Malory's work in *A Connecticut Yankee in King Arthur's Court*. For instance, the end of Twain's story is almost directly taken from Malory, with some modifications: Arthur finds out about Launcelot and Guenevere, orders her burned at the stake, Launcelot rescues her, and there is a fight for the kingdom between King Arthur's men and Launcelot's. Through the ages, each generation has taken Malory's story and expanded on it, reflecting the morals of contemporary society.

Critical Overview

Twain is considered to be one of the most significant novelists in American history, but *A Connecticut Yankee in King Arthur's Court* is generally thought of as an unstable effort. In his lifetime, Twain was greatly admired and immensely popular as a humorist, and he was widely read in newspapers. This popularity dwindled in his later years, from about the turn of the century until his death in 1910, when his writing became increasingly dark and his vision of humanity bleak. After his death, Twain received the attention that had been waning in his later years. Typical of this attention was the great journalist H. L. Mencken's observation (quoted in *A Mencken Chrestomathy*) in 1919: "The older I grow the more I am convinced that Mark was, by long odds, the largest figure that ever reared itself out of the flat, damp prairie of American literature." Perhaps the greatest single boost to Twain's reputation came when Ernest Hemingway, himself a deeply respected novelist and an eventual Nobel Prize winner, is said to have declared Twain's *Adventures of Huckleberry Finn* to be the source of all modern American fiction.

One of the things that has always maintained the reputation of *A Connecticut Yankee in King Arthur's Court* is its appeal to many different political perspectives, even gathering together those who do not agree with one another. Some, particularly those of Twain's own time, have seen the book as a "celebration of modern values," as Robert Keith Miller put it in his book *Mark Twain* in 1983. Others, Miller points out, have considered it a condemnation of all optimism. One good example of this flexibility is the way Charles L. Sanford, in an article originally published in *American Quarterly* (reprinted in *Readings on Mark Twain*) called "A Classic of Reform Literature," calls the novel Twain's "symbolic attempt to persuade himself that all was right in the American garden after all." Although Sanford says that this statement "takes into account both those critics who interpret *The Connecticut Yankee* as a veiled attack upon American business practices and those who take his praise of modern times at face value," there are very few critics who would agree in characterizing Mark Twain as wishing to be self-deluded.

While Twain has always had a reputation as a master satirist, critics have had trouble identifying just what is being satirized in *A Connecticut Yankee in King Arthur's Court*. John C. Gerber, writing in his book *Mark Twain*, refers to the novel's problem as "literary schizophrenia," noting that "[o]n the surface it is a tall tale that lampoons chivalric romances, while underneath it is a compendium of Mark Twain's increasingly gloomy thoughts about human behavior in both the past and the present." Because of its inherent contrasts, Robert Keith Miller tells his readers, "Clearly, this is a work that deserves to be read closely."

Criticism

David Kelly

Kelly is an instructor of literature and creative writing at two schools in Illinois. In this essay, Kelly examines how the character of Hank Morgan makes Twain's story difficult for modern readers.

Reading and becoming informed about the past is part of a well-rounded education. Still, it is not always easy. An especially difficult task for modern readers is to determine the proper approach to a work that was not only written decades prior, but whose setting is centuries in the past. Published in the late 1880s, the book is about history; at the same time, for the contemporary reader, it *is* history. Twain wrote about the Middle Ages, setting his novel in the year 587. His central idea concerns explaining the changes that had come over the world over the course of thirteen centuries. There is nothing in the novel to explain the changes of the past hundred and fifteen years .

Contemporary readers are presented with the world Twain was writing about and also the world that he assumed his readers would know. That is a lot of information to synthesize. To make matters worse, a good case can be made that in the twentieth century the rate of social change accelerated at a pace quicker than it did in many of the pre-technological centuries that separated Twain from his subject. The book focuses on the developments that occurred between King Arthur's time and Twain's, such as the locomotive, the telephone, the newspaper, and the gun; these are all significant advances, but they do not really hold up in magnitude to the automobile, airplane, television, laser, DNA mapping, and thousands of other achievements that have occurred. The time that has passed since Twain lived might easily be characterized as the age of the nuclear bomb and the computer. Both destruction and knowledge have become global, not provincial, realities.

It is common to blame contemporary American students for their lack of historical perspective; studies regularly quote students saying that they do not see how incidents in the distant past matter to their lives, and tests show that they cannot identify the dates for milestones in world history like the French Revolution, the Renaissance, or even the First World War. In the case of a novel like *A Connecticut Yankee in King Arthur's Court*, it would be easy to sympathize with their sense of alienation. Readers of this book are not only required to look backward through history, but also have to line up two separate historical points and determine their relationship to each other. Students might approach the book armed with a dictionary, but an astrolabe might be more appropriate.

Students will commonly express their frustration with fiction that was written long ago or about ancient times and their inability to relate to the strange settings and surroundings depicted in both. The standard response is that good readers will look beyond the cultural differences and concentrate on the work's characters. Literature is about the human condition. Regardless of where a story takes place or what happens in it, the characters should still, at heart, be human. No one says that a reader has to be a student of the sixth century or of the nineteenth century in order to appreciate *A Connecticut Yankee in King Arthur's Court*. The behavior of Hank Morgan, the Yankee of the title, is all that one really has to relate to. In some regards, Twain makes it easy for readers of any generation to join Hank in his adventure, but in other regards, Twain complicates things by making Hank more complex than people expect to find in an adventure yarn or satire.

This type of story should be familiar to anyone who has ever read a book, seen a movie, or watched TV. It is a standard stranger-in-a-strange-land myth, a variation on the old fish-out-of-water formula, which throws its protagonist into an unfamiliar environment and studies how he reacts to what he finds there and how the people there react to him.

In *A Connecticut Yankee in King Arthur's Court*, Twain continually refines this formula. When Hank becomes a familiar figure around Camelot, he leaves it to travel across the country on several extended journeys. While Hank is out on his travels, a war breaks out in King Arthur's realm. Hank returns to find a devastated landscape where almost all of the people he has come to know over the years are dead and the social order he personally constructed no longer exists. Rather than seeing him act throughout the downfall of Arthur's court, readers see him plunged into another unfamiliar situation, learning about what kind of man Hank Morgan is by watching how he reacts.

It would be easier for readers to float through this book, experiencing new worlds with Hank Morgan, if Hank were the ordinary man that he is often assumed to be. Twain does not give much background about his life before being transported back in time. Readers are told only that he was a foreman in the Colt firearms factory; that his father was a blacksmith and his uncle a horse doctor, and he has practiced both trades; that he had a girl in his time that he was "practically engaged to," although she seldom passes through his thoughts; and that he considers himself "a practical Connecticut man." From these details, one can assume a penchant for problem-solving and a high degree of impatience with sentimentality and romance. What one does not assume is the fact that Hank Morgan is not a very nice man.

Hank tells the story and, therefore, readers tend to identify with him. When he looks at the barbaric practices of Camelot, from the inequity of ownership to the government-supported cruelty of nobles to the people's ignorance of the physical world, his directness is admirable. When Hank sees problems, he sets about fixing them, which is a huge improvement over the people who are accustomed to accepting their troubles because of tradition or fear. And, in fact, one sees a few benefits when Arthurian society begins to run the Hank Morgan way. Slavery is abolished, prisoners are freed, and

> " Readers of this book are not only required to look backward through history, but also have to line up two separate historical points and determine their relationship to each other."

despots learn that they are accountable for the suffering of their subjects.

What is not as openly pronounced in the novel is the weakness of Hank's reforms. Readers hear about railroads, gold currency, a stock market, newspapers, etc., but, really, what effect do these have? The ones that are shown to have any value have value to Morgan, for securing his claims of being a great sorcerer, like his fixing of the pump at the Holy Fountain or his synthesis of gunpowder specifically to destroy Merlin's castle. Some reforms, like his miller-gun for dispensing currency, seem to have been forced on the Middle Age peasants because Hank, a gunsmith, thought to invent them. Hank does not comprehend that his reforms might never be appropriate for these particular people. His faith is in technology and machines, not in the democratic spirit that he so often evokes.

The idea of understanding a strange social setting by relating to the protagonist of the book is much more difficult in this book than it is in other novels because the protagonist has been written to be ignorant of his own flaws. Hank is aware of the shortcomings of Camelot and, like any good mechanic, he can suggest means to fix particular problems, but he cannot see beyond the repairs he suggests. He does not think about the problems that he might create when his programs fall into place. Hank is not a social planner. Twain himself was unimpressed with Hank. Edmund Reiss (in his afterward to *A Connecticut Yankee in King Arthur's Court*) quotes Twain as having said "this Yankee of mine has neither the refinement nor weakness of a college education; he is a perfect ignoramus; he is boss of a machine shop; he can build a locomotive or a Colt's revolver, he can put up and run a telegraph line, but he's an ignoramus, nevertheless." Readers who find it difficult to understand King Arthur's society and who are unfamiliar with

What Do I Read Next?

- At about the same time that Twain was writing his version of the Arthurian legend in America, Great Britain's poet laureate, Alfred, Lord Tennyson, was working on his masterful poem about the same subject, *Idylls of the King* (begun in 1859, completed in 1885). Tennyson's version of the story is beautifully lush, dreamy, and considerably more reverent than Twain's version.

- The version of the story of Camelot that Twain used as a basis for his novel was Sir Thomas Malory's *Le Morte d'Arthur* (1485). In 2003, Cassel published a complete version of Malory's work called *Le Morte D'Arthur: Complete, Unabridged, Illustrated Edition*, which is edited by John Matthews and lushly illustrated by Anna Marie Ferguson.

- Journalist T. H. White retold the story of King Arthur in his book *The Once and Future King* (1958), which made the tales accessible for modern readers. White's version became a bestseller and is considered by many critics to be a masterpiece of fantasy literature.

- Twain's own masterpiece is considered to be *The Adventures of Huckleberry Finn* (1884). Similar in episodic plot and political indignation to *A Connecticut Yankee in King Arthur's Court*, this work is considered by many to be the elusive "great American novel."

- Twain was a well-known personality of his day and has become almost as recognizable to readers of American literature as any of the characters he created. *The Autobiography of Mark Twain* (1959), edited by Charles Neider, gives Twain's story directly. This book was assembled from various autobiographical writings and is available in paperback from Harper Perennial.

- Of the many biographies of Twain that are available, one of the most user-friendly is *Mark Twain* (2001), by Geoffrey C. Ward and Dayton Duncan. This book was produced to be the companion piece to Ken Burns's documentary miniseries about Twain and reflects the most current (at the time) research on his life.

---

the way people thought in the eighteen hundreds will find Hank Morgan himself no less perplexing. He thinks that he knows more than he does so readers who take him at his word are bound to misinterpret the book's overall significance.

In Twain's time, it would be easy to judge Morgan as a meddler who has gone and interfered in another culture, finding them to be too lacking in modern conveniences, forcing his own social standards on them. Modern readers, though, see two historic cultures at work, each one with its positives and negatives, but neither one our own. Contemporary readers therefore tend to miss out on the story's careful moral balance.

The story of the stranger finding himself suddenly catapulted into an unfamiliar culture has been told time and time again. Usually, writers focus their attention on the clash of the cultures, and so

they make their protagonist either benign, so as to not draw too much attention away from the cultural issues, or wise, so that the author can use the story to show how the world ought to work. In *A Connecticut Yankee in King Arthur's Court*, Twain takes the more difficult path by having two cultures converge in the life of one complex character. This gives modern readers a lot to analyze, and they understandably might fail to notice just how much Twain expects of them.

Source: David Kelly, Critical Essay on *A Connecticut Yankee in King Arthur's Court*, in *Novels for Students*, Thomson Gale, 2005.

Scott Dalrymple

In the following essay, Dalrymple explores how Twain's immersion in the events of the U.S. Civil War at the time of his writing A Connecticut

Yankee *influenced characterization and events in the novel.*

1

We are able to document the genesis of Mark Twain's *A Connecticut Yankee in King Arthur's Court* quite precisely. During Twain's "Twins of Genius" reading tour with George W. Cable in December 1884, the two entered a Rochester, New York, bookstore where Cable introduced his friend to Malory's *Morte D'Arthur*. Alan Gribben has convincingly shown that this episode was not Twain's first encounter with Malory—his daughters owned an 1880 children's version of Malory, which their father must have known about, and in a letter dated August 1883 Twain had alluded to Sir Kay and Sir Launcelot—but the first notebook entries for the novel did appear in December 1884, just after the Cable incident. The first entry reads "Dream of being a knight errant in the middle ages," followed by a hilarious exploration of what it was like to wear medieval armor. Serious work on the manuscript of *A Connecticut Yankee,* however, did not begin until mid-December 1885 and January 1886. After Howard G. Baetzhold's solid and informative genetic study, it has been accepted that Twain wrote the novel in sporadic bursts until publication of the first British and American editions in December 1889.

Apparently a dark cloud hung over the novel's ending from the start of its composition. As early as December 1884, Twain had jotted a note about a battle between a "modern army, with gatling guns. . . 600 shots a minute, . . .torpedoes, balloons, 100-ton cannon, iron-clad fleet &c & Prince de Joinville's Middle Age Crusaders" (*Mark Twain's Notebooks and Journals*, 86). And although the artistic seams and contrasts may be visible between the bulk of the book and its shocking conclusion in the Battle of the Sand-Belt, strong evidence leads us to think that Twain thought of the ending as tragic all along.

In a notebook entry of December 1885, Twain wrote about his newly created Sir Robert Smith, later to be called Hank Morgan:

> He mourns his lost land—has come to England & revisited it, but it is all changed & become old, so old!—& it was so fresh & new, so virgin before. Winchester does not resemble Camelot, & the Round Table. . . is not a true one. Has lost all interest in life—is found dead next morning—suicide. (*Mark Twain's Notebooks and Journals*, 216)

Twain's early intent seems consistent with the final version: the ending sounds a tragic note. Hank

" But in many ways Hank is also a superhuman likeness of General Grant, leading the 'Republic' in battle against the archaic, slave-holding, non-technological South."

does not commit suicide, but he apparently dies of a broken heart as he "mourns his lost land."

During the period from 1885 through 1889, while he was writing the book, Twain had other relevant concerns. Not least among them was money; his obsession with the Paige typesetting machine, which he financed and thought would revolutionize the printing industry, would combine with other business blunders and drive him to bankruptcy. James Cox has shown how this obsession manifests itself in *A Connecticut Yankee.* But perhaps of greater importance during 1885 was Twain's major literary project: publication of *Personal Memoirs of U.S. Grant,* of which Twain speaks at some length in his autobiography. Twain had encouraged the aging hero, who was then living in near-poverty, to relate his experiences to the world. He convinced Grant to decline the Century company's offer and to accept that of his own publishing house, Charles L. Webster. Twain's only literary accomplishment that year was "The Private History of a Campaign That Failed" (first titled "My Campaign Against Grant"), a short and ostensibly true account of Twain's own Civil War experience. The article appeared in the December 1885 issue of *Century* magazine. This short work stands as his only memorable literary achievement in the five year period immediately before and during the composition of *A Connecticut Yankee.*

Early in 1885, Twain had been asked to write an article for *Century's* "Battles and Leaders" series, a collection of personal reminiscences of the Civil War. But he did not finish "The Private History" until November. During the nine months from inception to finished work, the essay changed from a lighthearted anecdote to a more serious, realistic, disturbing record of his experiences. Justin Kaplan finds this shift directly related to Twain's close contact with General Grant and with the manuscript and proofs of his *Memoirs.*

Much of what Twain has to say about the Civil War regards Grant; Twain was fascinated by him. It seems inevitable that Grant would surface somewhere in Twain's fiction. Kaplan has pointed out the importance of the General, mentioned both as a historical figure and possibly as the symbolic "stranger," in "The Private History." Grant and the Civil War seem to have had a largely unrecognized influence, however, on *A Connecticut Yankee* as well. During the composition of the book, when Grant's *Memoirs* were part of Twain's everyday life and when "The Private History" was his most recent literary output, the American Civil War was both consciously and unconsciously at the forefront of his imagination. Civil War imagery pervades the strange and oft-criticized conclusion of *A Connecticut Yankee.* Viewing it in this light, we may shed light on one of Twain's most fascinating novels.

2

After the novel's two picaresque sequences, which relate Hank's travels with Sandy and then with King Arthur, there is a civil war in sixth-century England that ultimately leads to the catastrophe of the book's conclusion. As Clarence explains, King Arthur has learned of the love between Launcelot and Guenever; when a trap is laid, and Launcelot falls into it, the knights divide into parties loyal either to the King or to Launcelot. Friends take up arms against friends, and Launcelot even mistakenly kills Sir Gaheris and Sir Gareth, whose "love for Launcelot was indestructible." Clarence tells Hank "the rest of the tale is just war, pure and simple." This medieval civil war eventually prompts a Church edict, under which Hank has been condemned. Clarence recognizes the seriousness of the situation and provisions Merlin's old cave for a siege against all of England's remaining knights, now under the unified command of the Church. The ensuing Battle of the Sand-Belt not only suggests parallels to the American Civil War, but it so surprisingly and particularly resembles a specific campaign—Grant's siege of Vicksburg, Mississippi—that it seems likely Twain's creative mind was reshaping this crucial siege in his novel.

Grant's long but successful siege of Vicksburg was seen by many, including President Lincoln, as the key to Union victory in the War. With control of the city, located on a bluff overlooking the Mississippi River, came command of traffic on the river's southern half. Grant led a six-week bombardment and siege upon Vicksburg that ended on July 4, 1863. "The fate of the Confederacy," Grant wrote in his *Memoirs,* "was sealed when Vicksburg

fell." Twain knew precise details about the siege of Vicksburg and its crucial impact on the war. In *Life on the Mississippi,* he devoted an entire chapter, "Vicksburg During the Trouble," to the siege, and originally he had planned more. He was fascinated by the survivors' tales of the siege and he questioned them in detail about their experiences.

Many specific details which Twain relates about Vicksburg reappear, with imaginative transformation, in the Battle of the Sand-Belt. Most apparent is the use of caves as hiding places during a civil war siege. Twain tells us of his first impressions of post-war Vicksburg in the following observation from *Life on the Mississippi:*

> Signs and scars still remain, as reminders of Vicksburg's tremendous war-experiences; earthworks, trees crippled by the cannon balls, cave-refuges in the clay precipices, etc. The caves did good service during the six weeks' bombardment of the city—May 18 to July 4, 1863. They were used by the non-combatants—mainly by the women and children; not to live in constantly, but to fly to for safety on occasion.

In an interview with a civilian survivor, Twain was told of the often "desperately crowded" conditions in the caves during a heavy bombardment, with "air so foul, sometimes, you couldn't have made a candle burn in it." In *A Connecticut Yankee,* when Clarence tells Hank about the cave he has picked for the siege, he is careful to say "that old cave of Merlin's—not the small one, the big one," even though there is no reason for Twain to distinguish for readers since we know nothing about either cave. And in Clarence's postscript to the novel he tells of the "poisonous air" that pervades the aftermath of the battle, sickening the Boss and his followers who are trapped in their cave.

Even exact numbers cited in Twain's novel are suggestive: in *Life on the Mississippi,* Twain says the people of Vicksburg numbered "twenty-seven thousand soldiers and three thousand non-combatants," or 30,000 in all. Hank says that the mounted host of mailed knights is, significantly, "30,000 strong." The fact that Twain keeps the number of 30,000, but reverses the sides (in the novel there are 30,000 attackers, rather than 30,000 under attack) suggests an unconsciously-made correlation between the 30,000 medieval chivalric knights and the 30,000 citizens of Vicksburg. The latter belonged to a society that turned back progress "with decayed and degraded systems of government; with sillinesses and emptinesses, sham grandeurs, sham gauds, and sham chivalries of a brainless and worthless long-vanished society." What better description of the society Twain derides in *A Connecticut Yankee?* In the novel, however, caves are more than places of occasional refuge for non-combatants. Unlike the people of Vicksburg, Hank and Clarence and their fifty-two young followers want the enemy to strike. The group under siege here is not composed of women and children (though it is a group of boys between 14 and 17 who are "as pretty as girls"), and their strength as warriors is great. During the battle, Hank is in total control. It has been suggested that here Hank is a kind of wish-fulfilling figure of Mark Twain, because "both are showmen who love gaudy effects."

But in many ways Hank is also a superhuman likeness of General Grant, leading the "Republic" in battle against the archaic, slave-holding, non-technological South. Hank and Grant are similar in some very specific ways. The terms of surrender that Hank, at one point, intends to offer the knights resemble those originally offered by Grant at Vicksburg. Hank orders the English knights to "surrender unconditionally to the Republic." Grant was famous for his demand of unconditional surrender, which was considered uncivilized by Confederate generals; Northern newspapers dubbed him "Unconditional Surrender" Grant. There is also another, more intriguing parallel between Hank and Grant. Grant had tried repeatedly to create a new river channel by cutting into the west bank of the Mississippi, hoping to bypass Vicksburg altogether; he was unsuccessful. Twain knew about this effort from Grant's *Memoirs,* and he mentioned the effort in his notebook. In a compelling similarity, Hank does succeed in re-routing what he first describes as a "mountain brook," but which later approaches with "a sudden rush and roar," and a thousand knights are drowned by the water, now "raging through the big ditch and creating a river a hundred feet wide and twenty-five feet deep."

But in addition to these circumstantial images, a similarity of narrative style also reveals Hank's and Twain's debt to the General. The Connecticut Yankee and General Grant—called by Confederate forces "The Yankee"—begin their stories the same way. "My family is American," reads the first sentence of Grant's *Memoirs,* "and has been for generations, in all its branches, direct and collateral." Similarly, the first sentence of *A Connecticut Yankee* is, even more simply, "I am an American." Such opening statements seem fitting for full-blooded Yankees who are proud of their heritage—and Hank describes himself as "a Yankee of Yankees," just as Grant was a Yankee of Yankees during the American Civil War.

Both men, as narrators, often recount grotesque scenes with realism and impassivity. The following is a passage about the mining of Vicksburg from Grant's *Memoirs:*

> On the 25th of June at three o'clock, all being ready, the mine was exploded. A heavy artillery fire all along the line had been ordered to open with the explosion. The effect was to blow the top of the hill off and make a crater where it stood. . .[A]ll that were there were thrown into the air, some of them coming down on our side, still alive. (Grant, I, 551)

And of the bloody battle of Shiloh, Grant writes:

> I saw an open field, in our possession on the second day, over which the Confederates had made repeated charges the day before, so covered with dead that it would have been possible to walk across the clearing, in any direction, stepping on dead bodies, without a foot touching the ground. (Grant, I, 356)

Such passages represent Grant's detached, unemotional tone in the face of extraordinary actual events. The images of a hill turned into a crater by a massive explosion, of human bodies flying through the air or littering the ground, are related with only as much emotion as an inventory of food rations. Such detachment is certainly necessary in a great war general; Grant's willingness to engage in combat, while harboring no love for it, was the reason he finally replaced George McClellan *et al.* as commander of the Union forces.

These realistic passages resemble many in *A Connecticut Yankee.* Take, for example, Hank's description of the scene outside his electric fences:

> One could make out but little detail; but he could note that a black mass was piling itself up beyond the second fence. That swelling bulk was dead men! Our camp was enclosed with a solid wall of the dead—a bulwark, a breastwork, of corpses, you may say.

Both Hank and Grant offer subjective comments in their narratives, but these statements are usually secondary to the major purpose of giving a detailed, realistic account of experience. Although Hank stretches the truth to his own ends, his eye for detail commands respect. After the first wave of knights reaches the torpedoes hidden under the Sand-Belt, Hank describes the scene. It is not sufficient to mention a large ditch created by the blast; he must tell us its precise dimensions:

> No living creature was in sight! We now perceived that additions had been made to our defenses. The dynamite had dug a ditch more than a hundred feet wide, all around us, and cast up an embankment some twenty-five feet high on both borders of it. As to destruction of life, it was amazing. Moreover, it was beyond estimate. Of course we could not count the dead, because they did not exist as individuals, but

merely as homogeneous protoplasm, with alloys of iron and buttons.

Although Twain allows Hank an exclamation point to show some emotion, it does not lessen the effect of his cold report of the "homogeneous protoplasm" of the slaughtered knights. In fact, the exclamation point, along with many of the other expletives in this section of the novel, were late manuscript additions. The above passage was originally followed by an even more graphic image describing "some trifle over 4,000,000 pounds of meat, that is, knights" on the battlefield; this phrasing was later deleted.

Grant's writing style—attacked by Matthew Arnold and vigorously defended by Twain—is simple, unaffected, and effective. And like Hank's narrative, Grant's "Personal" memoirs are, on the whole, not very personal at all. His narrative is filled with direct statements, supporting dates and facts, and a great deal of tactical explanation and justification. More personal details, such as mention of his family, are inserted almost apologetically within the text. Grant recounts details of his marriage with military succinctness, as if he feels guilty of rambling. Hank offers even less detail; when he speaks of his marriage to Sandy, rather late in the book, it comes as quite a surprise to the reader.

Although both narrators are fierce competitors in battle, they are not ashamed to show compassion afterward. Grant writes that during battle "one can see his enemy mowed down by the thousand, with great composure," but when the battle is over, "these scenes are distressing, and one is naturally disposed to do as much to alleviate the suffering of an enemy as a friend" (Grant, I, 521). Hank, at the very end of *A Connecticut Yankee,* seems modeled after Grant in this way, but his humane feelings lead to sinister results. Clarence tells us that Hank insists on helping the wounded after the Battle of the Sand-Belt, even though he had been advised against such actions. The first wounded man he comes across "was sitting, with his back against a dead comrade. When the Boss bent over him and spoke to him, the man recognized him and stabbed him."

On the whole, Grant's *Memoirs* give the impression of an honest, humble, realistic account of a great leader's life. Grant constantly downplays his accomplishments, unlike the proud Hank, who glories in his. Hank is a sort of amalgamation of Grant's and Twain's personal characters in this regard. Perhaps ultimately it is this sense of hubris

that makes the great "effect" of Hank's baffle morally offensive to some readers. His victory is a hollow one; very soon it will become a defeat. Still, Grant could almost be speaking of the aftermath of the Battle of the Sand-Belt when he writes: "The enemy fought bravely, but they had started out to defeat and destroy an army and capture a position. They failed in both, with very heavy loss in killed and wounded, and must have gone back discouraged and convinced that the 'Yankee' was not an enemy to be despised" (Grant, I, 356–7).

One final detail strengthens the Civil War imagery in *A Connecticut Yankee*'s conclusion. After the first onslaught of the knights, and after the destruction of thousands by the "torpedoes" (the contemporary name for land mines) in the Sand-Belt, Hank addresses his followers:

> SOLDIERS, CHAMPIONS OF HUMAN LIBERTY AND EQUALITY: Your General congratulates you! In the pride of his strength and the vanity of his renown, an arrogant enemy came against you. You were ready. The conflict was brief; on your side, glorious. This mighty victory having been achieved utterly without loss, stands without example in history. So long as the planets shall continue to move in their orbits, the BATTLE OF THE SAND-BELT will not perish out of the memories of men. THE BOSS.

This proclamation alludes to and contrasts with certain phrases from Lincoln's "Gettysburg Address." Lincoln spoke of a nation "conceived in liberty, and dedicated to the proposition that all men are created equal," much like Hank's "champions of human liberty and equality." Lincoln, with characteristic humility, thought "the word will little note, nor long remember what we say here, but it can never forget what they did here," but Hank, with characteristic self-aggrandizing "effect," is emphatic about the planetary consequences of his accomplishment. Furthermore, the final words of Lincoln's speech express a hope that democratic government "shall not perish from the earth," a phrase quite similar to "General" Hank's assessment that his battle "will not perish out of the memories of men." Twain was very familiar with Lincoln's Address; he once quoted a passage from Malory and said its "noble simple eloquence had not its equal until the Gettysburg Speech took its lofty place beside it." Appropriately, the Battle of Gettysburg was decided on the very same day as the siege of Vicksburg: 4 July 1863.

3

It seems inexplicable to many readers that *A Connecticut Yankee,* for most of its length an enjoyable "good read," could end in the tragic, grisly, and bizarre Battle of the Sand-Belt. One critic has called the ending "one of the most striking representations of aborted effort in our literature." What does it mean, if anything? On the surface, there certainly seems to be a boyish playfulness at work in the Battle. As David Sewell has recognized, using all of the neatest modern weapons to blow up an enemy is a typical boyhood fantasy. In the absence of any strong evidence to the contrary, we might be cautious in assigning great meaning to the destruction wreaked by Hank's forces. After all, when modern audiences see an action film, they witness dozens of violent deaths in the span of two hours; but viewers don't necessarily find (nor do the filmmakers imply) any great significance in them.

But two pieces of evidence seem to make the Battle of the Sand-Belt fundamentally different. The first is contextual. There simply were very few nineteenth-century novels that dared to include graphic descriptions such as the "homogeneous protoplasm" of the dead knights. Therefore the images of the Battle were that much more shocking to Twain's contemporary audience. Second, and more importantly, it is clear that Twain took great care to construct his ending, and it seems evident that he based many of its details on American Civil War facts. Given the amount of thought he apparently invested in it, it seems unlikely that Twain intended the Battle of the Sand-Belt merely as a Tom Sawyeresque diversion.

If indeed Twain was alluding to Grant and the Civil War, then we should view the Battle of the Sand-Belt as a parallel with the bloody war between Union and Confederacy: a clash between a chivalric, slave-owning, agrarian society and a modern, technologically advanced republic led by a general-president. As such, it is utterly consistent with the rest of the novel. Throughout, the object of Twain's satire has been primarily the culture of sixth century England, which parallels the ante-bellum American South. Knights, the icons of chivalry, are reduced to wearing sandwich boards. The Church is portrayed as power-hungry and evil. Arthur himself is a well-meaning buffoon. It so happens that most objects of satire in the novel lend themselves to such comedy.

But when it comes to war, even Twain can find little humor. He wrote in "The Private History of a Campaign That Failed," which appeared in the December 1885 issue of *Century:*

> And it seemed an epitome of war; that all war must be just that—the killing of strangers against whom you feel no personal animosity; strangers whom, in other circumstances, you would help if you found them in trouble, and who would help you if you needed it. My campaign was spoiled. It seemed to me that I was not rightly equipped for this awful business; that war was intended for men, and I for a child's nurse.

This is the voice of the author who writes about the carnage of the Battle of the Sand-Belt. As the American North and South tragically learned, and as Twain and his audience well remembered, real war feels nothing like the romantic battles of Sir Walter Scott's heroes. It truly is an "awful business." Men do not engage in grand oratory on the battlefield; instead they are more likely to be blown into "homogeneous protoplasm" by land mines. This graphic realism leaves the reader disturbed, but as Robert E. Lee observed, "It is well that war is so terrible, else we should grow too fond of it." Far from a failing, Twain's relentlessly realistic portrayal of war may be recognized by future readers as one of the novel's triumphs.

Source: Scott Dalrymple, "Just War, Pure and Simple: *A Connecticut Yankee in King Arthur's Court* and the American Civil War," in *American Literary Realism, 1870–1910,* Vol. 29, No. 1, 1996, pp. 1–11.

Lawrence I. Berkove

In the following essay, Berkove contends that A Connecticut Yankee *is "a successfully united novel of tragic vision—specifically a vision of universal damnation."*

A Connecticut Yankee in King Arthur's Court is centrally important to the effort to identify and chart a level of basic consistency in the life and works of Mark Twain. The novel should bring us much closer to the goal of establishing that there arc particular ideas and values which are characteristic of Mark Twain, and that they exist in an unbroken chain from the formative years of his youth to the end of his life. However, the prevailing critical position on *A Connecticut Yankee,* that it fails because excessive autobiographical intrusions by Twain destroy its fictional unity, leaves the thrust of the novel in doubt. As a consequence, what almost all commentators agree has the makings of a major novel is instead regarded as a disappointment, and its author is seen as being in a state of vacillation or declining power. This critical position is based on a great deal of evidence, especially biographical, which indicates what Twain's overt attitudes and intentions probably were at various stages of the novel's composition.

Although this position is valid as far as it goes, it is not necessarily compelling for it does not account for other evidence that points to the novel's

> " . . . a close look at
> almost any episode in which
> dreams play a part will reveal
> that dreams are even more
> important as message than they
> are as structure."

unity. More importantly, it either underestimates or overlooks entirely the deep control of the brooding concerns that were always on Twain's mind but were seldom—until his late period—explicitly discussed at length. Alan Gribben has recently encouraged scholarship that would peel away Twain's mask and "curtail Twain's posthumous control of his own legend, however compelling the works he left behind to imprint forever *his* version of people and events." In this spirit, therefore, I wish to advance an interpretation of *A Connecticut Yankee*'s structural and thematic unity and to indicate how much more is to be gained by pursuing this approach than by continuing to assume the incompatibility of its parts, and hence its artistic failure.

A full treatment of this powerful novel's complexity is beyond the scope of a short discussion, but enough may be said of its deep structure and artistic strategies to support a claim of its internal unity and its integral consistency with Twain's life. It is my contention that *A Connecticut Yankee* is a successfully unified novel of tragic vision—specifically a vision of universal damnation. This is achieved by the novel's pointed use of dreams first to undercut the notion of objective reality and then to replace it gradually with the growing sense that this world is truly hell.

The idea that one can be in this world and literally in hell also is one that other authors have also proposed. In Marlowe's *Dr. Faustus,* for example, occurs the following exchange:

> Faust: How come it then that thou are out of hell?
> Meph: Why this is hell, nor am I out of it.

What is unique in *A Connecticut Yankee* is that Twain, raised in Calvinism and acutely in mind of its doctrines all his life, has generalized Mephistophilis' condition to all humans. But unlike Mephistophilis, who understands his situation, none of the humans in this novel are quite conscious of the true nature of their existence. All live

and struggle in a dream. Some move from one dream to another, but they remain deceived about their state. The novel blurs and dissolves first the distinctions between dream and reality and then between reality and hell. At the end, when Hank Morgan in his delirium speaks of the "strange and awful dreams" that were "as real as reality" ("Final P.S. by M.T."), he is summing up the main point of the novel: that there is no difference between the nightmare of hell and what is thought of as reality; they are one and the same.

The blurring of the distinctions between reality and dream is an important motif in Twain's writing, one that grew out of the lifelong importance he attached to dreams, and his susceptibility to nightmares. There were originally two different kinds of dreams that disturbed Twain: dreams of the night and waking dreams. The night dreams were more obviously alarming, but Twain appears at an early stage in his career to have come to regard the waking dreams as both more insidious and more ominous. Even in so early a work as *Roughing It* (1872), for example, all of the references to the waking dreams which are frequently mentioned in it have some negative connotations. Beneath the humorous anecdotal level, the entire phenomenon of the silver fever's infectious hope of striking it rich is exposed by Twain as only a dream, but a mad one which wasted the lives of the miners deluded by it. And Twain's experience in the Eden of Hawaii could not be better summed up than by his own rueful description of it "It was tranced luxury to sit in the perfumed air and forget that there was any world but these enchanted islands. It was ecstasy to dream, and dream—till you got a bite. A scorpion bite" (Ch. 63).

Twain's apprehension of romantic daydreaming appears frequently in his middle period, in forms as diverse as his open diatribe against Sir Walter Scott in *Life on the Mississippi* (1883) or his more subtly disparaging characterization of Tom Sawyer in *Huckleberry Finn* (1884), especially in the climactic evasion chapters. The ground of Twain's animosity is not that such daydreaming is immature, foolish, or even unrealistic, but that it is perilous. The great danger of waking dreams consists of their taking control of the actual lives of the persons affected and fatally misleading them.

The preoccupation with dreams in the literature of Twain's late period is well known, but the most chilling feature of this tendency is its focus on the tangible takeover of reality by dream. In "The Great Dark" (1898), for instance, not only does dream appear to usurp reality but reality itself is relegated to the status of dream. A mysterious and sinister character called the Superintendent of Dreams appears to the narrator Edwards first in a service role, but soon assumes more power and dominates him. When commanded by Edwards to end the dream sea voyage which has become a nightmare, he stuns Edwards with his retort: "The dream? *Are you sure it is a dream?* . . . You have spent your whole life in this ship. And this is *real* life. Your other life was the dream!" Twain repeated this idea in *The Mysterious Stranger* manuscripts. Discussing the last chapter of "No 44, The Mysterious Stranger," Gibson sums up its central paradox: "mold your life nearer to the heart's desire; life is at best a dream and at worst a nightmare from which you cannot escape."

As we have seen, this gloomy meditation was not a late development in Twain's thought, but the culmination of an entire lifetime of brooding on the nature of dreams and their portents. Against this background of a distinctive thought pattern, which affected Twain even before his writing career began and lasted until his death. *A Connecticut Yankee* must be seen as a natural link in the pattern. The novel's abundant references to dreams are purposeful and crucial parts of both its structure and its themes. It is obvious at the very least that the dream motif is the structural frame of the novel. But a close look at almost any episode in which dreams play a part will reveal that dreams are even more important as message than they are as structure.

By the novel's end, for example, Hank Morgan dreams a final dream—that he is with his wife Sandy again and is telling her of some "hideous dreams" he had had: of a revolution against him, of his extermination of England's chivalry, and of his flight forward into the "remote unborn age" of the nineteenth century. And that last dream was the most torturous of them all ("Final P.S. by M.T."). Given Twain's supposd attack in the novel upon the barbarities of the sixth century, one might have expected something different than Hank's total alienation from his real or, rather, his original era.

Hank cannot be looked to for help in understanding what has happened to him. Like the Ancient Mariner, he has had a strange and distressing experience and has brought back a detailed report—but he doesn't understand the full meaning of it. This is evident from the lack of reflection he gives to the dreams which massively dislocated his existence in the first place and more subtly shaped it thereafter.

His first, contradictory impressions of sixth century England bear this out. He notices that before him was "a soft, reposeful summer landscape, as lovely as a dream, and as lonesome as Sunday." This pair of contradictory impressions (reposeful but lonesome) is immediately reinforced when a young girl appears, her head adorned with "a hoop of flame-red poppies"—beautiful but suggestive of opium "She walked indolently along, with a mind at rest, its peace reflected in her innocent face" (Ch. 1). Again, pairs of contradictory judgments: indolence and innocence, a mind at rest (by implication drugged) but peaceful.

Later in his tale, Hank observes how lack of thought characterized the inhabitants of this dreaming age. Of the knights at the Round Table he notices that "there did not seem to be brains enough in the entire nursery, so to speak, to bait a fish-hook with; but you didn't seem to mind that, after a little, because you soon saw that brains were not needed in a society like that, and indeed would have marred it, hindered it spoiled its symmetry—perhaps rendered its existence impossible" (Ch. 3). Once again, a contradictory judgment a brainless society but an attractive one in which brains would have been a blemish. And although the "child-like improvidence of this age and people" (Ch. 13) prevented the development of civilization—as Hank knew it—on the other hand, it had a symmetry and a peace, a charm, that Hank increasingly grew to prefer to his own age. Because these contradictions escape his consideration, or even his notice, Hank becomes absorbed in developing his schemes to modernize England. He admits that they are dreams but never suspects that they are just as illusionary as the dreams of everyone else, whom Hank loftily assumes to be his inferiors in perception and acumen. Thus blinded by hubris, Hank quickly accepts his new situation at face value. Once he does this, he unwittingly seals his doom, for by accepting his situation so unreflectively he forfeits his only opportunity of understanding it. Hank also becomes an unreliable narrator when he abandons himself to his dreams. The perceptive reader, therefore, can no longer look to Hank for a satisfactory account of objective reality but must seek it through interpretation, by paying closer attention to Twain's strategies.

At first, Hank does keep in mind that he is dreaming. As he awakens in the dungeon of Camelot he thinks at first, "well, what an astonishing dream I've had," but with the re-appearance at Clarence, he resigns himself: "All right. . .let the dream go on; I'm in no hurry" (Ch. 5). However,

Clarence brings news that Hank will be burned on the next day and evokes a reaction from Hank which unexpectedly discloses an essential similarity between "dream" and "reality," and illuminates how arbitrary and unimportant the distinction between the two states may be. "The shock that went through me was distressing. I now began to reason that my situation was in the last degree serious, dream or no dream; for I knew by past experience of the life-like intensity of dreams, that to be burned to death, even in a dream, would be very far from a jest, and was a thing to be avoided . . ." (Ch. 5). Hank's pregnant insight is paralleled by a comment that Twain made in an 1893 letter to Mrs. Theodore Crane: "I dreamed I was born and grew up and was a pilot on the Mississippi and a miner and a journalist in Nevada and a pilgrim in the Quaker City, and had a wife and children and went to live in a villa at Florence—and this dream goes on and on and sometimes seem so real that I almost believe it is real. I wonder if it is? But there is no way to tell, for if one applies tests they would simply aid the deceit. I wish I knew whether it is a dream or real." However it was in "real life" for Twain, for Hank at this point the distinction between dream and reality dissolves. Once he boldly steps forward into the dream to defend his existence, the dream becomes his reality from then on and his former reality the dream. He soon finds the exchange gratifying and by Chapter 8 "wouldn't have traded it [the sixth century] for the twentieth." His optimism, however, is blind. It is one of the major ironies of *A Connecticut Yankee* that while Hank boasts about his shrewdness, and compliments himself on his successes in remaking sixth century England into his dream of a nineteenth century republic, he is at the same time fatally insensitive to the implications of living in a dream.

In contrast to Twain who, inwardly at least, constantly questioned the accuracy of his perceptions and the truth of his experiences, Hank never doubts himself nor the world of appearances. As a consequence, Hank chronically over-estimates himself and under-estimates his situation. Twain's scorn for this brash cockiness can be inferred from the pattern of ironies which turn every one of Hank's "successes" into sad failures.

A case in point is the old married couple whom Hank releases from Morgan le Fay's dungeons They had been imprisoned on their wedding night in separate and lightless cells and kept there for nine years. Their cells are opened but the woman sits dumbly on the ground, unable to disturb "the meaningless dull dream that was become her life"

(Ch. 18); the man is no better. Hank brings them together, rhapsodically predicting that they will renew their love and lives. But after looking curiously at each other they resumed their "wandering in some far land of dreams and shadows" (Ch. 18). Hank's naively unintentional cruelty in trying to awaken them from their dream refuges to a sharp and painful reality contrasts strongly with Twain's very different way of handling a similar situation in his own family. In a letter to his brother Orion on July 2, 1888, on the care of their aged mother, whose senility was at least dulling the pains of her infirmities, Twain chided Orion for attempting to disrupt the comfort of her "dream" and urged him to take pity on her and restore it. The incident in the novel represents more than a chiding of Hank by Twain; it is an ominous exposure of a significant weakness in a man who would change history. He is not only unable to awaken the captive couple from their dreams, he is shown as being in the grip of a dream himself, a dream of his own power and importance.

It is this dream which manipulates Hank through most of the novel, and it is this dream which is his ultimate undoing. Believing himself free and powerful, Hank focuses his efforts on realizing his "dream of a republic" and remains enthusiastically hopeful about this dream until it collapses violently in the debacle of the Sand-Belt. That this dream was a delusion and not only could not happen but was never meant to happen can be demonstrated both by the logic of the dream structure of the novel and by the plot itself. All dreams in the novel lead to the same event: the Battle of the Sand-Belt. How that happens and what its significance is will now be made clear.

The inevitabiliy of that battle and its true meaning are established as early as Chapter 10. In a passage dense with ironies, Hank, while bragging about his surreptitious achievements, unconsciously prophesies the frightful consequences, totally unforeseen by him, that would attend England's "awakening" from its sixth century dream to Hank's dream of nineteenth century civilization. "Unsuspected by this dark land, I had the civilization of the nineteenth century booming under its very nose. It was fenced away from the public view, but there it was, a gigantic and unassailable fact . . . and as substantial a fact as any serene volcano, standing innocently with its smokeless summit in the blue sky and giving no sign of the rising hell in its bowels . . . I stood with my finger on the button . . . ready to press it and flood the midnight world with intolerable light at any moment" (Ch. 10). The passage, of course, conveys Hank's intended meaning that sixth century England was sleeping or dreaming ("dark land"—"midnight world") and that he was about to awaken it. Hank's boastful pride, however, is undercut by Twain's irony. For one thing, the internal logic of the passage is marred by contradictory impressions: *a serene* and *innocent* volcano *hiding* the *rising hell* within it, and an *unsuspecting dark* land about to be *surprised* by *intolerable light*. But if the passage is compared to the account of the Battle of the Sand-Belt, the point is quickly seen. The verbs "booming," "fenced," and "flood" and the adjective "unassailable" anticipate what happens in that awful holocaust, and "flood" even does triple duty suggesting the fatal spotlights, the surge of current through the electric fences, and the release of the torrent that drowns three-fourths of the besieging army. What Hank reveals when his hand touches the button in Chapter 42 is nothing less than the "rising hell" that is the nineteenth century.

Twain's famous—and sincere—references to the "damned human race" were expressions of the deeply characteristic gloom that was implanted or reinforced in him by his early Calvinistic training. It is present in all stages of his writing career, though it tends to be somewhat submerged in his early and middle periods. It surfaces openly and frequently in the works of the last two decades of his life, and has unmistakably theological associations despite his avowed attraction to determinism. In 1896 he suggested that humans had "no need of any hell 'except the one we live in from our cradle to our grave.'" And should anyone believe that Twain seriously subscribed to the belief in the progress of civilization, it might be well to recollect a relevant passage in Chapter 8 of "The Chronicle of Young Satan" (1897–1900). It is 1702 and Young Satan is speaking of the history of the human race:

> It is a remarkable progress. In five or six thousand years five of six high civilizations have risen, flourished, commanded the wonder of the world, then faded out and disappeared; and not one of them except the latest, ever invented any sweeping and adequate way to kill people. They all did their best, to kill being the chiefest ambition of the human race and the earliest incident in its history, but only the Christian Civilization has scored a triumph to be proud of. Two centuries from now it will be recognized that all the competent killers are Christian; then the pagan world will go to school to be Christian: not to acquire his religion, but his guns.

Twain might have had some illusions, but nineteenth century life was not one of them. Hank carried his dream of a modern republic to Merlin's cave in the midst of the fortifications in the Sand-Belt. One more, and very important, clue to *A Connecticut Yankee*'s essential unity is implicit in the symbolic significance of those fortifications. They are set in the midst of a belt of sand, itself a symbol of transience of time. They consist of twelve fences around a cave; thirteen concentric circles in all, one for each century from the sixth to the nineteenth. In Chapter 39, "The Yankee's Fight with the Knights," just after he used guns for the first time and killed nine knights with them, he crowed "The march of civilization was begun." If the march of civilization was begun with the shooting of nine knights in a tournament then it must be that the slaughter of twenty-five thousand men in the Battle of the Sand-Belt meant that the nineteenth century had arrived in its fulness. Each circle was filled with men; the closer they got to the center, the cave where the future extension of their civilization was now concentrated, the more their doom was sealed.

One of Dan Beard's illustrations of Morgan le Fay's dungeons shows a barred slit window with an arch over it bearing the inscription, "All hope abandon ye who enter here" (Ch. 18). The line, from Dante's *Inferno,* is not in the text; Beard supplied it as part of his graphic interpretation of the first edition, in 1889. But Twain knew of Dante and he certainly approved the illustration. Dante's hell consists of nine circles and is a function of sin. Twain's hell has thirteen circles and is a function of the human condition and time. Dante's hell is complete; Twain's is not; it is as endless as time. The story begins in the deepest circle of the nineteenth century, moves across thirteen centuries to the circle of the sixth century, then returns again to the nineteenth. In this scheme, there is nothing, no time that is outside of hell. All human beings are in it, all are damned and "progress," therefore, is a delusion. As in the *Inferno,* the closer one gets to the center, the deeper and more awful is the damnation. The innocent little girl with the "mind at rest" whom Hank saw when he first arrived in Camelot is damned, born into a cruel and barbarous age and destined to a hard life. Her damnation is ameliorated, however, by her inactive—her dreaming—mind. By the same token, the married couple in Morgan le Fay's dungeon have achieved some degree of peace by the escape of their minds into dull dreams; they would have been caused additional torment by the restless but chimerical plans such as those Hank devises to change his environment to his liking (Ch. 7). In Twain's circles, the more the human mind is exercised, the more it conceives of hell; the more conscious it is of its situation, the more hell it suffers.

Mark Twain, like his contemporary Dostoevsky, pondered what hell was. In *A Connecticut Yankee,* Twain used a pattern of dreams to intimate, by analogy, that human civilization's nightmarish decline to hell is more plausible as a model of reality than is the familiar daytime world's dream of progress ever onward and upward. Dante described hell as a place where the last kind ward that damned souls receive before entering it is the advice to abandon hope, because in hell hope is a delusion, a burden, and therefore even a form of needless punishment. Were Hank not in hell he would not have dreamed such cruelly impossible dreams. Not from the first page of the novel was there ever any chance of his realizing the slightest degree of success in his endeavors to reform society and bring modern civilization to the sixth century; it was not meant to be; it had not been predestined. The course of past history is, by definition, fixed, beyond change. Thus when Hank found himself in sixth century England, he was in an era whose events had already occurred and whose history had already been whiten.

Twain therefore represents the process of time as having already been determined by some superior decree, fixed into an inflexible pattern of eternal repetition, and completed in advance. This view of time is shocking in its remorselessness and the enormity of its deceit. But it is a view that is consistent with the idea that this world is hell. It is a view, moreover, that could have had its origins in Twain's Calvinist past or, even more basically, in the gloomy reflections of the Preacher. "The thing that hath been, it is that which shall be; and that which is done is that which shall be done; and there is no new thing under th sun" (Ecclesiastes 1:9). The eclipse of the sun, therefore, which Hank "providentially" remembers at the beginning of the novel is an event doubly ironic and ominous. Hank's very ability to predict it implies a fixed order in which it was already an accomplished fact. And the very existence of such a fixed order of accomplished fact implies that not only are eclipses predictable, but also all other events—because they had already happened. Hank knew from the beginning details of the historical period in which he found himself names, dates, and events. In other words, they had already happened and were fixed. But when he was unable to understand the consequences of his knowledge of the "future"—that he was in no way free to alter what had been decreed

(and also accomplished), he was doomed to a dream existence, in reality a Sisyphean labor of the damned.

A Connecticut Yankee is the last of Twain's major works in which his artistry veils the deep-rooted and desperate pessimism that was always central to both his inner life and his art. After 1889, the awful dreams which he had hitherto successfully suppressed or contained, and which are still subordinated with brilliant subtlety in *A Connecticut Yankee,* finally surfaced and increasingly became the overt subject matter of his writings. Though Twain fought Calvinism, he did not defeat it. The doubts it implanted in him about the truth of the objective world and the nature and destiny of man were supported over the course of his lifetime by his own observations and reflections and became near-convictions. In his inner and artistic life, Twain was not divided. His distinctive note was the edged jest; it was a peculiarly appropriate talent for one whose deepest and most persistent purpose was to expose life as a cruel jest.

A Connecticut Yankee, therefore, is not really about Hank, or sixth century England, or nineteenth century America either, for that matter. Twain has proposed in it a paradigm whose extrapolations bear upon his readers, whose present could be as immutably fixed to the people of "a remote unborn age, centuries hence" as that of the sixth century was to the people of the nineteenth century. In a life where individuality is only a sole "microscopic atom" (Ch. 18) or just a thought, and existence, in Hank's words, is a "plodding sad pilgrimage. . .[a] pathetic drift between the eternities" (Ch. 18), he who hopes the most is plunged into the deepest torment. As Mark Twain portrayed hell in *A Connecticut Yankee,* the best that can be done is to submit to it humbly, put one's mind at rest, and perhaps be allowed to dream of life in one of its outer circles.

Source: Lawrence I. Berkove, "The Reality of the Dream: Structural and Thematic Unity in *A Connecticut Yankee*," in *Mark Twain Journal,* Vol. 22, No. 1, Spring 1984, pp. 8–14.

Sources

Gerber, John, *Mark Twain,* Twayne's United States Authors Series, No. 535, G. K. Hall, 1988, p. 115.

Mencken, H. L., "The Man Within," in *A Mencken Chrestomathy,* Knopf, 1967, pp. 485–89.

Miller, Robert Keith, *Mark Twain,* Frederick Ungar, 1983, p. 113.

Reiss, Edmund, "Afterward," in *A Connecticut Yankee in King Arthur's Court*, Signet Classic, 1990, p. 320.

Sanford, Charles L., "A Classic of Reform Literature," in *Readings on Mark Twain*, Greenhaven Press, 1996, p. 170.

Further Reading

Cox, James M., "The Ironic Stranger," in *Mark Twain: The Fate of Humor*, Princeton University Press, 1966, pp. 222–46.

> Cox considers this novel's place in Twain's long career and finds it to be the point at which he started entering the final, worst stage of his writing life.

Davis, Sara de Saussure, and Philip D. Beidler, eds, *The Mythologizing of Mark Twain*, University of Alabama Press, 1984.

This book is a compilation of essays by and about Twain, charting the growth of his reputation.

Michelson, Bruce, "The Quarrel with Romance," in *Mark Twain on the Loose: A Comic Writer and the American Self*, University of Massachusetts Press, 1995, pp. 95–171.

> This long chapter from Michelson's excellent examination of Twain's career looks at the American Romantic tradition and Twain's relationship to it.

Robinson, Douglas, "Revising the American Dream: *A Connecticut Yankee*," in *Mark Twain*, edited by Harold Bloom, Modern Critical Views series, Chelsea House Publishers, 1986, pp. 183–206.

> Robinson's analysis of the book is steeped with philosophy and complex literary theory.

Snyder, Christopher, *The World of King Arthur*, Thames and Hudson, 2000.

> Snyder has assembled a richly-illustrated book filled with thousands of details about the time that Twayne was exploring.

Hard Times

Charles Dickens

1854

Hard Times, by Charles Dickens, was first published in serial form in the weekly magazine *Household Words*, from April to August of 1854. Set in fictional Coketown in the industrial north of England, the novel follows the fortunes of a variety of characters, including Thomas Gradgrind, who believes only in the utilitarian, "hard facts" school of thought; his dishonest son, Thomas; and his emotionally stifled daughter, Louisa. Other central characters are the boastful manufacturer, Josiah Bounderby; the manipulative idler, James Harthouse; and the virtuous but persecuted worker, Stephen Blackpool; and his saintly friend, Rachel.

Dickens's purpose in *Hard Times* was to satirize the utilitarian philosophy that recognized only the value of human reason, neglecting not only what Dickens calls in the novel "fancy" but also the values of the human heart. Dickens also wanted to highlight the harsh, monotonous lives of factory workers and to criticize the laissez-faire economic philosophy of the marketplace.

Hard Times has not usually been regarded as one of Dickens's finest novels. While some critics do regard it highly, others argue that the characters do not fully come to life. According to this view, Dickens's didactic purpose stifled his comic genius and his ability to tell an entertaining story. Be that as it may, *Hard Times* remains a powerful exposure of the ills of nineteenth-century industrialism and the philosophy that turned a blind eye to its inadequacies and injustices.

Author Biography

One of England's greatest novelists, Charles Dickens was born in Landport, Hampshire, on February 7, 1812, the son of John and Elizabeth Dickens. In 1814, the family moved to London and then to Chatham, in Kent. John Dickens, a clerk in the Naval Pay Office, was imprisoned for debt in 1824, and Charles was sent to work in a shoe-blacking warehouse for five months.

After attending Wellington House Academy in London from 1824 to 1827, Dickens became a solicitor's clerk and studied shorthand. Within a few years he had become a freelance newspaper reporter, and he published his first short story in 1833. *Sketches by Boz*, his sketches of London life, was published in 1836, the same year he became editor of a new monthly magazine, *Bentley's Miscellany*, a post he held for three years. Dickens also married Catherine Hogarth in 1836. They were to produce ten children, but the couple separated in 1858.

Dickens then began publishing novels, all in serial form, at a prolific rate. His first novel was *The Pickwick Papers* (1836–1837), followed between 1837 and 1839 by *Oliver Twist* and *Nicholas Nickleby*. Next were *The Old Curiosity Shop* (1840–1841) and *Barnaby Rudge* (1841).

In 1842, Dickens toured the United States and Canada giving lectures in which he advocated the abolition of slavery. He published *American Notes* in October 1842. Over the remainder of the decade, Dickens wrote *Martin Chuzzlewit* (1843–1844), *A Christmas Carol* (1843), *Dombey and Son* (1846–1848), and *David Copperfield* (1849–1850).

In 1850, Dickens established the weekly magazine *Household Words*, which he edited and contributed to until it ceased publication in 1859. During the 1850s, Dickens published *Bleak House* (1852–1853), *Hard Times* (1854), and *Little Dorrit* (1855–1857). *A Tale of Two Cities* (1859) appeared in *All the Year Round*, a new weekly edited by Dickens.

In 1858, Dickens gave a series of public readings from his works in London and elsewhere. Public readings became a feature of Dickens's life throughout the 1860s, including a reading in Paris in 1863 and a tour of America, which began in December 1867, in Boston. That tour continued through to April 1868, in East Coast cities, in spite of the fact that Dickens was in poor health.

During the 1860s, Dickens published *Great Expectations* (1860–1861) and *Our Mutual Friend* (1864–1865). His last book, *The Mystery of Edwin Drood*, had begun publication but remained unfinished at the time of his death at Gadshill, near Rochester, Kent, on June 9, 1870, of a stroke.

Plot Summary

Book the First—Sowing

Hard Times begins in a classroom in the fictional English industrial town of Coketown, where Thomas Gradgrind is explaining his educational principles. He believes education should be based on facts and nothing else. On his way home, Gradgrind passes a circus and is shocked when he finds his two children, Thomas and Louisa, amusing themselves there. He scolds them and takes them home.

At Gradgrind's home, Bounderby is taking pride in explaining to Mrs. Gradgrind about his deprived childhood, when Gradgrind returns and worries about his children's interest in the circus. He and Bounderby decide this is probably because Cecilia (Sissy) Jupe, one of the pupils at the school, is the daughter of one of the circus men. Bounderby gives instructions for Sissy to be dismissed from the school.

Intending to meet Sissy's father, Gradgrind and Bounderby visit the circus folk at the Pegasus's Arms. But Sissy's father has deserted her. Gradgrind agrees with Mr. Sleary, the circus owner, to take Sissy into his own house and educate her.

Bounderby tells Mrs. Sparsit, his housekeeper, that he intends to employ young Tom Gradgrind after he has finished his education. Later, Tom tells Louisa he hates the education he has received. He plans to enjoy himself more when he lives with Bounderby because he knows Bounderby is fond of Louisa, and he plans to use that to his advantage. Meanwhile, Sissy finds it hard to settle down in her new life, with her education in facts alone. She waits every day for a letter from her father, but it never arrives.

Stephen Blackpool, a weaver at a local factory, meets his friend Rachel in the street and walks her home. When he returns to his own house, he finds that his drunken wife has returned to him again. Stephen makes an appointment with Bounderby and asks whether he can divorce his wife. Bounderby says he must live with the situation. On his way home, Stephen is accosted by a mysterious old woman, who asks him about Bounderby, offering no

Media Adaptations

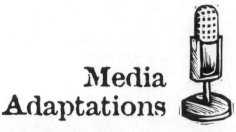

- *Hard Times* has been recorded on audiotape by The Audio Partners. The unabridged edition (2003) is read by Martin Jarvis.

explanation of why she wants the information. When Stephen arrives home, he finds Rachel attending his wife, who has been injured. During the night his wife wakes up and almost drinks some poisonous medicine. Rachel stops her in the nick of time.

Some time passes. Tom goes to live with Bounderby; Gradgrind becomes a member of Parliament, and Bounderby marries Louisa, even though she does not love him. Bounderby then dismisses Mrs. Sparsit but gives her an apartment in the bank.

Book the Second—Reaping

Bitzer, the bank messenger, informs Mrs. Sparsit that he does not trust Tom. A well-dressed stranger arrives to speak to Mrs. Sparsit, inquiring about Bounderby and his wife. The stranger is James Harthouse, who has been trained in the "hard facts" school of political thought and sent to Coketown by Gradgrind. Harthouse befriends Tom and takes a liking to Louisa, whom he realizes does not love her husband.

A union representative, Slackbridge, gives a fiery speech to the factory hands, in which he condemns Stephen Blackpool for refusing to join their union. Stephen is thereafter scorned by the other factory hands, who refuse to speak to him.

Stephen is summoned to see Bounderby, who fires him, and Stephen decides he must leave town. The mysterious old woman visits Stephen and Rachel and says she is Mrs. Pegler. Louisa and Tom also visit. Louisa gives Stephen a small amount of money to help him on his way, while Tom lays a plot that will result in Stephen being accused of robbery.

Harthouse ingratiates himself with Louisa by revealing that he knows her brother has gambling

debts. Harthouse convinces Louisa that he wishes to help Tom, but his purpose is to win over Louisa's heart for himself. Later, Tom confesses to Harthouse that he is in desperate need of money and resents his sister for not giving him more.

Bounderby reports that some money was stolen from Tom's safe at the bank. He suspects that Stephen is the culprit, since Stephen was seen lurking in the vicinity of the bank for several nights. Bounderby also suspects the mysterious old woman he has heard about. But Louisa fears that Tom might have had something to do with it.

Aided by the meddling Mrs. Sparsit, who is jealous of Louisa, Louisa and Harthouse become closer, and Louisa becomes alienated from her husband. When Bounderby is absent, Mrs. Sparsit observes Harthouse and Louisa in earnest conversation. Harthouse tells Louisa he is in love with her. Mrs. Sparsit thinks they are planning to meet in town, and she follows Louisa on the train to Coketown but then loses track of her.

Louisa confesses to her father that she hates her husband. She also confides that she may be in love with someone else, who is waiting for her to meet him. After appealing to her father for help, she faints at his feet.

Book the Third—Garnering

Louisa wakes up in her old bed at her father's house. She is comforted by her younger sister, Jane. Gradgrind is distressed about her condition and begins to doubt the wisdom of his "hard facts" philosophy.

Harthouse, who is disturbed about why Louisa has not come to meet him as planned, is confronted by Sissy at his hotel. She knows what has happened between Harthouse and Louisa, and she takes it upon herself to demand that Harthouse leave town immediately. Harthouse reluctantly complies.

In the meantime, Mrs. Sparsit has reported her suspicions to Bounderby. Summoned by Bounderby, Gradgrind refutes Mrs. Sparsit's allegations by informing him that Louisa is at his house and has no intention of acting improperly with Harthouse. Gradgrind requests that Louisa be allowed to stay a little longer at his house, but Bounderby is insulted by this suggestion. He sends Louisa's belongings along and resumes life as a bachelor.

Bounderby offers a reward for the arrest of Stephen, who is then publicly denounced by Slackbridge, the union delegate. Rachel writes to Stephen, asking him to return to clear his name.

She expects him within two days, but many days go by and Stephen does not appear.

Mrs. Sparsit confronts Mrs. Pegler, who turns out to be Bounderby's mother. It also transpires that Bounderby lied about his deprived childhood. He was, in fact, well provided for.

Sissy and Rachel walk in the country. By chance they find Stephen's hat, which lies near an old mine shaft. They realize that Stephen must have been walking back to Coketown when he fell down the shaft. They summon local villagers for assistance. After much preparation, two men are lowered into the shaft, and they return with Stephen, who is badly injured. He dies before he can receive proper medical attention.

Gradgrind is now sure that Tom is guilty of the robbery. Tom has disappeared, but Sissy knows he is hiding with the circus. Louisa, Sissy, and Gradgrind travel to the town where the circus is, where Tom confesses. The circus owner, Mr. Sleary, agrees to have Tom conveyed to Liverpool and then shipped to America. But Bitzer arrives and tries to take Tom back with him to Coketown. Sleary arranges to have them intercepted on the way, and so Tom escapes as planned.

Bounderby punishes Mrs. Sparsit by sending her away to live with her relative.

Five years later, Bounderby dies of a fit in the street. Gradgrind repudiates his former philosophy and is derided by his political associates. Rachel continues to work hard and shows compassion for Stephen's wife. Lonely, Tom dies of fever on his way home to see his sister. Louisa, although she never has children of her own, is loved by Sissy's children and does her best to stimulate in others a sense of beauty and imagination.

Characters

Bitzer

Bitzer is a boy who attends Gradgrind's school and later becomes a porter at the bank. He is clear-headed and calculating, without emotion. Near the end of the novel, when Gradgrind tries to arrange for Tom's escape, Bitzer attempts to thwart their plans by taking Tom back to Coketown. He hopes to be rewarded by Bounderby, his employer, with a promotion. In this incident, Bitzer shows he has fully absorbed his education in the "hard facts" school and acts heartlessly in his own selfish interests.

Stephen Blackpool

Stephen Blackpool is a worker at the factory. He is industrious and virtuous, showing no malice to anyone despite how badly he is treated. Stephen is trapped in a bad marriage to an alcoholic wife, who makes his domestic life a nightmare. He has a loyal friend, Rachel, but they are unable to marry because Stephen cannot afford a divorce. Stephen is ostracized by the other workers at the factory because he refuses to join their union. Bounderby decides Stephen is a troublemaker and fires him. Without any means of livelihood, Stephen leaves Coketown, only to find that he has been accused of a robbery he did not commit. Returning to Coketown to clear his name, he falls down a disused mine shaft. He dies shortly after being rescued.

Josiah Bounderby

Josiah Bounderby is one of Coketown's most important citizens. He is a rich, self-made man in his late forties, although he looks older. He is a banker, a manufacturer, and a merchant. Bounderby is an arrogant, conceited, boastful man who takes pride in endlessly repeating how he dragged himself up by his own efforts after he was abandoned by his mother as a child. He practices a kind of inverted snobbery, in which the more wretched and poor he makes his childhood out to have been, the more moral credit he can claim for himself for becoming the important, respected man he is. Bounderby has no understanding of human nature and is content to hold his bigoted opinions. He thinks all the factory workers are idlers who want a life of luxury. He badly misjudges Stephen Blackpool and has no ability to communicate with his young wife, Louisa. When she goes to stay with her father, he angrily rejects her and returns to living as a bachelor. Bounderby's ultimate humiliation comes when his mother appears and reveals in the presence of others that his claim to have been abandoned is untrue. He was in fact well provided for as a child by a loving mother.

Louisa Bounderby

Louisa Bounderby is Thomas Gradgrind's daughter. She is an imaginative child, but she is emotionally stifled by the rigid education she receives in her father's school and household. She is strongly attached to her brother Tom. She agrees to marry Bounderby, even though she does not love him. She does this in part to please Tom, who is living at Bounderby's house and wants to see more of her. Louisa resigns herself to her fate and keeps her emotions under control. She seems to expect nothing more from life than what she receives, since her father has never allowed her to dream. Her life is disrupted when James Harthouse arouses her affections. In turmoil, she goes to stay with her father and confesses how unhappy she is. Bounderby considers that she has left him, and the marriage is in effect over, although there is no divorce. Louisa lives the rest of her life trying to encourage others to live a more balanced life than mere facts can provide.

Thomas Gradgrind

Thomas Gradgrind is a local businessman who made money in the hardware trade. He prides himself on being "eminently practical" and values only facts and figures. He raises his children according to these principles, refusing to let them indulge in "fancy." He even admonishes them when he finds them trying to peep into a circus booth. Gradgrind becomes a Member of Parliament and only begins to realize the error of his ways when he discovers how unhappy his daughter Louisa is. His misery is compounded when he learns that his son, Tom, is a thief. Realizing that his "hard facts" philosophy is deeply flawed, he tries to amend his life, paying more attention to the virtues of faith, hope, and charity. He is then scorned by his former political associates.

Tom Gradgrind

Tom Gradgrind is Thomas Gradgrind's son and Louisa's brother. He dislikes the education he receives from his father and becomes a failure by his father's standard. Put under Bounderby's wing, he becomes a clerk at the bank, but he is lazy and also accumulates gambling debts. To escape from the debts, he steals money from the bank and tries to frame Stephen Blackpool for the crime. To escape justice, he is forced to emigrate to the United States.

James Harthouse

James Harthouse is a charming but cynical gentleman who has found no true mission in life. He has been a cavalry officer and has traveled around the world, but he always gets bored with what he is doing. He is recruited by Gradgrind for the utilitarian cause and sent to Coketown. But Harthouse only pretends to be a utilitarian and merely idles his time away. He ingratiates himself with Tom Gradgrind and tries to seduce Louisa, but when confronted by Sissy, he agrees to leave town.

Cecilia Jupe

Cecilia Jupe, known as Sissy, is a young girl whose father is a member of the circus. When her father deserts her, Gradgrind takes her into his house and allows her to attend his school. Sissy does not fare well at school because she is too much in touch with her heart and does not understand the school's emphasis on mere facts and figures. She and Louisa become friends, and when Louisa is pursued by Harthouse, Sissy confronts him and demands that he leave town.

Mr. M'Choakumchild

Mr M'Choakumchild is the teacher in Gradgrind's school. He is well trained and knowledgeable, but the narrator does not believe he is a good teacher.

Mrs. Pegler

Mrs. Pegler is Josiah Bounderby's mother. She appears mysteriously in Coketown without at first disclosing her identity. But when she meets her son, she discloses the true details of his upbringing, which he has falsified.

Rachel

Rachel is Stephen Blackpool's longtime friend. She shows great love and loyalty to him, even though she knows they will never be able to marry. She is with him when he dies.

Sissy

See Cecilia Jupe

Slackbridge

Slackbridge is the union delegate who gives a rabble-rousing speech to the factory workers. He excoriates Stephen Blackpool for not joining their union and later on is quick to condemn Stephen again when Stephen is accused of robbery.

Mr. Sleary

Mr. Sleary is the owner of the circus. He is a kindly old man who suffers from asthma and is frequently the worse for drink. His philosophy is the opposite of Gradgrind's; he believes that people cannot spend all their lives working and learning because they must also have their amusements. Near the end of the novel, he shelters Tom Gradgrind and makes arrangements for Tom to leave the country.

Mrs. Sparsit

Mrs. Sparsit is Bounderby's housekeeper. She comes from the distinguished Powler family, but a long time ago she entered a disastrous marriage and has since come down in the world. She takes a dislike to Louisa and takes great pleasure in the breakup of Louisa's marriage to Bounderby. Bounderby eventually dismisses her, and she goes to live with her irascible great aunt, Lady Scadgers.

Stephen Blackpool's Wife

Stephen Blackpool's wife is never named. She has been married to Stephen for nineteen years, but the marriage deteriorated early because of her love of drink. She remains a drunk who brings her husband nothing but misery.

Themes

Fact versus Fancy

Mr. Gradgrind's educational philosophy is based on the utilitarian idea that only facts and figures are important. This excludes all other values, especially "fancy." Everything in Gradgrind's world is based on facts, measurement, and strict order. Even his house, with its rigidly symmetrical design, reflects his principles, as do the grounds. Lawn, garden, and walkway are all "ruled straight like a botanical account-book."

Fancy, on the other hand, is embodied in the child's sense of wonder, which Gradgrind attempts to eradicate in his children. Tom and Louisa are not allowed to read poetry, learn nursery rhymes, or indulge in other childish amusements. Instead of toys, their nursery contains cabinets in which various metallurgical and mineralogical specimens are neatly arranged and labeled. Once, when Louisa began a conversation by saying, "I wonder," her father had replied, "Louisa, never wonder!" For him, all questions in life can be solved by calculation, by arithmetic. Anything that is not amenable to such analysis, that does not have a tangible reality, does not really exist.

Gradgrind's world of "hard facts" also excludes all the values of the heart. This is amusingly depicted when Louisa deliberates about how to respond to Bounderby's marriage proposal. Gradgrind invites her to consider only the facts. Regarding the thirty-year difference between her and Bounderby, Gradgrind offers some statistics. He informs her that a large proportion of marriages in England and Wales are between people of very unequal ages and that in three-quarters of these cases, the elder party is the man. Similar statistics apply, according to Gradgrind, to British possessions in India and in China. Having established these facts, Gradgrind asserts that the difference in

Topics for Further Study

- Should all students today receive an education in the arts as well as the sciences? How does cultivation of the imagination help a person succeed in life?

- How do the circus folk differ from Gradgrind and Bounderby? What are their values? Are they characters to be admired and emulated?

- Write a character sketch of Mrs. Sparsit. How does Dickens make her into a witchlike figure?

- Critics often argue that Stephen Blackpool and Rachel are not believable characters because they are too good to be true and that Bounderby is not believable because he is too bad to be true. Is there any truth in these views? How do you react to these characters? Why do you think Dickens created them the way he did?

the ages of Louisa and Bounderby virtually disappears. For Gradgrind, there is nothing else to consider. Louisa's feelings in the matter are not important.

Facts and statistics are at the heart of the curriculum in Coketown's school. This is why Sissy, who was raised in a circus family (the embodiment of fancy, according to Gradgrind), does not fare well there. The schoolmaster, the appropriately named M'Choakumchild, tries to convince her with statistics about how prosperous a town is if, out of a million inhabitants, only twenty-five starve to death in the streets each year. Sissy replies that it must be just as hard on the twenty-five, however many people there are who are not starving. Sissy always gives common sense answers that show she is in touch with the feeling level of life. She converts statistics into real people with real lives, which is not the way to flourish in Gradgrind's model school.

Gradgrind's dedication to facts does not work because it deprives people of vital aspects of their humanity. Louisa is forced to live an emotionally stifled life and finds herself trapped in a loveless marriage. Tom resents his education and says he would like to take all the facts and figures he has been taught and all the people who had taught them and blow them up with gunpowder. In Book Three, everything Gradgrind represents unravels. Louisa's marriage fails, and Tom is revealed as a thief. Such are the fruits of Gradgrind's "hard facts" approach to education.

The only person who thrives on the education he receives is Bitzer, who shows in his confrontation with Gradgrind in Book Three how well he has absorbed his lessons. When Gradgrind, trying to save Tom, asks Bitzer whether he has a heart, Bitzer replies in true Gradgrindian fashion: Since the blood cannot circulate without a heart to pump it, he certainly does have a heart. But it operates only according to the dictates of reason. Bitzer wants to take Tom back to Coketown because he expects Bounderby to reward him by promoting him at the bank. When Gradgrind tells him he has only his own interests at heart, Bitzer reminds his mentor that the whole social system is set up as a matter of self-interest. He is only repeating what he was taught. Gradgrind, to his distress, is hoisted on his own petard.

Evils of Industrialism

Dickens's critique of industrialism is apparent in his physical descriptions of Coketown and in his presentation of relations between owners and workers.

Coketown is an unnatural, blighted place, constructed according to the utilitarian philosophy that Dickens refers to as Fact. Everything in Coketown is designed to maximize industrial output. Nothing else matters. The town itself is disfigured by all the smoke that belches from the factory chimneys and which turns the red bricks of the houses black. The river has been polluted by bad-smelling dye, and the canal is black. All the houses are exactly like one another, and all the other buildings resemble one another, too. (The jail, the infirmary and the town hall all look the same.) Everything, including the people, has been reduced to drab conformity. The place runs according to clockwork; everyone's routine is the same, day after day, year after year. It is a place not fit for humans to live in. This is symbolized by the variety of crooked and stunted chimneys on the houses, which proclaim that anyone born under these roofs is likely to be stunted in some way, too.

Industrialism, with its emphasis on efficient production and nothing else, has ruined the lives of the workers in the factories, who toil long, monotonous hours, with little relief. Relations between the classes in Coketown are abysmal. The employers have a contemptuous opinion of the workers. They think the factory hands drink too much or stupefy themselves with opium. This hostile attitude is represented by Bounderby, who regards all the workers as ungrateful and restless, forever dissatisfied with their lot, even though, in his mind, they can afford to live well. Bounderby assumes the factory hands are all lazy and that anyone who complains simply wants a life of luxury, with "a coach and six, and to be fed on turtle soup and venison, with a gold spoon." He dismisses legitimate complaints as the work of external agitators.

Stephen Blackpool expresses the situation between the two groups in a nutshell when he says the bosses consider themselves "awlus right," while the workers are "awlus wrong," no matter what they say or do. Stephen regards the economic and political system in Coketown and beyond as a "muddle." He can offer no solution to the problem (and neither does Dickens), but he does tell Bounderby the approaches that will not work. It is no use the employers trying to defeat the workers by force. Nor will the economic policy of laissez faire favored by the utilitarians accomplish anything. Stephen calls this "lettin alone"; it refers to the policy of allowing market forces to dictate economic arrangements without interference by government. According to Stephen, this will only create a "black unpassable world" between the two groups. Most of all, Stephen says, it will not work to treat the workers as machines rather than as human beings with feelings and hopes. Bounderby's response to this is to fire Stephen.

Dickens, although often accused of writing a didactic work, offers no prescription for redeeming places like Coketown or changing economic systems that put men like Bounderby in charge of them. His final image is of Louisa doing what she can in her own small sphere to keep alive the hope of a balanced life, one not ruthlessly circumscribed by the worship of purely utilitarian considerations.

Style

Satire

Satire is the literary technique of exposing someone or something to ridicule. The intent is to arouse contempt or amusement in the reader. Gradgrind, M'Choakumchild, Bounderby, and

Mrs. Sparsit are the principle targets of satire in *Hard Times*, as well as the powers-that-be in Coketown.

For example, in Book 1, chapter 2, the description of the rigors of M'Choakumchild's training and the long list of the subjects he has studied are not meant to impress the reader with his knowledge and wisdom. On the contrary, they are set out only to mock him, as the facetious tone suggests and as the last sentence explicitly states: "Ah, rather overdone, M'Choakumchild. If he had only learnt a little less, how infinitely better he might have taught much more!" The point is that M'Choakumchild may know a lot, but he has neither the wisdom nor the skill to know how to impart it to young minds.

Sometimes Dickens uses satiric irony, in which the satire is carried out by implying the opposite of what the surface meaning of the words states. This technique can be seen in the way Gradgrind mentally introduces himself to virtually anyone he encounters:

> Thomas Gradgrind, sir. A man of realities. A man of facts and calculations. A man who proceeds upon the principle that two and two are four, and nothing over, and who is not to be talked into allowing for anything over.

The irony is that Gradgrind thinks this shows what an intelligent, "eminently practical" man he is, but of course to the reader it means the exact opposite.

Imagery

Coketown is always enveloped in clouds of smoke, which are belched out from the chimneys of houses and factories. They are described as "serpents of smoke," primarily because they trail out in a coiled shape that never uncoils. The image, which is repeated several times in the novel, suggests the ominous, life-denying quality of the industrial town, as if an evil, serpent-like spirit hovers over it. The serpent-smoke image is used in conjunction with an elephant image. The pistons of the steam engines in the factories as they move up and down are likened several times to "the head of an elephant in a state of melancholy madness," an image that gives to inanimate objects the sinister, aggressive quality of great animal power trapped in endless repetitive activity.

Symbols

Pegasus, the winged horse from Greek mythology, is used in the novel as a symbol of fancy, as opposed to fact. The circus folk, who embody the fancy-principle, live at the Pegasus's Arms, which has a picture of Pegasus on its signboard. Inside, behind the bar, is a framed portrait of "another Pegasus," one of the circus horses, "with real gauze let in for his wings, golden stars stuck on all over him, and his ethereal harness made of red silk." The circus performers make their living by riding horses and performing feats of balance, strength, and horsemanship on them. The horses are a vital part of the entertainment that the circus offers, giving people a sense of wonder, something other than facts and figures. Horses can make the human imagination soar.

The Pegasus symbol offers a devastating comment on Gradgrind's directive to the children in class (Book 1, chapter 2), to define a horse. Bitzer offers a purely factual definition, which includes this: "Quadruped. Graminivorous. Forty teeth, namely twenty-four grinders, four eye-teeth, and twelve incisive." This definition pleases Gradgrind, but of course it excludes everything symbolized by Pegasus. The point is driven home further if the flying Pegasus is seen in light of the comment made by the government gentleman to the children in Gradgrind's class. He tells them that they would never paper a room with representations of horses because such a thing would contradict reality: "Do you ever see horses walking up and down the sides of rooms in reality—in fact?" The government gentleman cannot conceive of a horse like Pegasus, but "fancy" can.

Historical Context

Industrial Conditions

During the early nineteenth century, the use of the power loom, which had been patented in 1785, rapidly became more widespread. This had a deleterious effect on the hand loom weavers, who could not compete with the power loom and could no longer find sufficient work. By the time Dickens wrote *Hard Times*, power looms were the norm and hand weaving was almost extinct. Because of this development, weavers were gradually driven from their home-based weaving to the factories in the towns, which grew rapidly in population. The new factory workers put in ten-hour days. Conditions were often dangerous, and industrial accidents were common. This subject gave rise to a heated article written by Henry Morley and published in Dickens's own magazine, *Household Words*, in April 1854. Morley claimed that over the previous three years, there had been a hundred deaths and

Compare & Contrast

- **1850s:** The groundwork is laid for universal compulsory education. In 1858, the British government appoints a commission to inquire into the state of education. The commission recommends an increase of state grants to schools, as long as the schools pass an inspection test regarding teaching standards.

  Today: All children in Britain up to the age of sixteen must, by law, receive full-time schooling. Over 90 percent of pupils receive state-funded education; the rest choose independent schooling. National targets are set for raising literacy and numeracy standards.

- **1850s:** Workers in textile mills are so poorly paid that they are forced to send their children to work in the factories as well. Government legislation reduces working hours to ten a day; weekly work hours amount to sixty.

  Today: The British government introduces a statutory minimum wage in April 1999 to reduce exploitation of low-paid workers and to ensure greater fairness in the workplace. The maximum working week is fixed by the European Union at forty-eight hours.

- **1850s:** The laissez-faire economic philosophy advocated by the utilitarians puts faith solely in the market forces of supply and demand, believing that this will deliver the greatest benefit to the greatest number of people. Utilitarians therefore oppose government regulation of economic and industrial conditions, although this does not prevent the passing of the Factory Acts in 1844, 1847, 1850, and 1867, regulating such things as the length of the working day.

  Today: Like all modern industrial nations, Britain has long ago abandoned laissez-faire economic principles. Instead, the economy is guided by government fiscal policy, which aims to produce economic stability that cannot be produced by relying solely on market forces.

---

nearly twelve thousand accidents in factories in England. These figures were disputed by other contemporary commentators, but there is no doubt that many serious accidents did occur, often caused by unguarded machinery. In *Hard Times*, there is a reference to people being "chopped up" by machinery (Book 2, chapter 1).

Factory workers sought to protect their own interests by joining trade unions, which were growing in power in the 1850s. But the unions often faced fierce opposition from employers. A notorious example of industrial conflict took place in Preston, a textile-manufacturing town in northwest England, not far from Dickens's fictional Coketown. In October 1853, between fifteen and sixteen thousand weavers went on strike for better pay. The mill owners responded by closing the mills. A bitter struggle ensued, in which the strikers were sustained only by contributions from union members in other manufacturing towns. Union leaders were arrested and charged with conspiracy. (This recalls Bounderby's threat in *Hard Times* to have Slackbridge and other union delegates arrested on felony charges and shipped off to penal settlements.)

Dickens took an interest in the conflict and visited Preston to get an idea of the mood and the conditions of life there. He attended a union delegate meeting, which gave him material for the Slackbridge episodes in *Hard Times*, and in general he gained a favorable impression of the workers and their representatives, as he recorded in his article, "On Strike," which was published in *Household Words* in February, 1854. Dickens wrote in conclusion:

> [T]his strike and lock-out is a deplorable calamity. In its waste of time, in its waste of a great people's energy, in its waste of wages, in its waste of wealth that seeks to be employed, in its encroachment on the

means of many thousands who are laboring from day to day . . . it is a great national affliction.

The Preston strikers found it increasingly difficult to survive on what they were receiving in contributions from other unions, and when the contributions began to fall off in April 1854, the strike collapsed. The strike leader was thrown into jail for debts he incurred during the strike.

Education

In 1854, there was no system of compulsory schooling in England. This was not to be established until the Elementary Education Act of 1870, the year of Dickens's death. However, there was at the time a large number of schools, differing widely in quality, methods of funding and organization, and the type of pupil who attended. The school that Gradgrind is so proud of was a non-fee-paying school for students of the lower classes, of which there were many. There was a general feeling among the educated classes that universal literacy should be achieved and that the poor should be better educated. Recognizing that teachers were often incompetent and untrained, the government had set out in the 1840s to improve teaching standards. Teacher training colleges were set up, and the first graduates emerged in 1853. In *Hard Times*, M'Choakumchild is one such newly trained teacher, although from Dickens's satirical treatment of him it is apparent that Dickens was not impressed with the results of the training program.

A review of *Hard Times*, published in the *Westminster Review* in 1854, questioned whether any school like Mr. Gradgrind's actually existed anywhere in England. The reviewer claimed that the English educational system gave as free a rein to the imagination and the study of the arts as any in the world. Dickens, as might be expected, claimed otherwise. In a speech given in 1857, he claimed to have seen too many schools in which the imagination of the children was discouraged and the pupils trained as "little parrots and small calculating machines" ("Schools I Do Not Like"). In *Dickens and Education*, Philip Collins shows that many educators at the time expressed views similar to those of Dickens. They believed there was too much emphasis on cramming the children full of names, dates, and facts but not allowing enough time for them to digest the information. There was also plenty of complaint that the schools were failing to develop the whole child and that the teacher-training curriculum was too mechanical and tried to achieve too much in too short a period of time.

Critical Overview

When first published in 1854, *Hard Times* did not receive the same praise that was customary for Dickens's other novels. Reviewers, with a few exceptions, were reluctant to hail it as an example of his best work. Some reviewers thought the book too didactic, too intent on conveying the evils of industrialism, and lacking Dickens's customary humor. Richard Simpson, in the *Rambler*, described it as a "mere dull melodrama, in which character is caricature, sentiment tinsel, and moral (if any) unsound." On the other hand, the novel did have its defenders. Well-known social critic John Ruskin called it "in several respects the greatest [Dickens] has written," although he faulted it for exaggerating the characters of Bounderby and Stephen Blackpool, making the former into a monster and the latter too perfect. But Edwin P. Whipple, in the *Atlantic Monthly*, took issue with Ruskin's positive assessment and accused Dickens of exaggerating the evils he opposed. According to Whipple, Dickens made "rash and hasty judgments on the whole government of Great Britain. . . . He overlooked uses, in order to fasten on abuses."

The status of *Hard Times* in the canon of Dickens's work has been problematic ever since. For nearly a century, it was in general regarded as one of Dickens's minor and less successful novels (although it was championed by no less a critic than Bernard Shaw). In the mid-twentieth century, however, the novel underwent a reevaluation. This was stimulated by one of the century's most influential critics, F. R. Leavis, who claimed in 1948 that *Hard Times* was a "masterpiece" and Dickens's finest novel. According to Leavis, *Hard Times* was different from other Dickens novels in the sense that Dickens's social criticisms are casual and incidental. But in *Hard Times*, "he is for once possessed by a comprehensive vision, one in which the inhumanities of Victorian civilization are seen as fostered and sanctioned by a hard philosophy, the aggressive formulation of an inhumane spirit."

This reassessment generated some controversy, and a number of critics attempted to refute Leavis's claims. Since then, *Hard Times* has had its share of detractors and defenders. It is fair to state that the novel will probably never be most readers' favorite work by Dickens. However, it seems unlikely also that the novel will fall into the neglect it had suffered before Leavis. As Paul Edward Gray states in his "Introduction" to *Twentieth Century Interpretations of "Hard Times": A Collection of Critical Essays*, "If . . . *Hard Times* is a limited success, it is also an endlessly fascinating work, fascinating both despite and because of Dickens's ambivalence toward the demands of art and argument."

Criticism

Bryan Aubrey

Aubrey holds a Ph.D. in English and has published many articles on nineteenth-century literature. In this essay, Aubrey discusses Dickens's attack, in Hard Times, *on the restrictive divorce laws in England.*

In the midst of his satiric attack on the philosophy of the utilitarians, Dickens found space in *Hard Times* to take aim at another target: the highly restrictive divorce laws that operated in England at the time.

The institution of marriage does not emerge from *Hard Times* with any credit. Three marriages are presented: the Gradgrinds, the Bounderbys, and Stephen Blackpool and his unnamed wife. Not one of these marriages is a good one (and that is not even to mention the allusions to the disastrous marriage of Mrs. Sparsit many years earlier). The worst marriage by far is between Stephen and his drunken wife. They have been married nearly twenty years, but the wife, as Stephen puts it, though he was not unkind to her, "went bad—soon." She became a drunkard, sold all the furniture, and pawned their clothes, presumably so she could get the money to keep buying alcohol. This happened again and again, in spite of Stephen's best efforts to help her. She keeps leaving him, only to return, since she knows that he must take her in. He has even tried paying her to stay away, without success. Stephen's bad marriage has turned his life into a nightmare; he has even contemplated suicide. The situation is made worse by the fact that he has a long-term friendship with Rachel, who appears to be everything his wife is not: loving, loyal, saintly. They appear to be perfectly suited, but there is no future for them, which means that Rachel's life is wasted as well as Stephen's. It is, as Stephen might say, a "muddle," and a tragic one at that.

The matter of the divorce laws was a highly topical one at the time Dickens was writing *Hard Times*. There was widespread agreement amongst the educated classes that the divorce laws were badly in need of reform. In 1853, a Royal Commission had been appointed to investigate the matter, and the following year the commission recommended that divorce be made a matter for the civil courts rather than the ecclesiastical courts. A bill incorporating the recommended changes was introduced into the House of Lords in 1854, but it faced powerful opposition and was quickly withdrawn.

Dickens's own magazine, *Household Words*, published several articles on the subject of the divorce laws, including one by Dickens himself. This was entitled "The Murdered Person" and appeared in October 1856. It was a comment on the trial, a few months earlier, of a working-class man who was convicted and hanged for murdering his wife. Dickens used the case to attack the divorce laws. He pointed out that there was no escape from a bad marriage except in certain very restricted circumstances and then "only on payment of an enormous sum of money." He cited drunkenness (the besetting sin of Stephen's wife) as one of the ills that was considered insufficient to "break the chain" that bound a man and a woman together in marriage. He continued as follows:

> The most profligate of women, an intolerable torment, torture and shame to her husband, may nevertheless, unless he be a very rich man, insist on remaining handcuffed to him, and dragging him away from any happier alliance, from youth to old age and death.

This, of course, is exactly the position that Stephen Blackpool is in. Dickens went on to point out that this kind of situation was harder on the working classes than on the wealthy. A wealthy couple trapped in a bad marriage could arrange to inhabit separate quarters in a large house and live virtually independent lives (a point that Stephen makes to Bounderby in the novel). But this was not possible for working-class couples who lived in cramped conditions, often a single room, as Stephen and his wife do. It was this situation, Dickens argued, that produced the sort of crime that, in the case he was discussing, cost two lives: the murdered wife and the executed husband.

Traditionally in England, divorce was a matter for the ecclesiastical courts. These courts would grant an absolute divorce (as opposed to a judicial separation, without the right to remarry) only in cases in which the marriage was found to be invalid due to age, mental incompetence, sexual impotence, or fraud. The only other way a complete divorce might be obtained was through a private act of Parliament. During the nineteenth century, there were usually about ten such acts passed each year, but they were not for the likes of Stephen Blackpool, because the procedure was extremely expensive. Only the wealthy could afford it. There was a case in 1845 (reported in Mary Lyndon Shanley's *Feminism, Marriage, and the Law in Victorian England, 1850–1895*) in which a working-class man was convicted of bigamy. He said in his own defense that his wife had robbed him and run away with another man. He had therefore decided to take another wife. But this argument did not influence Mr. Justice Maule, who presided over the case. He told the unfortunate defendant that he should have first brought a suit in an ecclesiastical court and then petitioned the House of Lords for a complete dissolution of the marriage bond, which would have enabled him legally to remarry. The procedure, said the judge, would not have cost the man more than £1,000. The man replied, "Ah, my Lord, I never was worth a thousand pence in all my life," to which the judge responded, "That is the law, and you must submit to it."

This interesting exchange was widely reported at the time, and Dickens would surely have known about it. This perhaps explains why Justice Maule sounds rather like that other defender and upholder of the status quo, Mr. Bounderby, who tells Stephen Blackpool that "There's a sanctity in this relation of life [marriage] . . . and—it must be kept up."

When Dickens devoted a whole chapter (Book 1, chapter 11) to Stephen's interview with Bounderby, in which Stephen seeks a way of divorcing his wife, he was making an important contribution to the contemporary debate about divorce.

Stephen reads the newspapers and is well informed. He is fully aware that in matters of divorce (as in many other matters) there is one law for the rich and another for the poor, and he points this out to Bounderby with almost the exact argument that Dickens would make two years later in his article in *Household Words*. And when Bounderby explains to Stephen that if he wants a divorce he will have to file suit with two different courts, then go to the House of Lords, and then get an act of Parliament to enable him to remarry, he is again echoing the words of Justice Maule, although Bounderby's estimate of costs is somewhat higher than that of the justice: "[I]t would cost you (if it was a case of very plain sailing), I suppose from a thousand to fifteen hundred pound. . . . Perhaps twice the money."

Dickens leaves his reader in no doubt that Stephen's marital situation is one of the chief causes of his despair. A short time after his unsuccessful interview with Bounderby, he reflects

> " In 1857, three years after the publication of *Hard Times*, the clamor for reform of the divorce laws bore fruit in the passing of the Divorce Act."

mournfully on how different things might have been, both for him and for Rachel, had he been able to marry the woman he truly loves. He thinks of how his bad marriage, in which he is "bound hand and foot, to a dead woman, and tormented by a demon in her shape," has forced him to waste the best part of his life. It changes his character for the worse every single day.

In 1857, three years after the publication of *Hard Times*, the clamor for reform of the divorce laws bore fruit in the passing of the Divorce Act. A civil court with jurisdiction over divorce was established, and the number of reasons for which a divorce might be obtained was increased. There was little comfort for the working classes, however. Although one of the stated aims of the reformers was to remove the perception that there was one law for the rich and another for the poor, the new act made it no easier for people from the lower classes to divorce, since there was only one court, in London, authorized to deal with such matters.

The refusal to ease the situation of the lower classes was deliberate on the part of the framers of the Divorce Act. Members of the House of Lords that debated the issue expressed widespread fear that easier divorce for the lower classes would unleash rampant sexual immorality. The Bishop of Oxford, for example, (quoted in Shanley) believed that such a measure would endanger "the moral purity of married life." No doubt Stephen Blackpool, had he survived his unfortunate encounter with an unused mine shaft, would have had some interesting reflections about the moral purity of married life. It was Dickens's achievement in *Hard Times* to show the realities that lay underneath the bland pieties of the ruling classes and their ignorant prejudice against the men and women on whose labor their wealth was built.

Source: Bryan Aubrey, Critical Essay on *Hard Times*, in *Novels for Students*, Thomson Gale, 2005.

What Do I Read Next?

- Dickens's *Great Expectations* (first published in serial form in 1860–1861) tells the story of young Pip and his mysterious benefactor. It has always been one of Dickens's most popular and critically acclaimed novels.

- *What Jane Austen Ate and Charles Dickens Knew: From Fox Hunting to Whist, The Facts of Daily Life in Nineteenth-Century England* (1994), by Daniel Pool, is a guide to Victorian life. The first part covers topics such as marriage, law, class, and Parliament; the second part is a dictionary of terms that commonly occur in Victorian novels and need to be explained to the modern reader.

- *Mary Barton: A Tale of Manchester Life*, the first novel by Elizabeth Gaskell, is based on a real event, the murder in 1831 of a progressive mill owner in Manchester, England. The story follows the life of Mary Barton through adolescence, love, and marriage. Set in Manchester (which was Dickens's model for Coketown) from 1837 to 1842, it presents a sympathetic portrait of working-class people as they struggle through the period known as the "hungry forties."

- *The World of Charles Dickens* (1970), by Angus Wilson, is regarded by many as the finest one-volume study of Dickens's life and work. Wilson is a novelist, and he writes with vigor, penetration, and astute judgment. The book is illustrated with a large number of engravings and color reproductions.

Anne Humpherys

In the following essay, Humpherys explores Louisa's role as daughter, wife, and single woman in Hard Times.

> "Is it possible, I wonder, that there was any analogy between the case of the Coketown population and the case of the little Gradgrinds?" Charles Dickens, *Hard Times*

In Nathaniel Hawthorne's gothic story "Rappacini's Daughter" (1844), a brilliant scientist "instruct[s his daughter] deeply in his science, [so] that, as young and beautiful as fame reports her, she is already qualified to fill a professor's chair" as her would-be lover Giovanni learns. But the father has done more: in a diabolical experiment he has had his daughter tend poisonous flowers through which she, Beatrice, becomes literally lethal: her kiss, her very breath kills. Though he has also arranged to give her a lover by infecting Giovanni with the poison, Beatrice, knowing that the antidote will be fatal to her, both sacrifices herself for her unworthy lover and rejects her father's gifts by killing herself.

The parallel between Hawthorne's gothic story and Dickens' most ungothic novel of hard facts is close. Louisa Gradgrind, like Beatrice, is the victim of a terrible fatherly experiment that the fathers justify in the same way: they intend to make their daughters more powerful. The experiments, however, are fatal both to the women and to others. Louisa's equally insufficient lover Harthouse is humiliated by his contact with her and disappears into Egypt, and though the sudden and untimely deaths of her husband and her brother are not her doing directly, they are at least metaphorically the result of their relationship with her. And in the most resonant connection, the innocent and idealized working-class hero, Stephen Blackpool, dies painfully as a result of two brief encounters with her. In a further parallel, Louisa's failure to remarry after Bounderby's death is a kind of death; like Beatrice's suicidal rejection of her father's gifts, Louisa, though she had accepted the husband her father gave her, lives out her life in the shadow of other people's happiness and fulfillment.

The father-daughter plot in these two works is archetypal—present in Western culture from the Old Testament Jeptha, Lot, and Dinah to *Iphigenia in Aulis* to *King Lear* to Jane Smiley's *A Thousand Acres*. There is a conflict in all these stories between social needs and private desires that usually surface—indeed usually generate narrative—at the point of the daughter's marriage. Daughters must move out of the family and make new alliances through marriage to keep the biological, political, and economic health of the community, but the dynamics, particularly the sexual dynamics, within the family itself resist the moving out of the daughter. Sometimes the desire to keep the daughter grows out of the father's romantic attachment to her as she supplants the woman he first loved, who has dwindled into a wife, a fictional pattern seen in *Oedipus at Colonus*, in *King Lear*, and in "Rappacini's Daughter" and *Hard Times* (Louisa is her father's "favorite child" and "the pride of his heart"). The father of Western father-daughter narratives frequently tries to negotiate his desire to keep the daughter by selecting the man she marries (not uncommonly she is given to his relative or friend), thus giving an additional turn to Eve Sedgwick's thesis of homosocial desire. But there is another reason the daughter needs to stay within the family in these narratives. She is also needed to serve, save, redeem, ultimately to sacrifice herself for the father, as does Iphigenia, Cordelia, Florence Dombey, or Louisa Gradgrind. To the degree that the Western narrative of the father-daughter concerns the redemption of the patriarch, the daughter's continued presence in the family is essential. So, as Fred Kaplan in his biography of Dickens states, Louisa's return to her father's house is the means of redeeming him even as the patriarchy in general in that novel is redeemed by sisterhood.

This benign thesis places the center of interest in *Hard Times*, as in most Western narrative, in the development of the father's story. But there is another story possible, that of the daughter. From her point of view, the sacrifice that might redeem the father can be fatal, as with Iphigenia or Cordelia. The daughter's story is not frequent in Western narrative, but "Rappacini's Daughter" suggests where we might find it, that is, in the gothic. For though Hawthorne's gothic story is centered on a representation of male abuse of knowledge and power, the daughter's story—the conflict between her desire for her father's love and her desire for self-fulfillment and autonomy—vies for center stage with the father's, particularly at closure, as it does in many gothic novels. In that most ungothic novel, *Hard Times*, Louisa's story is less visible and more problematic, but it is present intermittently, injected into the narrative not through the gothic but through the 1860s version of the gothic, the sensation novel and its interrogation of the institution of marriage.

> **Louisa's repressed feelings and self-assertion not only cause havoc among the men in her life (not to mention her own life), but they cause a little havoc in the text as well."**

The sensation novel in *Hard Times* is similar to the under-narrated sensation novel at the heart of *Bleak House* (the illicit affair of Honoria and Captain Hawden) and the undeveloped sensation novel at the bottom of *Great Expectations* (the story of Estella's mother Molly) in that, like these other marginalized women's stories in Dickens' novels, Louisa's story of the explosive potential of a woman's repressed desires generates the narrative and powers its development. Even though the novel's overt interest is in the father's story and his need for redemption, Louisa's repressed feelings about her father, her marriage, her husband, and her lover, and the actions she takes as a result of these repressions cause the reversals of fortune for both Bounderby and Gradgrind that make up both the plot and the overt themes of *Hard Times*. That is, through her self-assertive action Stephen is suspected of robbing the bank which ultimately leads to the unmasking and humiliation of Bounderby, and also through her return to her father's house, Gradgrind experiences doubt about his life's work and is turned into a "wiser man, and a better man." It is important to note that these changes in the fortunes of Bounderby and Gradgrind are not the result of the essentially passive ministering affections of a "good daughter" such as Florence Dombey or Little Dorrit. This version of the father's story in *Hard Times* is represented by Sissy, not only by her nursing presence in the Gradgrind house but also by her unquestioned forgiveness of her own father's abandonment of her. On the other hand, Bounderby and Gradgrind's fortunes change because of Louisa's subversive self-assertion—in other words, because of her similarity to a sensation novel heroine.

Louisa's repressed feelings and self-assertion not only cause havoc among the men in her life (not to mention her own life), but they cause a little havoc in the text as well. From the point of Louisa's marriage, there are a number of puzzling gaps in the story. One such gap, though a common one in Victorian fiction, is the configuration of the sexual nature of Louisa's marriage. There has been vigorous critical controversy over this subject. Louisa's physical repugnance for Bounderby (as in the scene where she tells Tom she wouldn't mind if he cut out the place on her cheek where Bounderby kissed her) and the clear sexual desire that motivates him suggests there might be some sexual trouble between them from the start. But when we meet them months after the honeymoon, Louisa and her husband appear to live calmly together, which suggests to me that, however unsatisfactory, there has been conjugal sex.

Does it matter? We know that no Victorian novel could directly depict the sexual nature of human experience even in marriage. Why should we care whether or not Louisa and Bounderby have had sex? It matters because the uncertainty about Louisa's sexual knowledge is one of a number of puzzling elements about her marriage. Her sexual experience or lack of it certainly would help us understand her feelings for Harthouse, which are rather mystified in the text. Why do her feelings for Harthouse result in her leaving her husband and returning to her father? Further, what does she have in mind in that return, and what does her father intend when he asks Bounderby to permit her to stay in her father's house "on a visit"? Finally, why does Louisa not remarry after Bounderby's death, that is, why does Bounderby die if by that Louisa is not freed to find happiness and fulfillment?

Of course, there are explanations for these events in the father's story. Louisa has to return and stay in her father's house to save him through her self-sacrifice. But in order for that story to dominate, questions about what Louisa might want must be suppressed. However, Louisa's story is not totally absent because it is part of another concern in the novel—that of marriage and divorce.

Though the introduction of the issue of divorce into *Hard Times* is as much the result of personal and political forces as narrative ones, once in the novel, it takes on a life of its own, as it were, and begins to disrupt the coherence of the narrative. Through the issue of divorce, parts of Louisa's story enter the narrative and vie for center stage with her father's story.

It is a critical truism that Dickens expressed his own boredom with his wife and marriage through Stephen Blackpool's desire for a divorce.

Kaplan says that in the portrayal of Stephen's wife, Dickens gives vent to his feelings about his wife Catherine's "incompetence, clumsiness, withdrawal from responsibility." But there was also considerable contemporary interest in the subject, for the first divorce reform bill was being debated in Parliament at the same time that Dickens was writing *Hard Times*. (The actual bill was not passed until three years later.)

The need for some reform was widely felt. As Bounderby makes clear to Stephen, divorce in 1854 was difficult, complicated, and costly. The only "cause" for divorce was adultery, which for women suing had to be "aggravated" by incest or bigamy, though, in fact, legal separations were granted women for abandonment and cruelty. (There were only four full divorces granted women prior to 1857.) Three separate legal actions, including a bill in the House of Lords, were necessary. Legal separation "from bed and board" was possible, but women in that position had no legal rights, nor a right to their own earnings, nor to custody of their children, nor could either party remarry.

But even though part of the stated motivation for reform was to protect women and increase access to divorce, the debates over the Matrimonial Causes Bill, as it was officially called, had a large element of bad faith in them. For example, efforts to scuttle the Bill entirely were cynically based on arguments that it did nothing for the poor or to equalize the position of women. In the end, divorce law reform essentially continued the status of divorce as an instrument primarily for well-off men to assure that, as Lord Cranworth put it, women not be able to "palm spurious offspring upon their husbands."

Nonetheless, given his personal situation and the current debates about divorce reform, there is nothing surprising in Dickens introducing the issue of divorce through Stephen. But once in the text, the issue of divorce, like the debates in Parliament, threatens to shift the discussion of a man's issue to women's issues. That is, in Parliament the desire to make it easier for men to get divorces opened the door to a vigorous campaign for changes in the Married Women's Property Law, while in *Hard Times* Stephen's desire to get out of a bad marriage invites us to look at all the marriages in the text and to see that, in fact, nearly all are abusive not to husbands but to wives.

Take Mrs. Sparsit, for example. The novel's plot would work as well, in fact better because more consistently, if she had been a social-climbing, money-grubbing husband hunter. Such bad behavior would justify Bounderby's humiliating treatment of her. But in fact, she was manipulated into a marriage with a boy fifteen years her junior by Lady Scadgers, probably because she thought he was a good match. In the event he is a very bad husband: he spent all his money and "when he died, at twenty-four . . . he did not leave his widow, from whom he had been separated after the honeymoon, in affluent circumstances." If Mrs. Sparsit were not so much in Bounderby's camp and so hostile to Louisa, we might notice how badly she has been treated.

More troubling, however, is Mrs. Gradgrind. Though she is generally represented dismissively throughout the novel (the list of characters refers to her as "feeble-minded"), it takes very little to see that she is in a terrible marriage. Her imbecility in fact appears to be a product of her marriage. Gradgrind chose her because "she was most satisfactory as a question of figures" and "she had 'no nonsense' about her." Though she may have been weak-minded to start with, she was presumably not at the time of her marriage an "absolute idiot." When we meet her later in her life with five children, she is close to being one. How did that happen? She herself describes the process by which she has been turned into an idiot as "never hearing the last of it," that is, when she ventures to say anything she is instantly and abruptly put down. So that "the simple circumstance of being left alone with her husband and Mr. Bounderby, was sufficient to stun this admirable lady . . . so, she once more died away, and nobody minded her." The repeated use of the word "died" in connection with Mrs. Gradgrind's ceasing to talk throughout the novel indicates the brutality of her suppression. When she is literally dying she tells Louisa "'You want to hear of me, my dear? That's something new, I am sure, when anybody wants to hear of me'" and later "'You must remember, my dear, that whenever I have said anything, on any subject, I have never heard the last of it; and consequently, that I have long left off saying anything.'"

Mrs. Gradgrind is a particularly troubling character because her brutalization is articulated (if never actually represented), but her story, like Mrs. Sparsit's, is systematically undercut by laughter, and both are meted out punishment: Mrs. Sparsit has to go live with the woman who made her marriage, Mrs. Gradgrind dies without even a claim to her own pain. While for the most part we think Mrs. Sparsit more than deserves her blighted life, the discomfort in our responses to Mrs. Gradgrind is a

sign of a disruption in the narrative that is the result, I would argue, of the interrogation of marriage introduced by the divorce plot.

But Mrs. Sparsit and Mrs. Gradgrind are minor figures. The most serious gaps in the narrative introduced by the issue of divorce concern Louisa. Most of Louisa's story is unnarrated, but one possible version is suggested, nonetheless, through the systematic analogy drawn between her and Stephen. In the structure of the novel her story alternates and contrasts with Stephen's. Louisa's questions to Sissy about Sissy's parents and their marriage were answered not only by the young girl's description of their compatible and happy marriage but also both by contrast and repetition in the two following chapters in which Stephen tells Bounderby about his own miserable marriage and wish for a divorce and then fantasizes about an ideal marriage with Rachael. More metaphorically, Stephen's subsequent murderous thoughts about his wife are followed by Louisa's capitulation to Bounderby's "criminal" proposal. Another contrast represents the emotions that bring both Louisa and Stephen to the brink of disaster: Louisa's assertion of herself in intimate, dangerous, but underrepresented conversations with Harthouse are followed by Stephen's equally dangerous self-assertions to Slackbridge and Bounderby. Louisa has two important scenes with her father; Stephen has two with his "father" Bounderby. Louisa's aborted "fall" from the bottom of Mrs. Sparsit's staircase into "a dark pit" is completed by Stephen's fall into the dark Old Hell Mine shaft. Finally, Louisa's leaving her husband and "dying" to the story is followed by Stephen's actual death.

Louisa and Stephen are further linked to Tom's betrayal of them both, while Tom's robbery of the bank acts out retribution on Bounderby for him, his sister, and Stephen (and also substitutes for Harthouse's intent to "rob" Bounderby of his wife). However, in a crucial scene in which the three are brought together by Louisa, Tom displaces his guilt and perhaps his sister's, too, onto Stephen. (Certainly both Stephen and Rachael initially think that Louisa is as guilty of using Stephen as Tom is.)

The most telling connection between Stephen and Louisa is in their equally dreadful if quite different marriages. Stephen and Louisa's responses to their bad marriages are similar: both turn to sympathetic others though they both resist acting on the needs and desires released in them by these others. The four illustrations for the novel reflect this linking of Louisa and Stephen in their responses to their marriages: two are of Harthouse, Louisa's would be lover; a third is of Stephen and Rachael with Stephen's wife, who is reaching out from the bed curtains for the poison. The fourth is of Stephen rescued from the Old Hell Mine Shaft, Rachel's hand in his while he delivers his unlikely speech on class relations. The first three point to Louisa's and Stephen's failed marriages; only the fourth relates to the industrial theme, though as we shall see, that theme is integrated with the marriage question as well.

But this parallelism between Louisa and Stephen is broken at a crucial point; Stephen's desire to end his marriage is sympathetically treated, but not achieved. On the other hand, Louisa's marital situation, while it is never narrated directly and poses a number of unanswered questions, actually ends in a permanent separation.

The steps leading to this outcome show the imbrication of the divorce plot with the father/daughter plot. Tom tells Harthouse that Louisa married Bounderby to do her brother a service, but Louisa also accepted Bounderby's proposal to please her father, whose heart was set upon it, as her mother tells her. Gradgrind for his part has given Louisa to a man "as near being [his] bosom friend" as possible, an exchange that is in the process of being repeated by Tom "giving" Louisa to his bosom friend Harthouse. But though the second exchange negates the first, it ultimately leads to the fulfillment of both Louisa's need for a "divorce" *and* the archtypal fatherly desire expressed in Gradgrind giving Louisa to Bounderby in the first place—to keep the daughter for himself.

Because the two narrative forces have the same drive—to separate Louisa from her marriage—they work together and climax in a single scene—that between Gradgrind and Bounderby that achieves the separation and makes Louisa's return to her father permanent. In that scene, Gradgrind tells Bounderby that he wants Louisa to remain with him "on a visit," a request he justifies by suggesting that Louisa, like Lady Audley, is mentally unbalanced, thus offering the strongest reason he can for the unorthodox arrangement he desires. But Louisa has never behaved in a selfish or improper way—not to Stephen to whom she gave money, not to Tom who from the very beginning recognized that he did not "miss anything in [her]," not to her father or mother, nor to her husband, and in fact she has been the soul of kindness and propriety to all (in this she resembles Oliver Twist or Florence Dombey more than Esther Summerson or Tom

Gradgrind). During her courtship by Harthouse, the narrator as much as admits that she has an incorruptible good heart: "in her mind—implanted there before her eminently practical father began to form it—a struggling disposition to believe in a wider and nobler humanity than she had ever heard of, *constantly* (my italics), strove with doubts and resentments."

But in spite of all this, her father in his justification to Bounderby says she has qualities that are "harshly neglected, and—and a little perverted." Gradgrind has to assert Louisa's mental imbalance because the separation between her and Bounderby is entirely contrary to legal definitions of separation and the attitudes that underlay the law, as articulated in this *London Times* comment on the aborted 1854 Matrimonial Causes Act: "Beyond all doubt, it is for the general public interest that marriage should be practically considered an immutable condition of life, to the end that it should not be hastily contracted, and that those placed in it should be stimulated by the pressure of necessity to accommodate themselves to one another" (15 July 1854).

Bounderby, thus, is quite correct to refuse the separation. In fact, in his response he actually uses a key word from the divorce debates. "I gather from all this" he says to Gradgrind, "that you are of the opinion that there's what people call some incompatibility between Loo Bounderby and myself," a sentiment frequently used derisively as in this *London Times* comment that "Society would be unhinged, and the next generation would be strangely educated if mere incompatibility of temper were a ground for divorce" (27 January 1857).

Nonetheless the main effect of Bounderby's ultimatum that Louisa be home by noon the next day is that Gradgrind is saved from having to explain what he means by her "perverted" qualities or to expand on his "visiting proposition" as Bounderby puts it. Louisa returns permanently to her father. It is if she never left her father's house, a situation forshadowed by both Mrs. Sparsit and her husband Bounderby's insistence on continuing to call her Miss Gradgrind and Tom Gradgrind's daughter after she is married. She thereby fulfills the father's plot of redemption, even as she acts out Stephen's desire "to be ridded" of his spouse—and perhaps Dickens' desire for the same thing as well.

But it is a hollow victory for *her*; she suffers a kind of narrative death, essentially disappearing from the narrative, dissolving into her father's story. What *her* feelings about her marriage and her husband and her return might be are unnarrated, though they have been vaguely suggested in the fire symbol and in her earlier conversation with her father about Bounderby's proposal (a chapter tellingly entitled "Father and Daughter"). Even in the climactic scene when she confronts her father and appears to speak her heart and mind, she still cannot name her own desire. In this Louisa is perhaps closer to Dickens' inner turmoil about marriage and divorce than Stephen ever is.

Even so, in this climactic confrontation between father and daughter, the daughter's story, released by the divorce plot, is the closest it ever comes in the novel to breaking through the father's story and entering fully into the text. Though Louisa does not voice her feelings about Bounderby nor her thoughts about her marriage, she admits her strong feelings for Harthouse: "There seemed to be a near affinity between us . . . If you ask me whether I have loved him, or do love him, I tell you plainly, father, that it may be so. I don't know!" she says, but "I have not disgraced *you*" (my italics).

The confrontation between a forgiving father and a sinning daughter was a familiar trope in Victorian popular literature, particularly in melodrama. Dickens' use of it here, while it keeps the titillating possibility of the daughter's "fall," significantly revises the scene. Instead of the erring daughter begging for forgiveness from the father, the almost-erring daughter accuses the father of responsibility for her faults. By this revision, the daughter's story for a moment overpowers the father's story. The emergence of the daughter's story is further strengthened by the way in which the final tableau is aborted. Catherine Gallagher, who first pointed out the melodramatic reversals in this scene, says that the conventional melodramatic father/daughter scene ends in a tableau in which the father forgives the daughter with a full embrace between them, in other words a visualization of the dynamic of the father's plot in which the daughter returns to his arms. But as Gallagher also points out, in *Hard Times* this resolution is violently disrupted; rather than seeking a forgiving embrace, Louisa begins to fall to the floor; as her father "tightened his hold in time to prevent her sinking on the floor . . . she cried out in a terrible voice, 'I shall die if you hold me! Let me fall upon the ground!'" Like Beatrice Rappacini, Louisa rejects the conventional relationship and insists on controlling her own story.

Finally though, I differ from Gallagher's reading of this scene. She sees in the failure of the confrontation to end in the loving embrace a sign that Gradgrind saves Louisa by letting her go. That certainly would be the way the daughter's story should develop. But unfortunately it does not really happen that way in the novel. It is true that Gradgrind does not embrace Louisa; instead he passes her off to Sissy, who puts her to bed, and after a subdued exchange in which the daughter forgives her father, the two women act out the melodramatic trope precisely. Louisa "fell upon her knees" and cries "Forgive me, pity me, help me! Have compassion on my great need, and let me lay this head of mine upon a loving heart." Sissy acts for the father by reintegrating Louisa into the paternal sphere through *her* embrace: "O lay it here! . . . Lay it here, my dear." Sissy then somewhat astonishingly continues to act for the father by sending Louisa's lover away. (Gradgrind is willing to play the father's role to the husband he has chosen for her, but not to the lover she has picked for herself, showing perhaps once again the power of Eve Sedgwick's model of homosocial desire.) One reason the scene between Sissy and Harthouse has struck most readers as unbelievable—even ridiculous—is because this melodramatic confrontation is conventionally acted out by either the father or the brother. As the good daughter, Sissy's assumption of the father's role here cannot really work.

Daniel Deneau has argued that Louisa must have had no real feelings for Harthouse because he is never referred to again after Sissy sends him away. But Sissy's "second object" in her conversation with Harthouse suggests something different, for there seems little reason to make him leave immediately and forever if Louisa, who has given Sissy "her confidence," is not still in some danger from her own heart and Harthouse's presence. The fact is, we have no idea *what* is on Louisa's mind; from the point she returns to her father's house, her story remains untold. Not only is Louisa not "saved," her story essentially disappears from the text.

With the return of Louisa to her father and the disappearance of Stephen, the father's story emerges as the only story and the issue of marriage and divorce is also erased from the text. This narrative move is achieved more or less seamlessly because of the imbrication of Stephen and Louisa—he representing the industrial theme, she the education theme and the divorce theme moving between them. In fact, issues of class and gender frequently were substituted for issues of marriage and divorce in the divorce reform debates. The reason for making divorce more difficult for the poor and for wives, members of Parliament argued, was that "the poor and women [are] particularly susceptible to moral lapses," as Mary Lyndon Shanley says. "Parliament's fear of the disruptive potential of female sexuality was as great as its distrust of the unrestrained passions of the poor." However, the debates on divorce reform achieved precisely what Parliament feared; they inevitably opened the way for women's issues and working-class issues to enter the arena of public concern.

The sensation novel worked in a similar way, though the development is reversed. These novels examine women's desires and the inadequacy of middle-class marriages to fulfill them, but in the conclusion they reinscribe the "heroine" into conventional roles. Lady Audley, who dared to make her own destiny, is declared even by herself to be "mad" and thrust out to die in a lunatic asylum; the self-reliant and adventurous Magdalen Vanstone in Collins's *No Name* falls into a death-like illness to be reborn as the passive wife of a sea captain.

The ending of *Hard Times* resembles in a general way these sensation novel's endings. Both Louisa and Stephen end badly, arguably Stephen worse than Louisa though her brother Tom's rejection of her compounds her lonely future. Louisa, even though she has not fully acted on her desires—she has not run away with Harthouse—lives unpartnered, a guest at the banquet of Sissy's domestic happiness, doing her father's work, atoning for his sins. Stephen dies painfully by falling down a mine-shaft.

The gratuitousness of Stephen's death and the underexplained events that lead up to it suggest how difficult it is in the end to integrate the gender and class issues involved in the divorce plot into the conventional father's story which dominates the last pages of *Hard Times*. In his final words, Stephen seems to lay the blame for his death on the misunderstandings between capital and labor—fathers and children—but actually his death has come about because of his terrible marriage and frustrated relationship with Rachael. The focal point for both this relationship and his death is his promise to Rachael. As many critics have pointed out, this promise is inexplicable, but even more puzzling is why Rachael does not release him from it when she sees what the result of his adhering to it is. And why does Stephen, whose refusal to join his fellow workers is based on this promise to Rachael to avoid trouble with the masters, then insist on justifying his colleagues to Bounderby, thereby essentially provoking his master into

dismissing him, thus achieving precisely what Rachael made him promise to avoid? And most importantly, why are these actions followed by such a painful and gratuitous death?

Stephen's death has been justified as Dickens' recognition that there is no way out of the class war. Nicholas Coles says "Stephen is killed off by the combined forces of both classes . . . and there is no manner of hope in either of them." However, if we think of Stephen's story as it connects to Louisa's through the marriage and divorce plot, we may see an additional reason for his death. Though overtly Stephen is the only one whose miserable marriage seems to call for divorce, the linking of Louisa and Stephen has opened a crack through which we see that for women much less dramatic situations than Stephen's make marriage a repressive institution. Though intermittently in evidence, this insight has been downplayed through laughter at Mrs. Sparsit and Mrs. Gradgrind and through narrative silence about Louisa. But in order to completely erase this story so the father's story can dominate the closure, the divorce issue must be killed *in* Stephen, who has been its overt spokesman.

This is Louisa Gradgrind's secret: she killed Stephen Blackpool, though unlike Lady Audley she did not personally push him down the well. Louisa's action of seeking Stephen out in his home, accompanied by her brother as an escort, has led to the suspicion of Stephen's robbing the bank, his hurried return, and ultimately his death. Further, Louisa also narratively necessitates Stephen's death. Though she is the embodiment of the sensation heroine's story of repression and lack of fulfillment in marriage, Stephen has carried the weight of her story. So even as she cannot remarry, though the healthy Bounderby dies five years after the separation, Stephen cannot live to marry Rachael. The sick Mrs. Blackpool survives, the healthy Stephen dies, thereby removing the last vestige of the divorce plot. The novel ends where it began—with the now-chastened father and sacrificed daughter together again, and for all time.

Dickens' letters emphasized what a strain the writing of *Hard Times* was for him, and when he finished he remarked "Why I found myself so 'used up' after *Hard Times* I scarcely know." Usually this is understood in terms of his struggle with the weekly number format. But I think that there are other tensions at work as well: the introduction of divorce into the novel (for whatever reasons Dickens did so) is a disintegrating force. Perhaps the struggle to contain and ultimately eliminate that force also contributed to Dickens' creative exhaustion. (Of course, Dickens had personal reasons for not wanting to concentrate on divorce from the woman's point of view.)

Kaplan remarks that the subject of divorce was still on the novelist's mind even after he finished *Hard Times* when he made an entry in his notebook about a proposed story of "a misplaced and mismarried man." While the "mismarried" is perfectly understandable to us in terms of Dickens' own situation, the "misplaced" is a more curious expression. It suggests a helplessness in the unfolding of one's life, a definition of life as one of accidental placement and lost possibilities rather than fatal choices or actions, a sense that life's miseries as well as its happinesses are the result of where one is placed and not of what one is. And even as the word "misplaced" perhaps gives poignant insight into Dickens' state of mind, it can also serve as a kind of coda to the glimpses of another "misplaced" person—Louisa. Thinking of himself perhaps but speaking for Louisa even as she has spoken for him, Dickens says, as he develops the idea for his story of the "misplaced and mismarried man," that he—or she—is "Always, as it were, playing hide and seek with the world and never finding what Fortune seems to have hidden when he was born."

Source: Anne Humpherys, "Louisa Gradgrind's Secret: Marriage and Divorce in *Hard Times*," in *Dickens Studies Annual*, Vol. 25, 1996, pp. 177–95.

Stanley Friedman

In the following essay, Friedman explores the many connections between Stephen Blackpool and Louisa Gradgrind in Hard Times, *focusing especially on their emotional states and the inability of society to support them.*

In *Hard Times*, the initial eight chapters, originally published as the first four of twenty weekly installments, start a narrative that seems as though it will be primarily concerned with Mr. Gradgrind, the apostle of facts. Moreover, a number of the titles originally considered for this novel definitely imply such an emphasis: for example, "Thomas Gradgrind's facts," "Hard-headed Gradgrind," "Mr. Gradgrind's grindstone," and "Our hard-headed friend." But Gradgrind, despite the importance of his eventual conversion, is not the focal center of *Hard Times*. In the fifth installment, two shifts of interest occur: the ninth chapter suggests that Sissy Jupe, the abandoned daughter of a circus clown, may become the main figure, and Chapter 10 introduces a new character who strongly commands our attention, Stephen Blackpool. Sissy, however, quickly fades from view and returns to prominence only late in the narrative. During the last fifteen of the original twenty installments, the role of protagonist appears to be divided between Stephen and Louisa, Gradgrind's restless oldest child, two persons whom Dickens connects in a truly extraordinary number of ways, their differences in age, sex, class status, and temperament notwithstanding. An odd couple, "Old Stephen," the forty-year-old mill-worker who has led "a hard life," and young Louisa, the pretty daughter of the wealthy Mr. Gradgrind and later the wife of the even more affluent Mr. Bounderby, Stephen's employer, serve as paired protagonists, alike in some respects, complementary in others, victims of an ethos that cherishes facts, statistics, and reason, while showing a concomitant disregard for imagination and feeling. As the fates of both Stephen and Louisa demonstrate, men and women in diverse social strata may suffer greatly in a nation marked by an insensitivity to basic emotional needs.

Stephen's difficulties with his debased, alcoholic wife, his co-workers, and Bounderby, as well as his falling under suspicion of bank theft and his accidental death, make up a story that Dickens interweaves with an account of the perils faced by Louisa because of her upbringing and the actions of her brother Tom, Bounderby, and James Harthouse. Although the narrator gives much more attention to Louisa than to Stephen, the latter's death-scene seems to be the novel's main climax. Furthermore, throughout most of *Hard Times* both of these characters are very closely linked, not only by the obvious fact that each is caught in a disastrous marriage, but also by many other parallels in situations and in relationships, as well as by similar details in settings and imagery. A reader may not consciously note each connection, but the cumulative effect of these numerous ties helps to unify the story. While Dickens wishes to make *Hard Times* an attack on some features of utilitarianism, he seems not wholly comfortable writing a "thesis-novel." Consequently, he seeks to give his narrative coherence and impetus by inducing us to care about the interwoven destinies of Stephen and Louisa.

* * *

Just as David Copperfield is susceptible to the antithetical influences of a "good angel" and a "bad" one—Anges and Steerforth—so each of the

> " Both Stephen and Louisa can be seen as victims of the 'Facts' philosophy's effects on the nation and on individuals."

two protagonists in *Hard Times* is menaced by a diabolical character and assisted by a saintly one. Stephen, contemplating his marital plight, thinks that he is "bound hand and foot, to a dead woman, and tormented by a demon in her shape," and the narrator later calls this person Stephen's "evil spirit." Similarly, when James Harthouse, the man who will try to seduce Louisa, first appears to Bitzer and Mrs. Sparsit, we are told "that he was a thorough gentleman, made to the model of the time; weary of everything and putting no more faith in anything than Lucifer." After meeting Tom, Harthouse behaves "as if he knew himself to be a kind of agreeable demon who had only to hover over him, and he must give up his whole soul if required." The narrator refers to this character as Tom's "tempter" and "powerful Familiar," but the diabolic qualities are given even more emphasis in the account of the ways in which Harthouse approaches Louisa: "When the Devil goeth about like a roaring lion, he goeth about in a shape by which few but savages and hunters are attracted. But, when he is trimmed, smoothed, and varnished, according to the mode; . . . then, whether he take to the serving out of red tape, or to the kindling of red fire, he is the very Devil." When subsequently reproached by Sissy, Harthouse concedes, "I . . . have glided on from one step to another with a smoothness . . . perfectly diabolical."

Stephen is tortured by his "evil spirit," a woman who suddenly just "went bad," as the weaver expresses it. In the original installment version of the novel in *Household Words*, Bounderby opens a very brief description of her decline with the statement that she "found other companions," but later editions omit this detail, the only semblance of an explanation for the great change (Ford and Monod 250). As Stephen's "long, troubled dream" indicates, his anguish over this abusive woman tempts him to violate the divine commandment against murder. Soon after, when his wife is about to make the fatal error of drinking a

poisonous liniment, the weaver finds himself powerless to speak or move.

Stephen is, of course, saved from the guilt of his inaction by Rachael, whom he twice tells, "Thou art an Angel," and then adds, "it may be, thou hast saved my soul alive." Earlier, the narrator has mentioned that, to Stephen, Rachael "looked as if she had a glory shining round her head." Later, speaking to Luisa in his room, the weaver once more calls Rachael "th' Angel" of his life.

Rachael, at a time before she prevents Stephen's wife from drinking the poison, had ministered to the ailing woman and then remarked, "When she gets better, Stephen, 'tis to be hoped she'll leave thee to thyself again, and do thee no more hurt," a hope that is later evidently fulfilled. In a sense, therefore, the good angel tends to the bad one and then dismisses her.

While Stephen's "evil spirit" tempts by tormenting, Louisa's devil torments by tempting. Harthouse, learning from Tom of her strange upbringing and marital discontent, uses her affection for her brother in trying to lead her to break the commandment against adultery. Although Louisa has the strength to resist and flee to her father's home, the prospect of love brings her to a mental crisis. Telling Gradgrind for the first time that she grew up with "a hunger and thirst . . . which have never been for a moment appeased," she refers to the conflict his system created by requiring her to struggle to suppress her instincts: "In this strife I have almost repulsed and crushed my better angel into a demon." This remark refers to her own inner qualities rather than to persons—to her angelic desire for emotion and imagination and to the demonic traits of doubt and aloofness—but the comment seems to recall the very recent escape from Harthouse, a diabolical seducer, and to anticipate the renewal of Louisa's relationship with the saintly character who will assist in her recovery, Sissy.

Although Sissy is not explicitly called an angel, she clearly deserves this appellation. An early review of *Hard Times*, after noting that Rachael, "a fellow 'hand' of pattern goodness," is Stephen's "guiding star," adds, "A star of the same kind is supplied to poor Louisa, in her trouble, by Sissy Jupe." Gradgrind himself senses Sissy's mysterious power: "Somehow or other, he had become possessed by an idea that there was something in this girl which could hardly be set forth in a tabular form." When Sissy subsequently comes to offer comfort to the remorseful, distraught Louisa, the latter "fall upon her knees, and clinging to this stroller's child looked up at her almost with veneration," before making a prayer-like request: "Forgive me, pity me, help me! Have compassion on my great need, and let me lay this head of mine upon a loving heart!" Significantly, just as Rachael, Stephen's good angel, handles his problem with his "evil spirit," so Sissy, Louisa's good angel, performs the task of persuading the devil, Harthouse, to retreat. Sissy's angelic status is again emphasized when Louisa, seeking to comfort Gradgrind after Tom's crime has become known to him, promises that his three younger children "will be different," then adds, "*I* will be different yet, with Heaven's help," and gives "her hand to Sissy, as if she meant with her help too." Upon later learning that Sissy has found a means of saving Tom from arrest, Gradgrind "raised his eyes to where she stood, like a good fairy in his house."

Of course, the two good angels—Rachael and Sissy—eventually join forces to find Stephen and to seek assistance for him. After the mortally injured Blackpool is brought up from the mine-shaft, Sissy induces Sleary's troupe to shield Tom, whose attempt to cast blame for the bank theft on Stephen caused the weaver to embark on the trip leading to the fatal accident. Being victimized by Tom further ties Stephen to Louisa, since she has also been betrayed by this "whelp," who induced her to marry Bounderby, extracted money from her, and then made Harthouse aware of her marital unhappiness.

Stephen and Louisa are additionally linked in that each is caused anguish by an outsider who comes to Coketown, the ugly Slackbridge and the handsome Harthouse. In the chapter in which Harthouse first appears, he is referred to only as a "stranger." Although we are meant to laugh at Bounderby's later attempt to attribute the workers' unrest to Slackbridge, whom the employer calls one of "the mischievous strangers who are always about," the organizer ironically is a mischievous stranger, and he encourages the ostracism of Stephen, a punishment that leads directly to the weaver's second interview with Bounderby, his dismissal from the mill, the visit to his room by Louisa, the plot concocted by Tom, whom Louisa took as an escort, and Blackpool's subsequent death. When Stephen is suspected of complicity in the bank theft, belief in his guilt is expressed by both Harthouse and Slackbridge. Both outsiders also leave Coketown suddenly, Harthouse being persuaded to depart by Sissy and Slackbridge seeming simply to disappear from the scene after convincing the union members to condemn the missing Stephen as a "proscribed fugitive."

Just as Stephen's close escape from committing murder occurs soon after he has a nightmare about being on the executioner's scaffold, so Louisa's avoidance of adultery is preceded by descriptions of Mrs. Sparsit's frequent daydreams expressing a desire for the younger woman's sexual disgrace. The narrator observes that Mrs. Sparsit, although "not a poetical woman," develops "an allegorical fancy": "She erected in her mind a mighty Staircase, with a dark pit of shame and ruin at the bottom; and down those stairs, from day to day and hour to hour, she saw Louisa coming." This figurative "dark pit," towards which Louisa gradually descends, is analogous to the "black ragged chasm," the abandoned mine-shaft, into which Stephen suddenly drops. Even though Louisa avoids a "fall," which would have made her an outcast like Blackpool, she does collapse, "an insensible heap," at Gradgrind's feet, and Stephen is later brought up from the pit "a poor, crushed, human creature," a "form, almost without forth."

Other parallels also connect Stephen and Louisa. The watchful Mrs. Sparsit first sees Blackpool lurking near the bank, an observation that leads to his unjustly falling under suspicion of theft, and Mrs. Sparsit subsequently, after extensive spying on Louisa, wrongly accuses her of adultery. During the rainstorm, Louisa has fled to her father and avoided misconduct, and we may recall the earlier rainstorm during which Stephen, with Rachael's assistance, escapes from the temptation to commit murder.

When the distressed Louisa asks Gradgrind to shelter her, the meeting provides an ironic contrast with the prior scene between father and daughter in the same room, at the time that they discussed Bounderby's marriage proposal. These two highly significant interviews between Louisa and her father seem balanced by the two climatic confrontations between Stephen and his employer: during the first meeting Blackpool is told there is no help for his marital problems, and during the second he is dismissed from his job. Although Stephen requests the first meeting, he is summoned to the second, a pattern that is reversed in Louisa's two interviews with her father. For each protagonist—Stephen and Louisa—the second meeting leads to a separation from Bounderby. During Stephen's first interview, Bounderby's callous indication that the law cannot help a poor man seeking divorce leads the weaver to remark several times "'*tis* a muddle," an assessment that he restates during the second meeting with Bounderby and reiterates when dying. Louisa's first long discussion with her father leads the young woman to a comparable expression of moral confusion, her repeated query, "What does it matter?" a question to which she returns when she afterwards wonders how to respond to Harthouse's overtures. Of course, Blackpool's view of life as a "muddle" gives way to his dying affirmation of faith in a guiding star, while Louisa eventually finds strength and comfort in the love offered by Sissy.

These two sets of interviews are also connected by a few other features. Stephen's initial meeting with Bounderby takes place during a rainstorm, as does Louisa's second interview with her father. Stephen's temptation to murder occurs on a night soon after the first discussion with his employer, while Louisa's near-seduction directly precedes her second climactic scene with Gradgrind.

During this second meeting, Gradgrind experiences a conversion, a change that leads him to acknowledge the inadequacy of his prior philosophy. Shaken and sorrowful, he seeks to offer reparation to Louisa, beseeching her, "What can I do, child? Ask me what you will," and then arranging for her to stay in his home and be cared for by Sissy. Similarly, Gradgrind is later the one to whom the dying Stephen turns for reparation: "Sir, yo will clear me an' mak my name good wi' aw men. This I leave to yo."

The vulnerability of each protagonist—Stephen and Louisa—is increased because of affection for another person. Since Stephen adores Rachael, he promises her not rejoin the union, a promise that results in his being ostracized, while Louisa's love for her brother Tom induces her to marry Bounderby. To underscore the resemblance, the narrator ends one of the two chapters in the seventh weekly installment with a night scene in which Stephen, in the road outside the building where he dwells, watches Rachael walk away, while the other chapter in the installment concludes its Louisa stands at night outside the door of her father's home and listens to Tom's "departing steps."

* * *

Nearly all of the dramatic intensity in the tenth through the nineteenth of the twenty original weekly installments is created by two immoral schemes: Harthouse's attempt to seduce Louisa and Tom's plot to have Stephen blamed for the theft from the bank. Although both plans ultimately fail. Tom's leads, as we have noticed, to Stephen's death, while Harthouse's ironically produces a beneficent result, since the crisis it creates for Louisa brings about her reconciliation with Sissy and her separation from Bounderby. But although

Louisa then proceeds to cultivate the emotional life that she was previously trained to suppress, Dickens stresses the fact that her future happiness remains limited.

Both Stephen and Louisa can be seen as victims of the "Facts" philosophy's effects on the nation and on individuals. Blackpool suffers because a political system made insensitive by excessive enthusiasm for rationality, statistics, and the doctrine of *laissez-faire* fails to assist him in three important areas: Parliament tolerates unfair divorce laws that can be used only by the very wealthy but offer no redress to the poor; it does not provide adequate supervision of working conditions, a neglect exemplified by the lack of legislation requiring proper fencing in of dangerous machines (like the one that maimed Rachael's younger sister); and it does not compel owners of coal mines to close up abandoned pits. In addition, Stephen is betrayed by the callous cruelty of Bounderby and the calculating treachery of Tom, two coldly selfish men who also do great harm to Louisa.

Nevertheless, while the sufferings of Stephen and Louisa support the validity of Dickens' views about the danger of Gradgrind's philosophy, these two victims also make us notice some of the limitations of this thesis. Although Louisa has been damaged by her father's destructive system of education, she nevertheless shows notable kindness in her early relations with Sissy. When the latter, speaking of her father's recent deterioration, starts to sob, Louisa "kissed her, took her hand, and sat down beside her." Later, when the young child asks Gradgrind if he has received information about her missing father, Louisa's eyes "follow Sissy with compassion." Louisa's subsequent withdrawal from Sissy seems prompted mainly by shame at having accepted Bounderby's proposal. Moreover, despite the change in behavior towards Sissy, Louisa continues to display generous impulses. Stephen Blackpool, harassed during his second interview with Bounderby, begins "instinctively addressing himself to Louisa, after glancing at her face," for he correctly senses her sympathy.

Stephen himself is also kind and considerate. Despite his "instinctive propensity to dislike" Mrs. Pegler, an impulse undoubtedly attributable to his unwitting recognition of some physical resemblance to Bounderby, her son, Stephen treats this strange old woman with great gentleness and tact, apologizing when his question, "Onny children?," seems to cause distress. Very soon after—in the same chapter—Louisa, after asking Stephen whether Rachael is his wife, blushes and states re-assuringly, "it was not my meaning to ask a question that would give pain to any one here," another minor detail tying the two protagonists together. Even though Stephen has not, as far as we know, been oppressed by an education like Louisa's, we may wonder if his upbringing included any specific nourishment of his fancy, the kind of instruction that Dickens believes will lead to compassion and unselfish concern for others. Bluntly denying that Stephen is "a particularly intelligent man," the narrator nonetheless notices that the weaver's room includes a "few books and writings . . . on an old bureau in a corner," but we never learn what these texts are. Certainly, the daily environment of Coketown is not responsible for Stephen's unselfishness and sensitivity.

As Blackpool is dying, he mentions his prayer "that aw th' world may on'y coom toogether more, an' get a better understan'in' o' one another," a reference to the need to close the rift between classes in mid-Victorian England. In responding, Louisa affirms, "your prayer is mine," as the novel's two main victims join in hoping for national redemption.

* * *

The account of Stephen's final comments and of his death may be regarded as the major climax of *Hard Times*, for most of the one remaining weekly installment (the novel's last three chapters) seems somewhat perfunctory, despite the excitement of Bitzer's last-minute apprehension of Tom, the amusement provided by Sleary's story of the ensuing escape, and the pathos in the ringmaster's speculation that the reappearance and demise of the dog Merrylegs are an almost certain sign of the death of Sissy's father. In Dickens's brief concluding chapter, the dismissal of Mrs. Sparsit is followed by a short survey of the subsequent lives of this woman, Bitzer, Bounderby, and Gradgrind. We then are asked to contemplate Louisa, "watching the fire as in days of yore, though with a gentler and a humbler face." Asking what she sees of the future, the narrator notes the broadsides and the tombstone epitaph exonerating Stephen, the continued saintly serenity of Rachael, and the remorseful death of Tom. But the three final paragraphs in *Hard Times* are strangely unsettling. First, we are teased by a possible prospect for Louisa: "Herself again a wife—a mother—lovingly watchful of her children, ever careful that they should have a childhood of the mind no less than a childhood of the body . . . ?" We are soon

surprised, however, by the stern, severe words, "Such a thing was never to be."

The fate then described—the view of Louisa winning the love of "happy Sissy's happy children" and of "all children" through her dutiful efforts to foster "imaginative graces and delights"—reminds us not of the future awarded to Esther Summerson, the protagonist of Dickens's immediately preceding novel, *Bleak House*, a heroine who gains happiness despite her dismal childhood, but of the lot assigned to Em'ly, the tarnished fallen woman in the yet earlier *David Copperfield*, a character whose life in Australia is celibate and saintly, a model of penance.

Both Stephen and Louisa remain victims, characters whose destinies are lamentable, since the emphasis is on loss, not fulfillment, even though the narrator provides religious consolation for Stephen and some degree of secular solace for Louisa in the redemptive satisfactions of her vicarious maternal role. The sad life and premature death of one figure, as well as the unfortunate youth and limited later happiness of the other, illustrate the shortcomings of a society that hinders instead of assisting the search of men and women for emotional nourishment. By skillfully keeping our attention fixed on these two examples of suffering humanity, Dickens seeks to win for them a sympathy that will induce us to stand against the forces that diminish sensitivity and compassion. As Stephen and Louisa confront nearly simultaneous crises, their fates are intricately interwoven, for *Hard Times* finally stresses not the differences that divide the social classes but the kinship that unites.

Source: Stanley Friedman, "Sad Stephen and Troubled Louisa: Paired Protagonists in *Hard Times*," in *Dickens Quarterly*, Vol. 7, No. 2, June 1990, pp. 254–62.

Lewis B. Horne

In the following essay, Horne seeks to define "the quality of the special period and place" in Hard Times *and exposes Dickens's deep-rooted criticism of utilitarianism.*

Although the Times referred to in the title *Hard Times for These Times* apply to a special period and place, the term also suggests Time in the sense of continuous duration—through past, present, and future. Recent studies point up the extent to which a consideration of Time can bear on Dickens's work, as well as some of the problems involved. George Ford, for example, suggests that Dickens shares with George Orwell a sense of 'divided allegiance toward past and future,' but goes on to demonstrate most forcefully how this divided allegiance—through Dickens's changing attitude toward the past—contributed so powerfully to his art. Such a contribution can be seen, I believe, in *Hard Times*. To demonstrate this I would like to apply to the novel one of the ideas Carlyle presents in 'Natural Supernaturalism,' probably the climatic chapter of *Sartor Resartus*. Here through the character of Diogenes Teufelsdröckh, Carlyle discusses those obstacles that block man's sense of the miraculous and wonderful, pointing among other hindrances to Space and Time. These 'two grand fundamental world-enveloping Appearances' blind 'our celestial ME,' he writes. It is the impact of the second of these Appearances on the world of *Hard Times* that I wish to investigate here. I wish to define further the quality of the special period and place described in the novel and to clarify certain features of character, and in doing so to point out in another way how deeply Dickens's criticism of utilitarian belief runs.

In *Hard Times* both city and citizen are bound by Time. Coketown with its 'interminable serpents of smoke' and its elephant-machines moving 'in a state of melancholy madness' is fettered by Time. It is inhabited by people 'who all went in and out at the same hours, with the same sound upon the same pavements, to do the same work, and to whom every day was the same as yesterday and tomorrow, and every year the counterpart of the last and the next.' Many of its effects are apparent. In Coketown, like its machines, 'Time, with his innumerable horse-power, worked away, . . . and presently turned out young Thomas a foot taller than when his father had last taken particular notice of him.' After passing 'Thomas on in the mill,' Time 'passed him on into Bounderby's Bank, made him an inmate of Bounderby's house . . . .' Likewise, 'the same great manufacturer . . . passed Sissy onward in his mill, and worked her up into a very pretty article indeed.'

A second force in the novel, more frequently noted and dramatically more powerful than Time, is that which views life as governed by Fact. This force, too, is connected with Time.

Fact exists in the present. Once it acquires being, once it is fully verified, Fact does not require its past. As statement, Fact is not concerned with how things *were* or how things *will* or *ought to be*. A fact is a result, a conclusion, an end—finished with its past, without need of its future. 'Two plus two equals four': the Fact exists. A statement dependent upon the future for proof is not Fact but

speculation. A statement looking to the future for fulfillment is not fact but Wish. For Gradgrind, Fact is immediately verifiable: 'Why, then, you are not to see anywhere, what you don't see in fact; you are not to have anywhere, what you don't have in fact.' To see, to have: the activities exist in the present tense and nullify what a person 'would' do with carpets and flowers and wallpaper and horses. Like the titles of the first two chapters of *Bleak House*—'In Chancery' and 'In Fashion'—the phrase 'in fact' comes to denote a state of being. Consider Mr Gradgrind's statement:

> You are not to have, in any object of use or ornament, what would be a contradiction in fact. You don't walk upon flowers in fact; you cannot be allowed to walk upon flowers in carpets. You don't find that foreign birds and butterflies come and perch upon your crockery; you cannot be permitted to paint foreign birds and butterflies upon your crockery. You never meet with quadrupeds going up and down walls; you must not have quadrupeds represented upon walls.

In *Hard Times* to act as one would *in* (according to) *Fact* is—of necessity—to bind one's self to the present, to be one of those 'to whom every day was the same as yesterday and tomorrow, and every year the counterpart of the last and the next.'

If one is fettered by Time, he is without the great Time-piercers, Memory and Hope, that Teufelsdröckh describes in *Sartor Resartus:* 'already through those mystic avenues' of Memory and Hope, Carlyle writes, in a statement more striking in expression than originality, 'thou the Earth-blinded summonest both Past and Future, and communest with them, though as yet darkly, and with mute beckonings.' In this state of Fact, noting the relationship of characters to Time—whether they are people of the Present or people for whom the curtains of Past and Future open through the workings of Memory and Hope—becomes another way of describing their positions between the two poles that set the thematic borders of the novel. A person with a sustaining memory of the past or a consoling hope for the future will hold out in a stronger manner against the imprisoning present than one without them. Concordant with this, one weaned on Fact, without some taste of romance or fancy, will have trouble holding his place in the sun, will be trapped in the narrowness of his own vision. A reader sees this readily in the examples of the children raised in the Gradgrind system.

Two of the children who offer illustrative contrast are Sissy and Louisa. In Chapter 9 of Book the First, whose title 'Sissy's Progress' connotes movement and change, the narrator suggests that, even though Sissy grows and develops through the years, life at Stone Lodge, going 'monotonously round like a piece of machinery which discouraged human interference,' is not in its essentials changed by Time. Positions shift—Gradgrind, for example, becomes a member of Parliament—but Time in Stone Lodge remains benumbed in the Present, turning seldom backward or forward. What sustains Sissy Jupe is a belief that amounts to religious faith, and a hope that keeps open the curtains of the Future: 'the girl believed that her father had not deserted her; she lived in the hope that he would come back, and in the faith that he would be made the happier by her remaining where she was.' Sissy's belief keeps her from running away. Her memories of her father and Merrylegs, though not exclusively happy ones, fortify her affection for him and strengthen her hope. She tells Louisa: 'I keep the nine oils ready for him, and I know he will come back. Every letter that I see in Mr Gradgrind's hand takes my breath away and blinds my eyes, for I think it comes from father, or from Mr Sleary about father.' Although Mr Gradgrind does not approve of such 'fantastic hopes,' the narrator comments that 'it did seem . . . as if fantastic hope could take as strong a hold as Fact.'

Louisa has no such sustenance. Others look to her future—her father with a well-intentioned but matter-of-fact plan for her marriage, her brother with his own selfish plan for helping his situation with Bounderby. Louisa has little to hope for. She cannot imagine ways of doing for Tom what other girls might do for those they love. 'I can't play to you, or sing to you,' she says, 'I can't talk to you so as to lighten your mind, for I never see any amusing sights or read any amusing books that it would be a pleasure or a relief to you to talk about, when you are tired.' Such feelings of helplessness are not expressed only to Tom. In talking to her father Louisa says, 'Father, I have often thought that life is very short'; she wishes 'to do the little I can, and the little I am fit for.' If the second statement expresses a hope, it is a short-term, highly limited one, so hesitant a step along that avenue to the future as scarcely to offer any glimpse at all. Indeed, her statement, 'What does it matter!' repeated twice during the conversation, suggests more of despair than hope, of drawing in than moving out.

When she sits before her fire watching the dying sparks, Louisa embodies the situation of the person closed solely within the present, the person without hope. The red sparks 'made me think . . . how short my life would be,' she tells her mother,

> Failure to cope with the movement of time, the effort to freeze time, to render existence static, results in a kind of life-in-death . . . and finds embodiment in Dickens's comic-grotesque figures."

'and how little I could hope to do in it.' Although a personal outburst appears to threaten when she later tells her father that 'when the night comes, Fire bursts out,' her own bursting-out—i.e., the temptation to run away with Harthouse—is severely contained. As a rebellion against her restrictive background, it appears weak because she overcomes it without significant difficulty (although it does bring her and her father to an important point of conciliation and understanding); as a moral victory, it appears weak because Harthouse is too much of a dandy to be a very strong temptation for a woman of her temperament and (presumed) intelligence—whatever kind of husband Bounderby is. But even more, by this time the fires of Louisa's spirit have faded and are not to be stoked by a shabby and illicit romance. When she stood at the door of Stone Lodge earlier as her father listened to Mr Bounderby's offer of marriage to his daughter, Louisa found little to look forward to. References to Time and fire come together:

> It seemed as if, first in her own fire within the house, and then in the fiery haze without she tried to discover what kind of wool Old Time, that greatest and longest-established Spinner of all, would weave from the threads he had already spun into a woman. But his factory is a secret place, his work is noiseless, and his Hands are mutes.

Louisa does not look toward the future with hope, but simply speculates, quietly and passively.

With his wishes grayed, Stephen Blackpool is Louisa's counterpart among the Hands, reflective individually of the mindless and mechanical treadmill of Time followed by all the Hands in the Coketown factories. Sometimes alone, sometimes with Rachael, he paces that treadmill without ever approaching the fulfilment of love or of fortune. He is without the opportunity for 'play' that Ruskin found 'necessary' for workmen—'this stretching of the mental limbs as their fetters fall away,—this leaping and dancing of the heart and intellect, when they are restored to the fresh air of heaven, yet half paralyzed by their captivity, and unable to turn themselves to any earnest purpose.' He is without the capacity to hope strongly. He can only dream. In his enlightening article, 'A Missing Childhood in *Hard Times*,' Edward Hurley considers Stephen's blacked-out childhood wishes, focusing on the dream Stephen has the night he sits in the same room with both his wife and Rachael. Dickens describes the dream this way:

> He thought that he, and some one on whom his heart had long been set—but she was not Rachael, and that surprised him, even in the midst of his imaginary happiness—stood in the church being married. While the ceremony was performing, and while he recognized among the witnesses some whom he knew to be living, and many whom he knew to be dead, darkness came on, succeeded by the shining of a tremendous light. It broke from one line in the table of commandments at the altar, and illuminated the building with the words. They were sounded through the church, too, as if there were voices in the fiery letters. Upon this, the whole appearance before him and around him changed, and nothing was left as it had been, but himself and the clergyman. They stood in the daylight before a crowd so vast, that if all the people in the world could have been brought together into one space, they could not have looked, he thought, more numerous; and they all abhorred him, and there was not one pitying or friendly eye among the millions that were fastened on his face. He stood on a raised stage, under his own loom; and, looking up at the shape the loom took, and hearing the burial service distinctly read, he knew that he was there to suffer death. In an instant what he stood on fell below him, and he was gone.

Hurley's analysis of the dream is detailed and probing and connects the details of the dream with the theme of his article—'childhood's confrontation with adult reality.' What is important for our purpose, however, is the dream's manifestation of a buried but living hope in Stephen Blackpool, a dreadful hope in many ways, one that cannot find strong outward expression in act or words or art but can come only out of the subconscious, in an event ridden with desire and taboo. Such a variety of hope, though, cannot part the curtains of the Future. Stephen's major expression of hope is the one connected with the star and imparted as he dies— 'that aw th' world may on'y coom together more'— but as many readers have felt, the circumstances and message are so strongly sentimental, so operatic in staging, that the idea scarcely seems to belong to Stephen Blackpool. The curtains of eternity

presumably part for him at this point, but he observes them from the same point in time where he has always stood.

Failure to cope with the movement of time, the effort to freeze time, to render existence static, results in a kind of life-in-death—an existence 'which does not allow anything whatever of novelty or change to come in from the outside'—and finds embodiment in Dickens's comic-grotesque figures. But if these characters are active and deliberate in their proceedings—as Miss Havisham, for example, is deliberate—characters like Louisa or Stephen Blackpool scarcely have enough self-drive, generated either by memory or hope, to invigorate their lives. Louisa lapses into the single long moment, while Stephen's history is simply a repetition of old events as steady and dreary as his drunken wife's cry: 'And back agen. Back agen ever and ever so often.'

A more active awareness of Time is shown by two other key figures of the novel—Bounderby and Harthouse. Both men misuse Time. By falsifying his past Bounderby misrepresents himself, puts on in Carlylean terms, a false vesture; both body and vesture work upon each other, one distorting the other. As Hurley puts it: 'Bounderby has tried to destroy his own childhood and thus made himself the most flagrant public hypocrite in the novel. In the eyes of the reader he is almost no one, since the childhood and history out of which he has created himself do not exist.' Nothing from the past can support him. He is unable to project himself into 'much of futurity.' Aside from Mrs Sparsit's sparring existence both with Lady Scadgers and with exigency, he 'probably' has little 'prescience,' as we hear in the final chapter, of the things to come.

Like Bounderby Harthouse professes his worst. He does not so much live for the moment as take advantage of it, unanchored, drifting with it in his world-weary manner. His philosophy is expressed in the repeated phrase, 'What will be, will be,' while he acknowledges to Louisa that 'the only difference between us and the professors of virtue or benevolence, or philanthropy . . . is, that we Know it is all meaningless . . .' Although reminiscent of Carlyle's Dilettante, as William Oddie has pointed out, his name from which one can coin— among other things—the phrase 'House of Art' reminds one of Carlyle's description of the Dandy. The obtuse Editor of *Sartor Resartus* calls the Dandy 'a poet'—an artist, one might say—and asks, 'Is not his body the (stuffed) parchment-skin whereon he writes, with cunning Huddersfield dyes, a Sonnet to his mistress' eyebrow? Dandy, an example of the artist Ruskin describes as indulging in 'unnecessary play,' Harthouse lacks the energy or will to burn with that hard gem-like flame of the late nineteenth-century aesthete. In the world of *Hard Times*, the moment is too numbing and deadening, drained of its vital qualities.

All of these characters and others—Gradgrind with the 'deadly statistical' clock in his study, his son Tom, the unpleasant Bitzer to name only three—are victims of Fact in one way or another and the limitations such a system imposes on a view of Time. Or if they are not victims, those—aside from Sissy Jupe—who evade the moment do it not through either Memory or Hope; rather, they evade the moment through indifference or through deliberate falsification. What such an observation means is that Dickens's criticism of a thoroughly Fact-oriented view of life runs more deeply than it might at first appear to do. If fancy is important to Memory and Hope and hence is a means of escaping Time, it is also a means of resisting Time. Using the term Imagination rather than Fancy, Samuel Johnson noted that 'time is, of all modes of existence, most obsequious to the imagination; a lapse of years is as easily conceived as a passage of hours.' To show how deeply Dickens's criticism runs we might turn to a statement deriving from the 1960s. It is drawn from a series of lectures delivered by Peter Hughes for the Canadian Broadcasting Corporation. In the first of these, entitled 'The Moment,' Hughes says:

> By resisting time, poetry gives its meaning. And by apparently defying time, as [Samuel] Johnson noticed, the imagination gives it existence. The memory in its turn, through history, philosophy, and religion, gives time an order and sequence it would otherwise lack. A trained memory strikes people nowadays as an old-fashioned, even primitive possession: 'Why write it down?' as the Watusi said to the anthropologist, 'can't you remember?' . . . But the decay of memory leads to the fading of those mental images that are necessary for thought. The decay of memory—which we tend to encourage—leads quickly to the decay of both the historical and poetic imagination, which we say we prize. The decay of memory also makes us forget that time is not the tyranny of clocks, schedules, and calendars; but rather *our perception* of duration, of the effects of duration on persons and things, especially living things.

Although his references in the passage are largely contemporary, Hughes's description of what is lost when the faculty of memory deteriorates describes what we see in *Hard Times*—that is, a situation in which many of his characters stand in solitude,

separate from each other, however much they may speak to one another, single figures inhabiting a single space with narrow, heavily shrouded horizons. They see nothing beyond. A sense of the past enriches the present, a *fact* of which Bounderby is fraudulently aware. But aside from Mrs Sparsit and Sissy, different as they are, the space inhabited by other characters in the novel is temporally impoverished, and even for these two figures barren.

When finally the power of Time penetrates, it does so with all the force of Aristotelian discovery, as the example of Gradgrind shows when he faces his runaway and unhappy daughter. In such a shattering event, the legacy of his past provides no enrichment through memory. Consequence directs his gaze backward over deed to show him the present he has created for himself. By restricting his vision of Time, he has made for himself a greater prison; for even though the curtains on Past and Future have for him been *torn* apart, as it were, the vision is of small comfort. Abused, Memory and Hope get back their own.

Dickens was gentler with another of his characters, though in a different work. A letter in which he explains his intention in *The Christmas Carol* can be used to summarize the importance of Time in *Hard Times*: 'I converted Mr Scrooge by teaching him that a Christian heart cannot be shut up in itself, but must live in the Past, the Present, and the Future, and must be a link of this great human chain, and must have sympathy with everything.'

Source: Lewis B. Horne, "Hope and Memory in *Hard Times*," in *Dickensian*, Vol. 75, No. 3, Autumn 1979, pp. 167–74.

Sources

Collins, Philip, *Charles Dickens: The Critical Heritage*, Routledge and Kegan Paul, 1971, pp. 300–21.

———, *Dickens and Education*, Macmillan, 1963, pp. 144–59.

Dickens, Charles, *Hard Times*, Norton Critical Edition, edited by George Ford and Sylvàre Monod, W. W. Norton, 1966.

———, "The Murdered Person," in *"Gone Astray" and Other Papers from "Household Words," 1851–59*, The Dent Uniform Edition of Dickens's Journalism, edited by Michael Slater, Vol. 3, Ohio State University Press, 1999, pp. 396–402.

———, "On Strike," in *Hard Times*, Norton Critical Edition, edited by George Ford and Sylvàre Monod, W. W. Norton, 1966, pp. 286–99, originally published in *Household Words*, February 11, 1854.

———, "Schools I Do Not Like," in *Hard Times*, Norton Critical Edition, edited by George Ford and Sylvàre Monod, W. W. Norton, 1966, pp. 310–11, originally given as a speech, November 5, 1857.

Gray, Paul Edward, ed., *Twentieth Century Interpretations of "Hard Times": A Collection of Critical Essays*, Prentice-Hall, 1969.

House, Humphry, and John House, *Dickens World*, 2d ed., Oxford University Press, 1965, pp. 203–11.

Leavis, F. R., "*Hard Times*—An Analytic Note," in *Hard Times*, Norton Critical Edition, edited by George Ford and Sylvàre Monod, W. W. Norton, 1966, pp. 339–59, originally published in *The Great Tradition*, 1948, pp. 227–48.

Morley, Henry, "Ground in the Mill," in *Hard Times*, Norton Critical Edition, edited by George Ford and Sylvàre Monod, W. W. Norton, 1966, pp. 299–301, originally published in *Household Words*, April 22, 1854.

Review of *Hard Times*, in *Hard Times*, Norton Critical Edition, edited by George Ford and Sylvàre Monod, W. W. Norton, 1966, pp. 286–99, originally published in *Westminster Review*, 1854.

Ruskin, John, Review of *Hard Times*, in *Charles Dickens: The Critical Heritage*, edited by Philip Collins, Routledge and Kegan Paul, 1971, pp. 303–04, originally published in *Cornhill Magazine*, August 1860.

Shanley, Mary Lyndon, *Feminism, Marriage, and the Law in Victorian England, 1850–1895*, Princeton University Press, 1989, pp. 22–48.

Simpson, Richard, Review of *Hard Times*, in *Charles Dickens: The Critical Heritage*, edited by Philip Collins, Routledge and Kegan Paul, 1971, pp. 303–04, originally published in *Rambler*, October 1854.

Whipple, Edwin P., Review of *Hard Times*, in *Charles Dickens: The Critical Heritage*, edited by Philip Collins, Routledge and Kegan Paul, 1971, pp. 351–21, originally published in *Atlantic Monthly*, March 1877.

Further Reading

Dyson, A. E., *The Inimitable Dickens: A Reading of the Novels*, Macmillan, 1970, pp. 183–202.

Dyson argues that *Hard Times*, Dickens's "angriest" novel, differs from his other novels because it is devoid of hope. There is no happy ending for any of the characters.

Monod, Sylvàre, *Dickens the Novelist*, University of Oklahoma Press, 1968, pp. 440–52, 456–65.

Monod discusses *Hard Times* and *A Tale of Two Cities* as examples of the least Dickensian of Dickens's novels. Monod faults Dickens for not providing a positive element in his social criticism and for the inconsistency in his thinking.

Nelson, Harland S., *Charles Dickens*, Twayne's English Authors Series, No. 314 Twayne, 1981, pp. 197–201.

Nelson discusses *Hard Times* in the context of the limitations of reason and intellect, namely that reason excludes love, which is needed for any solution to the world's problems.

Spector, Stephen J., "Monsters of Metonymy: *Hard Times* and Knowing the Working Class," in *Charles Dickens*, edited and with an introduction by Harold Bloom, Modern Critical Views series, Chelsea House, 1987, pp. 229–44.

Spector examines what he calls Dickens's failure to create a convincing portrayal of industrial workers, which he attributes to Dickens's faith in the power of language. While analyzing the novel's failings, Spector also praises its moral and intellectual honesty.

The House of the Seven Gables

Nathaniel Hawthorne
1851

The House of the Seven Gables, published in 1851 by the notable Boston publisher Ticknor, Reed & Fields, is Nathaniel Hawthorne's third novel. Some of the novel's themes can be found in his previous writings, specifically in *Legends of the Province House* (1830s) and "Peter Goldthwaite's Treasure" (also written in the 1830s). In both of these tales, as in *The House of the Seven Gables*, Hawthorne explores issues of class and the pursuit of wealth against the backdrop of decaying residences. Interestingly, in terms of plot, *The House of the Seven Gables* reflects actual events in Hawthorne's life and his family's history. He came from a long history of privilege in New England, yet faced poverty following the death of his father. Some critics have drawn parallels between Hepzibah's reticence to open the cent-shop and Hawthorne's own angst about publishing his writing. Further, Hawthorne's great-grandfather, John Hathorne (as the family's name was then spelled), was one of three judges who presided over the witchcraft trials of 1692. Like Colonel Pyncheon, John Hathorne played a role (a direct one in fact) in putting people to death for alleged witchcraft practices. Some writers have commented on Hawthorne's interest in the legacy of past family sins, which is a central theme in The House of the Seven Gables, because of his great-grandfather's involvement in the death of twenty wrongfully accused people. In the end, the characters in *The House of the Seven Gables* appear to be freed from the curse that has haunted their families for centuries. Though some speculate that

Nathaniel Hawthorne

Hawthorne forced a happy ending to this work to satisfy his publisher, and ultimately his readers, perhaps Hawthorne himself believed in the possibility that people have the ability to escape their pasts.

Author Biography

Nathaniel Hawthorne was born in Salem, Massachusetts on July 4, 1804 to an esteemed family headed by Nathaniel Hathorne and his wife, Elizabeth Manning (The author added the "W" to his name later in life). Hawthorne had two sisters (one older and one younger), and after his father's death of yellow fever in Surinam in 1808, the family lived for ten years with his mother's side of the family. Hawthorne and his immediate family lived in the third story of a house that was also home to his grandparents and eight unwed aunts and uncles. In 1818, his mother moved the family to Raymond, Maine, where they lived in the home that Hawthorne's Uncle Richard built in anticipation of making Maine the new center for the Manning family.

Hawthorne attended Bowdoin College and, following his graduation in 1825, returned to the Manning house in Salem to pursue his writing. In 1828, Hawthorne anonymously self-published his first novel, *Fanshawe*, which was a resounding failure. He remained in Salem until 1836, when he moved to Boston and worked as an editor of *American Magazine of Useful and Entertaining Knowledge* and later as the editor of *Peter Parley's Universal History on the Basis of Geography*. In 1837, Hawthorne published his first collection of stories, *Twice-Told Tales*, which launched his literary career. In 1837, he also met his wife-to-be, Sophia Peabody. The couple married in 1842 and had three children: Una, Julian, and Rose.

Despite his growing notoriety, Hawthorne was forced to pursue alternative means of supporting his family. In 1842, he took his first political appointment with the Boston Customhouse. In 1846, Hawthorne became the surveyor of the Salem Customhouse. During this time, Hawthorne published his second book of stories, *Mosses from an Old Manse*. When Zachary Taylor took the presidency in 1849, Hawthorne lost his appointment in Salem and again turned to writing. He published *The Scarlet Letter*, one of his best-known novels, in 1850. The novel was a bestseller and was quickly followed by *The House of the Seven Gables* (1851), which proved to be another success. In 1852, Hawthorne published *The Blithedale Romance*. When Franklin Pierce, Hawthorne's friend and former classmate at Bowdoin College, took the presidency in 1853, he appointed Hawthorne the consulship in Liverpool, England. Pierce failed to be reelected for another term; as a result, in 1857, Hawthorne lost the consulship in England. Hawthorne then moved to Italy for the next two years writing his final novel, *The Marble Faun*. He returned to the United States in 1860 and struggled with both his health and his writing. Hawthorne passed away in his sleep on May 19, 1864 while visiting Pierce in Plymouth, New Hampshire.

Plot Summary

Preface

The House of the Seven Gables begins with a preface in which Hawthorne makes a point to tell readers that the tale they are about to read is a "Romance" rather than a traditional "Novel." He proceeds to say that because the story is written as a Romance, it gives him creative license to present reader's with his selective understanding of the truth instead of binding him to being true to life. He notes

Media Adaptations

- An unabridged reading of *The House of Seven Gables* read by Roslyn Alexander is available through http://www.audible.com for purchase. Produced in 1993 by Recorded Books, Inc., this reading runs for over twelve hours.

- A second reading of *The House of the Seven Gables*, which runs six hours and is narrated by Joan Allen, is also available. This abridged reading was produced by Dove Audio, Inc. in 1997.

- Http://www.audiobooks.com also offers a recorded reading of *The House of Seven Gables* performed by Buck Schirner and produced by Brilliance. This 1995 version runs eleven hours.

- J. Searle Dawley directed a silent film adaptation of *The House of the Seven Gables* in 1910. This adaptation starred Mary Fuller as Hepzibah Pyncheon and was produced by the Edison Company.

- *The House of the Seven Gables* was adapted as a film by Joe May in 1940. The adaptation starred George Sanders, Margaret Lindsay, Vincent Price, Dick Foran, Nan Grey, Cecil Kellaway, Alan Napier, Gilbert Emery, Miles Mander, and Charles Trowbridge. Universal Studios re-released the video in June 1998.

- In 1951, Robert Montgomery and the production company Neptune produced a fifty-minute adaptation of the novel starring Gene Lockhart, June Lockhart, Leslie Nielson, and Richard Purdy.

- In 1963, Admiral released a two-hour production of Hawthorne's works starring Vincent Price. *Twice Told Tales* includes two of Hawthorne's short stories, "Doctor Heidegger's Experiment" and "Rappaccini's Daughter," as well as *The House of the Seven Gables*. Additional cast includes Sebastian Cabot, Mari Blanchard, Beverley Garland, Brett Halsey, Richard Denning, Abraham Sofaer, Joyce Taylor, Edith Evanson, Jacqueline DeWitt, Floyd Simmons, and Gene Roth.

---

that Romances give writers a creative and subjective license to "mellow the lights and deepen and enrich the shadows of the picture." Hawthorne also tells readers that the moral purpose of his work is to convey the notion that "the wrong-doing of one generation lives into the successive ones." Despite this claim, however, he notes that he has not tried "to impale the story with its moral." Finally, Hawthorne concludes that he did not intend to correlate the location or events in the story with any particular place or happenings in the County of Essex.

I: The Old Pyncheon Family

The first chapter opens with a description of the House of the Seven Gables, its history, and that of the Pyncheon and Maule families. In the mid-1600s, Matthew Maule (the elder) settles in the County of Essex and establishes a homestead. Soon thereafter, Colonel Pyncheon decides he would like to build his familial estate on Matthew's land.

Matthew refuses to surrender his land. He is then put on trial for witchcraft and with Colonel Pyncheon's full support, is hung. Just before dying, Matthew places a curse on Colonel Pyncheon, saying that "God will give him blood to drink." Colonel Pyncheon acquires the land, builds his house using Thomas Maule, Matthew Maule's son, as the architect. The day of his house-warming feast, to which he has invited the entire community, including many very esteemed society people, Colonel Pyncheon is found dead in his study with blood dripping from his mouth. Subsequent generations live in the house, believing that they are entitled to a large piece of land in Maine that Colonel Pyncheon was in the process of acquiring before he died. Many try to acquire the land, but fail.

More years pass, and thirty years before the beginning of the novel's action, another wealthy Pyncheon (Jaffrey Pyncheon, the elder) dies. His nephew (Clifford) is accused, tried, and convicted of the murder and is sentenced to life imprisonment. Jaffrey Pyncheon (the elder) believed that Matthew Maule was wrongly robbed of his land and put to death and intended to make restitution to the Maule descendents. Following Clifford's incarceration, Jaffrey Pyncheon's other nephew (Judge Jaffrey Pyncheon) inherits the dead man's wealth. Clifford's sister (Hepzibah) remained living in the House of the Seven Gables, per her uncle's will. Meanwhile, Maule's descendents have all but died out. They long inhabited the town and were a "quiet, honest, well-meaning race of people, cherishing no malice done them," who were said to have the power to influence people's dreams.

The chapter concludes with a description of the giant elm tree in the yard, the flowers that grow between two of the gables, and the door on the front gable that leads to a once used retail space.

II: The Little Shop-Window

Hepzibah Pyncheon rises from bed, dresses, examines herself in the mirror, and pulls out a miniature (very small portrait) of a young man, who readers later learn is her brother, Clifford. She cries as she readies herself for the day and notices how cross she looks as a result of the scowl caused by her near-sightedness. Despite her almost permanent scowl, Hepzibah is said to have a "heart that never frowned. It was naturally tender, [and] sensitive." Hepzibah faces the day in low spirits as she sets up the shop that she intends to open. Opening the shop is mortifying for her because she is an aristocrat by birth; however, she has no choice and must commence a business of her own in order to save herself from starvation. When she finally opens the shop door, she immediately runs inside the house to cry.

III: The First Customer

The first person to enter Hepzibah's shop is her boarder, Holgrave. The daguerreotypist comes to the store to offer Hepzibah help with her preparations. He congratulates Hepzibah on her endeavor, noting that this venture is a promising new beginning for her that will give her a "sense of healthy and natural effort for a purpose." Hepzibah views the situation quite differently and laments that she is no longer a lady. Holgrave counters that no Pyncheon lady has ever acted more heroically or nobly. Holgrave attempts to buy biscuits, but Hepzibah insists on giving them to him free. Holgrave departs and Hepzibah overhears two workmen discussing her shop. They discuss her disagreeable looks and the likely failure of her shop. As Hepzibah considers the possibility of

failure, the shop-bell rings and a boy (Ned Higgins) enters. As with Holgrave, Hepzibah gives the child a gingerbread cookie for free. He shortly returns to request another cookie, for which Hepzibah takes his payment. Other customers follow and in several cases, Hepzibah does not stock their needs. At the end of the day, she has a poor opinion of the temperament and manners of people who she sees as part of the lower classes. At the same time, after seeing a wealthy lady pass by, she wonders about the purpose of such a person.

IV: A Day Behind the Counter

Toward the afternoon, a large, elderly gentleman (Judge Jaffrey Pyncheon) passes by the shop and gazes upon it with both a frown and a smile. When he sees Hepzibah his "smile changed from acrid and disagreeable to the sunniest complacency and benevolence." Hepzibah shows dislike for the man and draws a comparison between his likeness and that of the portrait of Colonel Pyncheon, which hangs in the house. The shop bell rings when Uncle Venner enters the shop. He is the oldest resident of Pyncheon Street and is happy to see that Hepzibah has opened a shop instead of remaining idle. He discusses the possibility of his retirement to what he calls his farm. Although he praises Hepzibah for working, he tells her that it is an embarrassment that her wealthy cousin lets her do so. Hepzibah tells him that the judge is not to blame. Uncle Venner leaves Hepzibah after inquiring when Clifford will be home. Hepzibah is quite jarred by Uncle Venner's question and spends the remainder of the day dazed and clumsy. Just after she closes the shop for the day, an omnibus arrives, bringing Phoebe to Hepzibah's doorstep. Phoebe's letter was unfortunately delayed and thus her arrival is a surprise to Hepzibah, who decides that her country relation cannot stay lest she upset Clifford.

V: May and November

When Phoebe awakes in the morning, she arranges her quarters, "throwing a kindly and hospitable smile over the apartment." Her "sweet breath and happy thoughts" remove "all former evil and sorrow" from the room. Phoebe joins Hepzibah, who tells her that she unfortunately cannot stay. Unaffected by the comment, Phoebe assures Hepzibah that she will earn her keep and be a cheerful addition to the house. Hepzibah accedes and after telling Phoebe that Clifford is soon to arrive home, she fetches his miniature (a very small portrait). Phoebe, who thought that Clifford was dead, admires the miniature, commenting on Clifford's sweet and childlike face. The two women sit down to tea, and when the shop-bell rings, Phoebe jumps up. To Hepzibah's great pleasure, Phoebe serves the customer with ease and skill. Despite her being a country girl, Phoebe is praised by the narrator for her lady-like qualities. Phoebe's presence is known in the town and inspires a steady stream of shop customers. Uncle Venner praises her and likens her to one of God's angels. Hepzibah talks at length to Phoebe about Alice Pyncheon, who is believed to haunt the house and whose harpsichord Hepzibah had shown Phoebe earlier. Changing the subject, Hepzibah then tells Phoebe about Holgrave, the daguerreotypist with questionable politics who lives in one of the gables. Noting his strange hold on her mind and his agreeable and kind disposition, Hepzibah says that she is disinclined to send him away simply for his strange companions.

VI: Maule's Well

After having tea, Phoebe goes out to the garden, which she finds in a state of decay that has been only slightly modified by a small effort of evident care. While in the garden, she is happy to find flowers, vegetables, a robin's nest in a pear tree, a fountain, and a hen-coop. Within the hen-coop, she finds a rooster, two hens, and a chick, all having seen better days. Holgrave surprises Phoebe as he enters the garden. Holgrave notes the positive way the hens react to Phoebe, who approaches the conversation hesitantly. Holgrave tells Phoebe that he has been caring for the garden and offers to show her one of his daguerreotypes. He shows her one of Judge Jaffrey Pyncheon, and she mistakes it for Colonel Pyncheon. Holgrave continues the discussion by saying that it has been impossible for him to create a pleasing rendering of the judge despite more than one attempt. Pictures apparently cannot cover up the truth of a man's character as a subjective painter might. Holgrave asks Phoebe if she would care to tend to the flowers and the hens while he cared for the vegetables. Although her reticence about Holgrave remains in tact, she complies with the request and weeds the flower-bed. As Holgrave leaves, he warns Phoebe not to drink or bathe in the fountain, which is called Maule's well, because the water is believed to be bewitched. Phoebe also goes inside and finds Hepzibah in the dark. Phoebe has a strange feeling that someone else is in the room with them, and after she goes off to bed, she continues to think that she hears Hepzibah talking with someone.

VII: The Guest

Phoebe awakes to find Hepzibah already busy in the kitchen attempting to find something savory to make for breakfast. Hepzibah purchases the best mackerel available from the passing fish-dealer. Phoebe assists by roasting coffee and making an Indian cake. Hepzibah is emotional during the preparations, laughing and crying. Phoebe is aware of Hepzibah's strange behavior and inquires what has happened to affect her so, when Hepzibah signals that "he" is coming to the table. Clifford arrives, looking elderly and spiritless. He weakly greets Phoebe, and Hepzibah explains that Phoebe is their cousin. The three sit down to eat, and Clifford notices how changed Hepzibah is and wonders if she is angry with him because of her scowl. Hepzibah assures him that she has nothing but love for him. He eats voraciously as the narrator continues to describe his disposition toward all that is beautiful. He is pleased with Phoebe's presence but cannot look at his sister because of her unattractiveness. Clifford enjoys the beautiful rose presented by Phoebe and remarks about the dismal house. When the shop-bell rings, Phoebe gets up to attend to the customer, and Hepzibah explains to her brother that they are now quite poor. She fears the disgrace she has brought to them by opening the shop; however, Clifford apologizes for his previous disapproval and bursts into tears. Shortly thereafter, he falls asleep, leaving Hepzibah to weep quietly as she looks at him.

VIII: The Pyncheon of To-Day

When Phoebe enters the shop, she finds Ned, the young boy who favors the shop's gingerbread cookies. Before leaving, Ned asks Phoebe how Clifford is. Phoebe learns through the inquiry that the man at breakfast is Hepzibah's brother. Just as the boy leaves, Judge Jaffrey Pyncheon enters. He introduces himself and attempts to give Phoebe a kiss, which she instinctively rebuffs. He turns cold in response and then thinking better of it, warms again. She apologizes, yet is struck by the similarity between the judge and Colonel Pyncheon. Noticing her ill-ease, the judge asks if she is afraid of something. She tells him no and asks if he would like to see Hepzibah. He delays her and surmises that she fears Clifford. She assures him to the contrary and says that Clifford is not frightful in the least. He goes to enter the house just as Hepzibah comes out and prevents him from doing so. The judge offers Hepzibah anything he has to make Clifford comfortable and asks to see him. Hepzibah refuses his request. The conversation escalates with the judge offering more and more and Hepzibah refusing everything. The two are interrupted by Clifford's cry to not let the judge enter the house. The judge is deeply angered and tells Hepzibah that when she and Clifford realize their injustice, he will simply hope that they will accept his generous offers. He leaves and, while Hepzibah laments his evil ways, Phoebe questions if he is truly ill intentioned. Phoebe goes off to tend to Clifford, confused by the events of the day and certain that Hepzibah's contempt for the judge is rooted deeply in the past.

IX: Clifford and Phoebe

Despite her ongoing attempts to care for Clifford, Hepzibah realizes that because she so horribly lacks the beauty he so adores, Phoebe is better equipped to tend to him. Clifford brightens in Phoebe's refreshing and purifying presence and although he does not act on it, he finds himself attracted to her. For her part, Phoebe is likely unaware of her impact on Clifford. She finds the mysteries of his past annoying and is brought down a bit by the heavy atmosphere. Nonetheless, she perseveres, and the three settle into a daily routine. While Clifford sleeps in the morning, Phoebe works in the shop, which the public seems to enjoy. In the afternoons, Hepzibah takes over in the shop while Phoebe spends time with Clifford.

X: The Pyncheon-Garden

Phoebe often takes Clifford into the garden, where she reads to him. Clifford prefers poetry and is deeply delighted by the flowers in the garden. He is particularly fond of the scarlet blossoms found on some of the bean-vines, which Holgrave planted after finding the presumably ancient seeds in one of the garrets. The blossoms attract an ongoing stream of hummingbirds, which Clifford watches with childlike enthusiasm. Hepzibah is both happy and sad to see her brother's reaction. She remembers that the hummingbirds had the same effect on him in his youth, yet she is saddened by his present state. For his part, Clifford wants to be sure that what he is experiencing is real and sometimes asks Phoebe to pinch him or to give him a rose so that he can prick himself with the thorns. One day, Clifford asks that the hens be freed from their enclosure. When Hepzibah cooks one of the hen's recently layed eggs, the rooster "delivered himself of a harangue that might have proved as long as his own pedigree." Clifford likes to spend time looking into Maule's Well, where beautiful faces formed from the colored pebbles at the

bottom greet him. Occasionally, dark faces appear and hamper his mood for the remainder of the day. On Sundays after Phoebe attends church, Clifford, Hepzibah, Holgrave, and Uncle Venner gather for picnics in the garden. Clifford feels young in Uncle Venner's presence and is uncharacteristically social with him. Holgrave tries to engage with Clifford as well, but seems to be motivated by something other than beneficence. One Sunday, Clifford sadly declares that he wants his happiness. The narrator calls Clifford part crazy and part imbecile and cautions him to enjoy what he has because happiness other than this may always elude him.

XI: The Arched Window

In addition to taking Clifford to the garden, Phoebe often brings him to sit in front of the window that faces the street. From there, he watches passersby. Clifford finds all of the new inventions strange, including the omnibus, the water-cart, the cab, and the railroad steam-devil. He prefers the things of his past, like the butcher's cart, the fish-cart, and the scissor-grinder. One afternoon, an organ player stops in front of the house. While the greedy monkey plies the crowd for money, the organ player turns the crank, which plays music and also sets a host of small figures into action. The narrator notes that despite the actions engaged in by each figure, when the music stops, they have come no further than when they started. The cobbler does not finish making his shoe, the blacksmith's iron is not shaped, and the milkmaid has fetched no milk. Clifford enjoys the music but finally cries about the monkey because of its physical and spiritual ugliness. On another day, a procession passes the house and while watching the throngs of people, Clifford makes an attempt to jump into the crowd from the balcony. He is stopped by Phoebe and Hepzibah, but the narrator notes that such a plunge into the sea of humanity may have been a help to him. One Sunday, Clifford and Hepzibah decide to go to church. The two ready themselves but are unable to step out of the house. Clifford claims that they are ghosts whose only place is right there in the house. On yet another day, Clifford blows bubbles off the balcony, and one bubble lands and pops on Judge Jaffrey Pyncheon's nose. The judge mocks Clifford for still partaking in childish endeavors. Clifford is overcome with fear.

XII: The Daguerreotypist

When Clifford retires for the day, Phoebe spends her time shopping and reading the Bible.

She has grown pensive and more mature under the influence of her relations and her stay in their home. Her only social outlet is Holgrave, who despite their almost daily encounters she feels she does not really know. Holgrave was independent early in life and has held many jobs, including schoolmaster, salesman, peddler, and dentist. He has traveled in Europe and lectured about mesmerism. Despite such experiences, he is not learned and is marked by youthful passion more than intellect. In one of his meetings with Phoebe, with whom he appears smitten, Holgrave shares his views about the past and the future. He argues that everything in the past should be discarded and that before men can make their own mark on the world, they must rid themselves of the influence of previous generations. He believes that each new generation should start fresh, building their own public buildings and even homes. He argues that the House of the Seven Gables should be burned and cleansed of its awful past. Toward the end of their conversation, the legend of Colonel Pyncheon and Matthew Maule surfaces, and Holgrave tells Phoebe that he means to publish some of the Pyncheon history in a magazine. After Pheobe accedes to hearing it, he produces his manuscript of the story and begins to read.

XIII: Alice Pyncheon

The thirteenth chapter presents the text of Holgrave's story. Gervayse Pyncheon, having recently returned from Europe, requests that Matthew Maule (the younger) come to the House of the Seven Gables. Gervayse believes that Matthew may know the whereabouts of the deed to the land in Maine that Colonel Pyncheon was in the process of acquiring at the time of his death. Matthew is described as an unpopular man and despite his lower class status, enters the Pyncheon house through the front door. Gervayse offers Matthew money in exchange for information about the missing deed; however, Matthew refuses. When Matthew eventually agrees to give Gervayse the information in exchange for the House of the Seven Gables, the two confirm their agreement in writing and with a drink. Before leaving, Matthew asks to see Gervayse's daughter, Alice. When Alice looks at him admiringly, Matthew misconstrues her look as disapproval. Matthew mesmerizes Alice in an attempt to summon the spirits of his father, grandfather, and Colonel Pyncheon. Gervayse intervenes and attempts to stop the process; however, on Alice's insistence, Matthew continues. Once summoned, the Maule spirits prevent the spirit of

Colonel Pyncheon from telling where the deed is hidden. Matthew Maule (the younger) tells Gervayse that the secret must be kept until the deed is worthless and awakes Alice. Alice remains under his spell, however, and at any time, he can simply command her to laugh, be sad, or dance, and she does his bidding. On his wedding day, Matthew summons Alice to wait on his bride. She does so, and finally Matthew releases Alice from her spell. Alice kisses the bride and walks home in the snow in inappropriate clothes. She catches a cold and ultimately dies. Matthew attends the funeral procession, noting that he only meant to humble her and now she was dead.

XIV: Phoebe's Good Bye

Having listened carefully to Holgrave's detailed story, Phoebe is mesmerized. Holgrave is attempting to keep Phoebe under his spell; however, his integrity and value of the individual inspires him to awaken her. As the two watch the moon come up, Holgrave comments on his current happiness while Phoebe reflects that she has seen gayer days. Her time with Hepzibah and Clifford has aged her and, she hopes, made her wiser. Holgrave assures her that she is simply maturing and that what she is experiencing is an important part of the development of her soul. Phoebe gets up to help Hepzibah with the day's accounts when Holgrave acknowledges that she will briefly be returning to her country home. He tells Phoebe that her presence has much improved the lives of Hepzibah and Clifford, who for the most part are dead souls. When Phoebe wonders if he means well by the Pyncheon siblings, he responds that unlike her, he is not compelled to help them, but rather to observe them. Holgrave says that he believes that Judge Jaffrey Pyncheon is ill-intentioned and that trouble is brewing. Two mornings later, Phoebe is tearful as she leaves, and Hepzibah notices that the young woman's smile is not as bright as it was upon her arrival. Clifford bids her goodbye, telling her that she has matured into a beautiful woman. Phoebe passes Uncle Venner, who like Holgrave, tells her what a boon she has been to the Pyncheon siblings. He likens her to an angel and hopes she will return quickly.

XV: The Scowl and the Smile

The days following Phoebe's departure are dreary and stormy. Hepzibah's business falls off, and Clifford takes to his bed. Making matters worse, Judge Jaffrey Pyncheon arrives and insists upon seeing Clifford. He at first tries to sweet talk

Hepzibah with words of kindness and love about her and Clifford. Hepzibah remains cold and bitter and refuses to let him see Clifford, whom she fears would be unable to handle the encounter. Eventually, the judge becomes enraged. He tells Hepzibah that Clifford knows the whereabouts of certain necessary paperwork about the large remaining portion of their uncle Jaffrey Pyncheon's estate and threatens to have Clifford committed to an asylum if Hepzibah does not let him talk with him. Hepzibah insists that Clifford could not possibly know anything about the hidden wealth, but fearing her cousin's intentions, goes to summon Clifford. The judge sits in the chair that Colonel Pyncheon occupied upon his death and waits.

XVI: Clifford's Chamber

While Hepzibah slowly ascends the stairs to Clifford's room, she wonders if he could possibly know anything about the missing portion of their uncle's estate. She concludes it is impossible and ponders going for help. She knows the community would favor the judge and instead attempts to find Holgrave, who she discovers is not in his room. Giving in to the inevitable meeting, she knocks on Clifford's door and after receiving no answer, she enters to find that he is not in bed. Fearing he may have left and drowned himself to escape his cousin's inquiry, Hepzibah returns to the parlor to summon the judge for help. Despite Hepzibah's emotional and animated outbursts, the judge does not move or respond. Clifford appears and pointing into the parlor, tells Hepzibah that they are now free to dance, sing, play, and be as happy as Phoebe. Going into the parlor, Hepzibah realizes that the judge is dead. Clifford tells Hepzibah that they must go and the two leave the house.

XVII: The Flight of Two Owls

Clifford and Hepzibah board the train. Hepzibah feels as though she is in a dream while Clifford feels exhilarated by the events. Clifford begins a conversation with a fellow passenger, noting the merits of the railroad and its ability to take people away from their homes and parlors. Contrary to his previous favoring of the things of yore, Clifford expounds that the railroad is one of the greatest modern inventions for it will enable people to return to their nomadic routes. He argues that men need to be on the move rather than cooped up in their homes. Speaking of the House of the Seven Gables, Clifford deems that it should be burned because of the image of the dead man that it conjures in his mind. Hepzibah asks Clifford to be quiet for

fear that the traveler may think he is crazy. Enlivened by his thoughts, however, Clifford continues, pointing to the merits of mesmerism and the telegraph. He likes that friends and lovers can be more connected via the telegraph, yet expresses disdain for its use to catch criminals. Clifford and Hepzibah depart the train and all of Clifford's energy drains away. He tells Hepzibah that she must now take charge of their future. Hepzibah prays that God will guide them.

XVIII: Governor Pyncheon

Judge Pyncheon remains motionless in the parlor. Despite having open eyes, he is not breathing. His watch continues to tick as the narrator inquires why he lingers. The narrator addresses him, asking if he has forgotten his appointments for the day, especially his dinner with important personages from throughout the state who he was hoping to persuade to nominate him as a candidate for governor. The narrator encourages the judge to make haste; however, he of course does not. A procession of Pyncheon spirits then enters the room, starting with Colonel Pyncheon followed by the next six generations. Noticing that Judge Pyncheon's son is among the spirits, the narrator notes that the judge's wealth will now go to Clifford, Hepzibah, and Phoebe. When the next morning comes and the judge still does not stir, the narrator gives up the address just as the shop-bell rings.

XIX: Alice's Posies

The storm has ended, and the neighborhood is alive. The flowers on top of the house are in bloom. Uncle Venner arrives at the House of the Seven Gables to pick up the food Hepzibah sets aside for his pigs, and Holgrave tells him that no one is home. When Mrs. Gubbins comes to the shop, a neighbor tells her that she will not be able buy anything because Hepzibah and Clifford left yesterday to go to Judge Pyncheon's. Ned Higgens also comes to the shop to find it closed. The two laborers pass and speculate that Hepzibah has run off because her shop has failed. When the butcher comes, he peeks inside and believes he sees Clifford sitting in the parlor rudely ignoring his knocking. The organ player also arrives and after playing for a bit is warned to move on because rumor has it that the judge has been murdered in the house. Finding Judge Pyncheon's card with his datebook items for the previous day on the back of it on the porch, one of the laborers deems that they should take it to the City Marshal. Phoebe arrives and is warned by Ned Higgins that something wicked is inside. As Phoebe knocks at the door, it opens before her. She assumes it is Hepzibah opening it. She steps inside, and it closes behind her.

XX: The Flower of Eden

Holgrave, not Hepzibah, leads Phoebe into what had been the grand reception room. He tells her that Hepzibah and Clifford are gone and shows her the daguerreotype of the judge he made some time ago. He then shows her one he just completed, and she surmises that the judge is dead. Holgrave tells Phoebe that he has not told anyone about the death because he believes that with Hepzibah and Clifford gone and the similarity between the judge's death and uncle Jaffrey Pyncheon's, the two will be implicated. Holgrave believes that the judge's death, if evaluated properly, will show that his death occurred because of an inherited family condition. He also tells Pheobe that he believes the judge made uncle Jaffrey Pyncheon's death look violent after the man had already died of the same affliction. Holgrave then professes his love for Phoebe and vice versa. Just then, Hepzibah and Clifford return home. Clifford is glad to be home and seems stronger than Hepzibah, who is in tears.

XXI: The Departure

The judge's death creates a stir until the public learns that he died of natural causes. They seem to easily forget him except for the rumors that now surface about his less than benevolent past. A rumor now prevails that the night of old Jaffrey Pyncheon's death, the younger Jaffrey rummaged through the elder man's papers. Part way through the task, old Jaffrey surprised his nephew. As a result of the shock and his hereditary disposition, the elder Jaffrey died of apoplexy. The younger Jaffrey continued to look through the papers and destroyed a new version of his uncle's will, which left a favorable portion of the man's estate to Clifford. To avoid suspicion, the judge arranged clues that pointed police to Clifford as the assailant. Jaffrey did not intend Clifford be tried for murder; however, he never told authorities about his own part in his uncle's death. In subsequent years, the younger Jaffrey wrote the incident off to youth and rarely thought about it. Next, readers learn that the judge's only heir, his son, has died of cholera while traveling and that as a result, Clifford, Hepzibah, Phoebe, and Holgrave are now to enjoy the judge's riches. Though Clifford is never restored to his former self, he is greatly brightened by the judge's death. Clifford, Hepzibah, Phoebe, and Holgrave move to the judge's country estate as do the Pyncheon hens, who become prolific egg layers. In the face of the change, Holgrave's progressive views seem to be becoming more conservative. On the day of their departure, the foursome and Uncle Venner gaze upon Colonel Pyncheon's portrait and Clifford comments that he has a hazy remembrance about the portrait holding a secret about wealth. Holgrave taps a hidden spring on the portrait, which sends the picture toppling to the floor. In the open space that is revealed, everyone sees the legendary deed to the land in Maine. Hepzibah comments that Clifford must have mentioned something in his youth about the portrait to the judge, who then mistakenly believed that Clifford knew something about the whereabouts of their uncle's remaining estate. Holgrave reveals that he knows of the spring because he is the son of Thomas Maule, who hid the parchment behind the portrait when he built the house. Uncle Venner ventures that the claim is now worthless. Phoebe insists that Uncle Venner come live in the cottage on the judge's property. Clifford seconds the invitation and when the foursome prepare to depart, Uncle Venner is to follow them a few days later. Children gather around the carriage, and Hepzibah notices Ned Higgins, to whom she gives some money. The two laborers pass and acknowledge Hepzibah's good fortune. Leaving the house, Uncle Venner fancies he hears Alice Pyncheon playing her harpsichord as she ascends to heaven.

Characters

Ned Higgins

Ned Higgins, a young boy, is Hepzibah's first shop customer. He is a repeat customer who enjoys the shop's gingerbread cookies. When Phoebe returns from her visit home and later discovers that the judge has died in the parlor, Ned warns her that something wicked has happened in the house. As Hepzibah, Clifford, Phoebe, and Holgrave leave to take up residence at the judge's country estate, Hepzibah gives Ned money.

Holgrave

Holgrave is a resident in one of the gables in the House of the Seven Gables. The narrator describes him as "a slender young man, not more than one or two and twenty years old, with a rather grave and thoughtful expression, for his years, but likewise a springy alacrity and vigor." He is exceptionally supportive of Hepzibah's opening of the cent shop.

Holgrave falls in love with Phoebe and, in the final chapter, reveals that he is a descendent of Matthew Maule. Toward the end of the story, Holgrave tells Clifford, Hepzibah, and Phoebe where the now worthless deed to the Maine land can be found. Holgrave is a young and passionate character whose politics run contrary to the conservative ideals that the aristocratic Hepzibah embraces. Both professionally and personally, he represents the coming of the modern age and the retiring of past traditions. Although he has dabbled in several occupations, including dentistry and teaching, Holgrave is now a daguerreotypist, or a photographer. His profession represents the way in which he is a forward thinker who enjoys the changes brought by technology. Unlike Clifford, who is at first nostalgic about the past, Holgrave favors the future. Like his ancestor, Matthew Maule, Holgrave has the power of mesmerism, or the ability to hypnotize people. Unlike the younger Matthew Maule, Holgrave does not use this power in harmful ways against other people, specifically Phoebe.

Matthew Maule (The Elder)

Matthew Maule is the first owner of the land upon which the House of the Seven Gables is eventually built. He is not a man of great wealth or power, yet he stands up against Colonel Pyncheon and refuses to give him his land. As a result, Maule is put on trial for practicing witchcraft and is ultimately convicted and hung. Just before his death, Maule curses Colonel Pyncheon, who watches the proceedings from horseback. Maule says, "God will give him blood to drink." When Pyncheon dies mysteriously after building a home on Maule's land, the curse is believed by some to be the reason. Maule's son, Thomas, served as the architect of the House of the Seven Gables.

Matthew Maule (The Younger)

The younger Matthew Maule is the grandson of Matthew Maule (the elder). His father, Thomas Maule built the House of the Seven Gables. The younger Matthew Maule makes a deal with Gervayse Pyncheon, telling him that he will tell him where the legendary deed is for the land in Maine in trade for the House of the Seven Gables. Using his powers of mesmerism, Matthew hypnotizes Alice Pyncheon, Gervayse's daughter, and conjures the spirits of Colonel Pyncheon, the elder Matthew Maule, and Thomas Maule. The Maule spirits thwart his efforts and refuse to let the Colonel tell him where the papers are hidden. Matthew Maule

(the younger) cancels the deal with Gervayse but keeps Alice Pyncheon under his spell. He makes her do humiliating things and eventually, releasing her from his spell, allows her to walk home improperly clothed for snow. She dies as a result.

Thomas Maule

Thomas Maule is the son of Matthew Maule (the elder) and the father of Matthew Maule (the younger). He is the architect that built the House of the Seven Gables. When Thomas builds the house, he hides the deed to the legendary land in Maine behind the portrait of Colonel Pyncheon.

Alice Pyncheon

Alice Pyncheon is the daughter of Gervayse Pyncheon, the granddaughter of Colonel Pyncheon, and Phoebe's great-great-grand-aunt. Hepzibah describes her as "exceedingly beautiful and accomplished." Alice is hypnotized by the younger Matthew Maule and forced to act in embarrassing and humiliating ways, including waiting on his bride. Once Alice is released from Matthew's spell, she walks home inappropriately clothed for the snow and dies. The flowers that grow in between two of the gables are said to have been sprinkled there by Alice. They are called Alice's Posies. Sometimes the sounds of her harpsichord are said to be heard in the house.

Clifford Pyncheon

Clifford Pyncheon is Hepzibah's brother and Judge Jaffrey Pyncheon's cousin. After being framed by his cousin for the murder of his uncle, Old Jaffrey Pyncheon, Clifford is imprisoned for thirty years. He returns to the House of the Seven Gables following his imprisonment and is cared for by Hepzibah and Phoebe. Prior to his incarceration, Clifford is a man of privilege who enjoys all that is beautiful. This quality persists in him and is evident in his inability to look at his unattractive, scowling sister and his desire to quit the "dismal house" for finer accommodations in the South of France and Italy. He fancies Phoebe and seems to lose himself in the sensual undertaking of eating. Following his imprisonment, Clifford is a changed man. No longer masculine or mature, he is characterized by the narrator as feminine and childlike. When readers first meet Clifford, he is described as elderly and spiritless. The narrator writes "It was the spirit of the man, that could not walk" as though he "must have suffered some miserable wrong from its earthly experience." Early in the novel, Clifford is enamored of the past and watches wistfully from the arched window as modern inventions pass. He wishes to recover the life that is symbolized by the "antique fashions of the street." His past, however, is lost. After finding Judge Jaffrey Pyncheon dead, Clifford seems more equipped to embrace the future. As he and Hepzibah flee by train, he talks with a fellow traveler and lauds the advances of modern science and technology. Clifford's new attitude toward technology and his inherited wealth from Judge Jaffrey Pyncheon foretell a brighter future for him as well as for Hepzibah, Phoebe, and Holgrave, who all move out of the House of the Seven Gables to the judge's estate.

Colonel Pyncheon

Colonel Pyncheon is the man who had the House of the Seven Gables built 160 years before the action of the story takes place. He built the house on a piece of land that first belonged to Matthew Maule (the elder). Colonel Pyncheon was instrumental in having the elder Matthew Maule put to death for witchcraft. As a result of Matthew's death, Colonel Pyncheon was able to seize the land that he had long tried to obtain from Matthew. On the day that Colonel Pyncheon hosts a grand house warming party with many important community members in attendance, he is found dead in his study. In the story that unfolds, Colonel Pyncheon's portrait still hangs in the house and the legend of the Pyncheon and Maule conflict serves as the basis for one of Hawthorne's themes, which is that the sins of the past are carried down through successive generations. Like the Colonel, two other Pyncheon men die of apoplexy, an unexpected hemorrhage.

Gervayse Pyncheon

Gervayse is Colonel Pyncheon's son and Alice Pyncheon's father. In the story that Holgrave relates to Phoebe, Gervayse is said to have returned from Europe and begun to search for the deed to the land in Maine that the Colonel was in the process of acquiring at the time of his death. Gervayse summons the younger Matthew Maule to the house and makes a deal to give him the House of the Seven Gables in exchange for information about the missing deed. Matthew (the younger) then hypnotizes Alice, who eventually dies due in part to his mistreatment of her. Gervayse's greed can be blamed for his daughter's death.

Hepzibah Pyncheon

Hepzibah is the struggling spinster heroine of the novel. She resides in the House of the Seven Gables. She is Clifford's sister and Judge Jaffrey Pyncheon's niece. In the novel, she represents "old Gentility" with a reverence for the past and her previously well-to-do life. The narrator describes her "cherished and ridiculous consciousness" of her privileged ancestry, "her shadowy claims to princely territory." He recounts her accomplishments as having "thrummed on a harpsichord, and walked a minuet, and worked an antique tapestry-stitch on her sampler." As an aristocrat who has fallen into poverty, Hepzibah must save herself from complete financial destitution by opening a cent-shop in her home. The townspeople have little compassion for her and suspect her enterprise will fail. For the most part, the residents of the town seem to dislike Hepzibah. The narrator writes "they cared nothing for her dignity, and just as little for her degradation." She is an unattractive woman who has a perpetual scowl. Her rough and unapproachable exterior, however, hides a tender heart. She is deeply devoted to her brother and holds deep hatred and contempt for her cousin. Hepzibah's impoverished existence seems to better her. The narrator writes "she had been enriched by poverty, developed by sorrow . . . and endowed with heroism, which never could have characterized her in what are called happier circumstances."

Judge Jaffrey Pyncheon (The Younger)

Judge Jaffrey Pyncheon is Hepzibah and Clifford's cousin and the nephew of old Jaffrey Pyncheon. The judge dies toward the end of the book, and because his son dies from cholera, Clifford inherits the judge's riches. Prior to becoming a judge, the younger Jaffrey Pyncheon facilitated the death of his uncle. While the young Jaffrey was rifling through the old man's papers, the elder Jaffrey Pyncheon happened upon him and died of apoplexy. The younger Jaffrey destroyed a newly revised version of the elder Jaffrey's will, which favored Clifford, and successfully framed Clifford for their uncle's death. The judge later assists in Clifford's release from jail and his return to the House of the Seven Gables in hopes that he can help him locate papers that will point him to the remainder of their uncle's estate. As the narrator tells us, the judge was "reckoned rather a dissipated youth, but had at once reformed, and made himself an exceedingly respectable member of society." He served in an "inferior court" and later "served a part of two terms in Congress." Despite living a life "befitting the christian, the good citizen, the horticulturist, and the gentleman," Judge Jaffrey Pyncheon's status as a good man is a farce. Hawthorne evidences this fact by drawing strong comparison's between the judge and Colonel Pyncheon. When shown Holgrave's photograph of the judge, Phoebe mistakes him for the Colonel, and the narrator comments of their likeness:

> It implied that the weaknesses and defects, the bad passions, the mean tendencies, and the moral diseases which lead to crime, are handed down from one generation to another, by a far surer process of transmission than human law has been able to establish, in respect to the riches and honors which it seeks to entail upon posterity.

Like the Colonel, the judge is motivated by his own greed and strong desire for self-aggrandizement. He is a selfish, deceitful, and cruel man. His apparently benevolent attempts to help Clifford and Hepzibah are as false as the smiles he presents to the public. In the end, the public learns (albeit) through rumors, about his hand in the old Jaffrey Pyncheon's death and Clifford's imprisonment.

Old Jaffrey Pyncheon

Old Jaffrey Pyncheon is the uncle of Judge Jaffrey Pyncheon, Clifford, and Hepzibah. Like Colonel Pyncheon, old Jaffrey Pyncheon dies of apoplexy. His affliction is triggered when he finds the younger Jaffrey rifling through his personal papers. The younger Jaffrey Pyncheon inherits the elder's wealth. Old Jaffrey Pyncheon believed that "Matthew Maule, the wizard, had been wronged out of his homestead, if not out of his life," and intended "to make restitution to Maule's posterity" before his death, but was unable to do so.

Phoebe Pyncheon

Phoebe is a Pyncheon relation from the country. She comes to visit Hepzibah after her (Phoebe's) mother remarries. She falls in love with Holgrave, cares for Clifford when he cannot bear to look at his sister, and much to the neighborhood's delight, works in Hepzibah's cent-shop. Whereas Judge Jaffrey Pyncheon (the younger) can be seen to represent all that is evil, Phoebe represents all that is good. The narrator describes her as "very pretty; as graceful as a bird, and graceful much in the same way; as pleasant, about the house, as a gleam of sunshine." In sum, she is the epitome of "feminine grace." The narrator stresses Phoebe's good nature and ability to transform the places and people she encounters by her sweet disposition and charming voice. Like the sunshine, she has a refreshing influence on all of the characters, particularly Hepzibah and Clifford. When Phoebe first arrives at the House of the Seven Gables, she fixes up her living quarters. The narrator notes that it had now "been purified of all former evil and sorrow by her sweet breath and happy thoughts." Such is her effect throughout the narrative. For all of her beauty, Phoebe is not an intellectual and is naöive about the evil's of human nature; however, she becomes wiser as the novel progresses.

Uncle Venner

Uncle Venner is one of the oldest habitants of Pyncheon Street who befriends Hepzibah, Clifford, and Phoebe. He is one of Hepzibah's first customers. Clifford finds his company agreeable as well, and he joins the two along with Phoebe and Holgrave for picnics. The narrator says that he "was commonly regarded as rather deficient, than otherwise, in his wits," but that there was "something like poetry in him." In sum, Uncle Venner is described as "a miscellaneous old gentleman, partly himself, but, in good measure, somebody else; patched together, too, of different epochs; an epitome of times and fashions." In the end, Uncle Venner joins Clifford, Hepzibah, Phoebe, and Holgrave in their move to the judge's country estate.

Themes

Subsequent Generations Inherit the Sins of Their Ancestors

As stated in the preface, one of the primary themes in *The House of the Seven Gables* is that "the wrong-doing of one generation lives into the successive ones." In this case, Colonel Pyncheon's support of Matthew Maule's prosecution and ultimate execution start the chain of events that seem to carry down through the generations. Just before his death, Matthew Maule (the elder) curses Colonel Pyncheon, stating that "God will give him blood to drink." During the Colonel's first house warming festivities, he indeed dies with blood covering his beard and shirt. This first death is followed by the similar deaths of old Jaffrey Pyncheon and his nephew, Judge Jaffrey Pyncheon. Although these deaths can be attributed to a family predisposition for apoplexy, the existence of the curse and the similar nature of each death suggest something supernatural about the way in which such sinful behavior resurfaces within a family's lineage. This supernatural element conveys the idea that individuals are somewhat unable to control their own destinies. Another way to read Hawthorne's suggested theme, however, is that in this case, the

Topics For Further Study

- Much has been said by critics about the ways in which Hawthorne's life is evidenced in his fiction. Research Hawthorne's life and discuss which people and events in his life seem to surface in this novel. To what extent do you believe that writing this novel helped Hawthorne explore issues of sin and poverty? After writing this novel, do you think he felt better or worse about his ancestors and current social position?

- Some reviewers have been critical of the ending of this novel. Is the pairing of Phoebe and Holgrave believable to you? Does it seem to be too much of a Hollywood ending that neatly cleanses the families of their sordid past? If you could write a new ending, what would you have happen?

- Hawthorne states early on that one of the main themes in this novel is that the sins of the past are passed down through generations. Do you agree or disagree? Can you point to any examples in society today where something like crime seems to persist from generation to generation?

- Can you cite any examples to the contrary where perhaps people have overcome their pasts and made successful lives for themselves?

- Hawthorne named this novel after the house in which most of the action takes place. Why do you think he did this? What does the house symbolize? Can you think of any other titles that he might have given the novel?

- Watch the 1940 film version of the novel. How does the film differ from the book? If you directed the movie, are there sections of the book that you would emphasize or leave out? How would you decide what to include and what to exclude?

- Research the witchcraft trials of 1692 in Salem, Massachusetts. Can you make a case that Colonel Pyncheon may have believed that Matthew Maule was actually a wizard? Or does it seem more likely that the Colonel supported Maule's execution because he wanted to claim Maule's land as his own?

Pyncheon family was not cursed by Matthew Maule and his supernatural powers as much as they were by their own folly. Colonel Pyncheon, old Jaffrey Pyncheon, Alice Pyncheon, and Judge Jaffrey Pyncheon all die because of either their own avarice or that of one of their close family members. To this extent, then, the responsibility for evil or wrong doing lies with the individual rather than with the ancestors who may have made similarly poor decisions and had similar personality and character flaws.

Class Distinctions and the Fall of the Aristocracy

Hawthorne devotes much of his commentary in this novel to the discussion of class. This theme is first introduced by the distinctions between the Pyncheon and Maule families and their descendents. The Pyncheons were a prominent, wealthy, and successful family while the Maules were "generally poverty-stricken; always plebian and obscure; working with unsuccessful diligence at handicrafts; laboring on the wharves, or following the sea." Despite the general financial success of the Pyncheon family, one of its members, Hepzibah, has strikingly fallen from grace. Through her struggle about opening and running the cent-shop readers learn about aristocratic views of the lower classes and vice-versa. Now impoverished, Hepzibah represents both the aristocratic viewpoint and that of the working class. In the third chapter, the narrator writes of her:

> On the whole, therefore, her new experience led our decayed gentlewoman to very disagreeable conclusions as to the temper and manners of what she termed the lower classes, whom, heretofore, she had looked down upon with a gentle and pitying complaisance, as herself occupying a sphere of unquestionable superiority.

Within moments of this thought, however, she expresses disdain for "a lady, in a delicate and costly summer garb, with a floating veil and gracefully swaying gown." She says "for what good end, in the wisdom of Providence, does that woman live? Must the whole world toil, that the palms of her hands may be kept white and delicate?" Although the narrator, and by extension Hawthorne, writes that "since there must be evil in the world . . . a high man is as likely to grasp his share of it as a low one," he seems in part to favor the working class. Of Hepzibah, he writes:

> Truly was there something high, generous, and noble, in her native composition of our poor old Hepzibah . . . . she had been enriched by poverty, developed by sorrow . . . and endowed with heroism, which never could have characterized her in what are called happier circumstances.

Greed's Costly Consequences

Another predominant theme in this novel is greed. Colonel Pyncheon's original motivation for supporting the execution of Matthew Maule (the elder) involved his strong desire to obtain the property that had long belonged to him (Matthew). Ultimately, the Colonel builds his home on Matthew's land and meets his death during his first house-warming feast. Successive generations of Pyncheons also seem to be afflicted with this trait. Gervayse Pyncheon's desire to find the deed to the legendary land in Maine leads to the death of his daughter, Alice. Likewise, Judge Jaffrey Pyncheon's pursuit of his uncle's estate leads to his death and that of his uncle, old Jaffrey Pyncheon. In each case, Pyncheons suffer because of their desire to obtain wealth. This desire blinds them and prohibits them from making moral decisions. Thus, the cost of greed can be seen not only as the loss of morality, but of life itself.

Style

Gothic Romance

The House of the Seven Gables is a Gothic novel, which is a type of novel that was popularized in England in the late eighteenth and early nineteenth centuries. Gothic romances trace back to Horace Walpole's 1765 novel, *The Castle of Otranto* and were often mysteries that involved the supernatural. Characteristically, novels of this type take place in haunted castles or other remote and isolated locations. Often, gothic romances involve a heroine in peril and are peppered with horror and

violence. *The House of the Seven Gables* clearly takes after this genre. Though not a castle, the House of the Seven Gables is a desolate home that has a seemingly ongoing history of violence within its walls. The house is haunted by the curse that Matthew Maule (the elder) placed on Colonel Pyncheon in 1692 just before the former's execution for witchcraft. The mysterious deaths of Colonel Pyncheon, Jaffrey Pyncheon, and Judge Jaffrey Pyncheon, along with Matthew Maule's alleged witchcraft, his grandson's ability to mesmerize Alice Pyncheon, and later Holgrave's ability to do the same with Phoebe all can be seen as supernatural elements within the text.

Third-Person Omniscient and First-Person Plural Point of View

The House of the Seven Gables is told primarily in the third-person omniscient point of view. This means that the narrator, who is not a character in the story, tells the events of the story from a "godlike" perspective. The narrator knows everything about the characters and the events, past and present, relating to the action of the story. Interestingly, there are times that Hawthorne's narrator lapses into the first-person plural point of view, referring to himself and an unknown other person (perhaps the reader, perhaps not) as "we." While the third-person omniscient point of view suggests that the narrator is all-knowing and perhaps reasonably objective, the first-person plural narrative style suggests that the narrator may be telling the story from a more subjective position. In the preface, the narrator makes a point to tell readers that the story they are about to read is a "Romance" rather than a "Novel." The narrator makes this distinction in order to alert readers that the tale is a truth being told in a manner reflecting the "writer's own choosing and creation." This claim and the presence of the first-person plural narration suggests that the narrator is likely imparting his personal take on the events rather than depicting them as a wholly objective narrator might.

Light and Dark Imagery

Light and dark imagery permeates *The House of the Seven Gables*. As Richard Harter Fogle notes in *Hawthorne's Imagery: The Proper 'Light and Shadow' in the Major Romances*, the house as well as the characters are all cast in a reoccurring pattern of lightness-darkness or sunshine-storm. For Fogle, light and sunshine stand for "general good fortune, for material prosperity, and for harmonious kinship with society." On the other hand, he likens

Compare & Contrast

- **1850:** The population of the United States is 23,191,876.

  2000s: In 2000, the population of the United States is 281,421,906.

- **1850:** Hawthorne purchases a house in Concord, Massachusetts for $1,500.

  2000s: In 2004, with prices ranging from $275,000 to $4.8 million, the average home price in Concord, Massachusetts is $600,000.

- **1850:** Working women often work as shopkeepers, seamstresses, domestic servants, teachers, or hat and fan makers.

  2000s: Working women can be found in most every occupation, including corporate management, medicine, dentistry, construction, marketing and communications, trucking, accounting, small business ownership, and software programming.

---

the storm or darkness to "misfortune and the isolation of the original Pyncheon sin." With this observation in mind, one can readily place the characters within their respective realms. Phoebe is associated with light. While Hepzibah and Clifford were once associated with light, they have fallen into darkness. Judge Jaffrey Pyncheon, as Fogle notes, is "a false sun god" who "passes from one extreme to the other." First, he beams smiles and is a picture of beneficence incarnate; then, he changes and exposes his darker, greedier, and ill-intentioned self.

Historical Context

The United States: The Mid-Nineteenth Century

At the beginning of the second half of the nineteenth century, Americans were optimistically looking forward to the future. Opportunity was the buzzword of the day as territorial expansion and the industrial revolution continued to sweep the nation. The gold rush was on in California and with such economic opportunity feeding their dreams, Americans continued to seek land, wealth, and individual success.

Despite such hope and enthusiasm, the country was becoming increasingly divided on the issue of slavery. The debate about abolition was closely linked to the issue of territorial expansion. During

President James K. Polk's term in office, the United States nearly doubled in size, but with this expansion came questions of the status of blacks in the new territories. With the Compromise of 1850, California was admitted to the United States as a "free" state, yet other territories were allowed to decide whether they wanted to permit slavery or not. Also in 1850, the Fugitive Slave Act went into effect, which stated that fugitive slave commissioners could issue arrest warrants for fugitive slaves and order their return to their masters. The act enraged anti-slavery states, and also in 1850, states like Vermont began to pass their own personal-liberty legislation. This legislation stated that fugitive slaves who escaped to free states did not have to be turned over to federal officers for return to their masters. Ultimately, the nation's deeply divided consciousness on the issue of slavery led to the American Civil War, which began in 1861.

While the nation's attention was largely focused on issues of slavery and territorial expansion, the women's rights movement continued to gain strength. The United States Constitution of 1787 lacked specifications about who had the right to vote, and thus left the question up to the states, who largely granted such rights only to landowning white men. In 1848, a group of women who supported abolition met in Seneca Falls, New York, and sought to change this preference. The group, which included Elizabeth Cady Stanton and Lucretia Mott, officially set the Woman's Rights Movement in motion, calling for suffrage and equal

1912 painting depiction of the house as described in Nathaniel Hawthorne's The House of the Seven Gables

rights for women and blacks. In 1850, the first national women's rights convention was held in Worcester, Massachusetts, with Susan B. Anthony, Soujourner Truth, and Lucretia Mott all in attendance.

Witchcraft and the Salem Witchcraft Trials of 1692

In 1692, a group of young women in Salem Village, which is now called Danvers, became hysterical after engaging in fortune telling rituals. The group, which included the minister's daughter, Ann Putnam, were eventually diagnosed as being under the spell of witchcraft and were pressed to tell who it was that had bewitched them. The girls began to accuse people, starting with three neighborhood women. The fervor took hold of the community and with a growing number of imprisonments resulting, the newly appointed Massachusetts governor (Sir William Phips) convened a special court to try the accused. In the months that followed, one hundred and fifty arrests were made, and many people were imprisoned. In the end, twenty individuals were hanged for the crime of practicing witchcraft. Hawthorne's great-grandfather, John Hathorne, was one of the three judges to preside over the trials.

In 1711, the Massachusetts General Court financially compensated the families of some of the victims and their families for the wrongdoing.

Critical Overview

Like much of Hawthorne's work, *The House of the Seven Gables* has received ongoing attention from critics and scholars since its publication in 1851. The Nathaniel Hawthorne Society (http://asweb. artsci.uc.edu/english/HawthorneSociety/nh.html), which was formed in 1976 for scholars interested in his work, reflects the degree to which Hawthorne's writing is still very much alive and vital in present day academia. To Hawthorne's credit, his work remains in print and remains part of the core curriculum taught in American literature courses.

Of his critics, Hawthorne himself was likely one of the strongest. In the introduction to *Hawthorne: The Critical Heritage*, J. Donald Crowley quotes Hawthorne writing to Longfellow:

> As to my literary efforts, I do not think much of them—neither is it worthwhile to be ashamed of them. They would have been better, I trust, if written under more favorable circumstances. I have no external excitement—no consciousness that the public would like what I wrote, nor much hope, nor a very passionate desire that they should do so. Nevertheless, having nothing else to be ambitious of, I have felt considerably interested in literature.

Of *The House of the Seven Gables*, Crowley quotes Hawthorne again:

> Sometimes, when tired of it, it strikes me that the whole is an absurdity from beginning to end . . . my prevailing idea is, that the book ought to succeed better than "The Scarlet Letter," though I have no idea it will.

In fact, *The House of the Seven Gables* did succeed better than *The Scarlet Letter* and both have continued to be some of Hawthorne's best-known and studied work.

As can be expected, the reviews, commentary, and critical analysis of *The House of the Seven Gables* have varied in focus over the past one-hundred and fifty-three years and will likely continue to do so. In *"The House of the Seven Gables": Severing Family and Colonial Ties*, Peter Buitenhuis notes that "each age has to reevaluate the classics and read them in the light of its own cultural and critical assumptions, which gradually change over time."

Upon its publication, *The House of the Seven Gables* garnered much praise. Writing for *Graham's Magazine* in 1851, Edwin Percy Whipple wrote "Taken as a whole, it is Hawthorne's greatest work, and is equally sure of immediate popularity and permanent fame." Henry Fothergill Chorley would agree. In his review of the novel for *Athanaeum* in 1851, Chorley wrote that Hawthorne "possesses the fertility as well as the ambition of Genius." He further commented that "few will dispute his claim to rank amongst the most original and complete novelists that have appeared in modern times."

In his day and beyond, however, Hawthorne has had his dissenters. He has been criticized for his characterizations, the novel's lack of plot structure, its point of view, and the somewhat too neatly tied up ending. In *Rage for Order: Essays in Criticism, 1948*, Austin Warren wrote "The characters do not really develop or change; and we do not find it easy to remember their speech, for Hawthorne has no considered notion of what parts of his story to put into dialogue, what not." He further criticizes the novel's point of view, stating:

> The point of view is clumsily managed, for the novel professes to be narrated by an "I" who presently passes into "we." ... The mind of no character is consistently used.... He never really gains by his liberties of omniscient commentator.

Despite its weaknesses, *The House of the Seven Gables* continues to be regarded as one of Hawthorne's greatest works and has served as fodder for a continuing diverse range of critical study. Critics have analyzed the work from divergent perspectives, evaluating its autobiographical, psychological, social, emotional, mythical, historical, and political implications. To be sure, such a wide range of interpretations will continue, for as Buitenhuis reminds "there is never an end to interpretation."

Criticism

Dustie Robeson

Robeson is a freelance writer with a master's degree in English. In this essay, Robeson explores the ambiguous views expressed in the novel about the aristocracy and the working classes.

Class distinctions permeate *The House of the Seven Gables*. The story commences with an immediate contrast between the wealthy Colonel Pyncheon and the farmer, Matthew Maule. Later, at Colonel Pyncheon's housewarming party, guests are either ushered into the kitchen or into the home's more stately rooms depending on "the high or low degree" of each person. Through these early images, readers have an immediate sense that issues of social class are one of Hawthorne's central themes. In that the novel is considered to reflect much of Hawthorne's own life, one must wonder to what degree his views about the aristocracy and the working classes are embedded within the story.

On the one hand, one might readily conclude that Hawthorne held contempt and disdain for the aristocracy for their idleness and unwavering interest in the acquisition of material wealth. The first villain of the story, Colonel Pyncheon, exemplifies all that is reprehensible in men of questionable morals who are self-indulgent and motivated simply by the desire to build their estates, figuratively and literally. At the same time, the characterization of Hepzibah serves to point out the lack of purpose or function that can sometimes epitomize the upper classes. While Hepzibah's shame about falling into poverty and being forced to open a cent-shop is an absolute horror to her, the narrator at times adapts a somewhat mocking tone in regards to both her angst and her understanding of her previously privileged social position. The narrator describes Hepzibah as having a "deeply cherished and ridiculous consciousness of long descent" from wealthy ancestors. Further, when the narrator notes her "accomplishments," which include "having formerly thrummed on a harpsichord, and walked a minuet, and worked an antique tapestry-stitch on her sampler," one can almost hear the laughter in the description. Of the shop opening, Hepzibah concludes "I never can go through with it! Never, never, never! I wish I were dead, and in the old family-tomb, with all my forefathers!" She no longer considers herself a lady of gentility and fears that she has brought a terrible disgrace upon her family. Yet, through Hepzibah's dialogue with Holgrave, readers glean a different perspective, one perhaps embraced by Hawthorne. Holgrave encourages Hepzibah, telling her:

> These names of gentleman and lady had a meaning, in the past history of the world, and conferred privileges, desirable and otherwise, on those entitled to bear them. In the present—and still more in the future condition of society—they imply, not privilege, but restrictions!

He further assures her:

> I look upon this as one of the fortunate days of your life. It ends an epoch and begins one. Hitherto, the lifeblood has been gradually chilling in your veins, as you sat aloof, within your circle of gentility, while

> Hawthorne's ambiguous representation of the two classes and his imagery of the procession suggest that his disdain and admiration is not for one class or the other, but rather for all of humanity."

the rest of the world was fighting out its battle with one kind o necessity or another. Henceforth, you will at least have the sense of healthy and natural effort for a purpose.

For Hawthorne, there is something almost laughable in Hepzibah's dramatic feeling of loss, for to him, the aristocratic ways are a thing of the past, and valor and honor are now born of self-determination rather than inherited good fortune. Hawthorne's strongest opinions about the aristocracy's ongoing concern for the accrual of wealth seem to be conveyed best by the narrator's view of the monkey who accompanies the organ player. Of the monkey, the narrator says that he symbolized "the grossest form of the love of money. Neither was there any possibility of satisfying the covetous little devil." Through allusions to the devil and the Ten Commandments ("Neither shall you covet your neighbor's wife. Neither shall you desire your neighbor's house, or field . . . or anything that belongs to your neighbor.": Deuteronomy 5:21), Hawthorne shows not just a great disdain, but a moral aversion to aristocratic motivations. Through Uncle Venner, Hawthorne reinforces this perspective: "Men make a wonderful mistake in trying to head up a wonderful mistake in trying to heap up property upon property."

While the aristocracy seems to be looked down upon in this novel, the working class representatives seem to be respected, if not lauded. Phoebe is a perfect example. Although she is a Pyncheon, she is not part of the aristocracy, and yet, she is described by the narrator as more of a lady than Hepzibah. Further, because of her experience as a working class person, Hepzibah is viewed by the narrator as a better person: "She had been enriched by poverty, developed by sorrow, elevated by the strong and solitary affection of her life, and thus endowed with heroism, which never could have characterized her in what are called happier circumstances." Indeed, Hepzibah is improved by the experience. Once the shop is under way, she is filled with "a thrill of almost youthful enjoyment." The narrator notes:

> It was the invigorating breath of a fresh outward atmosphere, after the long torpor and monotonous seclusion of her life. So wholesome is effort! So miraculous the strength that we do not know of! The healthiest glow, that Hepzibah had known for years, had come now, in the dreaded crisis, when, for the first time, she had put forth her hand to help herself.

Holgrave's assessment of the situation again perhaps reveals Hawthorne's own opinion. Of the shop opening, Holgrave tells Hepzibah, "This is success—all the success that anybody meets with!"

While the above seems to clearly indicate Hawthorne's distaste for the aristocracy and more favorable impression of the working classes, the novel also offers examples that would lead readers to question this assessment. For example, despite his position as a wealthy Pyncheon, old Jaffrey Pyncheon was compelled to right the wrongs of his ancestor, Colonel Pyncheon. Unlike the Colonel, old Jaffrey Pyncheon was a man of morals, who wanted to do right by the farmer whom he (old Jaffrey) believed suffered unjustly. Similarly, although his ancestor, Matthew Maule, used powers of hypnotism in mean spirited ways, Holgrave is not compelled to do the same. He is instead a man of integrity who argues that individuals have the power to direct and create their own future. In these instances, the behavior expected from old Jaffrey Pyncheon and Holgrave runs counter to that of their ancestors. In another interesting reversal, Hepzibah changes her opinion both of the aristocratic and lower classes. After opening her shop, Hepzibah finds herself struggling "against a bitter emotion . . . towards the idle aristocracy," and at the same time coming to "very disagreeable conclusions as to the temper and manners of what she termed the lower classes, who, heretofore, she had looked down upon with a gentle and pitying complaisance, as herself occupying a sphere of unquestionable superiority."

In addition to the above, one must also consider the novel's ending in order to further flush out Hawthorne's message about social classes. In the end, Clifford and Hepzibah, once aristocratic and then destitute, inherit great wealth. Clifford, who earlier favored the things of the past, comes to expound the virtues of modern technology. Additionally, Phoebe and Holgrave, two characters whose bloodlines symbolize the historic conflict

What Do I Read Next?

- One of Hawthorne's best-known and respected novels is *The Scarlet Letter* (1850).

- Hawthorne self-published his first novel *Fanshawe* in 1828.

- Following the publication of *The House of the Seven Gables*, Hawthorne completed two additional novels: *The Blithedale Romance* (1852) and *The Marble Faun* (1860).

- Herman Melville and Hawthorne shared a brief friendship from 1850 until 1856. The two reviewed each other's work publicly and even after Hawthorne's death, Melville continued to read and annotate Hawthorne's work. Melville's character Vine in his long poem *Clarel: A Poem and Pilgrimage in the Holy Land* (published by Northwestern University Press in 1991) is believed to be based on Hawthorne.

- Another poem by Herman Melville that is believed to be about Hawthorne is "Monody," which first appeared in *Timoleon* (published by Folcroft Library Editions in 1976) and can also be found in *American Poetry : The Nineteenth Century: Herman Melville to Trumbull Stickney, American Indian Poetry, Folk Songs and Spirituals* (published by the Library of America in 1993).

---

between the Pyncheons and the less well-to-do Maules, fall in love and marry. Holgrave, once a progressive and liberal man, finds himself becoming more conservative. Interestingly, the social and political extremes that seem so well articulated in the beginning of the novel all seem to reverse themselves or blend and merge toward the end. In several instances, Hawthorne hints at this tendency toward homogenization. When the parade passes the House of the Seven Gables, it is described as follows: Seen from above, the procession "melts all petty personalities, of which it is made up, into one broad mass of existence—one great life—one collected body of mankind, with a vast, homogenous spirit animating it." Earlier, he notes that "Since there is evil in the world, a high man or a low man are just as likely to grasp it."

Thus, although the novel seems to suggest a preference toward the working classes, one can certainly also conclude in a closer reading, that neither the privileged or the working classes are above reproach or solely worthy of praise. Hawthorne's ambiguous representation of the two classes and his imagery of the procession suggest that his disdain and admiration is not for one class or the other, but rather for all of humanity. He presents men's weaknesses and strengths and in the end seems to suggest that just evil-doers can be found in all walks of life, so can ladies and gentleman. Hawthorne's proscription for humanity ends well. Holgrave's belief that each person is empowered to create a good life for him or herself independent of their past and perhaps their personal foibles is a lasting message of hope. Although he says, "For, what other dungeon is so dark as one's own heart! What jailer so inexorable as one's self," the flip side of this is also true. There is nothing brighter than one's personal passions and convictions, nor it there anything more freeing than striving to live well in the world.

Source: Dustie Robeson, Critical Essay on *The House of the Seven Gables*, in *Novels for Students*, Thomson Gale, 2005.

Joyce Hart

Hart has degrees in English and creative writing and is the author of several books. In this essay, Hart explores Hawthorne's use of environment to emphasize the psychological state of his characters.

The settings, or environments, that surround Hawthorne's characters in his novel *The House of the Seven Gables* are not only as fully detailed as the people in the novel are, but they make up an integral part of the story itself. For example, Hawthorne uses the rooms in which his characters sleep, the houses in which they live, as well as the light and darkness that surround them as a way to further describe and define the people he has created

> "The thought of locking the door to block Phoebe is symbolic of Hepzibah making sure that her own heart and soul remain closed."

in this story. By exploring these environments, readers gain a deeper understanding of his characters and appreciate more fully how Hawthorne uses this technique to fully develop and enrich his story.

Beginning with the maiden lady, Hepzibah Pyncheon, Hawthorne introduces this main character and then describes an old dresser whose drawers Hepzibah has to struggle to open. Like this antiquated piece of furniture, Hepzibah creaks and groans, her joints cracking and her loud sighs filling the room with noise. Also like her furniture, or more specifically like the drawers of the dresser, Hepzibah has a hard time opening her heart and soul. She has closed herself off to the outside world and only with difficulty will she open up, even to her soon-to-arrive relative, Phoebe. Hepzibah is a rigid old woman, set in her ways, which Hawthorne describes by mentioning the stiffness of her silk skirt. She is like an old dress, stored in a suitcase filled with mothballs. When she finally opens the door to her room to go downstairs, she releases a deep sigh, which Hawthorne likens to "a gust of chill, damp wind out of a long-closed vault."

Almost everywhere this old woman walks, lives, and breathes, darkness, stiffness, and a sense of being boxed in follow her. She wears black-colored clothes and passes through hallways and rooms that are bleak and darkened by time. Where there once was color in the rugs, there are now only thin and worn-out shades of gray. Doors to rooms around her are locked and bolted. In one room through which Hepzibah passes, Hawthorne purposefully describes a set of chairs that are "straight and stiff, and so ingeniously contrived for the discomfort of the human person that they were irksome even to sight." Hawthorne uses the description of these chairs to further depict the discomfort of Hepzibah's physical and psychological essence. Neither she nor the people who come into her presence are at ease.

Hepzibah is not a worldly woman. She has lived a sheltered life and has seldom left her home. She is like her house, whose front door has not provided entry to stranger or kin for a long time. But necessity forces Hepzibah to make concessions. Although she does not go out into the world, facing it head on, she does admit the public through a side room, the small discarded shop that she has renovated. Because she is desperate for money, Hepzibah will force herself to face the public. But, she does so reluctantly. As she has done with most of her emotions, hiding them in the dark recesses of her psyche, she also will do with her physical self. While Hepzibah has placed herself in a vulnerable position by inviting the public into her shop, she is not without escape. The shop is connected to her house, allowing her to quickly dart into the confines and the darkness of its privacy whenever her emotions overwhelm her; whenever the public comes too close.

Furthering the relationship between Hepzibah and the shop, Hawthorne informs his readers that a change is taking place. The shop, which had been heavily curtained to keep its interior out of sight, has been recently transformed. The cobwebs and rust have been cleared away. The shelves and bins have been filled with "merchantable goods." Likewise, Hepzibah is experiencing a transformation. She is, in Hawthorne's words, stepping "down from her pedestal of imaginary rank." Hepzibah's life is changing in more ways than she can imagine. One of those major adjustments will come to her in the person of Phoebe Pyncheon, a character who is as bright as Hepzibah is dull. To emphasize this contrast, Hawthorne portrays Hepzibah's first encounter with Phoebe by having Hepzibah stand in a darkened hallway, staring through a "dusty" window to see Phoebe, who is standing outside in the light.

Phoebe, in contrast to Hepzibah, is described as "fresh" and "unconventional" and far too beautiful to have come to this house with its "sordid and ugly luxuriance of gigantic weeds that grew in the angle of the house, and the heavy projection [of the door frame] that overshadowed her." Phoebe brings to this dark and dank home of Hepzibah the exuberance of spring and country air. At first, this throws Hepzibah back into the deep shadows as she considers not only not opening the door but also locking it so Phoebe cannot come in. It is as if Hepzibah realizes in advance that Phoebe's light will affect her, and this idea frightens her. The thought of locking the door to block Phoebe is symbolic of Hepzibah making sure that her own heart and soul remain closed.

Hepzibah, however, gives in and allows Phoebe to enter. Later that night, Phoebe sleeps in a room that is heavy with dark. An old canopy is stretched over the bed, which Hawthorne describes as being like a brooding cloud. However, in the morning, the light steals into the room, and upon finding Phoebe there, Hawthorn states that "the dawn kissed her brow." In other words, Phoebe's appearance has brought the sun into the once-dark house. Hawthorne has positioned this room in which Phoebe will stay as one that overlooks the garden. Phoebe, a country girl, needs the fresh air and sun, just as a flower does. She will, accordingly, spend much of her time in the garden, restoring the health and vigor of the plants and animals she finds there. It is in the garden, too, that Phoebe first meets Mr. Holgrave, a young man she will later marry. Their love blossoms as do the ancient plants that had previously been deteriorating due to a lack of care. In contrast to the negative attributes of the color black that Hawthorne uses to describe the interior of the house, in the garden, the color black designates something positive. Hawthorne describes the fertility of the black soil, which has been enriched from years and years of compost. As Hawthorne puts it, this soil has been enriched by "the decay of a long period of time; such as fallen leaves, the petals of flowers, and the stalks and seed vessels of vagrant and lawless plants." Death and decay in the house, or in Hepzibah's world, is morbid and unhealthy; but in the garden, death is the source of renewed life. The fallen garden debris will provide nutrients for the new plants, much as Phoebe will supply a new source of energy for Hepzibah.

Also in the garden are some chickens, which Hawthorne uses to reflect on the decaying lineage of the Pyncheons. These chickens were once a proud breed. Their meat was succulent, and their eggs were of enormous size. But, the fowl have withered over the years and are now gouty. Even their clucking noises sound despondent and depressed. So, too, have the Pyncheons withered. Only a few descendants are left. Their fortune is dwindling; their ancestral house is falling apart; and, they have yet to rid themselves of the curse of Matthew Maule, the old wizard from whom the first Pyncheon stole property. Like the chickens, the Pyncheons are shrinking in size, and their output (like the chicken's once succulent meat and eggs) is paltry in comparison to what it used to be.

But there is hope. Phoebe weeds the flowerbeds and cultivates the heirloom blossoms, encouraging them to perfume the air. As she does so, she weeds the misery out of Hepzibah and her brother, Clifford. "Little Phoebe," writes Hawthorne, "was one of those persons who possess . . . the gift of practical arrangement . . . a kind of natural magic that enables these favored ones to bring out the hidden capabilities of things around them." Phoebe will change and rearrange the lives of Hepzibah and Clifford to the point that they no longer recognize themselves. She will open them up to their potential by just being herself: a young woman full of light and love.

Clifford is another character upon whom Hawthorne throws metaphors through the immediate environment. Clifford, as readers find out toward the conclusion of the novel, was unjustly imprisoned for a crime he did not commit. Even upon his release, Clifford remains a prisoner, this time a prisoner of his own psychology. Like Hepzibah, Clifford remains locked up, so to speak, in the house of the seven gables, refusing to, or afraid to, leave the premise. However, there is one delightful scene in which Hawthorne places this brother and sister. It is their short-lived run for freedom upon a train. As the train rushes them from their home to some unknown destination, the usual metaphor of travel, that of taking someone into the future, is turned on its head. Clifford and Hepzibah have so long lived in the past that the train ride they take actually delivers them to the present. So taken by the speed and newness of her situation, Hepzibah asks: "Clifford! Clifford! Is not this a dream?" To which her brother replies: "A dream, Hepzibah . . . on the contrary, I have never been awake before!"

The speed of the train not only takes Clifford to the wide-awake present moment, it inspires his thoughts and moves his tongue. He cannot help but express himself out loud in clear sentences and profound thought. It is as if modern technology, of which Clifford had previously had little experience, stirs him from his somewhat walking-dead state and tries urgently to make up to him all the spirit that was stolen from him by his imprisonment. For a few moments, it is successful. Once Clifford steps off the train and back onto the motionless soil, his exuberance fades a bit, but his life, as he will soon learn, is forever changed. He returns home, as an adult, ready to face his consequences.

As the brother and sister make their way home, Hawthorne turns the reader's attention to young Holgrave, who shares the house of the seven gables. It is interesting to note that although Holgrave lives in this house, he does so only precariously. He stays in a wing of the house that is shut off from the main portion by doors, locks, and deadbolts. So, too, is Holgrave's existence, in association with the Pyncheons, only vaguely connected. His ancestors' lives are intertwined with those of the Pycheons, but he is not related by blood. His life is related to theirs in about as much as his status as a roomer in the same house with them. He is there. He observes them, hears them, knows them, but that is about as close as he gets. That is, until he meets Phoebe. She is the bridge, the one who rids her family of Holgrave's family curse. Phoebe will undo the locks so the doors can be opened, which is exactly how Hawthorne ends this story.

Hograve and Phoebe decide that the best thing they can do is to open the front doors so the magistrate can enter the house. With the opening of the house, not only does the public enter in, but the Pyncheons are able to go out. Thus ends the long habitation of generations of Pyncheons in the house of the seven gables. Symbolic of this change is the portrait of Colonel Pyncheon that lies on the floor. With the removal of this portrait, light exposes the hidden document of wealth. The iron-clad rule and all the curses of the older generations have been put to rest.

The newest generation, represented by Holgrave and Phoebe, will move to a house made of stone. Such a house, Holgrave claims, will allow future generations to alter the interior "to suit its own taste and convenience." And, the stony façade will add "venerableness to permanence."

Source: Joyce Hart, Critical Essay on *The House of the Seven Gables*, in *Novels for Students*, Thomson Gale, 2005.

John L. Idol Jr.

In the following excerpt, Idol discusses The House of the Seven Gables *as an example of Hawthorne's "theory of romance composition."*

. . . Although Hawthorne's introductory essay to *The Scarlet Letter* was written after he completed the romance, besides being an engaging personal essay and a consummate display of his talents as humorist and satirist, it has two important links to the romance. One link is that Hawthorne pointedly insists upon his Puritan heritage, beginning with the "bearded, sable-cloaked, and steeple-crowned progenitor" William Hathorne, "soldier, legislator, judge," who was "likewise a better persecutor," remembered for his severity toward a woman of the Quaker sect and continuing with William's son, John, who never recanted his decision in the Salem witch trials. Hawthorne confides that "strong traits of their nature have intertwined themselves with mine." The second link arises from the literary game that Hawthorne plays with his readers by pretending that the work he offers to them is only his edited version of a dusty account stashed away by a predecessor in the Custom House, Jonathan Pue, whose pastime as a local antiquarian led him to uncover the story behind a scrap of cloth bearing a scarlet letter.

More important, however, is Hawthorne's statement about the workings of his imagination, which he describes as a kind of spiritualizing agent working upon actualities, somewhat like the transformation of objects seen by moonlight rather than sunlight. For the writer of romances, unlike the writer of novels, photographic realism is not the object but rather something "invested with a quality of strangeness and remoteness, though still almost as vividly present as by sunlight." The romancer, Hawthorne asserts, requires a "neutral territory, somewhere between the real world and fairy-land, where the Actual and the Imaginary may meet, and each imbue itself with the nature of the other." He enlarged upon this theory of romance composition in later works, particularly *The House of the Seven Gables* (1851) and *The Marble Faun; or, The Romance of Monte Beni* (1860; first published in London as *Transformation: or, The Romance of Monte Beni*, 1860).

Appearing under the imprint of Ticknor, Reed, and Fields, with Fields crediting himself with having prompted Hawthorne to enlarge his draft of a tale about Hester to the length of a romance, *The Scarlet Letter* won instant praise but failed to bring in funds sufficient for the Hawthornes to remain in Salem. They found more economical quarters in the Berkshires, at Stockbridge, near Lenox. Celebrated for its summer colony of intellectuals and writers, the area attracted such literary figures as James Russell Lowell, Oliver Wendell Holmes, and Fannie Kemble. Not far away, in Pittsfield, Herman Melville had his permanent home.

Once the family settled in, Hawthorne enjoyed one of his most productive periods, writing *The House of the Seven Gables* and *A Wonder-book for Girls and Boys* (1851), adding a preface to a new edition of *Twice-Told Tales* (1851), and drawing together seventeen previously uncollected tales, among them "My Kinsman, Major Molineux" and "Ethan Brand," under the title *The Snow-Image, and Other Twice-Told Tales* (1852). This flurry of creativity and editing enabled him, for the first time, to meet the family's expenses.

Although he bade "forever farewell to this abominable" Salem, upon leaving for the Berkshires he instantly returned to his ancestral city for the setting of *The House of the Seven Gables*, not, he insists, "to describe local manners" nor to draw upon real personages there, his characters being, he asserts, "really of the author's own making." The claim is a smokescreen, since traits of Charles Wentworth Upham, the man most eager to remove Hawthorne from his customhouse position, were obvious to persons in Hawthorne's circle when they read his presentation of Judge Pyncheon. Hawthorne's sister Elizabeth has confirmed Upham was the model.

A brighter tale than his first romance, notably because Hawthorne shaped it to have a happy ending, *The House of the Seven Gables* traces events that stem from the rapacious deeds of the earliest Pyncheon, who forced the Maule family from its well-situated lot to build a home grand enough to match his aristocratic yearnings. The displaced Maule uttered a curse upon being ousted from his property, a curse passing from generation to generation and ending only with the union between descendants of the original disputants—Holgrave, the Maule descendant, and Phoebe Pyncheon.

Before presenting the characters upon whose shoulders he places the burden of ancient wrongs and within whose hearts he fixes remedies to cure past misdeeds, Hawthorne gives an account of the house and the family that inhabited it—a proud family with aristocratic pretensions that gradually had lost position and sunk into the near poverty it had reached as the story opens. A salient detail from this background information is that the original builder, Colonel Pyncheon, died quickly and mysteriously on the day he opened his grand new home for his fellow townsmen to see. His grim-faced portrait has remained in the house ever since his untimely death. Unknown to his descendants, behind that portrait repose a map and deed that might have helped the family secure aristocratic standing. The quest for them continues until the present moment, and that is where the principal action of the romance begins.

Now inhabiting the house are Hepzibah Pyncheon—ladylike, proud, and virtually penniless, forced by necessity to open a portion of the house as a shop; Holgrave, a renter—social reformer, man of various pursuits in his attempt to establish himself; and Clifford Pyncheon—a shell of a man just released from prison after serving a sentence as the (wrongly) convicted killer of his uncle. To the house come two others, Phoebe Pyncheon, a country cousin not brought up as a Pyncheon, and Judge Pyncheon, a modern embodiment of the worst family traits. Phoebe ultimately teams with Holgrave

> **" The drama of the romance arises from a conflict involving forces representing the past and energies directed toward living within the present and looking toward the future."**

to be a liberating force to end the curse, while Judge Pyncheon remains enslaved to the family's dream of aristocratic standing to the last—dying just as the governor's post seems within his grasp.

The drama of the romance arises from a conflict involving forces representing the past and energies directed toward living within the present and looking toward the future. Hepzibah—scowling, ugly, isolated, but compassionate in her dealings with her brother, Clifford, a devotee of beauty incapable of dealing with life as it is—desperately wishes to remain a lady and cannot cope with her new station as a shopkeeper. Falsely accused by Judge Pyncheon of killing his uncle, Clifford, on his release from prison, returns to his ancestral home and breaks free from his past only upon the untimely death of Judge Pyncheon. Whether he will be capable of dealing with freedom without the help of Hepzibah and Phoebe is uncertain, since there is something suicidal in his desire to rejoin humanity— he almost leaps from an upper-story window.

The dark, moldering house and the diminutive chickens remaining in the yard symbolize the fall of the Pyncheons from high estate to low. Yet, decayed as the house is, Judge Pyncheon believes that it somewhere conceals a map that will enable him to lay claim, at last, to a princely tract of land in Maine. That belief brings him to the house, motivates his wish to speak with Clifford, and precipitates his clash with Hepzibah. The judge's imperial ways offend Phoebe, the ray of sunshine that brightens the house and Clifford's life, and she helps Hepzibah delay the judge's inquisition of Clifford. As he waits in Colonel Pyncheon's old chair, the judge suddenly dies in the same manner as his rapacious forebear. His death not only proves psychologically liberating but also allows Hepzibah, Clifford, Phoebe, and Holgrave to leave the dilapidated house and move to the judge's country estate.

This happy ending seems forced to many of Hawthorne's readers, especially the final decision of Holgrave and his parting words, for, from a position asserting that one generation should not be burdened with houses and property passed down from a preceding one, Holgrave has turned conservative, expressing a wish that the Judge had built the house of stone rather than wood. As Terence Martin has pointed out, Holgrave did qualify his statement by saying that the exterior should have been stone and that future inhabitants should be free to redesign and furnish the shell as they see fit. Thus, Hawthorne suggests that certain conservative forces are necessary to guarantee stability and that if future generations need to make changes to keep a society viable, there should be no impediment to desirable adjustments. Perhaps that is why Hawthorne told his friend Horatio Bridge that he considered *The House of the Seven Gables* "better than" *The Scarlet Letter. The House of the Seven Gables* became a vehicle for his political views as it afforded him the opportunity to dramatize the moral of his romance: "namely, that the wrongdoing of one generation lives into successive ones, and, divesting itself of every temporary advantage, becomes pure and uncontrollable mischief."

Herman Melville, whom Hawthorne had met at a picnic outing some months before completing *The House of the Seven Gables* and with whom he had exchanged visits as well as philosophic ideas, wrote to praise the romance and to share an assessment of Hawthorne's nature: "There is a certain tragic phase of humanity which, in our opinion, was never more powerfully embodied than by Hawthorne. We mean the tragicalness of human thought in its own unbiased, native, and profounder workings.... There is the grand truth about Nathaniel Hawthorne. He says No! in thunder; but the Devil himself cannot make him say *yes*." In both thought and artistry Melville reaped a rich harvest from his association with Hawthorne; the most significant outcome was Melville's rewriting of *Moby-Dick; or The Whale* (1851), which Melville dedicated to Hawthorne. Hawthorne's sympathetic reading of that novel and his letter of congratulations (now lost) lifted Melville's spirits: "Your heart beat in my ribs and mine in yours, and both in God's. A sense of unspeakable security is in me this moment, on account of your having understood the book."

Even as he was touching another writer's heart with his latest romance, Hawthorne turned his hand to children's literature again, adapting Greek myths for a collection titled *A Wonder-book for Girls and Boys*. He created as his narrator, an energetic, playful, and articulate Williams College student named Eustace Bright, who, over a stretch of autumnal days, recasts tales of Perseus, Midas, Pandora, Hercules, and Philemon and Baucis for charmingly named children, among whom are Periwinkle, Sweet Fern, Squash-Blossom, Milkweed, and Buttercup. They are eager, spirited listeners who assume personalities as their imaginative young mentor spins his tales. The book had original illustrations done by Hammat Billings and enjoyed sales brisk enough to encourage Hawthorne to adapt a second set of myths, which appeared as *Tanglewood Tales for Girls and Boys: Being a Second Wonder-book* (1853)....

Source: John L. Idol Jr., "Nathaniel Hawthorne," in *Dictionary of Literary Biography*, Volume 223, *The American Renaissance in New England Second Series*, edited by Wesley T. Mott, Gale, 2000, pp. 183–218.

Sources

Buitenhuis, Peter, "Critical Reception," in his *"The House of the Seven Gables": Severing Family and Colonial Ties*, Twayne's Masterwork Studies, No. 66, Twayne Publishers, 1991, p. 11.

Chorley, Henry Fothergill, *"The House of Seven Gables,"* in *Athenaeum*, Scarecrow Author Bibliographies, No. 82, Scarecrow Press, 1988, p. 88.

Crowley, J. Donald, "Introduction," in *Hawthorne: The Critical Heritage*, Barnes & Noble, 1970, pp. 7, 9.

Fogle, Richard Harter, "III: *The House of Seven Gables*," in *Hawthorne's Imagery: The Proper "Light and Shadow" in the Major Romances*, University of Oklahoma Press, 1969, pp. 49, 50, 52.

Hawthorne, Nathaniel, *The House of the Seven Gables*, Modern Library, 2001.

Meeks, Wayne A., ed., "Deuteronomy 5:21," in *The Harper-Collins Study Bible*, New Revised Standard Version, HarperCollins Publishers, 1989, p. 278.

Warren, Austin, "Nathaniel Hawthorne," in *Rage for Order: Essays in Criticism*, 1948, reprint, University of Michigan Press, 1959, pp. 84–103.

Whipple, Edwin Percy, *"The House of Seven Gables,"* in *Graham's Magazine*, Vol. XXXVIII, No. 6, June 1851, pp. 467–68.

Further Reading

Boswell, Jeanetta, *Nathaniel Hawthorne and the Critics: A Checklist of Criticism, 1900–1978*, Rowman & Littlefield, 1982.

> As the title suggests, this volume provides a selection of criticism about Hawthorne through the greater part of the twentieth century.

Martin, Terrence, *Nathaniel Hawthorne*, rev. ed., Twayne Publishers, 1983.
> In addition to providing biographical information, Martin explores Hawthorne's major works.

Mellow, James R., *Nathaniel Hawthorne in His Times*, Houghton Mifflin, 1980.
> Mellow's biography is an important resource for all students interested in learning more about Hawthorne and his contemporaries.

Person, Leland S., *A Historical Guide to Nathaniel Hawthorne*, edited by Larry J. Reynolds, Oxford University Press, 2001.
> In addition to providing bibliographic information, Person's collection of essays includes a chapter about mesmerism in *The House of the Seven Gables*, a chapter about Hawthorne and history, and an illustrated chronology of history that maps Hawthorne's life to relevant historical events.

Rosenthal, Bernard, ed. *Critical Essays on Hawthorne's "The House of the Seven Gables,"* G. K. Hall, 1995.
> In this collection of essays, Rosenthal provides readers with an in-depth and readable look at one of Hawthorne's best known novels.

Scharnhorst, Gary, *Nathaniel Hawthorne: An Annotated Bibliography of Comment and Criticism before 1900*, Scarecrow Press, 1988.
> This volume provides a comprehensive bibliography for criticism about Hawthorne's works through 1900. Each entry includes a brief quote from the article. All mentions of the *The House of the Seven Gables* can be conveniently found through the index, which cross references the entries by topic.

Wagenknecht, Edward, *Nathaniel Hawthorne: The Man, His Tales and Romances*, Ungar, 1989.
> Wagenknecht takes a close look at the relationship between Hawthorne's life and his fiction, including a section dedicated to *The House of the Seven Gables*.

Wineapple, Brenda, *Hawthorne: A Life*, Knopf, 2003.
> In this lengthy biography of Hawthorne, Wineapple traces the writer's life—his marriage, friendships, politics, religious beliefs, and career—to its end in 1864.

The Hunchback
of Notre Dame

Victor Hugo

1831

By the time Victor Hugo wrote *The Hunchback of Notre Dame* (published in French as *Notre-Dame de Paris*), he had already made a name for himself as a poet and dramatist. Although he had written one other novel (*Han d'Islande*, 1823), he had not really been known as a novelist. *The Hunchback of Notre Dame* was to change all that. Even more popular than it became throughout the twentieth century and into the early 2000s, this romantic story grabbed the imagination of the French people who embraced it for its melodramatic storyline and Hugo's detailed rendering of the life and culture of fifteenth-century Paris.

On the surface, *The Hunchback of Notre Dame* is a story of unrequited love between a man horribly disfigured and a beautiful woman who loves someone else. But Hugo was a very complex writer who gave his readers a much more complicated story. Underneath the unfolding of Quasimodo's love of La Esmeralda is a historical drama set in 1482, a time that in many ways mirrored the times and political struggles of Hugo's nineteenth-century world. With almost the entire novel set in the cathedral of Notre Dame, the novel also conveys a spiritual element not only in its setting but in its characters. There is a priest who has lost his spiritual path; there is a physically disfigured man who is shunned and must find solace not in the material world but deep within himself; and there is the beautiful woman, innocence personified, who searches for a spiritual form of love.

Although his contemporaries applauded his novel, in many ways Hugo's *The Hunchback of Notre Dame* was also shocking in its time. Hugo was, after all, a central figure of the Romantic Movement in literature. Readers, prior to Hugo's works, were used to literature that was influenced more by the classical form, which emphasized rational rather than emotional topics and points of view. Also, Hugo's main character, Quasimodo, is physically repulsive, whereas in classical works, writers focused on idealized form. *The Hunchback of Notre Dame* also focuses on the personal rather than on classical universal themes, which may be one of the reasons why the novel retained its popularity for almost two hundred years.

Author Biography

Victor Hugo was one of the most influential of early French Romantic writers, a man who so dominated French literature that the French refer to the nineteenth century as the century of Victor Hugo. He was born in Besançon on February 26, 1802, the third son of Leopold, an apparently ruthless soldier who rose in rank to general, and Sophia, who because she was unhappily married, eventually separated from Leopold and took her children to Paris where she raised them. Hugo turned to poetry early in life and by the age of seventeen was with the help of his brothers publishing a magazine, *Conservateur Litteraire*. Three years later, he had published a collection of poems that gained the attention of, as well as a royal pension from, King Louis XVIII. By the time he was thirty, his name was both well known and well respected.

Much involved with the new literary movement, Hugo was one of a group of writers who argued against French classicism and in favor of French romanticism. Eighteenth-century classicism was a more conservative movement that emphasized the art and literature of ancient Greece and Rome and valued form tightly regulated by rules; nineteenth-century French romanticism, on the other hand, valued the emotional and more personal experience, as demonstrated in many of Hugo's works, especially *The Hunchback of Notre Dame*. After marrying Adele Fucher, his childhood sweetheart, in 1822, Hugo's house became the meeting place for the early French romantic writers. The couple eventually had four children.

Between 1826 and 1843, Hugo experienced a great rush of creativity, producing three novels,

Victor Hugo

numerous essays, and five volumes of poems, as well as many dramatic pieces. However, tragedy stuck in 1843, when his daughter and her husband died, draining Hugo of inspiration and initiating a long period in which he did not write.

Then in 1851, after Napoleon III seized full power, Hugo, who was a strong proponent of democracy, feared for his life and left Paris with his mistress Juliette Drouet and lived in exile for almost twenty years. He returned to Paris in 1870, after the fall of the Second Empire and was elected a senator of the Third Republic six years later.

Hugo continued to write despite his political activities and the deaths of his wife, his mistress, and his sons. His health slowly declined and in 1878, Hugo suffered a stroke. Then on May 22, 1885, he died. The people of Paris honored him by coming out in the millions for his funeral. He was given a national funeral and was buried in the Pantheon. As Laurence M. Porter, in his book *Victor Hugo*, describes him, as "a master of the lyric poem, the novel, the theater, and the essay, deeply committed to social reform, and the major symbol of resistance to Napoleon III's empire, Hugo became a national monument during his lifetime." After his death, Hugo's life works were collected in a forty-five-volume edition.

Plot Summary

Chapters 1–11

Hugo begins *The Hunchback of Notre Dame* with a detailed account of the life and culture of fifteenth-century Paris. There is to be a royal wedding, and the city is alive with performances and pomp. One of the main characters is introduced in the person of Pierre Gringoire, a poet and playwright, whose drama is presented amidst noise and many interruptions.

One of those interruptions is caused by La Esmeralda, a woman whose beauty attracts crowds and cheers. After the play is finally abandoned, Gringoire follows La Esmeralda, watches her dance, and later witnesses Quasimodo attempting to kidnap her. Claude Frollo has prompted Quasimodo to take the woman back to the cathedral. When Gringoire tries to rescue La Esmeralda, Quasimodo hits him and knocks him out. In the meantime, the handsome captain of the king's archers, Phoebus, arrests Quasimodo as Frollo sneaks away.

Chapters 12–20

Gringoire searches for a place to sleep and ends up with the gypsies, whose leader Clopin Trouillefou threatens to kill him unless a woman in their midst agrees to marry him. La Esmeralda, who recognizes Gringoire, agrees to save him. After they are married, La Esmeralda tells him she wants only a platonic relationship. Gringoire accepts but secretly hopes that one day he will win her love.

Hugo then describes the cathedral of Notre Dame. Great details are provided about the church's history and its architecture. Next Hugo offers a broader view of fifteenth-century Paris, its buildings and its various centers. There is a flashback to the time when Quasimodo was abandoned as an infant and left in the church. The history of priest Frollo is then provided. Readers learn about Frollo's singular focus on an intellectual life as well as his concern for Quasimodo and for Frollo's younger brother Jehan, whose care Frollo undertook upon the death of their parents. Jehan has turned out to be a disappointment, and Frollo plans to do a better job with Quasimodo.

A fuller description is offered about Quasimodo's life, which is fairly well cloistered in the cathedral. Not being able to socialize because people are fearful of him, Quasimodo makes friends with the statues and the bells, which are his

responsibility to ring on special occasions. The bells, however, have deafened him.

Chapters 21–30

King Louis XI makes a surprise visit (under disguise and using the name Compère Tourangeau) to Frollo, who has gained a reputation as a learned scholar not only in the spiritual realm but also in medicine and alchemy. The king's physician, Jacques Coictier, does not trust Frollo and insists that Frollo is a madman. Frollo discusses the power of the new printing presses, which he suggests to the king will eventually undermine the authority of the church as well as diminish the other arts such as architecture, which in classical and medieval times was decorated to display in stone sculpture and relief the stories of ancient civilizations.

Then the scene changes to the trial of Quasimodo for having kidnapped La Esmeralda. The trial is led by Provost d'Estouteville and the deaf auditor, Master Florian. When the crowd mocks both the auditor and Quasimodo for the coincidence of their deafness, Florian becomes indignant and eventually d'Estouteville sentences Quasimodo to a public beating. Because of his deafness Quasimodo does not sufficiently answer the provost's questions, thus leading the provost to believe that Quasimodo is being disrespectful. This scene demonstrates that the king's men are heartless, and the public is disgusted with their awkward authority.

The story of Pacquette, La Esmeralda's mother, is then told in flashback. Pacquette's mother was forced to raise her in poverty, and when her mother dies, Pacquette becomes pregnant and gives birth to a beautiful girl whom she names Agnes. Later, her child is stolen by the gypsies, and although Pacquette does not know it, they name her La Esmeralda.

The beating of Quasimodo then takes place. He is left on the platform after the beating, and the crowd throws stones at him. Quasimodo sees Frollo in the crowd and believes Frollo will save him. But the priest walks away. When Quasimodo begs for water, La Esmeralda steps forward to help him.

Spring arrives, and readers learn that Captain Phoebus has been matched up with Demoiselle Fleur de Lys, who happens to notice Phoebus's attraction to La Esmeralda. Demoiselle Fleur de Lys suggests that Phoebus invite La Esmeralda to the party they are going to. Once there, La Esmeralda receives too much attention from all the men, and the women become jealous. Frollo, also attracted to La Esmeralda, goes to Gringoire and asks about her. Gringoire tells Frollo that La Esmeralda is in love with Phoebus.

Chapters 31–40

Frollo overhears Phoebus talking about La Esmeralda and convinces Phoebus to let him join him as Phoebus plans to meet her. They enter a house and Phoebus locks Frollo in a closet. Frollo finds a hole in the closet and watches Phoebus and La Esmeralda embrace and kiss. This infuriates Frollo, and he breaks out of the closet, stabs Phoebus, and leaves. La Esmeralda faints. When she awakens, she cradles Phoebus in her arms believing he is dead. La Esmeralda is arrested, put on trial, and tortured for killing him. After her torture, she signs a confession and is sentenced to death. Frollo comes to visit her and tells her he loves her and can save her if she chooses him. He also tells her that Phoebus is dead. La Esmeralda refuses Frollo and says she is ready to die. As she is led outside, she sees Phoebus and faints. Quasimodo steals her away and takes her into the cathedral. There is a law that allows people asylum, or protection from secular law, so long as they take sanctuary in a church, so no one can take her.

Chapters 41–50

Frollo cannot stand to watch the execution of La Esmeralda, so he has not witnessed her rescue. But when he returns to the cathedral and sees the shape of a woman and a goat walking in the shadows of the towers, he thinks he is seeing a ghost. The scene then focuses on Quasimodo and his care of La Esmeralda. Quasimodo brings her clothing and food and tells her of his feelings. La Esmeralda can barely stand to look at him, although she does recognize the warmth of his heart. Later, she sees Phoebus and asks Quasimodo to go and bring him back to her. Quasimodo tries, but Phoebus will not come. La Esmeralda is visibly disappointed, which hurts Quasimodo even further. He knows that Phoebus does not deserve La Esmeralda's love.

Frollo finally realizes La Esmeralda is in the cathedral and seeks her out. He pleads once again for her to love him and forces himself on her. Quasimodo pulls Frollo away and refuses to leave when Frollo commands him. Instead Quasimodo offers Frollo his knife, telling him he will protect La Esmeralda until he dies. Frollo leaves, muttering that no one will have La Esmeralda. Frollo goes to Gringoire, tells him the king's men are planning to take La Esmeralda out of the cathedral in three days. He asks Gringoire to help him rescue La Esmeralda.

Media Adaptations

- *The Hunchback of Notre Dame* has been produced as a movie several times, first in 1923, starring Lon Chaney as Quasimodo; then in 1939, starring Charles Laughton as Quasimodo. In 1977, a British production starred Anthony Hopkins in the same role, and finally the Disney-made version appeared in 1996. There are books on tape, DVDs, and toys and games that use Hugo's original work as their inspiration.

Gringoire enlists the help of the gypsies. They march toward the cathedral under the cover of night, but Quasimodo spies them. He throws wooden beams, rocks, and molten metal at them. Many are killed but the group persists.

Chapters 51–57

King Louis hears that the citizens are revolting against him. He orders his men to capture and hang them all. He also orders La Esmeralda's immediate execution because he is told she is the reason the people are revolting. The king's men, led by Phoebus, force the gypsies to retreat. Quasimodo thinks he is safe now and turns to look for La Esmeralda, but she is gone. Unbeknownst to Quasimodo, Gringoire and Frollo (in disguise) have taken her away. Gringoire disappears after they take La Esmeralda outside the cathedral. Frollo once again reminds La Esmeralda that her life is in his hands and begs her to love him once again. La Esmeralda again refuses, so Frollo takes her back into the cathedral and locks her in the tower cell with Pacquette (Sister Gudule). As the women talk, they unfold their stories and realize they are mother and daughter. When soldiers come to take La Esmeralda away, her mother hides her. But La Esmeralda hears Phoebus' voice and comes out of her hiding place, still believing he loves her. Instead, Phoebus takes her away. Fighting to save her daughter, Pacquette bites the other officer. He knocks her away, and she hits her head and dies with La Esmeralda watching.

 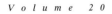

Quasimodo searches for La Esmeralda but only finds Frollo, whom he follows up the tower. Frollo stares out over the city as does Quasimodo and that is when he sees La Esmeralda being hanged. He hears Frollo laugh at her death and lifts Frollo up and throws him over the edge to his death.

Hugo then sums up the lives of the remaining characters. The king dies; Phoebus marries; and Gringoire becomes a famous writer. Quasimodo is later found in the cemetery vault where La Esmeralda was buried. He is recognizable only by the twisted skeleton of his form. His bones are intertwined in a death embrace with those of a female skeleton.

Characters

Jacques Coictier

Coictier is the king's physician who accompanies the king to visit Frollo to ask him about his medical knowledge.

Jacques Coppenole

Coppenole is a hosier who travels with the royal party from Brussels. Although he is a mere maker of hoses, he is announced as if he too were royalty. Coppenole has a way with the crowds in the opening of the novel, giving the reader a contrast between how the populace related to royalty and how royalty related to them, emphasizing the gap between them. Coppenole is the bridge. It is Coppenole who also suggests the election of the pope of fools, which introduces Quasimodo.

Robert d'Estouteville

Robert d'Estouteville is the provost of Paris and presides over the trial of Quasimodo, finally sentencing him to a severe public beating.

Demoiselle Fleur de Lys

Demoiselle Fleur de Lys is the betrothed of Captain Phoebus. When she notices that Phoebus is interest in La Esmeralda's dancing, she suggests that he invite La Esmeralda to the party they are going to. At the party, La Esmeralda becomes the center of attraction with all the men, making all the women jealous.

Master Florian

Florian, the king's auditor, is deaf like Quasimodo. The crowd finds the shared deafness hilarious, which makes Florian indignant. When he demonstrates his annoyance, Provost d'Estouteville blames Quasimodo and sentences him to a beating.

Claude Frollo

Claude Frollo is the priest (later becoming the archdeacon at Notre Dame) who adopts Quasimodo. He starts off a somewhat softhearted individual who not only cares for Quasimodo but also Frollo's orphaned younger brother Jehan. But as time passes Frollo's heart hardens, and his pursuit of knowledge does not completely fulfill him. He is somewhat an outcast himself, having spent most of his youth studying. His adoption of Quasimodo draws him further away from other people, who think Quasimodo is related to the devil.

Frollo finds himself distracted by his lust for La Esmeralda. He has Quasimodo kidnap La Esmeralda in a desperate attempt to conquer her. Then he demonstrates his lack of morals when he allows the authorities to punish Quasimodo for the crime that Frollo technically perpetrated. When Frollo realizes that no matter what he does, he cannot possess La Esmeralda because the only man she wants is Phoebus, Frollo stabs Phoebus and allows, once again, someone else to be punished for his crime; this time it is La Esmeralda who must suffer. After Quasimodo helps La Esmeralda escape from being hanged, Frollo employs Gringoire to help him take La Esmeralda away from Quasimodo's protection. Frollo then turns La Esmeralda over to the king's authorities and laughs when La Esmeralda is hanged. This outrages Quasimodo, who then throws Frollo out of the tower. The character of Frollo is the most complex, filled with contradictions. He raises orphans but allows others to be punished for his crimes. He is a priest, who should be committed to purity and devotion, but he lusts after La Esmeralda and is the cause of her death.

Jehan Frollo

Jehan is the younger brother of Claude Frollo. Upon their parents' deaths, Claude takes upon himself the raising of his younger orphaned brother, hoping that Jehan will become scholarly. Jehan does not, thus disappointing his brother. Jehan lives with the gypsies and constantly begs for money from his brother. However, his brother's caring for Jehan represents the softer side of Claude.

Pierre Gringoire

Gringoire is a poet and dramatist, who was orphaned and later educated by Claude Frollo. It is with Gringoire's play that Hugo opens his story. Gringoire is not a successful playwright by any means. His play is scarcely even listened to. He wanders the streets in search of food and a place to sleep and ends up in a sanctuary of gypsies, who threaten to kill him unless one of the females agrees to marry him. La Esmeralda comes to Gringoire's rescue but after the marriage ceremony is performed lets Gringoire know that their relationship will never amount to more than that of brother and sister.

Sister Gudule

See *Paquette La Chantfleurie*

Pacquette La Chantfleurie

Pacquette, as a young mother, has her baby stolen from her. In her baby's place, she is given Quasimodo, whom she abandons in the church. Pacquette's baby was stolen from her by a band of gypsies, and she finds out toward the end of the novel that her baby is none other than La Esmeralda. Pacquette's sorrow drives her crazy, and she is locked up in Rolande's Tower where she takes the name Sister Gudule. Later, Frollo locks La Esmeralda in the same cell in Rolande's Tower with Pacquette. While they share the cell, Pacquette and La Esmeralda discover they are mother and daughter. When the soldiers come to take La Esmeralda away, Pacquette fights to keep her daughter with her. In the process, one of the soldiers knocks her away, killing her.

La Esmeralda

La Esmeralda is the physical antithesis of Quasimodo. She is so beautiful crowds form around her just so they can see her walk by. Despite this physical disparity, La Esmeralda and Quasimodo have much in common. They are both outcasts (Quasimodo because of his physical infirmities and La Esmeralda because of her lack of proper standing in the community) and they both have pure hearts. They are also individuals who reach out to others in time of need. Both are depicted as innocents, people who are filled with complete trust, often even blinded by it.

La Esmeralda, like Quasimodo, knows little of her parentage. She was stolen by Egyptian gypsies when she was a baby. But unlike Quasimodo, La Esmeralda, as she matures into full womanhood, loves to be around people. People respond to her in positive ways. Because of her beauty, men cannot help but want her for their own. Gringoire falls in love with her for her beauty. Frollo and Phoebus lust after her. And Quasimodo falls in love with for her generous heart. But La Esmeralda wants

only Phoebus. She thinks only he can give her the love that she craves. After Frollo stabs Phoebus, La Esmeralda is left with his body. When the king's authorities arrive, she is accused of the crime and sentenced to death. Quasimodo saves her by stealing her away, but Frollo eventually turns her in. She is hanged for the crime. La Esmeralda affects many of the characters in this novel, but her character is not well developed. She enters the story and leaves it unchanged—beautiful and innocent.

King Louis XI

King Louis, the reigning monarch, visits Frollo to find out how much he knows about medicine. After interviewing him, the king is satisfied that Frollo knows what he is talking about and decides to study under him.

Captain Phoebus

Phoebus is the captain of the king's army, a handsome man who seduces women, including La Esmeralda. In a desperate act of jealousy, Frollo stabs Phoebus, leaving La Esmeralda with the bleeding body and allowing La Esmeralda to be charged with the crime. Unknown to La Esmeralda, Phoebus does not die but actually heals from his wounds and is later responsible for arresting a band of gypsies, which includes La Esmeralda.

Quasimodo

Quasimodo is the hunchback, a man so disfigured that many people believe he is no less than the devil. He is abandoned in the church by his mother who cannot confront his ugliness and is taken under the care of Claude Frollo, one of the priests. To keep him busy, Quasimodo (whose name is given him because he is left in the church on Quasimodogeniti Sunday, the first Sunday after Easter), is given the task of ringing the bells of Notre Dame, a task that eventually causes him to go deaf.

Quasimodo is totally devoted to Frollo, the only person who befriends him. Therefore when Frollo asks him to kidnap La Esmeralda, Quasimodo does so without hesitation. He later suffers the punishment for this crime, surprised and totally dejected that Frollo does not come to his aid. When La Esmeralda shows affection toward him, Quasimodo falls madly in love with her and proves that he will do anything for her by saving her from a death sentence for a crime she has not committed. Then he takes her into the cathedral and shelters her. At one point Quasimodo must choose between his first love, Frollo, and his love for La Esmeralda when

Frollo attempts to rape her. Quasimodo turns against his first master and saves the woman he loves. In the end, however, Quasimodo is incapable of protecting her. When he realizes that Frollo is the cause of her death, he throws Frollo from one of the cathedral towers. Quasimodo then realizes that the only two people he ever loved are dead, and he dies in the vault of Mountfaucon, holding onto the dead body of La Esmeralda. Quasimodo is the so-called beast in this story but only on a physical level. His beauty lies within, in his love and in his loyalty.

Compère Tourangeau

See King Louis XI

Clopin Trouillefou

Clopin appears in the opening scene of the novel as a beggar who climbs one of the pillars and cries out for alms. He fakes infirmities in order to attract more charity. Later, readers learn that Trouillefou is the leader of the band of gypsies of which La Esmeralda is a member. He calls himself the King of Thunes. Trouillefou in his capacity as leader threatens to kill Gringoire, stating that he can only be saved if a female gypsy agrees to marry him. La Esmeralda accepts the bid.

Themes

Abandonment

The theme of abandonment plays out in different ways in Hugo's *The Hunchback of Notre Dame*. The most obvious is the abandonment of Quasimodo by his mother, who steals the more beautiful child, La Esmeralda, and exchanges her malformed son, who is left in the halls of the cathedral. And that is just the beginning of abandonment in Quasimodo's life. The public abandons him in many ways, mocking and jeering him every time he appears outside his cloistered shelter. In more subtle ways, some of his physical senses also abandon him, leaving him without the power to hear or speak, pushing him deeper into isolation.

The priest Frollo and his brother Jehan are also abandoned by the death of their parents; as is Gringoire, another orphan in this story. On another level, all the poor of Paris are portrayed as having also been abandoned by the fabulously rich monarchy which has grown out of touch with not only the needs of the poverty stricken populous but with its subjects' humanity. This theme of abandonment

makes the loyalty of Quasimodo and La Esmeralda all the more intense by contrast.

Physical Appearance

The theme of the power of physical appearance in affecting others is played out at its fullest in the characters of Quasimodo and La Esmeralda. Quasimodo is scorned, mocked, abandoned, ridiculed, and beaten for having been born in a twisted body. Whereas La Esmeralda is loved, lusted after, praised, and celebrated for her innate beauty. It is, however, interesting to note that neither Quasimodo's ugliness nor La Esmeralda's beauty grants a better outcome. Although Quasimodo must seek refuge in isolation because of his physical appearance, La Esmeralda suffers from the jealousy of others when she exhibits herself in public.

Disguise of one's physical appearance is also used throughout Hugo's story. Frollo often tries to disguise himself either in a common cloak or in the clothing of his priesthood. His cloak is used to give him an advantage in getting closer to La Esmeralda, who has resolved to resist him. But his priestly habit, if one takes the highest ideals of spirituality that his religious outfit represents, also disguises Frollo's carnal lust.

Obsession.

There are many men who want to be close to La Esmeralda. Each man has his own reasons. Of all of them, Quasimodo and Frollo have the strongest desires, and those desires are born from opposite feelings. Quasimodo is sincerely in love with La Esmeralda. He demonstrates this by his ability to satisfy her needs without receiving anything in return. He wants to be able to look at her, but he turns his head so she will not have to see his ugliness. He serves her and then leaves her alone. He protects her although he knows that she does not love him.

By contrast, Frollo is obsessed with La Esmeralda. Or more precisely, he is obsessed with the thought of her. He really does not know her. He is merely aroused by her beauty, by her female form, how she moves, how she laughs, and as a result he wants to own her. His obsession drives him away from his own rational thoughts and his vows of spirituality. His lofty ideals are corrupted by his carnal desires, and he will do anything, even break his God's commandments, to possess her. His obsession controls his body and his mind, pointing him in the direction of the darkest evil rather than toward the spiritual light. He, who is dressed in the garb of the priest, Hugo seems to be saying, is

Topics For Further Study

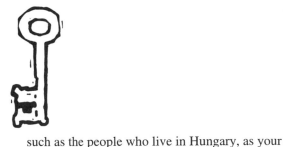

- Write a research paper on the construction of the cathedral of Notre Dame. Include descriptions of the architectural designs and how they changed, as well as the effects on the cathedral of the wars that raged around it and the influences of the monarchies. Conclude with the status of the cathedral in the early 2000s.

- Gypsies, or the Roma people, have been persecuted throughout their history. Write a paper about their struggles to exist in Europe, including a description of their background, culture, lifestyle, and music. Since there are various groups of the Roma, chose one particular section, such as the people who live in Hungary, as your focused topic.

- Hugo was very much involved in politics. What political causes did he pursued? How did he engage in them in the political arena? What did he have to say about them in his writings, both in fiction and in nonfiction?

- Hugo's play *Hernani, ou l'Honneur Castillan* was first produced in 1830 and is said to have dramatized the conflict between French classical authors and romantic ones. Read the play, then explain how these two literary philosophies are demonstrated in the play.

---

really the devil. While Quasimodo, who has been accused of being the devil because of his physical garb, is more like a saint.

Intolerance

Intolerance abounds in *The Hunchback of Notre Dame*. The most obvious is the intolerance that surrounds Quasimodo. From his birth to his death, people cannot bear to look at him let alone to be around him without mocking him. Even when he is in a court of law, the judge is so prejudiced by Quasimodo's looks, he has no tolerance of Quasimodo's inability to hear and therefore to express himself. The judge mistakenly believes that Quasimodo is acting disrespectfully instead of realizing that Quasimodo's communication skills are limited.

The king also demonstrates intolerance when he hears there is an uprising among his people. He, as well as the people who report to him, believe that the uprising is against the king. Rather than attempting to find out why the people are revolting, the king, almost like the Queen of Hearts in *Alice in Wonderland*, in essence shouts out, Off with their heads. There is also the general intolerance against the gypsies who are accused of every crime from theft to sorcery, whether or not they have committed them.

Betrayal

Quasimodo portrays the most sincere form of loyalty and is therefore the most sympathetic character to experience betrayal. Since Frollo is the only person who shows any signs of affection toward him, Quasimodo would do anything for his master. Frollo asks him to kidnap La Esmeralda, and Quasimodo does so, neither understanding the motives nor the consequences. But when Quasimodo is tried and convicted of a crime whose penalty is a severe beating, he does comprehend that he does not deserve that punishment. He is not the perpetrator of that crime, since he has only followed the dictates of his beloved Frollo. But Frollo's loyalty is nowhere near as exemplary as Quasimodo's, and although he sees his adopted child suffering unjustly, Frollo does not come to Quasimodo's defense.

Moreover, it is Frollo again, who exhibits another lethal form of betrayal in another circumstance, this time with La Esmeralda, when he stabs Phoebus and allows La Esmeralda to pay with her life for this crime. Phoebus, too, is guilty of betrayal when he pretends to love La Esmeralda only to win a few hours of physical passion. He watches as La Esmeralda is about to be hanged for a crime that he knows she did not commit. La Esmeralda, herself, or rather her blind love of Phoebus, betrays her own safety when she comes out of hiding upon hearing Phoebus' voice. Believing Phoebus loves her, she in essence turns herself in to those who want to see her dead.

Style

Gothic Novel

Typically, a gothic novel includes a dark setting preferably in an old castle; tension created through suspense; the appearance of mysterious signs that act as warnings or prophecy; the stirring of strong emotions; and of course a threatened woman in need of rescue. Hugo's *The Hunchback of Notre Dame* contains all of these elements and more. First there is the gothic cathedral of Notre Dame with its castle-like structure and embellishments of gargoyles, dark shadowy staircases, towers, and hidden rooms. This setting emphasizes mystery and foreboding. Then there is the constant flow of emotions, including despair, brief happiness, surprise, shock, disappointment, and fear. Finally there is La Esmeralda, the beautiful woman in distress.

Hugo also includes elements of the irrational, such as sorcery, black magic, alchemy, obsession, and devilry. He even adds a bit of prophecy or omen when he has Frollo write the word ΑΝΑΓΚΗ on the wall of his room. The word means fate and reflects both the gripping effects from which the characters appear unable to free themselves as well as the derivative form of the word, which is fatality, thus making the word a prophecy of the short time remaining for Hugo's main characters. As in other gothic novels, mystery abounds in Hugo's novel, too, from the unknown parentages of many of the characters to the motivation of Frollo who seems bent on fouling the lives of Quasimodo and La Esmeralda. The overwhelming power of the male is also present, another gothic ingredient. From the king, who has the power to execute anyone who disagrees with his thoughts, to Phoebus, who takes what pleasure he can find in women without caring about them in return, to Frollo, who exerts his power over both Quasimodo and La Esmeralda.

Tragedy

If one were to sum up the overall theme of Hugo's novel, it would be easy to refer to it as a melodramatic tragedy. A tragedy is a work that shows a conflict between an individual and a higher force that ends badly for the individual. There is the tragic form of Quasimodo that makes his life a living hell. There is the tragic figure of La Esmeralda, whose beauty should have given her easy access to a life of love but instead gives her nothing but disappointment and suffering. In Frollo, readers witness a tragic flaw—his inability to control his lust—which eventually destroys his life. The tragedy of poverty is also provided in regard to the masses of people going hungry while grand feasts and opulence of every kind are enjoyed inside the monarch's hall. And then there is Pacquette, who is driven mad after the theft of her beautiful baby girl, only to be reunited with her in the last moments of both of their lives. The book ends with misguided, bloody battles, murders, and executions, and the most tragic image of all—that of Quasimodo's skeletal remains wrapped around his dead beloved.

Privileging the Outcast

Quasimodo reflects the romantic tendency to privilege the outcast (the ugly, powerless, common) while discounting the heads of hierarchy. In a sense, Quasimodo is something of the "noble savage," one who exhibits higher virtue and greater compassion than the so-called leaders of the society, a figure that appears repeatedly in nineteenth-century romantic literature.

Complexity and Elaboration

Hugo's style is filled with very long, highly descriptive passages. For instance, he might, in the midst of describing a scene, point out the curvatures of scroll-topped columns in the architecture of the room in which the scene is being played out. He also provides long digressions about the history of a building or a place. Extended flashbacks present backgrounds for some characters, and some chapters are devoted to his personal philosophies, such as the discussion on the potential effect of the printing presses. He describes the cathedral of Notre Dame in fine detail, as well as the buildings in the surrounding area and the view of the city from one of the cathedral's towers. Modern readers may be impatient with this elaborate style, accustomed as they are to quick camera shots in movies and the scaled down writing of popular twentieth-century and early 2000s narrative styles. But it is through Hugo's extensive details that readers are given a deeper understanding of the life and times of fifteenth-century Paris. His attention to detail provides a lot of information beyond the plot of the novel, particularly regarding the setting, background, and fifteenth-century topics.

Historical Context

King Louis XI

Louis XI (1423–83) was king (he was crowned in 1461) during the time of Hugo's novel *The Hunchback of Notre Dame*. His reign was characterized by diminished prestige of the courts, intervention in the affairs of the church, and imposition of heavy taxes to support a powerful army. Louis XI tended to turn away from nobility, preferring the common man in his ranks. The nobility, in turn, tried several times to dethrone him. But the lesser gentry and the bourgeois classes, with whom Louis had won favor, refused to revolt against him. His reign, however, was filled with battles for land and power. He had many political enemies, many of whom were imprisoned in very poor conditions for long periods. In the latter years of his reign, Louis feared for his life. He sensed he might be assassinated. For this reason, during the last two years of his monarchy, Louis hid, in self-exile, in Touraine. He died in 1483 of cerebral arteriosclerosis. He was succeeded by his son, Charles VIII.

Cathedral of Notre Dame

Construction on the cathedral of Notre Dame was at least in the planning stages in 1160, when Maurice du Sully envisioned its design. The cornerstone was laid three years later. The original design was Romanesque. But the cathedral was built in three stages, and before it was completed, advances in architectural design allowed more freedom in how weight in large buildings could be supported and walls opened in to let in light. As construction continued, the cathedral design was increasing affected by the new gothic style. This style can be seen in the ribbed vaults (arched ribs that support the nave ceiling) and flying buttresses (arched supports built outside the nave walls that direct the weight of the roof outward along the ribs and down the buttresses outside the church, thus relieving the foundation of weight and making possible a higher vault in the nave). Because the weight was channeled this way, the wall space between the buttresses could be opened up with stained glass windows. The gothic cathedral also had ornate spires and ornate exterior sculpture. On the roof top, sculpted gargoyles symbolically were intended to scare away devils but practically functioned as downspouts. The gothic style was magnificent, and under the financial support of King Louis VII, the cathedral located on an island in the Seine River, rose in grandeur, the pride of Paris. The church was completed between 1250 and 1300 but went through major reconstructions thereafter. Over the years, the cathedral was the site of many coronations and royal weddings.

During the reigns of Louis XIV and Louis XV (late seventeenth and eighteenth centuries) some of the cathedral's tombs and stained glass windows were destroyed. At the end of the eighteenth century, revolutionaries plundered many of its valuables. Gradually the great building deteriorated, but major restoration programs in both the nineteenth and twentieth centuries restored it.

Gypsies

The term gypsy was applied to a group of nomadic people, more properly known as Roma, who were believed, according to linguistic research, to have their origins in northwest India. There are historical records that indicate that the Roma lived in Arabic, Byzantine, and Persian countries as well as all over Europe. They first appeared in Europe in the 1400s. Wherever they went, they were considered outsiders and were often persecuted. Some countries enslaved them; others used them for entertainment, music and dancing being two of their gifts. Harsh laws against them often deterred their travels. In 1502, King Louis XII banished all gypsies from France. Even more severe, in Great Britain, Queen Elizabeth I (1533–1603) actually signed a law that stated gypsies could be hanged just for being gypsies. During the Nazi control of Germany, large groups of Roma were tortured and killed along with the Jewish population. Although people of Roma descent can be found all around the world, the largest populations of Roma are found in Russia and in Hungary.

Napoleon III

Louis Napoleon Bonaparte (1808–1873) reigned during Hugo's life, and after returning from exile after the French Revolution of 1848, Napoleon III won the presidency and served as leader of the Second Republic. Then in 1851, he overthrew the Second Republic and gave himself dictatorial powers. A year later, he named himself ruler of France's Second Empire. He ruled France with a tight fist but also invested a lot of money in rebuilding the country. He was responsible for building railroads and authorizing the first banks. His strict rule led to his unpopularity among his citizens, so he attempted to liberalize his government, giving his general assembly broader powers. This measure did not, however, save him. His downfall resulted from his ambitions to be a great military

Compare & Contrast

- **1400s:** France's civil war, referred to as the Hundred Years' War, begins in 1407.

  1800s: Napoleon I, after victorious battles across Europe, establishing a vast French Empire, is defeated at Waterloo.

  2000s: President Jacques Chirac refuses to join the coalition in support of the U.S. pre-emptive military strike on Iraq.

- **1400s:** Anti-gypsy laws are enforced throughout most of Europe, making it a crime for the Roma people to live in such countries as Britain, Holland, and Germany. Spain tries gypsies as heretics.

  1800s: Gypsies come to the United States to flee European discrimination, but many are turned back at Ellis Island.

- **2000s:** Norway's largest religious group, the Lutherans, officially apologizes for its role in past discrimination against the gypsies.

- **1400s:** The influence of Italian Renaissance art is imposed on French gothic architecture after Charles VIII returns from his conquest of Naples.

  1800s: While King Louis XV (who is crowned when he is only five years old) matures, Phillipe d'Orleans supervises the French government and influences art and architecture in France with an emphasis on individualism.

  2000s: Many modern French architects vow to renew Paris and its urban setting with buildings that break out of the box form and incorporate triangle shapes or a fragmented layout.

---

leader, like his uncle, Napoleon I. In 1870, after taking to the battlefield during the Franco-Prussian war, he was captured by the Prussians and declared by his citizens at home to be dethroned by the then-authoritative powers of the Third Republic in Paris. Napoleon III died in exile in 1873 in Great Britain where he was buried.

Critical Overview

According to his biographer, Graham Robb, in his award-winning book *Victor Hugo*, "by the time he fled the country in 1851, Hugo was the most famous living writer in the world . . . His influence on French literature was second only to that of the Bible." Although Hugo's life's work included "seven novels, eighteen volumes of poetry, twenty-one plays," and as Robb writes, "approximately three million words of history, criticism, travel writing and philosophy," Hugo's *The Hunchback of Notre Dame* retains the honor of being one of his two most famous works. *The Hunchback of*

Notre Dame was very popular in France when it first came out despite the fact, as Robb states it, "the immediate effect on readers of the time was horror verging on intense pleasure." The book shocked Hugo's readers with its "extreme states," Robb concludes, which included those of poverty and ugliness as well as the evils of power and the consequences of extreme debauchery. Ironically, it was also these extreme states that made the book so popular. This popularity spread across Europe and the United States and soon tourists were flocking to Paris to visit the sites depicted in Hugo's novel. Many were disappointed at first, writes Robb, with the sad state of the old cathedral, which was in need of a major renovation. But when the literary tourists were shown the word ΑΝΑΓΚΗ carved into the wall, some of their disappointment was allayed. They began to look at the cathedral as Hugo presents it in his novel.

A century and a half after its publication, *The Hunchback of Notre Dame* retained its popular appeal, and, although not claimed as Hugo's best novel (*Les Miserables* usually claimed that prize), it was praised for Hugo's detailed account and

Maureen O'Hara as Esmeralda and Charles Laughton as the Hunchback in the 1939 film depiction of Victor Hugo's The Hunchback of Notre Dame

description of the cathedral as well as a glimpse into fifteenth-century France culture. The novel was deeply embedded in twentieth-century French culture, and the popularity of the novel, no doubt, played a significant part in influencing the French government to finance a restoration of the cathedral. Its effect could also be seen in the many interpretations that movie producers give it about every thirty years. Popular all over the world, Hugo is especially revered in France. As his biographer, Laurence M. Porter, in his book *Victor Hugo*,

explains, Hugo's writing has sometimes been referred to as simplistic because of his "dualistic rhetoric of light versus darkness," which implies an uncomplicated and noncomplex view of life. Although the characters in Hugo's novel may seem simplistic, Porter writes, closer study of his novels show that "[Hugo] repeatedly implies a cosmic vision deeper than the limited visions of his characters. Hugo finds a hidden God revealed not through the rites of a church but through nature and the human heart."

Criticism

Joyce Hart

Hart has degrees in English and creative writing and is the author of several books. In this essay, Hart explores the role of La Esmeralda and the force she portrays in uniting the characters and moving the story forward.

There has been much discussion about the protagonist of Hugo's *The Hunchback of Notre Dame*, and many believe that Quasimodo is the protagonist. After all, the title of the novel specifically refers to him. But other critics believe that the true focus is the cathedral of Notre Dame, pointing to the French title of this work, which is *Notre-Dame de Paris*. Whether Quasimodo or the cathedral is argued to be the protagonist or focus, it is quite clear that the ultimate motivating force in the plot is La Esmeralda. She is the spark that sets this story in motion and continually inspires the other characters to act out their roles.

The novel begins with a lot of commotion. The city is in the throes of a large celebration. There are parades and visiting dignitaries. There are parties and plays. But the action is scattered and constantly interrupted until one defining moment, when La Esmeralda makes her first appearance. Suddenly everyone's attention is focused as people run to the streets or to the windows and doorways of buildings calling out her name as she passes by. Her beauty and innocence draw their attention: the women wish they could be her and the men desire her touch.

As she moves through the streets, she draws the story forward. Gringoire, the poet and playwright, follows her, taking readers along with him. Gringoire is driven to find out who this beautiful woman is and why she demands so much attention, pulling his audience away as they have more interest in her than in Gringoire's play. Gringoire soon becomes obsessed with this woman, whose magic turns out to be more than just her beauty. She also has the gift of music and dance, and she seems to have mesmerized a goat just as she has captivated those who watch her. Gringoire is the first to be struck and motivated by La Esmeralda. He tries to save her from the hunchback who attempts to kidnap her, and thus Hugo, through this gypsy beauty, pulls his readers into the next phase of the story.

Gringoire is later saved by La Esmeralda. She marries him, and it is through this marriage and her subsequent demand that her relationship with Gringoire remain platonic, that she neutralizes Gringoire. He becomes a shadow in the story, flitting in and out of the background, not to fully reappear until the end, when he becomes unknowingly a catalyst for La Esmeralda's death. The story continues without him, as it now focuses on Quasimodo who attempts to kidnap La Esmeralda. Quasimodo does not fully comprehend why he has been asked to do so, nor does he completely understand the consequences when he is caught. Quasimodo is the blind follower of his master's will. Frollo is, after all, the first person Quasimodo learns to love. But once Quasimodo sets his eyes on the beautiful La Esmeralda, and once he witnesses her gentle spirit (offset by Frollo's betrayal), when La Esmeralda offers Quasimodo water, he, like all others, has trouble taking his eyes off her. But Quasimodo, who has suffered much rebuke because of his physical appearance, sees much deeper than La Esmeralda's surface beauty. He sees that she alone has looked at him (despite her repulsion of him) not solely as a beast but as a person who has physical needs. And it is through her gift of water that the story takes another turn. Up till now, Quasimodo has done as he has been told to do. But from now on, because of La Esmeralda's innocent heart, Quasimodo discovers thoughts and feelings all his own. He learns to act instead of to react. He will do what he concludes must be done. He will fight to the death to save his queen. In contrast to what La Esmeralda has done to Gringoire, quieting him and sending him to the back of the stage, she has brought Quasimodo to life. He, who has lived in seclusion, in silence, in the darkness and shadow of near nonexistence, has been pushed forward into the light through the power of La Esmeralda.

But the story has not yet progressed that far. Hugo has yet to fully expose the complete contradiction in Frollo caused by La Esmeralda. Frollo has existed on the food of thought. Frollo has not only committed his life to the intellect, he has surrendered his soul to the church. He has sworn to remain celibate as his religious vows dictate. His mind, throughout his adult life, has been focused on books and the care of two orphaned children. He is sought after as a master of reasoning and understanding. His knowledge far exceeds the dogma of his church; he studies medicine and science and alchemy. And yet, beneath the mantle of intellect is Frollo's Achilles heel, his mortal character flaw. Frollo melts at the sight of La Esmeralda. He not only is affected by her beauty, his passions for her controls his behavior. La Esmeralda has turned this great angel of intellect into a devil of lust. Because of his need of her, Frollo will abuse Quasimodo and will attempt to assassinate his rival Phoebus. He will lie, cheat, and scheme. In other words, because of La Esmeralda, Frollo is, along with the story, transformed.

It should be pointed out that La Esmeralda is powerful in spite of herself. Although her god-given beauty incites the characters of this novel and moves the story along, La Esmeralda herself lacks personal power. Or maybe this should be stated in another way. La Esmeralda has her own Achilles heel, her own point of weakness. She desires a perfect love. And her definition of perfect love comes to her in the form of Phoebus, a vain, shallow soldier, whose own beauty inflates his ego and overshadows his heart. Whether it is the handsomeness of this king's archer that captivates La Esmeralda or it is his rank, the young gypsy woman cannot see beyond what she thinks he is to the real dangers that he presents. He is the one she wants no matter how heartlessly he treats her. Thus La Esmeralda is blinded. But even in her weakest state, even in spite of herself, La Esmeralda exerts power. As ruthless as Phoebus is, how can he not be affected by the innocent La Esmeralda. He has no doubt wronged many women in his lifetime, but who among even the most cynical of men could watch the hanging of this woman, knowing that his voice of truth could save her life and not be affected by her innocence? Hugo writes that after La Esmeralda's death, Phoebus marries, but Hugo leaves undetermined the idea that the young couple lived happily ever after. There is another option available, one more plausible, one that rings more true. Phoebus, in his inability to speak out and save La Esmeralda, is a marked man. Let there be no doubt of the psychological consequences of his missed actions. Although Phoebus may witness and maybe even cause, many deaths in his lifetime, La Esmeralda's will be the one that will haunt him for the rest of his life.

In the dramatic conclusion of this story, it is not through Frollo, in his vow to either have La Esmeralda or to destroy her, that the final turn in the story takes place. It is not really Phoebus, in his role of king's deputy, whose order it is to find La Esmeralda and bring her to the hangman's rope, who moves the novel to its final resting place. Even Quasimodo, in his deep love to save La Esmeralda, is helpless to shift the story from one path to another. And what about Gringoire? He does reappear, and he is instrumental in helping to bring the story to a conclusion, but his actions do not define

> " La Esmeralda has her own Achilles heel, her own point of weakness. She desires a perfect love. And her definition of perfect love comes to her in the form of Phoebus, a vain, shallow soldier, whose own beauty inflates his ego and overshadows his heart."

the final swing. Rather, as in all other parts of the story, in all the other transitions, it is La Esmeralda who casts the final dice in determining how the story concludes. Whether one wants to portray La Esmeralda in the light of power or in the consequence of her weakness, it is for her unselfish love of Phoebus, her blind desire for a perfect love that this story takes its last turn. She has found her mother at last, and her mother, in the last few breaths of her life is determined to save her daughter—this child who was stolen from her and for whom the mother has grieved all of her life. The mother hides La Esmeralda, but La Esmeralda cannot hide from her lover. She cannot protect herself from the wrath of this man. She is willing to give him one more chance. She believes that his love of her is much greater than the love of her mother. La Esmeralda will offer herself to Phoebus, believing that he alone can save her. But she is mortally wrong.

And so the story takes its final turn. La Esmeralda has led the story along its path, turning and twisting its fate, persuading and evading its characters, challenging and tempting its motives from beginning to end. And in that end, she once again has a profound effect, not just on the storyline and the fictitious people who play out their created roles. This time, if in no other portion of the novel, La Esmeralda uses her power to affect readers. Even in death, after the flesh of her beauty has been eaten away, after her pure heart has shriveled out of sight and all that remains is her skeleton, La Esmeralda leaves her readers with a disturbing image that will revisit them and possibly drive them to

What Do I Read Next?

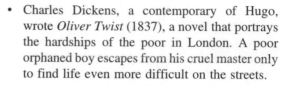

- Some critics believe that Hugo's *Les Miserables* (1862) outshines *The Hunchback of Notre Dame*. The book exposes the struggles of the underclass in France. It is interesting to note that the year this book was published, Hugo began financing a weekly dinner for fifty poor children, reflecting the sentiments he expresses in this story.

- Mary Shelley's *Frankenstein* (1818) focuses on a hideous-looking monster with fine feelings. The book is an example of the gothic horror novel.

- Charles Dickens, a contemporary of Hugo, wrote *Oliver Twist* (1837), a novel that portrays the hardships of the poor in London. A poor orphaned boy escapes from his cruel master only to find life even more difficult on the streets.

- *The Strange Case of Dr. Jekyll and Mr. Hyde* (1886), one of Robert Louis Stevenson's classic works, features a well-mannered gentleman who struggles against his anti-social desires in this novel of two opposing forces fighting for the soul of one man.

---

visit Paris in irrational hopes of catching a glimpse of the dancing gypsy. Hugo gives La Esmeralda the last moment, demonstrating the power of this female character, who may not be the protagonist but without her the story would lack the energy to propel itself to the end. Who would not be moved by the final sight of Quasimodo's skeleton embracing his only true love, the giver of strength and inspiration of change? Of course, it is La Esmeralda.

Source: Joyce Hart, Critical Essay on *The Hunchback of Notre Dame*, in *Novels for Students*, Thomson Gale, 2005.

Elizabeth McCracken

In the following introduction, McCracken discusses the strengths of the novel as great literature.

For a moment, let us forget Quasimodo.

You know him already, of course. He is one of the most famous fictional characters of all time, a creation so indelibly described that—even if you have never seen an illustration, on paper or canvas or celluloid—you would recognize him walking down the street. Like Hugo, I "shall not attempt to give the reader any idea of that tetrahedron nose, of that horseshoe mouth, of that little left eye, obscured by a bristly red eyebrow, while the right was completely overwhelmed and buried by an enormous wart; of those irregular teeth, jagged here and there like the battlements of a fortress; of that horny lip, over which one of those teeth protruded . . ." The bell ringer of NotreDame requires no introduction at all.

I mean to introduce the entire book, which is *a great work of literature*. Those words once suggested a book you had to read; now they suggest one you needn't bother with, because so many generations have done it for you. Surely by now the plot of *The Hunchback of Notre-Dame* (or *Robinson Crusoe*, or *A Tale of Two Cities*) is encoded in our DNA, a kind of evolutionary Cliff's Note.

The fact is, most novels, great and bad, are best read in a state of near ignorance. You are always more easily and pleasantly seduced—even by a brilliant seducer—without the voice of your mother or your eighth-grade English teacher in your ear. Perhaps the only proper introduction for a Great Novel is: Reader, here is your book. Book, here is your reader—

—except we often know just enough about great novels to dissuade us from reading them. In the case of *The Hunchback of Notre-Dame*, I blame Quasimodo. Not the one who lives between the covers of the book but the one who haunts the world at large, the sweet Beast who falls in love with the unattainable Beauty, that whiff of melodrama about him, the human heart awoken by love. Actors want to play him, in movies and musicals. They've made him into a g——d—— Disney character, in a cartoon whose moral is that good triumphs, evil fails, and people will accept you for your essential niceness even if your face is, well, a little lopsided.

This book, this great book, is not nice. It is merciless. It is full of poetry and ideas, tragedy and moments of laugh-out-loud comedy. *The Hunchback of Notre-Dame* is a Gothic cathedral of a novel, as endlessly beautiful, instructive, tragic, and brilliantly formed, as darkly funny, diverting, and entertaining. It's as interested in small things as grand, as crammed with detail, and as rigorously organized: broad-shouldered, full of gargoyle-topped alcoves and saint-filled niches you can find your way back to without much trouble, if you have paid attention.

And Quasimodo is only one of these treasures. He isn't even the true eponymous hero of Victor Hugo's novel, which was called by its author *Notre-Dame de Paris*. The English title, which Hugo hated, narrows the book down to one character and one building. In fact, this is a book full of heroes and monsters, saints and gargoyles, and saints-turned-gargoyles. For quite a while, the book seems to be a wandering mass of characters, though slowly we meet the essential players: Pierre Gringoire, luckless poet, who leads us through Paris and to Esmeralda, who saves him from being ordered hanged by the King of the Tramps at the Cour des Miracles; Claude Frollo, the archdeacon of Notre-Dame, who took in the foundling Quasimodo; Frollo's dissolute younger brother, Jehan; Esmeralda's exquisite goat, Djali; and the mysterious and wrenching recluse Sister Gudule ("Sack Woman"), formerly known as Paquette la Chantefleurie, who has shut herself in the Rat Hole, a basement cell with no door that has been expressly designed for women "who should wish to bury themselves alive, on account of some great calamity or some extraordinary penance." She has cast herself out of society, which makes her somehow more monstrous than even Quasimodo.

There is, of course, no actual aimlessness—you cannot discern the architecture of a cathedral by examining the carving on one doorjamb, exquisite though it might be. Slowly, as you read along, you see the brilliant organization. The structure is one of the true pleasures of the novel. *Notre-Dame de Paris* is broken into eleven books, which are in turn broken into smaller titled chapters. Some titles are charming and comic—for instance, "The Danger of Trusting a Goat with a Secret"—and others named for characters or locations whose natures are described therein. Some cover essential plot points and some are more digressive, some are a single page, and some thirty pages long, but each is beautifully shaped and satisfying. Your tour guide will lead you up a circular stone staircase, or

> " This book, this great book, is not nice. It is merciless. It is full of poetry and ideas, tragedy and moments of laugh-out-loud comedy. *The Hunchback of Notre-Dame* is a Gothic cathedral of a novel, as endlessly beautiful, instructive, tragic, and brilliantly formed, as darkly funny, diverting, and entertaining."

into the rose-window-lit apse; he will point out the smallest cautionary serpent carved into a threshold stone. Serpent, stained glass, the iron bars over a window: no one can say exactly what architectural detail holds a cathedral up, what makes it a cathedral and not a warehouse. Not just size, not just decoration; not merely those spaces that remind us of God because they leave us awestruck, nor those that are homely and holy. *Every* detail is essential, though they seem too numerous to absorb.

Which is, after all, why you need a tour guide. Hugo's narrator is funny and mocking and mordant, and one of the first things that is lost in movie adaptations. That's the problem with filmed versions of books: they take out the poetry and replace it with recorded music. Here on every page is Hugo's brilliance with metaphor (Quasimodo looks like "a giant who had been broken in pieces and badly soldered together again"); his attention to his characters' physicality, whether Clopin Trouillefou, King of the Tramps, or Louis XI, King of France; his ability to be simultaneously chilling and laugh-provoking with the merest twist of tone, to educate and to mock—I don't even know how to begin to catalog all he accomplishes in one paragraph composed of a single sentence in a chapter discussing the former public gallows at La Place de Grève, which ends explaining that in civilized nineteenth-century Paris, there is "but one miserable, furtive, timid, shamefaced guillotine, which always seems as if fearful of being taken in the act, so speedily does it hurry away after striking the fatal blow."

It is a wicked, compassionate, enticing voice.

When you have finished reading the novel, you can go back. I always do. I love to revisit the third book, which is composed of the chapters "Notre-Dame" and "A Bird's-eye View of Paris." No human characters appear in Book III; no dialogue is spoken; the plot is not, it seems, advanced a pace. Mostly the narrator laments urban renewal, renovation, man's need to tear down the old and replace it, the "thousand various barbarisms" visited upon Notre-Dame, the fact that Paris is "deformed day by day." The narrator's voice is sometimes didactic, sometimes satirical—there's a long and hilarious riff on buildings in Hugo's own nineteenth-century Paris. He jumps over steeples and centuries, and sometimes he seems to do so only because he can.

But something happens at the end of "A Bird's-eye View of Paris." The voice turns seductively imperative. He instructs the reader, the very dear reader, to "build up and put together again in imagination the Paris of the fifteenth century," and then, step by step, the voice tells you how. It shows what a narrator like this can do: all those imperative verbs are like a great pianist taking your hands in his, and placing your fingers on the keys, and—look! what extraordinary music you can make: you almost believe that you've done it yourself, dear reader, most beloved reader. In a book full of sadness and sudden death and good, futile human works and cruelty and fear and disappointment, all those reliable jerkers of tears, it is the end of the bird's-eye view—accompanied by the bird's-tongue song of church bells (written long before bird's-eye views were as cheap and easy to obtain as footage shot from a plane)—that reliably makes me cry, for its beauty, and its brilliance, and the loss of that world, and then again for its beauty.

Small wonder Hollywood's so fond of this book; for those of us born since the dawn of cinema, it's hard to not think, from time to time, What a movie this would make! We'd recognize single-handedly staving off the Tramps who are attempting to storm the cathedral: that is what the hero of an action movie *always* does. We instinctively hear dramatic music as Claude Frollo hangs from the edge of the cathedral, begging his adopted son for rescue.

But, of course, this is not cinema: this is genius. It's the kind of peculiar mobile imagination that is rare enough throughout history and may now be rendered *impossible,* now that we have seen how plausibly (though imperfectly) cameras can mimic it. Can a post-1900 intellect think without being informed by camera angles? Hugo's eye and sensibility went everywhere. He saw things from Quasimodo's monocular point of view, and through the Recluse's barred windows; he could think like the frivolous and yet endearing Gringoire; he could think like an educated goat; he could be sympathetic with an entire mob of people; and he could distance himself from all of these points of view and mock them or instruct the reader. He could think like Paris itself: he could fly over rivers and creep behind gargoyles.

Cinema has other flaws. With enough pancake and spirit gum and prosthetics, any actor can turn himself into a credible Quasimodo: physical ugliness is easier to mimic than physical beauty. Which is, of course, the problem. So much of Hugo's book, it seems to me, is about how we are imprisoned by our physicality (how else do you explain Frollo's descent from earnest, loving priest to Esmeralda's tormenting admirer?) but also how we transcend it. In the movies we are always reminded of Quasimodo's ugliness and Esmeralda's beauty: he is always half-made, she always a shining gem, as their names suggest.

But Quasimodo is sometimes beautiful, and not just metaphorically. In one of the book's most famous scenes, he rescues Esmeralda from the gallows and spirits her into the cathedral, yelling, "Sanctuary! Sanctuary!" And, says Hugo, "at that moment Quasimodo was really beautiful. Yes, he was beautiful—he, that orphan, that foundling, that outcast." The crowd outside the cathedral sees it, and cries and laughs and cheers.

This is something a movie can never accomplish: he *really is beautiful.* Everyone sees it.

I recommend the 1939 Charles Laughton version for Laughton himself, who acts more with his one visible eye in five seconds than most other men with their whole bodies in three hours. He is extraordinary. But I cannot forgive the makers of the movie for letting him live, or for sending Esmeralda off in the arms of—good grief!—Gringoire.

In the book, Gringoire's fate is Djali, the goat. It's the only happy marriage of two living things in the entire book. Do not scorn the love of a goat: it is a powerful, touching thing, at least in Hugo's hands. Flaubert, some years later, named Madame Bovary's lap dog Djali, and small wonder: Djali is one of the greatest animal characters in all of literature, the role any goat actor would give up a hoof to play. (The best portrayal of Djali is in the 1957 Anthony Quinn *Hunchback,* which has little else to recommend it, apart from Gina Lollobrigida's really impressive corseted torso; Quinn plays Quasimodo like a five-year-old with a backache.) When Gringoire and Djali are reunited near the end of the book, she rubs against his knees, "covering the poet with caresses and white hairs." Anyone can see this is true love. When he is faced with the choice of saving the goat or his former wife from the now quite mad Frollo, Gringoire's eyes fill with tears. The goat will be hanged alongside Esmeralda. In anguish, he looks into his heart and finds the answer: he shakes off Esmeralda's pleading grip and spirits away the goat. It's such an odd moment, comic and moving at once. Hugo manages to suggest that only a much more noble man would have tried to save the woman, and that the much more noble man would then have paid with his life. And who's to say that a man who lives with a goat is less admirable than a man who dies with his dignity?

But to unite in love Gringoire and Esmeralda? It's ludicrous in the way of all forced happy endings, because it ignores the Greek word carved on the wall of Claude Frollo's cell: ANÁΓKH. Fate. Doom. Necessity. In a preface written for the book, Hugo said he'd seen that particular graffito on a visit to the cathedral; after the success of the book, tourists added it themselves so often the various *fates* began to obscure each other.

Fate is powerful, and its greatest weapon—not a gift, *never* a gift in the book—is love. In a book full of prisons and pseudo-prisons—Frollo's cell, the Recluse's rat hole, the pillories, the bell tower, Quasimodo's own body—love of another person is the worst.

Love is lethal. Love will pick you up and fling you from Paris's tallest building. It will lead you to the gallows. It will lock you in a tower, and when it finally releases you, it will smash your head on a paving stone. If you love your brother, he will disappoint you at every turn; if you love your baby, she will be taken from you. If you love Esmeralda, you will be tortured and rebuked, and then you will die for love.

No Hollywood happy endings here.

—

There is one beautiful love story in the book— far lovelier than anyone's pining over the beautiful gypsy girl, more moving than the Recluse's love for her daughter—and that's the romance between Quasimodo and his bells. It is returned, it is not fruitless, it has lasted, when the book begins, for years.

"He loved them, he caressed them, he talked to them, he understood them"—and they do so likewise. The bell ringer and the rung bells shout endearments to each other in the bell tower—they have to shout, because the bells deafened Quasimodo some years before. A small price to pay for requited love, though he's already half-formed and half-blind. He can still hear the bells, just not human beings. Perhaps they have deafened him out of jealousy.

And then he meets Esmeralda, and forsakes them.

For me, the most tragic moment of the book comes when Quasimodo, at the top of the north bell tower, looks down and sees Esmeralda on the gallows and says, "There is all I ever loved!" It is awful because it isn't true: behind him are six of his once beloved bells. Across from him, in the south tower, is his favorite, the largest, Mary, and her sister, Jacqueline. He has forgotten them; they would take him back even now. But Hugo has already foreseen the cathedral's own heartbreak: after Quasimodo, Notre-Dame seems dead: "It is like a skull: the sockets of the eyes are still there, but the gaze has disappeared." If he, like Gringoire, had honored requited love, he would not need to die for love at all.

But it is his fate to do so. Love makes him no better than any of those people with more usual souls housed in more usual bodies.

Which is, in the end, why Quasimodo haunts us, as he haunts the cathedral and the book itself. He embodies a basic human fact: we are neither the container nor the thing contained. We exist somewhere on the pulsating edge between the two. "His spirit expanded in harmony with the cathedral," Hugo writes of Quasimodo. "His sharp corners dovetailed, if we may be allowed the expression, into the receding angles of the building, so that he seemed to be not merely its inhabitant but its natural contents." Our salient angles are always shaped by the physical world, by our bodies and the spaces our bodies inhabit. Our souls change when our bodies do, as we age and improve and decline, when we suffer accidents and when we heal, when people look at us and judge us beautiful or abnormal— whether we are awarded the Golden Porpoise or the crown of the Pope of Fools. When Pierre Gringoire happens into the Cour des Miracles and finds, there in the middle of the forest, beggars casting off afflictions, blind men seeing, the legless acquiring legs, it as though he really *is* watching miracles, and not the end of a long day of fraud. And he is: they are different people when they see and walk, as surely transformed as if they'd been truly afflicted, and truly cured. How people look at you changes everything, no matter how you may wish otherwise.

We are more than our bodies, always; but we require them to bind us to the earth, and each body is binding in a different way. The body is a bucket; without it, we would be nothing but puddles on the paving stones, noble puddles, beneath notice, beneath use.

—

So Quasimodo's deformed body is what we first see in Hugo's novel; it is pages and pages before we see his soul. Hugo's patience with his characters is astonishing. Frollo is drawn the opposite way, a human who eventually turns monstrous. They are both more moving and realistic for being inconsistent, though *The Hunchback of Notre-Dame* would probably never be considered a realistic novel. It is too unlikely. These days novels tend to be classified as either Realistic Fiction—books that take place in an average world, with average characters—or Unrealistic: magic realism, science fiction, our old fables, our new ones. I wonder, really, whether that's an offshoot of several generations of readers and writers raised on the movies. Having seen the fantastic on the movie screen, people better looking than our neighbors, richer, in more peril, in deeper love—maybe now we're more likely to go to books to learn about people somewhat like ourselves, people who are neither vagabonds nor kings but somewhere between the two.

But there is a much wider spectrum. Real people, actual living people, are bizarre, full of eccentricities (both physical and spiritual) and sudden hatred and wells of love. Quasimodo has an actual hump, but we are all deviant somehow. We are not average. We are not normal. I can't imagine why we spend so much time trying.

Every day on this planet is full of occurrences and people so unlikely that we would not believe them for a moment unless presented with concrete evidence. What we think of as realism—in books and in movies—is too often a very sad kind of averaging of the human experience. It is plot based on statistical probability, personality shaped out of what feels familiar. And, strangely enough, that means that the element so-called realism most often removes from the world of the book is Hugo's ΑΝΆΓΚΗ. Fate. Things happen because there's no reason—if we examine the actuarial tables—for them *not* to happen. Perhaps we don't believe in

Fate anymore, now that we are able to run so many numbers in so many ways.

But Fate—that which must come to pass, despite our best wishes for a happy ending—occurs to the individual, not the demographic group, and great art is *about* what occurs to the individual, not the demographic group. Just because something happens less often, does that make it less realistic?

Life is implausible. Novels distill what is possible, what is inevitable, what is shocking, what is true, so that at the end we are clobbered over the head by ΑΝΆΓΚΗ. Fate: that which is surprising and inevitable. Fate is different in every work of art, will play out on stages as small as kitchens or as large as Paris, will exact its price subtly or explicitly, will save one character and kill another, and there is no way to tell, on page one, how it will happen. That is realism. We may have fate inscribed upon us when we are born, but we will be ignorant of the details.

The characters in *The Hunchback of Notre-Dame* suffer at the hands of their passions, and their passions change in an instant—which is, in fact, human nature; only in fiction are characters so resolute that they are not able to despise someone half a second after they have declared their love, as Frollo does; or vice versa, as does the Recluse of the Rat Hole. Do I believe that every day a superhumanly strong hunchback falls in love with the beautiful dark-haired girl who is also beloved by his adoptive father, the priest? Do I believe that a woman who has imprisoned herself in a tower grabs her mortal enemy by the wrist and discovers that her enemy is in fact her long-lost daughter? Do I believe that two brothers are killed falling from the same cathedral, that two people die because they have clung to the same woman, or that a goat will fling herself into the arms of the poet she loves?

Not every day, or course, or every year, or every century. But that it happened almost six hundred years ago, beginning on the sixth of January, 1482: yes. I do believe it happened.

—

"The book will kill the building," Frollo declares in Book V, Chapter I, and then Hugo's narrator elucidates in the next chapter. The printing press will change everything, has changed everything, is an endless architectural monument producing bricks for a tower, and replaces monuments like Notre-Dame itself. And, of course, he is right, because here is this novel, safe from weather, fire,

Nineteenth century illustration capturing the Notre Dame cathedral, located in Paris, France

revolutions, renovations, earthquakes. It cannot be blown up by man or toppled over by God; it fits in your hand but is larger than a cathedral.

Reader, here is your book.

Source: Elizabeth McCracken, "Introduction," in *The Hunchback of Notre Dame*, Modern Library, 2002, pp. xi–xx.

Timothy Raser

In the following excerpt, Raser presents decline in many aspects of society as the "deep subject" of Hugo's novel.

... *Hernani* was a great success, but this success was achieved only after as "battle" during which Hugo's proponents, young members of the Romantic movement, systematically cheered the play and drowned out its opponents—literary conservatives—for the first week of its performance. In the success following those first performances, Hugo neglected to give the option of first refusal to Gosselin, publisher of *Le Dernier Jour d'un condamné*, and in order to rectify this breach of contract, promised Gosselin a new novel for January 1831, thus agreeing to write a major work in less than a year. The July Revolution (1830), during which the Bourbon monarchy was replaced by the house of Orléans, interrupted this work, and Gosselin granted Hugo a short respite. The manuscript was published on 16 March; it was entitled *Notre-Dame Paris*.

The novel, set in Paris in [1482], recounts three men's love and one woman's hatred for a young Gypsy dancer, Esmeralda, who in turn loves a fourth man: the handsome soldier Phoebus. The men incarnate different classes of medieval society: Quasimodo, the cathedral's hunchbacked bell ringer, represents the lower classes; Claude Frollo, the cathedral's deacon and Quasimodo's guardian, represents the clergy; Pierre Gringoire, an unappreciated author, is marginalized, as unable to participate in society as he is to consummate his marriage of convenience to Esmeralda. Complementing the three men is an old woman, Paquette Chantefleurie, whose baby was stolen years ago by Gypsies, and who has vowed an undying hatred for that group. Phoebus wins Esmeralda's heart and, at the moment of fulfilling his passion for her, is struck by Frollo, but Esmeralda is the one who is charged with murder (even though Phoebus survives) and sorcery. Tried and convicted, Esmeralda is rescued by Quasimodo, only to fall into the hands of Paquette, who recognizes her as her long-lost daughter Agnès, but too late. Esmeralda is arrested again and hanged; Quasimodo, understanding Frollo's role in this judicial murder, throws his master from the cathedral's tower, only to wander off to Esmeralda's pauper's grave, and to die with her body in his arms.

The plot is undoubtedly both sentimental and melodramatic. The diabolical priest, the handsome, free-living soldier, and the devoted but deformed hunchback all spring from the repertory of popular fiction, and it is easy, reading for the plot alone, to dismiss the novel. Indeed, English critic John Ruskin was so outraged by Hugo's portrait of his cherished medieval city that he labeled the book "disgusting." Nonetheless, it was an immediate success, going into several editions in two years; the "eight" edition (published by Renduel) includes three chapters Hugo had withheld from Gosselin in hopes of raising the book's price.

Critics agree that it is not the plot, but the evocation of the Middle Ages that constitutes the center of the novel's interest, and the statement that the cathedral is its main character is of great validity. Two chapters in particular are singled out for praise: "Notre-Dame de Paris" and "Paris à vol d'oiseau" (A Bird's-eye View of Paris). In the first Hugo claims to evoke the cathedral, not as it is in 1832, but as it was in 1482, before the ravages of time and man. Then, it was incomparably more beautiful than now, and if it has suffered through the centuries, it is not due to any weathering, but to revolutions, restorations, and changes of fashion. Notre-Dame appears as a worn masterpiece from another era, a work bridging two periods (Romanesque and Gothic), and bringing that sense of transition to the present day. The other chapter describes Paris as it was 350 years prior to the book's publication and evokes the many quarters, churches, and monuments of the medieval city, its narrow confines and its outlying towns. Hugo opposes this vision to the more recent developments of Parisian geography and deplores the Renaissance and its effects. Just as time has damaged the cathedral, each century has taken with it much of Paris's medieval beauty.

What becomes more apparent as one reads *Notre-Dame de Paris* is that its deep subject is decline: that of the cathedral and Paris, to be sure, but also that of the monarchy (in an often-noted scene, the king asks when his time will come), of architecture (Claude Frollo foretells the demise, with the advent of the printed book, of the cathedral as a source of knowledge), and of individual resolve (Frollo slowly gives in to his diabolical impulses). Hugo refers to this process as 'ANAΓKH, or fate: this is the word Frollo scratches on the wall when Esmeralda haunts his thoughts; this is the principle the priest invokes when, fascinated, he watches a fly perish in a spider's web. The fly's predicament symbolizes his own passion for Esmeralda as well as Esmeralda's own inability to extricate herself from the judicial system, the cathedral's demise in the web of printed words, and the monarchy's futile struggle in the web of history. It is important here not to confuse fate with progress: to be sure, the decline of the monarchy or of superstition can be understood as the coming of a better order. The force that Hugo describes as " ANAΓKH, however, is blind, careless of whether it produces good or evil. Fate brings the printed book but also the guillotine; Frollo's death but also Esmeralda's; the end of monarchy but also revolution.

Even in this work "d'imagination, de caprice et de fantaisie" (of imagination, caprice, and fantasy), there is a strong current of social commentary, and the themes of judicial cruelty, of institutional blindness, and of social upheaval are never far from the surface. At the very moment that Louis XI's Flemish visitor reassures him (ironically, in the fortress of the Bastille) that monarchy will last for some time to come, the criminal rabble of Paris is assaulting Notre-Dame—nominally the king's responsibility to defend—and this violence must be put down with even more violence. When Esmeralda is tried for sorcery, she at first denies knowledge of the black art but, upon being tortured, confesses to having killed a man still alive and is condemned to death on the basis of this confession, citations from books of necromancy, and the testimony of her pet goat. The comedy of this trial only makes its tragic outcome more poignant. However one looks at the novel—from the point of view of its description, or its characterization, or its social commentary—Hugo tells a story of relentless fatalism, of a vanishing world's resignation to its own disappearance.

When *Notre-Dame de Paris*, was published, Hugo's friend Vigny expressed his pleasure at the novel. The poet Alphonse de Lamartine called its author "le Shakespeare du roman" (the Shakespeare of the novel) but faulted it for its insufficient expression of religious belief. Charles de Montalembert criticized it for the quality that Hugo deliberately sought in his plays: "ce mélange continuel du grotesque au tragique" (this continual mixture of the grotesque and the tragic). . . .

Source: Timothy Raser, "Victor Hugo," in *Dictionary of Literary Biography*, Volume 119, *Nineteenth-Century French Fiction Writers: Romanticism and Realism, 1800–1860*, edited by Catharine Savage Brosman, Gale Research, 1992, pp. 164–92.

Sources

Porter, Laurence M., "Preface," in *Victor Hugo*, Twayne Publisher, 1999, pp. vii–xviii.

Robb, Graham, *Victor Hugo: A Biography*, Norton, 1997.

Further Reading

Baguley, David, *Napoleon III and His Regime: An Extravaganza*, Louisiana State University Press, 2000.
>   In this book, readers meet Napoleon III who dismantled France's republic and took it upon himself to establish a dictatorship. This nephew of the more famous Bonaparte lived in his uncle's shadow but tried desperately to outshine him.

Erlande-Brandenburg, Alain, *Notre-Dame de Paris*, Harry N. Abrams, 1998.
>   Critics highly recommend a slow reading of this beautiful book that portrays the long history and the architectural accomplishments of one of the Middle Age's most magnificent buildings.

Kelly, Linda, *The Young Romantics: Victor Hugo, Sainte-Beuve, Vigny, Dumas, Musset, and George Sand and Their Friendships, Feuds, and Loves in the French Romantic Revolution*, Random House, 1976.
>   Kelly provides a good background study of the early authors of the French Romantic Movement.

Yors, Jan, *The Gypsies*, Waveland Press, 1989.
>   When he was only twelve years old, Jan Yors ran away from his home in Belgium and lived with a group of gypsies, following them from one country to another, learning their culture from the inside. This book has won praise from the critics for its first-hand account of life with one group of gypsies.

Maggie: A Girl of the Streets

Stephen Crane

1893

Stephen Crane's *Maggie: A Girl of the Streets* was first published at his own expense in 1893. Literary critic William Dean Howells was so impressed with the novel that he helped get it published by D. Appleton and Company in 1896. *Maggie* came to be regarded as one of Crane's finest and most eloquent statements on environmental determinism.

The story centers on Maggie Johnson, a pretty young woman who struggles to survive the brutal environment of the Bowery, a New York City slum, at the end of the nineteenth century. Abused by an alcoholic mother and victimized by the overwhelming poverty of the slums, Maggie falls in love with a charming bartender, who, she tells herself, will help her escape her harsh life. Maggie's relationship with Pete compounds her suffering, however, when her family and her neighbors condemn her. Eventually abandoned by her lover, as well as her family, Maggie is forced to make a living on the cruel city streets. Crane's unblinking depiction of the devastating environmental forces that ultimately destroy this young, hopeful woman was celebrated as one of the most important documents of American Naturalism.

Author Biography

Stephen Crane was born on November 1, 1871, in Newark, New Jersey, the last of fourteen children to Jonathan and Mary. His father was a Methodist

Stephen Crane

minister and his mother was an active member of the church and reform work, including the temperance movement. Crane's upbringing in this religious household profoundly influenced his own worldview, which he eloquently expressed in his works. James B. Colvert, in his article for the *Dictionary of Literary Biography*, notes that Crane's poetry especially reflects "the anguish of a spiritual crisis in which he attempted to exorcise the Pecks' God of wrath and, beyond that, to test his faith in general against the moral realities" of the 1890s, which he recorded during his years as a reporter. His religious questioning was a primary subject in much of his fiction.

Crane began his career as a newspaper reporter after his father died and the family moved to Asbury Park, New Jersey, where his brother Townley ran a news agency for the *New York Tribune*. Townley and another brother, Will, encouraged Crane to rebel against his strict, religious upbringing and helped him develop a secular worldview, which was reinforced during his years at Lafayette College and Syracuse University. During his college years, Crane continued to write newspaper articles and began writing fiction.

After leaving college without obtaining a degree, Crane moved to New York City where he continued his work as a newspaper reporter. When he

was twenty-two, he wrote under the pseudonym Johnston Smith and published at his own expense, his first novel, *Maggie*. He did not, however, gain fame until the publication of his second novel, *Red Badge of Courage*, which was heralded internationally as one of the finest war novels ever written.

During this time, Crane continued to work as a reporter in the west and in Mexico. In the late 1890s, he moved with Cora Taylor, a hotel/brothel proprietor, to England where he met Joseph Conrad, H. G. Wells, and Henry James. He continued writing fiction there and worked occasionally as a reporter, since his later novels were not well received. His travels, however, caused his health to deteriorate. Crane died of tuberculosis in 1900 when he was twenty-eight. In his short lifetime, he had produced a remarkable volume of work, including numerous newspaper articles, six novels, more than a hundred stories and sketches, and two books of poems.

Plot Summary

Part 1

The novel opens with young Jimmie in the midst of a street fight "for the honor of Rum Alley," a tenement street in New York City at the end of the nineteenth century. Jimmie is caught up in the "fury of battle" as he is continually assaulted by a gang of children from nearby Devil's Row. He alone defends his street after his compatriots have run off. Some workmen watch the bruised and bloody-faced boy with mild interest and no intervention until a sixteen-year-old boy named Pete approaches and, after recognizing Jimmie, pulls the assailants off of him. When Jimmie's friends return, the child upbraids them for leaving him to fend for himself until he gets into a fight with one of them. Jimmie's father soon arrives and breaks up the fight by kicking his son and his combatant. The battered boy then sullenly follows his father home. On the way, they meet his younger brother Tommie and his sister Maggie. When she complains that his fighting angers their mother, Jimmie slaps her.

At home, their drunken mother explodes in anger after seeing Jimmie's bruises and begins to inflict some of her own on the boy. When Mr. Johnson complains that she beats the children too often, she turns on him, and they engage in a fierce quarrel that ends with his departure to the local pub. During this brutal scene, the children cower in the

Media Adaptations

- A recorded version of the novel *Maggie: A Girl of the Streets and Other New York Stories* was produced in 1997 by the American Library Association.

corner. Mrs. Johnson flies into a new rage after Maggie accidentally breaks a dish and Jimmie escapes to the hallway, where an elderly female resident joins him, listening to the shrieks emanating from the Johnson's apartment.

The old woman asks Jimmie to slip down to the pub and buy her some beer. After completing his mission, his father spots him and steals the beer from him, drinking in down in one gulp. When Jimmie returns to the apartment later that night, he discovers that his parents are engaged in a new fight, and so he waits in the hallway until the noise dies down. After returning home to find his parents passed out on the floor, Jimmie and Maggie sit in fear, watching their mother's prostrate body until dawn.

Part 2

Some years later, Tommie has died and Jimmie has grown into a hardened young man who has "clad his soul in armor." He takes a job as a truck driver, which gives him a measure of pride, and gains a reputation as a troublemaker with the police. Jimmie easily lives up to that estimation, determining "never to move out of the way of anything, until formidable circumstances, or a much larger man than himself forced him to it." After his father dies, he becomes the head of the household.

Maggie "blossomed in a mud puddle" into a rare sight in the tenements—a pretty girl. She gains employment at a shop where she makes collars and cuffs along with several other young women of "various shades of yellow discontent." The "eternally swollen and disheveled" Mrs. Johnson has become famous in the neighborhood, especially at the police station and the courts, where she offers a continual stream of excuses and prayers for her troubles.

One day Jimmie brings Pete home, and Maggie is immediately impressed by his dress and his confident air, as he gestures like "a man of the world." She is an attentive audience for his tales of valor in his position as bartender, which involves dealing forcibly with anyone who disrupts his bar, and soon determines that he is "the ideal man." She admires his elegance and the way he defies the hardships of tenement life. Pete also takes notice of Maggie, declaring eventually to her, "I'm stuck on yer shape." The two begin to go out on dates.

On their first evening out, Maggie is embarrassed by her mother's drunken state and the disheveled apartment that her mother has wrecked in one of her tirades that afternoon. Maggie has only a shabby black dress to wear and is "afraid she might appear small and mouse-colored" in contrast to Pete and his crowd, which she is certain will be quite elegant.

Pete takes Maggie to a vaudeville show, where he displays a confident indifference to all. His attitude impresses Maggie and reinforces her vision of his superiority. Pete showers attention on her, which she revels in, along with the performances on stage. After the show, Pete asks for a kiss, but Maggie declines, insisting "dat wasn't in it." On the walk home, Pete wonders if he has "been played fer a duffer," expecting Maggie to offer some more tangible form of gratitude.

As Maggie and Pete continue to date, she becomes more critical of her clothes, her home, and her job, and Pete becomes more like "a golden sun" to her. The two attend plays and museums, which excite Maggie but bore Pete.

One evening, Jimmie finds his mother staggering home from a bar from which she has just been ejected, jeered on by the local children and her tenement neighbors. An embarrassed Jimmie yells at her to shut up and get into the apartment. Inside, the two begin a fierce battle that ends with broken furniture and Mrs. Johnson in her usual position in a heap on the floor. When Pete arrives, he shrugs and tells Maggie they will have a good time that night. Mrs. Johnson curses her daughter, insisting that she is a disgrace to the family and tells her not to return, which causes Maggie to tremble. Pete insists that her mother will change her mind in the morning and the two depart.

Part 3

Jimmie is decidedly upset that Pete has "ruined" his sister. The old neighbor tells him that she saw Maggie return home one evening, crying to

Pete, asking him if he loved her. Jimmie determines to kill him while Mrs. Johnson curses her. Soon all of the neighbors are discussing Maggie and her ruin, insisting that they knew that there was always something wrong with her.

One evening, Jimmie and a friend enter Pete's bar and begin to harass him. Pete tries to calm him down but Jimmie and his friend back him into a corner and a fight breaks out. Soon all of the bar's patrons join in, smashing the mirrored walls, bottles, and glassware. When the police appear, Jimmie dashes out just in time.

On a subsequent evening, Pete and Maggie attend a show. She has changed markedly, her sense of self now lost in her complete dependence on Pete, whose confidence has grown as Maggie's has diminished. Pete is proud of the effect he has on Maggie, who fears any sign of anger or displeasure from him. Others at the show treat her with the same lack of respect as her neighbors have.

When Jimmie returns home several days after the fight, he discovers that Maggie has not been home either. He and his mother are shamed by her behavior, but Mrs. Johnson uses her tale of woe as an effective method to gain leniency when she is arrested for drunkenness.

Three weeks after she leaves her home, Maggie accompanies Pete to another show where he runs into an old friend, who pays no attention to Maggie. As Pete shows his obvious pleasure in the other woman's company, Maggie can think of nothing to say. When the woman asks Pete to leave with her, he initially refuses to abandon Maggie, hinting that she is pregnant. However, when he goes outside to discuss his situation, he never comes back for Maggie, stranding her at the show. An astounded Maggie waits for quite a while until she accepts the fact that Pete is gone and then leaves.

Part 4

The narrative jumps here to a time in the future when an unidentified "forlorn woman" wanders the streets in search of someone. As Jimmie walks up the street and the woman greets him, the reader learns that the woman is Hattie, apparently someone who is in a similar situation to that of Maggie. Jimmie turns his back on her, just as Pete has done with Maggie, departing with an admonition to "go t'hell." When he arrives home, he finds Maggie suffering her mother's wrath and ridicule. Neighbors join in the torment until Maggie turns to Jimmie for support and is rebuffed.

The narrator now focuses on Pete, who has not given a second thought to Maggie's fate. He determines that he has never really cared much for her and was in no way responsible for her. The evening after he leaves her at the show, Maggie walks by his bar, and he feels a temporary twinge of guilt. When he speaks with her, though, he shows no mercy, telling her to leave before she gets him in trouble. She asks him where she should go, and he answers, as Jimmie had done to his similar "problem," "oh, go t'hell."

Afterwards, Maggie wanders the streets, looking for some support but finds none. Several months later, she is still walking the streets, willing to offer herself to anyone in order to survive. Initially, she frequents the more well-respected areas of town, but the men there soon realize her lack of refinement and so reject her advances. Even when she walks on to the poorer sections of the city, she has no luck. She moves onto the worst sections near the river where she encounters "ragged" men "with shifting, blood-shot eyes and grimy hands." The narrator suggests at this point that Maggie is drawn to the river, where the "sounds of life . . . came faintly and died away to a silence" and jumps in.

Pete and several women, including the woman who lured him away from Maggie, participate in a drunken revelry in a local saloon. They all seem to be thoroughly enjoying themselves. Pete gets too drunk, however, which eventually disgusts the women who leave him in a heap on the floor. The woman whom he has admired so much concludes on her way out of the bar, "what a damn fool."

The novel closes with Mrs. Johnson's tearful response to Jimmie's report that Maggie has died. At last, Mrs. Johnson expresses tender feelings toward her daughter and swears she will forgive her.

Characters

Jimmie Johnson

Jimmie, Maggie's brother, appears at the opening of the novel. At a young age, he has become as savage as the little "true assassins" he battles in the streets. His survival on these mean streets depends on his ability to dodge fists and stones as well as to develop an exalted sense of himself, which he displays in the opening fight when he tells

all comers that he can lick them "wid one han'"
The world hardens him at an early age, and he gives
it no respect "because he had begun with no idols
that it had smashed."

As he grows older, he becomes a bully, menacing "mankind at the intersections of streets,"
afraid of nothing. His sneering attitude toward
everything and everyone deepens in his "down-
trodden position which had a private but distinct
element of grandeur in its isolation." He has a few
friends but is not loyal to them, as he illustrates after the bar fight with Pete. As he escapes, he thinks
of returning to rescue his friend, but he immediately dismisses the idea with, "ah, what d'hell?"
His lack of character also emerges in his behavior
toward his sister. Initially he appears to be concerned about Maggie's welfare when he determines
to punish Pete for his treatment of her, but he proves
to be driven more by a sense of shame than of responsibility. He turns his back on Maggie as cruelly as does his mother. When she dies, he reports
the news dispassionately.

Maggie Johnson

The central character in the novel, Maggie
Johnson has retained her innocence and virtue
within her brutal environment and has "blossomed
in a mud puddle." She longs to escape her abusive
family and dreary job at the collar and cuff factory
but does not have the confidence or the opportunity to succeed on her own. She has an active imagination that she uses to escape the crushing despair
of her world. When Pete appears, she becomes
filled with hope that she will succeed. "Under the
trees of her dream-gardens there had always walked
a lover"; Pete becomes that "ideal man."

Her imaginative and illusory vision of Pete,
however, causes her to feel pale by comparison. As
he displays his confident assurance of his superiority to all who come into contact with him, Maggie begins to feel insecure in her relationship with
him. She often finds herself at a loss for words, intimidated by the glamorous world in which, she believes, he operates. Her naiveté and clouded vision
of reality causes her to be too dependent on Pete,
which eventually leads to her destruction.

Mr. Johnson

Maggie's sullen father has been beaten down
by society and by his wife. He often retreats to the
local saloon to drink away his troubles, or he takes
out his resentment on his children. Evidence of both
behaviors emerges in the opening pages when he
kicks Jimmie for fighting and flees the apartment

after a row with Jimmie's mother. His lack of
concern for anyone other than himself is further
illustrated when he steals the neighbor woman's
beer from Jimmie, who has just paid for it. His
weak character perhaps precipitates an early death.

Mrs. Johnson

Maggie's mother is a monstrous woman who
harbors a vindictive hatred for anyone who gets in
her way. She walks with a "chieftain-like stride"
as she beats her family and curses them, continually insisting they should all "go t'hell." Sometimes
when drunk, she falls into "a muddled mist of sentiment" but the shallowness of this emotion is revealed when during one episode, she reverts
immediately into a murderous rage when Maggie
breaks a plate. Her utter lack of love or concern for
her children emerges in her treatment of Maggie
when the neighbors begin to regard the young
woman's behavior as immoral. Mrs. Johnson responds not by defending her daughter, but by kicking her out on the streets. As a result, when Pete
also abandons her, Maggie is forced to prostitute
herself in order to survive.

Nellie Johnson

Nellie appears as a female version of Jimmie
and Pete—someone who has developed an attitude
of confident superiority as a means of survival.
When she comes across Pete and Maggie at the
club, her "brilliance and audacity" dazzle the couple. Her own shallowness emerges when she convinces Pete to abandon Maggie. Later she abandons
Pete in much the same way when she grows tired
of his drunkenness.

Tommie Johnson

The youngest Johnson, Tommie becomes more
of a plot device than a fleshed out character. He
first appears on the street as Maggie drags him
home, adding to her already overwhelming burdens. She tries to look out for him, but a vulnerability to their harsh environment leads to his death.
Maggie seems to be the only one who is affected
by his death when she places a flower inside his
"insignificant" coffin.

Pete

Pete is as immoral as Jimmie, but he has hidden it more effectively under a respectable appearance. Like Jimmie, he has developed a superior
persona in order to survive the inhumanity of tenement life. As he struts in front of Maggie at her
apartment when they first meet, the room seems "to

grow even smaller and unfit to hold his dignity, the attribute of a supreme warrior." At first he behaves like a gentleman as he becomes attentive to Maggie's desires on their first date, but his true intentions emerge when she refuses to kiss him goodnight, and he thinks he has "been played for a duffer." Pete quickly rejects Maggie as unsuitable when a more interesting and confident companion arrives. He heartlessly turns his back on her when her presence and most likely her pregnancy have become tiring.

Themes

Poverty

The impetus for the misery the characters endure in the novel is the abject state of poverty in which they live. Their tenement is inhabited by "true assassins" who prey on anyone in their path. Nearby "a worm of yellow convicts . . . [crawl] slowly along the river's bank." The Johnsons' building "quivered and creaked from the weight of humanity stamping about in its bowels." In this atmosphere, children like Maggie's younger brother Tommie die. Family life is destroyed as Mr. And Mrs. Johnson drink themselves into oblivion to escape the reality of their lives and then take their drunken wrath out on their children. The streets become schoolyards where Jimmie and his friends learn how to foster within themselves the brutality they must endure. Maggie's dreams of escaping her impoverished existence lead her to the mind-numbing work at the collar and cuff factory and eventually to Pete. When Pete and her family reject her, she is forced to prostitute herself in order to survive.

Hypocrisy

The atmosphere of the novel breeds a moral hypocrisy as the characters struggle to justify their own immoral actions. Mr. Johnson yells at his wife to stop always "poundin' a kid" after he has just savagely kicked Jimmie in an attempt to break up the street fight. Mrs. Johnson, who is more brutal to her children than her husband, declares Maggie to be a disgrace to the family and questions "who would t'ink such a bad girl could grow up in our fambly." Jimmie, who has abandoned many young women in the same manner as Pete has done with Maggie, declares that he will kill Pete for his treatment of her. Yet, he wonders only "vaguely" whether "some of the women of his acquaintance had brothers. Nevertheless, his mind did not for an

Topics for Further Study

- Why do you think *Maggie* has never been made into a film? What difficulties would a filmmaker face in trying to create a cinematic version of the novel? Try to address these difficulties as you write a script for one scene in *Maggie*.

- Crane's *Red Badge of Courage* has been heralded as one of the finest war novels ever written. Although the novel's subject matter is quite different from that of *Maggie*, scholars have found many thematic and stylistic parallels. Read *Red Badge of Courage* and compare its themes and style to those of *Maggie*.

- Research Irish immigration to the United States in the late nineteenth century and discuss the difficulties the Irish faced as well as how they were eventually able to establish themselves in America.

- Investigate working conditions and regulations in New York City at the end of the nineteenth century, and compare them to working conditions and regulations in New York City today.

instant confuse himself with those brothers nor his sister with theirs."

A subtle social hypocrisy is revealed in Maggie's relationship with Pete. Survival for men in this atmosphere depends on them gaining an exaggerated sense of their own superiority coupled with an attitude of complete independence. That avenue is not open for women like Maggie, whose only escape is through utter dependence on a man. Ironically, when she adopts the illusory vision that Pete promotes, she loses her own sense of herself and as a result reduces her standing in Pete's eyes. When her family turns her out because of the neighborhood's condemnation of her relationship with Pete, she is forced to become what they insist she already is and always has been. Her inability to endure this life prompts her to commit suicide.

Style

Structure

Colvert writes that in the novel, Crane "eschewed the conventional plot, shifting the focus from the drama of external event or situation to the drama of thought and feeling in the mental life of his subjects." There are important events in the story, usually marked by their violence, but they serve mainly as a catalyst for the characters' internal responses, which adroitly focus the narrative on the effect the environment has on them. For example, few details are given of Jimmie's fight with the neighboring gang, while more time is spent detailing the animalistic rage he feels coupled with a sense of heroism. A few sentences provide a description of what Maggie sees on stage, but her response to it mingled with her feelings toward Pete, reveal Crane's ironic depiction of the tension between illusion and reality.

Imagery

Crane's use of imagery reinforces the novel's themes. His focus on the illusory and fragile world his characters inhabit is symbolized in Pete's saloon by "a shining bar of counterfeit massiveness" and the mirrored walls that multiply the "pyramids of shimmering glasses" lined up on the shelves. During Jimmie and Pete's fight in the saloon, the mirrors "splintered to nothing" along with Maggie's dreams of escape. The tenement becomes filled with images that reflect its danger and brutality. "A dozen gruesome doorways gave up loads of babies to the street and gutter" while "withered persons . . . sat smoking pipes in obscure corners." Colvert notes that these images prompted Frank Norris in his review of the novel to write that the picture Crane makes is not "a single carefully composed painting, serious, finished, scrupulously studied, but rather scores and scores of tiny flashlight photographs, instantaneous, caught, as it were, on the run."

Historical Context

Naturalism

Naturalism is the name of a literary movement that emerged in the late nineteenth and early twentieth centuries in France, England, and the United States. Writers included in this group, like Stephen Crane, Emile Zola, and Theodore Dreiser, described in their works a biological and/or environmental determinism that prevented their characters from exercising their free will and thus controlling their fates. Crane often focused on the social and economic factors that overpowered his characters. Zola's and Dreiser's works include this type of environmental determinism coupled with an exploration of the influences of heredity in their portraits of the animalistic nature of men and women engaged in the endless and brutal struggle for survival.

Irish Immigration

Thousands of Irish men and women immigrated to the United States during the nineteenth century to escape the hardships of their native land. America became a dream for these people who fled poverty and disease as well as English oppression as they packed themselves tightly into ships, referred to as coffin ships due to the harsh living conditions on board, heading for their new home. Being in the United States, however, would hardly live up to their vision of the good life. Most settled in their arrival ports and were soon herded into the city's tenement sections, where they had little chance of escape. Each major city, including New York, had its Irish section or shantytown where, due to the prejudice against them, immigrants were confined to cellars and shacks. Ridiculed for their dress and their accents and blamed for increases in the crime rate, they were often greeted with "No Irish Need Apply" signs when they looked for employment.

A Woman's Place

At the close of the nineteenth century, feminist thinkers began to engage in a rigorous investigation of female identity as it related to all aspects of a woman's life. Any woman who questioned traditional female roles was tagged a "New Woman," a term attributed to novelist Sarah Grand, whose 1894 article in the *North American Review* identified an emergent group of women, influenced by J. S. Mill and other champions of individualism, who supported and campaigned for women's rights.

Many women insisted that marriage and motherhood should not be the only choices available to women. The more conservative feminists of this age considered marriage and motherhood acceptable roles only if guidelines were set in order to prevent a woman from assuming an inferior position to her husband in any area of their life together. This group felt that a woman granted equality in marriage would serve as an exemplary role model for her children by encouraging the development of an independent spirit. Women, however,

Compare & Contrast

- **Late Nineteenth Century:** In 1888, the International Council of Women is founded to mobilize support for the woman's suffrage movement.

  Today: Women have made major gains in their fight for equality, although the Equal Rights Amendment Bill that was intended to codify the equality of men and women has yet to be passed. It was introduced to every Congress between 1923 and 1972. In 1972 it was passed and then sent to the states to be ratified, but it failed to gain the approval of the required number of states. It has been introduced to every Congress since 1972.

- **Late Nineteenth Century:** Feminist Victoria Woodhull embarks on a lecture tour in 1871 espousing a free love philosophy, which reflects the women's movement's growing willingness to discuss sexual issues.

  Today: Women have the freedom to engage in premarital sex and to have children out of

wedlock. The issue of single parenting caused a furor in the early 1990s when then vice president Daniel Quayle criticized the television character Murphy Brown for deciding not to marry her baby's father. In the early 2000s, however, single parenting is more widely accepted.

- **Late Nineteenth Century:** Samuel Langhorne Clemens (also known as Mark Twain) dubs the 1870s "The Gilded Age," due in large part to the industrialization of the West. During this period, a handful of large industries gains control of the economy in the United States. Those industrialists who make profits see their fortunes grow at a rapid rate, while the working class suffers from low wages and dangerous working conditions.

  Today: Public awareness of major companies who exploit foreign workers has grown. Many fear that the current push for economic globalization reinforces the imbalances between the rich and the poor.

---

especially in lower socio-economic classes, found it almost impossible to break away from traditional female roles until the second wave feminist movement in the 1970s.

Critical Overview

After completing *Maggie* when he was twenty-two, Crane had the novel published privately under the pseudonym Johnston Smith in 1893. This version caught the eye of literary critics Hamlin Garland and William Dean Howells, who championed it and eventually, after its rejection by *The Century Magazine*, convinced D. Appleton and Company to publish the novel in 1896. *Maggie* did not gain much success with the reading public, however, until Crane toned down the more violent scenes in the revised 1896 version.

Theodore Dreiser, in a letter to Max J. Herzberg, printed in the *Michigan Daily Sunday Magazine*, declared *Maggie* to "bear all the marks of a keen and unblessed sympathy with life, as well as a high level of literary perception." He concluded that Crane was "one of the few writers who stood forward intellectually and artistically at a time when this nation was as thoroughly submerged in romance and sentimentality and business as it is today." In a 1922 piece on Crane printed in *Friday Nights: Literary Criticism and Appreciation*, Edward Garnett described the novel as a "little masterpiece" in its "remorseless study of New York slum and Bowery morals." Garnett insisted *Maggie* is not "a story *about* people; it is primitive human nature itself set down with perfect spontaneity and grace of handling." He found the "aesthetic beauty" of the work unsurpassed.

The support of Dreiser and Garnett, along with that of Amy Lowell and Willa Cather, helped

1895 photograph capturing a desolate view of the New York Bowery, the setting of Maggie: A Girl of the Streets

rediscover Crane and *Maggie* in the 1920s. In the early 2000s, the novel is regarded as one of the finest examples of American literary naturalism.

Criticism

Wendy Perkins

Perkins is a professor of English at Prince George's Community College in Maryland and has published articles on several twentieth-century authors. In this essay, Perkins examines Crane's exploration of the naturalistic themes in Maggie.

> [The wind-tower] was a giant, standing with its back to the plight of the ants. It represented in a degree . . . the serenity of nature amid the struggles of the individual—nature in the wind, and nature in the vision of men. She did not seem cruel to him then, not beneficent, not treacherous, not wise. But she was indifferent, flatly indifferent."

This famous passage from Stephen Crane's short story "The Open Boat," which focuses on four men in a small dinghy struggling against the current to make it to shore, is often quoted as an apt expression of the tenets of naturalism, a literary movement in the late nineteenth and early twentieth

centuries in France, the United States, and England. Naturalist writers like Crane, Emile Zola, and Theodore Dreiser argued in their works that human destiny is controlled by biological and/or environmental factors. Their characters enjoy no free will as they struggle to survive their often brutal lives. As in "The Open Boat," in his first novel, *Maggie: A Girl of the Streets*, Crane examines naturalistic tendencies in the harsh lives of the novel's main characters. Their fate, however, is not determined by natural forces. Through his story of a young Bowery woman's experiences within a destructive and indifferent social environment, Crane raises important questions about endurance and survival.

Crane wrote on early copies of the novel that the story "tries to show that environment is a tremendous thing in the world and frequently shapes lives regardless." He succeeds admirably. Crane's depiction of Maggie's tragedy reveals an ironclad biological as well as environmental determinism, as is noted by Edward Garnett, in an essay on Crane. Garnet writes that the characters' "human nature responds inexorably to their brutal environment" and concludes "the curious habits and code of the most primitive savage tribes could not be presented with a more impartial exactness, or with more sympathetic understanding."

The biological forces that shape the characters' destinies emerge in their adaptive response to their harsh environment. The novel opens with an apt illustration of this cause and effect relationship in the description of Maggie's brother Jimmie, who is engaged in a fight with the neighborhood boys. Street fighting was commonplace in the Bowery at the end of the nineteenth century, as one gang of boys would battle another for a dominant position in the neighborhood. Boys like Jimmie joined gangs for a sense of belonging and protection. Ironically, though, in the opening scene, Jimmie's friends have abandoned him, and as a result, he is being brutally beaten by a rival gang. His instincts for survival take over as he does anything he can to defend himself. The "fury of the battle" turns him into "a tiny, insane demon" as he uses every method available to fend off his attackers.

Jimmie's fists, however, are not the only tools he employs to survive his savage environment. In order to endure the beatings doled out by his parents as well as the neighborhood children and the devastating, abject poverty of the tenements, Jimmie along with his sister Maggie must invent comforting illusions. Jimmie survives because he creates a vision of himself as a god within the neighborhood, vastly superior to all the other inhabitants. This vision begins to take shape from an early age, when Jimmie has dreams of becoming "some vague soldier, or a man of blood with a sort of sublime license." His false sense of the heroic is reflected in the opening scene when Jimmie stands "upon a heap of gravel for the honor of Rum Alley."

Later, when he gains employment in the city as a truck driver, he determines that only he has "the unalienable right to stand in the proper path of the sun chariot." As he drives through the streets, he wonders at the inhabitants' "insane disregard for their legs and his convenience." His sense of superiority causes him to encase his soul in armor as he sneers at the world and becomes "so sharp that he believed in nothing."

Jimmie's friend Pete has adopted a similar sense of grandeur, which has not only helped him survive the mean streets of the Bowery; it also has earned him a respectable position as a bartender. Pete's "mannerisms stamped him as a man who had a correct sense of his personal superiority." James B. Colvert, in his article on Crane for the *Dictionary of Literary Biography*, writes that "the swaggering Pete and Jimmie apprehend a world of menace which challenges their assumptions about

> "Ironically, while Pete's illusory vision of himself enables him to survive his harsh world, Maggie's embracement of that same vision eventually destroys her."

their special virtues and their dreams of heroic destinies." As a result they must cover themselves in an armor of scorn, as is indicated by Pete's assumption that "he had certainly seen everything and with each curl of his lip, he declared that it amounted to nothing."

Pete's superior sense of himself and his nonchalant disregard of his surroundings causes Maggie to deem him "the ideal man." Unfortunately for her, however, Pete does not live up to these expectations. In her relationship with Pete, Maggie adopts a similar defense mechanism, as does Pete and her brother—the creation of comforting illusions. Her fantasies, however, do not involve an exaggerated sense of self; they revolve around her distorted vision of Pete, who proves himself to be as morally bankrupt as others in Maggie's world. Ironically, while Pete's illusory vision of himself enables him to survive his harsh world, Maggie's embracement of that same vision eventually destroys her.

Maggie's desperate need to escape the brutality of her family life and the monotony of her position at the collar and cuff factory becomes apparent at the theater, which she frequents with Pete. There, she is transported by "plays in which the dazzling heroine was rescued from the palatial home of her treacherous guardian by the hero with the beautiful sentiments." These melodramas, with their "pale-green snow-storms," "nickel-plated revolvers," and daring rescues, are "transcendental realism," removing her from the sordid reality of her own life. Pete gains so much power over Maggie because he becomes her method of transport to this charming and safe world, where "the poor and virtuous eventually overcame the wealthy and wicked."

What Do I Read Next?

- *The Awakening* (1899) is Kate Chopin's novel of a young woman who struggles between the prescribed role of wife and mother and the desire to act independently and inevitably suffers the consequences of trying to establish herself as an independent spirit.

- In the play *A Doll's House* (1879), Henrik Ibsen examines a woman's child-like role as wife and mother in the nineteenth century and the disastrous effects those limitations have on her marriage when she attempts to help her husband.

- Stephen Crane's short story "The Open Boat" (1898) depicts the struggles of four shipwrecked seamen to reach shore.

- George Bernard Shaw's play *Mrs. Warren's Profession* (1898) focuses on a daughter who struggles to deal with her discovery that her mother has been running successful brothels, the source of her family's income.

After her mother throws her out in response to Maggie's relationship with Pete, Maggie becomes completely dependent on him, a situation reinforced by her illusory vision of him as "a golden sun." In his rarefied presence, she feels "small and mouse-colored" as she "beseeches tenderness of him." Soon, her "air of spaniel-like dependence" becomes magnified and shows its "direct effect in the peculiar off-handedness and ease of Pete's ways toward her." Pete inevitably is drawn to Nellie, a woman of "brilliance and audacity," more fitting, he assumes, to a man of his stature. When Nellie joins Pete and Maggie at the club, Pete's "eyes sparkle" and Maggie is ignored by all.

Pete's ultimate rejection of Maggie results in her ruination. Her vision of her necessary escape from her brutal life has been dependent on a rescue by this "ideal man," and when that vision is shattered, "her soul could never smile again." Her devotion to Pete, which prompted her to disregard her reputation, has stripped her of her physical as well as emotional shelter when her mother refuses to allow her back into her home.

Crane's focus on the tension between illusion and reality in *Maggie* provides an adeptly ironic vision of the naturalistic world of the Bowery. Colvert quotes Crane's declaration in 1896, "I do not think much can be done with the Bowery as long as the people there are in their present state of conceit." Colvert concludes that Crane's "stinging verbal irony constantly chastises" the novel's characters "for their moral blindness, which clearly is caused by their absurd and self-indulgent illusions about their world and themselves." Crane's artistry also inspires our sympathy for Maggie, whose innocence is destroyed by the disease of poverty and the moral vacuity that surrounds her.

Source: Wendy Perkins, Critical Essay on *Maggie: A Girl of the Streets*, in *Novels for Students*, Thomson Gale, 2005.

Annette Petruso

Petruso has a bachelor's degree in history and a master's degree in screenwriting. In this essay, Petruso compares and contrasts the characters of Maggie, the purported heroine of Crane's novel, and Jimmie, Maggie's brother who also plays a large role in the novel. Both are creatures of the street for different reasons, and their differing sexes and lives result in very different life paths.

In Crane's novel *Maggie: A Girl of the Streets*, he writes of circumstances both very familiar to contemporary audiences, but also very specific to his late nineteenth-century readers. Set in a slum in an urban area, the naturalistic novel describes in detail the effect of living there—with alcoholic parents, no real direction in life, and many other issues—on Maggie, Jimmie, and other young characters. Siblings Maggie and Jimmie seem to be about the same age, and both face many of the same issues. They include how Maggie and Jimmie deal with family life, relationships, sex, employment, and violence. While both face many obstacles in their lives, Jimmie survives and is relatively up-right while Maggie's life is more compromised and ends early. The reasons for the difference are complex and often gender specific, but are also revealing and give Crane's story depth.

One of the biggest differences between Jimmie and Maggie is that from the beginning of the novel, when the reader meets Jimmie as a "very little boy," he lives out a masculine role by standing up for himself, often with his fists. In contrast, Maggie is given the female role of caretaker who should be protected by her family, primarily her father and brother but also her mother, but is not. Throughout *Maggie: A Girl of the Streets*, Maggie cares for others, but no one, save Pete, ever shows interest in her until she is forced to live on the streets. Pete, her brother's friend and the man with whom she becomes involved, uses her for a sexual relationship and some standing among other men because of Maggie's comely appearance. But even Pete leaves Maggie when Nell, a somewhat classy prostitute, questions his choice to be with Maggie and convinces him to leave with her (Nell). Maggie, as always, loses, which leads to her ultimate demise.

Jimmie and Maggie have a very difficult home life. Both of their parents are alcoholics who beat them and ignore them, focusing more often on drink than being a parent. Crane draws their mother, named Mary, worse than their father. He holds a job (probably at a factory), while the mother does not really care much for the children. She cooks for the family, at least in the early chapters, but also breaks objects in the kitchen and living area, including cookware, plates, and tables, when drunk. Crane depicts no real concern with their children's welfare, unless it has to do with sexuality and reputation where Maggie is concerned.

After Jimmie and Maggie's father dies, Jimmie soon steps into his role as primary provider and head of the small family. He finds work as a truck driver where he can continue to act as an angry young man. Like his father before him, Jimmie does not protect Maggie. When Pete shows interest, then begins to see his sister, Jimmie becomes upset that the older man has taken advantage of their friendship. Crane writes at the beginning of chapter ten, "Jimmie had an idea it wasn't common courtesy for a friend to come to one's home and ruin one's sister. But he was not sure how much Pete knew about the rules of politeness." After Maggie leaves the family and lives with Pete, Jimmie follows his mother's lead and condemns her.

> **Until she meets Pete, Maggie is most certainly not a girl of the streets."**

While Jimmie thinks about killing Pete or bringing harm to him, he does not try to find his sister or convince her to come home. Though Jimmie considers rescuing Maggie in chapter 13, his mother says she will not let her daughter come home. Still, he is conflicted between how it looks to have a sister who has a compromised reputation, and his feeling that his mother might be wrong and he should protect her. In the end, he lives up to the example set by his parents and does nothing for Maggie.

In contrast to her brother, Maggie stays out of the way at home. There is no mention of education for her or her brother, yet she did not play in the streets as her brother did as a child. Maggie tries to help her family, both as a child and as an adult. In chapter two, for example, she performs a simple household task of moving dishes, but when she breaks one, her mother beats her. She often makes an effort to avoid her mother's wrath, as well as her father's anger and, later, her brother's anger, after he takes over as head of the family, but fails on all counts. Maggie is obedient to Jimmie. When her brother takes over as the head of the family, he tells Maggie to take a job. She finds work at a small sweatshop factory making collars and cuffs for clothing. Until she meets Pete, Maggie is most certainly not a girl of the streets.

Despite this kind of family life, Maggie possesses something that Jimmie does not. She is physically attractive. At the beginning of chapter five, Crane describes the young woman: "The girl, Maggie, blossomed in a mud puddle. She grew to be a most rare and wonderful production of a tenement district, a pretty girl." Pete notices how Maggie looks, which leads to their relationship. He shows an interest in Maggie when no one else has. Because of his interest, Maggie comes to realize that there is more to life than what happens in the family's tenement apartment. Pete takes her to places where she is entertained and amused. Pete is also different than her father and brother in where he works and his outward appearance. Instead of driving a truck, Pete works as a bartender in a local saloon. It is cleaner than any job the men in her family hold, though Pete has to keep order and break up fights.

As soon as Pete enters Maggie's life and Maggie decides that she is attracted to him, her mother belittles her daughter and immediately assumes the worst. In chapter six, before Maggie has even gone out with Pete, her drunk mother accuses her of not coming home from work right away. The mother yells at Maggie, "Why deh hell don' yeh come home earlier? Been loafin''round deh streets. Yer getting' teh be a reg'lar devil." When she leaves with Pete the first time, Crane writes that Maggie's mother "blasphemed and gave her daughter a bad name." Yet Maggie would not even kiss Pete after the first time he took her out.

The turning point in Maggie's family life comes in chapter nine. After her mother comes home drunk and gets into a scuffle with Jimmie, Pete picks up Maggie to take her out. Her mother curses her and tells her to get out and do the things that her mother assumes her daughter will do. Her mother repeats ideas like this over and over again: "Mag Johnson, yehs knows yehs have gone teh deh devil. Yer a disgrace teh yer people, damn yeh." After Maggie has left with Pete, her mother believes she is blameless. She says "When a girl is bringed up deh way I bringed up Maggie, how kin she go teh deh devil?" Her mother believes that Maggie has always been bad, and her brother, perhaps not wanting to argue, agrees at first. He comes to buy into his mother's condemnations himself. Maggie is attacked for bringing shame on the family for her sexual relationship with Pete, though she never speaks one word against her mother or brother at any point in the story.

Thus, there are different standards for sexual relationships for Jimmie and Maggie. Before Maggie even met Pete, the adult Jimmie stayed away from home for days at a time with no real denunciation from his mother. On two occasions in *Maggie: A Girl of the Streets*, Jimmie reflects on some of the women he has had sexual relationships with. At least two women have accused him of fathering their children. No one questions what Jimmie does with these women, except himself, and these relationships do not affect his social status in his family or at work. As the situation with Maggie and Pete evolves, Jimmie wonders if the women he has been with have brothers or fathers, and why they have not gone after him for his actions. Crane writes in chapter ten, "He was trying to formulate a theory that he had always

unconsciously held, that all sisters, excepting his own, could advisedly be ruined." After Maggie leaves home with Pete, Jimmie does get into a fight with Pete at his bar, though Maggie's name is not mentioned. After the fight with Pete, he does not return home for many days. When he does, his mother is still angry that Maggie has not come home; Jimmie's absence hardly mattered.

Maggie idealizes Pete and believes he can take her away from her empty life. She does not come home after she leaves with him at the end of chapter nine. It is implied that they have a sexual relationship, and Maggie becomes very dependent on him. After a few weeks, when Nell challenges Pete in a public place and he chooses her, Maggie tries to go back home. In chapter 15, Maggie's return to the tenement is unsuccessful. Her mother calls her names, cursing her to hell and condemning her for bringing shame on the family. Jimmie agrees with his mother's statements. The neighbors offer only backhanded support. A lady who lives there offers Maggie a place to stay for the moment. She tells Maggie, "So 'ere yehs are back again, are yehs? An' dey've kicked yehs out? Well, come in an' stay wid me tehnight. I ain' got no moral standin'." Maggie tries to go back to Pete in chapter 16, but he throws her out of his saloon.

Because of the family's and society's condemnations, Maggie finally turns to an unrespectable life on the street, while her brother continues to live his somewhat respectable one with a job and a little responsibility. She takes up a new kind of employment. Maggie becomes a somewhat successful prostitute for several months, and while her clothing is nicer, she ends up serving a customer whom Crane describes in negative terms. This encounter leads directly or indirectly—Crane is obtuse—to Maggie's death. After Maggie has passed away, the other ladies in the tenement convince her mother to forgive her. Jimmie reluctantly claims her body.

Crane depicts the world that Jimmie and Maggie live in as a chaotic disorderly mess, where violence is accepted as a part of every day life. Both Jimmie and his mother have police records, and Jimmie learned from a young age to appreciate the power of violence. Yet, it is the most nonviolent person—rivaled only by Jimmie and Maggie's little brother Tommie who dies as a toddler—who suffers the most. The streets that Jimmie embraced from an early age end up taking the life of his sister, after she spent much of her life avoiding them. Maggie and Jimmie never rise above the circumstances they were born into and the mistakes both made along the way. Crane uses *Maggie: A Girl of the Streets* to show how easily both sexes' lives can be wasted in such an environment.

Source: Annette Petruso, Critical Essay on *Maggie: A Girl of the Streets*, in *Novels for Students*, Thomson Gale, 2005.

Henry Golemba

In the following essay, Golemba examines how Crane and other realist writers "developed a language of food in order to give an impression of being 'inside' the social topic, of seeing deeper than the surface," and the problems associated with that approach.

Pete's first words to Maggie are: "Say, Mag, I'm stuck on your shape. It's outa sight." Maggie's response: "She wondered what Pete dined on." These two quotations encode an enormous problem for Stephen Crane's *Maggie: A Girl of the Streets,* and it reflects a crucial anxiety for American writers in the last decades of the nineteenth century who were attempting to transform new social phenomena into literary, journalistic, and photographic constructions. Pete's words reflect the realist's worry that aesthetic aims become "stuck on shape." Realism's attempt to achieve an objective point of view risks turning its subjects into objects, transforming groups of people into statistics, changing individuals into things. More drastically, realism's technique turns reality into "tecnic," and ontology becomes nothing beyond surface. The realist's motivation, welcomed by many American writers as excitingly new, once again truly "novel," was soon perceived as extremely limiting. A style that was hoped to be transcendentally "outa sight" became merely shapes and shadows, and what you saw was what you got.

On July 3, 1896, Crane inscribed a copy of *Maggie:* "It is indeed a brave new binding and I wish the inside were braver." While realists triumphed at giving their works a sense of "photographic realism," their text's "inside" remained problematic, The closer artists came to achieving their technical goal of surface representation, the more their works bordered on voyeurism. This essay examines how Crane, as well as other literary and reform writers, both developed a language of food in order to give an impression of being "inside" the social topic, of seeing deeper than the surface, and how a language of food created problems even as it answered the problem of voyeurism. In so doing, I invite a slightly different reading of Crane's now famous letter to John Northern

> " *Maggie,* the novel itself, points downward, feeding readers' interests in how the poor literally starved and figuratively hungered for the refined and safer existence which Maggie envisions and the average reader already enjoys."

Hilliard, celebrated for its romantic heroism (as in "personal honesty is my supreme ambition [even though] "A man is sure to fail at it"). I explore instead how closely we should attend to Crane's admission in that same letter that "Personally I am aware that my work does not amount to a string of dried beans" and further inquire what relationship this sentence has to his goal of seeing life with only his "own pair of eyes."

Frank Norris, using his review of *Maggie* to vent his frustration at realism generally, complained that it seemed "written from the outside" (Wertheim 54–62; McElrath 87–90). Critics since Norris have considered this quality a virtue, whether as an early example of reification, or tragedy in a Realist mode, a representation of subjectivity within economic matrixes, or an achievement of objective vision. But Norris more faithfully reflects the anxiety of realists, torn between their ambition and achievement, and their frustration and fear. A later theorist like Raymond Williams would articulate the need for realistic art to include "the essential forces and movements underlying" objects and surfaces, not the "mere surface" or "appearances only."

Though one of the writers who had once waved realism's banner most proudly, Norris, anticipating Williams, had come to condemn realism for "entertaining with its meticulous presentation of teacups, rag carpets, wall-paper and haircloth sofas, stopping with these, going no deeper than it sees." Realism, he observes, "notes only the surface of things. For it, Beauty is not even skindeep, but only a geometrical plane, without dimensions and depth, a mere outside. Realism is very excellent so far as it goes, but it goes no further than the

Realist himself can actually see." More specifically, Norris's anxiety centers on a lack; as a realist, he longs for "an instrument, keen, finely tempered, flawless—an instrument with which we may go straight through the clothes and tissues and wrappings of flesh down deep into the red, living heart of things" ("A plea for romantic fiction, 1901; quoted in Pizer 75–78).

Writers like Kate Chopin in *The Awakening* (1899) had managed to pierce through surfaces and probe the "red, living heart" by having their characters transforms themselves into that emblem of pulsing subjectivity which Chopin represented as the "throbbings of desire" (32). Her Edna

> . . . stretched her strong limbs that ached a little. She ran her fingers through her loosened hair for a while. She looked at her round arms as she held them straight up and rubbed them one after the other, observing closely, as if it were something she saw for the first time, the fine, firm quality and texture of her flesh.(39)

Edna's auto-communion as both host and celebrant creates a new hunger for life. She had had no appetite when dining with her husband and had felt no satisfaction in writing a weekly menu (39), but after her new vision she drains her glass of wine and devours her food. In her auto-communion she rips into "a crusty brown loaf, tearing it with her strong white teeth" and avows, when told that her dinner of broiled fowl has dried out, that "If it turned to stone, still will I eat it" (40–41). Her appetite becomes gargantuan, much like the triumph that Bakhtin envies in Rabelais: "This victory over the world in the act of eating was concrete, tangible, bodily. . . . In this image there was no trace of mysticism, no abstract-idealistic sublimation. This image materializes truth and does not permit it to be torn from the earth" (285).

Though Edna is ensconced in circumstances that Chopin frequently calls "luxurious," a setting that did not suit self-conscious realist writers attempting to address the vast social phenomena of the hungry, the homeless, the poor "huddled masses" as Emma Lazarus labeled them for the world, realists did, like Chopin, choose food as a way to delve below surfaces. Realistic writing is stocked with a language of food, from Norris's "Epic of the Wheat," where individuals drown in grain aimed at relieving world famine, to William Dean Howell's dinner parties as tests of social standing and Theodore Dreiser's postponement of Hurstwood's suicide in *Sister Carrie* because he happens to be given enough money to eat; from Charles Waddell Chesnutt's delicious grapes that speculators will convert to wine in *The Conjure Woman* (1899) to Jack London's equation of mass behavior with fermenting yeast and of morality with a full stomach in *The Sea-Wolf* (1904). Paul Laurence Dunbar's *The Sport of the Gods* (1902) uses food to represent everything from racist theories about theft to "The Universe" setting "Berry" up "to taste all the bitterness" (587). Indeed, the entire careers of non fiction reform writers can be summarized by their book titles—as with Thomas DeWitt Talmage's *Around the Tea Table* (1888), *The Battle for Bread* (1889), and *Crumbs Swept Up* (1897); Jewish life in New York tenements is captured in well-known late realist works like Anzia Yezierka's *The Bread-Givers* (1925) and Samuel Ornitz's *Haunch, Paunch and Jowl* (1923); and even later realists dream of Old World wheat fields as in Henry Roth's *Call It Sleep* (1934) and hope for New World success as in Rose Pesotta's *Bread Upon the Waters* (1944). Indeed, food is so integral to realistic fiction that Chester Wolford, in response to Eric Solomon, argues that *Maggie's* structure is an inverted vegetation myth with Mary as a twisted Proserpine who lays waste to the land because of Dis, personified by Pete (78–87). In this sense, Crane's comparison of his works to "a string of dried beans" seems more than a fortuitous cliche.

Of course, one reason realistic depictions of slum life are filled with a language of food is the sheer, raw reality of starvation. Reform writings catalogue starving children, diets of moldy bread, offal in the streets, goat carcasses that decompose over the course of weeks, and the bad food of "two-cent restaurants" (Jacob Riis, *How the Other Half Lives,* 56–58). One Victor Hugoesque Riis chapter titled "The Man with the Knife" describes how a father is driven to madness and murder by the sight of rich people feasting as he pictures "those little ones crying for bread around the cold and cheerless hearth" (263–64).

Moreover, many of the reform writers of the 1890s were reverends or related to ministers and thus already had a long tradition of mingling religion, food, and reform. Crane's parents are an obvious example of the blending of religion with reform, a characteristic of the reform movement that Ann Douglas and other biographers have noted. As William James observed, food had been a natural language in both reform and religious discourse in America ever since the earliest Puritans wrote of the Old and New Testaments as the twin breasts from which we suck nourishment. In addition, as Steven Mailloux has argued, the relationship between food and language changed in children's literature and conduct books from a figurative to a literal level by the late nineteenth century. In popular literary genres, food shifted from being a metaphor for words to an equation with language. Mailloux impressively demonstrates that by the 1890s it had become commonplace for authors to advise their readers, as Annie H. Ryder did in *Go Right on Girls!* (1891), "to digest your books, turn them into nourishment, make them a part of your life that lives always" (13357).

Crane was writing within an established tradition, then, when he used food to create an impression of depth—what he called a "braver inside"—contrasted with realism's surfaces and "outside look." When Maggie wonders how Pete dined, her imagination points upward, signalling transcendence of home, the slum, individual powerlessness, and a dog-eat-dog universe. *Maggie,* the novel itself, points downward, feeding readers' interests in how the poor literally starved and figuratively hungered for the refined and safer existence which Maggie envisions and the average reader already enjoys. Whether one adopts the vantage point of reformer or novelist, photographer or reader, the point of view is privileged; reality is observed from on high. How then does a reader avoid replicating the hypocrisy and self-deception which are blatantly attacked in the novel? As an example of 1890s social realism, Crane's challenge in *Maggie* was to make readers consume a text, not merely gaze at or patronize social issues raised by the text. The aesthetic challenge was to cause readers to make a text part of their selves as though they had eaten it, not to allow readers to dine elegantly on literary fare. However, the solution was not without problems, and Crane soon leapt from the frying pan into the fire. In breaking the planes of realism by imagining his words as food, Crane created new difficulties in the way his texts were consumed. As will be shown, problems with voyeurism yielded to problems about consumption.

Chapter XV graphically demonstrates how the text *Maggie* might be read voyeuristically, that is, read much the way Mary in this chapter turns her daughter into spectacle. "Lookut her! Lookut her!" Mary shouts nine times in succession. Expounding "like a glib showman at a [sideshow] museum," she draws a "doorful of eyes" that gaze upon Maggie, their gaze objectifying her, proving her powerlessness. Even a "baby, overcome with curiosity concerning this object," crawls near to gaze, personifying Crane's fear that his novel may be read in an infantile way, or that the text might remain nothing but spectacle. Rather than empathizing with

and absorbing the vision, a reader might remain mere spectator, mere voyeur, like Pete stuck merely on shapes, attracted only to form and surface. It is no surprise that the text avenges itself upon Pete by reversing the motif; surface yields to savagery as Pete's supposed friends pick him apart cannibalistically in a kind of devourment that is as far removed from voyeurism as can be. The depth of the anxiety represented in these scenes could be missed by modern readers less steeped in humanistic background and reform impulse than were the realists. But the major source of the anxiety under study here is how realists, seeking a cure for realism's weaknesses, find that the cure is intricately connected with the problem; devourment is intimate with voyeurism. Dunbar certainly constructs that problem in *The Sport of the Gods* when Skaggsy and The Universe set Berry up, as Dunbar says, to "taste all the bitterness." As a realist, Dunbar replicates the crushing racist powers of life; it is no wonder that his preacherly voice so often intrudes to wish that life and the text could be other than realistic. When the choreographer, an arranger of music and dance if not words on a page, is shown to dislike the taste of his own words, one wonders how much Dunbar intends him self-reflexively to be an emblem of the realist author (547).

My contention is that, for Crane, the problem was more about ontology and aesthetics than humanism, closer to photography and the problem of the Other. Why is the first reform book to include documentary photographs titled *How the Other Half Lives?* What is the connection between the ability of photographic realism to bring the Other right before readers' eyes and the insistence of this technique on the Other remaining alien? In 1904, for example, Henry James, no friend of the poor by any stretch, watched in repugnance as "the inconceivable alien" was admitted to his native country. "It is a drama that goes on, without a pause, day by day and year by year, this visible act of ingurgitation on the part of our body politic and social, and constituting really an appeal to amazement beyond that of any sword-swallowing or fire-swallowing in the circus." What precisely is the difference between James's contemptuous "inconceivable alien" and Jacob Riis's "Other Half"? Dunbar's *Sport,* if one recalls, muddies this matter by alleging that reformers, at least in the variety of yellow journalism, feed upon the poor and keep them on the lowest rungs of society as effectively as do the rich, the powerful, and the power-hungry.

Recent research on representations of the homeless further blurs the distinction between sympathy and disdain. Even the most humane motives cannot avoid realism's alienation of the Other as its technique asks people to "Lookut her, Lookut her." The most empathetic gaze still alienates the Other, confirms the distance separating seer from the seen, and flattens the foregrounded with its scene. Voyeurism is always ideological. Documentary photographs insist upon the difference between those who look and those looked at; they privilege positions of who can show and who cannot speak for themselves, thus through technique reinforcing the charity model—"the imbalance of power and the division between self and other," as Allen Carey-Webb puts it (701). One recalls the sermon in *Maggie* where the minister distances the hungry in sermons full of "yous" to which, in one draft, Crane had added: "Once a philosopher asked this man why he did not say 'we' instead of 'you.' The man replied, what?" The question is also the answer, just as Maggie becomes a "what" when she is objectified by the text and passes "before open doors framing more eyes strangely microscopic" and just as the text, through its technic of microscopic inspection, becomes an instrument of alienation. In modern times, reformers sometimes deconstruct their own speeches, as when Jim Hubbard's motivation in his documentary *American Refugees* to "urge you to see the similarities between you and the people shown here" is called into question by the text's use of "you" and "me" separated from "they" or "these people" (xiii). To say "They are like you and me" contradicts the sentiment as soon as it is uttered.

One event early into *The Other Half* illustrates the point clearly. Riis wanted to photograph "a particularly ragged and disreputable tramp" smoking a two-cent clay pipe. The man agreed to pose for a dime but cunningly put away his pipe, the one item that Riis thought looked particularly picturesque in an urban slum sort of way. The man had sized Riis up nicely and insisted that his pipe made his picture worth a quarter. Though incensed, Riis says, "I had to give in. The man scarce ten seconds employed at honest labor, even at sitting down, at which he was an undoubted expert, had gone on strike. He knew his rights and the value of 'work,' and was not to be cheated out of either" (78). Though phrased in praise this is a complaint; the newly-hired working man was treating Riis as any businessman or shopkeeper might, negotiating the value of commodities. What is more, the working man was abridging the unilateral power relationships; he was metaphorically stepping out of the photograph, refusing to be framed, at least not at the framer's price.

This revelation of a "tramp's" remarkable intelligence, understanding of market realities, and insight into the psychology of the Other slips out of Riis's picture and into the text where we can read the meaning between the lines in spite of Riis's interventions and rhetorical directions, but the photograph tames and domesticates the incident. Its caption tells us what we see, a "tramp, who sat smoking his pipe on the rung of a ladder with such evident philosophic contentment in the busy labor of a score of rag-pickers all about him" (79). From the photograph and its caption one would never know that there was a fascinating "brave inside" to this posed manikin. In 1891, the year after *The Other Half* was published and while *Maggie* was still in early drafts, Crane discussed photography in a *New York Tribune* article: "The photograph is false in perspective, in light and shade, in focus. When a photograph can depict atmosphere and sound, the comparison [of literary communication with photography] will have some meaning, and then it will not be used as a reproach." Pamela Yates and Peter Kinoy would agree, for their film *Takeover,* a documentary of the homeless occupying vacant homes repossessed by HUD on 1 May 1990, shows active, vigorous subjects who are far from exhibiting "philosophic contentment on the bottom rung" of society. Far from being objectified, they work together, develop strategies, act collectively, and insist upon their own voice. As Carey-Webb says, "They threaten to tear down the fence that separates them from the podium, and voices shout, 'We can speak for ourselves! The homeless can speak for themselves!'" (707).

In 1891, Crane's images of absorption made his brand of literary realism seem more like the subjective presentation claimed by Yates and Kinoy and Carey-Webb than the objectification and alienation of Riis's photographs. Like most of the reform writers of the 1890s, Crane used metaphors of food and eating to smudge the lines that separated viewer from object, reader from text, the self from the Other. The various functions of food in *Maggie* begin with Jimmie's mouth filled with curses and smashed by stones and conclude with a twin communion: Pete's cannibalistic anticommunion and Mary's mock communion. Along the way the author "forgets" that food is a metaphor and begins to think that his words literally are an equation, that literacy is a form of eating. But to analyze that transformation one should survey the discourse of reform on this score to understand that Crane's "confusion" was actually an aesthetic ideal among reformers and self-conscious realists.

Marcus Cunliffe, Eric Solomon, Thomas Gullason, David Halliburton and other scholars have persuasively argued that *Maggie* is one strand of a vast literary fin-de-siecle web spun by urban novelists like Hall Caine, Brander Matthews, Edward Townsend, and Edgar Fawcett as well as reform writers like Jacob Riis, Charles Loring Brace, Reverend Thomas De Witt Talmage, and Crane's own parents. The bulk of scholarship concentrates on similarities of scene, imagery, name, theme, and event. However there also exists the curious and all but inevitable combination of poverty, literacy, and food, of reading and diet, with the urban setting and social problems in a way that transcends any sheer transaction of realistic phenomena. Food imagery may begin as stereotype and convention, but it soon becomes more interesting and complex.

With Riis, for example, one finds literary quotation (Thomas Hood's "The Song of the Shirt"), Biblical allusion (Chapter XIX: "The Harvest of Tares" from Matthew 13:25), and Reform Movement slogans and songs ("Bread so dear, And flesh and blood so cheap!") used as stock literary techniques, but Riis's writing often goes beyond this treatment to link poverty, crime, and literacy. In his discussion of "The gang [as] the ripe fruit of tenement-house growth" (82), Riis prefers the gang member over the meek pauper because the gang member's appetites are "those of the wolf rather than the tiger," giving him the energy to become something better "with different training." Riis not only presumes that gangsters are avid readers, but he also insists that their reading not only "affects" but causes their behavior. (Riis would probably be attracted more to the Swede than to the others in Crane's "The Blue Hotel," not only because he has more vitality but because we know that he reads, and because we knew that he reads exciting, sensationalist fiction.)

For a reformer like Charles Loring Brace, "the literature she reads" is only one of several factors that "degrade and defile" a prostitute, but to Riis a city tough's "inordinate vanity" is a direct "result of his swallowing all the flash literature and penny-dreadfuls he can beg, borrow, or steal (220). Reading is not mearly an influence upon his character; it is as integral to his biological system as breast-feeding or medicine: readers are "nursed by such a diet into rank and morbid growth" (83).

Reverend Talmage's *The Night Sides of City Life* also clearly blends food with reading and the city. Whenever *Night Sides* addresses political or social approaches to urban problems, the imagery tends to medicine, cleanliness, clothes, and engineering; but, when Talmage begins to talk about his readers' feelings or personal attitudes toward the poor, his associations shift to eating and reading. Thus when he comes to praise those who recognize poverty as owing as much to circumstances as to abulia, his discussion immediately widens to include spiritual truth and the reception of The Word. And so, he sides with the poor and hungry but good woman who tells the preacher that "The great want of our city is the Gospel and something to eat! . . . you have to go forth in this work with the bread of eternal life in your right hand and the bread of this life in your left hand . . ." (173).

What Talmage calls "the bread of this life" includes not only actual food but literacy; the secular word is as significant as the holy word. Authors and publishers possess a power marvelous in its capacity to nourish but dangerous in its potential to corrupt:

> Every time the cylinders of Harper or Appleton [*Maggie's* 1896 publisher] or Ticknor or Peterson or Lippincott turn, they make the earth quake. From them goes forth a thought like an angel of light to feed and bless the world, or like an angel of darkness to smite it with corruption and sin and shame and death.

Indeed, Talmage, as a preacher and reform writer, openly envies the power of the novelist and the journalist. When he sees that "Almost every man you meet has a book in his hand or a newspaper in his pocket," he worries that they are more welcome to readers than the word of God. "This hungry, all-devouring American mind must have something to read" (73), and he realizes that the more novels like *Maggie* are lashed for their brutality and lurid melodrama the more readers will be eager to taste them.

Crane hoped his works would be read, but a greater worry was that his first novel might fail to fulfill the kind of profound literacy depicted in Riis, Brace, and Talmage. His focus was the communicative problem of how to make literacy as profound an activity as eating and nourishment. How was an author to make readers feel that they were doing something beyond merely gazing upon a fictional representation of reality, that they were engaged in a fundamental literary process, that they were feeding upon words and not just looking at them? The problem was not so much how to get readers "inside" the story, but how to get the text inside them—or, at least, to create that illusion, at least to encode textual signs to signal that this was the anxiety troubling the author enough to create fiction.

The two most obvious signals in *Maggie* are the stove and the saloon. The stove's first and literal function, of course, is for feeding the family as well as for warmth. Symbolically it functions as the urban surrogate for the domestic hearth, the psychological site where the family is supposed to center, as it does for the "hurrying men" in Chapter XV who do not notice the "forlorn woman" because they have "their thoughts fixed on distant dinners." But for the Johnsons, that basic function fails; the stove is treated disgracefully, as when the supposed head of the family plops "his great muddled boots on the back part." Although massive, or at least the heaviest object in the home, it takes a beating, sometimes bounced around as though it were made of cardboard instead of iron. It is also the site of the characters' only effort at art when Maggie, attempting to give her family class and to attract Pete's courtship (and thus start another family centered at its own stove), makes "with infinite care" a lambrequin of alternate wheat and roses for the shelf above the stove. Her choice of pattern indicates her humble desire to combine simple food with plain beauty, and her future efforts to restore the lambrequin to its place create sympathy. Her longing for art is also lonely in this harsh environments. Pete does not notice the lambrequin, and the mother of the family destroys it in one of her drunken rampages.

Most of all, the stove stands no more chance against the saloon than the past has against the future. As in *George's Mother* where the saloon's fraternity attempts to be a surrogate mother, the barroom offers a substitute family in the midst of an urban chaos that is as fragmented as the collars and cuffs in Maggie's workplace. As Riis wrote, "in many a tenement-house block the saloon is the one bright and cheery and humanly decent spot to be found" (79). In *Maggie's* Chapter XI, alienation is commented on in a fittingly oblique way with a stranger whose presence seems as irrelevant to the text as it is in the tavern. The first time he is mentioned, Pete is "bending expectantly toward" him, but each of the next six times the stranger appears he is farther from the center of the bar. Finally, he is "sprawled very pyrotechnically out on the sidewalk," and the usual crowd of spectators is there to gawk.

If the crowd were a community as represented by the chorus in Greek tragedy (or by the women "like a choir at a funeral" on the last page), their remarks would be apt commentary on the action, but here in the chaotic city there is no empathy; they come merely to feast greedily on spectacle.

"The crowd bended and surged in absorbing anxiety to see," and they read everything wrong. Instead of seeing a fight between Jimmie and Pete (allies in the first chapter's fight), and instead of noticing that Jimmie now abandons his new-found ally, they jump to the conclusion that "Dey've t'rowed a bloke inteh deh street." The atmosphere of alienation is thickened also by the fact that aliases are wise in the saloon's supposed fraternity, where Billie (if that is indeed his name) pretends that Jimmie's name is Mike (just as in Nellie's bar Freddie uses a false name to protect himself from the friends he is trying to make). Even Maggie's first publication was under the false name Johnston Smith. The problem extends beyond false names, however; the saloon's very appearance is deceptive and false.

At first, Crane's introduction of the saloon sounds as if he will merely echo the reform writers' stereotyped depictions or Zola's *L'Assommoir* with its dram-shop entrance framed by lush but poisonous oleander plants. (In *Maggie,* "The open mouth called seductively to passengers to enter and annihilate sorrow or create rage.") But Crane goes further: the saloon's insides are false as well. Its walls are papered and its leather imitation, and even the massiveness of its shining bar somehow seems "counterfeit." Mirrors are everywhere, multiplying and misleading, feeding vanity with less than skin-deep images. Unnatural, it is geometrically manipulative and deceptive. Liquor bottles stand at "regular intervals" and the cash register (the chief icon of this altar) sits in "the exact center of the general effect. The elementary senses of it all seemed to be opulence and geometrical accuracy."

Most telling of all, the saloon subdues and subjugates food to an auxiliary role. Even exotic lemons and oranges are deprived of nutritive value and reduced to decoration, "arranged with mathematical precision" along with the paper napkins. Across from the bar, the food counter is much smaller and much less attended, full of vitality but without any control through diet or etiquette. Upon it "swarmed frayed fragments of crackers, slices of boiled ham, dishevelled bits of cheese, and pickles swimming in vinegar. An odor of grasping, begrimed hands and munching mouths pervaded." Although frantic, this food scene has vitality, unlike the situation at home where "The fire in the stove had gone out. The displaced lids and open doors showed heaps of sullen grey ashes. The remnants of a meal, ghastly, like dead flesh, lay in a corner." A page earlier, Maggie, realizing the inability of the home to nourish growth and coming to understand how a life of toil in the factory will soon begin to devour her and drain her vitality, hears the ticking of the clock more clearly than ever before. With time running out, she creates a fiction: "She wondered what Pete dined on."

Maggie hopes for a life that is nourishing, not merely one in which one feeds with grasping hands and munching mouths as in the saloon, but one that shows a more positive relationship between individuals and their environment wherein individuals desire a harmonious and balanced, a controlled yet energetic interaction, with the world as symbolized by eating and dining, the most basic connection one has to life. Thus, it is fortunate that when Pete realizes Jimmie wants to fight and growls "what's eatin' yehs?" Jimmie merely replies, "Gin," because there are so many other powerful forces threatening to devour Rum Alley residents that they would be overwhelmed with rage or depression if they realized it.

That is, liquor is but one of their problems, or is simply symptomatic of other diseases. In fact, even if there were no alcohol at all in the saloon, one could tell just by glancing at the vandalized food table that there was an intense and distorted hunger, a hunger that causes the saloon's inhabitants to put unhealthful things in the mouth—liquor, pipes, cigars, curses—not only to cope, but also because it seems a fitting representation of how poorly life is feeding them. Jimmie vaguely suspects that edenic happiness and secular well-being are at "a hopeless altitude where grew fruit." He might as well, like his companion, ask for "a million dollars and a bottle of beer." Nellie might think Maggie is a "pale little thing with no spirit" expressive of "pumpkin pie and virtue," but pumpkin pie is as hard to come by as virtue in this text, and the last "meal" offered Maggie is a glass of beer and a charlotte-russe, fancier but less nourishing. Filled with toxic chemicals and poisonous relationships, the saloon-goers naturally spew maledictions in return: as the "breaths of fighters came wheezingly from their lips," they gave "vent to low, labored hisses, that sounded like a desire to kill."

These "hisses" of destructive violence are not confined to the saloon; they are heard as readily in the home, where Mary brandishes "a frying-pan full of potatoes that hissed." For this non-communion, the father is absent, the mother drunk. The baby "gorged his small stomach. Jimmie forced, with feverish rapidity, the grease-enveloped pieces between his wounded lips. Maggie, with side glances of fear of interruption, ate like a small pursued

tigress." As the mother consumes potatoes and liquor, she reciprocates by "deliver[ing] reproaches" in return for what she puts into her body.

This kind of scene caused *The Nation* in 1896 to complain of Maggie's animalism and the *New York Tribune* to say that it was like having "one's face slapped twice a minute for half an hour." Donald Pizer said of this scene that it "combines both the warfare and cave images into one central metaphor of primitive competition for food," exposing "an instinctive amorality, a need to feed and to protect themselves." This observation is certainly true enough, and I like Pizer's suggestion that the scene both draws and repels by making the characters seem so vulnerable yet alien. But another way to look at the scene is as a cluster of metafictional signals to readers wherein what Crane says as the author behind the text is something like the following: in this scene I am trying to give you the impression that we are really delving into the essentials of reality. This scene is not meant to be received as an "Experiment" in misery, but rather as an expose of awful ordinariness among the poor. As my characters eat, you should feel that unguarded moments at home like this dinner scene seem more real than most representations that call themselves Realism. That is, I hope this kind of eating scene makes readers sense that they are engaged in a deeper literary experience than simply gazing at artifacts; that they are actually absorbing the linguistic reality of words in these moments when characters are taking in reality in the form of food. Readers should feel that they are internalizing these literary experiences even as "The shutters of the tall buildings [close] like grim lips" against them (53).

What Crane explicitly says is much more and less direct. When he mentions the father's pipe for the second time and calls it "the apple-wood emblem of serenity between his teeth," the repetition and observation disrupts the narrative flow, thereby drawing attention to a major distinction. The phrase tells us that this is a piece of realistic writing that differs dramatically from sociology, sermons, reform writing, journalism. A pipe is more than a pipe. In *Maggie*'s realism, aurorae of meaning are meant to emanate from and surround key objects in the reality being transcribed from life. Moreover, these symbolic values may be distorted, skewed, or ironic. The pipe-smoker, for example, is not serene; his mouth is also full of threats.

Another turn of the screw makes us consider that the presence of this one sign stating that a symbol exists makes as wonder about the other ingredients in the text. Without being attached to directional signs, when are they to be taken as standing flatly for their referent and when are they to be read for symbolic import? Tommie chewing on a "bit of orange peeling" seems to be a fairly literal re-presentation of a bit of folklore: babies pacified with orange rinds. But how much should we link it with other food imagery where fruit stands for Jimmie's dream of happiness at an "impossible altitude"? To what degree are we being invited to tie the pipe that is not just a pipe but is made of "apple-wood" into the web of meaning we have created around the stove? The argument would then run: just as the stove has supplanted the family hearth, an apple tree instead of being valued for its healthful fruit has been cut down and reshaped so that Mr. Johnson can put something unhealthful into his mouth. How much do any of these interpretations relate to the later apple reference which emphasizes how Pete turns everything into spectacle when he sees Maggie as "the apple of his eye?" Readers are instructed that there is much in this text beyond the literal, that there is meaning deeper than the surface. Maggie's ontology includes both the sensible and the symbolic. Readers are assured that they have the author's blessing, that his motivations are the opposite of the curses of Maggie's mother. "May Gawd curse her forever," Mary shrieked. "May she eat nothin' but stones and deh dirt in deh street."

Crane had hoped to achieve a fiction which would not only be read and looked at but consumed. He had hoped to strike an equation between words and food, but that equation kept returning to metaphor. "Is" kept becoming "like." Reading tended to remain, after all, a spectator sport. As the novel progresses, the abstractness intensifies. Crane increasingly uses words like "apparently" to increase the distance between the reader and the event (Halliburton 45). By the last chapter, Crane takes the strongest emotions and turns them into simile and simulation. Crane first describes the keening of the women at the wake in realistic transcription but then intrudes and turns their keening into simile; instead of crying at a funeral, they are crying "like a choir at a funeral." An "expose" of the "bare facts" of the "naked truth" stays sensationalistic—a peep at urban instead of Polynesian life. Maggie undercuts the humanistic aspiration it articulates about the nature of literary communication. Reading is, after all, different from eating. This humanistic aspiration, however, is very noticeable. In Children of the Poor in 1892, Riis had

hoped readers could identify with the poor even if the police called them criminals and the pietistic said they were sinners. He hoped that the power of his words would make readers realize that "After all, [the poorman] is not so very different from the rest of us. Perhaps that, with a remorseful review of the chances he has had, may help to make a fellow-feeling for him in us" (Alland 86). However, it would appear that familiarity bred contempt in Riis. His desire for "fellow-feeling" does not stand much chance against his language that calls the poor "scum," labels workhouse inmates "human wrecks," complains that beggars "prey upon our charities," and wars against "a standing army of ten thousand tramps." In his autobiography, The Making of an American, Riis explained that he left the city to seek refuge in the country, putting "the backbone of Long Island between New York and us. The very lights of the city were shut out. So was the slum, and I could sleep" (Alland 212).

Almost eighty years later, Joseph Katz echoed the same sentiments when he compared Maggie's lot with Mary Magdalene. The problem in Maggie is greater, Katz claimed, because "there is no one save the reader to forgive the transgressor" (196). Even today, misreadings are normal in that readers have so taken up Maggie's story that they believe that Maggie is the well-dressed prostitute who drowns herself in Chapter XVII, even though there is no evidence that it is so. It could be Hattie (with whom Maggie had already been confused in XV) or any "girl of the streets." Halliburton suspects it might simply be a literary echo of Edgar Fawcett's The Evil that Men Do (1889), where a fat man murders a well-dressed prostitute (68). At any rate, Crane's aesthetic has hit another wall. His novel can build reader sympathy for one character (the first part of the title) but not more broadly for a class problem like prostitution or poverty (suggested in the second part of the title).

Or so Crane fears, if the characters he has invented stand for reading relationships. He has created Pete who is stuck on shapes and surfaces when he reads his environment, Mary who will not or cannot read just as she refuses to take Maggie in and who becomes like the city itself which has shut its lips against its victims. Jimmie is the only reader in the text who comes anywhere close to fulfilling Crane's rhetorical ideal. While Riis refers to "fellow-feeling" and Katz calls it love or forgiveness, Jimmie labels the reading situation "confusion": "Again he wondered vaguely if some of the women of his acquaintance had brothers. Nevertheless, his mind did not for an instant confuse himself with those brothers." Jimmie alone comes close to seeing others as being like him, but he quickly rejects the thought, just as he alone wishes to take Maggie in but quickly concedes to objections. Such softness would lessen his chances for survival in this harsh, naturalistic environment of eat or be eaten.

Hence, no one but the reader exists to take Maggie in, to have communion with her or at least to confuse our identities with her and with the helpless and the homeless whom Crane used her to represent. However, when Maggie is indeed taken in, the prospect is repulsive. When a passer-by in the text ceases to shun her, or ceases to treat her as mere spectacle (as does the music box lady), Maggie seems doomed. That is, when Crane's communication model is to be fulfilled, he loads the text with the most sensationalistic material of his entire tale. I refer of course to the only major exclusion of any substantial length in the 1896 edition, and I am not so sure that it was deleted only because of Appleton's censorship. It is the paragraph in Chapter XVIII when Maggie (presumably) is approached by the last of a series of Johns, a "great figure" of a "huge fat man" with "great rolls of red fat" and "brown, disordered teeth gleaming under a grey, grizzled moustache from which beedrops dripped. His whole body gently quivered and shook like that of a dead jelly fish." Certainly leaving this paragraph in made the "inside" a much "braver" book, as Crane had expressed in his note to a friend. The "great figure" is not only a disgusting John, but he is also, technically, a fulfillment of the equation between literacy and eating. He is a gross Whitmanian, waiting to take Maggie in, to absorb her, to swallow her up, but his actions are worlds away from the rhetorical ideal and communication model which Crane and other reform and realistic writers of his generation articulated. This "great figure" represents Crane's contrary worry that Maggie might not draw crowds to look at her; it also represents Crane's dread at being devoured by his readers, of his text playing Jonah to our whale.

The anxiety that one's greatest authorial ideal might also be connected with great dread, that the "great figure" of a reader might also be the fat, devouring sea creature of one's nightmares, begins the first of three bizarre communions. The last chapter features Mary's false communion where she's "at a table eating like a fat monk in a picture." She continues to eat while others try to tell her of Maggie's death; her forgiveness is patently insincere, her mouth filled with a vocabulary "derived from mission churches," a vocabulary also similar to and as superficial and trite as the words of reform writers. There is something wrong about a fat monk for Crane, just as there is something wrong about having his communion between reader and text take place. There has been no progress since we first heard someone "shrieking like a monk in an earthquake," nor has there been movement toward spiritual acceptance or humanistic fellow-feeling since Jimmie heard the sermon in the soup-kitchen and "confused the speaker with Christ." The only moment that promises to escape this era's materialistic definitions of the self and deterministic explanations of social realities comes in the previous chapter when Pete's friends are metaphorically cannibalizing him. Striving to prove "the purity of his motives" and the "fervor of his friendship," Pete tries to force money on a waiter Who "kept his hands on his tray. 'I don' want yer money,' he said." But this moment is no sharing of food and spirituality in common communion. Its transcendence, instead, is born of disgust. Crane had hoped that fiction might enable readers to consume a text and feel that they were nibbling "the sacred cheese" of life itself, as expressed in "The Open Boat," the equation to achieve the same absorptive feelings of camaraderie, fellowship, and correspondence between individuals. However, his initial aesthetic goals predicated on an equation of eating and literacy resulted in disgust, devourment, or metaphor and spectacle.

Source: Henry Golemba, "Distant Dinners in Crane's *Maggie*," in *Essays in Literature*, Vol. 21, No. 2, Fall 1994, pp. 235–50.

Sources

Colvert, James B., "Stephen Crane," in *Dictionary of Literary Biography*, Vol. 12, *American Realists and Naturalists*, Gale Research, 1982, pp. 100–24.

Dreiser, Theodore, Letter to Max J. Herzberg on November 2, 1921, in the *Michigan Daily Sunday Magazine*, Vol. XXXII, No. 54, November 27, 1921, p. 1.

Garnett, Edward, "Stephen Crane and His Work," in *Friday Nights: Literary Criticism and Appreciations*, Knopf, 1922, pp. 201–17.

Further Reading

Howard, Jane, *Form and History in American Literary Naturalism*, University of North Carolina Press, 1985.
    Howard discusses *Maggie* and other naturalist works in context.

Nagel, James, *Stephen Crane and Literary Impressionism*, Pennsylvania State University Press, 1980.

> Nagel examines aspects of this literary school in Crane's work alongside the traditional focus on naturalistic elements.

Solomon, Eric, *Stephen Crane: From Parody to Realism*, Harvard University Press, 1966.

> Solomon suggests that Crane parodied conventional literature of the nineteenth century as a means of developing his own fiction.

Stallman, R. W., *Stephen Crane: A Biography*, Brazillier, 1968.

> Stallman presents a comprehensive look at Crane's life and work.

The Phantom of the Opera

Gaston Leroux

1910

Gaston Leroux's novel *The Phantom of the Opera*, first published in 1910, remained a perennial favorite throughout the twentieth century and into the early 2000s. It was adapted to several popular motion pictures and into one of the most successful stage musicals of all time. Its main character, Erik, is a romantic figure whose appeal reaches across different cultures and times. He is a sensitive soul, an accomplished composer and musician whose great unfinished work, *Don Juan Triumphant*, is described as breathtakingly beautiful by the one person he allows to hear it; he is an object of pity, whose face has been disfigured from birth, causing him to hide behind a silk mask; and he is hopelessly in love with a young woman whom he can never seriously hope will love him back. At the same time, he a dangerous, menacing figure, lurking in the hidden catacombs beneath the opera house and blackmailing those who will not bow to his whims. He can hear things said in privacy and can create catastrophes that might or might not be the accidents that they seem to be.

Like other precursors of modern superheroes, such as the Hunchback of Notre Dame and Frankenstein's creature, Erik balances sympathy with horror, admiration with revulsion. Set in one of the most beautiful buildings in Europe, this story of the love triangle between the phantom, the young peasant-born opera singer he loves, and the dashing viscount who she loves, was written as a thriller, and it continued to excite the imaginations of readers into the twenty-first century.

Author Biography

Gaston Leroux was born in Paris on May 6, 1868, a month before his parents, Dominique Alfred Leroux and Marie Bidault, were married. His father was a public works contractor. After Gaston was born, his parents went on to have two more sons and a daughter.

Gaston Leroux went away to school when he was twelve, graduating with honors at age eighteen. He then went to Caen to study law. In the meantime, his mother died, and his father died soon after Leroux turned twenty. As head of the household, he returned to Paris, where he reluctantly finished studying to be a lawyer, passing the tests required for his license. He preferred writing, however, and began covering trials for smaller papers, which led, in 1893, to a full-time position as a reporter for *Le Matin*. Tremendously successful as a newspaper reporter, he stayed at *Le Matin* for nearly thirteen years. It was an exciting life of global travel, for which he became a celebrity. Soon after he married Marie Lafranc, he realized that the marriage was a mistake; they separated, but she refused to grant him a divorce. He fell in love with another woman, Jeanne Cayatte, and they had a son together, although they were not able to marry until Marie Lafranc died in 1917.

His journalistic career ended suddenly, in 1907, when, after his return from covering a volcano eruption, he sought to relax with a few days of vacation time: his editor ordered him to go out on another assignment, and he spontaneously quit. Having already published one minor novel, he turned to writing fiction. From 1907 until his death in 1927, he published thirty-three novels, as well as twelve short stories and six screenplays.

Leroux died suddenly, unexpectedly, of natural causes on April 27, 1927.

Plot Summary

Preface

In the Preface to *The Phantom of the Opera*, the book's narrator tells of the methods he used to research the legend of the phantom. Writing roughly thirty years after the events conveyed in the novel, he tells of his research in the library at the Paris Opera house; his interviews with people who were present at the time; his reliance on the memoirs of one of the opera's directors at that time; and his own study of the opera house.

Chapters 1–5

The first three chapters take place on the night that the old opera directors are retiring and turning over the directorship to Armand Moncharmin and Firmin Richard. While the performers are preparing for the night's show, several of the dancers claim to have seen the phantom. In the basement, Joseph Buquet, the chief stagehand, is found hanged.

At the retirement party, all attention is drawn to the mature, nuanced performance of Christine Daaé, previously an obscure understudy. Raoul de Chegny, attending the opera with his older brother, Count Phillippe de Chegny, falls in love with Christine. When she faints, Raoul pushes his way into the crowd in her dressing room and tells her that he is the little boy who chased her scarf into the sea. After the room is cleared, he listens outside the door and hears a male voice talking with her inside, saying that he has made her a star.

The retiring directors tell the new directors about the phantom and his demands: he is to have Box 5 always left available to him, and he is to have 20,000 francs paid to him each month. Moncharmin and Richard think this is a joke, and they rent Box Five. Soon after they receive a letter from the phantom, expressing his displeasure about his rules being broken.

Chapters 6–10

The novel gives background information. Christine traveled as a child with her father, an accomplished violinist, settling in the French seaside town of Perros-Guirec. It was there that she first met Raoul de Chegny when her scarf blew into the water, and he dived in to retrieve it. They were separated until he saw her on the stage at the opera.

Christine sends a note to Raoul, telling him to meet her in Perros. When he arrives, she is mysterious and aloof. She explains that the voice he heard in her dressing room was the Angel of Music, whom her father said would watch over her. Raoul follows her to the cemetery at midnight, where, at the tomb of her father, he hears violin music. The next day, he is found unconscious at the tomb, having been attacked by a mysterious cloaked figure with a face like a blazing skull.

Messrs. Richard and Moncharmin investigate Box 5 and are convinced that the whole phantom story is a hoax. They receive a note insisting that Mme. Giry be rehired; that Christine be given the lead in *Faust*; and that Box 5 be left abandoned: otherwise, the performance will be cursed. Instead, they hire a new box attendant, give the lead role to

Media Adaptations

- The 1925 silent film version of *The Phantom of the Opera* was one of the first horror films ever made and remains one of the most influential movies in film history. Lon Chaney Sr. played Erik, the phantom, and Mary Philbin played Christine. The film was directed by Rupert Julian. It was re-released in 1929, with edits and a new score. Both versions are available on DVD in a package called *The Phantom of the Opera— The Ultimate Edition*, from Image Entertainment.

- A second movie was made in 1943, with Claude Rains and Nelson Eddy. This one used all of the sets from the original silent film and augmented them with sound and color. It is available on DVD from Universal.

- The version of this story that is perhaps most familiar to late twentieth-century and twenty-first century audiences is the musical version that debuted at Her Majesty's Theater in London on October 9, 1986, and as of 2004 was still running. The music is by Andrew Lloyd Weber, and the lyrics are by Charles Hart and Richard Stilgoe. By the early 2000s it had been in more than fifty major theaters worldwide and had won more than ninety major awards.

- In 1989, a theatrical motion picture version of *The Phantom of the Opera* was released, starring Robert Englund and Jill Scholen. It is available on videocassette and DVD from Columbia Tristar.

- In 1990, Tony Richardson directed a miniseries of the phantom story for USA network, featuring Charles Dance, Burt Lancaster, and Teri Polo. It is available on DVD from Image Entertainment.

- An unabridged audio reading of this book, read by Barrett Whitener, is available for download from Audible.com.

Carlotta, and sit in Box 5 themselves. During the performance, Carlotta's voice croaks like a frog's, and the house chandelier drops onto the audience, hurting dozens and killing the woman hired to replace Mme. Giry.

Christine disappears after that performance. Hearing that she has been seen riding in a carriage at night in the Bois de Boulogne, Raoul goes there and sees her ride past. She sends him a note, telling him to meet her at a masked ball at the opera house, and what costume to wear. He meets her at the ball, but lurking about there is also a mysterious figure wearing a feathered costume and skull mask. Christine tells Raoul that she cannot see him any more, and when he follows her to her dressing room he sees her disappear into her mirror.

Chapters 11–16

The next day, Raoul goes to Mme. Valerius, who is Christine's guardian, and Christine is there, acting as if nothing had happened the night before. She says that she loves Raoul but cannot see him any more.

When he tells her that he must leave within a month, Christine agrees to a secret engagement with Raoul. She explains to him that the phantom, Erik, is in love with her and insanely jealous and that he is dangerous. She leads Raoul to the roof of the opera house, assuming that Erik cannot hear them talk there. She tells him about being fooled by Erik into thinking that he was the Angel of Music her father talked about, about being held in the basement by the phantom, about listening to his beautiful violin playing and then removing his mask and seeing his grotesque, death-like face. She explains that he finally agreed to let her go hoping to win her love freely. While on the roof, they have a feeling that they are being watched. The next day, Raoul talks with his brother, Philippe, and tells him that he is running away with Christine; Philippe does not approve.

The following night, in the middle of a performance, the lights go out at the opera. When they come on again, Christine is missing from the stage.

Chapters 17–21

The managers have locked themselves in their office, trying to figure out how the phantom could have changed an envelope of money to counterfeit bills. Mme. Giry explains that she switched envelopes and put the real bills into M. Richard's coat pocket, so they pin an envelope of cash into his pocket, only to find, soon after hearing of Christine's disappearance, that the envelope is mysteriously empty.

The Persian, a mysterious figure who has been seen around the opera house, stops Raoul from telling the police about Erik. He leads Raoul to Christine's dressing room and shows him the mechanism by which she appeared to disappear into her mirror. Then he leads Raoul into the cellars of the opera house.

Walking through the cellars, they pass the furnaces and the opera's rat catcher leading a small army of rats to their doom, but they do not see the phantom.

Chapters 22–26

These chapters are told as passages from the Persian's written account of that night. He leads Raoul to a secret panel that will drop them into Erik's house from the cellar above it, without having to cross the lake that he rowed Christine across. They land, however, in a room called the torture chamber and are trapped there. Erik, demanding that Christine agree to marry him, hears them in there and turns the chamber on: bright electric heat lamps and mirrored walls make it seem like a tropical jungle. When the Persian finds a release switch, they escape down into Erik's wine cellar, only to find that the barrels there are not filled with wine, but with enough gun powder to blow up half of Paris.

Above them, Christine is told to turn one knob if she accepts Erik's proposal and another if she rejects him, unaware that the rejection knob will trigger the gunpowder. She turns the one to accept him, and the wine cellar floods with water. At the last minute, Erik has a change of heart and saves Raoul and the Persian from drowning.. Erik goes to the Persian while he is recuperating from that night and says that he set Christine and Raoul free to marry each other and that he is dying of heartbreak. He asks him to place an obituary in the paper after his death, so that the young lovers will know.

The book's Epilogue tells the history of the phantom: how he learned about magic and construction and ventriloquism, how he came to work at the construction site of the opera building, and how he was able to elude detection for so long.

Characters

Joseph Buquet

Joseph is a stagehand who has seen the phantom in the opera house's third basement. He is found hanged in the cellar, but when people go to retrieve his body, the rope is missing. Later in the book, the Persian guesses that the phantom killed Buquet with a device called the Punjab lasso.

Carlotta

Carlotta is the opera's female lead, for whom Christine Daaé is an understudy. Carlotta is a technically accomplished singer but does not sing with soul. The phantom threatens her if she goes onstage as Marguerite in *Faust*, but she refuses to be intimidated; as a result, the sound of a croaking frog comes out when she sings.

Christine Daaé

Christine in Sweden was raised by her father, a traveling violinist. As he was dying, he explained to her that he would remain with her and guide her through the Spirit of Music. As a young singer with the Paris Opera, Christine heard Erik speaking to her from behind a wall; she asked if he were the spirit that her father had told her about, and for a while he said that he was. He taught her to sing well, so that, given her first chance for public attention, she sings so beautifully that much of Parisian society takes notice of her. That night, though, she runs into Raoul de Chagny, whom she met and fell in love with as a child; her love for Raoul makes Erik jealous, who does what he can to make her his. He promises her the freedom to leave him but then, unable to let her go, kidnaps her and gives her a short time to consent to marry him before killing her. She tries unsuccessfully to fool him into thinking that she will love him, but he is still moved by her love for Raoul enough to let them leave.

Philippe de Chagny

Forty-one-year-old Count de Chagny, whose given name is Phillippe-Georges-Marie, is the oldest of his family and since the deaths of his parents has been responsible for one of the oldest families in Europe, which includes his brother Raoul, who is almost half his age. He disapproves of his brother's romance with Christine Daaé, so that when she disappears from the opera stage Count de Chagny is a primary suspect. Later, he is found drowned in the lake that protects the phantom's house from the outside world, but the phantom denies any responsibility for his death, saying that

Philippe fell out of his boat by accident even before any of the lake's traps could get to him.

Raoul de Chagny

As the youngest member of the prestigious de Chagny family, Raoul has been raised by a sister and old aunt. At the time of the novel he is twenty years old and scheduled to go into the navy and, while waiting for his orders, is spending a few weeks in Paris with his brother Phillippe. He sees Christine Daaé on the stage of the opera and remembers her as the little girl whom he met and fell in love with years earlier, when her scarf blew into the water and he dove in to retrieve it. He can tell that Christine loves him, too, but she tries to send him away frequently, worried that Erik, the phantom, will hurt him. He and Christine agree to a secret engagement, but when their engagement becomes publicized the phantom abducts Christine. The novel's last chapters are about how Raoul, with the help of the stranger known as the Persian, infiltrates the phantom's hidden underground house in an attempt to free Christine. They fail, and Raoul is in danger of drowning before the phantom has a change of heart and agrees to let Christine leave with him, even though it breaks his heart and he dies as a result.

Monsieur Debienne

With Monsieur Poligny, Debienne is one of the directors of the Paris Opera who is retiring in the opening chapters of the novel.

Erik

Erik is the name that the phantom of the Opera has taken for himself; his real name is never revealed in the book. He was born deformed, and it was his mother, whom Eric refers to several times, who gave him his first mask. He was born in a little town near Rouen but ran away as a young man, sometimes exhibiting his gruesome looks at country fairs under the title of the living dead man. As a performer, he learned to become proficient as a musician, a magician, and as a ventriloquist. Summoned by a shah to Persia, he designed a palace with hidden panels and trap doors. The shah ordered him executed, to keep the palace's secrets unknown, but the Persian helped Erik escape.

In Paris, Erik was part of the construction team that helped Charles Garnier build the Paris opera house. Because he knows where the secret passageways are, he is able to move about the opera house without being seen. Because he is proficient in ventriloquism, he is able to speak from hidden places and to make people think that his voice is coming from the empty air beside them. And he uses his musical skill to compose a masterful violin opus, *Don Juan Triumphant*, which he has worked on for decades in his home in the opera house's cellars.

As the phantom, Erik demands that the managers of the opera give him an annual stipend and a private box. Erik falls in love with Christine when he meets her. For a while, he pretends to be the Spirit of Music that her father once told her about, and he trains her to become a great singer. When he is unable to make her love him, though, he becomes insane. He kidnaps her and eventually threatens to blow up a quarter of the town with all of the gunpowder he has hidden beneath the opera house. In the end, though, his heart is softened by her promise to love him, and he lets Christine and Raoul go free to marry each other. When he last appears in the novel, it is to tell the Persian that he is dying of a broken heart.

Mme. Giry

The mother of the girl known as Little Meg, Mme. Giry is also the attendant of Box Number 5, which is reserved for the phantom. She has never seen him, but she does services for him, like bringing a program and a footstool to the box. In return, he leaves her tips and gifts. When she is fired by the opera's directors, a huge chandelier falls on the audience, killing just one person: the woman hired to replace Mme. Giry. She is assigned to deliver money to the phantom, and when the money in the envelope is changed for counterfeit money, the directors threaten to turn her over to the police until they find out that she could not possibly have stolen it. They do find out why she is so interested in helping the phantom; in addition to the tips that he gives her, he has predicted that Little Meg will be the empress by 1885.

La Sorelli

One of the opera's featured dancers, La Sorelli is a diva who expects to be the center of attention. When she dances, the narrator explains, "she appears to be in a tableau so lascivious that it could drive a man to blow his brains out." But she is also presented as a vain, stubborn woman.

Monsieur Lachenal

Monsieur Lachenal is the stable master of the opera house, in charge of the horses that are trained to perform in operas.

Armand Moncharmin

One of the new directors of the opera, Moncharmin has no musical training but is rich and socially connected. His working relationship with

M. Richard is threatened when the phantom is able to steal an envelope of money from Richard's pocket. The book's narrator relies on Moncharmin's autobiography, *The Memoirs of a Director*, as a primary source for the events reported in the book.

The Persian

The Persian is a witness of the events at the opera house, whom the narrator interviews about what happened to Raoul de Chegny and Christine Daaé. The Persian is so famous that he cannot be referred to by his real name. He is a shadowy figure throughout much of the story, until the final chapters. Then, it turns out that he has known Erik, the phantom, for years, from the time when he was the *daroga*, or chief of the national police. In Persia, he saved Erik from execution and lost his government position because of it. He knows many of the secrets of the phantom's underground world, having followed him and observed him and once having nearly been killed by one of his traps in the underground lake.

When Christine is kidnapped, the Persian steps forward to help Raoul find his way through the underground world to the place where she may have been taken. In the course of the rescue mission, his advice is invaluable, but he nearly loses his life when the cellar he is in is flooded. The phantom saves him, though, and, after making sure he is all right, knocks him out with drugs and deposits him in a doorway.

Monsieur Poligny

With Monsieur Debienne, Monsieur Poligny is one of the directors of the Paris Opera who is retiring in the opening chapters of the novel.

Firmin Richard

One of the opera's new directors, Richard is an accomplished musician and composer. He is characterized as loving all types of music and all musicians. He is skeptical of the existence of the phantom and hesitates about giving in to his demands. When the money disappears from an envelope that is pinned in his pocket, he and his partner, M. Moncharmin, become suspicious of each other, a suspicion that seems, according to Moncharmin's memoirs, to last throughout their professional relationship.

Madame Maudie Valerius

Christine is staying at the house of Mme. Valerius, an old friend of her father. Raoul de Chagny goes to the house when Christine disappears the first time, but Mme. Valerius cannot tell him where she is. She is convinced that Christine has gone away with the Spirit of Music.

Themes

Appearance and Reality

The fact that *The Phantom of the Opera* takes place behind the scenes of the opera almost automatically draws readers' attention to the disparity between reality and appearances. Leroux gives backstage details, starting with the dancers who line up in the first chapter, gossiping, and continuing on to point out the backdrops and the business arrangements that few opera goers are allowed to see. Unlike most backstage stories, though, this novel also goes into details about the Paris opera house that few of the average workers would be aware of, such as the complicated system of tunnels underneath the building, with furnaces and prisons and hoards of rats and even a lake. Some of these details might be exaggerated from reality, but they are plausible as the reality of the novel. They clearly indicate that, as much as the sets and costumes create a false world on the stage, the opera house that visitors enter only reveals part of the story regarding what it takes to put on a grand spectacle.

The phantom himself is also used as a symbol to represent the ways that reality and appearance differ. The most obvious example of this is, of course, the mask that he wears. When he is wearing his mask, Christine can believe that he is a poor, misunderstood man who has just not been given the attention he deserves. When he represents himself to her as the Spirit of Music, she responds to his musical gift and really does see him as angelic. Once she sees Erik without his mask, however, she is so horrified that she can never think fondly of him again.

In addition to the phantom's looks, however, his whole existence is one big charade. He is greatly gifted, but his talents are in making voices seem to appear where no one is actually talking; in coming and going without being seen; in overhearing conversations that seem to be private; and in making people think that they see things that are impossible, as in when his torture chamber turns out to be a hall of illusions. He is known as a phantom for a reason: no one is ever really sure that he exists.

Innocence

The phantom's anger with the society that has rejected him is balanced in this novel with the simple innocence of the love between Christine Daaé and Raoul de Chagny. Christine's life story is surrounded by the sort of heartwarming and fantastic details that are common in fairy tales. Her father,

Topics For Further Study

- Examine the history of the Paris Commune, which Leroux says lived in the jails upon which the Opera House was built. Find out how much the underground life led in the 1870s corresponds to the underground life that Raoul discovers while going to find the place where the phantom lives.

- This story centers on the opera company's performance of *Faust*. Read a version of the Faust story and write a short play in which Erik and Faust meet, telling each other about their common experiences.

- One of this story's conceits is that, through the use of ventriloquism, Erik is able to make it seem as if his voice is coming out of places that are far from where he is hiding. Prepare a report on ventriloquism: its capabilities, its shortcomings, and its greatest practitioners. In what ways would proficiency in ventriloquism help Erik in pretending to be the Opera ghost?

- Study another opera house, either in person or on the Internet. Report on what areas behind and under the stage would be handy for this house to harbor its own phantom.

---

for instance, is a kindly old soul and an incredibly talented musician. He fills her childhood with the sweet view of the world that is found in folk stories. Before he dies, he tells Christine that she will be watched over by the Spirit of Music, which at first serves to give her comfort but later, as is common with innocence carried into adulthood, causes her to fall victim to Erik, who uses his talent for ventriloquism to make her loyal to him. Mme. Valerius is another example of the innocence that surrounds Christine's life. She never questions that the younger woman is doing the right thing even when others doubt her, supplying a level of sweetness and naiveté that reflects on Christine's understanding of the world.

The romance between Christine and Raoul is particularly untouched by the harsher elements of reality. From their first meeting as children, when Raoul puts his life at risk in service to her as he swims out into the ocean to retrieve her scarf, to their chance meeting years later at the opera house when they recognize each other, they are true to each other. A few times, Raoul questions Christine about her purity, but he always accepts her word that such questions are misguided. Readers believe so firmly in the couple's innocence that, when the narrator has bystanders remark that it is scandalous for them to go into her dressing room together and close the door, it is the bystanders who seem ignorant of the reality of true love.

Horror

This book uses several standard horror elements to make the phantom threatening and mysterious. The most obvious of these is the opera house itself, with its high, shadowy ceilings and miles of tunnels beneath. When Raoul and Christine go up to the roof, they are among the swooping gables and heavy statuary that set the ominous mood in other works, such as *The Hunchback of Notre Dame*. In its cellars readers are introduced to fantastic sights that are hard to believe: legions of forgotten workers who never see the light of day or swarms of rats that are at the command of the Rat Catcher.

The most distinct horror device is Erik's face. Though he is described as having a skin disease, its manifestation gives him the exact semblance of a skull, so that even as a young man he was able to travel to county fairs and bill himself as the living dead man. His eyes, too, are described as glowing in the dark, like a cat's. These details might be unlikely in the real world, but they are not at all out of place in a horror story.

Style

Narration

The Phantom of the Opera is told from the point of view of a narrator whose name is never given, who is examining the events of the novel thirty years after the fact. The Preface gives details of his search: how he examined the records of the opera library, interviewed people who had been present at the time of the story (including Little Meg Giry and the Persian, whose name is withheld but who proves to be a major part of the action in the book's final chapters), and examined a skeleton found in the catacombs under the opera house, assuming it to be the remains of the phantom. Throughout the course of the novel, this narrator sometimes makes his presence felt, with statements like "I assume" and "we know now that," but for the most part he stays out of the story and relates the facts as a third person narrator would.

There are several ways in which this narrator gives over the telling of the story to other participants. One way is in quoting songs that were sung at the opera while the story was being lived, giving readers a greater sense of immediacy than they would get from a scholarly recap of the events. The most striking example occurs when he gives the narrative over to the Persian in chapters 22 through 26, using the excuse that these are the exact words that the Persian wrote in his memoir of the events. It is significant that, at the height of this suspenseful story, the narrator changes to one of the two people who is actually involved in the action.

Historical Context

Belle Époque

The long stretch of time between the collapse of the empire of Napoleon III in 1871 and the start of the First World War in 1914 was a relative peaceful and prosperous period for France. Napoleon, like his predecessor Napoleon Bonaparte, had sought to remake Paris on a grand scale, restructuring its centuries-old layout and adding outlying provinces to the city proper. He had also, however, tried to leave his mark as a great military leader, which ended up in his defeat by the Prussians. The fall of the emperor was followed by a four-year period of political anarchy, marked by the uprising known as the Paris Commune (discussed in *The Phantom of the Opera* for the rebels who hid under the tunnels under the opera house). Stability was established under the Third Republic, which came to power in 1875, the same year that the magnificent opera house designed by Charles Garnier was completed.

During the final decades of the nineteenth century and the first decade of the twentieth, Paris saw a burst of technology that was integrated into ordinary daily life with ease. Electric lighting became available in the early 1880s and spread quickly; in the 1890s, automobiles became available; and, just before the turn of the century, the first moving pictures were exhibited. The 1900 Paris Expo, a large party to herald in the twentieth century, hosted nearly fifty-one million visitors: more than the population of the entire country. While France had spent much of the nineteenth century under the rule of Napoleon and his heir, Paris entered the twentieth century as one of the world's great capital cities. This period was known as the Belle Époque, also called the Banquet Years or the Miraculous Years.

Popular Entertainment

When *The Phantom of the Opera* was published in 1910, opera was still a popular diversion in Paris, but other forms of entertainment were more accessible to the masses. The theater world was all overshadowed by the genius of Sarah Bernhardt, one of France's most popular actresses, who started her career in the 1860s at the Comédie Française, the national theater company. Even more threatening to the high prices and formality of the opera was the ascent of the motion picture. Though Americans usually credit Thomas Edison with inventing movies in 1893, his kinetoscope projector was limited to one viewer at a time in a small booth. The first motion picture theater opened in Paris in 1895, using a process that was developed by two French brothers, Louis and Auguste Lumière. The Lumière method became the standard that was to be used in motion picture projection for decades. When this novel was published, the city of Paris already had over thirty-five movie theaters.

While motion pictures made shows available to the people who could not afford tickets to the opera or even to the theater, there were also a number of low-budget music venues that could be enjoyed for very little money. Paris had a tradition of being an artists' city and in particular a city for starving artists, and these artists frequented music halls and provided the talent for their stages. The majority of Parisians, to say nothing of the rest of the world, had never stepped foot inside of the opera house, and learned of its intriguing design through Gaston Leroux's novel.

Compare & Contrast

- **1880:** Transportation within Paris is by horse carriage; for cross-country trips, the locomotive is available.

  1910: In the year following the first flight across the English Channel by Louis Blériot, Parisians realize that the age of aviation has arrived. Automobiles are common on Parisian streets.

  Today: Paris's streets, designed in the 1870s, are choked with automobile traffic. For travel on the continent, the TGV, or bullet train, travels at speeds often exceeding 186 miles per hour.

- **1880:** Paris is the artistic center of the world, home to impressionist painters such as Alfred Sisley, Auguste Renoir, Edouard Manet, Edgar Degas, and Paul Cézanne.

  1910: Paris is the home of the influential and challenging Cubist artistic movement, promoted by painters such as Pablo Picasso and Georges Braque.

  Today: The best-known Parisian artists, such as Jean-Marc Bustamante and Sophie Calle, are photographers.

- **1880:** The Garnier Opera building is less than five years old and is revered as an architectural triumph.

  1910: At the advent of the age of Modernism, the Garnier Opera building is seen as an ornate and almost gothic structure.

  Today: The Garnier Opera building is considered to be one of Paris's most important cultural landmarks.

- **1880:** Interior light is provided by open gas flames, lanterns, or candles.

  1910: Large gathering places such as the opera are lit with incandescent lighting.

  Today: Lighting of stage productions such as operas has become an art form in and of itself.

Critical Overview

It is unlikely that Gaston Leroux's novel *The Phantom of the Opera* would be read today if it were not for the ways that other artists have adapted it to visual media. When Leroux's story first appeared as a newspaper serial in 1909, it was popular enough to be carried in papers in France, Great Britain, and the United States, but the subsequent release as a novel was only modestly successful. It was considered just another thrill story by a competent writer who churned out entertainment stories for a living. The book fell out of print quickly. In 1925, however, while looking for a film vehicle to match the success that he had just had with Lon Chaney in *The Hunchback of Notre Dame*, film producer Carl Laemmle purchased the rights to *The Phantom of the Opera*. The film took great liberties with Leroux's story, but it was a great success, a groundbreaking horror film, and its following continued over the decades and stirred interest in the novel that spawned it.

Modern audiences are familiar with the story of the phantom through the immensely popular stage musical, written by Andrew Lloyd Weber. That play opened in London in October of 1986 and as of 2004 had not yet closed, making it as of that year the second-longest running musical in the history of the theater (after Weber's own *Cats*).

One reason that the novel is so seldom discussed on its own terms is that its story is, in the words of Leonard Wolf, who edited a contemporary, annotated edition, a "strange sort of masterpiece." Wolf points out the conventions of gothic fiction, such as the perils faced by the young, beautiful heroine, pursued "from one cold, dark, dank, and macabre place to another by a tall, dark stranger who is infinitely more interesting than the good-looking and (often) wealthy or titled young hero

1925 motion picture version of Gaston Leroux's The Phantom of the Opera, *with Lon Chaney as the Phantom and Mary Philbin as Christine Daaé*

who rescues her." While many readers have dismissed the book as a hack job, Wolf credits Leroux with weaving "a tapestry of myth that frequently feels both complex and moving."

In his 2002 study titled *The Undergrounds of "The Phantom of the Opera": Sublimation and the Gothic in Leroux's Novel and Its Progeny*, Jerrold E. Hogle shows that it is in fact possible to give serious critical consideration to the phantom's story. Heavy on psychological and sociological interpretation, Hogle's book observes aspects of the story that

have never been noted before. His discussion of the underground catacombs, for example, is common of the tone of the whole book: "As both the principle creditor and himself a debtor in this novel, Leroux's phantom thus occupies yet another symbolic position with many layers, this time in the way the book exposes and disguises the economic roots behind a world of simulation." It is notable that, while taking Leroux's work seriously, still the majority of Hogle's book is concerned with adaptations, from the silent film to the stage musical.

Criticism

David Kelly

Kelly is an instructor of literature and creative writing at two schools in Illinois. In this essay, Kelly examines the reasons why The Phantom of the Opera *has been more successful in film and on stage than the original novel ever was.*

It is something of an adage among film critics that great movies can be made from bad novels but that great novels very seldom yield great movies. When screenwriters try to adapt a great novel, they are almost sure to have their work met with the tired old line, "The book was better." Great books are considered great because readers care about them: screen adapters of these books have to know that their every move is being scrutinized, lest they leave out some important, treasured element. At the same time, those adapting weaker sources might feel free to leave out whole plot lines, move the action to another continent, or tack on a happy ending, all without much fuss being raised.

Gaston Leroux's novel *The Phantom of the Opera* does, in fact, fit this general rule. The book has never been taken very seriously, having been serialized in newspapers, having been bound into novel form in 1910, and then having withered away from the shelves into the dustbin of obscurity. Most readers of its time dismissed it as just another potboiler churned out by a former journalist who was striving to bring in an income by freelancing, willing to write whatever the public would pay to read. It took the 1925 silent film to bring that book back to life. The film starred Lon Chaney, who was one of the most sought-after stars of its day, and it, along with F. W. Murnau's 1922 vampire film *Nosferatu*, defined the horror film for decades to come. Throughout the decades, there were various remakes of the Chaney film, and then, in 1986, there came the stage musical by Andrew Lloyd Weber. As of the early 2000s, the musical had broken records for ticket and soundtrack sales and had played all over the world to sellout crowds. Its version of the story, emphasizing the romantic angle and de-emphasizing the macabre, had defined *The Phantom of the Opera* for late twentieth-century and early twenty-first-century audiences.

Since Leroux's novel had both the horror and the romance that the subsequent adaptations were able to capitalize on so well, it is interesting to ask why they were able to succeed so well with his ideas. The novel is not without its skills, but it also has its weaknesses. The core issue seems to be that

> At any given moment he brings Erik's sense of love, anger, or compassion to the fore, depending on whether Leroux wants the action to move toward murder, kidnapping, or, in the end, sudden forgiveness."

its strengths all tend to lend themselves to the visual arts, while its weaknesses all fall in areas where great writing usually shines.

There are many elements of true wit and originality in the novel, twists that show Leroux to be a talented writer, distinguishing him from others who are more willing than able when it comes to producing literature. Of these, one of the strongest elements is the consistency of the narrator's voice. Leroux provides an inquisitive narrator on a quest in this book: he (or, conceivably, she) starts out with the question of whether the legendary opera ghost was real and chases the evidence down to its one deductive conclusion. The triumph of this narrator lies in the lengths that Leroux goes to in order to plausibly give him access to information. The book's Preface gives a list of sources that the narrator is said to have contacted for this inquiry, some thirty years after the fact: names that mean nothing to the reader who has just cracked the book's cover but that establish a sense of honesty. Other narrative techniques include references to printed sources such as police interviews and the journals left by the Persian (whose true name is withheld, simulating a connection to late nineteenth- or early twentieth-century society) and facts about the way the opera house came to be built. As a former journalist, Leroux does a meticulous job of feeding his story through this plausible, objective narrator, one that could possibly have access to the information and, more importantly, the feelings of those who participated, more than a generation earlier. Still, the narrator is the first element that the successful adaptations leave out, and rightfully so.

Although the narrator is skillfully constructed, it turns out to be a hollow accomplishment. The narrator does not really *do* anything in the novel

What Do I Read Next?

- In his entertaining 1993 novel *The Canary Trainer*, Nicholas Meyer, writing as Sherlock Holmes's confidant Dr. Watson, has Holmes interact with characters from Leroux's novel, as he tries to capture the opera ghost.

- There are many comparisons to be made between the story of the phantom and Mary Shelley's 1818 novel *Frankenstein*, which also deals with an outcast from society. In Shelley's novel, though, the philosophical questions of what it means to be human are much more significant.

- The costume ball with the mysterious death's head figure in attendance is an almost exact copy of the scene Edgar Allan Poe used in his short story "The Masque of the Red Death." This story is available in most anthologies of Poe's works, including the one published by the Library of America.

- Readers who enjoy Leroux's style might want to read more of his writings. His 1907 detective novel *The Mystery of the Yellow Room*, which was one of his most popular works during his lifetime, is available in a 2002 release from Indypublish.com. Also, a number of his macabre stories were collected in *The Gaston Leroux Bedside Companion: Weird Stories by the Author of the "Phantom of the Opera,"* but as of 2004 this collection was out of print.

- This novel is closely associated with Victor Hugo's *The Hunchback of Notre Dame*. Like Leroux's Erik, Hugo's Quasimodo is a deformed genius who occupies the hidden spaces of a grand Parisian building, pining for the beautiful woman whom he loves. Hugo's novel was available as of 2004 in a Tor Classics edition.

- Robert Louis Stevenson's 1886 novel *Dr. Jekyll and Mr. Hyde* is similar to the tale of the phantom in that it takes place in the late Victorian era and in mostly urban settings, mostly at night.

---

other than gathering information. He has the same function that a third-person narrator would have, though a third-person narrator could explore people and places without having to explain how the information became available. Though there may have been some benefit to having the story told by a man living in 1910, in order to show the contrast between the modern world and the shadowy world of the past, little is lost in leaving this person out of films and plays. The narrator's main function of shrouding the events with mystery is taken up by light and shadow and set designs.

Which leads to Leroux's other great accomplishment in the novel, his sense of scene. Of the thousands of patrons who sat in the Paris opera house after it was built, he was the one with a sense of mystery who could see the inherent drama that it evoked, presenting culture and refinement built over former prisons. So strong was his sense of scene, in fact, that readers can see the lengths he was willing to go, just to raise the right atmosphere.

In Chapter XIII, for instance, he has Christine and Raoul move out of the opera house to talk but places their conversation on the roof, amid a gloomy background of imposing statuary that is just as spooky as anything down below—a setting that makes no sense, given that they are still within range of the phantom's influence. But even that brief change of venue is mild, compared to the way that, in Chapter VI, Leroux has Christine and Raoul travel cross-country to Perros, apparently just to take them to a graveyard at midnight. The book is full of vivid but structurally unnecessary moments, from the appearance of the rat-catcher underground (to tease the audience with an infestation of rats) to the amazing coincidence of Raoul going to Bois de Boulogne on a vague tip, only to see the phantom and Christine drive by in a carriage (apparently added for the visual effect of a carriage at night).

Though Leroux was brilliant at producing frightening visual effects in this book, his execution was not always so impressive. Readers have difficulty *seeing* the statue of Apollo's Lyre, the carriage, or the gravestone that Raoul was apparently found spread out on in the morning. One of the most chilling sights to come from the book, the appearance of a masked death-head at a costume ball (which was itself openly appropriated from Edgar Allan Poe's story "The Masque of the Red Death") is glided over in two paragraphs of dense narrative, muting its power and making readers wonder what it was they have just seen and why. This very image plays an impressive role in both the movie and the play, capitalized on by storytellers who understood the value of the scary images that Leroux seems to have conjured up by the dozens without restraint.

As a writer, Leroux was weakest in handling characterization. He just seems to have had no interest in the inner workings of the human beings. The other characters in the novel do not prove to be much more substantial than the narrator. The book's male lead, Raoul, is so lacking in personality that Leroux brings in the Persian at the end to take over the traditional chores of the hero, such as finding and confronting the monster. Christine is a little more complex, but her complexity results from her being tricked by the phantom into associating him with a guardian angel: it is not until the screen and stage adaptations that her dual attraction and revulsion are acknowledged. As for the phantom himself, Erik: in the abstract, he could be considered a complex character, with his hatred for humanity clouded by his love for Christine, his beautifully artistic soul defied by the shadows that he is forced to live in. The problem is that, having established these elements of character, Leroux does not follow through with them. At any given moment he brings Erik's sense of love, anger, or compassion to the fore, depending on whether Leroux wants the action to move toward murder, kidnapping, or, in the end, sudden forgiveness.

The problem is that Leroux's writing is all elements and no details. He is like a land developer who can see a field built up into blocks of houses, but he does not know what particular houses should go where, much less what should go in them. This is why adaptations of his book work better than the book itself. His horror-story elements are visual and, therefore, work more effectively when played out visually, but that is only half of the explanation: his work was so unrefined that anybody who took the time to rework it, to pay closer attention to the implied meaning behind the phantom's mask, the falling chandelier, the rooftop encounter, the caverns of forgotten laborers and the rest would

almost have to produce an impressive artistic work. In fact, the characters from *The Phantom of the Opera* were appropriated by several writers over the course of the twentieth century, who cast them into their own fiction. The fact that the most popular forms of this story have been a movie and a play has something to do with Gaston Leroux's sense of the visual and his sense of the broader movements that make characters, but it has even more to do with the fact that he seems to have left the telling of his story undone.

Source: David Kelly, Critical Essay on *The Phantom of the Opera*, in *Novels for Students*, Thomson Gale, 2005.

Contemporary Authors Online

In the following essay, the author discusses the critical reception of Leroux's The Phantom of the Opera *and his contribution to the fields of detective and horror fiction.*

Several motion picture adaptations (the first in 1925) and stage adaptations have kept French author Gaston Leroux's original novel *Le Fantome de l'Opera* (*The Phantom of the Opera*) alive in the minds of readers throughout the world for over eight decades. Published in 1996, *The Essential "Phantom of the Opera": The Definitive Annotated Edition of Gaston Leroux's Classic Novel*, edited by Leonard Wolf is merely one of numerous, more recent editions published in the United States since the first English translation appeared in 1911. Through the book and its offspring in other media, this story of a disfigured singer who haunts the labyrinthine opera house in Paris and his love for the young and beautiful Christine has become a part of modern culture, a legend that has taken on a life of its own. The Phantom "is a figure of power and poignance, horror and mystery," explained Richard Corliss in *Time* magazine." He dwells in the fetid cellar of the subconscious; from those depths rises the music of passions we hardly dare attend. He is the Id aching for the Ideal, loathsomeness wanting to be loved, unknown fear reaching up to touch or break our hearts." Corliss added, "He is kin to Pygmalion, Cyrano, Quasimodo, Dracula, the Elephant Man and King Kong—artists isolated in their genius, Beasts pining for a Beauty."

Leroux's classic novel was first serialized in France and Britain before being published in book form. It was based in part on actual events. Leroux had visited the Paris Opera House several times while working as a drama critic and was familiar with its architecture and history. Begun in 1861, the Opera was finished in 1879 and was comprised of seventeen stories with mazes of corridors and stairways, private suites for then-Emperor Napoleon III, stables for horses, dressing rooms for 500 performers, storage cellars for costumes, and an underground lake on its lowest level. The atmosphere of the building was made more mysterious by rumors that a ghost or strange being haunted its depths and had been responsible for several unexplained deaths. Leroux worked many of these details into his novel, including how the opera house's main chandelier had fallen upon an audience in 1896.

Influenced by Victor Hugo's *Hunchback of Notre Dame*, Leroux created for his book a horribly disfigured central character named Erik. Erik is a wonderful musician with a beautiful voice, but he is so ugly that from birth his mother required him to wear a mask. He builds a home for himself on the underground lake beneath the Opera and prowls its corridors unseen, leaving notes signed "O.G." (for Opera Ghost) instructing the management on how the theater is to be run.

To his underground residence the Phantom brings young Christine Daae, a beautiful understudy he has fallen in love with and whose career he is advancing. But Christine is in love with Raoul, a young nobleman she has known since she was a child, and is terrified of the Ghost. Eventually, however, she begins to understand Erik's longing and comes to pity him. In Leroux's final scenes, writes Drake Douglas in *Horror*!, "when Erik speaks of the wonder of being looked upon without fear by a beautiful woman, of actually feeling the warmth of a woman's kiss on his horrible face, surely then we cannot feel too much fear and hatred for this monster who had the misfortune to be born with a great heart and a terrible ugliness."

The Phantom of the Opera was not an overwhelmingly successful novel in a critical sense. At the time of its original publication, a contributor to the *New York Times Book Review* noted it as an interesting "ghost story . . . but when the phantom ceases to be a phantom, and things begin to be accounted for, one's interest sensibly weakens." Even so, the *New York Times Book Review* contributor positively remarked on the novel's description of the Opera House and found the book "effective" and stated that "its style is picturesque and vivid." And although at times almost "ridiculous," a *Nation* reviewer concluded that the story is "ingenious" and "despite the incredibility of the whole situation, M. Leroux succeeds in piquing the reader's curiosity, and ... [the novel contains some] 'breathless suspense.'"

Despite the novel's reception among critics, the Phantom's story has transcended its evaluations. Each new adaptation of the book, from the 1925 classic silent movie starring Lon Chaney to the award-winning 1986 musical created by Andrew Lloyd Webber and Richard Stilgoe, has intrigued the public and lured them back to rediscover the original novel.

Leroux may forever be remembered as the creator of *The Phantom of the Opera*, but in his day, he was recognized as an innovative creator of detective and horror fiction. The only child of well-to-do shop owners, he acquired a taste for literature at an early age. Although sent to Paris to study law as a young man, he preferred to spend his time writing stories and verse; his first published work consisted of a sequence of sonnets about Parisian actresses. At the age of twenty-one, he inherited nearly one million francs from his father, but Parisian night life—drinking and gambling—quickly reduced his inheritance. Within six months he was penniless, and turned to his writing as a means of support. He became a court reporter on the staff of *L'Echo de Paris*, combining his legal training with his writing skills.

Tired of simply reporting court cases, Leroux launched a career as an investigative reporter by trying to solve a case before the verdict came in. "He was convinced the accused man was innocent, and the reason he was being kept under such tight security before his court appearance in the town of Bourges was to protect some incompetent officials," explained Peter Haining in his introduction to the Dorset Press edition of *The Phantom of the Opera*. Passing himself off as a prison inspector, Leroux obtained access to the prisoner and interviewed him. Haining quoted Leroux from a 1925 interview: "I got my paper to publish a full report which completely exonerated the prisoner—and as a result the Prefect of Police was disgraced and the Prison Director was sent packing! Curiously, it was my newspaper colleagues who were the most annoyed. I had interviewed an accused man in prison before his trial—it was something that had never been heard of before in law reporting!"

This case established Leroux's reputation as a reporter, and led to many other interviews with influential figures, including the Duc d'Orleans, pretender to the throne of France, and the Swedish Antarctic explorer Nils Nordenskjold. It also led to a job with *Le Matin*, a major daily newspaper, and assignment as a roving reporter. Over the next fifteen years, Leroux became famous for his adventurous reporting from crisis spots throughout Europe, Africa, and Asia. A master of disguise, he covered the Russian Revolution of 1905 and posed as an Arab while reporting on European imperialism in Morocco—an assignment that could have cost him his life.

Because of these escapades, Leroux became known as a reporter "who could get a story out of even the most unlikely situation," wrote Haining. For example, in an attempt to interview British Colonial Secretary Joseph Chamberlain during the Boer War, Leroux slipped into the minister's private study without permission. When he was discovered by a secretary and ejected, Leroux composed an article titled "How I Failed to See Chamberlain," which, according to Haining, "delighted French readers and was widely hailed as 'a masterpiece of good humour and wit.'" Eventually, however, Leroux tired of the traveling and hazards that his journalism demanded and turned to writing fiction and plays. Much of his work drew on his experiences as a reporter, and "right from the start," declared Haining, "he proved himself an ingenious storyteller with a flair for pace and excitement."

Leroux's first success as a novelist came with the 1908 publication of *The Mystery of the Yellow Room*, which introduced his amateur detective hero, Joseph Rouletabille. Like the author himself, Rouletabille is a mentally sharp reporter whose reasoning ability far outpaces that of the police officers he meets. With his assistant Sainclair, Rouletabille solves one of the first "locked-room" mysteries, in which a crime is committed in a place no one could have entered or left. Leroux also wrote mysteries in which the least-likely character is cast as the culprit and is credited with introducing this plot device to the genre.

The Mystery of the Yellow Room was translated into English and established Leroux as a major figure in the field of mystery writing. "*The Mystery of the Yellow Room*," wrote Howard Haycraft in 1941 in *Murder for Pleasure*, "is generally recognized, on the strength of its central puzzle, as one of the classic examples of the genre. For sheer plot manipulation and ratiocination—no simpler word will describe the quality of its Gallic logic—it has seldom been surpassed. It remains, after a generation of imitation, the most brilliant of all 'locked room' novels."

The sequel to the *The Mystery of the Yellow Room—The Perfume of the Lady in Black*—featured the second appearance of Rouletabille and confirmed his reputation as an amateur sleuth who out-thought professional detectives. Although popular, *The Perfume of the Lady in Black* did not receive the acclaim that had greeted *The Mystery of the Yellow Room*. Rupert Ranney wrote in *Bookman*: "*The Perfume of the Lady in Black* is no better than its predecessor, and it is no worse, which implies neither high praise nor serious disparagement. The faults and merits of one book are the faults and merits of the other." Other adventures of Rouletabille failed to duplicate the success of the first volume. Leroux later penned another series of detective novels starring a magician named Cheri-Bibi.

The creator of Rouletabille, Cheri-Bibi, and numerous other intriguing characters, Leroux continued to be a prolific writer of fiction until his death in 1927. Although his creation *The Phantom of the Opera* currently overshadows his other works, Gaston Leroux is still remembered in the fields of detective and horror fiction for his unique contributions to these genres.

Source: Contemporary Authors Online, "Gaston Leroux," in *Contemporary Authors Online*, Gale, 2003.

Philip J. Riley

In the following excerpt, Riley examines the historical background which led to the conception and writing of The Phantom of the Opera.

Gaston Leroux is known to the American audience today as the author of *The Phantom of the Opera*, but in France he is known as one of the most popular and well read mystery writers in the country.

In April of 1907, Leroux had just returned from another exhausting journey to Morocco when the phone rang at 3 a.m. The editor of *Le Matin*, Maurice Bunau-Varilla, was on the line. He was ordered to take the next train to Toulon, where the largest French battleship had just sustained extensive

Parisian film poster for The Phantom of the
Opera, *circa 1925*

damage in an explosion. He looked at Jeanne, at
his children, at the warm bed in which he had been
peacefully sleeping for the first time in weeks. With
a few well chosen words to the editor, Leroux
quit—hung up the phone—went back to bed and
became a novelist.

He immediately began to write *The Mystery of
the Yellow Room*. The inspiration for the novel he
freely admitted, was Edgar Allen Poe's, *The
Murders in the Rue Morgue* (first published in
Graham's magazine in April 1841). Poe's story had
been written only 12 years after the establishment
of the world's first professional police in London.
The word "detective" did not exist—at least in
English until its use by Poe.

Murders in the Rue Morgue was a new form of
fiction, called by Poe himself, "tales of ratiocination". (The only example of any type of deductive
reasoning in a fiction work, before that time, was
Voltaire's *Zadig*, published in 1748). Poe invented
the gentleman-detective, who acts through his own
intellect to solve a crime that has baffled the official
police. The story is written in narrative as told by
the reporter, and written down by a colleague.

French novels, especially mysteries, were over-
burdened with self analyses when Leroux announced

to Jeanne that he was going to "Out-Poe-Poe," in
writing a "locked room" mystery. He certainly did.
It became an overnight sensation and confirmed
Leroux's belief in himself. The only concession he
had to make was to change the name of his character from the original, Boitabille, to Rouletabille—a
name that would make him as famous in France, as
Sherlock Holmes made Arthur Conan Doyle in
England or C. Auguste Dupin made Poe in America.

After the newspaper serialization of the work,
it was published in novel form by Pierre Lafitte—
who, through 1924, would eventually publish 26
more volumes written by Leroux.

At some point in 1909, assured of an income,
he and Jeanne and son, Miki, and daughter
Madeleine (Leroux and Jeanne Cayette were still not
married at this time) moved to the French Riviera
and set up a home on Mont-Boron, overlooking the
Casinos at Nice. It was there that he was to write his
most famous novel, *The Phantom of the Opera*
which he dedicated to Joseph, his closest brother.

The Opera *Faust* did not become the center-
piece of the "Phantom" story by mere chance. Just
as Leroux's avant garde use of italics to convey
"thoughts" holds far-reaching action together, Eric,
the Phantom is always kept in our minds while
reading about scenes from the Opera. Eric is Faust
turned inside out—or sideways. In Leroux's research, he found that Faust was, at first, all that is
admirable and uplifting in a man, and yet his physical appearance was hardly one that would attract
a beautiful girl to love him . . . an old man. He was
intelligent, giving and full of love for his fellow
man until he made his pact with Satan. Then,
through the medium of boredom, the line between
good and evil disappeared in the self-serving life
in which he had trapped himself through his bargain. He became a master of music, architecture,
medicine, but with his soul now owned by Satan,
the dark side became the source of his power. Erik,
his counterpart, was hideous on the outside. But his
mistreatment by man, from childhood, was the
cause that turned him away from his God. His intelligence gave him the means to become his own
law, living outside acceptable social society. As his
soul got blacker and blacker, a beautiful young girl
came into his life, and soon, a single act of kindness towards him destroyed the only things that
kept his reality intact, the hatred of man; the belief
that love did not exist in him; that there was no
God and therefore no good in the world.

A theologian of the 17th century recorded
meeting the real Faust at a dinner party. Faust

arrived attended by two devils, in the form of a dog and a horse. Later in his story he states:

"The wretch came to an end in a terrible manner; for the Devil strangled him."

Whomever he was, the real Faust disappeared in time to be replaced by the legend. The first publishing of the legend came from Spiess Publishers of Frankfurt in 1587. The actual title of the book?—

History of Dr. Joh. Faust, the notorious sorcerer and black-artist: How he bound himself to the Devil for a certain time: What singular adventures befell him therein, what he did and carried on until finally he received his well-deserved pay. Mostly from his own posthumous writings; for all presumptuous, rash and godless men, as a terrible example, abominable instance and well-meant warning, collected and put in print. James, IIII., Submit yourselves therefore to God: resist the Devil, and he will flee from you.

There doesn't seem much reason to read the book once you get past the title, but apparently it was well received, reprinted several times and in every language of Europe.

From this book Christopher Marlowe obtained the material for his play "Dr. Faustus," which appears to have been first performed in London in 1593.

This text of *Faust* remained the foundation of one of Europe's most popular tales for the next 200 years until the next character in our history appears . . . Johann Wolfgang Goethe.

Goethe (pronounced Ger-ta) was born on August 28, 1749 at Frankfort-on-the-Main and he died in Weimar, (Saxony) at the age of eighty-two, on March 22, 1832.

At the age of 21, he met a 15 year old girl named Frederike Brion, the daughter of a Lutheran Pastor. Captivated by his good looks and fame as a poet, they soon had a passionate affair. No record has been found of a child born from their affair, but the very next summer Goethe left. Frederike went away for a year to a retreat. Goethe saw her only once more, three years later and even that was just a brief uncomfortable encounter at a dinner. Frederike never married and died at the age of 61.

By the mid-19th Century, Goethe's epic poem "Faust" was a national German treasure, but it would not be a German that would eventually bring "Faust" to the Opera stage.

The Opera *Faust*, which plays a big part in the novel and the 1925 film, was written by Charles Gounod. When it premiered, *Faust* was the first notable success by a French composer in a Paris,

> " The maze of labyrinths amazed him and possibly the thought that 'the man who designed all of this must be in a madhouse' planted the seed for a fascinating villain."

which had for 50 years been dominated by foreign composers. The premiere, however, was not at the Paris Opera as we know it today but in a small theater. By the time *Faust* reached the new *Place de l'Opéra* in 1875, it would be in its third revision.

While *Faust* was being fine tuned by Gounod between 1859–1861, one of the greatest structures in the world was being considered—the setting for our story, The Paris Opéra.

Before Gounod had his first version of *Faust* underway there had been several changes in the Government of France and there had been no less than thirteen different National Opera Houses.

France was now governed by the nephew of Napoleon Bonaparte, Napoleon III. Although Napoleon III was responsible for the design for the city of Paris, as it exits today, he was not a popular ruler with the citizens of that time. His plan of large tree-lined boulevards which radiated like the spokes of a wheel from a cultural and governmental center were put into action, along with a modern sewer system, bridges and artificially lighted streets. The results were that the century old slums of Paris were eliminated. Most of the working class lived in those slums. While they were being continually pushed out of the city, they were also drafted into many of the foreign wars of Napoleon III in his search for new sources of wealth in Mexico and the Middle East.

In the early months of 1858, Napoleon III left the palace to attend a performance at the "Opera-house-of-the-day" which was located on the edge of the diminishing slum line. As they neared the theater several bombs exploded around the imperial carriages. The anarchist killed 150 people, but the Emperor and the Empress Eugénie were unharmed. They continued on to the performance where he was hailed for his bravery.

When he arrived back at the Palace after the performance, he summoned the city planner, Baron Haussmann, and told him it was time for a new opera house, one so grand that it would be the envy of the world [and one that would have a fortified side entrance, with plenty of room for security guards—close to the palace.]

It would take two years for the planning board to finally approve the designs of a young architect, Charles Garnier, out of almost 200 submissions.

The Opera House was conceived for not only the stage performances but also state occasions, balls and artistic festivals of all types.

The mechanics of the modern Opera House were not the only phase of creation in which Garnier showed amazing forethought. Knowing that the future of opera would demand more extravagant productions, as technology progressed, he designed a stable for horses in one of the lower basements. A long series of arch-supported ramps gave the stable master easy access. As Garnier and his talented staff were in the excitement of creation, outside world events were to bring frustration and more delays.

Napoleon's expansion program in the Middle East was draining the countries resources. For Garnier, nine years had now gone by and still the Opera House was far from finished. In 1870, the losses caused by the Franco-Prussian war pushed the people to the breaking point. When Napoleon III's army was defeated in the Sudan he lost the support of the upperclass and was exiled. A new republic was declared by the parliament, but this was not enough. Prussia marched into France and encircled the capital, when the new government was unable to pay the war debt caused by Napoleon III. Inside Paris, the working class took the law into their own hands and formed their own army called the Communards, in an attempt to oust the temporary government.

The first place chosen for the headquarters of the Communards was the unfinished Opera House. Built like a fortress and centrally located, it was stored with ammunition, food and wine. The Prussian siege lasted a year and a half. Food began to run out. The animals of Napoleon III's zoo were slaughtered for those willing to pay the price, and for those who could not, there were the cats, dogs and rats of the sewer. Finally, the National Guard was moved into action. Not only would they rid the city of the Communards but they ran out the "New Republic". The Communards were no match for the well armed National Guard and they were soon routed, but not without attempts to destroy the great creations of the past. The *Louvre* was set on fire as

well as the magnificent *Hotel de Ville*. The Opera House became a prison for the enemies of the people.

France now had its Third Republic and it was to take three more years before construction resumed on the Opera House. First, the sanitation crews had to remove the remains of the slaughtered animals and dead prisoners. The immense basements and lower labyrinths made it impossible to find all of the prisoners and many died and rotted in forgotten dungeons. Rumors began to spread of ghosts of former soldiers and of forgotten prisoners, reduced to animalistic levels from their isolation in the dark cellars for so many years.

Finally in January of 1875, the "Gala Opening" of the Opera was announced. After years of waiting, Garnier was now rushing to meet the deadline. Many areas had not even been painted! The musicians faced a Wagnerian orchestra pit for the first time and almost went on strike. They were used to being seen by the audience along with the action on stage. Being a politically promoted affair, no one dared protest. The new French government wanted to show the rest of the world that Paris had not only changed for the better, but it was again, the center of world arts. Garnier, after all his labor, was given a seat with the public instead of a place of honor.

One of Garnier's admirers was the newspaper journalist, Gaston Leroux, who had settled down to write novels, rather than continue the time-consuming and dangerous life of a reporter. Through one of his many contacts from those press days, he gained permission to explore the depths of the Opera House.

With a few guides, Leroux covered the upper scene docks, admired the beauty and subtle art, the frescos and statues. Then he wished to go into the lower levels, almost 70 feet down into the ground. There was little or no light and few who would even dare glance at the door to the levels below, let alone go through it. Some levels had not been inspected for 25 years.

He remembered the hundreds of prisoners who had died there during the Franco-Prussian war. The maze of labyrinths amazed him and possibly the thought that "the man who designed all of this must be in a madhouse" planted the seed for a fascinating villain. Early notes on the *Phantom* indicate just that. Leroux imagined a child who had been forgotten when the Commune prisoners were freed. The boy eventually went mad and made the underworld his home. Maybe as an adult he became an architect who purposely designed all types of secret rooms, with the intent of using the old torture chambers on any accidental visitors who stumbled into his hidden rooms.

At various times, his attention was broken by a call from his friend, who was moving on to a new area. When they reached the lower levels, the dampness became more prominent. They came upon the lake, five stories below the opera stage. It was nearly full and could only be viewed from above through barred grills. He was shown the mechanisms by which the lake could be drained and the walls inspected. When this was done, the lofty arches were exposed and the workmen used a small boat to travel from area to area. It was rumored that there was a secret room, now under water, that could only be entered when the lake was drained. It was at this level that a morbid discovery was made. He was about to join his guide, when he stumbled upon the remains and bones of the victims of the torture chambers. His foot kicked a skull as he scrambled to remove himself from this ghastly vision! Once he regained his composure the opera ghost was born. (Fact, or just legend propagated by Leroux's wonderful sense of humor?)

In the eerie underworld of the Opera House, Leroux began to formulate what type of person could survive in such a morbid tomb-like land of shadows. Certainly, a prisoner of this darkness would eventually be driven insane. Years of journalism and practicality imbedded in Leroux, kept him from the consideration of making his Phantom a real monster, (in the manner of Stoker's Dracula). So it would have to be a character within the realms of possibility.

Leroux always kept a large library. Consulting his medical reference books he noted the effects on the human body when deprived of sunlight, clean water and sanitary conditions over a period of years. Leprosy was one disease that came from these conditions, but it usually occurred in tropical areas. Also in 1909, he had obtained copies of recently published papers from London, in which, Dr. Treves' patient Joseph Merrick, known as the Elephant Man, was finally diagnosed as having von Recklinghausen's neurofibromatosis. Although Dr. Treves' own account of Joseph Merrick were not published until 1923, one of the transcripts in Leroux's library told how Merrick cried when a woman visitor politely shook hands with him. The overwhelming emotion taxed his weak heart to the point where he almost had a seizure and died from the joy of the moment. It was the first time that a woman had ever smiled at him and shaken his hand. The horrible deformities of the Elephant Man were *too* much. Leroux's

character had to draft blueprints, draw and be athletic. The hand shaking incident, however, gave him some insight as to how kindness affects one whose life has been littered with abuse and rejection due to his physical appearance.

It was to a visit by an unnamed physician, a guest of Leroux's, that he credits the physical and mental requirements of his mad-genius.

A disease, which is known today as congenital porphyria produced tragic symptoms in its sufferers. The disease itself becomes progressively worsened by exposure to sunlight. In an early German medical Journal supplement called *Strahlentherapie*, he discovered photographs of the victims, plus descriptions of the symptoms. An excerpt from *The Proceedings of the Royal Society of Medicine #57* published in 1964 provides some insight:

1. Severe photosensitivity in which a vesicular erytheman is produced by the action of the light.

2. There is a tendency for the skin lesions to ulcerate, and these ulcers may attack cartilage and bone. Over a period of years, structures such as nose, ears, eyelids, and lips undergo progressive mutilation.

3. Hypertrichosis of pigmentation may develop.

4. The teeth may be red or reddish brown due to the deposition of porphyrins.

5. Nervous manifestations may be referable to any part of the nervous system, and include mental disorders ranging form mild hysteria to manic-depressive psychoses and delirium.

6. In cases a jaundice produces pale yellowish excoriated skin.

The plausible yet horrible figure of an architect, once a prisoner of the Commune, who had been hired to design and create the underground labyrinths, formed in Leroux's imagination through these medical studies. Much like Arthur Conan Doyle's Professor Moriarity, this person's madness would also be his genius. Yet, if he were to contract this nervous disease, his symptoms would be a gradual mental breakdown, whereupon the mechanical training of the mind would remain, while the reasoning would cause whatever was happening at any particular moment to become the total of his reality. His physical characteristics would be, in layman's terms, loss of muscle bulk, which would make him almost skeletal. The jaundice would turn his skin pale yellow. Exposure to sunlight would cause the loss of his ears, nose, lips, eyelids, hair and cause the teeth to turn reddish brown.

That took care of the outer appearance. For the inner workings of Erik, he went back to the original *Faust* and developed a mind corrupted by evil and lack of discipline. But the lack of sympathy bothered him. Even Faust was redeemed in the legend.

Other pieces of the story were now beginning to fire his imagination. He remembered an accident at the Opera that had occurred in 1896 while he was still a reporter for *Le Matin.* During the first act of *Thétis and Pélée,* the cable, holding an 800 pound counterweight that was used for balancing the great chandelier, snapped due to an electrical short and crushed a woman to death. He imagined what would happen if the whole chandelier were to fall.

As the story line became clearer, the idea of an architect did not hold as much romance as that of a musician. What better than to have a mad genius who was not only an architect, but a musician as well; who used the old rumors of the commune ghosts as a means to keep people away from his hidden home. Then came the problem of motive. After taking such great pains to hide from society, what would bring this mad disfigured person up from his dark world?

The French classic *Beauty and the Beast* provided that answer. Love! Could the unbalanced nature of the Phantom be overcome by the love of a woman? Could his heroine—Beauty—be able to overcome the horrible appearance of the Beast to see the true inner beauty that he possessed?

AND. . . The object of the Phantom's affections could not be just a member of the ballet troupe or opera chorus. She would have to be a well known and beloved performer. Now . . . How could he work in the wonderfully dramatic chandelier tragedy?

Going back in his studies of the Opera House history, he found the progression of *Faust.* He found Mlle Carvalho, upon whom he based his Prima Donna, Carlotta; Carlotta's stranglehold on her husband, the manager of the Opera, plus the record of Carlotta having the understudy fired because *her* voice was better than her own. He now had his heroine, Christine Daaé, (pronounced Diea) a protégée, who would rise from a mere understudy to the Phantom's personal Prima Donna! AND . . . If the Opera Company did not comply with his wishes to present her voice to the Paris audience, here was the motive to drop the chandelier!

In staying within his literary history style, he even mentions Mlle Carvalho and his character Carlotta in the same paragraph, with references to the *Théâtre Lyrique,* where *Faust* was first performed. In the introductory paragraphs about Christine, he has Gounod, himself, conducting selections as Christine sings.

The gallant soldier Raoul De Chagny [pronounced Rah-ool Dee Shah-n-yay] provided the Phantom with an antagonist. But Raoul alone was not quite strong enough for such a powerful villain. Enter the Persian! With the Persian, a whole chapter of Leroux's past experiences in Morocco became available.

The opening of the mystery needed something special. Borrowing the name of the favorite performer of Méphistophélès for the period, M. Faure, Leroux had satisfied the public's expectations for an "official police Inspector" such as Doyle's Lestrade and for private "detectives" (such as Doyle's, Sherlock Holmes and Edgar Allen Poe's, C. Auguste Dupin) who would manage to solve the crime while the police stood by baffled.

Leroux now put himself into the story as the narrator. No longer would this be a mystery, but a report of an actual tragic, real-life occurrence. Inserting his massive file of facts, research and documented material into the plot, he presents it as a journalist would successfully giving the reader the proof that "The Opera Ghost really existed . . . "

The world respected the factual details of Leroux's newspaper articles. His ability to capture whole battlefield scenes in just a few paragraphs for his newspaper articles, and his vivid memory, worked much to his credibility in presenting his report of the Opera mystery. It was, however, not a "gimmick" that provides the thrills experienced by his fans for over 75 years, but his exceptionally visual style.

Leroux's remarkable ability to paint with words, gives you the feeling that you are standing alone in an empty theater not quite sure which shadow is a deranged maniac and which shadow is just. . . . .a shadow.

Near the end of 1909 Leroux completed the novel that was to bring him world-wide fame.

Source: Philip J. Riley, "Gaston LeRoux, Faust and the Phantom," in *The Making of "The Phantom of the Opera,"* MagicImage Filmbooks, 1999, pp. 21–29.

Sources

Hogle, Jerrold E., *The Undergrounds of "The Phantom of the Opera,"* Palgrave, 2002, p. 117.

Wolf, Leonard, "Introduction," in *The Essential "Phantom of the Opera,"* edited by Leonard Wolf, Plume, 1996, pp. 2–3.

Further Reading

Johnson, James H., *Listening in Paris: A Cultural History*, University of California Press, 1996.

Focused on the history of silence in the concert hall and opera house, this book gives a good sense of the cultural tendencies of opera goers at the time of the novel.

Perry, George, *The Complete "Phantom of the Opera,"* Henry Holt, 1991.

Though focused on the London musical, this book is filled with information about the novel and about the Paris opera house.

Skinner, Cornelia Otis, *Elegant Wits and Grand Horizontals*, Houghton Mifflin, 1962.

Skinner examines the social life of uppercrust Parisian society during the Belle Époque. These are the people who would have made up the opera audience during the time that this story takes place.

Zizek, Slavoj, "Grimaces of the Real, or When the Phallus Appears," in *October*, Vol. 58, Fall 1991, p. 46.

This analysis examines the correlation in some folk traditions between the size of a man's nose and his masculinity and the implications of this theory on Erik's physical deformity.

The Picture of Dorian Gray

Oscar Wilde

1891

Oscar Wilde's *The Picture of Dorian Gray* was published simultaneously in Philadelphia's *Lippincott's Monthly Magazine* and by Ward, Lock and Company in England, in July, 1890. In England, the novella was condemned by many reviewers as shocking and immoral. Wilde tried to address some of these criticisms as he worked on an expanded version of the story, which was published as a full-length novel in 1891, along with a preface in which Wilde stated his artistic credo.

The novel centers on Dorian Gray, a young man of great beauty. When he meets Lord Henry Wotton, Lord Henry inspires him with a vision of life in which the pursuit of beauty through sensual pleasure is valued above ethical or moral concerns. Another friend of Dorian, the artist Basil Hallward, awakens Dorian's vanity. After admiring a portrait of himself painted by Basil, Dorian declares that he would give his own soul if he could remain eternally young while the portrait grows old. He gets his wish, and the picture shows the gradual disfigurement of his soul as he sinks into a life of degradation and crime.

As a variation on the Faust legend, with echoes of the fall of man and the Adonis myth, and as an examination of the relationship between art and life, *The Picture of Dorian Gray* fascinated readers into the early 2000s and gave rise to many different interpretations.

Author Biography

Irish poet, novelist, and playwright Oscar Fingal O'Flahertie Wills Wilde was born on October 16, 1854, the son of Sir William Wilde, a distinguished doctor, and Jane Francesca Elgee, a poet and journalist. Wilde attended the Portora Royal School at Enniskillen, where he excelled at classics. In 1871, he was awarded the Royal School Scholarship to attend Trinity College in Dublin. He excelled there also, winning the college's Berkeley Gold Medal for Greek and being awarded a Demyship scholarship to Magdalen College in Oxford. At Oxford, Wilde won the Newdigate prize for his poem, "Ravenna," and was awarded a First Class degree in 1878.

After graduation, Wilde moved to London, where he became famous in fashionable and intellectual circles for his witty conversation and outlandish dress. He quickly established himself as one of the leaders of the Aesthetic Movement, and in 1881 he published his first collection of poetry, *Poems*. In January 1882, he began a lecture tour of the United States. On his arrival he famously told customs officers that he had nothing to declare but his genius. During the course of nearly a year, Wilde delivered over 140 lectures on aesthetics.

The following year, Wilde's play *Vera* was produced in New York, and Wilde became engaged to Constance Lloyd, whom he married in 1884. They had two sons, Cyril in 1885 and Vyvyan in 1886. To support his new family, Wilde became editor of *The Woman's World* magazine, from 1887 to 1889.

Wilde then embarked on the most creative period of his life. In 1888, he published a collection of children's stories, *"The Happy Prince" and Other Tales*. In 1890, *The Picture of Dorian Gray*, Wilde's only novel, was published in serial form in an American magazine. The following year it was expanded and published in book form. In 1892, another collection of children's stories, *The House of Pomegranates*, appeared.

Wilde then wrote a series of highly successful plays. The first of these society comedies was *Lady Windermere's Fan* (1892), followed by *A Woman of No Importance* (1893), *An Ideal Husband* (1895), and *The Importance of Being Earnest* (1895), all of which were highly acclaimed by public and critics alike. But *Salomé*, a poetic drama Wilde wrote in French in 1891, was refused a license by the Lord Chamberlain. It was never produced in England in Wilde's lifetime.

In 1895, the series of events that was to lead to Wilde's downfall began. Since 1891, he had been

Oscar Wilde

close friends with Lord Alfred Douglas, and Douglas's father, the Marquis of Queensberry, now accused him of homosexuality. Wilde responded by suing the marquis for criminal libel. The marquis was acquitted, but Wilde was arrested and convicted of gross indecency. He was sentenced to two years hard labor. After he was released, he traveled to France and never returned to England. *The Ballad of Reading Gaol* (1898) was a response to his prison experience. Wilde wandered around Europe, staying with friends, until 1900, when he returned to Paris. He died of meningitis on November 30, 1900.

Plot Summary

Chapters 1–5

The Picture of Dorian Gray begins on an afternoon in London, in the studio of the artist Basil Hallward. Basil discusses his latest portrait, of an extremely handsome young man named Dorian Gray, with Lord Henry Wotton. Basil says he will not exhibit the painting because he has put too much of himself in it. After they go into the garden, Basil explains how captivated he has been by Dorian since he first met him a couple of months earlier. Lord Henry makes some witty, cynical remarks about life,

Media Adaptations

- *The Picture of Dorian Gray* has been adapted to film in the following versions: the version starring George Sanders (Warner, 1945); the version directed by Glenn Jordan (1973); and the BBC version, directed by John Gorrie, with Sir John Gielgud as Lord Henry (1976).

and Basil chides him that he does not really believe what he is saying. Then Basil expands on how Dorian's personality has suggested to him an entirely new manner in art; he sees and thinks differently now and envisions a new school of art, in which soul and body are in perfect harmony.

They return to the house, where Dorian is waiting. Basil puts the finishing touches to his painting as Lord Henry expounds his philosophy of how to live a full life, which is not to be afraid of passion and sensuality as a way to fulfillment of the soul. Dorian is moved by Henry's words, and Henry goes on to speak of the beauty of youth and how it is destroyed by time. When Dorian looks at the finished portrait of himself, he is struck by his own beauty in a way he has never felt before. He feels sad that he will grow old and his beauty will be spoiled. He then says he would give everything, even his own soul, if he could always remain young, and the picture grow old instead.

A month later, Dorian informs Henry that he has fallen in love with a young actress named Sibyl Vane, who plays Shakespearean roles in a tawdry theater in the London back streets. Henry regards this attachment as an interesting psychological phenomenon, and he resolves to study the nature of Dorian's sudden passion. Later, he receives a telegram from Dorian announcing that he is engaged to marry Sibyl.

Sibyl explains to her mother about her love for Dorian, whom she calls Prince Charming. Her mother thinks she is too young to fall in love. James Vane, Sibyl's sixteen-year-old brother, who is about to leave for Australia, is concerned for her welfare. He is suspicious of Prince Charming and

tells his sister that if the man ever wrongs her, he will kill him.

Chapters 6–10

Dorian, Henry, and Basil go to see Sibyl play Juliet in *Romeo and Juliet*. Her performance is awful, and Henry and Basil leave after the second act. After the performance, Sibyl admits to Dorian that she acted poorly. She explains that now she is in love with him, she knows what real love is, and all the dramatic roles she has acted seem unreal. She can no longer believe in them. But Dorian says he only loves her because she is able to bring great art to life, and he does not wish to see her again. When he goes home he notices the picture of himself has changed. There is an expression of cruelty in the smile. He hides the picture behind a screen and resolves to go back to Sibyl, make amends, and marry her.

The following afternoon, Lord Henry brings him the news that Sibyl is dead. Henry makes some cynical remarks about love and encourages Dorian to view Sibyl's death as resembling a scene from a play. Dorian quickly overcomes his grief and vows to enjoy remaining young. He convinces himself he does not care what happens to the picture.

The next morning, Basil reproaches Dorian for his callousness and attributes it to the influence of Lord Henry. Dorian says he can never sit for him again and refuses to allow Basil to look at the picture he painted. Basil wants to exhibit it, but he reluctantly accepts Dorian's decision. Dorian arranges for the picture to be hidden away in an upper room that has not been used for years.

Chapters 11–15

As the years go by, rumors circulate in London about Dorian's lifestyle, but his charming appearance makes it hard for anyone to think ill of him. The picture, however, grows more horrible, as he continually searches for new sensations and frequents disreputable areas of London. People start to distrust him. There are whispers of scandals.

When he is thirty-eight years old, he meets Basil by chance in a London street. He has not seen the artist for a long time. Dorian invites Basil into his house, where Basil confronts him with the stories about how he has ruined so many people's reputations. Scandal follows him everywhere. Basil wonders whether he really knows Dorian and remarks that to find out, he would have to see his soul. Dorian says he will show Basil his soul, and he takes the bemused artist to the room where the picture is stored. He removes the curtain that covers the picture and shows it to Basil, who is horrified. Dorian feels a rush of hatred for the artist and stabs him with a knife, killing him. He goes downstairs to the library and ponders how he can get away with his crime.

The next day he summons Alan Campbell, who used to be his close friend, to his house. Campbell is an expert in chemistry, with a reputation for undertaking unusual experiments. Dorian tells Campbell that he has murdered a man and asks him to destroy the body so that no trace of it remains. Campbell refuses until Dorian threatens to blackmail him over some shameful secret that Dorian knows about him.

That night, after attending a dinner party, Dorian burns Basil's coat and bag. At midnight he goes out and hires a hansom cab.

Chapters 16–19

Dorian is taken to an opium den in a disreputable part of the city. There he encounters Adrian Singleton, one of his former friends who has been disgraced. As he leaves, a woman yells at him, calling him Prince Charming. A sailor hears this and follows Dorian outside. The sailor is James Vane, who accosts Dorian and intends to kill him. But when the still-youthful-looking Dorian points out that whoever deserted Sibyl must be many years older than he, Vane lets him go. But then the woman who called Dorian Prince Charming tells Vane that she first encountered him eighteen years earlier. Vane rushes after Dorian, intending to kill him, but Dorian has vanished.

A week later, Dorian is attending a dinner party when he thinks he sees Vane peering in at the window. He fears for his life and does not go out for three days. Then he joins a shooting-party led by Sir Geoffrey Clouston, the brother of the Duchess of Monmouth. The hunt is called off after Sir Geoffrey accidentally shoots and kills a man. The man turns out to be James Vane.

Dorian now bitterly regrets his life and desires to change. He tries to do good by breaking off a relationship with a working-class girl named Hetty, whom he has been deceiving. But Lord Henry mocks his desire to change, saying he is perfect as he is. Later, tormented by his corrupt life, Dorian takes a knife and slashes the picture. The servants then hear a terrible cry. Dorian is discovered dead, with a knife in his heart, but the picture is as perfect as the day it was painted, and shows Dorian in all his youthful beauty.

Characters

Alan Campbell

Alan Campbell is a former close friend of Dorian Gray. The friendship lasted for eighteen months and ended for unknown reasons. After the split between the two men, Campbell became melancholy and gave up playing music, which had been his delight. After he murders Basil, Gray summons Campbell, who is an expert in chemistry, to dispose of the body. Campbell agrees to do it only after Gray indicates he will blackmail him if he does not cooperate. Campbell later commits suicide by shooting himself in his laboratory.

Lord Fermor

Lord Fermor is the uncle of Lord Henry Wotton. He is a bachelor and former diplomat who devotes himself to what the narrator describes as "the great aristocratic art of doing absolutely nothing." He informs Lord Henry about Dorian Gray's family background.

Dorian Gray

Dorian Gray is twenty years old when the novel begins. He is the grandson of Lord Kelso, and his mother was the beautiful Lady Margaret Devereux. Margaret married a man Lord Kelso did not approve of, and her father arranged for the man to be killed in a duel. Dorian's mother died within a year, and Dorian was raised by his grandfather. When Dorian comes of age at twenty-one, he will inherit enough money to enable him to live comfortably.

Dorian possesses great physical beauty, and the artist Basil Hallward is infatuated with him. When Dorian meets Lord Henry Wotton, he falls under the influence of Henry's new hedonism, in which the goal of immediate sensual pleasure is valued above ethics or morality. Soon after Dorian meets Lord Henry he falls in love with the actress Sibyl Vane but rejects her when she declares that since she has fallen in love with him, she no longer cares for creating art. It is Dorian's callous response to Sibyl's resulting suicide that produces the first change in the portrait that Basil painted of him: a distinctly cruel expression appears on the face. After this, Dorian pursues a life of pleasure in which he courts all manner of sensual enjoyments, searching for beauty in fleeting sensations and objects of art.

But since he does not balance his love of beauty with a sense of morality, he sinks into selfish behavior. He leads many of his friends to ruin or disgrace, and as the years go by, rumors circulate in

London about his objectionable behavior, and people start to shun him. In his physical appearance, however, he remains as youthful as the day the portrait was painted. The degradation of his soul is registered only in the picture.

Dorian sinks to his lowest point when he murders his friend Basil, who has made the mistake of inquiring too closely into the nature of his activities. Dorian effectively covers up his crime, and when James Vane, who has been trying to kill him, is killed in a hunting accident, it appears that Dorian is safe. But he is weighed down by his dissolute life and desires to change it, a goal for which he receives no encouragement from his friend Lord Henry. Eventually, driven to desperation, Dorian slashes the picture on which his sins are visible, but in a mysterious act of transference, Dorian himself dies of a knife wound through his heart, and the picture is restored to its original condition.

Basil Hallward

Basil Hallward is an artist who paints the picture of Dorian Gray. He is completely captivated by the beautiful Dorian, whom he has known for two months, and paints him in many different guises. He secretly worships Dorian and later confesses this adoration to him. He believes that Dorian has inspired him to create the best work of his life. Through Dorian he has discovered a new style of painting and hopes it will be the beginning of a new school that will combine the best of the Greek and Romantic spirit, presenting a harmony of spirit and passion, body and soul. Basil does not intend to exhibit the painting because he says he has put too much of himself into it. Instead, he presents it to Dorian.

Unlike his friend Lord Henry, whose cynicism he regards as a mere pose, Basil does not take an amoral approach to life. He tries to console Dorian after the death of Sibyl Vane and is shocked by the callousness of his friend. He attributes Dorian's attitude to the bad influence of Lord Henry.

After this exchange, Basil and Dorian meet seldom. Eighteen years after their first meeting, they run into each other by chance. Basil demands to know from Dorian the truth regarding the many rumors about Dorian's bad behavior. Dorian resents his criticism. He decides to show Basil the real state of his soul, which is revealed in the picture. Basil only has time to express his horror at the alteration in the picture before Dorian stabs him to death with a knife. Since Basil had been due to depart for Paris that same night and planned to remain there for six months, he is not missed for some time.

Adrian Singleton

Adrian Singleton is a former friend of Gray's. Dorian encounters him again at the opium den, and it is clear that Singleton has been disgraced as a result of his association with Dorian. None of his friends will speak to him, and he takes refuge in an opium addiction.

James Vane

James Vane is the sixteen-year-old brother of Sibyl Vane. He becomes a sailor, but not before he has vowed that if Sibyl's aristocratic admirer, whom he knows only by the name of Prince Charming, ever wrongs her, he will kill him. Eighteen years later, he spots Dorian Gray in an opium den, follows him out to the street, and is ready to kill him, but Dorian convinces him that he has got the wrong man. Vane soon realizes his mistake, and eventually tracks Dorian down, but he is accidentally shot and killed when he intrudes on a hunting expedition.

Mrs. Vane

Mrs. Vane is the mother of Sibyl and James Vane. Like her daughter, she is an actress, but she is a tired woman who has had a hard life. The family lives in poverty because Mrs. Vane was not married to the father of her children, and he died without making provision for them.

Sibyl Vane

Sibyl Vane is a seventeen-year-old girl who excels as an actress. She performs many of the great Shakespearean roles in a tawdry theater in the back streets of London. Dorian Gray falls in love with her, and she with him. But he rejects her after she performs badly, and she is so distressed by his rejection she commits suicide.

Lord Henry Wotton

Lord Henry Wotton, an aristocratic man of thirty, is a friend of Basil Hallward. He has a languid manner and smokes cigarettes constantly. He is married, but later his wife runs away with another man. When he meets Dorian Gray, he makes such an impression on the younger man that Dorian tries to put into practice the kind of life that he thinks Lord Henry espouses. Lord Henry, however, although he advocates the pursuit of sensual experience for its own sake, tries to remain a spectator of life. Although he and Dorian become friends, he watches Dorian's life as if he is observing a psychological experiment conducted by himself. He is amoral and cynical in his attitudes and expresses no sympathy after the death of Sibyl

Vane or the disappearance of Basil. Lord Henry likes to apply his keen intelligence to making epigrams at dinner parties or in conversation with Basil and Dorian. He seems to prefer coming up with witty sayings that reverse conventional notions or morality than getting involved in the realities of life. Basil sometimes says that Lord Henry does not really believe a word he says. Late in the novel, Lord Henry does admit that he would like to be young again, but typically, he immediately takes refuge in a witticism that effectively disguises his real feelings: "To get back my youth I would do anything in the world, except take exercise, get up early, or be respectable."

Themes

Homoerotic Love

Although the theme of homoerotic love is never stated explicitly (and could not be, given the conventions of the day), it may be present in Basil's feelings for Dorian. He tells Lord Henry that he cannot be happy if he does not see Dorian every day. He is upset when Dorian becomes engaged to Sibyl. Later, he confesses to Dorian that from the first moment they met, he worshipped him. He says, "I grew jealous of every one to whom you spoke. I wanted to have you all to myself. I was only happy when I was with you." He is completely dominated by his feelings for the younger man, which also transfigure his perception of the entire world. Everything becomes wonderful to him because of Dorian. Basil presents what may be homoerotic attraction in different terms, as the lure of an aesthetic ideal. He worships Dorian because the beautiful young man allows him to fulfill his highest ideals as an artist. He tells Lord Henry that Dorian is to him "simply a motive in art."

The Indulgence of the Senses

Dorian attempts to live according to the view of life presented to him by Lord Henry. Lord Henry believes that nothing is gained by self-denial. He tells Dorian that people should not be afraid of their own desires and impulses, because in them lie the seeds of fulfillment and joy. His credo is "to cure the soul by means of the senses, and the senses by means of the soul." To live a full life, it is necessary to savor with the senses every passing moment. It is better to experience everything the world has to offer than to spend time worrying about ethics or morals. It is better to seek beauty, in the

Topics for Further Study

- Who is most to blame for the tragedy of Dorian Gray—Lord Henry, Basil Hallward, or Dorian himself?

- Research how attitudes toward homosexuality have changed over the last hundred years. How and why did the changes occur? What are the issues facing the United States today regarding homosexuality?

- What is the relationship between art and morality? Should art be moral? Should it serve some social good? Should the government have the right to censure works of art that it finds morally objectionable?

- Imagine that you are Lord Henry Wotton and write three epigrams of your own. Remember that an epigram is a short, witty saying that works by inverting conventional expectations and sometimes using a paradox to create a surprise effect.

contemplation of art and beautiful objects, than to tie up the mind in intellectual concerns and with education. Lord Henry calls this philosophy a "new Hedonism." (Hedonism is defined as pleasure-seeking as a way of life.)

The novel presents at least two different ways of interpreting this theme. Since Dorian, who attempts to follow Lord Henry's advice, ends up destroying many people's lives, committing murder and suicide, and also corrupting his own soul, there is either something intrinsically wrong with Lord Henry's new Hedonism, or Dorian has failed to understand it or erred in the way he has put it into practice.

Both views are possible. The novel can be read in moralistic terms as a condemnation of Dorian's self-indulgent life. In a letter to the *Daily Chronicle* on June 30, 1890 (quoted in *The Artist as Critic*), Wilde himself sought to counter charges that the book was immoral and stated that it did have a moral: "All excess, as well as all renunciation, brings its own punishment." Wilde refers not only to Dorian but also to Basil and Lord Henry. Basil (said Wilde) worships physical beauty too much and creates an overweening vanity in Dorian, whereas Lord Henry seeks to be merely a spectator in life and is even more wounded by that stance than are those, like Dorian, who enter into life with more vigor. However, Wilde's explanation is not in keeping with the preface to the novel, which he added after the negative reviews were published. The preface states in a number of different epigrammatic ways that art should have nothing to do with morality.

The second possible interpretation is that Dorian fails to understand Lord Henry's credo. Indeed, it seems that Lord Henry himself does not live according to it either. As Wilde stated, he remains largely a spectator in life. His manner is languid, and he cultivates an ironic detachment from everything, even as he advocates passionate involvement. Lord Henry seems to do very little during the course of the novel other than exert psychological dominance over Dorian and attend dinner parties for the sole purpose of shocking people with his epigrams. But near the end he confides in Dorian: "I have sorrows, Dorian, of my own, that even you know nothing of."

It seems that Lord Henry's ideal is to take exquisite pleasure in the experience of the senses, to be wide awake sensually in every single moment of existence, while at the same time remaining undisturbed, keeping an evenness of mind. This is a paradox, since the proclaimed ideal is to be simultaneously involved and uninvolved in life. Lord Henry's error is to cultivate one ideal—detachment—at the expense of the other. Dorian makes the opposite mistake. Neither is able to fulfill the theoretical goal of the new Hedonism.

Style

Epigram

An epigram is a short, witty statement in prose or verse. Wilde is famous for his epigrams, and the novel furnishes many examples, almost all of them uttered by Lord Henry Wotton. "A man cannot be too careful in the choice of his enemies," he tells his friend Basil. The humorous effect is gained by a reversal of the expected meaning, since it would be natural to expect to hear "friends" instead of "enemies." The reversal creates a comic surprise. Lord Henry uses the same reversal of expectations when he says, "The only way to get rid of a temptation is to yield to it." This can also be described as a paradox, which is a statement that appears to be contradictory or absurd but on examination may prove to

be true. Wilde's preface to the novel also contains many epigrams, many of which show his eagerness to undermine conventional ideas, as in "No artist has ethical sympathies. An ethical sympathy in an artist is an unpardonable mannerism of style."

Myth

Underlying the narrative are suggestions of several myths, including the fall of man as described in Genesis. Dorian, as an innocent, beautiful young man, newly created (in a sense) by Basil Hallward, the artist/God, is the equivalent of Adam in the Garden of Eden before the Fall. Lord Henry Wotton plays the role of Satan. He tempts Dorian with the promise of a fuller, richer life, if he will only follow his, Henry's, credo. Dorian has too much pride and egoism to resist the temptation, and so he falls.

There is also an allusion to the medieval legend of Faust. Faust is a man who sells his soul to the devil in exchange for knowledge and power, just as Dorian makes a bargain to keep his eternal youth even if it means the loss of his soul.

Another allusion is to the classical myth of Narcissus, who falls in love with himself after seeing his reflection in a pool. When Lord Henry first sees the picture he compares Dorian to Narcissus. This gives a clue to the vanity inherent in Dorian's nature. Lord Henry may tempt him, but in a sense he is only drawing out the qualities that are already present in Dorian.

Historical Context

Aestheticism and Decadence

Aestheticism was a literary movement in late nineteenth-century France and Britain. It was a reaction to the notion that all art should have a utilitarian or social value. According to the Aesthetic Movement, art justifies its own existence by expressing and embodying beauty. The slogan of the movement was "art for art's sake," and it contrasted the perfection possible through art with what it regarded as the imperfections of nature and of real life. The artist should not concern himself with political or social issues.

In France, Aestheticism was associated with the work of Charles Baudelaire, Gustave Flaubert, and Stéphane Mallarmé. In England, its chief theorist was Walter Pater (1839–1894), who was a professor of classics at Oxford University. In contrast to the usual Victorian emphasis on work and

Compare
&
Contrast

- **1890s:** Male homosexuality is a crime in England, punishable by imprisonment.

  Today: Homosexuality is no longer a crime. In law, homosexual people are treated the same as everyone else. However, many people holding conservative and religious views based on the Bible still regard homosexuality as a sin.

- **1890s:** Britain is the foremost power in the world but faces increasing rivalry from the growing industrial and military strength of Germany.

  Today: Britain and Germany, having fought against each other in two world wars, are now allies within the European Community and NATO. Britain is no longer the leading power in the world.

- **1890s:** Class divisions are emphatic in Britain, and there is a wide contrast in dress, manners, and way of life between those who are comfortably off and those who are poor. Families are large. Only working class women take employment outside the home. University education is not available for women of any class or for the working classes.

  Today: Britain is a more egalitarian society than at any time in its history. The influence of mass culture, through television, films, and advertising, has tended to erode differences between classes in dress and manners. Women of all classes now make up a large percentage of the workforce, and higher education is open to all.

---

social responsibility, Pater emphasized the fleeting nature of life and argued that the most important thing was to relish the exquisite sensations life brings, especially those stimulated by a work of art. The aim was to be fully present and to live vividly in each passing moment. As Pater put it in the "Conclusion" to his work *Studies in the History of the Renaissance* (1873), which is in effect a manifesto of the Aesthetic Movement in England, "To burn always with this hard, gemlike flame, to maintain this ecstasy, is success in life." This is in complete opposition to the prevailing Victorian mentality, with its emphasis on hard work, moral earnestness, and material success.

Wilde was an admirer of Pater, and it was Wilde who later became the representative figure of Aestheticism. Pater's influence on *The Picture of Dorian Gray* was profound. When Dorian adopts Lord Henry's belief that the aim of the new Hedonism "was to be experience itself, and not the fruits of experience" he is virtually quoting Pater's "Conclusion," in which he writes, "Not the fruit of experience, but experience itself, is the end."

Pater was a key figure in the emergence of the later movement in England and France known as Decadence. This movement flourished in the last two decades of the nineteenth century, a period also known as fin de siècle (end of the century). Decadent writers believed that Western civilization was in a condition of decay, and they attacked the accepted moral and ethical standards of the day. The theory of Decadence was that all "natural" forms and behaviors were inherently flawed; therefore, highly artificial, "unnatural" forms and styles were to be cultivated, in life as well as art. Many Decadent writers therefore experimented with lifestyles that involved drugs and depravity (just as Dorian does in *The Picture of Dorian Gray*).

One influential work of the Decadent movement was *À Rebours* (*Against the Grain*), a novel by French writer, J. K. Huysmans, published in 1884. The protagonist is estranged from Parisian society and continually seeks out strange and new experiences. It is generally accepted that *À Rebours* is the novel that Lord Henry sends to Dorian Gray and which fascinates and grips Dorian for years.

Another example of Decadent literature is Wilde's play *Salomé*, with its lurid subject and imagery of blood, sex, and death. In addition to Wilde, Decadence in England was associated with the poets Algernon Swinburne and Ernest Dowson, and the painter, Aubrey Beardsley.

1945 film rendition of Oscar Wilde's The Picture of Dorian Gray, *with Hurd Hatfield (left) as Dorian Gray and Lowell Gilmore as Basil Howard*

Critical Overview

When first published in England, *The Picture of Dorian Gray* met with a storm of negative reviews, many of which attacked the book in virulent terms for its alleged immorality. The *Daily Chronicle*, for example, assailed its "effeminate frivolity, its studied insincerity, its theatrical cynicism, its tawdry mysticism, its flippant philosophisings and the contaminating trail of garish vulgarity" (quoted in Norbert Kohl's *Oscar Wilde: The Works of a Conformist Rebel*). The anonymous critic for the *St. James's*

Gazette affected a manner of even greater disgust when he wrote, "not wishing to offend the nostrils of decent persons, we do not propose to analyse [the novel] ... that would be to advertise the developments of an esoteric prurience" (quoted in Michael Patrick Gillespie's "*The Picture of Dorian Gray*: What the World Thinks Me"). This critic even ventured the opinion that he would be pleased to see Wilde or his publishers prosecuted for publishing the novel.

In letters to the editor of the *St. James's Gazette*, Wilde defended himself against such charges. He insisted that *The Picture of Dorian*

Gray had a very clear moral and that his main problem in writing the book had been to keep the obvious moral from subverting the artistic effect.

Although not all early reviews were unfavorable, the negative impression created by those who denounced the book affected how people responded to it for decades. Passages from the novel were read in court by the prosecution during Wilde's trial for homosexuality in 1895. The habit of interpreting the novel, and other works by Wilde, in the context of his life dominated early scholarship about Wilde. Some twentieth-century and twenty-first-century critics continued to use biographical details to shed light on *The Picture of Dorian Gray*; others examined it in relation to the cultural context in which it was written or used archetypal criticism, in which the novel was analyzed in terms of myths and legends such as the Faust story. Some critics interpreted the novel by examining issues of sexual orientation.

Criticism

Bryan Aubrey

Aubrey holds a Ph.D. in English and has published many articles on nineteenth-century literature. In this essay, Aubrey discusses how the three main characters in The Picture of Dorian Gray *represent in different ways the relationship between art and life, contemplation and action, beauty and ethics.*

The Picture of Dorian Gray presents three intriguing characters, all of whom represent in different ways the relationship between art and life, contemplation and action, beauty and ethics. But neither Lord Henry Wotton nor Basil Hallward nor Dorian Gray embodies the ideal to which each aspires, and they all fail catastrophically in one way or another. *The Picture of Dorian Gray* is not a novel for the optimist.

Lord Henry is often pilloried by critics as a cynic who manipulates Dorian into doing the things that he advocates but is too withdrawn and too frightened to do himself. In this view, Henry is a tired man who wants to live vicariously through a younger, more beautiful specimen who has the ability (or so Lord Henry supposes) to experience life as Lord Henry believes it ought to be experienced.

No doubt all this is true. But Lord Henry certainly has his appeal, since he is the chief vehicle in the novel for Wilde's dazzling epigrammatic wit, and his aesthetic ideal needs to be taken seriously. What, then, does Lord Henry stand for? A clue to

> " In his attempt, following Lord Henry's dictum, 'to cure the soul by means of the senses, and the senses by means of the soul,' Dorian succeeds only in satiating the one and corrupting the other."

his governing aesthetic can be found in the opening scene of the novel, which takes place in Basil's studio. The door of the studio is open, and the rich sights, sounds, and smells of the adjoining garden, as the light summer wind blows, are vividly described. Henry is characteristically taking it easy by lying on the divan, but he is aware of all the sensory life going on around him—the heavy scent of the lilac, the almost unbearable beauty of the laburnum blossoms, the "sullen murmur" of the bees. Just as importantly, he is aware of the shadows cast on the curtains by the flight of birds, which reminds him of Japanese artists, who "through the medium of an art that is necessarily immobile, seek to convey the sense of swiftness and motion."

This passage suggests Lord Henry's ideal, which is to cultivate an intensity of experience whilst paradoxically remaining undisturbed and untroubled by it. This ideal is fully realized through the contemplation of art, which permits the observer the privilege of being at once involved and uninvolved in the experience. It is in this sense that art is superior to life, as Wilde so often claimed, and this is what Henry is driving at when he instructs the malleable mind of Dorian on how to react to the suicide of Sibyl. He must view it, says Lord Henry, from the perspective of art, as a scene from some Jacobean tragedy. What he means is that tragic drama has the power to evoke in the spectator a full and sympathetic response but one that does not engulf him or her in actual grief. Lord Henry is here a spokesman for the position Wilde staked out in his essay, "The Critic as Artist":

> Art does not hurt us. The tears that we shed at a play are a type of the exquisite sterile emotions that it is the function of Art to awaken. We weep, but we are not wounded. We grieve, but our grief is not bitter.

In this view, art shields people from the harshness of actual existence. It is to be preferred to life

What Do I Read Next?

- *The Importance of Being Earnest* (1895; first published, 1899) was the last of Wilde's four stage comedies and is generally regarded as his masterpiece. It sparkles with that unique Wildean wit. Wilde's aim in writing it was to treat the trivial things in life seriously and the serious things with triviality.

- Richard Ellmann's biography *Oscar Wilde* (1987) is indispensable for the study of Wilde's life. Ellmann presents Wilde as the tragic hero of his own life.

- *Dorian: [An Imitation]* (2004), by British novelist Will Self, is a retelling of *The Picture of Dorian Gray* set in the last two decades of the twentieth century. All the same characters appear. Henry Wotton is a gay heroin addict, "Baz" Hallward is a video artist, and the narcissistic Dorian Gray is a seducer of both men and women. By 1997, all three are HIV-positive, but Dorian shows no sign of illness.

- *Oscar Wilde: Myths, Miracles and Imitations* (1996), by John Stokes, shows how Wilde played a vital part in the development of modern culture. Stokes examines diaries, letters, dramatizations of Wilde's plays, and impersonations of the man himself, and discusses Wilde's relationship to fin-de-siècle and twentieth century ideas.

---

because, as Wilde writes earlier in the same essay, life, unlike art, lacks form:

> Its catastrophes happen in the wrong way and to the wrong people. There is a grotesque horror about its comedies, and its tragedies seem to culminate in farce. One is always wounded when one approaches it.

Dorian is convinced by Henry's argument. Changing his way of responding to Sibyl's death, he recovers his equanimity (or so he thinks). Of course, Dorian's fatal mistake, according to Lord Henry's philosophy, is to get his emotions tied up with Sibyl in the first place, because that has inflicted a wound on the invisible level of life (the level of soul, or conscience, as reflected in the changing picture) that extracts a bitter price further down the road.

It is to avoid wounds such as these that Wilde argues, in "The Critic as Artist," for the superiority of contemplation over action, being (or more precisely, becoming) over doing. And this is why art, he says, can have nothing to do with ethics, since ethics applies only to the sphere of action. This is why Lord Henry appears to withdraw from life and seek perfection only in art.

And yet there is another side to Lord Henry's philosophy. In contrast to the inward impulse is the push outward, the desire for the sensory world. He advocates a life of passionate personal experience, to be enjoyed most fully in youth, while the senses are at their sharpest. He will have nothing of self-denial. As he tells Dorian, "Every impulse that we strive to strangle broods in the mind and poisons us." Henry's "new Hedonism," in which novel sensations are sought in order to keep the flame of life from going out in the dullness of habit and routine, demands the courage to yield to temptation (another Wildean paradox). "Resist it," he explains to Dorian, "and your soul grows sick with longing for the things it has forbidden to itself, with desire for what its monstrous laws have made monstrous and unlawful."

To remain a spectator of life and at the same time to fulfill every desire of one's sensual nature is a paradox; it suggests the co-existence of opposite values. It is the art of feeling life without feeling it, the art of touching whilst remaining untouched. Paradoxes such as these lead often to the sphere of mysticism. Indeed, the book that Lord Henry gives Dorian, and which fascinates and influences him so deeply, sometimes seems to him like a work of mystical philosophy. But neither Wilde nor any of his characters were mystics. It is the concrete material form, shaped into beauty, which holds their attention. As Wilde put it, attributing the thought to Walter Pater, in "The Critic as Artist": "Who . . . would exchange the curve of a single rose-leaf for that formless intangible Being which Plato raises so high?"

If in his personal life, as opposed to what he advises Dorian, Henry embraces the first rather than the second part of the paradox—detachment rather than involvement—his protégé Dorian leans to the other side. Totally under Lord Henry's spell, this refined young man with high ideals adopts his mentor's words to the best of his ability. He tells Basil that he understands what Henry says about art and the "artistic temperament," and he quotes Henry approvingly that "To become the spectator of one's own life . . . is to escape the suffering of life." And even though Dorian has few original thoughts in his head, he still manages to think in lofty terms about the new Hedonism leading to the birth of a new spirituality, dominated by an instinct for beauty.

But Dorian does not succeed in living the paradox. More involved in the world than Lord Henry and giving full rein to his love of beauty and his quest for novel sensations, he allows himself to become a poisonous influence on those around him. He becomes indifferent to the effects of his actions, which not only destroy others (in ways never specified) but also leave him fatally marred, despite the illusion—for that, ultimately is what it is—generated by his unchanging youthful, beautiful appearance. Detached contemplation becomes callous disregard. In his attempt, following Lord Henry's dictum, "to cure the soul by means of the senses, and the senses by means of the soul," Dorian succeeds only in satiating the one and corrupting the other. In terms of the Art/Life dichotomy, he deserts the calm serenity of art in favor of the sordidness of life. This becomes crystal clear as Dorian takes the hansom cab to the opium den the day after he murders Basil:

> Ugliness that had once been hateful to him because it made things real, became dear to him now for that very reason. Ugliness was the one reality. The coarse brawl, the loathsome den, the crude violence of disordered life, the very vileness of thief and outcast, were more vivid, in their intense actuality of impression, than all the gracious shapes of Art, the dreamy shadows of Song.

The third main character in the novel, Basil Hallward, can also be analyzed in terms of this dichotomy between art and life, detachment and involvement. He confesses to Dorian in chapter 9 that when he first began to paint portraits of him, he managed to retain the proper artistic distance from his subject: "it had all been what art should be, unconscious, ideal, and remote." But then when he painted Dorian not in classical costume but as himself, his personal feelings entered into the painting; he revealed too much of himself in it. This is why he initially decides he cannot exhibit the painting.

When Basil allows himself to become infatuated with Dorian, he commits the same error (from Lord Henry's perspective, that is) that Dorian does with Sibyl Vane. He allows himself to be drawn out of the sphere of Art into that of Life, and no good results from it. As Dorian later reproaches him, "You met me, flattered me, and taught me to be vain of my good looks." Basil, then, must bear his share of responsibility for encouraging Dorian on the path that proves so destructive for him as well as others. However, Basil, unlike Lord Henry and Dorian, does not divorce his principles as an artist from his moral and ethical awareness. This is what makes him the most sensible, and perhaps also the least interesting, of the three main characters. His is the voice of conscience that speaks to Dorian when the younger man is intent on ignoring his own conscience. Basil is shocked by Dorian's callous demeanor after Sibyl Vane's death, and his moral concern about Dorian's dissolute life is what precipitates Basil's murder, since Dorian cannot bear to listen to Basil's insistence that Dorian should pray for repentance.

It is in this moment, through the agency of Basil, that a thematic framework quite different from the concerns of art and life, contemplation and action, beauty and ethics, enters the novel. This is the Christian scheme of sin, followed by repentance and the possibility of redemption. When Dorian finally does feel remorse and desires to change his life, he moves into a different sphere than Lord Henry, who refuses to take seriously anything Dorian says on that subject. Lord Henry, apparently ignorant of the course that Dorian's life has taken, believes him still to be as perfect as his handsome appearance suggests. This failure of Lord Henry to respond to the events of the real world is presented in extreme form when Dorian all but confesses to the murder of Basil; Lord Henry's response is prompted by his aesthetics, rather than any moral or practical concern. He says that Dorian does not have the vulgarity to commit a murder. This last glance at Lord Henry may be Wilde's way of demonstrating that Lord Henry's detachment involves him in illusions no less damaging than those which Dorian has for long entertained about his own life. The worship of art and beauty may have its place, but it proves to be an inadequate guide through the troubled maze of real human experience.

Source: Bryan Aubrey, Critical Essay on *The Picture of Dorian Gray*, in *Novels for Students*, Thomson Gale, 2005.

> " Wilde posited quite a simple plot. A remarkably attractive twenty-year-old, upper-class Englishman faces his future, and after the passage of time—twelve years in the short *Lippincott* version, eighteen years in the longer version published in book form the following year—concludes his development in abrupt and destructive fashion."

Robert Boyle

In the following excerpt, Boyle suggests that "Each chapter has a calculated task in the carefully planned whole."

. . . In the following two years he produced several reviews, essays, and lectures, and he and his wife produced two children, Cyril on 5 June 1885 and Vyvyan on 3 November 1886. In 1886 Wilde met a young Canadian, Robert Ross, and according to fairly well-accepted opinion began his involvement in the disordered, destructive homosexual life-style so luridly suggested in *The Picture of Dorian Gray* (1891) and catalogued in his sensational trials. In April 1887 Wilde became the editor of *The Lady's World* magazine. He stated that his aim was to provide "for the expression of women's opinions on all subjects of literature, art, and modern life" and changed the name to *The Woman's World*.

In 1887 some of his best short stories appeared, notably *"Lord Arthur Savile's Crime"* in the 11, 18, and 25 May issues of *Court and Society Review*. In this story the moral complications resulting from efforts to conform to the demands of a stagnant and corrupt society are grimly and satirically understated, with the spooky, suprarational involvement of a "Professional Cheiromantist." *The Picture of Dorian Gray* would develop a similar suprarational situation with far deeper and more complex personal and social effects. In 1888 his

fairy tales *The Happy Prince and Other Tales* and *"The Young King,"* revealing another approach to moral situations and human relationships, interested and delighted adults as well as children—and puzzled some, as they still do.

In 1889 the first of his critical essays, so deeply influential for some great artists of the twentieth century, appeared. All his most important critical essays were published on 2 May 1891 under the title *Intentions*. This collection forms one of the profoundest, healthiest, and most graceful nineteenth-century investigations into the nature of literary art. Victorian criticism subjected literature to the demands of morality and utility; Matthew Arnold was the best, and thus the worst, of such critics. Wilde strove to dislodge that burden.

Wilde was dismissed as editor of *The Woman's World* in July 1889; the same month saw the appearance of *"The Portrait of Mr. W. H.,"* a brilliant commentary on Shakespeare's sonnets. In this story Wilde created a character so vivid and alive that Shakespeare scholars, a solemn crew, still feel obliged to devote a footnote or two to killing him off—Willie Hughes. Wilde perceptively satirizes Matthew Arnold's "touchstone" approach to literature in developing from sonnet twenty a theory about Hughes. Cyril Graham, the central character in Wilde's story, which skillfully affects a documentary realism, intuits "on a kind of spiritual and artistic sense" that Willie was the sonnets' "Onlie Begetter," the "Mr. W. H." of the title page of Shakespeare's work. Many kinds of artistic trickery in poetry and in painting complicate the plot. There is no more detailed, more illuminating, and perhaps more eerily degenerate analysis of those glorious sonnets in all of the vast critical writing dealing with them.

"The Portrait of Mr. W. H.," usually classified with Wilde's critical essays, could equally well be approached as a story or novella. Its structure, involving a beautiful youth (Willie Hughes), two older men (Shakespeare and the Rival Poet), and a homosexual ambience (slightly disturbed by an interfering Dark Lady) foreshadows Wilde's only novel. The revised "Mr. W. H." of 1893 in turn shows a considerable influence of *The Picture of Dorian Gray* in its stressing of an intellectual nobility in the love of man for boy, in adverting to the influence of the unconscious, and in the development of a Platonic idealism in the fruitful "marriage of true minds."

The first version of *The Picture of Dorian Gray* appeared in July 1890 in *Lippincott's Monthly Magazine*. In his essays, Wilde had preached Pater's doctrine with glib grace and triumphant success. In his novel, that eloquent doctrine, mixing with human realities, ran into considerable trouble.

Wilde posited quite a simple plot. A remarkably attractive twenty-year-old, upper-class Englishman faces his future, and after the passage of time—twelve years in the short *Lippincott* version, eighteen years in the longer version published in book form the following year—concludes his development in abrupt and destructive fashion.

The *Lippincott* version has only three main characters; three others appear briefly. The novel begins with the artist Basil Hallward painting a portrait of Dorian; Lord Henry Wotton, an elegant man-about-town, a "Prince of Paradox," comes in to meet the subject of the picture. Basil fears that he is putting too much of his intense love for the young man into the painting; Lord Henry sees in the youth an opportunity to observe the higher life, the welcoming of every sensation, the fullest development of soul and sense in a beautiful human being.

The homosexual undertones of Wilde's development of his plot roused a critical eruption, mostly of indignation and vilification. The plot was reputedly (but probably not actually) based on an experience Wilde had had in the studio of Basil Ward, an artist friend, where Wilde expressed regret that a beautiful young man in one of Ward's paintings should ever grow old. (Another version places the incident in the studio of a woman painter who painted Wilde's portrait.) In the Gothic tone of his mother's granduncle, Charles Maturin—author of the model of all Gothic novels, *Melmoth the Wanderer*—Wilde introduces a painting which, after the subject of the painting offers his soul for the miracle, takes on the signs of age and moral decay while its lovely, criminal original remains unchanged.

The main characters, according to Wilde's later account, are three aspects of Wilde himself. Hallward is the suffering and sacrificed artist; Dorian is the youthful aesthete-about-town; Lord Henry is the mature philosopher and wit. Their tortuous and fascinating wanderings in obscure psychological depths have kept readers, viewers of movies, psychiatrists, and critics mildly agog for a hundred years—and will no doubt continue to do so, in the company of Hamlet, Balzac's *Peau de Chagrin*, Mary Shelley's *Frankenstein*, Edgar Allan Poe's Usher family, Bram Stoker's *Dracula*, and James Joyce's Stephen Dedalus.

Turning the *Lippincott* version of the novel into a book required more bulk, better balance, and tighter unity. Wilde added six chapters and other characters, increased the scope and depth of the

second half (Dorian's mature experience, James Vane's return), and toned down the homosexual implications of the first version. He also added a preface, to meet some of the charges made against the first version and to set forth some of the Paterian bases for the doctrine involved.

The preface upholds Pater's view of art as a reflecting function independent of the strictures of conventional morality. The surface of art, that smooth and lovely skin that all can see, conceals human experience; the symbol, the hidden meaning, of art expresses what the partaker of art finds beneath the surface if he dares to penetrate it—his own face confronting him. Those who rage and howl, like the critics of Wilde's novel, suffer from seeing their own savage faces reflected in the artist's creation. For the artist morality is of interest only as subject matter; ethics should not constrict his scope, nor does he concern himself with encouraging or discouraging moral behavior. The work of art is totally useless; it finds its goal within itself, a beautiful creation reflecting all things human. It should be contemplated for itself, and aims at no other use. Thus the critics who condemn it as having evil effects should look inside themselves for the causes of those effects, not in the work.

In his arrangement of the twenty chapters of his book, Wilde devotes ten chapters to the twenty-year-old Dorian, one remarkable bridge chapter to the eighteen following years, and nine chapters to Dorian at the age of thirty-eight. The ten chapters of the first section are divided into three groups. Chapters 1 through 3 establish the relationships among the three central characters. Chapters 4 through 7 set forth the effect of Sibyl Vane on the three men. Chapters 8 through 10 deal with the portrait—the change in it, the painter's attitude, the hiding of the picture.

Chapter 11 carries the reader by a most effective narrative device over eighteen years of Dorian's sybaritic life. Chapters 12 through 14 deal with Basil's murder, chapters 15 through 18 with James Vane's return. Chapter 19 echoes, in the talk of Henry and Dorian, the Paterian idealism of the early chapters, now with a sinister tonality. In the final chapter, Dorian kills his conscience.

Each chapter has a calculated task in the carefully planned whole. Chapter 1 sets forth, in the conversation of Basil Hallward and Lord Henry, their views on the aim of the artist, on the effect on the artist of his work of art, and on the danger for a young man of Henry's teaching of the value of the fullest possible self-development. Henry preaches "a new Hedonism" in which the doctrine of Pater is central.

In his *Studies in the History of the Renaissance* (1873), Pater urged response to all sensations, intense concern for keeping always burning the "hard gem-like flame" of self-fulfillment. Lord Henry's advice to Dorian in chapter 2 echoes Pater: "'Yes,' continued Lord Henry, 'that is one of the great secrets of life—to cure the soul by means of the senses, and the senses by means of the soul.'" The mature Dorian of chapter 16 finds those words ringing in his ears, continuously repeats them with savage intensity as if they were a talismanic formula, and desperately wonders whether or not his senses could, after a life of total self-indulgence, cure his sick soul.

In chapter 2 the twenty-year-old Dorian finds Henry's words a clarion call to a brave new world. An apprehensive Basil moves to destroy the picture, but Dorian stops him. At the end of the chapter, Dorian leaves Basil to join Lord Henry.

Chapter 3, the first of the new chapters added to the *Lippincott* version, develops Henry's growing control of both Dorian and Basil. He preaches Plato's reality, the intellectually perfect form which gives reality to shadows. Thus style, the surface, is of prime importance to every artist—to Michaelangelo in stone, to Shakespeare in sonnets. So Henry, as an artist, in living aims to dominate and fashion Dorian. Echoing the attacks on the first version of the novel, Wilde introduces the proper Sir Thomas, who condemns with "tight lips" Henry's Paterian advocacy of freedom from conventional moral restraints. Henry defends his idea, and the narrator describes Henry's method (which is also Wilde's) of using fancy and language in his campaign to repel mere facts: "He played with the idea, and grew willful; tossed it into the air and transformed it; let it escape and recaptured it; made it iridescent with fancy, and winged it with paradox. The praise of folly, as he went on, soared into a philosophy, and Philosophy herself became young, and catching the mad music of Pleasure, wearing, one might fancy, her wine-stained robe and wreath of ivy, danced like a Bacchante over the hills of life, and mocked the slow Silenus for being sober. Facts fled before her like frightened forest things. Her white feet trod the huge press at which wise Omar sits, till the seething grape-juice rose round her bare limbs in waves of purple bubbles, or crawled in red foam over the vat's black, dripping, sloping sides." Again, and more definitely, Dorian deserts Basil to follow Henry.

In chapter 4, Dorian has acquired "a passion for sensations." He has "collected" Sibyl Vane, who resembles Wilde's wife Constance (as Wilde described his fiancée in a letter to Lillie Langtry in

December 1883). Sibyl, Dorian thinks, escapes time; she is full of mystery, sacred. She is all great heroines, never an individual. Dorian seems to have persuaded himself that by joining her he, too, will exist in the world of art, the world created by Shakespeare. She seems divine to him, since she will lift him out of the crass world where imagination must be subject to animal necessities. Henry attempts to discourage Dorian: "Good artists exist simply in what they make, and consequently are perfectly uninteresting in what they are." Henry decides, however, to watch the situation as an experiment, to achieve "scientific analysis of the passions."

Chapter 5 is the second added chapter, and its mean style fits the situation—Sibyl's poverty-ridden and melodramatically sterile home life. The reader is told about her romantic dream, her mother's overacted apprehensions, her brother James's sincere concern and his violent threats to anyone who should harm her. In soap-opera terms, the reader learns, as James now finally does, that Sibyl and James are bastards, since the "highly connected" gentleman their mother had loved could not marry her. Mother and brother have listened to Sibyl declare her passion for a Prince Charming whose real name she does not know.

In chapter 6, Lord Henry and Basil discuss Dorian's determination to marry, and after his arrival, Dorian describes his infatuation. Henry doubts the quality of Dorian's "selfless" love, and asserts the superiority of selfish pleasure: "I should fancy that the real tragedy of the poor is that they can afford nothing but self-denial." They drive off to the theater, Basil gloomy and apprehensive.

Chapter 7 reveals that Sibyl's power of acting has deserted her. Dorian's love evanesces, his friends leave, he berates Sibyl as she sobs. She flings herself at his feet (people fling themselves throughout the novel). He coldly leaves her and wanders through the night. At dawn, returning home, he notes a new expression of hard cruelty on the face in the portrait. But maybe it is not so; maybe he can yet love Sibyl.

In the third subsection of the first half of the novel, chapter 8 sees Dorian, with Lord Henry's tutelage, transforming Sibyl's suicide into a triumph of art, a further help to his own self-development: "It has been a marvelous experience. That is all." The picture still mirrors his cruelty, bears "the burden of his shame: that was all." In chapter 9 Basil arrives at Dorian's house; they exchange views; Basil confesses the intense love he had expressed in the picture, the motive for his effort to destroy it. Dorian resolves to hide it away safely. He takes the painting in chapter 10 to the unused old schoolroom at the top of the house, where he had spent much of his childhood. Then he turns to the book Henry had sent to him, a volume resembling J. K. Huysmans's *A Rebours* (1884), a book written in "that curious jeweled style" which Wilde himself had admired. Here the voice of the narrator strongly suggests that he is Wilde himself; it is almost, but not quite, identical with the voice of Lord Henry: "There were in it [the book Lord Henry had sent to Dorian] metaphors as monstrous as orchids, and as subtle in color. The life of the senses was described in terms of mystical philosophy. One hardly knew at times whether one was reading the spiritual ecstasies of some medieval saint or the morbid confessions of a modern sinner. It was a poisonous book." This view of the operation of a work of art does not at all seem in accord with Wilde's preface.

For his bridge chapter, chapter 11, Wilde hit upon the effective device of merging Dorian's experience for the next eighteen years with the vast historical background, mostly deviously evil, of the beautiful objects he collects—manuscripts depicting sensual adventures and mystical theologies; perfumes; music of savage as well as of civilized traditions; exquisite jewels; embroideries, tapestries, and vestments; paintings; literature; poisons. Thus Wilde gives the effect of many passing years, bringing Dorian to the point at which he can look "on evil as a mode through which he could realize his conception of the beautiful." The chapter brilliantly deals with time on two levels: general human historical experience with beautiful and poisonous things, and Dorian's shifting interest in those same things.

The last half of the novel begins in chapter 12, on the eve of Dorian's thirty-eighth birthday. On his way home through the fog from a party at Lord Henry's, Dorian passes the hurrying figure of Basil Hallward, and attempts to avoid speaking to him. But Basil turns and requests an interview. He confronts Dorian with the stories of his moral corruption and urges him to reveal the truth. Dorian furiously agrees and invites Basil upstairs.

In chapter 13, Basil, horrified, sees the picture. He urges repentance. Dorian stabs him to death, then goes outside and rings the bell to establish an alibi (his valet had previously sent Basil on his way, and was unaware of his return with Dorian). Dorian looks into the Blue Book, a listing of notable persons, to find the address of Alan Campbell, a scientist.

In chapter 14 Dorian blackmails Campbell into destroying Basil's body, apparently by reducing it to its elements. The florid style of these chapters continues the atmosphere of the elegantly evil bridge chapter, chapter 11.

In the four following chapters, added to the *Lippincott* version, Wilde fleshes out the lean earlier ending, particularly by bringing back Sibyl's brother James to attempt to carry out his threat of vengeance. Wilde achieves far greater unity, as well, by reviving Dorian's first vicious cruelty and depicting the cowardice and fear of Sibyl's Prince Charming in his maturity.

In chapter 15 Dorian, fresh from his gruesome crime (or "tragedy," as the narrator puts it) goes to a party at Lady Narborough's. The narrator's voice here is closer than ever to Lord Henry's, and the narrator literally quotes Henry's statements. Lord Henry arrives late, notes something changed in Dorian, and amuses the company with a series of paradoxes: "She is very clever, too clever for a woman. She lacks the indefinable charm of weakness. It is the feet of clay that makes the gold of the image precious. Her feet are very pretty, but they are not feet of clay. White porcelain feet, if you like. They have been through the fire, and what fire does not destroy, it hardens. She has had experiences." The image has its application to Dorian, as does much of Henry's persiflage. (Wilde refers to this image in *De Profundis*, his long letter from prison to Alfred Douglas: "When I wrote, among my aphorisms, that it was simply the feet of clay that made the gold of the image precious, it was of you that I was thinking.")

After the party, Dorian returns home, disquieted and craving forgetfulness. He collects some drugs and takes a hansom for the opium dens of Chinatown. When, in chapter 16, Dorian enters the squalid den, he sees a sailor "sprawled over a table." An old crone, a woman Dorian had corrupted many years ago, calls after him, "Prince Charming." The sailor, who by strange coincidence turns out to be James Vane, hears the name his sister had called the man she loved. He follows Dorian, threatens him, and Dorian steps into light to reveal the face of "a lad of twenty summers." Vane subsides in confusion, and Dorian departs. The crone, creeping up, informs Vane that that "lad" had ruined her "nigh on eighteen years since. . . ." Vane stares at empty streets.

In chapter 17, a week later, at a hunting party in the country, Lord Henry is entertaining the guests, earning the title of "Prince Paradox" from Dorian. There are hints of the future *Importance of Being Earnest*: "That is the reason I hate vulgar realism in literature. The man who would call a spade a spade should be compelled to use it. It is the only thing he

Illustration portraying the death of Dorian Gray from the 1925 edition of The Picture of Dorian Gray

is fit for." Then Dorian, having seen through a window the white, staring face of James Vane, faints. In chapter 18, Dorian, though ill, goes out on the hunt. Over Dorian's protest, since he was charmed by the hare's grace of movement, Sir Geoffrey shoots into the bush—and kills the hiding James Vane. Dorian weeps with relief that he is now safe.

Chapter 19 returns to the material of the *Lippincott* version. Henry and Dorian return to the Paterian atmosphere of the first chapters, now without Basil. Dorian's determination to reform and be good, evidenced by his refraining from corrupting altogether a village maid who reminded him of Sibyl, meets with tolerant incredulity from Lord Henry: "Crime belongs exclusively to the lower orders.... I should fancy that crime was to them what art is to us, simply a method of procuring extraordinary sensations." They discuss Basil's disappearance, his possible murder, Dorian's life, the loss of the soul. For Dorian, Henry tells him, "Life has been your art." As he leaves, Dorian hesitates, as if he had left something important unsaid. "Then he sighed and went out."

In the final chapter, Dorian for the last time "throws himself" down on the sofa and thinks. The

past overwhelms him. He determines to be good. Having accomplished one minor triumph by resisting a sexual urge, he goes to see if the picture looks better. It is more disgusting. He stabs it with the knife that had killed Basil. When the servants break in, they find a picture of an exquisite youth and an old, withered, loathsome corpse with a knife in its heart.

This second version of *The Picture of Dorian Gray* is a well-balanced and unified novel, expressed in a musical, clear, and flowing style, if flowery and overstuffed like stylish Victorian furniture. The imagery well serves the central insight, which contemplates the goal of existence in human beings involved with art. Wilde formally disavows a moral aim, but his book frustrates that disavowal. The human who serves only self, as a perfect work of art may do, may end murdered in horror like Basil, suicidal like Dorian stabbing his conscience, or vapidly mouthing entertaining aphorisms like the seemingly self-sufficient Lord Henry.

Wilde's reputation as a novelist has to rest on this one work, but that is not a trivial base. The novel's solid structure and other virtues have kept it alive for a century, tempting filmmakers and playwrights, as well as a steady stream of interested critics and readers.

James Joyce understood why Wilde failed to achieve the highest literary merit and fell short of revealing the ultimate human secret in his novel. In a letter to his brother in 1906 after reading *The Picture of Dorian Gray*, Joyce laid his critical finger on Wilde's literary fatal flaw: "Wilde seems to have some good intentions in writing it—some wish to put himself before the world—but the book is rather crowded with lies and epigrams. If he had had the courage to develop the allusions in the book it might have been better." Wilde, in what he and Joyce both recognized as the goal of the literary artist—to express human experience in all its psychic complexity—lacked courage. In the young Joyce's view, Wilde feared self-revelation.

An illustration of the difference as well as the likeness between the flawed artist and the toweringly successful one might be discerned in a comparison of artistic achievement in the creation of the somewhat similar characters of Dorian Gray and Stephen Dedalus. For example, in chapter 11 the young Dorian contemplates the sinister transformation of his portrait: "He grew more and more enamoured of his own beauty, more and more interested in the corruption of his own soul. He would examine with minute care, and sometimes with a monstrous and terrible delight, the hideous lines that seared the wrinkling forehead or crawled around the heavy sensual mouth, wondering sometimes which were the more horrible, the signs of sin or the signs of age." In chapter 3 of *A Portrait of the Artist as a Young Man* (1916), Joyce says of Stephen Dedalus: "He stooped to the evil of hypocrisy with others, sceptical of their innocence which he could cajole so easily.... If ever his soul, re-entering her dwelling shyly after the frenzy of his body's lust had spent itself, was turned towards her whose emblem is the morning star, 'bright and musical, telling of heaven and infusing peace,' it was when her names were murmured softly by lips whereon there still lingered foul and shameful words, the savour itself of a lewd kiss." Joyce could powerfully and unashamedly depict hypocrisy; Wilde, according to Joyce, crippled his art by a concern for concealing his own hypocrisy....

Source: Robert Boyle, "Oscar Wilde," in *Dictionary of Literary Biography*, Vol. 34, *British Novelists, 1890–1929: Traditionalists*, edited by Thomas F. Staley, Gale Research, 1984, pp. 315–31.

Philip K. Cohen

In the following excerpt, Cohen examines moral symmetry and structure in The Picture of Dorian Gray.

The structure of *The Picture of Dorian Gray* is unambiguously, rigorously moral. Through the portrait, Wilde monitors Dorian's steady, irreversible progress toward damnation. The murder of Basil Hallward constitutes the crisis of the novel and divides it into two fairly symmetrical halves, the second of which also ends on the climactic note of murder—though this time it is self-murder—committed with the same weapon. Wilde builds upon this foundation a system of analogous and contrasting characters and character relationships that he apportions between the halves of the plot so as to augment and clarify its moral symmetry. And he further enhances the balance between halves by carefully choreographing the entrances, exits, and reappearances of key characters.

At the outset, Basil Hallward and Lord Henry Wotton, essentially positive and negative moral influences, compete for Dorian's allegiance. Wotton wins easily and, as the plot approaches the murder, his growing ascendancy is balanced by Hallward's increasing estrangement. These shifting relationships provide an appropriate backdrop for the murder, which sets in motion the novel's central irony. Prior to this crime, Dorian views his evil behavior as a positive means of self-realization. Using the portrait as a repository for his deeds, he thinks that

> Heaven and hell, pride and repentance, Christ and the devil—Wilde situates Dorian between these moral extremes and calls upon him to decide his fate."

he can act with impunity. He kills Basil in order to free himself from conscience, but his sense of guilt and spiritual anxiety increases instead. Too late he recognizes the validity of Basil's moral position, as the relative influences of Basil and Henry begin to reverse themselves. Behavior that before stemmed from a positive, if perverse, philosophy now has for its sole purpose the escape from guilt. Each venture toward oblivion yields instead a confrontation with past sins. And, as he sinks deeper in corruption, Dorian takes Basil's place in the moral debate with Harry. Just before the novel's central crisis, in which Basil loses his life, he returns after a long absence to confront Dorian with the rumors about his wickedness. Dorian confesses to Basil, who attains to full awareness of both his and Dorian's sins. When Henry returns prior to the novel's final crisis, Dorian tentatively confesses to him also. But Henry refuses to believe him and, blind to Dorian's spiritual anxiety, ironically expresses envy of the life Dorian has come to loathe.

Wilde carefully constructs the murder scene as the novel's moral fulcrum. Basil's confrontation with the altered portrait, which implicates him as well as Dorian, moves him to repent and seek mercy:

> "Good God, Dorian, what a lesson! what an awful lesson!" There was no answer, but he could hear the young man sobbing at the window. "Pray, Dorian, pray," he murmured. "What is it that one was taught to say in one's boyhood? 'Lead us not into temptation. Forgive us our sins. Wash away our iniquities.' Let us say that together. The prayer of your pride has been answered. The prayer of your repentance will be answered also. I worshipped you too much. I am punished for it. You worshipped yourself too much. We are both punished."

Moments after the unveiling, Basil and Dorian exchange the following remarks:

> "Christ! what a thing I must have worshipped! It has the eyes of a devil."

"Each of us has Heaven and Hell in him, Basil," cried Dorian, with a wild gesture of despair.

Heaven and hell, pride and repentance, Christ and the devil—Wilde situates Dorian between these moral extremes and calls upon him to decide his fate. He must either turn from false worship—a theme that incorporates both his initial Faustian pact and Basil's strange idolatry—to true, or be damned. Wilde stresses the possibility for salvation rather than the necessity for punishment. Basil calls upon Dorian to join him in the appeal for New Testament mercy. The artist represents and acts upon the positive force of conscience, which can bring about an inward change and lead to regeneration. But, at the crisis in his life, Dorian chooses rebellion rather than repentance, the hell rather than the heaven within. He blames Basil for the course his life has taken; and Wilde frames the accusation so that it extends implicitly to God:

"I wonder do I know you? Before I could answer that, I should have to see your soul.... But only God can do that."

A bitter laugh of mockery broke from the lips of the younger man. "You shall see it yourself, to-night!" he cried, seizing a lamp from the table. "Come: it is your own handiwork."

Dorian forces upon Basil the role of God, who alone can see the soul He has created. And he blames the divine surrogate for his evil nature rather than accepting responsibility for it himself. After he murders Basil, conscience, with its potential for salvation through repentance, becomes overpowering guilt that blocks out deliverance.

Dorian's symbolic rejection of the Christian dispensation appeared in the *Lippincott's* text. When Wilde added six chapters to form the book version, he contributed to the moral symmetry of the structure by developing that opposition between Old and New Testament codes which permeates his writings. By rejecting Basil, the spokesman for New Testament mercy, Dorian forces the confrontation with an angry God who judges and punishes. Since contrition can no longer be generated from within, vengeance must be imposed from above. In the added chapters Wilde therefore introduces James Vane, an agent of the Old Testament code who replaces Basil to become the living moral force in the novel's second half. Whereas Basil, Dorian's good angel, sought to lead him toward grace, Vane, the angel of wrath, increases the guilty man's terror as he attempts to avenge an infuriated deity. After the murder, anxiety, supported by the relationship between hunter and hunted, sets the tone of *Dorian Gray.* The protagonist

acknowledges the justice of Vane's moral code shortly before his own death:

Ah! in what a monstrous moment of pride and passion he had prayed that the portrait should bear the burden of his days, and he keep the unsullied splendour of eternal youth! All his failure had been due to that. Better for him that each sin of his life had brought its sure, swift penalty along with it. There was purification in punishment. Not "Forgive us our sins," but "Smite us for our inequities," should be the prayer of man to a most just God.

He explicitly recalls Basil's appeal and brings the New and Old Testament perspectives on sin into sharp contrast. Having denied the former, he unwittingly replaces James Vane as agent of the latter when he stabs the portrait.

Though Vane and Hallward function as contrasting manifestations of moral order, Dorian uses similar, and only temporarily successful, tactics to evade them. When Basil requests permission to exhibit the portrait, Dorian protects his own secret by shifting the burden of guilt; he forces the painter to make a confession. More blunt in manner than Basil, the sailor points a cocked pistol at Dorian's head and demands: "You had better confess your sin, for as sure as I am James Vane, you are going to die." But again Dorian turns the tables, this time by displaying his youthful countenance beneath a street lamp. Now he becomes the accuser and Vane the guilty party:

He loosened his hold and reeled back. "My God! my God!" he cried, "and I would have murdered you!"

Dorian Gray drew a long breath. "You have been on the brink of committing a terrible crime, my man," he said, looking at him sternly. "Let this be a warning to you not to take vengeance into your own hands."

"Forgive me, sir," muttered James Vane.

Dorian knows well what a "terrible crime" murder is, but he, who has committed it, never seeks forgiveness. And guilt can no more be transferred indefinitely to these two representatives of right than can the deeds that prompt it be forever imposed upon the portrait. The deceptive sense of release experienced by Dorian after the deaths of Basil and Vane soon gives way to renewed anxiety. He has denied the angel of mercy and tricked the angel of wrath. But he has wasted these efforts because he cannot, finally, escape himself. Dorian ironically punishes himself by an act characteristic of the very immorality through which he has tried to escape judgment.

Source: Philip K. Cohen, "The Crucible," in *The Moral Vision of Oscar Wilde*, Fairleigh Dickinson University Press, 1978, pp. 123–27.

Sources

Ericksen, Donald H., *Oscar Wilde*, Twayne's English Authors Series, No. 211, Twayne Publishers, 1977, pp. 96–117.

Gillespie, Michael Patrick, *The Picture of Dorian Gray: "What the World Thinks Me,"* Twayne's Masterwork Studies, No. 145, Twayne Publishers, 1995.

Kohl, Norbert, *Oscar Wilde: The Works of a Conformist Rebel*, translated by David Henry Wilson, Cambridge University Press, 1989, p. 138.

Pater, Walter, "Conclusion," in *The Norton Anthology of English Literature*, 4th ed., Vol. 2, Norton, 1979, pp. 1580–83, originally published in *Studies in the History of the Renaissance*, 1873.

Wilde, Oscar, "The Critic as Artist," in *The Artist as Critic: Critical Writings of Oscar Wilde*, edited by Richard Ellmann, Random House, 1969, pp. 340–408.

———, *The Picture of Dorian Gray*, Unicorn Press, 1948.

Further Reading

Cohen, Ed, "Writing Gone Wilde: Homoerotic Desire in the Closet of Representation," in *Critical Essays on Oscar Wilde*, edited by Regenia Gagnier, G. K. Hall, 1991, pp. 68–87.
    Cohen analyzes *The Picture of Dorian Gray* to show how even in the absence of explicit homosexual terminology or activity, a text can subvert the traditional standards and representations of appropriate male behavior.

Cohen, Philip K., *The Moral Vision of Oscar Wilde*, Fairleigh Dickinson University Press, 1978, pp. 105–55.
    Cohen argues that Wilde's recurrent themes are sin and salvation and a conflict between the moral perspectives of Old and New Testament, judgment and love. He explores these themes in *The Picture of Dorian Gray*.

Paglia, Camille, *Sexual Personae: Art and Decadence from Nefertiti to Emily Dickinson*, Vintage, 1991, pp. 512–30.
    As part of her celebrated, controversial, and wide-ranging examination of Western culture, Paglia treats *The Picture of Dorian Gray* as the fullest study of the Decadent erotic principle: the transformation of person into *objet d'art*.

Raby, Peter, *Oscar Wilde*, Cambridge University Press, 1988, pp. 67–80.
    This is an introductory essay that emphasizes two major elements in the novel: the Sybil Vane episode and the yellow book that Lord Henry sends Dorian.

Silas Marner

George Eliot

1861

Silas Marner: The Weaver of Raveloe, by Victorian novelist George Eliot, was first published in 1861. The idea for the short novel, which she described as "a story of old-fashioned village life," came upon Eliot suddenly and interrupted her plans for the writing of another novel, *Romola*. After the publisher John Blackwood read some of the manuscript and told her he found it somber, Eliot replied that it was not a sad story because "it sets in a strong light the remedial influences of pure, natural human relations."

Silas Marner is a story of loss, alienation, and redemption that combines elements of fairy tale and myth with realism and humor. Set in the fictional village of Raveloe, it centers on Silas Marner, a weaver who is forced to leave his hometown in the north after being falsely accused of theft by members of his chapel. His religious faith gone, for fifteen years Marner isolates himself from the life of the village and becomes a miser. But when the gold that he cherishes is stolen, and he adopts a child whose mother has just died, his life changes dramatically for the better.

Silas Marner has always been admired as one of Eliot's best and most appealing works. Not only is it a touching story that ends, like the fairy tale, happily ever after, it also presents a realistic portrait of nineteenth-century life in a traditional English village in which the spirit of kindness and cooperation overrule petty differences.

Author Biography

George Eliot, neé Mary Ann Evans, was born on November 22, 1819, in Chilvers Coton, in Warwickshire, England, the daughter of estate manager Robert Evans and his wife Christiana Pearson. Evans was educated at home and at various schools, including Mrs. Wallington's school in Nuneaton, where she became an Evangelical Christian. When her mother died in 1836, Evans became her father's housekeeper, while continuing her education through private tutors. She learned Italian, German, and Latin, and within a few years also studied Greek and Hebrew.

In 1841, Evans and her father moved to the outskirts of Coventry. There she met the philanthropist Charles Bray and his wife, Caroline Hennell, as well as Hennell's family, who introduced her to new political and religious ideas and under whose influence she rejected Christianity.

Evans translated and published David Friedrich Strauss's *The Life of Jesus* in 1846, and within three years she had also translated the work of the philosophers Spinoza and Feuerbach. After her father died in 1849, she moved to London and became assistant editor of the influential journal, *Westminster Review*. In the London literary circles in which she now moved, she met the man of letters, essayist and playwright, George Henry Lewes, and in 1853 she traveled to Germany with him. Lewes was estranged from his wife but was unable to obtain a divorce, and he and Evans lived together until Lewes's death in 1878. Their relationship shocked Victorian society; even Evans's brother Isaac refused to communicate with her in any way until after Lewes's death.

While Evans experienced social isolation because of her relationship with Lewes, she excelled as a novelist. In 1857, she published her first work of fiction, "The Sad Fortunes of the Reverend Amos Barton," in *Blackwood's Magazine*, under the pseudonym George Eliot, the name she used for all her subsequent works. The following year, "Amos Burton" was republished as one of Eliot's *Scenes of Clerical Life*, in two volumes.

Evans's first novel, *Adam Bede*, appeared in 1859, and achieved huge critical and popular success. Evans continued to maintain her anonymity, going to some lengths to disguise the fact that she was George Eliot. Over the next dozen years, Evans produced a series of novels that placed her in the front rank of English novelists. In 1860, after traveling with Lewes to Italy, she published *The Mill*

George Eliot

on the Floss. *Silas Marner* followed in 1861, and *Romola*, a historical romance, was published in serial form in the *Cornhill* magazine in 1862 and 1863. It appeared in three volumes in 1863. *Felix Holt: The Radical* appeared in 1866, after which Evans and Lewes traveled extensively in Europe, visiting Holland, Belgium, Germany, and Spain. These European travels were a regular feature of Evans's life for the next decade.

Evans began writing her greatest novel, *Middlemarch*, in 1869. It was published in serial form from 1871 to 1872, and then in three volumes. Evans's last novel was *Daniel Deronda* (1876).

In 1880, two years after Lewes's death, Evans married John Walter Cross, who was twenty years her junior. She died that year, on December 22.

Plot Summary

Part 1

Silas Marner begins in the early years of the nineteenth century, near the English village of Raveloe, where Silas Marner practices his trade as a weaver. He is a solitary man who is regarded as strange by the other villagers because he does not socialize with them. Marner first arrived in the

Media Adaptations

- The film *Silas Marner* (1985) was directed by Giles Foster and starred Ben Kingsley as Marner, with co-stars Jenny Agutter, Freddie Jones, and Angela Pleasence.

---

village fifteen years earlier, from a large town in northern England. In his hometown he had lived a pious life and was a member of a Dissenting chapel (that is, a Protestant sect not affiliated to the Church of England) that met at Lantern Yard. But when Marner was falsely accused of theft by another member of the church, his friend William Dane, he was forced to leave the town and make his life elsewhere. With his religious faith shattered, Marner turned inward and made himself hard. Now, fifteen years later, the only thing he loves is his money, which he hoards.

The chief family in Raveloe is that of Squire Cass. Cass has three sons, two of whom are important for the story. Dunsey, the youngest son is a dishonest ne'er-do-well, while Godfrey, the eldest, is good-natured but weak. Godfrey made the mistake of marrying secretly to Molly, a girl from a lower class. She became an opium addict and now threatens to betray his secret to his father. She also has a young child by Godfrey. Godfrey is terrified that his father will discover his secret and cut him off from his inheritance. He is also frustrated because he wants to marry Nancy Lammeter, a pretty girl from the village, but cannot do so as long as he is married to Molly. Dunsey knows his secret and blackmails him. Godfrey agrees to let Dunsey sell Godfrey's horse, Wildfire, to raise money, but Dunsey rides the horse foolishly, and it is killed in an accident. Dunsey walks home, and finding himself near Marner's cottage, he robs Marner, who has slipped out of his house on an errand, of all his gold. When Marner discovers the theft, he is distraught. Dunsey disappears, but no one connects his disappearance to the robbery. In the meantime, Marner's misfortune makes the villagers think more kindly of him.

On New Year's Eve, a dance is held at Red House, the home of Squire Cass. Molly decides to

walk there to reveal the truth about Godfrey, but drugged on opium, she collapses near Marner's cottage. Her two-year-old daughter wanders into the cottage, where Marner discovers her asleep. Then Marner finds Molly and rushes to Red House for assistance, taking the child with him. When Molly is later declared dead, Marner insists on keeping the child, while Godfrey is relieved that the death of Molly leaves him free to marry Nancy Lammeter. He also goes out of his way to show kindness to Marner and the child, who is his daughter.

Marner christens the child Eppie and raises her as his own. The presence of the child revives his spirits, and he becomes once more open to life. The villagers lose their suspicions of him and welcome him whenever he comes into the village. His long years of isolation are over.

Part 2

Sixteen years have passed since Marner first took in Eppie. Godfrey has married Nancy, and they are childless. They lost a child in infancy, and Nancy has resisted her husband's desire to adopt Eppie. Dunsey has never returned. Eppie has grown into a pretty young woman who is very fond of Marner, whom she regards as her father, even though he has explained to her the circumstances in which she arrived at his house. Eppie has a young male admirer named Aaron, and they are contemplating marriage. Marner, now a respected member of village society, says he will do nothing to prevent her marrying.

One day, the stone-pit near Marner's cottage goes dry, and the remains of Dunsey are found. Godfrey informs Nancy that it was Dunsey who robbed Marner, since the money was found in the pit. Godfrey also confesses that the woman Marner found dead in the snow was his wife and that Eppie is his child. He and Nancy agree that they will try to adopt her. But when they inform Marner and Eppie of their intentions, Eppie says she would prefer to stay with Marner. Even Godfrey's announcement that he is Eppie's real father does not change Eppie's mind, even though Marner says she is free to go if she wishes.

After his money is returned, Marner takes Eppie north to visit the town were he grew up. He wants to find out if he has ever been cleared of the crime he was falsely accused of, thirty years ago. But the chapel has been pulled down and a factory built in its place.

The novel ends happily with Eppie's marriage to Aaron. The young couple plans to live with Marner.

Characters

Dunstan Cass

Dunstan Cass is Godfrey's younger brother. He is a disreputable, dishonest, spiteful young man who uses his knowledge of Godfrey's secret marriage to blackmail him. Godfrey agrees to let Dunsey sell Godfrey's horse, Wildfire, to raise money, but Dunsey rides the horse foolishly and is responsible for the horse's death. As he walks home, Dunsey robs Marner of his gold and then disappears. No one is concerned by his absence, since he has left home for long periods before. His remains are discovered sixteen years later in a stone-pit that has gone dry. It is concluded that he drowned.

Godfrey Cass

Godfrey Cass is the eldest son of Squire Cass and heir to the estate. He is a good-natured man, but he lacks strength of character and does not like to face up to difficult situations. In a fit of drunkenness he made the mistake of marrying beneath his station, and he has kept his wife and child a secret. He lives in fear that his ill-willed younger brother Dunsey will tell their father about his secret, which would probably result in his being turned out of the family home and cut off from his inheritance. He is also bitterly frustrated by the fact that because he is already married, he cannot marry the girl of his choice, Nancy Lammeter. When his wife dies and Dunsey disappears, Godfrey's worries appear to be over, and he duly marries Nancy. But he is tormented by the fact that his unacknowledged daughter Eppie is being raised by Marner. He shows as much care and concern for her as he can without arousing suspicion, and he tries to persuade Nancy that they should adopt Eppie. But Nancy refuses. After Dunsey's remains are found, Godfrey tells Nancy everything about his past. They try to adopt Eppie, but she refuses to be parted from the man she regards as her father. Godfrey is forced to accept that he can never publicly acknowledge Eppie as his daughter, a blow for which his happy marriage is only partial consolation.

Molly Cass

Molly Cass is Godfrey Cass's first wife, whom he married secretly. She comes from a lower social class than her husband, and she is addicted to opium. She decides to walk to the Red House on New Year's Eve to betray Godfrey's secret, but she collapses and dies near Marner's cottage.

Squire Cass

Squire Cass, the father of Dunsey and Godfrey, is the most prominent landowner in Raveloe. A widower of sixty, he is a bluff, robust, quick-tempered man who never questions the superiority of his own family within the parish. He is a difficult man to deal with. He is indulgent with his tenants for a while and lets them get into arrears, but then when he gets short of money, he comes down on them hard for rent. Once he has made up his mind about something, he does not alter it.

William Dane

William Dane is a treacherous friend of Silas. When they are both young men, they are devout members of a religious sect that meets at Lantern Yard in a town in northern England. But Dane steals money from the church and deliberately arranges for Marner to take the blame. He then marries the girl to whom Marner had been engaged.

Dunsey

See Dunstan Cass

Eppie

Eppie is the daughter of Godfrey and Molly Cass. Since Godfrey will not acknowledge his marriage, it is left to Molly to raise the child. But she is unfit to do so, and when she dies of an overdose of opium, the child is adopted by Marner. He christens her Eppie. Eppie grows up in a loving home and regards Marner as her father. She is pretty, with golden curly hair. She is content with her position in life and has no interest in being adopted by Godfrey and Nancy, even when she is informed that Godfrey is her real father. She remains utterly loyal and devoted to Marner and is happy to be associated with the poor, working people of the village. When she is eighteen, Eppie marries Aaron, and they live together in Marner's cottage.

Mr. Kimble

Mr. Kimble is the village farrier (veterinarian), and he also serves as the town doctor. Because of his status he has a rather high opinion of himself. It is Kimble who takes charge of the situation in the Rainbow tavern after Marner tells the people he has been robbed.

Nancy Lammeter

Nancy Lammeter is the attractive young woman courted by Godfrey Cass. Nancy is well mannered, sincere, and always neat; at the New Year's Eve dance she is perfectly attired, with not a hair out of place. Although Nancy is a woman of good character, she also lives by some rigid, simple ideas, which she refuses to alter. She insists that her sister Priscilla dress in exactly the same way as she does, even though this does not set Priscilla off to best advantage. Nancy also refuses to adopt Eppie, even though Godfrey her husband greatly desires it, because she believes that Providence has decreed she remain childless. In Nancy's inflexible mind, adopting a child would be wrong, and the child would not turn out well. In spite of this fault, however, Nancy is a good, tender wife to Godfrey, and after he finally confesses his past indiscretions she agrees to try to adopt Eppie.

Priscilla Lammeter

Priscilla Lammeter is Nancy Lammeter's sister. Five years older than Nancy, she is not as pretty as her sister and describes herself as ugly. But she does not seem to mind this disadvantage. She is a cheerful woman, full of common sense, and she has no wish to marry.

Mr. Macey

Mr. Macey is the old tailor and parish clerk of Raveloe. He often tells stories about village history in the Rainbow, and the men listen to him with respect.

Silas Marner

Silas Marner is a weaver. As a young man living in a town in northern England, he is a member of a fundamentalist Christian sect that meets at a place called Lantern Yard. He is highly thought of by the other members of the sect, and the fact that during prayer meetings he sometimes goes into trances that last as long as an hour is seen as a sign of some special spiritual gift. But Marner is driven away from the town after his treacherous friend, William Dane, ensures that Marner is falsely convicted of theft. Marner settles in Raveloe, but his faith is shattered, and he isolates himself from the community. The villagers regard him with suspicion, which is not helped by the fact that Marner has knowledge of the healing properties of herbs. The superstitious villagers think this kind of knowledge may have something to do with the devil. Marner does not attend church and knows nothing of the village's church calendar because it is very different from the sect of Christianity practiced in Lantern Yard. The only thing he loves is his money. He earns a good income as a weaver, working alone in his cottage, and he hoards his gold, counting it lovingly. When the gold is stolen he is shattered. He seeks help from the villagers, and they begin to think more kindly of him. Marner's life changes completely when a child whose mother lies dead in the snow near his home finds her way to his cottage. He insists on raising her himself. The child, christened Eppie, brings out Marner's latent kindness and gentleness. Through Eppie he realizes that love is more valuable than money. He is then able to connect with the life of the community, and he becomes a respected and honored citizen of Raveloe.

Mr. Tookey

Mr. Tookey is the deputy parish clerk and is unpopular with the other men.

Aaron Winthrop

Aaron Winthrop is the son of Dolly Winthrop. He is a steady, good-hearted young man, and he marries Eppie while promising also to take care of Marner.

Dolly Winthrop

Dolly Winthrop is the mother of Aaron and the wife of Ben, the village wheelwright. She is a mild, patient, hard-working woman who is always ready to look after the sick and the dying. She is one of the first of the villagers to take pity on Marner after his gold has been stolen, visiting him with her young son and bringing lard-cakes. Dolly supports Marner's decision to adopt Eppie, and she is full of valuable advice and practical help about how to raise the child.

Themes

Moral Order

Although there are tragedies in *Silas Marner* (the death of Molly Cass, for example), the narrative emphasizes the moral order of the universe. The principal characters get their just desserts. Silas Marner is rewarded for the love he shows Eppie; Dunsey never lives to profit from his robbery; and Godfrey Cass, because of his deceitfulness and moral cowardice, can never publicly acknowledge that Eppie is his daughter. This moral order is at work through seemingly chance events. It seems to be chance, for example, that Marner happens to be away from his cottage on a short errand and has left his door unlocked (which he would never normally do) at the exact moment that Dunsey is walking by, thus giving Dunsey a chance to rob him. It also seems to be a chance event when Molly Cass

Topics For Further Study

- Does Godfrey Cass, Eppie's biological father, have the right to take her from Silas Marner, her foster father? What moral issues does this matter raise? How is this issue relevant in the early 2000s?

- Bearing in mind that Eliot has sometimes been criticized by feminists for being too conservative in her representation of women, discuss the characters Nancy Lammeter, Dolly Winthrop, and Eppie. Are they presented as dependent on men? How do they go about fulfilling their needs and desires? How do they support others?

- Discuss how Silas Marner rears Eppie. What principles does he follow? Does he follow Dolly Winthrop's advice? What role does punishment have in childrearing?

- Write a detailed analysis of the scene in Chapter 6 in which the male villagers meet at the Rainbow. Who are the main characters, and what do they discuss? What does this scene reveal about village life in Raveloe? Why is the scene placed at this point in the narrative?

---

collapses near Marner's cottage and Eppie wanders inside. The door to the cottage is once again open and Marner is in one of his strange trances, so he does not notice the girl until she is asleep on his hearth.

But there is more at work than chance. Almost as soon as he sees the child, Marner senses that some supernatural order is operating in his life, and he later thinks that the child must have been deliberately sent to him. Dolly Winthrop agrees with him, although neither offers any explanation as to who or what this benevolent power might be. Later, after Marner has explained his past life to Dolly, she struggles to articulate her intuitive feeling that there is a higher power that arranges everything for the best: "For if us as knows so little can see a bit o' good and rights, we may be sure as there's a good and a rights bigger nor what we can know."

The Need for Human Community

The novel presents pictures of two poles of human existence, isolation and community. For fifteen years Marner retreats into a solitude that denies life. He is redeemed only when events conspire to make him rejoin a human community.

In his years of isolation at Raveloe, cut off from the real springs of life, Marner makes the mistake of treating inert things as if they were alive. His delight in his gold is so great that it even gratifies his senses of touch and sight: "It was pleasant to feel them [the guineas] in his palm"; he enjoys looking at their "bright faces"; they offer him "companionship," and as he "bathed his hands" in them he "felt their rounded outline between his thumb and fingers." He even begins to think that the gold is conscious of him, as he believes his loom is. And Marner's life, with its ceaseless, monotonous, repetitive activity, has come to resemble the actions of the loom. His constant bending over his loom has also deformed him physically, making him curiously fitted to it, like a "handle or a crooked tube" that has no independent existence apart from what it is attached to. In his attachment to a machine, Marner has cut himself off from nature. He forgets all about his former interest in herbs and his skill in using them for healing. When he walks through the lanes on a work-related trip, he thinks only of his money and his loom. The life of nature goes on around him unobserved. As a miser, he has given to inanimate things a spurious life and forgotten what real life is. His own life has become "a mere pulsation of desire and satisfaction that had no relation to any other being."

The loss of his money is a blessing in disguise for Marner because it breaks his attachment to things that have no life. It also reveals that the human spirit within him is not quite dead. He has a dim sense that if any help is to reach him, it must come from outside. This is why, when the villagers become more sympathetic to him, "there was a slight stirring of expectation at the sight of his fellow-men, a faint consciousness of dependence on their goodwill." This faint channel of hope is symbolized by the fact that at Christmas, Marner, even though he is still full of grief, does not make any attempt to close the shutters or lock the door of his cottage. Moreover, he develops a habit of opening his door and looking out from time to time. He does this not because he is consciously inviting companionship, but because he has some irrational hope that his money will somehow be returned. But it is this habit of leaving his door open that allows the child to come into his life. It is a sign that he has begun his journey back from isolation to community.

The arrival of Eppie has an immediate effect on Marner. When he first sees the child, he thinks it may be his little sister, come back in a dream. He remembers how he carried his sister around in his arms for a year until she died. By recalling a tender time of childhood that he had closed off from memory, Silas begins the process of reconnecting with his past. The process continues when he tells Dolly Winthrop all the details of his early life. Through this process his fractured psyche starts to become whole again. And with Eppie taking his thoughts away from their endless circularity into a more outward direction, Marner is at last ready to become integrated into the community life of Raveloe.

Just as Marner is a case study in isolation, Raveloe is presented as an example of community. There are two centers of community in Raveloe: the Squire's Red House, which is generous in giving out food to the poor and hosts the New Year's Eve dance, and the Rainbow inn, where the villagers gather round the hearth to tell their stories. The inhabitants of Raveloe may not be perfect, but they are fairly easy going and do not make a habit of applying moral censure to others. Although the village is strictly divided along class lines, there is no envy of the rich by the poor. It is a community in which everyone knows his or her place, and a spirit of cooperation and tolerance is the norm. This is shown especially vividly when the men in the Rainbow immediately do everything they can to help Marner, a man they all regard as rather strange, when he informs them that he has been robbed. The villagers all know that they are dependent on each other, and when Marner also realizes this, he is ready to play his part in a wider community, instead of foolishly trying to be self-sufficient.

Style

Imagery

In becoming a solitary miser, Silas Marner has become almost less than human, a point which is brought out by the imagery that is associated with him. He is described as like a spider, weaving its web; his life is reduced to the "unquestioning activity of a spinning insect." After he has lost his money, the image changes to that of an ant. His mind is baffled like a "plodding ant" that on its way home finds that the earth has been moved.

The imagery changes when Marner is on the way to redemption. When he sits with Eppie on a bank of flowers listening to the birds, he starts to look for herbs again, as he did when he was younger. As a leaf lies in his palm, memories of the past come flooding back to him. His mind is "growing into memory," and his soul is "unfolding too, and trembling gradually into full consciousness." Instead of being compared to an insect, Marner is now implicitly likened to an unfolding flower.

Fairy Tale and Realism

The narrative combines elements of the fairy tale with realistic settings and characters. Fairy tales often tell of a man or woman who is unjustly banished from a kingdom or is otherwise the victim of great misfortune. The person then goes through many trials and much suffering and feels that all is lost. Chance events, often involving the supernatural, intervene, evil is punished, good is rewarded, a perfect marriage is arranged, and the characters live happily ever after.

The story of Silas Marner has clear affinities with the fairy tale. Silas is unjustly expelled from his hometown and arrives in what is to him an alien environment. As a miser hoarding his gold, he is like a stock figure in folklore and fairy tale. When the miser sees the child and mistakes her golden curls for his stolen gold, the narrative is firmly in fairy tale mode. Marner's restoration to happiness and the happy ending with Eppie marrying Aaron are also strongly reminiscent of the fairy tale.

But other elements in the story are realistic. Unlike fairy tales, which are set in unnamed places in unknown times, Silas Marner takes place at a definite time and in a definite place. It is anchored in rural England at the beginning of the nineteenth century. Village life and customs are described in realistic mode, and realism is also seen in the

Compare & Contrast

- **1810s:** Each parish in England provides a workhouse to accommodate and employ the destitute. Conditions in the workhouses vary. Some are relatively acceptable, but others are grim. In 1810, George Crabbe writes of one workhouse: "It is a prison, with a milder name, / Which few inhabit without dread or shame."

  1860s: Since the Poor Law Amendment Act of 1834, hundreds of new workhouses have been built. They are supervised by a local Board of Guardians. Conditions in the workhouses are intentionally made harsh and degrading, to deter all but the most desperate. They are inhabited mainly by the old, the infirm, the sick, the orphaned, and unmarried mothers. The largest of them house over a thousand people.

  Today: Workhouses no longer exist. They were abolished in 1930. People who in addition to being poor are sick, old, or mentally ill are cared for in hospitals and by social welfare organizations. Under the National Health Service, every British citizen is entitled to free health care, according to his or her need. No social stigma is attached to being an unmarried mother, and women in such situations are able to gain employment.

- **1810s:** The population of England and Wales, according to the official census, is 10,164,000. The population is rising rapidly. The increase is due largely to a falling death rate, which falls from 33.4 per 1,000 in 1730 to 19.98 per 1,000 in 1810. This is due to better living conditions and better diet.

  1860s: The population continues to increase. There is a continuing shift of population to cities and away from rural areas. London is the biggest city in the world, with a population in 1861 of 2,803,989. This is an increase of 19 percent in ten years. Manchester also becomes one of the largest industrial centers in the world. After 1860, mortality rates decline because of the reduction in deaths from scarlet fever, typhus, and consumption.

  Today: The population of the United Kingdom (England, Scotland, Wales, and Northern Ireland) at mid-2001 is 58.8 million. Nearly 84 percent of this total lives in England, mainly in the major cities. London is the largest city in Europe, with a population of 7.2 million. The population of the United Kingdom is increasing. It has risen by 10 million between 1950 and 2000, mainly due to rising immigration. The death rate has dropped to 10.35 deaths per 1,000 population.

- **1810s:** The Napoleonic Wars end in 1815. Britain's conservative government fears social revolution and represses civil liberties.

  1860s: Britain increases democracy by extending the franchise. In the 1850s, only 900,000 out of 5,300,000 adult males in England and Wales were eligible to vote, but the Parliamentary Reform Act of 1867 adds an additional 1,008,000 men to the voter rolls. An amendment for the enfranchisement of women is rejected by 196 to 73 votes in the House of Commons.

  Today: Like all Western democracies, all British citizens who qualify by age are eligible to vote. However, voter participation is in decline. In the general election of 2001, only 59.4 percent of the total electorate vote. This figure is down from 70.9 percent in 1997 and 76.7 percent in 1992. It remains higher than voter turnout in the United States.

---

dialect in the villagers' speech. The story of Godfrey Cass, as opposed to that of the miser, contains no fairy tale elements. Godfrey's marriages, his family relations, the secret he keeps that may ruin him are the stuff of realistic Victorian fiction.

Historical Context

Weavers in England

Historian E. P. Thompson, in his book *The Making of the English Working Class*, describes four different employment situations for weavers during the nineteenth century. The first was the "customer-weaver," like Silas Marner, an independent worker in a village or small town who fulfilled orders from individual customers. Although customer-weavers were diminishing in numbers, those who continued the practice made a good living. In *Silas Marner*, Mr. Macey guesses that the hard-working Marner may make a pound a week from his weaving, which would have been a fairly sizable income. (This would have been during the early years of the nineteenth century.) The second kind of weaver was self-employed, producing work for a number of different masters. The third type was the journeyman weaver, who often owned his own loom and worked in his own home for one master. This was probably the status of Silas Marner in his hometown in northern England, where he learned his trade. The last category of weaver was the farmer who worked part-time at the loom. From 1780 to 1830, according to Thompson, these groups tended to merge into one group, "the proletarian outworker, who worked in his own home, sometimes owned and sometimes rented his loom, and who wove up the yarn to the specifications of the factor or agent of a mill or of some middleman."

Thompson emphasizes the loss of status and security that accompanied these changes, although weaving could still be a profitable business for the weaver.

The business was changing, however. The power loom was invented in 1784 and patented the following year. It enabled the weaver to once more to keep pace with the spinner, who up to then had been able to produce more yarn than the weaver could use. The power loom was first used in Manchester in 1791. By 1813, there were 2,400 power looms in England. But weaving remained predominantly a domestic industry until 1820, when power looms came into general use.

Social Change

At the beginning of the nineteenth century, England was a largely settled and static society. Villages like the fictional Raveloe in *Silas Marner* were relatively self-sufficient, since the inhabitants were able to manufacture their own clothes and supply their own food. But social change accelerated during the course of the century. Agricultural laborers and manufacturers became willing to leave villages in search of work or of better paid work. This was not just a matter of a shift from the countryside to the nearest town, but of large-scale migrations. By the end of the century, workers were

moving to Lancashire, where the cotton industry was flourishing, at the rate of fifteen thousand a year. The town of Bolton, for example, increased its population from 5,339 in 1773 to 11,739 in 1789. New canals enabled raw materials to be transported more quickly and efficiently, and new roads facilitated the recruitment of a labor force. There was, however, a price to be paid for economic gain, and that was the creation of a new class of landless agricultural laborers, who had lost their independence.

By the beginning of the reign of King George IV in 1820, the huge growth in manufacturing towns that had little connection with the old rural communities had radically changed England. As social historian G. M. Trevelyan writes in *Illustrated English Social History*: "The harmonious fabric of old English society suffered a perpendicular cleavage between town and country, as well as expanding the old lateral cleavage between rich and poor."

Critical Overview

Although there have been occasional complaints that the first part of the book is too gloomy and the second part too sentimental, *Silas Marner* has always been highly regarded by literary critics. Initial reviews were all positive. In a review published in *The Times* in 1861, E. S. Dallas praised the novel for its truthful portrayal of village life. He pointed out that although the characters were not idealized they were given dignity by the author's treatment of them:

> The personages of the tale are common, very common people, but they are good and kind, hardworking and dutiful. . . . their lives are ennobled and beautified by their sense of duty, and by their sympathy with each other.

Many modern critics regard *Silas Marner* as a flawless work, although because it is only novella-length it is not regarded as Eliot's greatest novel. Critics have shown that the novel is far more than a simple moral tale about a miser who discovers through adopting a young child that love is more rewarding than money. Elizabeth Deeds Ermath analyzes the novel as a "double story about isolation and community," and points out the complex similarities and differences between the stories of Marner and Godfrey Cass. Q. D. Leavis, in her introduction to the Penguin edition of the novel, discusses it in terms of the social changes brought

Engraving of a weaver at his loom, circa 1889

about by the Industrial Revolution. She points out that Marner, brought up in a manufacturing town, has become a slave to his loom—a piece of machinery—whereas Raveloe still clings to the traditional way of life, "the organic community and the unified society."

Criticism

Bryan Aubrey
Aubrey holds a Ph.D. in English and has published many articles on nineteenth-century literature.

In this essay, Aubrey discusses the contrast between the approach to religion of the sect at Lantern Yard and that of the villagers of Raveloe.

The story of Silas Marner's life has a mythic dimension to it. Silas undergoes a spiritual journey that is a variation on the great religious myth of Western culture. In the Christian myth, man is expelled from a garden, saved by the birth of the Christ-child, and promised a life in bliss in the heavenly city of Jerusalem described in the Book of Revelations. Silas travels a similar path from expulsion to redemption, but the symbolism is reversed. He is expelled from a city, saved by a child, and ends up

> " The child that saves is not the divine child that the wise men came to honor, nor the angels of popular tradition, but a poor little orphan girl."

in a garden (as seen in the final chapter when Eppie and Aaron grow a garden just outside his cottage). In the course of this journey, which occupies over thirty years of Silas's life, he travels from a stern, Bible-centered Calvinistic religion, in which the central concern is the "Assurance of salvation," to a more tolerant, nondogmatic version of Christianity in which the emphasis falls not on the idea of salvation but on tolerance and solidarity with others in a cooperative human community.

Marner's spirituality is first awakened at Lantern Yard, where as a young man in the 1780s he is a member of a Dissenting Protestant sect. In nineteenth century England, those who rejected the doctrines and authority of the Church of England were known as dissenters. They included such groups as the Presbyterians, Congregationalists, Baptists, Quakers, Unitarians, and other minor sects. The most notable feature of the dissenters was that they were more democratic than Anglicans. They had no bishops or priests, and did not accept doctrines or policies handed down from above. Instead, they took responsibility for organizing, financing and running their own groups. Large towns like Birmingham and Manchester were dominated by dissenters, and many artisans, like Silas Marner, were members of dissenting sects. The sect to which Marner belonged has not been identified as of 2004, but from the clues given in the text, it was strongly Calvinistic in nature. Calvinist tradition was strong in parts of Yorkshire and Lancashire during this period. The tenets of Calvinism, as Q. D. Leavis points out in her notes to the Penguin edition of the novel, include the idea of a priesthood of all believers; marriage only within the sect (as Silas, who was engaged to a girl named Sarah, intended to do); and the necessity of personal salvation, accomplished through divine grace revealed through personal religious experience. Those who were assured of salvation became members of the Elect.

Silas, who by nature is humble and self-doubting, never manages to convince himself that he possesses that vital assurance, quite unlike his holier-than-thou, judgmental friend William Dane. From Dane's treachery to the subsequent unjust condemnation of Silas for theft, it appears that the members of this sect, that pride themselves on being among the Elect, do not possess much in the way of spiritual wisdom. And just in case events do not speak sufficiently for themselves, the narrator (whose voice is surely that of Eliot) adds this poignant description of the earnest discussions that take place between Silas and William Dane and others of their type: "Such colloquies have occupied many a pair of pale-faced weavers, whose unnurtured souls have been like young winged things, fluttering forsaken in the twilight." This description gives the impression of youthful purity of heart and intention that is given no guidance at all by the religious sects to which the young people entrust their spiritual lives.

It is a long journey, in more ways than one, from Lantern Yard to Raveloe, from dissenting chapel to village church. Not surprisingly, Silas, his faith shattered, does not go out of his way to discover what kind of religion might be available to him in his new place of residence. Lantern Yard was all he knew. Had he been of a mind to investigate, he would have discovered that religion in Raveloe is a different matter altogether than the fierce and narrow faith he has been fed at Lantern Yard. The narrator is at pains to point out that Raveloe has not only seen nothing of the Industrial Revolution, it has not been affected by "puritan earnestness"—the kind that flourished in many of the dissenting chapels. People in Raveloe are not in the habit of applying a stern morality to their own lives, and they do not judge their neighbors in that way either.

In Raveloe, religion is a much more easy-going, casual affair than it is at Lantern Yard. No one is expected to be fanatical about regular church attendance, for example. In fact, the opposite seems to apply:

> [T]here was hardly a person in the parish who would not have held that to go to church every Sunday in the calendar would have shown a greedy desire to stand well with Heaven, and get an undue advantage over their neighbors—a wish to be better than the "common run."

Whereas in Lantern Yard, religion has an element of competition in it—the urge to show that one is saved—in Raveloe, it is a more cooperative enterprise. It is valued primarily as a way of encouraging a sense of community. For example, Mr. Macey's purpose in telling Silas he should have a suit made

What Do I Read Next?

- Like *Silas Marner*, Eliot's novel *Adam Bede* (1859) is set in a fictional rural community in which the people adhere to traditional ways of communal living. Unlike the situation in *Silas Marner*, however, the villagers must learn to deal with the kinds of social change they are ill-equipped to face.

- *North and South* (1855), by Victorian novelist Elizabeth Gaskell, makes for an interesting comparison with Eliot's style and themes. Margaret Hale, a girl from southern England, is unwillingly sent to the northern industrial city of Manchester, where she must adjust to a rougher society than the one in which she was raised.

- Frederick Robert Karl's biography *George Eliot: Voice of a Century: A Biography* (1995) has been widely praised for bringing Eliot vividly to life. Giving full attention to issues of class and gender, he recreates the world in which she lived and shows how she became a great writer.

- Asa Briggs's *The Age of Improvement: 1783–1867* (1959; 2d ed., 1999) is a classic study of how and why Britain changed from the time of the French Revolution to the mid-Victorian era. Briggs covers sociological, economic, political and cultural history.

- Richard Muir's *The English Village* (1980) describes the history of the English village and provides many photographs.

---

so he can come to church on Sunday, is to enable Silas to "be a bit neighborly." It has nothing to do with salvation, which no one in Raveloe ever talks about. Indeed, Godfrey Cass, who perhaps has as much reason as anyone in the novel to fear God and ask Him for mercy and forgiveness, appears to be untroubled by any religious thought at all. He relies only on "chances which might be favourable to him."

"Favourable Chance," as Godfrey continually finds out, makes a poor god. Most people in Raveloe, if anyone were to ask them, would no doubt claim to believe in a better one, but few trouble themselves to inquire into His nature. Eliot gives no opportunity to the rector, Mr. Crackenthorp, to discourse on such a topic. A minor character, his sole contribution is to admonish Silas that his money has probably been taken from him because he thinks too much about it and also because he does not go to church. But Mr. Crackenthorp, like some of the other villagers, does bring Silas a gift of food, a gesture that shows his desire to include Silas in the community.

The real theologian of Raveloe is not the rector but the humble, inarticulate, unlearned Dolly Winthrop. Dolly understands almost nothing of Christian doctrine, but she has an intuitive faith that a higher force operates in human life that knows better than she does what is right for her and for everyone else. She goes to church because doing so makes her feel better. She trusts in "Them," as she puts it—the plural pronoun satisfying her need not to seem overly familiar with the divine persons. Dolly's faith is based on bits and pieces she has picked up from sermons and other aspects of the church services, as well as from her own experience. It serves her well enough. Like Mr. Macey, she has no interest in assuring Silas's eternal salvation; she simply wants him to go to church because it will make him feel better too, and will also enable him to participate in the community.

Such is religion in Raveloe. It offers comfort and a sense of community. In that respect it is perhaps no more important than the Rainbow or even the squire's Red House when it hosts a community event. The nearest the Raveloe church congregation ever gets to the kind of spiritual experience that the believers at Lantern Yard might value is during the special service at Christmas, which "brought a vague exulting sense . . . that something great and mysterious had been done for them in heaven above and in earth below, which they were appropriating by their presence."

The "something great and mysterious" in *Silas Marner* is of course the appearance of Eppie on Silas's hearth. This is the moment when salvation reaches out and touches the miser. But it is a this-worldly salvation, redemption of Silas's earthly life, not the promise of an afterlife in heaven. It has nothing to do with the Thirty-Nine Articles that constitute the orthodox doctrine of the Anglican Church. And just in case the reader misses the point, the narrator, who has earlier subtly conveyed her disapproval of the spiritual education provided at Lantern Yard, now tellingly comments on the events by which Silas's life is to be transformed. His salvation is not to be confused with anything transcendental or supernatural:

> In old days there were angels who came and took men by the hand and led them away from the city of destruction. We see no white-angels now. But yet men are led away from threatening destruction: a hand is put into theirs, which leads them forth gently towards a calm and bright land, so that they look no more backwards; and the hand may be a little child's.

This interpolation by the narrator might be seen as a kind of agnosticism or humanism. The child that saves is not the divine child that the wise men came to honor, nor the angels of popular tradition, but a poor little orphan girl. What counts in human life, the narrator seems to be telling the reader, is not man's relationship to God or his reliance on the panoply of divine helpers so beloved by true believers, but man's relationship with man. In place of empty speculation about "Assurance of salvation," which led the pious young Silas into the barren terrain of "hope mingled with fear," is the concrete reality, mediated to him by the innocent Eppie, of a man's connections to the human community in which he lives. Silas's salvation is found not in supernature but in nature, not in a future shining heavenly city but in a garden and a cottage and the comforting familiarity of daughter and son-in-law and neighbors well-known and loved.

Source: Bryan Aubrey, Critical Essay on *Silas Marner*, in *Novels for Students*, Thomson Gale, 2005.

Joyce Hart

Hart has degrees in English and creative writing and is the author of several books. In this essay, Hart examines the themes of Eliot's novel as they develop through a contrasting evaluation of the characters of Silas Marner and Godfrey Cass.

Some critics have dismissed Eliot's *Silas Marner* because it reads too much like a fairy tale. And true, there are many fairy-tale elements in the novel, but this is no reason to condemn it as lacking depth. Eliot uses the familiar story frame of fortuitous coincidence, clear-cut relationships between good and evil, as well as the novel's happy ending so as to avoid inventing a new kind of story structure. Using this simple form has allowed Eliot to concentrate on the themes she wants to explore. The fundamental form highlights Eliot's messages, making them stand out against the more basic background. Her point is not to tell a complicated story but rather to get her point of view across. Eliot's themes are her message, and her messages can be seen most clearly through an examination of the contrasting characters of Silas Marner and Godfrey Cass.

Although the title of this novel emphasizes Silas Marner as the main character, Marner would not be as fully developed if Eliot had not included Marner's mirror image, Godfrey Cass. Not only does Eliot flip back and forth between the circumstances of these men's lives throughout the story, she also compares and contrasts their images with one another long before their eventual meeting. So as readers travel through this novel, it is as if they are wearing stereophonic headphones through which they listen to two separate tracks of music that, though diverse, complement one another. Godfrey is like the bass to the melody of Silas. One offsets the other.

When Silas is first introduced, he is seen as an "alien-looking" man who lives near the village of Ravenloe. He has "mysterious peculiarities." He also does not invite people to his cottage, nor does he enter the village to seek company. Silas is a loner, who needs, or so it appears, nothing more than to work, which he does incessantly. He is, according to gossip, a "dead man come to life again," a man who might just as easily cure you from a malady as to cause you mischief. In the villagers' eyes, Silas is someone to talk about but not someone to talk to. He is a man with no known past and thus a man who cannot be trusted.

In contrast, Godfrey Cass is the son of "the greatest man in Raveloe" whose main weakness, according to village sentiment, is that he has "kept all his sons at home in idleness." Although Godfrey has his family's reputation behind him, he has not proven himself. He has yet to establish any worth other than his inheritance. Godfrey's history is well known, and so he is trusted. His path has been determined by the stature of his father and his grandfather. He has a path that the local citizens expect him to follow. Their only fear is that Godfrey might stray from that path, as did his brother. Thus, the comparison of Silas and Godfrey begins. Silas works hard but is criticized for not socializing while

Godfrey is deemed a "fine, open-faced, good-natured young man," but he is lazy. At this point, Eliot also begins to display her other major theme: the disparities between the working class and the wealthy landowners. Each group has its qualities; each has its weaknesses. At the beginning of the novel, Godfrey is given the benefit of the doubt because of his known ancestry. Silas is feared because he represents the unknown. As the novel progresses, however, the villagers become more acquainted with Silas as his humanity becomes exposed. In contrast, Godfrey's reputation begins to crumble.

Eliot gives both Silas and Godfrey adversaries. It is through the men's relationship with these antagonists that the novelist explores her dual theme of honesty and deception. Ironically for Silas, his enemy is his best friend, William Dane. Dane betrays Silas and is the reason Silas leaves his hometown and lives for many years in total isolation. Dane's dishonesty causes Silas to mistrust everyone. Silas eventually turns against himself. Instead of blossoming in his youth, Silas sinks deeper and deeper into a world of darkness.

Godfrey's adversary is his brother Dunstan, a fraudulent man who causes Godfrey a lot of distress. The circumstances surrounding the brothers' relationship are more complicated than that between Silas and Dane. Dane, in comparison to Silas, is a man of loose morals. The Silas and Dane relationship has very definite boundaries without any shades of gray. Silas is all good. Dane is all bad. Dane acts alone, without any communication with Silas. Dane is cruel and, as far as the story studies the matter, fully without repentance. Silas portrays the role of the innocent and is caught completely off guard when Dane betrays him. In contrast, Godfrey, even though at first it appears he is only trying to protect his brother from their father's wrath, turns out to be a silent partner in his brother's deception. Godfrey himself is dishonest and makes excuses for his own weaknesses in order to justify them. In this way, Eliot's contrast of the two main characters begins to deepen. Silas, Eliot demonstrates, is the better man.

The issue of money is another major theme of Eliot's story. She looks at it from several different points of view. There is, of course, the money that William Dane stole and then blamed its theft on Silas. This matter of pilfering a small bag of coins has as much to do with money as it does with religion and friendship, at least in terms of Silas's life. It was this theft and the blame for it that drove Silas away from his home, his church, and his friends.

> " So as readers travel through this novel, it is as if they are wearing stereophonic headphones through which they listen to two separate tracks of music that, though diverse, complement one another. Godfrey is like the bass to the melody of Silas."

This act was the catalyst that in the end would save Silas from a life of monotonous labor in an industrialized world. It might have also saved him from an unhappy marriage, as his betrothed ended up marrying Silas's best friend, the one who had betrayed him, implying that the young woman might not have been worth Silas's love. This money and the theft of it turned out to be Silas's ticket out of town. Looked at in this way, this first robbery foreshadows a greater and more significant crime, one that will once again change the course of Silas's life.

Silas is more personally involved in the second robbery. This time the money is his—savings he has accumulated over many years. Silas's devotion to and admiration of his wealth is as close as he comes to feeling love. There is nothing more precious to him than the gold that he hides under his loom and counts each night before going to bed. It is the reason for him to weave all day and night. It is what drives him to go out and sell his wares. This money is the motivation that makes him want to continue to live. It is his family, his friends, and his community. When Godfrey's brother steals it, Silas is devastated. He was like a "man falling into deep water," Eliot writes, and he "gave a wild ringing scream, the cry of desolation" when the full realization of the theft sunk deep into his consciousness. Silas had invested every thought, every hope in his golden treasure. His attention to his wealth might even have absorbed him to the depth of his identity, his soul. Who was he without the rewards he had earned through his labors? What worth remained in him? Or as Eliot puts it, the theft had "left his soul like a forlorn traveler on an unknown desert." This loss of money will once again turn Silas's life around. Only this time, instead of turning toward the dark, Silas will turn toward the light. His life will open up, as will his heart. He will become a part of the community. His past, both the good and the bad parts, will be reviewed. He will no longer have to hide. Money, Eliot seems to be saying, is not the proper goal in life. It is but currency and must move from one hand to another to provide food and shelter. The love of money can turn one's heart into an organ as cold as a rock.

Offsetting Silas's part of the story, Eliot presents Godfrey's problems once again. Godfrey has wealth but it is controlled by his father. This does not usually seem to concern Godfrey. His needs are always met. He has no need for a craft by which to earn a wage because he will one day rule the family estate. It seems that the only time Godfrey thinks of money is when he is forced to cover his brother's mishandling of it. Money, in Godfrey's case, is not associated with sweat, as it is with Silas. The only sweat Godfrey experiences is of a psychological nature. For one thing, Dunstan causes Godfrey great anxiety. So, too, does Godfrey's own deeds. Godfrey's real fear is that his secret will be found out, and he will lose both his father's and his sweetheart's respect. It is at this point that Eliot reveals further corruptions of Godfrey's integrity. For reasons of sexual passion, Godfrey has become involved with a poor, drug-addicted woman. She has born him a child for whom Godfrey shows little affection. He provides monetary easements but little else. With this, Eliot demonstrates again her theme that money is not related to love. She also shows the shallowness of Godfrey's feelings. Godfrey cares little for his wife, Molly. He wants only to be rid of her so that he can marry Nancy, a woman more suited to his social standing. Also with Godfrey's involvement with Molly, Eliot emphasizes the chasm that exists between the poor class and the rich. It is in contrast with these exposed elements of Godfrey's personality, his weaknesses and deficits, that Silas Marner begins to shine.

Finally there is Eppie, Godfrey's child, who has a head of gold curls that remind Silas of the pile of gold treasure he once had but has lost. Upon seeing Eppie, Silas immediately falls in love with her. It is his belief that the gods of fortune have replaced his lost money with this child. He feels he has finally been rewarded. Eppie now becomes the true reason for living. She opens Silas's heart. Silas had been misguided in the past, trying to amass a fortune of gold to dismiss his loneliness and make up for the false judgment of his character. It takes more than

gold, Eliot proclaims through Silas, to make a life worthwhile. Opening oneself to another is the most gratifying pleasure that exists. Then, Eliot takes this concept one step further by having Godfrey try to win the heart of Eppie through monetary things. Godfrey tries to buy Eppie's love. He will provide her a better home and bestow on her social status. Eppie exemplifies Eliot's message. Love, not money, is the way to open someone's heart. So in the end, Silas is victorious, and Godfrey berates himself for having failed. "It's part of my punishment," he says to his wife, "for my daughter to dislike me."

With this, the fairy tale ends. The bad are punished for their weaknesses and sins, and the good are provided benevolence. Through this fairy tale, Eliot has found a form upon which to display her message.

Source: Joyce Hart, Critical Essay on *Silas Marner*, in *Novels for Students*, Thomson Gale, 2005.

Robert Speaight

In the following excerpt, Speaight argues that while Silas Marner *may not be Eliot's best book, it may be her most well-structured.*

Silas Marner is not the most important, but it is perhaps the most perfect of George Eliot's novels. It is flawed by no failure of characterisation and no excess of moralism. Where *Adam Bede* had in parts the still beauty of an eclogue and where Maggie Tulliver expressed with great tenderness and truth the unsatisfied longings of her creator, *Silas Marner* represents a significant advance in objectivity. Even the familiar landscape is viewed with greater realism; nowhere, except in the passages between Marner and his foster-child Effie, is there the slightest effort to charm. George Eliot tells us that she once asked a dying labourer: "Is there anything that you can fancy that you would like to eat?" "No," he answered, "I've never been used to nothing but common victual and I can't eat that." It was out of her own experience of this plainness, this homespun simplicity, that *Silas Marner* was conceived. The Methodist atmosphere of Marner's youth, and of her own, is perfectly evoked:

> The whitewashed walls; the little pews where well-known figures entered with a subdued rustling, and where first one well-known voice and then another, pitched in a peculiar key of petition, uttered phrases at once occult and familiar, like the amulet, worn on the heart; the pulpit where the minister delivered unquestioned doctrine, and swayed to and fro, and handled the book in a long-accustomed manner; the very pauses between the couplets of the hymn, as it was given out, and the recurrent swell of voices in song: these things had been the channel of divine influences

to Marner—they were the fostering home, of his religious emotions—they were Christianity and God's kingdom upon earth.

This was [Latern Yard] with its courtyards and red-brick alleys and censorious congregations, where Marner had been unjustly pronounced guilty of theft. A sharp contrast is drawn between this industrial dinginess and the fat complacent countryside where Marner will always feel himself to be an exile.

> Orchards, looking lazy with neglected plenty; the large church in the wide churchyard, which men gazed at lounging at their doors during service-time; the purple-faced farmers jogging along the lanes or turning in at the Rainbow; homesteads, where men supped heavily and slept in the light of the evening hearth, and where women seemed to be laying up a stock of linen for the life to come.

And there is the prosperous Anglican Christmas, with its

> vague exulting sense, for which the grown men could as little have found words as the children, that something great and mysterious had been done for them in heaven above and in earth below, which they were appropriating by their presence. And then these red faces made their way through the black, biting frost to their own homes, feeling themselves free for the rest of the day to eat, drink, and be merry, and using that Christian freedom without diffidence.

These oppositions are more scenic than sociological; they prepare the reader's mind for the myth which is the core of the novel. Nothing is more dangerous for a novelist than an idea, and George Eliot was more than once defeated by them. But in *Silas Marner* the myth is so amply clothed by characterisation, so subtly aided by description, that we still feel that "this is life"—the acid test of fiction—even though we are made aware, as we are so often made aware in life itself, of symbols and purposes behind it. Marner is certainly presented to us as a wronged man, but there is a sin in his embitterment. Of this embitterment, this sterile turning in upon himself, the hoarded gold is the expression; and when he loses it, again unjustly, he loses a prop which had really been an obstacle. His material and spiritual poverty are now made one, and he is free to welcome the redemptive influence of Effie. These profound meanings are never overstressed and Marner himself is doubtless but half aware of them. He only knows that:

> The gold had kept his thoughts in an ever-repeated circle, tending to nothing beyond itself; but Effie was an object compacted of changes and hopes that forced his thoughts onward and carried them far away from their old eager facing towards the same blank limit.... The gold had asked that he should sit weaving longer and longer, deafened and blinded more and more to all things except the monotony of his loom and the

> *Silas Marner* is, technically, a very finished book. It is much shorter than George Eliot's other more important novels and one feels that she has put into it exactly the right weight of writing."

repetition of his web; but Effie called him away from his weaving and made him think all its pauses a holiday—re-awakening all his senses with her fresh life, even to the old winter-flies that come crawling forth in the early spring sunshine, and warming him into joy because *she* had joy.

Marner's redemption was neither automatic nor immediate. It was only when his love was perfected that the gold was given back to him. He sensed it with that clear moral intuition which belongs to all George Eliot's unsophisticated characters.

> At first, I'd a sort of feeling come across me now and then . . . as if you might be changed into the gold again; for sometimes, turn my head which way I would, I seemed to see the gold; and I thought I should be glad if I could feel it, and find it was come back. But that didn't last long. After a bit, I should have thought it was a curse come again if it had drove me from you . . .

George Eliot was never again directly to treat the theme of money. There is nothing sentimental in her opposition of gold and charity; indeed, her handling of it, though it lacks psychological complexity, has the pure simplicity of a parable. Behind it lies the mystery of being, the unpredictable design, and the permitted wickedness of Mammon. These are left in the twilight where the mind does its feeble best to apprehend them. There is no trace of pessimism in George Eliot's agnostic acceptance of Fate: "the gods of the hearth exist for us still; and let all new faith be tolerant of that fetichism, lest it bruise its own roots." And Marner has his own irrefutable reply to the problem of evil:

> There's good i' this world—I've a feeling o' that now; and it makes a man feel there's a good deal more nor he can see, i' spite o' the trouble and the wickedness. That drawing o' the lots is dark; but the child was sent to me: there's dealings with us—there's dealings.

This is more profound, because it is more realistic and less emotional, than Hardy's "the President of the Immortals had ended his sport with Tess." And Marner is helped to his conclusion by Dolly Winthrop, one of George Eliot's most triumphant character parts. She is the voice itself of naturalism, understood not as an accurate recording of dialect or photographic observation of idiosyncrasy—though she is both of these—but as nature's own comment upon life. The peasant common sense is finally prepared to accept Marner's rearing of Effie:

> It's like the night and the morning, and the sleeping and the waking, and the rain and the harvest—one goes and the other comes, and we know nothing how nor where. We may strive and scrat and fend, but it's little we can do arter all—the big things come and go with no striving of our'n—they do, that they do; and I think you're in the right on it to keep the little 'un, Master Marner, seeing as it's been sent to you, though there's folks as thinks different. You'll happen to be a bit moithered with it while it's so little; but I'll come and welcome, and see to it for you; I've a bit of time to spare most days, for when one gets up betimes i' the morning, the clock seems to stan' still tow'rt ten, afore it's time to go about the victual. So, as I say, I'll come and see to the child for you, and welcome.

Listen to the liturgical lilt of this speech and you will find it easy to imagine that Dolly was used to hearing the Authorised Version read aloud, and these Biblical echoes are mixed with native poetry. George Eliot is generally able to rise to a poetic apprehension of character, and Dolly Winthrop is a good example of this capacity. She is with Shallow and Touchstone and Mistress Quickly, giving to her setting as much as she takes from it.

Silas Marner is, technically, a very finished book. It is much shorter than George Eliot's other more important novels and one feels that she has put into it exactly the right weight of writing. She does here all her characteristic things supremely well. The scene at the Rainbow is justly celebrated, with Marner, crazy with the loss of his gold, shattering the bucolic humours of the bar. In a single image George Eliot gives us the whole picture, when "the long pipes gave a simultaneous movement, like the antennae of startled insects." The various social *milieux* are admirably related to each other—the small squires, the yeoman farmers, the tradesmen, the peasants. There is a rough equality here; the fabric holds easily together. Geoffrey Cass, weak, conscientious, and good-natured, quite without imagination, is first cousin to Arthur Donnithorne and Nancy, a step lower down in the social scale, is carefully differentiated by a touch of provincial dialect. But this was the last time that George Eliot was to

content herself with a rustic theme. The bloom of these Midland hedgerows was beginning to wear off; there was a world elsewhere; and even within the loved, familiar setting a more complex pattern of human relationships awaited her discovery.

Source: Robert Speaight, "George Eliot," in *George Eliot*, Lowe and Brydone, 1954, pp. 62–67.

Sources

Dallas, E. S., Review of *Silas Marner*, in *The Critical Response to George Eliot*, edited by Karen L. Pangallo, Greenwood Press, 1994, pp. 94–96, originally published in *The Times*, April 29, 1861.

Eliot, George, *Silas Marner*, edited and with an introduction by Q. D. Leavis, Penguin, 1985.

Ermath, Elizabeth Deeds, *George Eliot*, Twayne's English Authors Series, No. 414, Twayne Publishers, 1985, pp. 97–102.

Leavis, Q. D., "Introduction," in *Silas Marner*, by George Eliot, edited by Q. D. Leavis, Penguin, 1985.

Thompson, E. P., *The Making of the English Working Class*, Penguin, 1968, pp. 297–346.

Trevelyan, G. M., *Illustrated English Social History*, Vol. 3, *The Eighteenth Century*, Harmondsworth, Penguin Books, 1968, p. 139.

Further Reading

Beer, Gillian, *George Eliot*, Indiana University Press, 1986, pp. 108–46.
    In this feminist study, Beer discusses Silas Marner, Romola, and Felix Holt in terms of the displacement involved in proposing a conflict between natural parents and nurturing parents.

Johnstone, Peggy Fitzburgh, *The Transformation of Rage: Mourning and Creativity in George Eliot's Fiction*, New York University Press, 1994, pp. 68–94.
    This is a Freudian interpretation of the novel, including a discussion of what is called obsessive-compulsive disorder (repetitive actions and thoughts) and its cure.

McCormack, Kathleen, *George Eliot and Intoxication: Dangerous Drugs for the Condition of England*, St. Martin's Press, 2000, pp. 91–109.
    As part of her study of Eliot's drug metaphors, McCormack analyzes the novel as a parable of addiction and recovery.

Speaight, Robert, Review of *Silas Marner*, in *George Eliot*, 2d ed., Arthur Barker, 1968, pp. 61–67.
    This is a short review of the many outstanding aspects of the novel, including its characterization, its lack of excessive moralism, and its life-like realism that still allows for symbolic elements.

Summer

Edith Wharton
1917

Summer, published in 1917, is one of only two novels the prolific writer Edith Wharton set in rural New England. Wharton, who was both critically acclaimed and a bestselling author, was perhaps better known in her lifetime for her many novels set in New York City among the wealthy elite. In this novel, however, the author's keen attention to detail is turned away from fashion and manners and city life and instead directed at the wonders of the natural world as they echo the changes felt by the central character, Charity Royall. *Summer* was only a moderate success when it first appeared, but when Wharton's work was rediscovered in the 1960s the novel found a new, larger, and more appreciative critical audience.

Like the protagonist in *Ethan Frome*, Wharton's most widely read novel today, Charity yearns for a fuller life than the one she lives in her small town, but social restrictions and a certain weakness of character prevent her from realizing her dreams. One of the first American literary novels to deal frankly with a young woman's sexual awakening, *Summer* begins with a chance encounter, has a passionate affair at its center, and ends with a wedding. In this bare outline, *Summer* appears similar to hundreds of "sentimental" novels of the period, but critics agree that Wharton's depth of feeling and rich prose have turned a conventional plot into art. The novel's contemporary reviewers argued heatedly over the meaning of the wedding, and the question continued to interest critics in the twenty-first century.

Edith Wharton

Author Biography

Edith Wharton was born Edith Newbold Jones on January 24, 1862, in New York City. Her parents, wealthy members of New York's social elite, had a large home in Manhattan and another home in fashionable Newport, Rhode Island. From the time Edith was four until she was about ten, the family lived and traveled throughout Europe, avoiding the economic downturn that occurred in the United States after the Civil War. Edith developed an ear for languages and a taste for art and architecture that stayed with her for her entire life. When the family returned to New York, she did not attend formal school as her two brothers did but was encouraged by her father to study literature and philosophy on her own. Fluent in German, Italian, and French, she read widely. She also began to write, completing her first satirical fiction while she was only fourteen. Her first publication was a small volume of poetry, *Verses*, published anonymously in 1878 when she was sixteen.

In April 1885, Edith married Edward "Teddy" Wharton, who was fifteen years older than she. Wharton reveals in her memoir *A Backward Glance* (1934) that she and Teddy were friendly but not passionate with each other; the couple never had children, and Edith did not discover sexual passion

until an affair decades later. The couple settled in Newport, and Edith established the morning as her time to write. In 1891, the first story published under the name Edith Wharton appeared and was followed by dozens of stories in the most important magazines of the day. By the turn of the century, Wharton was an internationally renowned fiction writer. With the publication of the novel *The House of Mirth* in 1905, she became a celebrity. She and Teddy divorced in 1913, and Wharton lived an independent but not lonely life thereafter.

Over the next thirty years she published more than forty novels, collections of stories, and nonfiction books. A few, including *Ethan Frome* (1911) and *Summer* (1917), were set in rural New England among people of the middle and lower classes, but she is best known for her fiction exploring the lives and values of wealthy Americans in urban settings. In 1921 she became the first woman to win the Pulitzer Prize for fiction, for *The Age of Innocence*, a novel about the moral conventions of the nineteenth-century New York elite. In 1930, she was elected to the American Academy of Arts and Letters. As she grew older, her literary output and success increased; she was very wealthy and lived extravagantly, with lavish homes in New England and France. She died after a series of strokes and a heart attack, on August 7, 1937, at Pavillon Colombe, her home in Saint Brice-sous-Forêt, France.

Plot Summary

Chapter 1

It is a June afternoon in the early part of the twentieth century as *Summer* begins, and nineteen-year-old Charity Royall stands on the doorstep of her home, about to set off for her job at the library. As she looks over the small New England town of North Dormer, she notices a stranger, a young man clearly from the city. Something about him captures her imagination, and she feels, not for the first time, that her small-town life is unsatisfying. She is flustered when he enters the library to ask for books about the local architecture, and he appears flustered as well, struck by Charity's beauty. His questions about the library's holdings remind Charity how little she knows about books, and she is both disappointed and relieved when he leaves.

Chapter 2

To clear her head, Charity heads for a hillside, where she lies among the wild flowers and observes the many signs of summer. She often comes here when she has thinking to do, and the scented breezes on her skin always cheer her. On this day she reflects on her life since she came to live in North Dormer. She is the legal ward, though not the adopted daughter, of Lawyer Royall, whose wife died seven or eight years after they took Charity in. Charity has given little thought to the man who provides for her. Once, when she was seventeen, he approached her bedroom at night and made a feeble attempt to seduce her, but she rebuffed him and has had no fear that he will repeat his actions. However, she has taken the library position hoping that eventually she can earn enough money to get away from North Dormer.

Chapters 3–6

Over the next few weeks, Charity and the stranger, Lucius Harney, become friends. Harney lives alone down the street and has arranged to take his meals at the Royalls' home. The young architect is sketching and measuring the old houses in the area, and with the horse-drawn buggy he rents from Royall he has visited several remote areas of the region with Charity as his guide. Charity has kept the amount of time she spends alone with Harney a secret, though she is not sure why. She tells herself that she does not care what the neighbors think and that she does not care that Harney has never spoken of love. When she takes him to a house in which some of the poor Mountain folk live, she is ashamed to be reminded again of how different her background is from his.

Chapters 7–8

Now hopelessly infatuated with Harney, Charity looks forward eagerly to their meetings. One evening, he does not appear for supper, and Lawyer Royall tells Charity that he will not be coming again. Impetuously, Charity storms out and walks to Harney's house. Noticing a light, she goes to the back of the house and sees through a window that Harney is packing his bags and preparing to leave. Realizing that if she makes her presence known he will invite her in and their chaste relationship will become a physical one, she remains silent until Harney falls asleep and then returns home. The next day she learns that she was seen leaving the house after midnight, and the town gossips assume that she has had sexual relations. To protect her reputation, Lawyer Royall asks Charity to marry him and leave town, but she refuses. Harney comes to say goodbye to Charity and then sends a note asking her to meet him secretly in the next town.

Media Adaptations

- Books in Motion offers an unabridged audio recording of *Summer* read by Shaela Connor. It was published in 1992 on audiocassettes.

- Another unabridged audio presentation is available on audiocassette and CD from Blackstone Audio Books. Recorded in 1994, the novel is read by Grace Conlin. A 1999 edition includes the novel and excerpts from *A Backward Glance*.

Chapters 9–10

It is the Fourth of July, and Harney takes Charity to Nettleton for the celebrations. Everything is a wonder to Charity: the train ride, the shops and restaurants, the hotels full of glamorous and confident people, the doctor's office where an unfortunate acquaintance is said to have had an abortion. Harney shows her around the city, introduces her to the taste of wine, and even buys her a pin with blue stones—her first piece of jewelry. Later, they go to the lake where they watch a spectacular fireworks display and Harney gives Charity her first kiss. Flushed with excitement, Charity is stunned to run into Lawyer Royall, drunk and angry. He loudly calls her a whore and stumbles away.

Chapter 11

When she returns home after the Fourth of July celebration, Charity dreads encountering Lawyer Royall, but he does not return that day. Suddenly unable to bear society's condemnations, Charity decides to run away, to join her mother on the Mountain. She sets out on the fifteen-mile walk but does not get far before Harney finds her. He persuades her not to go to the Mountain, but she insists that she will not return home. Instead, they walk to an abandoned house in an orchard, and there their sexual relationship begins.

Chapters 12–14

At the end of August, the town of North Dormer is busily preparing for Old Home Week. Charity has been drafted to help make decorations, and Harney has returned to help design a stage for Town Hall. The two have been meeting secretly every afternoon. During the festivities, however, Charity sees Harney talking intimately with Annabel Balch, a sophisticated young woman from the city, and begins to doubt her hold over him. One afternoon, as she waits for Harney in the abandoned house, she is met instead by Royall, who has learned about the secret meetings. He urges Charity to break off the relationship before it is too late, but she refuses. When Harney arrives, Royall asks him whether he intends to marry Charity, but Harney will not reply.

Chapter 15

As he had planned, Harney leaves North Dormer the next day to return to his work in New York. He has made a vague promise that he will return and marry Charity when his affairs are settled, but has asked her not to tell anyone of their plans. Later, Charity learns that Annabel Balch was with him when he left town and that they are engaged. Charity also discovers that she is pregnant. When a letter from Harney seems to offer no hope of their eventual reunion, she decides to go to the Mountain at last and raise her child among her own people.

Chapters 16–17

With the added burden of her pregnancy, Charity finds the long trip to the Mountain exhausting. She is met on the way by the local minister, called to attend to Charity's mother, who is dying. When they arrive, Charity's mother Mary has died, and Charity sees for the first time how impoverished her existence has been. Mary's people are rough and unfeeling; they have had none of Charity's meager advantages. She knows that she cannot stay there to raise her child and heads wearily back for North Dormer. Before she gets very far, Royall, who has driven all night to rescue her, finds her. He picks her up, speaks kindly to her, and asks her once again to marry him.

Chapter 18

Royall and Charity take the train to Nettleton and are married. They take a room at a fashionable hotel in the city and have a nice supper in the hotel restaurant. Charity goes up to their room to go to bed. The lawyer comes up hours later to spend the night in the rocking chair, and Charity understands that he knows she is pregnant and that he will protect her. The next day, Charity sends Harney a letter telling of her marriage and returns to North Dormer with her new husband.

Characters

Annabel Balch

Annabel Balch, a young woman of about the same age as Charity, stands as the ideal type of womanhood to which Charity aspires, despite Charity's claims that she does not care what others think. Annabel is wealthy, educated, beautiful, and sophisticated. In contrast to Charity, who is described more than once as "swarthy," Annabel is blond and blue-eyed. A relative of Miss Hatchard, she visits New Dormer periodically, but she is a city girl from Springfield with all of the advantages that implies. Even when Charity feels that she is at her best—when she is preparing to wear her white satin dress and be admired by her lover—the specter of Annabel Balch is present, as it is Annabel's hand-me-down satin shoes that complete Charity's outfit. In the end Annabel wins what Charity cannot: Lucius Harney's true love and commitment to marriage. Annabel never speaks during the novel, but she is often seen from afar or remembered at a distance, as is appropriate for an unreachable ideal.

Lucius Harney

Lucius Harney is a young architect from New York who has come to North Dormer to stay the summer with his relative, Miss Hatchard, while he measures and sketches the important old houses in the area. Although when Charity first sees him he is clumsily chasing his windblown hat, his clothing marks him as a man from the city, and Charity develops an immediate infatuation with him. At the same time, even before she meets Harney she cannot help but compare herself to him and her life to his, making her feel small and dull. As soon as she sees him, Charity wants to be more than she is.

Harney uses Charity as his guide and driver. She shows him around the area, pointing out houses he might wish to sketch for his publisher. In turn, he is her introduction into a wider world she has only glimpsed. He speaks of books and architecture. He takes her to the city of Nettleton, buys Charity her first taste of wine and her first piece of jewelry, escorts her to her first fireworks display, and gives her her first kiss. For Harney, these pleasures are commonplace, but even though he meets them with a hint of superiority he does seem to enjoy sharing them with Charity. Later that summer, he initiates Charity into a sexual relationship, and though the double standard for sexual behavior is strong in North Dormer and the risk to Charity is much greater than it is to Harney, she cannot or does not resist his temptation. His very name, Lucius, derives from Lucifer, a name for the devil.

Harney is never quite honest in his dealings with Charity: he denies that he has given a bad report of her to Miss Hatchard; he prepares to leave town without saying goodbye; he fails to mention even once his engagement to Annabel Balch; and he promises to marry Charity once he has had time to "settle things." Clearly, he has no intention of speaking to her of marriage until Lawyer Royall forces his hand, and after his angry and embarrassing confrontation with the older man Harney abruptly leaves town. Still, Harney is not ultimately a bad person—simply a young and a weak one.

Miss Hatchard

Miss Hatchard is the elderly great-niece of Honorius Hatchard, the founder for whom North Dormer's library is named. As the town's most respected and respectable citizen, she reigns over Old Home Week. She is the very model of the unmarried innocent, who knows nothing of sex and desire and who avoids thinking or knowing about anything unpleasant. When Charity turns to Miss Hatchard for help in escaping Lawyer Royall, Miss Hatchard fails to understand the problem and can offer no assistance or advice. She is surprised when Charity asks for the position as librarian but grants the request when Lawyer Royall makes it. Still, Miss Hatchard places a great value on the library that bears her great-uncle's name, and she is ready to have Charity replaced when she believes that the library is not being well tended.

Ally Hawes

Ally Hawes is Charity Royall's best friend in North Dormer and the poorest girl in the village. The two do not exchange confidences, but they pass pleasant afternoons together making small talk. Ally, who seems content with her simple small-town life, earns money as a seamstress, occasionally helping Charity supplement her modest wardrobe with clever if not lavish designs. Ally also works for Annabel Balch, and it is she who tells Charity that Annabel and Harney are going to be married. Ally is sweet and innocent and has no idea of Charity's secret passion. And although Julia, Ally's older sister, has fallen into disgrace, Ally loyally and secretly visits her sister when she can.

Julia Hawes

Julia Hawes, a few years older than Charity and Ally Hawes, is the young woman from North Dormer who turned to the bad. Sometime in the past, before the action of the novel, Julia was seduced by a young man who did not marry her. She was forced to leave North Dormer and have an abortion, which nearly killed her; she now works as a prostitute in Nettleton. No one in town speaks her name in public. Ally Hawes, her younger sister, has maintained a secret correspondence with Julia, and the young women of the town whisper Julia's name as a warning about what can happen to a young woman who is not careful. When Charity and Lucius Harney visit Nettleton on the Fourth of July they meet Julia, with her heavy make-up, showy clothing, and "coarse laughter," on the arm of Lawyer Royall. Julia mocks Charity's innocence, hardly guessing that soon a pregnant Charity will find herself in Nettleton, visiting the same abortionist who attended Julia.

Charity Royall

Charity Royall is the novel's protagonist, a young woman of some nineteen years. Although she lives with her guardian Lawyer Royall and uses his last name, she is in fact the child of a drunken convict and a prostitute, and this heritage, which places her in an even lower socioeconomic class than the rest of North Dormer, shames her. Lawyer Royall and his wife rescued Charity when she was five years old, but Mrs. Royall died seven or eight years later. Since then, Charity has ruled the Royall home and has grown increasingly strong-willed. After Mrs. Royall's death, Charity refused to go away to boarding school, fearing that Royall would be too lonely without her. Six or seven years later, a drunken Royall approached Charity's room and attempted unsuccessfully to seduce her. Since that time, the older man and young woman have lived essentially separate lives under the same roof, and Charity has taken a job at the town library hoping to earn enough money to leave North Dormer.

When Charity meets and becomes infatuated with Lucius Harney, her dissatisfaction with her life becomes her essential reality. She sighs, "How I hate everything!" As her relationship with Harney deepens, and she spends more and more time alone with him driving him around the countryside, she knows she is violating convention, but she does not care. For the first time, she feels sexual yearning, and she finds it thrilling and puzzling. Her infatuation for Harney is mixed with awe, and she finds herself relying on his judgment more than on her own. When he takes her to Nettleton for the Fourth of July, she lets him order her food and drink and select her jewelry. When he is ready for sexual intimacy, she follows his lead, and she does not ask for any assurances from him.

In the end, Charity's attempt to be independent fails. She finds herself pregnant and abandoned, and while she may not care what the town thinks of her, she knows she cannot hope to live as a single mother in North Dormer. In her desperation she finally becomes willing to look for good qualities in Lawyer Royall, and she marries him. She will not have the excitement or the independence she dreamed of, but she will have stability and contentment.

Lawyer Royall

Lawyer Royall (his first name is never mentioned) is the guardian of Charity, whom he rescued from extreme poverty when she was five. Royall is a widower, an angry man who drinks too much, a lonely man who has too much education and experience to find close friends in the backward town of North Dormer. His only close relationship is with Charity, but the fatherly feelings he felt for her in the past have changed to feelings of love and lust. Since his one attempt to gain entry to her room, however, he has maintained an honorable distance from Charity. Knowing that she wants to leave him, he has nevertheless helped her obtain her job, hired a cook to stay in the house with them, and kept silent about his disapproval over her relationship with Harney.

Royall is the most complex character in the novel and the most mysterious. Earlier in his career, he worked in the city, but some unnamed disappointment brought him back to North Dormer. He does not reveal his thoughts and feelings to Charity—or perhaps she simply does not care to see them—so she is surprised at his depth of knowledge when he converses with Harney and at his eloquence when he speaks at Old Home Week. When he confronts Charity after she is seen leaving Harney's house late at night and again in the abandoned house where she has been meeting Harney, his concern seems to be for her welfare, though Charity cannot see it. Yet when he publicly calls her a "bare-headed whore" at the Fourth of July festivities, his concern seems to be only for his own wounded feelings.

Critics have argued since the book's first publication over the sort of marriage Royall and Charity may have. They point to his drinking, his temper, his violent changes in mood. They point also to his quiet compassion and understanding, revealed in his spending his wedding night in the chair beside Charity's bed. Royall can never be the exciting lover that Harney has been. But in the end, it is Royall, not Harney, who stands by Charity in her trouble, who goes looking for her when she is lost, and who brings her home again.

Themes

Sexual Awakening

More than anything else, *Summer* is the story of a young woman's discovery of sexual desire. At the beginning of the novel, Charity is completely inexperienced when it comes to men; she has seen other people in the village break off into couples, but the young men of North Dormer hold no attraction for her. Harney is the first man Charity feels an interest in, and as she spends time with him her feelings change and develop. But unlike the heroines of many other novels, Charity does not dream of a cozy cottage or the domestic life of a wife and mother. Her desire is for sexual fulfillment.

The Charity who opens the novel is bored with everything and everyone. Though tired and cold, when Charity steps down from the buggy after being tenderly and platonically held by Harney in the rain she feels as though "the ground were a sunlit wave and she the spray on its crest." As she watches him through the window of his bedroom, she feels "All her old resentments and rebellions . . . confusedly mingled with the yearning roused by Harney's nearness." And when they have begun their affair, she feels that "all the rest of life" has become "a mere cloudy rim about the central glory of their passion." As she waits for Harney in their secret meeting place, Charity, who has been wanting to get out of North Dormer since she was mature enough to frame the thought, feels that he has "caught her up and carried her away to a new world." Charity does not question how sex fits into the rest of her life, or whether the relationship might last, or what its consequences might be. For her, for now, the delights of sexual experience are enough.

In Chapter 3, just after she has met Harney for the first time, Charity does daydream about marrying him. She sees herself walking down the aisle in her wedding dress and imagines him kissing her. As she pictures the kiss, she puts her hands in front of her face "as if to imprison the kiss," and the daydream is interrupted. Beyond this glimpse of a wedding, Charity never imagines what married life might be like. In fact, once they become sexually intimate she stops wondering about marriage altogether and does not think of it again until Lawyer Royall raises the issue when he confronts Charity and Harney in the old house. When Charity finds her dress for Old Home Week laid out on her bed looking like a wedding dress, she remembers dreaming about marrying Harney but notes that "She no longer had such visions . . . warmer splendors had displaced them."

Topics For Further Study

- Research the tradition of Old Home Week in New England villages near the turn of the twentieth century. What purposes does this tradition seem to have served? In what ways is Old Home Week like and unlike homecoming as it is celebrated at high schools and colleges today?

- Research the availability of contraceptives and abortion in the early part of the twentieth century. What might Charity and Harney have done to avoid pregnancy? If Charity had decided to have Dr. Merkle perform an abortion, how safe might it have been?

- The pin Harney buys for Charity costs $10—the same as the fare to ride around the lake in an "electric run-about." Using 1910 as the year Harney bought the pin, calculate the approximate cost in dollars used in the early 2000s. How nice a gift did he buy her?

- Edith Wharton's original readers would have understood from the beginning that Charity and Lucius Harney would not last as a couple, because they come from different social classes. In the community you live in, what are the chances that two people from different social, ethnic or religious groups can form lasting bonds, supported by the larger community? Is the idea of sticking with your own kind outdated or still important?

- Are any old buildings in your town named after early citizens? Research the lives and contributions of one or more of these namesakes. What kinds of people are honored in this way?

Social Classes

In the early part of the twentieth century in the United States, social class was still an important factor in social interaction; that is, it was almost unheard of for members of different classes to become close friends or to marry. As her fiction demonstrates, Wharton believed that these conventions were especially strict among the very wealthy and among those rural people who found themselves cut off from the rest of the world. Towns like North Dormer, with no railroad station or telegraph, were likely to be conservative in regulating people with clearly understood but rarely articulated codes of behavior. In North Dormer, it is understood that the different classes do not mix.

Three different classes move through the world of *Summer*. Most of the residents are middle-class people who earn their living as shopkeepers and seamstresses. Lawyer Royall, by virtue of his profession, is slightly out of step with the rest of the community, and he is widely thought to be slightly above the others, but he is more similar than different. Below the people of North Dormer are the folk from the Mountain, "humblest of the humble." Charity was born on the Mountain, of a prostitute mother and a father who was a drunken criminal, and she knows she is fortunate to be in North Dormer because "Everyone in the village had told her so ever since she had been brought there as a child." She even looks different from the others, with her "swarthy" face and her yellowish eyes. The two classes do not mix. People from North Dormer do not talk much about the Mountain people but show their "disparagement by an intonation rather than by explicit criticism." For their part, the Mountain people do not tolerate any intrusion from North Dormer (with the occasional exception of the minister), and the people from town are afraid to go to the Mountain, for fear of the reception they would find. Charity, however, knows the Mountain people "would never hurt her," because she will always be one of theirs.

The third social class, represented by Miss Hatchard and her relatives Lucius Harney and Annabel Balch, is educated, wealthy, and urbane. They read books, they have fine clothes, travel freely between the cities and the countryside, and they feel at ease moving through different communities. As her friendship with Harney deepens, Charity's greatest fear is that he will learn of her origins, that her origin "must widen the distance between them." She understands but soon forgets, that "Education and opportunity had divided them by a width that no effort of hers could bridge."

In his anger when Harney will not speak of marriage, Lawyer Royall utters the assumption that most of North Dormer has presumably been making about Charity all along: that her parentage being what it is, she cannot be expected to be virtuous. He tells Harney, "They all know what she is, and what she came from. They all know her mother was a woman of the town." Charity has feared all along that Harney would find out about her parents and think less of her because of them, and she is right to be fearful. Clearly, he has never planned to commit to Charity but has seen her as available and of a lower class, perfect for a summer romance. Charity benefits from the sexual energy that Harney would never consider expending on an unmarried woman from his own world, just as she wears the white satin shoes that Annabel Balch no longer needs. In the end, Harney does what he has intended to do all along: he marries Annabel, a woman of his own class. The novel does not explicitly challenge the notion that one's social class determines one's personality or one's place in the world. It simply shows what happens in a world where this notion is assumed to be true.

Style

Bildungsroman

Summer is a *bildungsroman* (from the German for "novel about education"), the story of a young person's development into adulthood. The tradition of the *bildungsroman* in English literature is strong and includes such important novels as Charlotte Brontë's *Jane Eyre* (1847) and Charles Dickens's *David Copperfield* (1849–1850). Typical of the form, *Summer* begins with Charity, a relatively sheltered young person on the verge of adulthood. Charity has no real responsibilities, and her basic needs are provided for. She is independent-minded but still rather childish, as when she murmurs, "How I hate everything!" She is not curious about books or about other people, she keeps telling herself that she does not care what anyone thinks of her but cannot stop comparing herself to Annabel Balch and the Nettleton ladies, she falls head over heels in love with the first city-born man she sees— in short, she is a typical adolescent. As she moves through the novel, Charity is forced to consider

other lives than her own. As a jilted lover and finally as a wife and an expectant mother, Charity is finally forced to grow up.

By the beginning of the twentieth century, several novels had explored the maturation of a female protagonist. However, as Cynthia Griffin Wolff explains in an Introduction to *Summer*, Charity's story "is the first to deal explicitly with sexual passion as an essential component of that process." While Charity at first yearns, as earlier heroines had, for a safe and romantic soft-lens kind of love, her romantic fantasies pale beside her strong sexual urges, and in her passion she does not even wonder whether Lucius Harney will marry her. Knowing the difference between love and lust, or between a summer romance and a lifetime commitment, is an important lesson Charity must learn before she moves into adulthood.

Imagery

Unlike Lucius Harney and Lawyer Royall, who are primarily interested in books and buildings and ideas, Charity finds her most expansive self when she is alone in nature. When she has something to think over, she leaves the library and goes to a quiet hillside; while Harney sketches a historic house, Charity waits in a field. Throughout the novel, Wharton uses vivid imagery to draw parallels between the natural world and Charity, both, in summertime, bursting with life and energy and fertility. The novel is set in summer, the time of heat and growth. Everything around Charity is growing, bearing blossoms and seeds, throbbing with life: "a tuft of sweet-fern uncurle[s]," "a small yellow butterfly vibrate[s]," there is "bubbling of sap and slipping of sheaths and bursting of calyxes." She watches all of this carefully, perhaps sensing that the same process is alive in her. As Charity's passion increases, the air temperature does as well. But by the time of Old Home Week, when Charity is already pregnant and Lucius will soon be gone, autumn is already beginning, and in the jar on the table where Charity and Harney meet are not summer flowers but "purple asters and red maple-leaves." As Charity walks to the Mountain where she hopes to raise her child, she sees more signs of autumn in the apple trees heavy with fruit and rose bushes "strung with scarlet hips" rather than the flowers that would have come before. That afternoon, the first snow of the year begins to fall. A few days later, as Charity and her new husband drive back to the red house, it is in "the cold autumn moonlight." As the imagery makes clear, summer—Charity's time for youth and carelessness—is over.

Compare & Contrast

- **Early Twentieth Century:** In 1914, Margaret Sanger, a nurse, is prosecuted for publishing *The Woman Rebel*, a newsletter promoting birth control. The newsletter is banned as obscene literature. Two years later, she opens a birth control clinic in New York City, one of the nation's first. It is illegal in most parts of the United States even for physicians to prescribe or discuss birth control.

  Today: Although some religious groups oppose the use of birth control, it is widely available, and generally considered safe and reasonably (but not entirely) effective. Information about sex, conception, and contraception is easily obtained.

- **Early Twentieth Century:** In Pittsburgh, the first American movie theater opens in 1905. Within ten years, all major cities in the United States have cinemas, showing silent spectacles, comedies, and newsreels. By 1912, five million people in the United States go to the movies each day.

  Today: Most American cities have multi-screen cinemas showing full-length movies with color, sound, and big-budget special effects. Movies can also be seen on broadcast television or in various in-home video formats.

- **Early Twentieth Century:** Travel is difficult and expensive for rural people. Bicycles and horse-drawn vehicles are common but naturally limit the distances one can travel. Automobiles are still largely a novelty. Women are discouraged by social convention from traveling without chaperones. As a result, poor and rural women might spend their entire lives within a few miles of their homes.

  Today: There are more automobiles in the United States than there are licensed drivers. Airplanes, buses, trains, and cars make it easy to get from one town to another. Millions of Americans live in one town and are employed in another.

- **Early Twentieth Century:** Communication is cumbersome, making it difficult to send and receive private messages. Private homes in small towns like North Dormer do not have telephones or home mail delivery.

  Today: With telephones, email, instant messaging, and mail delivery, it is easy for couples to communicate quickly and privately.

Historical Context

Women's Rights and Women's Literature

The first part of the twentieth century was a heady time for many women in the United States. For some thirty-five years, since the end of the Civil War, debate throughout the nation about what the new political role for African Americans would be had spilled over into debate about new roles for women. Active women's rights groups began to emerge in the late 1860s, demanding new rights for women: the right to vote, the right to attend colleges and universities alongside men, the right to work in the professions, the right to respectful and appropriate medical care, including information about birth control and abortion, the right to control property. Along with these political and economic demands, women also developed a heightened interest in literature that dealt with their lives and concerns. The bestselling novelists of the late nineteenth century in the United States were women, writing stories about women. Although most of these writers were not recognized by the literary establishment as serious or important, they served an important need in giving voice to women's experience.

In 1899, novelist Kate Chopin published her novel *The Awakening*, about a young woman who comes to understand that the life of a wife and mother is not satisfying to her. For Chopin's heroine Edna, there are almost no acceptable alternatives to domesticity. She would like to express herself through painting, to earn her own living, and to have passionate relationships with men. During the novel, she does have an affair with one man and feelings of love for another, in addition to her tepid relationship with her husband. The novel was met with a fury of angry criticism and accusations of obscenity, and it was banned in Chopin's hometown of St. Louis, Missouri. The novel went quickly out of print and was forgotten for more than half a century; Chopin never wrote another novel.

Like Chopin, Edith Wharton was typical of what was called the New Woman. She earned her own living from her own work (and in fact became the highest-paid novelist in the country); she divorced her husband; she traveled freely; she spent time with male friends, including the writer Henry James. Wharton did not join any women's organizations or campaign for women's rights; she preferred to keep to herself and fulfill her own dreams. In her writing, however, she created characters who had minds and hopes of their own and who frequently behaved in ways that did not conform to the rigid societal expectations for women. When Wharton published *Summer* in 1917, the "woman question" was still very much in debate. A minimum wage law for women existed in Massachusetts but nowhere else. Doctors could not discuss or prescribe birth control. Women were routinely denied educational and career opportunities. Women could vote in certain states but would not get the right to vote in federal elections until 1920. Young middle-class women like Charity Royall might have romantic dreams of more exciting lives, but other than by marrying above their class (something frowned upon and rarely accomplished) there were few ways to achieve these goals.

Critical Overview

Although *Summer* never became as popular as some of Wharton's other novels, its author was important enough that the novel was widely reviewed when it was published in 1917. Many reviewers praised Wharton for her skillful description and characterization, while others regretted that *Summer* was overall a slighter work than the previous novels. Reviewers also disagreed about the ending of the novel. Lawrence Gilman, writing for *The North American Review*, found no satisfaction in Charity's marriage to Mr. Royall, stating that her story "ends

grayly, resignedly, with long anonymous years of kindly and terrible amelioration stretching vacantly before her." An unsigned review in *The Nation*, on the other hand, was among those that celebrated the marriage, stating that "Mrs. Wharton permits, nay, encourages, us to hope a good measure of happiness for them both." H. W. Boynton, a reviewer for *The Bookman*, agreed, noting that the marriage offers, "we really believe, some chance of happiness, or at least content."

Little critical attention was paid to *Summer* and Wharton's other work during the 1930s and 1940s. Wharton lived in France for the last years of her life and watched her reputation decline. As she herself noted somewhat bitterly in her 1934 memoir *A Backward Glance*, readers during the years following the Great Depression were less interested in stories of New York and New England wealth and manners and more interested in tales of the struggles of common laborers. The 1950s saw a cluster of Wharton studies, including Blake Nevius's overview *Edith Wharton: A Study of Her Fiction* and Josephine Lurie Jessup's *The Faith of Our Feminists: A Study in the Novels of Edith Wharton, Ellen Glasgow, Willa Cather*. Critics of this period took the opportunity, some fifteen years after Wharton's death, to examine her complete output and discern major themes and techniques that carried over from work to work. They paid little attention specifically to *Summer*. Nevius, observing Charity's "pride, willfulness, and ignorance," concludes that "Her clash with her guardian makes it clear that temperamentally they are akin." Jessup, on the other hand, sees the novel as a "feminine triumph," one of many examples in Wharton of stories in which "woman exceeds man."

The second wave of feminism in the 1960s and the opening of Wharton's sealed papers at Yale in 1969 led to a dramatic revival of Wharton studies which continued into the twenty-first century. Critics in this last period, more willing than their predecessors to explore the frankly sexual nature of Charity's awakening, published dozens of studies of *Summer*. Most of these studies grew out of a more fully realized conception of feminism than previous work. Kathy Grafton's essay in *Twentieth Century Literature* is one of several that trace Wharton's understanding of the work of Sigmund Freud and her use of sexual imagery to suggest "Harney's need for degradation and Charity's need for forbiddenness." Wharton's possible sexual attraction to her own father and the issues of incest suggested by Harney's marriage to Annabel Balch and Charity's to Lawyer Royall have been the subject of several

Edith Wharton's home in Lenox, the Berkshires, Massachusetts, also referred to as the "The Mount"

studies, including William E. Hummel's article in *Studies in American Fiction*. A different feminist approach is demonstrated by Rhonda Skillern's contribution to *The Cambridge Companion to Edith Wharton*, which draws on semiotics to "trace the process by which Charity Royall, who represents the resisting feminine, is drawn into the symbolic order" but also "does manage to express her resistance to the symbolic order."

Criticism

Cynthia Bily

Bily is an instructor at Adrian College in Adrian, Michigan. In this essay, Bily examines how Charity Royall receives and rejects clothing and other objects of adornment from men in Summer.

At the turn of the twentieth century there were strict social prohibitions against a gentleman giving a lady clothing or jewelry. An unmarried woman who received clothing from a man was considered to be "no better than she should be," a woman of loose morals. Married men could display their worth by the way they adorned their wives; a woman with expensive clothing and jewelry and the time to study

the latest fashions was evidence that her husband had enough disposable wealth to support such conspicuous consumption. These social conventions were a small part of a rigid system that worked against women having autonomy within or without the bonds of marriage. Young women like Charity Royall in Edith Wharton's *Summer* had few means outside marriage for leading satisfying lives: denied higher education, professional careers, even the right to participate in government, they relied on husbands to advance them socially and economically.

Charity would like to believe that she can do as she pleases without the approval of society, and it is in this spirit that she enters into an affair with Lucius Harney. But throughout the novel, Wharton shows Charity as struggling against societal expectations. Every time Charity looks in a mirror or decides she cannot bear looking in a mirror, she accepts the ideology that says her worth is in how she appears to men. If she is to find any happiness in her unhappy situation, Charity will have to learn to stop caring how men see her. Only if she can gain that much self-worth can she become a wife and a mother without losing her soul.

Charity does not read books, but she has internalized the belief that the world can be read in its appearance, and she tends to form judgments of

> " Charity knows instinctively that Lawyer Royall and Lucius Harney, the two men who want to dress her, also want to undress her."

people quickly based on what they look like. She gauges her own reception to romance based on her willingness or unwillingness to change her appearance for a particular man. As she understands, a woman makes herself appealing to a man by ornamenting herself. When she considers falling in love with the young men of the village, she puts it in these terms and realizes she cannot imagine "curling her hair or putting a new ribbon in her hat" for any of them. It is Harney's "city clothes" that first makes him worthy of attention, and she puts a great deal of thought into a new hat and dress for the Fourth of July.

In Charity's important moments with Lawyer Royall, his clothing indicates how she will respond to him. In her youth, on the day Charity decides not to go away to school, he waits for her on the porch. He is clean-shaven and has "brushed his black coat," and Charity notes that "at such moments she really admired him." She looks at him closely again on the day of the Old Home Week festivities, when his face wears "the look of majesty that used to awe and fascinate her childhood. His frock-coat had been carefully brushed and ironed, and the ends of his narrow black tie were so nearly even that the tying must have cost him a protracted struggle." As he gives his speech, Charity hears nobility in it that surprises her, and her willingness to hear the voice is connected with Royall's clothing. When Lawyer Royall looks his best, he is at his best, and vice versa. When Charity feels the most revulsion for him, he tends to be unshaven, and she attacks his appearance: "How long is it since you've looked at yourself in the glass?"

Charity knows instinctively that Lawyer Royall and Lucius Harney, the two men who want to dress her, also want to undress her. Twice, Lawyer Royall tries to dress up Charity, and twice she thwarts his attempts. The first time is when he has received payment from Harney for the use of

the buggy, and he gives Charity ten dollars, saying, "Here—go get yourself a Sunday bonnet that'll make all the other girls mad." He makes the gift by "tossing a ten-dollar bill into Charity's lap," symbolically demonstrating what he hopes to buy with his money. When Charity does buy a new dress and hat with the money, however, it is to impress Harney, and she leaves home with the hat and dress covered up so Royall will not see them. On the morning after their wedding, Royall gives Charity forty dollars for clothes, telling her, "You know I always wanted you to beat all the other girls.... If it ain't enough, there's more where that come from—I want you to beat 'em all hollow." Royall is among those men who use women as competition; in helping Charity "beat" the other girls he hopes to "beat" the other men. If Charity uses this gift to buy stylish clothing now, she will be accepting a role for herself as an ornament, a mannequin to be dressed up for Royall's pleasure. But as we will see, she does not.

When Charity comes home with her husband to North Dormer, she is wearing the only two pieces of jewelry she has ever received in her life. On her breast she wears the blue brooch Harney bought her on the Fourth of July, and on her finger she wears Royall's wedding ring. Each piece was chosen by the man who gave it, and neither is quite right. The brooch, fond as Charity is of it, is a reminder of her dependence on Harney, her willingness to bow to his judgment even in matters that concern her more than they do him. At the jewelry store, where she sees jewelry close up for the first time, she is attracted to "a gold lily-of-the-valley with white flowers"—an understandable attraction for a woman who loves the natural world as much as she does. Harney, however, has shown little interest in the flowers and fields Charity loves; he is dedicated to the symmetry and geometry of architecture. "Don't you think the blue pin's better?" he asks her, and immediately Charity feels ashamed at her lack of perception. Why should she feel this way? The gift of the pin is meant to give *her* pleasure, but Harney is more concerned with ornamenting the woman he appears with than with giving her what she would enjoy.

Harney, of course, does buy sexual intimacy with the brooch, however cold-bloodedly a reader may see his intent. When Charity has her first close-up look at jewelry, she is struck by the "dark blue velvet" on which "brooches glittered like the moon and stars." A few hours later, as Charity and Harney watch fireworks that resemble "jeweled light" interspersed with "velvet darkness" (Charity absent-mindedly crushing the hat she bought with Royall's

What Do I Read Next?

- *Ethan Frome* (1911) is Wharton's other short novel of rural New England. Its title character is an unhappily married man who comes to believe he has a chance at real love when his wife's cousin Mattie comes to stay.

- *The Age of Innocence* (1920) is Wharton's Pulitzer Prize–winning novel of social life in New York City during the 1870s. The novel's upperclass characters are just as bound by convention and just as fearful of gossip as the middle-class characters in *Summer*.

- *The Awakening* (1899), by Kate Chopin, tells the story of a young woman's gradual realization that being a dutiful wife and mother is not enough for her. The novel was greeted with anger and scorn because it did not condemn its central character for committing adultery.

- Among the most frequently borrowed material from the Hatchard Memorial Library is the poetry of Henry Wadsworth Longfellow, an immensely popular poet of nineteenth-century New England. His *Ballads and Other Poems* (1841) included "The Village Blacksmith," "The Wreck of the Hesperus," and other favorites which were still widely anthologized in the early 2000s.

- *North of Boston* (1914) is a collection of poetry by Robert Frost. Published shortly before *Summer*, it includes several poems, including "Mending Wall" and "The Death of the Hired Man," that depict life in rural New England.

- The *Ladies' Home Journal*, a magazine for women readers, has been published since the nineteenth century. Issues from the early part of the twentieth century, collected and available in many public libraries, offer fascinating looks at the advice given to women about their appearance, their responsibilities for maintaining a home, and their behavior.

---

money), Harney kisses her for the first time. Charity has considered earlier that the money for the brooch might have bought an engagement ring instead, but she knows Harney will never buy her one. Nevertheless, it is not long before she becomes his lover.

The blue brooch plays an interesting role in the second half of the novel. Because she has no money, Charity must give the brooch to Dr. Merkle in order to have her pregnancy confirmed. At this time, Charity does not mind giving up the brooch, because she is still confident that when she tells Harney about the baby he will choose her over Annabel Balch. Once she realizes that he has already chosen Annabel, she decides not to tell him about the baby and determines that she must get the brooch back. Ironically, the money she uses to get the brooch back comes from her new husband, Lawyer Royall. Charity almost lets the brooch go, "But how could she leave her only treasure with that evil woman? She meant it for her baby; she meant it, in some mysterious way, to be a link between Harney's child

and its unknown father." The pin "lay in her bosom like a talisman . . . It gave her strength." Actually, Charity's strength comes from her decision to buy back the brooch but not to take ownership of it; the brooch is for the baby, not for keeping a useless dream alive.

Charity's other piece of jewelry is her wedding ring, the sign that she belongs to Royall, not to Harney. (Unlike more recent customs, only women wore wedding rings at the early part of the twentieth century, as a sign that they—but not their husbands—were not available for sex.) Like the brooch, the ring was chosen for her, and it is only when she feels "a ring that was too big for her being slipped onto her thin finger" that she understands she is married. When did Royall buy the ring? How far in advance has he been preparing for this wedding to a woman who was not a part of the planning? Each time the ring is mentioned, it is as a symbol of loss, not of eternal love. When Charity looks out the window and sees the lake in

---

the distance, she realizes "what she had done. Even the feeling of the ring on her hand had not brought her this sharp sense of the irretrievable." The next day, sitting down to write Harney a last letter, Charity is "possessed with a fear which had haunted her ever since she had felt Mr. Royall's ring on her finger: the fear that Harney might, after all, free himself and come back to her."

Why does Charity fear Harney coming back? Perhaps she knows now what a life with him would be like: that if he came back because of the baby or because of his desire for Charity, he and Charity would quickly grow weary of each other. He would not take her to New York and present her as his wife among his society friends, and neither would the couple be accepted and happy in North Dormer. She has known since her last meeting with Harney that "the gulf between them was too deep, and that the bridge their passion had flung across it was as unsubstantial as a rainbow." Now that she wears Royall's ring she has a chance at stability and contentment, if not passion, and she fears that she would cast it aside for one more embrace.

As the novel draws to a close, the newlyweds Charity and Royall are in their hotel room packing for their return to the red house as husband and wife. Royall cheerfully asks, "Well, did you rig yourself out handsomely? I haven't seen any bundles round." Charity, who has spent the money he gave her to get back Harney's brooch, answers that she would rather see to her own modest needs. Royall contemplates this for a moment and says, "Well, I wanted you to go back looking stylisher than any of them; but I guess you're right. You're a good girl, Charity." In rejecting Royall's attempt to dress her up, Charity has claimed for herself some control over her own role in the marriage. She will not be an adornment for Royall; she will make decisions, she will be autonomous, she will be an equal. As for Royall (who, after all, has taken on a wife who does not love him and a baby that is not his), he accepts Charity's vision. When he says, "I guess you're right," Charity knows that marrying Royall was the right choice. "I guess you're good, too," she says.

Source: Cynthia Bily, Critical Essay on *Summer*, in *Novels for Students*, Thomson Gale, 2005.

Kate Covintree

Covintree is a graduate student and expository writing instructor in the Writing, Literature, and Publishing department at Emerson College. In this essay, Covintree explores how settings and landscape mirror the emotional/moral life of the novel's main character, Charity Royall.

According to Marilyn French in her introduction to Wharton's novel, *Summer*, "Wharton's main theme, her deepest concern, was the emotional/moral life, especially in the area of sexuality." Wharton created a story of a young woman's coming of age through sexual experience and love. In many ways, this novel was ahead of its time. Long before essays on female identity were being written, Wharton created a female character exploring just these things. Much of Wharton's approach to the taboo subject of sexuality was brought to the reader through the imagery and environment in which she placed her characters.

When the novel's main character, Charity Royall, first visits Nettleton it is with the church youth group. At this time, the sights and sounds of such a place are overwhelming to her. They make her aware of the plain life she lives in North Dormer. What she remembers from this first visit are the "plate-glass fronts, . . . cocoanut pie, . . . and a theater [where she listened to a lecture on] pictures that she would have enjoyed looking at if . . . explanations had not prevented her from understanding them." With this experience, Nettleton becomes a place of newness and excitement. Wharton describes the town in an abundance of sensory images: what Charity can see, taste, and hear. It becomes a town Charity can fantasize about.

Charity needs something to fantasize about. Already an outsider because of her history with "the Mountain," she remains closed off to the interactions with the boys of North Dormer. In her essay "Development of Female Identity," Phyllis Katz asserts that "the major sex-role task of [the phase of later adolescence] involves the development of heterosexual interactions." At the beginning of the novel, Charity's history of interactions is marred by annoyance and invasion. She is annoyed at the couples who use the library to make out. She herself does not entertain male visitors there. Only her adoptive father, Lawyer Royall, shows interest of a sexual or marital nature. This, of course, is unacceptable to her, and so she is starved for real attention and affection from a man.

Wharton makes it clear to the reader that "North Dormer is at all times an empty place." Living in such an empty place, Charity's own needs and desires are stifled. She is unable to consider her own sexual needs or development. There are no men that she imagines being with. Charity's newfound dislike for North Dormer correlates with her female development. As a child, she "had long supposed it to be a place of some importance." It is only after her visit to Nettleton that she is no longer satisfied. However, North Dormer is not changing; Charity is changing. She is becoming aware of her own desires.

Until the stranger comes to the library, she can only see her own sexual power as something that appeals to her adoptive father. Her own need to be admired, then, works against her in her own home. The response to her own sexuality becomes a re-action to Lawyer Royall's propositions of marriage. Charity demonstrates this in the quick way she sends Royall out of her room and her means to gain another female in the house. She can see her own sexuality has power, but it is one that compromises the comforts of her own home. In this way, Charity's sexuality is a burden to her life in North Dormer. Both are isolated and repressed according to the strictures of the time.

If it were not for the nearby fields, it could be possible to believe that Charity had no concept of her own sexual desire. But, like the town of Nettleton that peeks at North Dormer through the train route, Charity is aware of what she is not often exploring. "She was blind and insensible to many things, and she dimly knew it; but to all that was light and air, perfume and colour, every drop of blood in her responded." The external sensory experiences are able to arouse an internal emotion. Her visits to the hillside are an escape and is one in which she can explore her own thoughts and feelings. In the introduction to her book *Female Adolescence*, Katherine Dalsimer explores the "possibility of pleasure, delight, or pride on the part of the female in her own genitals *as they are*, and in her own feminity." Above her empty town, Charity can "feel" and Wharton makes this point clear by repeating this one word four times in one paragraph. It is here, while lying in the grass, she first fantasizes about Lucius Harney.

Charity's evening ritual of washing her face becomes an opportunity to imagine "herself a bride in low-necked satin, walking down the aisle with Lucius Harney." Lucius has made it possible for her to take the feelings and desires she can experience in nature and find them within herself. Therefore, the affair between Charity and Lucius begins in her mind. It would almost seem enough that this be the resolution for Charity, that she tastes such desire and then returns to normal life, but this is not the case. Wharton pushes the emotion further. She brings the affair to fruition.

An affair so highly charged with emotion and desire cannot happen in the towns of Wharton's time, and so Wharton creates for them

> **An affair so highly charged with emotion and desire cannot happen in the towns of Wharton's time, and so Wharton creates for them an environment where it is possible."**

an environment where it is possible. The little house in the woods becomes their summer home. Though the walls are "sun-bleached to a ghastly grey," it contained, for Charity, a "secret sweetness." This sweetness is parallel to Charity's own confidence with her budding sexuality, which comes before Lucius arrives and "before [his] first kiss [blots] it out," or erases it because he brings his own sweetness. The house has a door, a table, a bed, and even a vase of flowers. This is the home that Charity wants for herself. The simple freedom her landscape allows for more freedom between her and Lucius. Though it is all done in secret, it is a better representation of Charity's inner self. Here, she finds, "the wondrous unfolding of her new self, the reaching out to the light of all her contacted tendrils." She finds that love is not "something confused and furtive," but "as bright at the summer air."

Like the detail of the Mexican blanket on the mattress of the little house, their involvement with one another is filled with little intimacies. While they do not even kiss until late into their affair, they share experiences in places that are sensual or alluring. As Katherine Dalsimer points out in her introduction to *Female Adolescence*, Charity is making "decisions . . . which will define adulthood; . . . with respect to sexual intimacy, to values that are expressed in ways of living." Lucius's surveying work allows Charity to rest in the grass in the kind of freedom she most enjoys. They are able to ride through the area in a comfortable silence. Though the relationship is actually tenuous, Charity makes decisions about it that demonstrate her ideal and most fulfilled version of herself.

When she and Lucius visit Nettleton, Charity is keenly self-conscious of every move they make. Wharton is also keenly aware of what sights they could see in Nettleton to allude to their desire. On this visit, the shop windows are not just reflections of "plate-glass." Now, Wharton describes the contents of the windows: "waves of silk and ribbon . . . hats [rising] like tropical orchids. . . . wax ladies in daring dresses, . . . pink corsets and transparent hosiery." Again Nettleton is filled with sensual images, but this time they are also sexual. They mirror Charity's own sexuality, as each image applies most strongly to women. Wharton lists the exotic and the hidden, showing how Nettleton can put it all in full view. Even objects that might not initially appear sexual are sexualized as Wharton writes: "the pink throats of gramophones opened their giant convolutions in a soundless chorus."

Charity is a character who begins the novel despising her town. As the story progresses, however, she begins to move through the town with exhilarating secrecy. This is the secret of her burgeoning sexuality. Like the gramophone, she is pink-throated, waiting to open. Once Charity does open, her fulfillment brings a power and awareness that lets her finally find comfort in her own town. In an age when such ideas were not discussed, Wharton makes it clear how liberating and satisfying awareness of sexuality can be.

Source: Kate Covintree, Critical Essay on *Summer*, in *Novels for Students*, Thomson Gale, 2005.

Douglas Dupler

Dupler is a writer, teacher, and independent scholar. In the following essay, Dupler discusses the role of nature and culture in Summer, *with particular attention to the part played by shame in the society of the novel.*

Edith Wharton's novel, *Summer*, is a classic coming-of-age story about a young woman. This type of story, called a *bildungsroman* (which translates from the German as "novel of formation"), generally contains a hero or heroine who is set in opposition to society and his/her upbringing in order to find his/her place in that society. Themes of coming-of-age novels often deal with love, with the conflict between adolescence and adulthood, and with the process of maturation and all the introspection and experimentation inherent in that process. In *Summer*, the female protagonist, Charity Royall, embodies many of the themes of the coming-of-age novel. In particular, Charity's character reveals a young adult's emerging individuality, or nature, in conflict with the society that has nurtured her.

At the beginning of Wharton's novel, the external world of nature plays a significant role. The story begins on a June afternoon, and the splendor of summer is all around. Wharton uses the imagery of nature both abundantly and carefully. In scene after scene, there is lavish description of the blooming summer world that serves as the backdrop for her characters' interactions. These scenes of nature may symbolize elements of the human story. For instance, in the beginning of the story, when Charity begins to fall in love, nature reflects the passion and abundance of her feelings, overflowing with life as it does in early summer. Later in the novel, when much has changed for Charity and she has experienced an "unfolding of her new self," the season has changed to autumn, When Charity becomes most distraught and has seemingly been abandoned by the world, the world is cold and wintry, and the optimism of summer is but a memory.

When Charity leaves her library job early one day and goes to lie in a summer meadow, Wharton describes the scene in great detail with smells, colors, and textures. In this verdant setting, "every drop of blood in her responded." Thus, nature is not only on the outside but on the inside of Wharton's human characters as well. Indeed, although Charity is a willful and free-spirited young woman, throughout the story there is also present an "undercurrent as mysterious and potent" as the force that "makes the forest break into leaf." Charity feels this force when she falls in love and she knows that "something transient and exquisite had flowered in her." She also experiences this force when she feels "pitted against unknown forces," and is "slipping down a smooth, irresistible current," which later feels "overwhelming."

Charity's character is influenced both by nature and by culture, and it reveals the conflict between the two. She is a natural woman who has an "animal secretiveness" about her, while at the same time she is considered to be intelligent and attractive by the community around her. She is clever enough in social roles that "in her narrow world she had always ruled." While in nature Charity becomes "absorbingly interested in herself." This suggests that she experiences an increase in self-esteem when left alone in a natural setting. But when Charity is in human society, in culture, she feels most challenged; she has a pervasive sense of shame that is revealed throughout the story.

One way that society uses to shame Charity, to motivate her to conform and to stifle her individuality and her freedom, is to belittle her past. Charity has come from the "mountain," a "bad place" and "a shame to have come from." In the beginning, Charity exclaims, "How I hate everything!" which suggests her loss of self-esteem because of the shame of her origin; her very birth is considered unworthy by the town's arbitrary standards. Charity has been taught all her life that she should be indebted to Mr. Royall, the man who brought her down from the mountain and saved her from misery and poverty. This shaming mechanism subordinates Charity to the older and wealthier man who is her guardian.

On a number of occasions, Mr. Royall causes Charity to feel shame. When he speaks with Lucius Harney about Charity's humble beginnings, she is described as "choking with humiliation." When Charity tells Harney of Mr. Royall's presumptive advances, she is swept over by "a flush of shame." When Mr. Royall accuses Charity of improperly visiting Harney one evening, Charity's "shame weighed on her like a physical oppression." And when Mr. Royall sees Charity with Harney in the town of Nettleton, Mr. Royall shames Charity with profanity and disrespect. At the very end of the story, when Mr. Royall is trying to help Charity after she has been abandoned by Harney, his look makes her feel "ashamed and yet secure."

Although Lucius Harney at times seems to build Charity's self-esteem, nevertheless he brings out the deepest feelings of inadequacy in Charity. Next to him, Charity is painfully aware of her "ignorance of life and literature." Harney's worldly experience gives him an "air of power" that she is missing and that she is infatuated with. When attempting to write to Harney, Charity experiences an "inability to express herself." In another instance, lacking the proper words to write, Charity wonders "what a civilized person would have done," again pointing to her difficulties with culture. Harney represents a level of society that Charity, with her damaged sense of self, can only envy. Furthermore, Harney takes advantage of Charity, leading her to believe that he wants a permanent relationship with her but leaving her pregnant for another woman, which greatly increases Charity's sense of shame as a "leaden weight of shame" hangs on her, "benumbing every other sensation."

Others promote this sense of shame as well. An evangelist tells Charity that she must "confess her guilt," without having any specific reason for telling her to do so. Even the abortion doctor attempts to shame Charity, saying, "Ain't you ashamed," when Charity cannot make a payment. The community seems to be held together by the fear of shame. The town of North Dormer is described as full of "mean curiosities" and "furtive malice," ready to pounce on any citizens who dare

> **One way that society uses to shame Charity, to motivate her to conform and to stifle her individuality and her freedom, is to belittle her past."**

cross its "harsh code of conduct." Even Mr. Royall is not free from feeling shame: "he despised himself" after Charity refuses his advances toward her one night.

Just like nature in the story, there are both internal and external manifestations of the shaming mechanism. For instance, Charity at different times in her relationship with Harney feels shame coming from within as a response learned from immersion in North Dormer society. There is also shame that is enforced by the other members of the community. When Charity, for example, spies on Harney one evening, Mr. Royall tells her that her reputation is ruined because the rumor that she improperly spent the evening with Harney has spread through the whole town.

Charity feels oppressed by shame and struggles to break free. She finds strength to do this from within herself, asserting her true nature over the demands of her society and its sense of shame. Charity spends time alone in nature, restoring herself away from culture's demands. Her natural intelligence gives her power in the household that she shares with Mr. Royall. The first time her guardian offends her, she gains the upper hand and demands that another female be hired in the household. It also becomes apparent in her relations with Harney that "she was the stronger" of the two. She confronts the shame of her impoverished background, when she admits to Harney that she comes from the mountain. Thus, Charity's nature overcomes the disadvantages that she finds in her position in society. In addition, she performs acts of rebellion. In spite of the warnings from the small town against men from the city, Charity chooses to pursue a relationship with Harney. She and Harney find an abandoned house, away from the rest of society, in which to spend time together.

Charity's transformation in the story comes about as she struggles with the sense of shame that her society has associated with her place of birth and with the sense of shame associated with her relationship with Harney. Although she fears "unescapable isolation" when she gets pregnant outside of wedlock and the man she loves runs away with her arch-rival, she confronts her fears and decides to go back to the mountain. On the mountain she is finds more despair, as her mother has just passed away. But when she views her dead mother's body, from what is probably the loneliest and saddest point in her life, she experiences a release of her shame. She realizes that, contrary to acting in a shameful way that tainted Charity's life, her mother acted in a way that gave her an opportunity. With this realization Charity experiences an opening, a "softness at her heart" that seems to create a shift in her character. In the end, Charity's willful nature gives way to "complete passiveness," and she accepts the marriage offer from Mr. Royall. The reader is uncertain whether this is a positive act for Charity, but Mr. Royall does rescue her from the impending difficulties of her situation. As the novel closes, the reader senses that Charity is relaxing into a new and safer fate, while retaining her fundamental freedom, as she can see the life around her with a "sudden acuteness of vision."

Source: Douglas Dupler, Critical Essay on *Summer*, in *Novels for Students*, Thomson Gale, 2005.

Kathy Grafton

In the following essay, Grafton analyzes the relationship between Charity and Harney, particularly Harney's need "for a certain degradation of Charity," by referencing an essay by Sigmund Freud.

In Edith Wharton's 1917 novel *Summer* the relationship between the heroine, Charity Royall, and her lover, Lucius Harney, depicts a kind of feminine sexual awakening that is profoundly original in literature. As Cynthia Griffin Wolff notes in her introduction to the book, "*Summer* is not the first *Bildungsroman* to focus on this awakening to maturity as it occurs in a woman's life; however, it is the first to deal explicitly with sexual passion as an essential component of that process" (x). The precise way in which this sexual relationship is entered into by these young people has significant psychoanalytical ramifications. Specifically, Harney's need for a certain degradation of Charity to occur before he can find her sexually accessible, his subconscious need to separate feelings of sexual desire and attraction from feelings of genuine tenderness and high esteem, and Charity's own need to experience her sexuality as a forbidden pleasure, constitute driving forces in the revelation

of their relationship within the novel. Freud's 1912 essay "The Most Prevalent Form of Degradation in Erotic Life" proves insightful in a close analysis of the relationship between Charity and Harney—particularly with regard to the factors that contribute to Harney's perspective and involvement.

The assumption that Wharton knew Feud's work is almost inevitable. Like Freud, Wharton exhibited great appreciation for the works of Arthur Schnitzler (Lawson 46, 129), the late-nineteenth-century "Vienna-born Jewish doctor" who is known for "epitomizing" Viennese impressionism in his literary works (Johnson 171–72), and whose stories, novels, and plays revealed a "perceptiveness with which they laid bare the inner, mainly the sensual, world of their characters" (Gay 130) As well, both Freud and Wharton admired the works of Goethe and Schiller. Freud "could quote [them] by the hour" (128), while Wharton reaffirmed "her loyalty to the older German literature and the German language" by immersing herself in the correspondence between the two (Lewis 394) " 'Goethe always schillered when he wrote to Schiller, didn't he?' she observed" (394). Even more persuasive is the fact that Wharton often mentioned and discussed Freud among her friends during her excursion to Germany in 1913, as well as after her return to Paris that same year (352, 355). Freud's influence on Wharton . . . then, though not unequivocally documented, is apparent in that they often expressed similar concerns about cultural expectations and restrictions . . . and in that they were both interested in critiquing the "attitudes to premarital and extramarital sexual experience, [and] the precarious relation between parents and children" that they perceived in the societies in which they lived (134).

Summer tells the story of the romance that develops between Charity Royall, a relatively inexperienced young girl of humble beginnings, and Lucius Harney, an ambitious young man from the city. Charity is living with her guardian, Mr. Royall, in North Dormer, Massachusetts, when Harney comes to stay with his cousin, Miss Hatchard, for the summer. After their coincidental meeting in the library where Charity works part-time, Harney and Charity begin to see more and more of each other until their friendship evolves into a torrid affair. The romance of this seemingly mismatched couple "breaks, or stretches, many conventions of romantic love stories and in the process creates a new picture of female sexuality" (French xlii).

First of all, the relationship has only progressed so far as Harney's giving Charity her first real kiss when Charity is publicly degraded by Mr. Royall. The scene of the first kiss is in itself a foreshadowing of the sexual ecstasy that is soon to follow for the young couple. Having spent the day together in Nettleton, Charity and Harney are sitting in the bleachers at a Fourth of July fireworks display when the kiss takes place. As Charity leans back to view the display, she feels "Harney's knees against her head."

> After a while the scattered fireworks ceased. A longer interval of darkness followed, and then the whole night broke into flower. From every point of the horizon, gold and silver arches sprang up and crossed each other, sky-orchards broke into blossom, shed their flaming petals and hung their branches with golden fruit; and all the while the air was filled with a soft supernatural hum, as though great birds were building nests in those invisible tree-tops.

The sexual imagery in this passage is important to note; Charity is about to "break into flower" or "break into blossom" herself. She is at once becoming aware of her own sexual instincts and needs in response to her growing intimacy with Harney. She will soon "shed [her] flaming petals," so to speak, and enter into an awakening that will incur all the brilliance and excitement that the fireworks symbolize. In fact, she and Harney are soon to embark on building their own secret little nest where they may covertly experience this excitement.

This imagery becomes even more explicit in the succeeding paragraphs leading up to the actual kiss:

> For a moment the night seemed to grow more impenetrably black; then a great picture stood out against it like a constellation. It was surmounted by a golden scroll bearing the inscription, "Washington crossing the Delaware," and across a flood of motionless golden ripples the National Hero passed, erect, solemn and gigantic, standing with folded arms in the stern of a slowly moving golden boat.
>
> A long "Oh-h-h" burst from the spectators: the stand creaked and shook with their blissful trepidations. "Oh-h-h," Charity gasped: she had forgotten where she was, had at last forgotten even Harney's nearness. She seemed to have been caught up in the stars.

The obvious phallic imagery of the scroll and the replica of Washington, and especially the delight and "bliss" they evoke in the audience, again suggest the sexual delight and bliss that will occur for Charity as a result of a deeper physical intimacy with Harney.

The first kissing seems to arise out of Harney's genuine affection for and attraction toward Charity. It seems spontaneous enough on his part: "With sudden vehemence he wound his arms about her, holding her head against his breast while she gave

> **"**
> Although Harney does not himself degrade Charity, she suffers degradation in his eyes due to Mr. Royall's outburst. Harney also does not understand why this outburst makes her suddenly seem more sexually accessible to him in comparison to Annabel Balch, his well-brought-up fiancée."

him back his kisses" However, it later becomes apparent that Harney's mental assessment of Charity and her position in society at this point in the story perhaps gives him leeway, at least in his own mind, to be so aggressive. Charity feels "herself possessed of a new mysterious power" over him at this point. What she does not realize is that this "power" is about to be lost when she encounters Mr. Royal as they are leaving.

In the next scene Chasity is irrevocably degraded in Harvey's eyes. As they are leaving, they come in contact with the drunken Mr. Royall, who, annoyed at finding them together, berates and shames Charity in front of the crowd:

> He was just behind Julia Hawes, and had one hand on her arm; but as he left the gang-plank he freed himself, and moved a step or two away from his companions. He had seen Charity at once, and his glance passed slowly from her to Harney, whose arm was still about her. He stood staring at them, and trying to master the senile quiver of his lips; then he drew himself up with the tremulous majesty of drunkenness, and stretched out his arm.
>
> "You whore—you damn—bare-headed whore, you!" he enunciated slowly.

This particular scene of degradation prompts Harney to intensify his physical relationship with Charity soon afterward. In fact, the next time he sees her is the first time they retreat to the little house that becomes their hideaway.

At this point the correlation between the scene at the wharf with Mr. Royall and Harney's subsequent seduction of Charity may be unclear. Here

Freud's essay comes in handy in helping us better to understand the nature of this correlation in psychoanalytic terms. To begin with, according to Freud, the male's need to degrade the love object stems from a "psychical impotence" that has occurred due to an unacknowledged incestuous desire for his mother and/or sister. This desire is fundamentally unacknowledged because the male holds these two family members in very high esteem; thus, this type of desire seems entirely unacceptable to him. He then finds it necessary to separate feelings of desire from feelings of true affection and esteem. As Freud points out, "The erotic life of such people remains disassociated, divided between two channels, the same two that are personified in art as heavenly and earthly (or animal) love. Where such men love they have no desire and where they desire they cannot love" (207).

Freud claims that the most prevalent way in which the male then copes with his divided feelings is to create two love objects—one to love, the other to desire. He then degrades the desired love object in some way in order that his desire for her become acceptable to himself:

> The principal means of protection used by men against this complaint consists in *lowering* the sexual object in their own estimation, while reserving for the incestuous object and for those who represent it the overestimation normally felt for the sexual object. As soon as the sexual object fulfills the condition of being degraded, sensual feeling can have free play, considerable sexual capacity and a high degree of pleasure can be developed. (208)

Although Harney does not himself degrade Charity, she suffers degradation in his eyes due to Mr. Royall's outburst. Harney also does not understand why this outburst makes her suddenly seem more sexually accessible to him in comparison to Annabel Balch, his well-brought-up fiancée. Freud also addresses this problem:

> The man almost always feels his sexual activity hampered by his respect for the woman and only develops full sexual potency when he finds himself in the presence of a lower type of sexual object; and this again is partly conditioned by the circumstance that his sexual aims include those of perverse sexual components which with his well-brought-up wife, for instance, he does not venture to do. (210)

In light of this assertion, we need to examine the backgrounds of both Charity and Annabel as they are described in the novel, in order more fully to comprehend Harney's view of each.

The contrast between the backgrounds of the two young women is brought to our attention very early in the novel, even before we learn anything of significance about Harney. Charity, we discover, is from "the Mountain." She has no real family to speak of, aside from her guardian Mr. Royall, and she is keenly aware that her origins are ambiguous, her place in society mean, especially in comparison to the position of someone like the formidable Miss Balch. Charity knows that the Mountain is "a bad place, and a shame to have come from" and she feels "ashamed of her old sun-hat, and sick of North Dormer, and jealously aware of Annabel Balch of Springfield, opening her blue eyes somewhere far off on glories greater than the glories of Nettleton." Annabel, then, has undoubtedly been more privileged during her lifetime than Charity can even imagine.

For Harney, who comes from the same world of privilege as Annabel, the difference between the backgrounds and present social positions of the two women is more prevalent in his consciousness and more directive of his actions than he realizes. In applying Freud's ideas to this love triangle, we can see the way in which Harney's subconscious reasoning affects his decision to pursue a sexual relationship with Charity rather than with Annabel. For instance, I would posit that in choosing Charity, Harney, like Freud's exemplary male, exhibits his "need for a less exalted sexual object, a woman ethically inferior, to whom he need ascribe no aesthetic misgivings, and who does not know the rest of his life and cannot criticize him" (Freud 210). Indeed, Freud goes on to claim, "It is to such a woman that he prefers to devote his sexual potency, even when all the tenderness in him belongs to one of a higher type" (210). Though Harney is quite tender to Charity and finds her aesthetically pleasing and valuable, he does, in fact, unquestionably consider Annabel to be of a "higher type" than Charity.

The next time in the story that we hear of Annabel is when Mr. Miles mentions her to Harney in Charity's hearing at the library. Speaking of a garden party he has attended, he says, "I saw Miss Balch several times by the way . . . looking extremely handsome." The unprecedented mention of Annabel's name unnerves Charity, and we begin to understand the separate kinds of response that Harney reserves for his two love interests. Charity's intimidation and her sense of helplessness are revealed as her "restless imagination fasten[s] on the name of Annabel Balch." She notices a change in Harney's expression at the mention of this name, and though she does not fully comprehend the exact nature of a garden party she envisions "the flower-edged lawns of Nettleton" and enviously recalls "the 'old things' which Miss

Balch avowedly 'wore out' when she came to North Dormer." Indeed, "Charity understood what associations the name must have called up, and felt the uselessness of struggling against the unseen influences in Harney's life." Charity then automatically "fits the bill" for Harney as a woman "to whom he need ascribe no aesthetic misgivings, and who does *not know the rest of his life and cannot criticize him*" (Freud 210, italics mine). In other words, Harney does not feel as if Charity could possibly encumber the beautiful future he envisions for himself because, in the back of his mind, he knows that he will end up with a more "appropriate" mate. Even Charity perceives that her relation to Harney at this point is characterized by her inferiority.

However, perhaps the most telling of descriptions is Wharton's depiction of Annabel's appearance and behavior at the North Dormer "Old Home Week" celebration: "Miss Balch, in an unbecoming dress, looked sallow and pinched, and Charity fancied there was a worried expression in her pale-lashed eyes. She took a set near Miss Hatchard and it was presently apparent that she did not mean to dance." Annabel is here delineated as an "object" completely void of any sexual inclination, indeed rather inclined *against* sex, in that she looks "sallow and pinched." Her asexuality is accentuated even more by the fact that she does "not mean to dance." Wharton effectively stresses here that the kind of creature held in high esteem by Harney is one of respectable origin and social position, yet one who seems to lack any kind of sensual vitality. Harney's previous decision that Charity is a more acceptable and accessible choice for a sexual affair thus becomes more clear, and the degradation of Charity that he witnesses at the wharf then only confirms the ideas that have already been collecting in his mind.

However, the scene at the wharf is only the first major occurrence of Charity's degradation. As she reveals more and more about herself to him in later stages of their relationship, she becomes increasingly degraded in his eyes. In fact, each time a new threshold is crossed in this respect, Harney's estimation of Charity drops to a lower level. For example, when Harney overtakes Charity in her flight to the Mountain, she reveals the truth about her origins to him. When he questions her about why she is going "home" in this particular direction (away from North Dormer), she replies that she is going to her home "up yonder: to the Mountain." With this utterance "she became aware of a change in his face. He was no longer listening to her, he was only looking at her, with the passionate absorbed expression she had

seen in his eyes after they had kissed on the stand at Nettleton." Though Charity interprets his response to her admission as one of love, his response comes from a newly awakened sexual urge resulting from this new degradation. In fact, he immediately clasps her hands, embraces and kisses her, and leads her up to the little house that becomes their hideaway. Here the most important stage of her degradation takes place.

After they enter the little house and Charity seems to have calmed down, Harney tries to persuade her to go back to Mr. Royall's. Yet Charity vows that she will not go back, and in giving Harney her reasons she discloses an even more demeaning aspect of her circumstances. At Harney's insistence that Mr. Royall's drinking accounted for his rude behavior at the wharf, Charity replies that she understands "all that." But she also adds that Mr. Royall would not have dared to speak to her "that way" had he not wanted her "to be like those other girls" so that "he wouldn't have to go out."

> [Harney] stared at her. For a moment he did not seem to seize her meaning; then his face grew dark. "The damned hound! The villainous low hound!" His wrath blazed up, crimsoning him to the temples. "I never dreamed—good God, it's too vile," he broke off, as if his thoughts recoiled from the discovery.

Again, this sort of revelation motivates Harney to express sexual attraction toward Charity even as he attempts to console her. Indeed, almost immediately after proclaiming Mr. Royall's actions "too vile,"

> He came close and caught her to him as if he were snatching her from some imminent peril: his impetuous eyes were in hers, and she could feel the hard beat of his heart as he held her against it.
>
> "Kiss me again—like last night," he said, pushing her hair back as if to draw her whole face up into his kiss.

This ultimate degradation of Charity in Harney's eyes results in further lowering his estimation of her and thus inspires powerful feelings of sexual desire in him. According to Freud, "as soon as the sexual object fulfills the condition of being degraded, sensual feeling can have free play, [and] considerable sexual capacity and a high degree of pleasure can be developed" (208). In this case, the course of Charity's degradation ends in the sexual consummation of the relationship. However, the fact that Harney chooses to pursue more intimate sexual relations with his desired love object at this particular time and in this particular place, along with the fact that Charity willingly submits, not only reveals the phenomenon of degradation in their relationship but also points toward a similar phenomenon having to do with Charity's own sub-conscious needs.

The phenomenon I refer to is Charity's over-whelming fascination with the forbidden aspect of her intimacy with Harney. In the latter part of his essay Freud asserts:

> Women show little or no need to degrade the sexual object. . . . The long abstinence from sexuality to which they are forced and the lingering of their sen-suality in phantasy have in them, however, another important consequence. It is often not possible for them later on to undo the connection thus formed in their minds between sensual activities and something forbidden. (211–12)

Though we cannot seriously conjecture about the way it could affect Charity later, her need for for-biddenness is exemplified in several stages of the relationship.

Her desire really awakens the night she spies on Harney in his room. She is outside the window looking in and she is aroused not only by the sight and nearness of him, but also by the clandestine nature of her being there:

> Her heart jumped and then stood still. He was there, a few feet away; and while her soul was tossing on seas of woe he had been quietly sitting at his draw-ing-board. The sight of those two hands, moving with their usual skill and precision, woke her out of her dream. Her eyes were opened to the disproportion be-tween what she had felt and the cause of her agita-tion; and she was turning away from the window when one hand abruptly pushed aside the drawing-board and the other flung down the pencil.

Specific images of awakening in this passage ("The sight . . . woke her out of her dream," "Her eyes were opened") denote Charity's own sexual awak-ening. She is frustrated, "tossing on seas of woe," and she fantasizes while watching his hands move.

Nervous, yet excited, Charity continues to watch and becomes aroused by the sight of Harney's bare throat. She also continues to fanta-size as he reclines on his bed. As she watches him undress, she takes in "the vigorous lines of his young throat, and the root of the muscles where they joined the chest." When he sprawls out on the bed and stares up at the ceiling, Charity recalls see-ing him in the same position "at her side on the grass or the pine-needles, his eyes fixed on the sky, and pleasure flashing over his face like the flick-ers of sun the branches shed on it."

Yet the primary reason for Charity's stimula-tion is the knowledge of what *could* happen were she to alert Harney to her presence. This knowledge is particularly colored by her understanding of what had happened to Julia Hawes, the older sister of her friend Ally. Charity suddenly becomes afraid at the thought of what could so easily happen to her:

> It was the thing that *did* happen between young men and girls, and that North Dormer ignored in public and snickered over on the sly. It was what Miss Hatchard was still ignorant of, but every girl of Char-ity's class knew about before she left school. It was what had happened to Ally Hawes's sister Julia, and has ended in her going to Nettleton, and in people's never mentioning her name.

In this passage we see that it is not just Charity's sense of secrecy but her anticipation, mixed with apprehension, that contributes so much to her feel-ings of titillation. The forbiddenness of her own ac-tions, along with the knowledge of Julia Hawes's forbidden actions and fate, stirs up undeniable sen-sual urges in Charity. This need for forbiddenness also accounts for Charity's voyeuristic impulse to continue watching Harney and to remain, despite her "constrained position" and "weariness" even until he falls asleep. Though she is "beginning to grow numb," she felt she "could not move till he moved." She is "held there only by a vague weight of weariness" until "With a deep sigh he tossed the hair from his forehead; then his whole body re-laxed, his head turned sideways on the pillow, and she saw that he had fallen asleep." Only now does she feel that she can safely creep away. Her am-bivalent feelings at this point, a longing combined with a kind of fear, cause her to stay until her chances to show herself have passed. In other words, she is caught between her desire to reveal her presence and join Harney, and her knowledge of what could happen were she to do so. As she contemplates her options, she feels the need to re-main until the decision is basically made for her when Harney falls asleep. This initial need for for-biddenness, however, grows increasingly stronger as the relationship progresses.

Later, the first confidential correspondence oc-curs between Harney and Charity in the form of a note that he sends to her by way of a young farm boy from Creston. Through this note they arrange to meet secretly at the Creston pool, giving Harney the chance to explain his previous discussion with Mr. Royall. "When Charity, in response to Harney's message, had gone to meet him at the Creston pool her heart had been so full of mortification and anger that his first words might easily have estranged her. But it happened that he had found the right word, which was one of simple friendship" (Wharton 87). Harney breaks free, here, from sexual expectations and actually reveals his sensitivity. Still, this reconciliation, made covertly, contributes to Charity's need for forbiddenness and leads to plans for another secret outing—the trip to Nettleton.

Charity's careful calculations in preparing for this trip pointedly illustrate the necessary forbidden quality of her romance. Unlike the brief meeting at Creston pool, this excursion requires much forethought. Yet it clearly excites Charity to make these secret plans and deliberately conceal the true nature of her journey:

> She was determined to assert her independence, and if she stooped to fib about the Hepburn picnic it was chiefly from the secretive instinct that made her dread the profanation of her happiness. Whenever she was with Lucius Harney she would have liked some impenetrable mountain mist to hide her.

This passage clearly shows that Charity is much preoccupied with breaking the rules and doing something taboo in furthering her infatuation with Harney. Even the most trivial of preparations takes on this aspect of secrecy and forbiddenness for her: "Charity sat before the mirror trying on a hat which Ally Hawes, *with much secrecy,* had trimmed for her" (italics mine). Indeed, her dream of being totally secluded with Harney, hidden away from the rest of the world, soon comes true for her.

After the disastrous trip to Nettleton, the scene at the wharf, and Charity's subsequent attempt to run away to the Mountain, she and Harvey reunite and establish the little abandoned house on the road between North Dormer and the Mountain as their special meeting place. This secluded hideaway becomes very important to the progress of the sexual relationship, and definitely promotes the forbidden aspect of it. The connection in Charity's mind "between sensual activities and something forbidden" (Freud 212) is abundantly illustrated in the following passages:

> She was always glad when she got to the little house before Harney. She liked to have time to take in every detail of its secret sweetness—the shadows of the apple-trees swaying on the grass, the old walnuts rounding their domes below the road, the meadows sloping westward in the afternoon light—before his first kiss blotted it all out.

> Charity's heart contracted. The first fall of night after a day of radiance often gave her a sense of hidden menace: it was like looking out over the world as it would be when love had gone from it. She wondered if some day she would sit in that same place and watch in vain for her lover

For Charity the little house is a place shrouded with mystery—the mystery of the natural world and especially the mystery of sexuality that is unfolding before her.

Later Charity again delights in even the most minor clandestine actions. For instance, at "the triple click-click-click of a bicycle-bell under her window" ("Harney's secret signal as he passed on his way home"), she "stumbled to the window on her high heels, flung open the shutters and leaned. He waved to her and sped by, his black shadow dancing merrily ahead of him down the empty moonlit road; and she leaned there watching him till he vanished under the Hatchard spruces." She also tends to romanticize not only the seclusion of the place where her sexual initiation occurs but the little things that represent the secret understanding that exists between Harney and herself. The development of her sexuality is thus directly linked to the necessary condition of forbiddenness.

In drawing a correlation between Harney's need for degradation and Charity's need for forbiddenness, we must consider the standards of the society in which they lived and the ways in which they were educated by this society. In fact, Freud posits this cultural education concerning sexuality as the main catalyst for these tendencies in men and women. His sociosexual typology, dependent on Vienna, successfully maintains its validity when translated to Nettleton in that Wharton, in accord with Freud, perceives "the excessive self-denial that respectable middle-class society imposed on the sexual needs of ordinary humans" (Gay 338).

Indeed, Wharton had ample occasion to experience these excessive restrictions in her own life. For example, she "did not find out where babies came from until several weeks after her marriage" (Wolff *Feast* 40). Though she pleaded with her mother a few days before her marriage to explain the "facts of life" to her, Wharton met only with "icy disapproval" and the impatient reply, "You've seen enough pictures and statues in your life. Haven't you noticed that men are—made differently from women? . . . Then for heaven's sake don't ask me any more silly questions. You can't be as stupid as you pretend!" (Wolff 40). Wharton is, unquestionably, a perfect example of the kind of woman Freud is speaking of in his essay. Thus it is not surprising that Wharton's descriptions of the social milieu of Nettleton readily correspond to Freud's descriptions of late-nineteenth-early-twentieth-century Vienna, where "court preciosity found an equivalent in every bourgeois household, where girls were so sheltered from the fats of sexuality that many marriages foundered in frigidity"—indeed, where "[in] sex-starved young women, neuroses were commonplace" (Johnson 240). In short, Wharton seems to agree with Freud that "the unconscious . . . cannot escape culture" (Gay 338).

Freud wrote this essay in 1912, and *Summer* was published only five years later; Freud accurately describes the effects of society's standards on young people such as Charity and Harney. The class distinctions made by Freud and Wharton are also similar; both write of well-born men and lower-class objects of desire. In the following passage, Freud explains this correlation:

> In my opinion the necessary condition of forbiddenness in the erotic life of women holds the same place as the man's need to lower his sexual object. Both are the consequence of the long period of delay between sexual maturity and sexual activity which is demanded by education for social reasons. (212)

However, an even more significant part of this correlation has to do with the frustration that is experienced because of this delay. "It is certainly true in a general way that the importance of an instinctual desire is mentally increased by frustration of it" (213–14). In other words, social restrictions defer sexual activity and this deferral instigates these tendencies—to degrade the object of affection in the case of the male, and to experience love as a forbidden pleasure in the case of the female.

The fact that Charity is degraded in Harney's eyes allows him to lower his estimation of her; she thus becomes sexually desirable for him. However, his fiancée, Annabel Balch, remains untainted in his mind. Although she is portrayed as sexually repressed, Harney's esteem for her remains high as he reserves for her the feelings of tenderness and regard he theoretically reserves for his mother and/or sister. Because Harney is unable to feel sexual desire for Annabel, he needs Charity.

On the other hand, Charity has been educated to understand her own sexual desires as something that must remain unacknowledged and stifled because of society's expectations. She specifically learns this through the fate of Julia Hawes. Yet she chooses to break the rules, and the knowledge that she is doing so greatly contributes to her excitement. Because her sexual relationship with Harvey is taboo in the eyes of her society, an inevitable link is formed in her mind between the fulfillment of sexual desires and forbiddenness. The application of Freud's essay to the story of Charity Royall helps us to uncover and clarify many of the underlying factors and potent forces that are the catalysts for the sexual awakening that she and Lucius Harney experience.

It is interesting, finally, that Charity and Harney's relationship does not *completely* fit Freud's pattern. Specifically, Harney is *not* at a loss for tender feelings toward Charity, as Freud's male

is for his desired object. Neither does the need for forbiddenness continue to dominate Charity's sexuality, making her ultimately frigid. Instead, Harney displays a combination of tenderness and degradation in his actions toward Charity, and Charity develops an understanding of her own sexuality and affirms herself, no longer relying on forbiddenness, when she chooses to have her baby, believe in the love that she and Harney shared, and marry Mr. Royall. She becomes a powerful source of life in the end rather than the frigid woman exemplified by Freud's model.

Harney undoubtedly has feelings of tenderness for Charity, even as he desires her. Freud, however, in referring to the desired object, asserts that "It is to such a woman that he prefers to devote his sexual potency, even when *all* the tenderness in him belongs to one of a higher type" (210, italics mine). It becomes apparent that the situation between Harney and Charity is not quite as clear-cut as this, beginning with his words and actions toward her early in their relationship, as they begin to spend a great deal of time together after their meeting at the Creston pool:

> In most of the village friendships between youths and maidens lack of conversation was made up for by tentative fondling; but [Harney], except when he had tried to comfort her in her trouble on their way back from the Hyatts', had never put his arm about her, or sought to betray her into any sudden caress. It seemed to be enough for him to breathe her nearness like a flower's; and since his pleasure at being with her, and his sense of her youth and her grace, perpetually shone in his eyes and softened the inflection of his voice, his reserve did not suggest coldness, but the deference due to a girl of his own class.

In this passage Harney's initial feelings of tenderness toward Charity are undeniable. We must bear in mind, however, that these are developing well before the scene of degradation at the wharf takes place.

Later, during the trip to [Nettleton] (again *before* the scene at the wharf), Harney is still showing a propensity for genuine tenderness when he buys the pin that Charity has been admiring. "'You mustn't be afraid of looking at the blue pin any longer, because it belongs to you,' he said; and she felt a little box being pressed into her hand."

In the early part of this paper, Harney's need for a degradation of Charity to occur in order for her to become sexually desirable to him has been examined; now we must look at the combination of this need for degradation and his sincere tenderness. After the scene at the wharf takes place, Harney continues to treat her with tenderness even as he begins to make sexual advances. When

Charity runs away to the Mountain in shame, Harney catches up with her and tries to console her:

> "Did you really think you could run away from me? You see you weren't meant to," he said; and before she could answer he had kissed her again, not vehemently, but tenderly, almost fraternally, as if he had guessed her confused pain, and wanted her to know he understood it. He wound his fingers through hers.

He leads her up to the little abandoned house; yet as he seduces her he truly tries to comfort her. In a tone of "tender reassurance" he says, "'Let us go there now and sit down and talk quietly.' He took one of the hands that hung by her side and pressed his lips to the palm. 'Do you suppose I'm going to let you send me away? Do you suppose I don't understand?'" As I have mentioned, Freud does not allow for this compromise of degradation and tenderness in his essay. Harney departs from Freud's exemplary male in that he is able to sustain tender feelings for the desired object as well as the love object "of a higher type."

Just as Harney does not completely adhere to the Freudian model, Charity also surpasses it in her behavior. According to Freud, "It is often not possible for [women] later on to undo the connection thus formed in their minds between sensual activities and something forbidden, and they turn out to be psychically impotent, *i.e.* frigid, when at last such activities do become permissible" (212). However, though Charity certainly enjoys the element of forbiddenness in her relationship with Harney, this need is not carried over into her later involvement with Mr. Royall, and we can assume that she does not become "psychically impotent" in any way as a result of it. In fact, Wharton seems to suggest quite the opposite. Charity's understanding of her own sexuality progresses and she becomes at ease with herself. In the end she chooses to affirm herself and she begins to enjoy the element of openness rather than forbiddenness.

Charity's decision to reject the abortion option and have the baby is her first step in acknowledging and accepting her pregnancy, as well as her sexuality. The realization of her situation dawns on her after her visit to Dr. Merkle:

> On the way home, she felt an immense and unexpected quietude. It had been horrible to have to leave Harney's gift in the woman's hands, but even at that price the news she brought away had not been too dearly bought. She sat with half-closed eyes as the train rushed through the familiar landscape; and now the memories of her former journey, instead of flying before her like dead leaves, seemed to be ripening in her blood like sleeping grain. She would never again know what it was to feel herself alone.

At this point, though she still has hopes of reuniting with Harney, Charity begins to think of her pregnancy in a new way. She is no longer ashamed and discouraged; instead, she begins to understand the full potential of her own sexual maturity. More importantly, however, she begins to *appreciate* this potential. Through her decision to have the baby she becomes proud and affirms her sexuality, no longer relying on the secrecy linked to her need for forbiddenness, but experiencing the relief of acceptance and openness. Her outlook becomes positive as she strives to face her problems and the decisions she must make.

The next step in her acceptance of herself and her situation comes when she receives the letter from Harney confirming the fact that he is to marry Annabel Balch and thanking her for "understanding." Through all the hurt and pain she feels, Charity also begins morally to affirm her relationship with Harney. In other words, she does not regret anything with him. She refuses to feel shame or remorse or to let society project its values onto her personal experience. Though she feels anguish as she mentally relives each stage of her futile romance with Harney, she maintains a positive outlook:

> All these memories, and a thousand others, hummed through her brain till his nearness grew so vivid that she felt his fingers in her hair, and his warm breath on her cheek as he bent her head back like a flower. These things were hers; they had passed into her blood, and become a part of her, they were building the child in her womb; it was impossible to tear asunder strands of life so interwoven.

Again, she affirms herself not only by accepting her pregnancy, but by accepting her relationship with Harney and believing in what they shared together. She does not feel that she should have to spell out her choices for a society which does not understand her. Rather, she owns her individual power through self-affirmation, not the affirmation of others.

Her subsequent decision to marry Mr. Royall can also be seen as a positive one. We must keep in mind that the options for a young girl of her class in such a predicament during this time were few. Therefore, though marriage to Mr. Royall may at first seem like a kind of surrender on Charity's part, it actually further reveals her maturity and clear vision. Her true feelings for Mr. Royall, which, once realized, motivate her to consent to marriage, are best expressed in the thoughts she has when he brings her down from the Mountain, where she has once again fled in her distress: "Mr. Royall seldom spoke, but his silent presence gave her, for the first time, a sense of peace and security. She knew that where he was there would be warmth, rest, silence; and for the moment they were all she wanted." Here we can see how Charity realizes that many of her thoughts about how to handle her situation (such as going to Harney, or running away to the Mountain again) are unrealistic and self-defeating. She then understands that her most rational choice, the one that will allow her to continue to own her power in spite of society's mores, is marriage to Mr. Royall.

Thus, for all the tragic limitations that Freud spells out in his essay, Charity and Harney do at least partly transcend their culture's predilections. Though Harney clearly exhibits the split between the desired object and the esteemed love object, he does not fall into the one-sided show of affection and tenderness that this Freudian division suggests. And Charity surpasses the Freudian model even more because she overcomes her need for forbiddenness and becomes at ease with her sexuality. Though Freud's model of degradation and forbidden love in the erotic lives of men and women is ubiquitous in literature, the relationship of Charity Royall and Lucius Harney provides welcome relief to the old pattern.

Source: Kathy Grafton, "Degradation and Forbidden Love in Edith Wharton's *Summer*," in *Twentieth Century Literature*, Vol. 41, No. 4, Winter 1995, pp. 350–66.

Carol Wershoven

In the following essay, Wershoven argues that Summer *is "both Charity and Lawyer Royall's story, a dual conflict and ... a dual growth. . . ."*

When Bernard Berenson complimented Edith Wharton on her latest novel, *Summer,* and expressed admiration for its predominant male character, Lawyer Royall, Wharton replied, "of course *he*'s the book."

Wharton's statement has been largely ignored by critics who view the book as Charity Royall's story, and who classify Lawyer Royall as an old windbag, a pompous drunkard, or worse. The popular interpretation ignores not only Royall's central position in the plot, but Royall's central role in the novel's subtle and unfolding themes. For *Summer* is not just Wharton's variation on the old seduced-and-abandoned theme; it is a story of *two* protagonists, both of whom must come to terms with their destructive illusions in order to lead adult lives.

The ability to "look life in the face," to confront reality without flinching or evasion, was, for Wharton, an essential quality in mature conduct. She repeatedly traced the conflicts of characters faced with the choice of escape through evasion or

a more painful but adult recognition of things as they are. In the majority of her novels, Wharton chronicles this conflict through the use of an outsider heroine, one who exposes the reality of situation and self in confrontation with a weak male. This male figure, unable to face the truths the heroine reveals, rejects her. Such is the pattern of Ellen Olenska and Newland Archer in *The Age of Innocence,* of Lily Bart and Selden in *The House of Mirth,* as well as of Wharton's lesser-known novels. (Among them: *The Reef, The Custom of the Country* [where several heroes are drawn to an intruder heroine but reject what she reveals], *The Valley of Decision, New Year's Day.*) What is unusual about *Summer* is, as Wharton herself noted, that a man, Royall, is at the center of the book, that the conflict between suffocating illusions and painful but liberating reality is not expressed through Wharton's customary plot structure.

Granted the traditional elements of a Wharton novel—ineffective and evasive male and outsider female—are here, Lucius Harney qualifying as the first and Charity Royall as the second. But ... in *Summer,* Wharton departs from her usual pattern by splitting the character and conflict of the intruder into male and female, and by resolving the conflict through a union of the two. It is a union which not only satisfies the requirements of plot, but which delineates what, Wharton felt, an adult marriage must be. *Summer,* Wharton's most uncharacteristic book, is both Charity and Lawyer Royall's story, a dual conflict and, more importantly, a dual growth achieved through "looking life in the face."

As Blake Nevius has noted, Charity Royall and her guardian Lawyer Royall are twins. They share certain characteristics which set them apart from, and above, the stifling environment of North Dormer. Both are rebels, rejecting the restraints of village life: Royall, by his drunkenness and dissipation, Charity, in her affair with a city gentleman. Both are village outsiders: Charity, because of her ties to the Mountain; Royall, because he is too large a figure for small town life. They share a desire for more of an existence than North Dormer provides, and, in seeking that life, both resort to fantasies which are destructive and essentially paralyzing.

Trapped in a society they scorn and in lives they despise, Royall and his ward resort to a common consolation: the fantasy of escape. In a new place, they feel, they will become new persons. Royall laments his diminishing law practice and his own degeneration, but blames them both on his environment; had he stayed in Nettleton, he reasons, he would be a bigger man. He camouflages his own self-hatred by surrounding himself with younger men, men like Harney, in whom he sees his own wasted potential, and young drunkards, who will flatter him through their inferiority.

Charity has her own fantasies of escape—to Nettleton, to a larger world with Harney as guide, even to the Mountain. Anywhere is better than North Dormer, for Charity has "a childish belief in the miraculous power of strange scenes and new faces to transform her life and wipe out bitter memories." Royall and Charity both evade change from within, believing that a new place will make them new persons.

Charity's fantasy of escape from self by a change of place is paired with an even more destructive fantasy—the dream of deliverance through romantic love. Her affair with Harney is grounded on the classic feminine fantasy of romantic submission, on an abdication of will (and self) through absorption into the loved one. From their initial meeting, Charity feels inferior to Harney, and senses "the sweetness of dependence" on him. After her sexual initiation, Charity chooses a masochistic, servile role in Harney's life: "she could imagine no reason for doing or not doing anything except for the fact that Harney wished or did not wish it. All her tossing contradictory impulses were merged in a fatalistic acceptance of his will." Rather than resolve her conflicts and develop an adult identity through painful yet free choices, Charity hides in her dream of a self defined by her lover: "her own life was suspended in his absence." Their relationship becomes the stereotypical romance of patriarchy; Harney, the superior guide, educating, dominating, forming his inferior mistress, who has sold all sense of self in exchange for his protection. It is no wonder that Wharton associates Harney with a musty "vault" of a library, with decayed and empty houses, with manmade enclosure in the midst of natural, open beauty. For Harney, not Royall, represents the dangerous paternal power opposed to Charity; he fathers her child, thus making her a prisoner of her body. More importantly, he reduces her to the status of a dependent, both a child, relying on him for her very identity, and a prostitute, selling her emerging self for the security of his indulgent and patronizing care.

This destructive fantasy of love is shared by Royall. He, like his ward, seeks a way out of the prison of isolation through the avenue of romantic love. The love he envisions is, essentially, the same kind of love chosen by Charity, a relationship of master/slave, of woman submitting to man's superior

> " . . . in *Summer*, Wharton departs from her usual pattern by splitting the character and conflict of the intruder into male and female, and by resolving the conflict through a union of the two."

will. His fantasy is expressed, grotesquely, in his drunken assault upon Charity one lonely night, yet the model of love it expresses is, at bottom, the model of Charity and Harney's romance. The paternal lust of the father for the child only parodies the dynamics of Harney, representative of money, old New York and its suffocating superiority, seducing the poor and adoring country girl.

The subtle and hidden plot of *Summer*, then, is the revelation of these fantasies to the two main characters. It is a gradual exposure of destructive illusions accomplished, by Wharton, through the use of mirror images. Charity and Royall, twins in their weaknesses, must come to terms with themselves by repeatedly confronting one another. When Royall makes his sexual advance upon Charity, for example, she forces him to face himself, in shame. "How long is it since you've looked at yourself in the glass?" she asks, and she mocks his appearance, his age, his lecherousness. Similarly, Royall repeatedly shatters Charity's dream of Harney. When Royall refuses to board Harney any longer, suspecting Harney's motives regarding Charity, Charity surreptitiously observes her lover, and sees "a look of weariness and self-disgust on his face: it was almost as if he had been gazing at a distorted reflection of his own features. For a moment Charity looked at him with a kind of terror, as if he had been a stranger under familiar lineaments." Royall's action exposes Harney to himself and to his lover.

Two major episodes highlight the use of mirror images. The first is the Fourth of July celebration, where Harney and Charity, who is intoxicated by the fireworks, the crowds, and her first lingering kiss, meet Royall, drunk, on the arm of the local prostitute, Julia Hawes. When Royall calls

Charity a whore, she has "a vision of herself, hatless, dishevelled, with a man's arm about her," a whore confronted, ironically, by a whoremonger. The further irony is, of course, that while Royall calls her a whore, Harney will make her one.

And still the illusions persist, for Charity continues to believe in her deliverance through an all-consuming love, and Royall, though repeatedly shamed by Charity, undergoes no radical change of character. It is not until near the end of summer (the season and the book) that Royall, facing himself, reaches out to Charity, to force her to face herself.

The scene is the Old Home Week festivity, a time when North Dormer gathers to celebrate its sense of place and to welcome those who have left the village back "home." The keynote speaker for the occasion is Lawyer Royall, and his speech, delivered to the entire town, is symbolically directed at only two people—himself and Charity. It is an oral resolution of his own conflicts, an acceptance of his own shortcomings, and a plea to Charity to "come home" to reality, to abandon her fantasies and accept herself.

In a masterful speech of reconciliation, expressing his own dignity and courage, Royall confronts himself, exhorting his listeners with Wharton's favorite theme: "let us look at things as they are."

> Some of us have come back to our native town because we've failed to get on elsewhere. One way or other, things have gone wrong with us ... what we'd dreamed of hadn't come true. But the fact that we had failed elsewhere is no reason why we should fail here ... even if you come back against your will—and thinking it's all a bitter mistake of Fate or Providence—you must try to make the best of it, and to make the best of your old town; and after a while ... I believe you'll be able to say, as I can say today: "I'm glad I'm here."

For both Charity and Royall, who so closely associate self with place, the return "home," for "good," as Royall specifies, represents the return to one's self, an acceptance of one's self and of one's limitations. Royall, having faced himself, can only appeal to Charity to do likewise, to seek growth and identity in the real world of "home," rather than to escape into dangerous illusions.

Eventually, Charity does come home, to North Dormer and to herself. She begins to face the suffocating and deathlike nature of her romance: "she felt as if they were being sucked down together into some bottomless abyss"; "she had lost all spontaneity of feeling, and seemed to herself to be passively awaiting a fate she could not avert." Finally, pregnant, alone, deprived of the fantasy of a world of love apart from the real world, Charity seeks one last escape, one last place—the Mountain. It is Royall who must bring her down from the horror of the primitive place, and bring her home. And he brings her love, not particularly romantic love, not particularly passionate love, but a love that will allow her to be free of illusions and free to redefine herself.

Much has been said about the vile nature of Charity and Royall's marriage. It has been called sick, incestuous, and, superficially, it does signal Charity's return to the prison of North Dormer, where things never change, where people just get used to them. What such interpretations dismiss, however, are the changes which have taken place within the protagonists, and the subtle yet positive signs Wharton distributes through her final scenes. For what Wharton describes is not the incestuous marriage of father and child, the paradigmatic marriage of old New York, but a union of equals, of adults who have grown through confrontation and acceptance of themselves and of each other.

The marriage is, first of all, the marriage of two people who will never become model citizens of North Dormer. The pregnant girl has already scandalized the village, and the man who weds her knows full well that he is violating village norms. Both Charity and Royall will always be "too big" to fit comfortably into North Dormer, which Royall calls "a poor little place," but, as he said in his homecoming speech, a place which can become bigger "if those who had to come back ... wanted to come back for *good*." Rather than get used to North Dormer, Charity and Royall can work to change it.

Unlike the union of Harney and his society fiancée, Annabel Balch, the marriage of Charity and Royall is not incestuous. Charity is no innocent child-bride, no ornament to be displayed and broken by New York aristocrats. When Royall offers Charity his name and his life, he does so with sensitivity and compassion, so that Charity may salvage her dignity and pride from the shambles of her pain.

The man who had attempted to rape his ward sleeps in a rocking chair on their wedding night, and exhibits delicacy and tact by asking no questions about her pregnancy. He gives Charity money to spend as she wishes, and in Wharton's world, where money represents male power and female submission to that power, the incident is noteworthy. When Charity chooses to spend that money to preserve the memory of her summer with Harney, Royall makes no comment. At home, Charity has always ruled in Royall's house and she will continue to do so.

Spared the sexual violation of the traditional wedding night, spared the enslavement of economic control, Charity is given the liberty of a different kind of marriage. The young girl who "had never known how to adapt herself," and "could only break and tear and destroy," has broken herself and her romantic dreams. Now, like Royall, she must rebuild herself and must learn when to adapt, never forgetting when to rebel.

The young girl trapped in loneliness can change, and fight for good, with a new partner. Even Charity, in her misery, can see a new Royall, one from whom "all the dark spirits had gone out," and for whom she now feels "a stir of something deeper than she had ever felt." In the marriage of Charity and Lawyer Royall, Wharton proposes a new and radical union: not of father and child, but of adults, coming together without illusions but with tolerance and compassion, with appreciation of the others' strengths and acceptance of weaknesses. The marriage is nothing like a surrender to the status quo of Harney and old New York, but a coming home to a union built together out of loneliness and pain and shame, and dedicated to working together, as equals, for *good*.

Source: Carol Wershoven, "The Divided Conflict of Edith Wharton's *Summer*," in *Colby Literary Quarterly*, Vol. 21, No. 1, March 1985, pp. 117–22.

Sources

Boynton, H. W., "Some Stories of the Month," Review of *Summer*, in the *Bookman*, Vol. 46, September 1917, p. 94.

Gilman, Lawrence, "The Book of the Month: Mrs. Wharton Reverts to Shaw," in the *North American Review*, Vol. 206, August 1917, p. 307.

Grafton, Kathy, "Degradation and Forbidden Love in Edith Wharton's *Summer*," in *Twentieth Century Literature*, Vol. 41, No. 4, Winter 1995, p. 360.

Hummel, William E., "My 'Dull-Witted Enemy': Symbolic Violence and Abject Maleness in Edith Wharton's *Summer*," in *Studies in American Fiction*, Vol. 24, No. 2, Autumn 1996, pp. 215–36.

Jessup, Josephine Lurie, *The Faith of Our Feminists: A Study in the Novels of Edith Wharton, Ellen Glasgow, Willa Cather*, Richard R. Smith, 1950, p. 23.

Nevius, Blake, *Edith Wharton: A Study of Her Fiction*, University of California Press, 1953, p. 170.

"Plots and People," Review of *Summer*, in the *Nation*, Vol. 105, No. 2718, August 2, 1917, p. 125.

Skillern, Rhonda, "Becoming a 'Good Girl': Law, Language, and Ritual in Edith Wharton's *Summer*," in *The Cambridge Companion to Edith Wharton*, edited by Millicent Bell, Cambridge University Press, 1995, p. 119.

Wharton, Edith, *A Backward Glance*, D. Appleton-Century, 1934.

———, *Summer*, 1917, reprint, Perennial Library, 1979.

Wolff, Cynthia Griffin, Introduction, in *Summer*, by Edith Wharton, Perennial Library, 1979, p. x.

Further Reading

Lauer, Kristen O., and Margaret P. Murray, *Edith Wharton: An Annotated Secondary Bibliography*, Garland, 1990.
Although no longer up to date, this volume offers the most complete information about virtually every important piece of criticism of Wharton's work from original publication through 1987.

Lewis, R. W. B., *Edith Wharton: A Biography*, Harper & Row, 1975.
At well over five hundred pages, the Pulitzer Prize–winning *Edith Wharton* was a groundbreaking biography of Wharton, written with the help of thousands of pages of letters, journal, and other documents that were sealed for thirty years after Wharton's death. Lewis's biography offered the first substantive look at Wharton's relationships with the various men in her life.

Pennell, Melissa McFarland, *Student Companion to Edith Wharton*, Greenwood Publishing Group, 2003.
Part of Greenwood's Student Companions to Classic Writers Series, this volume is an introduction to Wharton's life and work written specifically for the general reader. Included are a biography and a critical overview of Wharton's place in American literature as well as a chapter dedicated to characters, plot, structure, and interpretation of *Summer*.

Singley, Carol J., ed., *A Historical Guide to Edith Wharton*, Oxford University Press, 2003.
This volume collects original articles about Wharton's place and time, providing a historical and cultural context for her works. Materials especially relevant for studying *Summer* include a brief biography by Shari Benstock, an analysis of women's fashions by Martha Banta, a narrative bibliography by Clare Colquitt, and an illustrated chronology.

Wolff, Cynthia Griffin, *A Feast of Words: The Triumph of Edith Wharton*, rev. ed., Addison-Wesley, 1995.
Wolff's biography is a thorough and insightful psychological study of Wharton's life and work.

This Side of Paradise

F. Scott Fitzgerald

1920

In the summer of 1919, after encouraging him to perform two revisions, Scribner's finally signed a contract with the unknown author F. Scott Fitzgerald to publish his first novel. Fitzgerald sold his first major short stories while waiting for the printing, but *This Side of Paradise* was his major debut, an immediate success that marked both the dawn of the Jazz Age and the dawn of Fitzgerald's turbulent career. An insider's satire of the American aristocracy and the social hierarchy of Ivy League universities, the novel turned Fitzgerald into a daring symbol for the Jazz Age, caused a sensation in the older generation, and inspired many in the younger generation to rush out and buy a copy.

The novel is much more than a sensation, however; it is a landmark in modernist fiction that challenged literary tradition and helped give a voice to a younger generation shocked by the horrors of World War I. An admittedly self-obsessed portrait of the "egotist" Amory Blaine and his intellectual development, Fitzgerald's novel is also a portrait of his own artistic development that led to his emergence as an author now considered perhaps the most important American modernist writer. Widely criticized as a haphazard collection of short stories that fail to cohere as a whole, *This Side of Paradise* does reveal some naivety in its young author, but its unique structure is also a vital part of what makes it a challenging and innovative text. In the early 2000s it was recognized as an enormously influential and compelling novel by an emerging legend of American literature.

Author Biography

Born in 1896 to an Irish Catholic family with connections to the American aristocracy, Francis Scott Key Fitzgerald grew up in the elite schools of St. Paul, Minnesota. He was a favorite of his mother's and loyal to his father despite Edward Fitzgerald's series of business failures in upstate New York that brought the family back to St. Paul. In high school, Fitzgerald wrote his first short stories and developed an intense interest in drama, but his poor grades forced him to transfer to the Newman School in Hackensack, New Jersey. He continued to write fiction and participate in drama when he entered Princeton University in 1913, and his experience there was very important to his writing, although he never graduated because of poor grades and illness and because he joined the army when the United States entered World War I.

While he was stationed in Montgomery, Alabama in 1917, Fitzgerald met his future wife Zelda Sayre, with whom he had a long and volatile relationship (due in part to Zelda's mental illness). He also began working on the first edition of *This Side of Paradise*, which was published by Scribner's in 1920 and effectively launched his success as a fiction writer. Because of his and Zelda's lavish lifestyle in New York, supported chiefly by the numerous stories he sold to magazines, Fitzgerald became known as a symbol of the Jazz Age. The couple and their daughter Scottie then moved to Paris, where Fitzgerald wrote his most famous novel, *The Great Gatsby* (1925), and the family remained there for the rest of the decade.

After the publication of *The Great Gatsby*, Fitzgerald's relationship with his wife grew increasingly problematic, his friendship with the writer Ernest Hemingway turned sour, he developed a drinking problem, and he failed to make significant progress on a new novel, although he continued to publish short stories. The Fitzgeralds returned to the United States in 1931, where Zelda continued to be in and out of sanitariums. In 1934, Fitzgerald published *Tender Is the Night*, but the novel failed to produce the critical acclaim for which he was hoping, and his drinking problem grew more severe. Financial burdens and a desire for success caused Fitzgerald to pursue a career in Hollywood, and in 1937 he signed a contract with the production company Metro-Goldwyn-Mayer. While working as a screenwriter, Fitzgerald battled alcoholism and fell in love with film columnist Sheilah Graham. He died of a heart attack on December 21, 1940, while working on his last, unfinished novel, *The Last Tycoon* (1941).

F. Scott Fitzgerald

Plot Summary

Book 1: The Romantic Egotist

The novel opens with a description of Amory Blaine's mother Beatrice and her exciting life of travel with her son Amory until his appendix bursts on a ship to Europe, and he is sent to live with his aunt and uncle in Minneapolis, Minnesota. While in private school there, Armory kisses Myra St. Claire on the cheek and takes on various elitist values before Beatrice gives in to his request to go to a boarding school. After enrolling at the school, where he is unpopular because of his arrogance, Amory meets his friend and mentor Monsignor Darcy. Amory is more popular during his second year because he succeeds at football and as a writer for the school paper, and he decides to enroll at Princeton University.

At Princeton, Amory once again gradually becomes a social success by acting in plays and writing for the college newspaper, and he meets some of his most important friends, such as Kerry and Burne Holiday, and Tom D'Invilliers. He travels back to Minneapolis to meet his first love, Isabelle Borgé, at a "petting party" for upper class daughters, and they exchange long letters while Amory is at Princeton with his elitist group of friends.

Media Adaptations

- A book-on-tape of *This Side of Paradise* is available unabridged from Bookcassette Sales, 1997.

Then, coming back from a night out in New York, Amory is shocked and dismayed to see his friend Dick Humbird die in a car accident.

When he next sees Isabelle at the prom, they quarrel and Amory leaves her, and this is followed by Amory's discovery that he has failed math and therefore will be expelled from the editorial board of the college paper. Amory's father then dies suddenly, but this does not affect Amory deeply, and it leaves him with an inheritance despite his father's somewhat ineffective investments. After returning to Princeton, Amory encounters a disturbing and devilish man with "queer feet" who terrifies him and from whom he flees through the streets of New York.

During Amory's final two years at Princeton, many of his peers, especially Burne Holiday, begin to challenge the social institutions and traditions of the college, but Amory does little himself. He falls in love with his third cousin, Clara Page, but this comes to nothing. Amory begins to be more interested in poetry at Princeton, but then the United States enters World War I and Amory enlists in the army. This is followed by the novel's "Interlude," which consists of a letter of advice to Amory from Monsignor Darcy and a letter to Tom from Amory with a plan to meet in New York after the war.

Book 2: The Education of a Personage

Book Two begins in the format of a play to introduce Rosalind Connage, the sister of Amory's Princeton friend Alec. Amory and Rosalind immediately fall in love and become consumed with each other, but their relationship is doomed because Amory is poor and without prospects, and Rosalind leaves him for the rich Dawson Ryder. Devastated, Amory falls into an alcoholic stupor, quits his job at a New York advertising agency, and dwindles his inheritance money. He does begin to write and read more, however, and he discusses philosophy and literature with his roommate Tom, but soon Tom must go home because his mother is ill, and they sell the apartment.

After narrowly missing Monsignor Darcy in Washington, Amory travels to Maryland to stay with an uncle, and while there he meets Eleanor Ramilly, an intelligent and passionate girl from an old Maryland family, with whom he begins a relationship. They discuss philosophy and literature, and they develop a bond that lasts long afterwards in the form of poems they send to each other, but Amory is still affected by his relationship with Rosalind, and he leaves Eleanor in a rather bitter mood. The next scene shifts to a party in Atlantic City, after which Amory wakes up in a hotel room he was supposed to be sharing with Alec Connage to discover that Alec has illicitly brought a girl back to the room and two house detectives are banging on the door to find them. Amory makes a "sacrifice" of himself in order to save Alec's reputation and then discovers in the paper that Rosalind has been married and Monsignor has suddenly died.

The last chapter of the novel describes the Amory's intellectual convictions during his attempt to walk from New York to Princeton. On the way, he is picked up by a "big man" who is revealed to be the father of his college friend Jesse Ferrenby, and with him and his companion Amory argues about socialism and the radicalism of his generation. Amory then leaves them and reflects on religion, philosophy, politics and literature, unsure about precisely what he believes or where exactly he should go with his life. As he exclaims in the last line of the book, " 'I know myself,' he cried, 'but that is all—.' "

Characters

Mr. Barlow

Mr. Barlow is the president of the advertising company in whose office Amory rudely quits his job.

Mr. Barton

Mr. Barton, Amory's family lawyer, advises Amory about his inherited and mainly unprofitable property in Lake Geneva, Wisconsin.

Amory Blaine

The main character of the novel in the process of becoming a "personage," Amory is chiefly characterized by his intense self-obsession and egotism. He changes markedly in the course of the plot, growing from a superficially clever and pretentious boy to a much more profound thinker, but his egotism remains his defining characteristic. His affairs with the four main young women of the novel, as well as his relationships with other adults and friends, are in many ways important to him only as they affect and influence his own development and desires.

Physically good-looking, but not conventionally so, and known for his "penetrating green eyes," Amory is very successful with young women and consistently manages to intrigue them. By the time of his relationship with Eleanor, however, Amory is not sure if he is able to love again after Rosalind affected him so deeply. Much of his taste for enigmatic and unobtainable women goes back to his unconventional relationship with his charming, indulgent, but often absent mother.

Like his other relationships, the young women in Amory's life represent the stages of his intellectual, artistic, and religious development, and they reflect that his own changing opinions and beliefs become more substantial as he reads more and explores himself more thoroughly. He retains something of an inability to persist in his endeavors, however, just as he remains an ambitious and romantic dreamer. Amory has become known as a Fitzgerald-type character, an elitist, ambitious, and daring youth of the Jazz Age based on the author himself.

Beatrice O'Hara Blaine

Amory's mother, with her "brilliant education," and the "exquisite delicacy of her features," is a beautiful woman from the American upper class. She is more of a companion to Amory than a mother, which is reinforced by the fact that he calls her by her first name. Nevertheless, she is extremely important to his development, babies him throughout his youth, and carefully arranges his education. With her brilliant charm, she is also a model for the elusive and intriguing women with whom Amory continually falls in love. A heavy drinker and socialite continually in danger of another nervous breakdown, Beatrice dies while Amory is in the army, leaving half of her possessions to the Catholic Church.

Stephen Blaine

Amory's father is an "ineffectual, inarticulate" man whom Amory does not know very well and who dies while Amory is at Princeton.

Isabelle Borgé

"Capable of very strong, if very transient, emotions," Isabelle is Amory's first love. He travels all the way to Minneapolis to see her at a "petting party," during which they flirt and begin a relationship of passionate letter writing until they fall out when she comes to the Princeton prom. Isabelle is something of an actress, and she fits in well with the vanity of Amory's pre-war Princeton period because she is quite vain herself. Nevertheless, she and Amory make an exciting pair during their relationship, and she enchants Amory as much as she infuriates him.

Phoebe Column

Phoebe is Fred Sloane's friend, and it is in her New York apartment that Amory has a severe fright due to the man with the queer feet.

Alec Connage

A "quiet, rather aloof slicker," Alec is Amory's friend from Princeton and Rosalind's brother. Amory's love for Rosalind puts a strain on his and Alec's relationship, as does the awkwardness after Amory takes the blame for Alec's having illicitly brought a young woman back to their hotel room.

Cecelia Connage

Cecelia is a sarcastic and "good-humored" girl who acts as a foil, or a character whose function is to reveal something about another character, for her sister Rosalind.

Mrs. Connage

Rosalind's mother Mrs. Connage keeps close tabs on her daughter and continually urges her to marry a rich gentleman.

Rosalind Connage

Amory's most important and intense love in the novel, Rosalind is an extremely striking character. Her long description shortly into the first chapter of "Book Two," beginning "Rosalind *is— utterly* Rosalind," emphasizes that all men fall in love with her except those that are afraid of her, claims that she is not spoiled despite her selfishness, and states that "*all criticism of* Rosalind *ends in her beauty*." She is spontaneous and intriguing, and her treatment of men in some ways represents a new type of liberated woman, since, she explains, she toys with men and leaves them as male lovers always used to do their female partners in the past.

Because of this pattern, Rosalind very frequently devastates men by leaving them, and there is much foreshadowing to her abandonment of Amory for the rich Dawson Ryder. Nevertheless, Rosalind seems entirely absorbed with Amory, as he is with her, during their brief and intense romance.

She seems to agonize over her decision to leave Amory because he is too poor, although there is the suggestion that she does not suffer from it later as he does.

Thomas Park D'Invilliers

Tom is a Princeton friend with whom Amory begins a friendship because of their mutual interest in poetry. They remain friends and confidants after the war, and they live together in New York, where Tom has a job as a reviewer. When Tom grows tired of Princeton, he becomes more cynical, and while they are living in New York, Tom is frustrated by what he sees as a dishonest and incompetent literary community. Amory sees him as "a blighted Shelley, changing, shifting, clever, unscrupulous," who represents "the critical consciousness of the race."

Monsignor Thayer Darcy

Monsignor Darcy, an influential and successful priest in the Catholic hierarchy, is Amory's confidant and father figure. He was Beatrice's passionate lover in his youthful romantic days, but when she abandoned him for the rich Stephen Blaine, Monsignor began his career in the priesthood. Because of his charm and ability to be adored by everyone, Father Darcy earns the title "Monsignor," which is a general term of influence in the Catholic Church, and tells Amory before his sudden death towards the end of the novel that he will soon become a cardinal. Monsignor exerts a great influence over Amory, and they are very close because of their many similarities, including their elitism and their taste in philosophy and literature.

Jesse Ferrenby

Part of Amory's Princeton group, Jesse eventually gets a place at the "Princetonian," the college's daily newspaper. He dies in World War I.

Mr. Ferrenby

Known as "the big man with goggles" until his identity as Jesse's father is revealed, Mr. Ferrenby is the impressive capitalist who gives Amory a ride in his car and argues with him about socialism.

Howard Gillespie

Howard is the unhappy young man of whom Rosalind has recently become tired when she meets Amory.

Thornton Hancock

The Honorable Thornton Hancock is a historian, advisor to famous politicians, and rich intellectual from an aristocratic Bostonian family. Amory meets him because of his friendship with Monsignor Darcy and afterwards considers that he is an example of an admirable atheist.

Burne Holiday

Burne is the chairman of the "Princetonian" and a social success at Princeton until he begins to radically challenge the social hierarchy. Although Burne is busy trying out for the "Princetonian" during their first year and Amory does not get to know him until later, Amory grows to admire his enthusiasm, stubbornness, and "earnestness." Flirting with ideas of socialism and pacifism, some of Burne's ideas are muddled, but he thinks seriously about intellectual issues in a way that inspires Amory's own development. Burne comes out as a pacifist during World War I and leaves Princeton, disappearing from the novel, although Amory speculates that he could have ended up in jail.

Kerry Holiday

Amory's first friend at Princeton and Burne's dark-haired older brother, Kerry is "the mentor of the house" and an elitist such as Amory. He becomes close with Amory by planning their social rise at Princeton, and they remain friends until Kerry leaves college to enroll in the war, in which he dies. Kerry's easygoing and charming personality makes him, with Alec Connage, the "life" of their Princeton social group, and Amory likes nearly everything about him, including his snobbishness.

Dick Humbird

Dick is Amory's "quiet" friend from Princeton, who admires him as the "perfect type of aristocrat." Amory is deeply shocked by Dick's death in a car accident, and his face comes back to haunt Amory while he is running from the man with the queer feet.

Mrs. Lawrence

"A type of Rome-haunting American" who is intelligent and dignified, Mrs. Lawrence is a friend and devotee of Monsignor Darcy.

The Little Man

"The little man" who offers Amory a ride is the assistant to Mr. Ferrenby. Amory insults him and uses him as an example of ignorance in his argument about socialism.

The Man with the Queer Feet

While at a club in New York, Amory has a strange and "inexpressibly terrible" experience with a middle-aged man in a brown suit who may represent the devil. Amory has a vision of the man in Phoebe's flat that frightens him and seems to chase him through the streets, and he remembers long afterwards the "wrongness" of the man's strange pointed shoes that curl up at the end.

Mr. Margotson

The senior master at St. Regis preparatory school, Mr. Margotson attempts to advise Amory about why the other boys dislike him, but Amory walks out of his office in a fury.

Axia Marlowe

Phoebe Column's friend, Axia chats and flirts with Amory until he runs away, frightened of the man with the queer feet, from Phoebe's apartment in New York.

Clara Page

Clara is Amory's third cousin, with whom he falls in love. She is a poor widow with two children and has led a "hurried life," but she is nevertheless charming and delightful, and everyone treats her with respect. Because of the vast "goodness" that he sees in her, and her ability to bring out a different side of his narcissistic personality, Amory proposes marriage to her. Clara brushes this off, however, and they lose touch with each other at the beginning of the war.

Frog Parker

"Froggy" is Amory's closest friend during his years of private school in Minneapolis.

Rahill

The "president of the sixth form" at St. Regis, Rahill becomes a friend and "co-philosopher" of Amory's during his second year.

Eleanor Ramilly

Eleanor is Amory's final love in the course of the novel, and she is associated with wildness and nature. From a very old Maryland family, Eleanor was brought up in France and is an extremely intelligent and well-read person who is intellectually challenging to Amory. She describes herself as a "romantic little materialist," and has an inclination towards paganism in thought and literature. Although her appearance is unclear at first, she is eighteen years old and beautiful, with pale skin and green eyes. She and Amory later write poems to each other, but their relationship ends when Amory leaves Maryland.

Dawson Ryder

The rich young man that eventually marries Rosalind, Dawson is a reliable choice, and Amory has to agree that he is "a good man and a strong one." Rosalind is never in love with him, however.

Fred Sloane

Sloane is part of Amory's group of Princeton friends. He has a "happy personality," likes to drink alcohol, and is the pitcher for the baseball team.

Myra St. Claire

Myra, a girl Amory meets while he is living with his aunt and uncle in Minneapolis, give Amory his chance for his first kiss. Myra is slightly spoiled and becomes upset when Amory refuses to kiss her more than once while they are alone at her "bobbing party."

Phyllis Styles

Phyllis Styles is the socialite that Burne Holiday embarrasses very awkwardly at a Harvard-Princeton football game.

Jill Wayne

Jill, in whom Amory sees the evil of "pride and sensuality," is the young woman who Alec illicitly brings back to a hotel in Atlantic City.

Sally Weatherby

Sally is Amory's acquaintance from private school in Minneapolis, and she sets him up with Isabelle.

Themes

Generational Conflict

Although Fitzgerald's novel may seem less shocking now, it created a sensation when it was published because of its representation of a younger generation that perceived itself as departing entirely from the tradition of the generations before it. Amory's vanity and egotism, his flirtatious affairs with young women, his startling ideas (such as about socialism), and his vague contempt for nineteenth-century tradition all struck a chord with a generation that blamed their parents, for example, for the horrors of World War I.

This generational conflict was a key motivation for the modernist literary movement in the United States. In *This Side of Paradise*, the intellectual and aesthetic aspects of the conflict are first

Topics For Further Study

- *This Side of Paradise* includes a number of poems by Amory and other characters, such as Eleanor. Reread these poems and discuss their style and themes. What role do they play in the novel, and what is their relationship to Amory's intellectual development? What do you think of the poems? Why do you think Fitzgerald includes them? How do they go about expressing themes such as traditionalism, radicalism, paganism, or other themes that you can see in them? Is their style similar to that of the novel itself? Are they modernist poems? Explain why or why not.

- Fitzgerald's personal life has long fascinated critics. Read Arthur Mizener's biographical work *The Far Side of Paradise* (1951) or another biography of Fitzgerald paying particular attention to his life before 1920, and discuss how what you have read affects your understanding of *This Side of Paradise*. How are the personalities and experiences in Fitzgerald's life directly or indirectly included in his first novel? Discuss why you think Fitzgerald used certain events

from his life in the novel, and how you think critics should treat knowledge of an author's life when they are discussing his or her writings.

- Amory is characterized as a self-absorbed egotist in the novel. Do you think this is an undesirable trait? What are its positive aspects? By the end of the novel, does Amory think it is undesirable? Does Fitzgerald? Do you think Amory's personality will change? Why do you think Fitzgerald wrote a book about such a character? How is egotism important to the novel's place in literary history?

- Two of the most important scenes in *This Side of Paradise* are written in the format of a play. Find a cast of characters and act out these scenes. Afterwards, discuss how this experience adds to your understanding of the novel, as well as how these scenes affect the rest of the book. Why you think Fitzgerald chose to use the dramatic form? Is it a success, and does it work well in the book? Why or why not?

---

revealed by Burne Holiday, who inspires many of Amory's own convictions against nineteenth-century tradition. And Amory's meditations and convictions in "The Egotist Becomes a Personage," although many critics have noted that they are not necessarily well informed or even coherent, are nevertheless something of an intellectual manifesto for his generation. As Amory says while he is arguing with Mr. Ferrenby about socialism, "I'm a product of a versatile mind in a restless generation." While his specific intellectual theories are unclear, and, for example, Amory does nothing but dabble without conviction in socialism, this wavering is consistent with Amory's previous statement: "I'm in love with change and I've killed my conscience."

Such a demand for progress away from the previous generation without a clear view about the direction that this progress should take led to criticism

of the novel such as that of Edmund Wilson in his essay, "F. Scott Fitzgerald": "In short, one of the chief weaknesses of *This Side of Paradise* is that it is really not *about* anything: its intellectual and moral content amounts to little more than a gesture—a gesture of indefinite revolt." Whether this revolt was "indefinite," however, it moved and excited many readers, and was key in defining Fitzgerald as a spokesperson for his generation.

Egotism

Amory's vanity and narcissism is more than a character trait; it is an emblem of the theme of "egotism" that pervades Fitzgerald's novel. When Amory says that he is an egotist, he does not simply mean that he is self-absorbed; he is revealing an essential philosophical trait of the novel, which is that the self is all-important. He best expresses this idea in the final chapter of the novel, "The

Egotist Becomes a Personage," with statements such as, "This selfishness is not only part of me. It is the most living part." Like many people in his generation feeling cut off from tradition and drastically changed after World War I, Amory comes to think that his self is, in a sense, all that he has.

This idea, which is common in other important modernist texts (such as Ezra Pound's famous magazine, the *Egoist*), is influenced by Freudian psychology, by the modernist generation's disavowal of past traditions, and by the individualism that was important to many writers of the time. Often, however, Fitzgerald is also critical and satirical of Amory's egotism, and he certainly mocks its more superficial form of vanity, a trait that characterizes Amory's youth as well as his first love, Isabelle. The egotism and snobbishness of many aristocrats in the novel is also something that Fitzgerald alternatively ridicules and admires. By the end of the novel, it is not necessarily clear whether Amory fully embraces egotism, although he does seem to recognize its valuable artistic and intellectual aspects.

Elitism and the American Aristocracy

Throughout *This Side of Paradise*, Amory encounters social hierarchies, aristocratic families, elitist standards of behavior, and vast amounts of wealth that allow a unique insight into the American upper class in the first two decades of the twentieth century. Since Amory is an elitist himself, he is continually coming into contact with the institutions and practices of upper class families such as the Connages, and upper class institutions such as Princeton University. Fitzgerald offers a thorough satire of the vanity and hypocrisy of the aristocracy (such as when Rosalind rejects Amory for a wealthy husband) at the same time as he suggests its enormous allure in the form of Beatrice, Monsignor Darcy, and Rosalind, despite their faults. His satire of the "petting party," in which young upper class girls kiss and make promises to a variety of men, was particularly shocking to the aristocracy, as was his ridicule of various Princeton clubs and elitist hierarchies.

Style

Dramatic, Poetic, and Epistolary Forms

This Side of Paradise is largely told by an omniscient or all-knowing, third person narrator, but many sections employ a variety of different and unique forms, from poems and songs, to lists, to letters and short notes, to the dramatic form or play that is used to portray the beginning and the end of Amory's relationship with Rosalind. These unconventional methods use a distinct style of text and layout, and they vary according to the situation that Fitzgerald is attempting to express. They are important for two reasons. First, they highlight the unsuitability of a more typical, straightforward narrative in a novel for the new generation of modernist authors; the dramatic form in particular is an innovative approach. And, second, they provide a reading experience that is slightly jarring and that inspires the reader to imagine the events and characters in a fuller, more evocative way.

Self-Conscious Narration

A predominant feature of Fitzgerald's style is the narrative voice's own insistent self-consciousness. One of the clearest examples of Fitzgerald's tendency to call attention to his own methods takes place in the "Young Irony" chapter of Book Two, after the narrator begins his story of Amory and Eleanor by describing how they remembered the affair afterwards. When he breaks off this description and states, "I see I am starting wrong. Let me begin again," the narrator surprises the readers greatly and makes them wonder why this false start has been included, if it really is "wrong."

Fitzgerald's showy style, including many of his romantic, elaborate descriptions and numerous epigrams, or brief witty sayings, is another method of drawing attention to himself as an author. Like Amory, the narrative voice often appears vain and superficially charming, and it is in this way that Fitzgerald presents himself as a daring, debut writer. In fact, this technique is part of the reason that such a large critical emphasis on *This Side of Paradise* has historically been placed on Fitzgerald's personal life. Most of the characters have some equivalent or near equivalent in real life: Amory is strikingly similar to Fitzgerald; most of Amory's Princeton friends are based on some of Fitzgerald's Princeton friends; Isabelle and Rosalind are both based, in part, on Fitzgerald's college obsession Ginevra King (although Rosalind also has much in common with Fitzgerald's wife Zelda); and Monsignor Darcy is based on Fitzgerald's friend, Father Sigourney Fay, to whom the novel is dedicated. All of these likenesses add to the intrigue of the novel, and the technique of self-consciousness is an important aspect of the period's aesthetic innovations.

Compare & Contrast

- **1920:** Many young soldiers have come home to the United States from a devastating war abroad to a mood of increasing isolationism and a desire to enjoy a prosperous economy.

  Today: American soldiers remain in Iraq and Afghanistan, and the United States military remains engaged in international initiatives, although they are nowhere near the scale of World War I.

- **1920:** The younger generation in the United States shocks parents with kissing and flirting that was very liberal for the time, as displayed in Fitzgerald's novel.

  Today: Although the United States has the highest rate of teen pregnancy in the western industrialized world and teenagers in the early 2000s might not find the romance in *This Side of Paradise* very shocking, younger generations are probably not any more sexually liberal than their parents were at their age.

- **1920:** Private Ivy League universities such as Princeton are elitist institutions dominated by and populated with the upper class.

  Today: Financial aid and diversity initiatives have made Ivy League colleges somewhat more accessible to high-achieving lower and middle class students.

- **1920:** Women make up one-fourth of the workforce (a dramatic increase from before World War I) and begin to vote for the first time.

  Today: Women make up nearly half of the workforce and show an increasing presence in managerial and professional positions.

Historical Context

World War I

With tensions running very high between the major European powers, the 1914 assassination of Archduke Ferdinand of the Austro-Hungarian Empire and his wife in Belgrade sparked the beginning of World War I. Germany, Austro-Hungary, and the Ottoman Empire formed the Central Alliance against Great Britain, France, Russia, and later many other countries, waging a devastating war on a number of fronts. The United States remained neutral for much of the war, but anti-German sentiment increased when passenger and commercial ships with American interests began to be attacked and sunk, and when Great Britain produced a decoded telegram from the German foreign minister promising Mexico control of areas of the United States if it entered the war on the side of the Central Powers.

President Woodrow Wilson declared war on Germany in April of 1917, and the American assistance on the Western front helped to overwhelm the Central Powers despite the Russian withdrawal from the war in the spring of 1918. By November of the same year, the Central Powers had been defeated, and in January Wilson delivered his idealistic "Fourteen Points" statement about international conflict resolution. Instead of adhering to Wilson's ideas, however, the embittered Allied Powers signed punitive treaties with Germany, Austro-Hungary, and the Ottoman Empire by 1919 that left these countries divided and in severe debt. The 1919 Treaty of Versailles also set up the League of Nations, a body intended to resolve international disputes, but opposition in the United States Senate blocked American entry into the organization.

The Dawn of the Jazz Age

In the years following World War I, the United States was beginning to enjoy the optimism and economic boom characteristic of the 1920s. Mass-produced goods and household technology were becoming available, and people were investing in the prosperous stock market. In the final period before the Eighteenth Amendment prohibiting alcohol took effect in early 1920, jazz music was popular and the social scene was notoriously flamboyant, particularly in large cities like New York. The beginning of the Jazz Age was also an important period for women's rights: women were increasingly involved in the social scene; they had a much larger presence in the workforce; and the Nineteenth Amendment, enacted in August of 1920, gave women the right to vote.

American Modernism

The literary movement of modernism is generally considered to have coincided with World War I, an event that caused many assumptions about the world to change drastically. Writers and artists across the western world, feeling that they could no longer express themselves in old forms, responded with experimental techniques that borrowed from a variety of other movements, most notably post-impressionism, which dealt with a simplification of form in the visual arts, and naturalism, which tended to present a deterministic universe that involved a brutal struggle for survival.

Modernism is most commonly associated with Europe, and the nucleus of modernist writers lived in Paris, where Fitzgerald later moved, and with the Bloomsbury group living in London. Perhaps the most influential modernist writer was James Joyce, an Irish author who became known for his efforts to deal with a multiplicity of viewpoints that lead to an "epiphany," or sudden moment of truth and understanding, as well as his later use of the stream-of-consciousness style. There was also, however, a group of American modernist writers, including Fitzgerald, Ernest Hemingway, and John Dos Passos, from the "lost generation" of an age to fight in World War I. Although many of them lived in Paris at some point, these writers often approached the literary movement by dealing with American social and political themes and did not necessarily identify with European modernism.

A specifically American modernist identity is noticeable in *This Side of Paradise*, for example, when Amory mentions that he did not take to Joyce's *A Portrait of the Artist as a Young Man*. In fact, Amory tends to group all European authors into one and deny them all, from the patriotic English poet of World War I, Rupert Brooke, to the traditionalist English writer H. G. Wells, to the visionary Victorian poet Algernon Charles Swinburne, who was known for being profoundly at odds with his age. Although it is not at all clear that Fitzgerald is actually interested in disavowing all of European tradition, his first novel does reveal a desire to be uniquely new and to develop a distinctly American literary identity.

Critical Overview

Although it took two years of revision before Fitzgerald finally obtained a publishing contract for his first novel, *This Side of Paradise* was an immediate critical and popular success. As the anonymous article, "With College Men" in the *New York Times Book Review* of May 9, 1920, read, "The glorious spirit of abounding youth glows throughout this fascinating tale," and most reviews were similarly enthusiastic. Heywood Broun's April 11, 1920, review in the *New York Tribune* found the novel little more than a "self-conscious . . . stunt," but almost all other critics acknowledged Fitzgerald's great promise as a writer.

The novel briefly topped bestseller lists, and it was particularly popular among the young generation and in colleges. But Fitzgerald's success as a short story writer and the intrigue about his personal life were equally responsible for the subsequent success that earned him a reputation as an icon of the "lost generation." Critical opinion of Fitzgerald fluctuated when his next novel, *The Beautiful and the Damned*, was largely received as a disappointment and when *The Great Gatsby* was more successful in 1925. However, the author, and his first novel, generally remained in vogue with the public and the literary community until Fitzgerald's rapid decline in reputation and subsequent bout of alcoholism that began with the tepid reception of *Tender Is the Night* in 1934. From this point until Fitzgerald's death, *This Side of Paradise* sold few copies and was largely ignored by critics.

The revival of interest in Fitzgerald began to blossom after 1951, when Arthur Mizener's analytical biography of the writer attracted attention to him and his wife Zelda. From this point onward, Fitzgerald's works were incorporated into the canon of American literature to the point that he was as of the early 2000s viewed as one of the most important novelists of the twentieth century. *This Side of Paradise* was perhaps less highly esteemed than *The Great Gatsby* or *Tender Is the Night*, and critics tended to find it slightly naive and less a novel than a collection of short stories. It was nevertheless viewed as a landmark achievement of the Jazz Age by the ambitious young modernist writer, however, and critics continued to write about the novel from nearly all analytical perspectives.

Criticism

Scott Trudell

Trudell is a freelance writer with a bachelor's degree in English literature. In the following essay, Trudell discusses the significance of Monsignor Darcy and the theme of religion and tradition in This Side of Paradise.

Sigourney Fay, the person to whom Fitzgerald's novel is dedicated, was a brilliant priest whom Fitzgerald met while he was in preparatory school in New Jersey, and with whom he remained close friends until Father Fay's sudden death in 1919. Fay is, of course, the basis for the character Monsignor Darcy, and although the purpose of this essay is not to speculate about the particulars of Fitzgerald's real life and their impact on *This Side of Paradise*, it is worth noting that Fay made an extraordinary impression on Fitzgerald. Their discussions greatly affected the author's intellectual and artistic development, and Fay's premature death assumed a unique significance in Fitzgerald's symbolic world.

Monsignor Darcy's death, on the other hand, is not in any way premature or untimely. It is exactly in line with Amory's development and, coming as it does in the lines immediately preceding the novel's last chapter, "The Egotist Becomes a Personage," it allows Amory to complete what the novel terms his "education." Monsignor is Amory's father figure throughout the novel; while Mr. Blaine does not so much as make an appearance, Monsignor is introduced in the first chapter as Beatrice's true passionate lover, and Amory's mother predicts: "Amory will go to him one day, I know." With Monsignor's death, which represents, in symbolic terms, the death of the father, Amory's religious faith dies as well, and he is finally able to contemplate artistic and intellectual ideas outside the European tradition.

Amory and Monsignor get along immediately when they meet during Amory's first year at St. Regis and discover an intense affinity with each other. Their relationship remains close enough for Monsignor to constantly compare their similarities and even write that he considers Amory the "reincarnation" of himself. Monsignor's description of a recurring dream of his in a letter to Amory during the novel's "Interlude" is particularly enlightening on this subject:

> I've enjoyed imagining that you were my son, that perhaps when I was young I went into a state of coma and begat you, and when I came to, had no recollection of it . . . it's the paternal instinct, Amory—celibacy goes deeper than the flesh. . . .

Sometimes I think that the explanation of our deep resemblance is some common ancestor.

Not only does this dream reinforce Monsignor's significance as Amory's father figure; it helps to establish the idea that Amory's deep connection to Monsignor has been passed down from an ancient tradition of spiritual, intellectual, and artistic ideas. Like many of Amory's relationships, Monsignor is chiefly important because of what he represents about Amory and Amory's relationship with the ancient European literary, cultural, and religious tradition. Although Amory is still fairly ignorant of literature when he arrives at Princeton (he does not know who Oscar Wilde is, for example), his interest in "English and history" sparks at about the same time he meets Monsignor, and from then on the priest serves as the cultural and intellectual mentor that Amory never finds among the faculty at Princeton. Monsignor advises him on what to read, whom to idealize ("some such man as Leonardo da Vinci," for example), and which philosophies to follow.

There is, however, a growing sense that Monsignor and Amory's ideological connection is breaking apart. Monsignor's letter in the "Interlude," while Amory is in the army, is the first and perhaps most important signal of this break. Beginning by pointing out that, "you will never again be quite the Amory Blaine that I knew," Monsignor then highlights the widening gulf between their generations: "your generation is growing hard, much harder than mine ever grew," and the letter ends with the mysterious thought: "curiously alike we are . . . curiously unlike." In his last letter to Amory, Monsignor stresses that Amory's last letter was "not a bit like yourself," and it includes the statement, "Beware of losing yourself in the personality of another being, man or woman," which refers to Rosalind but is ironic because it could be applied to Monsignor as well. Then, after Monsignor's death, Amory appears to renounce the priest's religion and moral system, counting instead on a newly discovered philosophy of reliance on the self and one's inner convictions.

In this egotistical break from tradition, Amory goes so far as to declare that the books of previous generation were all lies, and it is in ideas like these that the widening difference between him and Monsignor becomes clear. A "reincarnation" of a figure like Monsignor in Amory's generation will not, it seems, have a very similar life to the priest at all, and this is in fitting with the new artistic movement's radical goals and convictions. During the penultimate scene of the novel, when Amory finds himself in a cemetery at "the golden beauty of four," Fitzgerald reminds the reader of Monsignor's description of giving out "the genial golden warmth of 4 P.M." when he first introduces Amory to the idea of "personage." Unlike a personage of Monsignor Darcy's generation, when the egotist of Amory's age becomes a personage, it is by disavowing the generations that came before.

In addition to its generational significance, Monsignor and Amory's relationship is a metaphor for the relationship between Europe and the United States before and after World War I. American modernist writers such as Fitzgerald and Hemingway were part of the generation involved in a bloody and devastating war in Europe that, many felt, was the culmination of all that was wrong with the European tradition. The war destroyed thousands of American soldiers; it contributed to many in Amory's generation believing the "Gods dead"; and it was a significant factor in the death of the transatlantic cultural elite. Introduced as "rather like an exiled Stuart king" and a "Turner sunset," which refers to the popular nineteenth-century English painter J. M. W. Turner, Monsignor's identity as an American with firm European roots is what leads to the necessity of his death in a novel that envisions the collapse of this tradition.

The great shock of World War I led many young readers to sympathize fully with Fitzgerald's metaphor for this political break. But Fitzgerald envisioned something even more extensive than a break with Europe's politics and literary tradition; he very purposefully uses the image of a Catholic priest to represent the separation and, therefore, firmly connects it to a rejection of this faith. Indeed, the author's agenda is much more radical than the satire and frankness about upper class America that offended many readers, because he is rejecting the very basis of Christian faith and replacing it with a boundless egotism like Amory has. The last chapter of the novel makes this atheism explicit with certain phrases, such as "There was no God in his heart," and the stark newness and deep conviction of Amory's break from the past should make the reader doubt that this atheism is simply a temporary phase.

The chapter "The Supercilious Sacrifice," at the end of which Amory learns of Monsignor's death, is the key evidence of the central importance of atheism to the intellectual content of the novel. Amory's sacrifice by implicating himself with Jill, which he believes to be divinely inspired and later recognizes, in the form of something "featureless and indistinguishable" among the curtains, to be connected to Monsignor, is a religious sacrifice.

> " With Monsignor's death, which represents, in symbolic terms, the death of the father, Amory's religious faith dies as well, and he is finally able to contemplate artistic and intellectual ideas outside the European tradition."

However, it is not a selfless sacrifice as in the traditional Christian understanding; in fact, it is "supercilious," or disdainful and self-important, because Alec will "secretly hate [Amory] for having done so much for him," and because it is essentially a selfish endeavor. This is reinforced by the fact that the quotation that inspires Amory's action is an incorrect version of Luke 23:28, in which Jesus says, "weep not for me, but for yourselves, and for your children," and the fact that Amory leaves out the "for yourselves" in his version suggests that he misunderstands the place of the self in the sacrifice.

The point of Amory's selfish sacrifice, which is inspired by a religious impulse but turns out to be useless and misdirected, is that it results in the subheading, "The Collapse of Several Pillars." The last of these pillars is Monsignor Darcy and, with him, the pillar of religion in Amory's intellectual and moral life. As Fitzgerald goes on to discuss more overtly in the form of Amory's thoughts and conclusions in "The Egotist Becomes a Personage," as far as the modernist egoist is concerned, religion has no place in the philosophy of the younger American generation.

In his 1952 essay, "F. Scott Fitzgerald," Edmund Wilson famously describes *This Side of Paradise* as "a gesture of indefinite revolt," and this is true in the sense that the philosophical system offered as an alternative to the tradition represented by Monsignor is inconsistent and even incoherent. As Wilson points out, Fitzgerald's literary references are often uninformed, and many of Amory's intellectual conclusions have little substance. But the novel nevertheless has tremendous intellectual importance because its "gesture" is distinctly away

What Do I Read Next?

- Fitzgerald's most famous novel, *The Great Gatsby* (1925), is the story of the rise and fall of Jay Gatsby together with the boredom, seduction, and moral irresponsibility of the American aristocracy.

- Algernon Charles Swinburne's *Selected Poems* (1987), edited by L. M. Findlay, is an excellent introduction to the nineteenth-century visionary poet who refused to be categorized into his time.

- Ernest Hemingway's *A Moveable Feast* (1964) is a compelling autobiographical account of the expatriate modernist writing community living in Paris in the 1920s, and it includes stories of

Fitzgerald and his wife Zelda during their time in Europe.

- *The Time Machine* (1895), by H. G. Wells, is a science fiction novel about an inventor who claims to have traveled to the distant future to learn in what direction nineteenth-century ideas are taking humankind, and its political and social commentary influenced Fitzgerald.

- Virginia Woolf's *To the Lighthouse* (1927) is a brilliant modernist novel that, like *This Side of Paradise*, is divided into two parts in order to dramatize the political, social, and artistic break from the past that followed World War I.

---

from the European literary, political, and moral tradition. And one of the most important aspects of this revolt that is definite and substantial is its call for the modernist generation to turn away from religion.

Source: Scott Trudell, Critical Essay on *This Side of Paradise*, in *Novels for Students*, Thomson Gale, 2005.

Barry Gross

In the following essay, Gross argues that, despite critical contention to the contrary, there is intent, unity, and force in This Side of Paradise *if the novel is read as a bildungsroman.*

Considered opinion of F. Scott Fitzgerald's first novel has not changed much since 1924 when Edmund Wilson labelled it "a phantasmagoria of incident which had no dominating intention to endow it with unity and force, . . . really not *about* anything: intellectually it amounts to little more than a gesture—a gesture of indefinite revolt." Those critics who discuss the book at all verify Wilson's judgment; if the novel is at all significant, that significance lies in its stylistic place in the Fitzgerald canon or in its historic place in the Fitzgerald canon or in its historic place in the literary twenties. But *This Side of Paradise* does have unity and force, and it is about something. It is about what Fitzgerald's novels are always about: the realization

that "life is essentially a cheat and its conditions are those of defeat, and . . . the redeeming things are not 'happiness and pleasure' but the deeper satisfactions that come out of struggle." If the dominating intention is not as clear in *This Side of Paradise* as it is in *The Great Gatsby* and *Tender Is the Night,* that is because this first novel, for all of its attempted unconventionalities, is a traditional *bildungsroman.* Amory Blaine does not begin to appreciate the redeeming things or understand what he should struggle for until the end of the novel. And it takes him that long because, unlike Gatsby, he is not immediately one of the free dispossessed; he inherits a system that seems to him attractive and viable. Amory and the novel move from spiritual marriage to that system to spiritual divorce, from instinctive questioning of it to total rejection, from a casual to a deliberate and necessary search for an alternative.

At Princeton he acquires a distaste for the social system based on "the bogey 'Big Man'" and on "artificial distinctions made by the strong to bolster up their weak retainers and to keep out the almost strong." By the end of the novel, the "bogey 'Big Man'" has evolved into "the big man with the goggles" who gives Amory a lift to Princeton. The huge hedge and tall iron fence behind which Ferrenby lives are the barriers the socially strong erect for self-preservation. He represents "those who by inheritance or industry or brains or dishonesty have become the moneyed class," the class to which Amory originally belonged. For Amory, he is also a symbolic father: Ferrenby's son, a classmate of Amory's killed in the war, "had borne off the crown that [Amory] had aspired to" at Princeton. Ferrenby's invitation for lunch behind the huge hedge and iron fence is an offer to Amory of another crack at that crown, now the crown of class succession. But Amory knows this world has nothing to offer him; he tells Ferrenby he has got to get on.

He has to get on to Princeton. Although the university first attracted him because of its bright atmosphere and reputation for easy living, it is now a shrine to which Amory makes solemn pilgrimage. He wants to see if, in a world in which "all gods [are] dead, all wars fought, all faiths in man shaken," anything remains. He finds that something does:

> as an endless dream it went on; the spirit of the past brooding over a new generation, the chosen youth from the muddled, unchastened world, still fed romantically on the mistakes and half-forgotten dreams of dead statesmen and poets. Here was a new generation, shouting the old cries, learning the old creeds, through a revery of long days and nights; destined finally to go out into that dirty gray turmoil to follow love and pride.

The chosen youth cannot know that the world is muddled, unchastened, a turmoil because it has taken Amory the whole of *This Side of Paradise* to learn that this is, as Lionel Trilling terms it, "the condition, the field of tragedy" against which he must order his life.

Amory suspects that the world is a turmoil long before he knows that it is. He makes lists of all sorts of things in order "to get something definite." Fitzgerald was only half kidding when he referred to *This Side of Paradise* as "A Romance and a Reading List": there is a reading list for each stage of Amory's development, and there are lists of what interests him at twelve, of the contents of a trunk, of Eastern prep schools, of Princeton buildings and clubs. The same impulse to get something definite prompts his repeated attempts to classify himself. At thirteen he formulates "a code to live by," about as profound as any thirteen-year-old's "philosophy" is likely to be. His premature summations of himself—Amory plus Beatrice plus Minneapolis plus St. Regis plus Princeton etcetera—are tedious, ludicrous. But the impulse is more important than the act, the need to create such formulation is more significant than the formulations. He is searching for order. It can be said of Amory's lists and

> *Amory and the novel move from spiritual marriage to that system to spiritual divorce, from instinctive questioning of it to total rejection, from a casual to a deliberate and necessary search for an alternative."*

classifications what Tom Burnam says of Jimmy Gatz's schedule and resolves: they represent "the boyish effort to reduce the world to terms in the Chaucerian sense of 'boundaries,'" to impose "on the haphazard circumstances of life a purpose and a discipline."

The most significant classification is the "personality-personage" formulated by Darcy:

> Personality is a physical matter almost entirely; it lowers the people it acts on—I've seen it vanish in a long sickness. But while a personality is active, it overrides "the next thing." Now a personage, on the other hand, gathers. He is never thought of apart from what he's done. He's a bar on which a thousand things have been hung—glittering things sometimes, . . . but he uses them with a cold mentality back of them.

In itself, this is not very meaningful. But later, "personality" will evolve into the "spiritually married man" and "personage" into the "spiritually unmarried." Amory does not realize the implications of the personality-personage distinction because, at this point, he does not have to. The spiritually married-spiritually unmarried distinction, however, will be the product of a painful passage through disillusionment and of a deliberate and necessary search for meaning.

Also foreshadowed early in the novel is Amory's later conclusion that the problem of evil has to do with the problem of sex, that evil is inseparably linked with beauty because both beauty and sex have "too many associations with license and indulgence." License and indulgence become synonymous with evil, and their contraries—order, restraint, purposefulness—with good. Darcy correctly perceives that Amory is prudish about sex not because of convention but because he fears he "would run amuck." Concerning this problem of evil, Kenneth Eble maintains that Amory's "awareness is not directed toward or counteract human nature. His problem is harder. It is not life that's complicated, it's the struggle to guide and control life. That is his struggle. He is a part of progress—the spiritually married man is not.

The spiritually married man—Amory at the beginning—is wed to the system he inherits. Like personality, the system "lowers the people it acts on" because the spiritually married man is necessarily committed to the status quo and is, therefore, not a part of progress. But the spiritually unmarried man—Amory at the end—divorced from his inheritance, is, like the personage, "never thought of apart from what he's done." Having no system to preserve, he must seek one, not merely for the sake of having a system but in order "to guide and control life." In Fitzgerald's terms, that is always the hero's struggle and Amory commits himself to it.

The place of *This Side of Paradise* in the Fitzgerald canon should now be clear: it has the same "dominating intention" as *The Beautiful and Damned, The Great Gatsby, Tender Is the Night,* and *The Last Tycoon.* But it is not necessary to go outside the novel to find it worthy. *This Side of Paradise* is like the personage, "a bar on which a thousand things have been hung." Too many things—albeit "glittering things sometimes"—have been hung on the bar of Fitzgerald's first novel. But the bar is strong enough to hold them and emerges intact because Fitzgerald does use those things with a "mentality back of them." Amory's metamorphosis into the spiritually unmarried man should come as no surprise: from his first instinctive attempts to get something definite to his explicit commitment to the struggle to guide and control his life, that is where he is heading. Rather than "a gesture of indefinite revolt," *This Side of Paradise* is a mature affirmation that, although all gods are dead, all wars fought, all faiths in man shaken, man can—must—struggle to guide and control life, foredoomed though it may be.

Source: Barry Gross, "*This Side of Paradise*: The Dominating Intention," in *Studies in the Novel*, Vol. 1, No. 1, Spring 1969, pp. 51–59.

Margaret Emerson Bailey

In the following review, Bailey notes Fitzgerald's youthful vigor and individual style, and calls This Side of Paradise *"a convincing chronicle of youth by youth."*

"Just as the boiling pot gives off heat, so through youth and adolescence we give off calories of virtue." Since this, as Mr. Fitzgerald sees it, is the process of molten youth as it takes shape and hardens, his novel is less a history of its assumption of form than of its loss of radiance. Were this all, *This Side of Paradise* would contain little new. More tolerantly, certainly more humorously, the same process has been set forth by a score of English novelists. But though referred to still as "the younger group," they show by their very tolerance and humor that they have passed on, that their experiences have already become recollections. They are reviewing youth with a memory—not a sensation—of its joy and bitterness, and are looking back to its problems with a wistful patronage. Mr. Fitzgerald, in contrast, gives the impression of being still in the thick of the fight, and of having the fierceness of combat. The dust of conflict is still in his eyes and he does not even see very clearly. At times he cannot distinguish youth's friend from its foe or perceive where it has met with defeat and where conquered. The battle is on and the besetting forces loom very large. They take shape allegorically; it is their exaggeration and the very solemnity with which they are viewed that give the book value, for they make it a record at the very moment of the encounter.

Amory Blaine, the hero of this tale, starts life with a handicap. "From his mother he inherits every trait except the inexpressible few which make him worth while." An exotic she may no longer be called, for in novels her species has become indigenous to the Middle West and is constantly culled there whenever costly and poisonous beauty is needed to color the page. Unfortunately for her son, whose coming she had looked upon as a burden, she finds him a source of diversion and takes delight in the precocity developed by her companionship. Had it not been for his heritage from his father, the calories of his virtue must have been multitudinous to have held out. As it is, the worst that she does for him is to cut him off from his kind and from a normal boy's "roughing it," to make him acutely conscious of his good looks, and to give him a snobbish belief in himself as a personage reserved for special adventure. But once she has worked what havoc she may, she drops him with a swiftness amazing even in a person of her fleeting interest, and he is left to the leveling process of school and college. From both as well as from the war, he emerges with mind awakened and consequently with a lessened conceit, save where it is concerned in the *amourettes* which lead up to the tragedy, so splendidly black, of the lost Rosalind. It is in relation to these that the author sets himself the task of the social historian, presenting society in its mad reaction to war. For the hero does not need to go to the underworld in his quest for excitement. The débutante of old days, the Victorian "virginal doll," has been transformed

Treasure Island

Robert Louis Stevenson

1883

Treasure Island is considered one of the first adventure stories written specifically for adolescents without an obvious emphasis on teaching morals. This is not to say that Robert Louis Stevenson's novel about a young boy is without lessons but rather that its emphasis is a coming-of-age story filled with challenges, fears, and triumphs like any exciting and fun-filled journey of exploration. The lessons are learned through the characters' decisions and mistakes, which makes them more life-like and less didactic.

Stevenson has stated that the story was inspired by a detailed map he drew from his imagination. This map, Stevenson wrote in an essay called "Treasure Island," "was elaborately and (I thought) beautifully coloured; the shape of it took my fancy beyond expression; it contained harbours that pleased me like sonnets; and with the unconsciousness of the predestined, I ticketed my performance 'Treasure Island.'"

The more Stevenson studied this map of his creation, the more his imagination expanded. First, he could see the vegetation of the island. Then the island became peopled in his mind's eye, and their stories began to appear. "It was to be a story for boys," Stevenson wrote; and with excitement and ease, he produced the first fifteen chapters in as many days. But then the inspiration disappeared—the author claims that he was at a very low point in his life at this time. He was thirty-one and had yet to make a salary on his own. He was supported by his father, and he wanted to write something that not only

to the "baby vamp," who if she is too hard-headed to follow in morals the Queens of the Movies, has at least adopted their manners. Against her, Amory hasn't a chance. And when to disillusionment is added the loss of money and of his friends who are pushed out of the story in a way to which no vigorous characters would submit, he goes down like Brian de Bois Guilbert, "the victim of contending passions." One would think in such a moment that it would be small comfort to "know one's self," though it is with that triumphant if unconvincing protestation that the book closes.

Such a summary is undoubtedly too hard on the book, for it overstresses its failure to arouse sympathy. It also fails to take into account passages, sometimes whole chapters, of brilliant cleverness—those for example where the author takes a fling at modern literary movements or satirizes the already jaded débutante as she makes her curtsy to the world. Little, moreover, does Mr. Fitzgerald care for the conventions of form; and there is something very taking in the nonchalance with which he passes from straight narrative to letters, poems, or dramatic episodes. Quite as wilful is his style. But in all its affectations, its cleverness, its occasional beauty, even its sometimes intentioned vulgarity and ensuing timidity, it so unites with the matter as to make the book a convincing chronicle of youth by youth.

Source: Margaret Emerson Bailey, "A Chronicle of Youth by Youth," in the *Bookman*, Vol. 51, June 1920, pp. 471–72.

Sources

Broun, Heywood, "Paradise and Princeton," in *F. Scott Fitzgerald: The Critical Reception*, edited by Jackson R. Bryer, Burt Franklin & Co., 1978, p. 9, originally published in the *New York Tribune*, April 11, 1920, Sec. 7, pp. 9–11.

Fitzgerald, F. Scott, *This Side of Paradise*, edited by James L. W. West III, Cambridge University Press, 1995, originally published by Scribner's, 1920.

Wilson, Edmund, "F. Scott Fitzgerald," in *F. Scott Fitzgerald: A Collection of Critical Essays*, edited by Arthur Mizener, Prentice-Hall, 1963, pp. 80–85.

"With College Men," in *F. Scott Fitzgerald: The Critical Reception*, edited by Jackson R. Bryer, Burt Franklin & Co., 1978, p. 21, originally published in the *New York Times Book Review*, May 9, 1920, p. 240.

Further Reading

Bryer, Jackson, Ruth Prigozy, and Milton R. Stern, eds., *F. Scott Fitzgerald in the Twenty-First Century*, University of Alabama Press, 2003.
> This collection of critical essays, presented at the F. Scott Fitzgerald conference at Princeton University in 1996, offers a variety of new approaches to Fitzgerald's work.

Eble, Kenneth E., ed., *F. Scott Fitzgerald: A Collection of Criticism*, McGraw-Hill, 1973.
> Eble presents a useful collection of criticism on Fitzgerald, including the key essays from the 1960s and early 1970s.

Miller, James E., Jr., *The Fictional Technique of F. Scott Fitzgerald*, Nijhoff, 1957.
> Miller provides a sophisticated analysis of Fitzgerald's style and overall career.

Mizener, Arthur, *The Far Side of Paradise*, rev. ed., Houghton Mifflin, 1965.
> Winner of the National Book Award, this biographical and critical study of Fitzgerald is widely influential and highly respected.

would make money but would please his father. Much of his writing up to this point Stevenson referred to as a failure; he was afraid that this current story he was working on would become one too.

Stevenson took a break from his work and went on a short vacation. Upon arriving at his destination, he sat down at a desk, determined to free himself from his despair. With great discipline, he started writing again. "And in a second tide of delighted industry," Stevenson wrote, "I finished 'Treasure Island.'" The book turned out to be a huge success for Stevenson, bringing both money and fame. It was published first as a magazine serial before being produced as a book in 1883. But that is not the end of the story. When Stevenson sent his manuscript to his publisher, the map, which had inspired the pirate story, was missing. It was never found. Stevenson had to create another map, "but somehow it was never 'Treasure Island' to me," Stevenson wrote.

Author Biography

Robert Louis Stevenson was born in 1850 in Edinburgh, Scotland, the only son of a famed engineer and inventor. Stevenson's grandfather was also an engineer, known around the world for the many beautiful lighthouses he designed. The family expected the young Stevenson to follow in his grandfather's and his father's footsteps. But in his earliest years, Stevenson suffered from a lung disease and spent much time in bed. To pass the time, he made up stories. Some of the earliest literary influences, authors he tried to mimic, included Daniel Defoe (*Robinson Crusoe*, 1719), Edgar Allan Poe ("The Raven," 1845), and Nathaniel Hawthorne (*Scarlet Letter*, 1850).

When it came time to go to university, Stevenson enrolled in engineering classes but later changed his mind. He was more interested in literature. Stevenson's father did not approve of his son's writing, however, and insisted that Stevenson gain a more respected and more practical degree. So Stevenson studied law and passed the bar in 1875, but he never practiced. Instead, he began to write in earnest, publishing several short stories, essays, and travel sketches, which were only modestly successful and did not provide him with enough money to pay all his bills. So his father continued to support him well through his twenties.

Stevenson's travel sketches were the byproduct of his hopes of finding a climate that would prove more beneficial for his health. While he was

Robert Louis Stevenson

in Paris, where he found some relief in the warmer climate, he also found the woman who would later become his wife. Fanny Osbourne, an American, was older than Stevenson, was married and the mother of three children, and was apparently the inspiration of Stevenson's life and literary career. In 1879, three years after they met, Osbourne obtained a divorce, and she and Stevenson were married. He was twenty-nine; she was forty.

The couple traveled throughout Europe and the United States, still looking for a place that suited Stevenson's frail health. But it was during a visit to Scotland that Stevenson wrote *Treasure Island*, which first appeared in serialized form in a magazine between 1881 and 1882, before it was published as a book. *Treasure Island* finally made a name for Stevenson and provided him with a livable wage. The book also won the approval of Stevenson's father, who finally accepted his son's chosen vocation.

After living in Scotland for a short time, Stevenson and his wife moved to London. This move proved beneficial for Stevenson's career, as it was during this time that he made friends with the author Henry James and other literary figures. While in London, Stevenson wrote two more texts, which, together with *Treasure Island* became his most famous works. They were *The Strange*

Case of Dr. Jekyll and Mister Hyde (1886) and *Kidnapped* (1886).

Two years later, the Stevensons discovered the island of Samoa, which provided a tropical setting that suited Stevenson's health and the place in which he produced a very large collection of poems, short stories, essays, and novels before his early death. On December 3, 1894, while helping his wife fix dinner, Stevenson died of a brain hemorrhage. When his neighbors in Samoa heard the tragic news, they grabbed axes and machetes and cut a trail up the mountainside behind his house so as to honor Stevenson's final wish to be buried at the top of Mount Vaea.

Plot Summary

Part 1—The Old Buccaneer

Treasure Island is narrated by Jim Hawkins, the son of the owners of the inn, the Admiral Benbow. In the first pages, Billy Bones, a mysterious and ragged old seaman, appears at the doorstep of the inn, dragging a large sea chest. Bones decides to stay at the inn and asks Hawkins to warn him if he ever sees a one-legged man.

One day, while visiting Hawkins' father whose health has deteriorated, Dr. Livesey, local doctor and magistrate, inadvertently disregards Bones' demand for silence in the inn. Despite Bones' physical threats, Dr. Livesey calmly stands up to the old seafarer and even threatens to put him out of town if he hears of any more disturbances.

Bones dies by the end of this section; Hawkins discovers the map of buried treasure in Bones' sea chest and shares it with Livesey; and the two men, along with Squire Trelawney, begin their search for the buried treasure.

Part 2—The Sea Cook

Hawkins meets Livesey and Trelawney in Bristol, where a ship, the *Hispaniola*, has been purchased. Here Hawkins meets Long John Silver, a seaman with just one leg. Although Hawkins remembers Billy Bones' warning, Hawkins finds himself unconcerned about Silver, who puts on a show of gentlemanly manners, poise, and confidence.

Silver is hired as the sea cook for the *Hispaniola*; and once the voyage gets under way the majority of the pirate sea hands look to Silver as their leader. There is little trouble on the ship as it makes its way toward Treasure Island. However, one night, while Hawkins climbs into a huge apple barrel to retrieve a fruit, he happens to overhear Silver talking to some of the men. It is upon this conversation that the story takes a major turn. Before this point, Silver has been painted as a reliable, intelligent, and fair-minded man. But after overhearing Silver, Hawkins has a new perception of this man, who is proving to be dishonest, cunning, and possibly murderous. Hawkins discovers that Silver is planning a mutiny. Hawkins tells Dr. Livesey, Squire Trelawney, and Captain Smollot about Silver's plans. The group makes counter plans as the ship heads toward the island.

Part 3—My Shore Adventure

A depressive mood descends upon the crew once the ship is anchored in the harbor of Treasure Island. In order to ease this mood, the captain tells the crew that they can go ashore. The captain hopes this will keep them preoccupied so they do not mutiny prematurely, catching the captain and his cohorts off guard. Hawkins, aware that he is unneeded on board and overly excited about exploring the island, slips off the ship and heads toward land in a small dingy without waiting for his companions.

The first sign of trouble is the sound of a gun being shot. Upon hearing it, Hawkins, who hides in the bush, sees Silver kill one of his own men. Having witnessed the murder, Hawkins starts running. In his desperate need to put distance between himself and Silver, Hawkins runs into Ben Gunn, a sailor who has been marooned on the island for three years. He was left there by a Captain Flint, the pirate who hid the treasure on this island to begin with. Gunn had been a mate on Flint's ship, along with Billy Bones and Long John Silver. Gunn tells Hawkins about his experiences and about the treasure and a hidden boat that Gunn has made. He tries to tell Hawkins more but a volley of cannon balls is hurled at the island, and both men run for their lives.

Part 4—The Stockade

In the beginning of this section, the narration is taken over by Dr. Livesey. Livesey relates the events that were happening on his part of the island while young Hawkins was experiencing his own. As Livesey and the trusted members of the crew are about to leave the *Hispaniola*, Livesey learns that Hawkins has already left the ship. He fears for Hawkins' safety. Upon arriving on the island, Livesey finds an old stockade, a six-foot-high structure made of logs. Inside he discovers a fresh water spring. The doctor concludes that this is a good place to make the stand against the pirates.

The doctor and his men return to the *Hispaniola* and tell the captain the new plan. Then the men load supplies—food, medicine, and guns and ammunition—into several small boats and set their course for the island. Once they land on shore, they carry their crates to the stockade. After several trips, Dr. Livesey returns to the *Hispaniola* and announces that they have completed their plan, and all but a handful of men leave the ship. The small boats they are using for the last trip are overloaded, and the tide is working against them. In their hurry to prepare for a confrontation with the pirates, they have failed to realize until it is too late, that the only men left aboard are Silver's men. When they look back to the *Hispaniola*, the captain suggests that they kill Silver's men. Trelawney takes aim. He misses his intended target but wounds another. At this moment, the little boat in which Captain Smollot's men are rowing suddenly sinks. Since they are in only three feet of water, no one drowns, but some of the guns and half the supplies are lost. They have little time to reclaim anything as the pirates on the *Hispaniola* begin shooting cannon balls at them. The captain's crew barely makes it to the stockade before gunshots are fired and the battle on the ground begins. As the first battle comes to an end, Hawkins returns to the scene.

Hawkins takes over the narration and tells the men about Ben Gunn. They discuss their plans. This section ends with Long John Silver making a surprise visit to the stockade with a white flag in hand. Silver suggests that the captain turn over the treasure map. Then he suggests that the treasure be divided between the two sides. The captain scoffs at these suggestions and tells Silver to have his men come to the stockade and surrender. Silver spits into the fresh water spring in disgust. He leaves and shortly afterward, the next battle begins. In the process, several are killed and the captain is wounded.

Part 5—*My Sea Adventure*

Once again, Hawkins decides to leave his group without telling anyone. He grabs some food and a gun and heads east toward the shoreline. He finds Ben Gunn's boat, rows it out to the *Hispaniola*, and frees the anchor, thus setting it adrift. He hears drunken noises from the pirates and climbs aboard to investigate. He finds the men quarreling and quickly returns to his small boat. He is tired, so he lies down and falls asleep. When he awakens, he sees that the waves have increased in size and when he sits up, his boat almost capsizes. In order to stay afloat, he must lie low at the bottom of the boat. He then notices the *Hispaniola* about

Media Adaptations

- *Treasure Island* has been produced as a movie several times. There is Paramount Studios' 1920 version; MGM's 1934 production; Disney's 1950 presentation; and the 1972 UK project that starred Orson Wells as Long John Silver. In the 1990s, several animated versions of this story appeared on DVDs. Frank Oz and his muppets even made their version of this classic in 1996.

- *Treasure Island* was produced by Books on Tape, Inc. in 2002, read by Richard Matthews.

---

one-half mile away from him and makes up his mind to board it again.

The only man conscious onboard the *Hispaniola* is Israel Hands. Hawkins acts boldly, taking down the pirates' flag and telling Hands to call him captain. Hands is wounded, so Hawkins brings him food and drink in exchange for Hands helping Hawkins navigate the ship to a safe harbor. Once the boat is all but safe, Hands lunges for Hawkins but is thrown overboard by a sudden twist of the ship. However, before falling off the ship, Hands thrusts his knife into Hawkins' shoulder, thus nailing him to the mast. Hawkins is at first mortified, but then he realizes that it is just a superficial wound and frees himself. He then leaves the ship and runs to find the doctor and the captain. He runs to the stockade but is startled to find Long John Silver and his men there.

Part 6—*Captain Silver*

Silver stands up for Hawkins, although some of his men want to kill him. Hawkins admits everything to Silver, telling him that he was the one who overheard their plan to rebel against the captain. Silver tells Hawkins that the doctor gave the treasure map to him, and he has deserted Hawkins. Of course, Hawkins is confused. Silver's men then turn against Silver because they no longer trust him.

Coincidentally the doctor shows up to administer to the wounded pirates. He talks in private to Hawkins and reprimands him for running away.

The doctor urges Hawkins to run away with him now, but Hawkins has given his word to Silver and tells the doctor he must remain a prisoner to the pirates. Before the doctor leaves, Hawkins tells him about rescuing the *Hispaniola*.

The pirates head out to look for the buried treasure. When they finally figure out the map and follow its directions, they come upon an empty pit. Someone has already dug up the treasure. The pirates believe they have been tricked and decide to kill Silver. But the doctor and Ben Gunn, who have been hiding in the bushes, shoot at the pirates. After the pirates run for their lives, the doctor, Hawkins, Silver, and the others retreat to Ben Gunn's storage cave, where the treasure has been hidden. It appears that Silver has been working with the captain. But Hawkins has seen both sides of Silver and suspects that the old pirate chooses any side from which he will benefit.

A few days later, the *Hispaniola* is set to leave. Silver is in custody, but the captain has guaranteed him a fair trial. They leave food for the three remaining mutineers and sail for the nearest city to get fresh supplies and a new crew. When they anchor in a "Spanish American" city, Silver escapes, and most of the men are relieved. Only five men of the original crew make it back to Bristol, where they share the treasure.

Characters

Mr. Arrow

Mr. Arrow is the first mate on the *Hispaniola* but not a good one. His weakness is alcohol. He tries to befriend the pirates not so much because he likes them but because he does not know how to separate himself from them and therefore to regulate them. One day, while upon the open seas, he disappears. It is not known if he is thrown overboard or if he falls overboard in a drunken stupor.

Black Dog

Black Dog, whose distinguishing mark is two missing fingers on his left hand, is the first pirate to find Billy Bones. Black Dog fights with Bones and is injured but manages to run away. He is later seen with the blind man Pew who wants to find the treasure map. Later in the story, when Jim Hawkins first meets Long John Silver, Black Dog is sitting in the pub. When Hawkins points him out, Silver denies knowing him. This is Stevenson's first hint that Long John Silver might not be as honest as he pretends.

Billy Bones

Billy Bones appears in the beginning of this story and is the first pirate Jim Hawkins meets. Bones stays at the Hawkins' inn, the Admiral Benbow, scaring all the villagers with his sea stories and his dictatorial meanness. Bones pays Hawkins to watch for a man with one leg, someone who is obviously searching for Bones. Eventually Bones is discovered by a roving band of pirates, who give him the "black spot," a pirate sentence of death. Although the pirates do not kill him, Bones dies of some unknown cause, which the doctor assumes is related to Bones' alcoholism. After his death, young Hawkins finds a treasure map inside Bones' trunk, a map that sets up the premise of the story.

Captain Flint

Captain Flint, a notorious pirate, leaves Ben Gunn on Treasure Island. He never appears in the story but is mentioned by several pirates, who both praise and curse him. Long John Silver also names his parrot Captain Flint.

Ben Gunn

Ben Gunn is discovered on Treasure Island by Jim Hawkins. Gunn has been marooned there for three years and is a bit eccentric by the time Hawkins finds him. Despite his peculiarities, Gunn has figured out how to survive on the island and is instrumental in saving Hawkins and the rest of the crew of the *Hispaniola*. Gunn has a store of food that he shares with them and has built a crude rowboat, which Hawkins uses to save the *Hispaniola*. Despite the fact that Gunn has found the buried treasure, what he desires most when rescued is a piece of cheese. In the end, Gunn is given part of the treasure once the ship returns to England, but readers are told that Gunn spends his fortune quickly.

Israel Hands

Israel Hands is one of Long John Silver's men. During the mutiny, Hands is left on the ship. When Jim Hawkins returns to the ship and releases the anchor and climbs aboard, it is with Hands that Hawkins must deal. Hands helps Hawkins navigate the *Hispaniola* to a safe harbor. Once the ship is anchored, Hands tries to kill Hawkins but is thrown from the ship and drowns when the current abruptly changes. Before that fatal accident, Hands impales Hawkins with his dagger. Hawkins' wound, however, turns out to be superficial.

Jim Hawkins

Jim Hawkins is the young boy who narrates most of this story. He is observant of events that occur around him and of the people with whom he becomes involved. His observations at times get him into trouble but more often than not also save his life and the lives of his companions. He fortunately happens to be in the right place at the right time. The knowledge he gains through his good fortune is put to good use. Hawkins is both lucky and clever.

Hawkins' youthful curiosity leads him into the adventure of his lifetime after he gains possession of a treasure map. With a crew of less than respectable sea hands and a group of professional men at the helm, Hawkins eventually sails off to search for the buried bounty. It is through this treasure-hunt adventure that Hawkins experiences a rite of passage from adolescent to adult, as he learns to distinguish right from wrong, good from evil, and all shades in between. The story is told mostly through his eyes.

Mr. Hawkins

Mr. Hawkins is Jim's father. He is sickly and dies early in the story, leaving Jim the only man available to help his mother run the pub.

Mrs. Hawkins

Mrs. Hawkins, mother of Jim Hawkins, is present only in the first chapters of the book, in which Jim helps her run the Admiral Benbow.

Dr. Livesey

Dr. Livesey enters the story when Jim Hawkins' father is dying. He appears again at the Admiral Benbow when Billy Bones falls ill. It is to Dr. Livesey that young Hawkins gives the treasure map once he has discovered it in Bones' trunk. Dr. Livesey understands the importance of the map and helps to organize the ocean trip to find the buried treasure.

Livesey is honest and honor-bound. He is the mirror image of Long John Silver in many ways. While Silver pretends to be honest, sincere, and honor bound, Livesey really is. Livesey is also a humanitarian while Silver cares little for anyone but himself. In contrast, Livesey, even in the midst of the mutiny, treats the wounded pirates with as much care as he treats his own friends. Livesey is cool headed and intelligent and plays out the role of a father figure or older brother for young Hawkins.

Old Man Pew

Old Man Pew is a blind pirate who comes looking for Billy Bones at the Admiral Benbow. Jim Hawkins must personally deal with Old Man Pew and is frightened by the experience. Pew is strong and threatens Hawkins physically so that Hawkins does what Pew tells him. Pew also frightens Billy Bones. Bones sees him as a bad omen. After Bones dies, Old Man Pew is trampled by horses while citizens try to keep order in their village by chasing the pirates away from the town.

Old Redruth

Old Redruth, a friend of the squire's, is loyal to the professional crew on the *Hispaniola* but is the first to be killed when the pirates mutiny.

Long John Silver

Long John Silver, hired as the cook for the ship *Hispaniola*, is a chameleon, changing his "colors" depending on the situation. He is working in a pub when first introduced, a place he and his wife own. When Jim Hawkins encounters him, Silver pretends to be a legitimate businessman. In fact, Silver has gained all of his wealth from piracy and, despite the loss of a leg, has a reputation of being a successful pirate. He is an intelligent man and well aware of the psychology of the people around him. Silver uses this knowledge to manipulate the circumstances in which he finds himself, with an intense loyalty to no one but himself.

It is through Silver that the crewmembers, most of whom have histories of piracy, organize a mutiny. They plan to either kill or maroon the legitimate leaders of this expedition and claim the treasure for themselves. Silver, compared to the other pirates, is easily the most conniving. He charms everyone from the lowliest pirate to the captain of the ship. He stresses that all men must display honor and makes a grand show to prove that he is the most respectable of them all. His bright intelligence and quit wit help him turn every situation to his advantage. Given that Stevenson originally wanted the title of this book to be *The Sea Cook*, readers can be assured that Long John Silver, in many ways, was meant to be the main character.

Captain Smollet

Captain Smollet, the officer in charge of the *Hispaniola,* is hardworking and understands the power of rank, not for the power but rather for the discipline. He demonstrates his intelligence and understanding of human nature by recognizing Long John Silver's power over the pirates on his ship. He is wounded during a battle on Treasure Island, but Dr. Livesey saves him. Smollet is patriotic and often makes grand statements about his country.

Squire Trelawney

Squire Trelawney's strength is organization. He is the one who arranges the ship, the *Hispaniola* and its crew. Trelawney is loyal and hard working, but he does have a couple of faults. First, his judgment of people is in question, since he hires a bunch of ruffians to man the boat. Second, he has trouble keeping a secret. Perhaps Trelawney is the person who let it be known that the people who organized the crew of the *Hispaniola* were sailing in search of treasure.

Themes

Honor

There is much made of the concept of honor in Robert Louis Stevenson's novel *Treasure Island*. Whether it is the honor of gentlemen or the honor of thieves and pirates, this concept is interwoven throughout the story. Even though the pirates in this story steal other people's fortunes, killing many sailors and villagers in the process, they have a code of conduct and are expected to obey that code or lose honor among their peers. For example, when Long John Silver protects young Hawkins, Silver's mates grow suspicious of him. They believe Silver might be in cahoots with Dr. Livesey or Captain Smollet. If this is true, then Silver is a traitor and has committed an act that is contrary to the pirates' code. Likewise, there is a bond of honor between Hawkins and Silver. Hawkins gives his word to the old pirate that he will not run away once Silver holds Hawkins hostage. Silver later praises Hawkins for keeping his word. Dr. Livesey is also an honorable man. He is particularly honorable in reference to his vocation. He cares for the wounds of the pirates despite the fact that the pirates have tried to kill him.

Adventure

This story was written for one of Stevenson's stepsons. So its targeted audience is young. Stevenson wanted to give the young boy something exciting to read; thus this tale filled with high adventure and thrilling challenges in each chapter was born. Throughout the story, the young narrator bears the threats of seafarers like Billy Bones and Long John Silver. At other times he is sneaking around Billy Bones' bedroom to retrieve the treasure map or going against the orders of the ship's captain and devising daring plans of his own. Hawkins has led a simple life before this story begins. But suddenly he finds himself sailing across an ocean in search of treasure and having to defend himself. He faces mutiny, several gun battles, uncouth pirates who try to kill him, and the constant threat of being marooned on an island—all the right ingredients for keeping young readers reading to find out what happens next.

Coming of Age

As the story begins, young Hawkins lives in a small village and works each day in his parents' inn. He is devoted to his parents and at first afraid of the pirate Billy Bones. Hawkins trembles when Bones touches him. Hawkins is also somewhat naïve, trusting other people's interpretations rather than trusting his own. For example, when Hawkins recognizes a pirate in Long John Silver's inn, he believes Silver when he says he has no idea who the man is.

Hawkins' gullibility slowly fades as the adventure progresses and his experiences widen. For instance, when Hawkins climbs into the apple barrel and overhears Silver planning a mutiny, he begins to understand that there is real evil in the world. As the story continues, there are more rites of passage as Hawkins passes through adolescence to adulthood. He sneaks off the ship once it is anchored and takes off on a journey all by himself. He fights in a battle against the pirates and sees many men die. He conjures up a plan to rescue the ship from the pirates. At this point he feels the full strength of his power. He tells the only conscious pirate onboard that he, Hawkins, should be referred to as the captain of the ship. It is as if Hawkins is stating he is a man. He orders the pirate to help him steer the ship through dangerous currents and anchor the boat in a safe harbor. At the end of this scene, Hawkins receives his first wound. It is a superficial cut, but with it Hawkins faces his own mortality.

Conflict

The themes of man against man, man against nature, and man against himself help to structure this novel. For example, Hawkins must overcome his fear of the pirates, beginning with Billy Bones and later with Long John Silver. Hawkins must also face nature, especially when he pulls the anchor on the *Hispaniola* and is first thrust about in the ocean waves in the small boat of Ben Gunn's and then later in the great ship itself as he tries to navigate the strong currents in the island's narrow harbors. Moreover, Hawkins faces conflict when he must make very difficult choices, such as when he decides to desert his crew. Through conflict and its consequences Hawkins matures. Furthermore, conflict

Topics For Further Study

- Investigate modern forms of piracy. What do they have in common with the piracy of the eighteenth and nineteenth centuries? How do they differ? Where does piracy occur other than at sea? Is it committed through the Internet? In the fashion trade? In the stock market?

- Stevenson wrote much poetry. Read some of his more famous works, such as *A Child's Garden of Verses* (1885). Compare his work to that of modern-day children's poet Shel Silverstein. How do their works differ? What is the tone of their writing? How is the subject matter the same?

- Read *Treasure Island* and Louis Sachar's *Holes* (2000), a modern adventure and coming-of-age story. Then write a short story about the main characters, Jim Hawkins and Stanley Yelnats, as if they were friends who were sharing a common adventure. Set the story in any time you choose. Demonstrate through your story how the two young boys are alike and how they differ. Make sure you understand each character's strengths and weaknesses.

- Write a travel piece on Samoa. Include descriptions of the island, the history of its people, and interesting aspects of the culture. Include as much information as you can find on what Stevenson experienced there. Assume your readers want to visit the island because they are fans of Stevenson's. Include a description of Stevenson's house and the reaction of the native people to his being there.

- Stevenson's grandfather was a famous designer of lighthouses. Find out where his lighthouses are located and provide pictures of them and their history.

---

draws in readers, as they attempt to second-guess the outcome of conflicts and read on to discover them.

Style

Serialized Novel

Stevenson's novel *Treasure Island* was first published in a serialized form. This means that it was published chapter by chapter in separate small units. Serialization imposed its own form on plot design, dictating chapters that practically stand on their own with inconclusive endings. In other words, each chapter is a mini-adventure but designed to leave the reader wondering what will happen next. In Stevenson's book, the stories are collected in parts, and within each part are separate sections. This arrangement intensifies the tension. The first part of the book, for example, is divided into six sections. At the end of the first section, it is hinted that Dr. Livesey and Billy Bones will meet again, and readers are left to wonder how the next confrontation between them will take place. The second section is called "Black Dog Appears and Disappears," which sums up the action. But again, the reader senses at the end of this section that Black Dog will reappear, and when he does, something catastrophic will probably occur. By the end of the first part of the book, the reader has been introduced to most of the major characters. Readers are primed, much like Hawkins himself, and ready for the next part of the journey. The serialized form helps readers experience the excitement in sequence as Hawkins experiences it.

Point of View

The majority of this story is told by young Hawkins, who tells readers in the first few sentences that he has been asked by Dr. Livesey, the squire, and the rest of the professional crew of the *Hispaniola* to write this story with all its details. Readers watch the boy's growth as he develops from a naïve teenager to an experienced man. It is clear what Hawkins is thinking, whether he is making bold decisions or stupid mistakes. Stevenson only changes

Compare & Contrast

- **1800s:** Captain Kidd, a privateer, hired by the British to protect their ships, is accused of piracy and is hanged. He is said to have captured a ship with a British captain and a boatload of jewels. No treasure is ever uncovered.

  1900s: The International Maritime Bureau praises Indian government officials and several ships' crews for helping to recover a hijacked ship (an act of piracy) loaded with aluminum ingot.

  2000s: The term *piracy* is often used when software, music, or movies are copied illegally.

- **1800s:** Rumor has it that $300 million worth of treasure, stolen from mines in Lima, Peru, is buried on the island of Cocos off the Pacific coast of Costa Rica. August Gissler buys half of the island and spends nineteen years searching for the missing goods but never finds any of it.

  1900s: In 1988, the treasure of the *S.S. Central America*, a U.S. mail ship that sank in 1857, is recovered. Its huge shipment of freshly minted gold coins and gold bars, approximately one-third of the accumulated wealth of the gold rush years, is found intact.

  2000s: Civil War era *S.S. Republic* a paddle-wheel steam ship that sunk off the coast of Georgia in 1865 with a cargo of approximately $180 million of gold coins is located. Plans are underway to salvage the sunken treasure.

- **1800s:** Doctors gain a better understanding of tuberculosis and begin to recommend the importance of fresh air and wholesome climates as treatment. Robert Koch discovers the microorganism that causes this disease.

  1900s: Scientists determine that tuberculosis is not hereditary, and the disease can now be detected in its earliest stages through x-rays. By mid-century, antibiotics to combat the disease are in use.

  2000s: Two million people worldwide still die of tuberculosis each year.

---

point of view when Dr. Livesey recounts events that young Hawkins does not participate in. Stevenson uses the doctor, for instance, to tell about what happens on the ship when Hawkins is on shore. This shift gives readers a little advantage because they know more than Hawkins, but this gap is quickly closed. Once the doctor and Hawkins are reunited, Hawkins continues the narration of the story.

Historical Context

Piracy

Piracy, which can be loosely defined as lawlessness and usually at sea, has a long history, dating as far back as the Phoenicians (1200 to 800 B.C.) Piracy occurred on almost every body of water from the China Sea to the Mediterranean and eventually along New World's Atlantic shores and in the Caribbean. Pirates were both feared and romanticized as heroes. They thrived on the booty (or stolen wealth) they stole from merchant ships and shoreline villages. Their practice lasted well into the nineteenth century when British and U.S. naval forces eventually overwhelmed them. Nonetheless, some piracy continued throughout the twentieth century and into the early 2000s. Beyond crimes committed on the high sea, the term has been applied to many different types of theft, including the illegal downloading of material from the Internet.

One famous pirate is Blackbeard, whose real name was Edward Teach, a British man who scoured the Caribbean and the Atlantic coast of the United States during the eighteenth century. His outpost was on the North Carolina shoreline, where he was eventually hunted down and shot to death in 1718.

Although most stories and movies about pirates feature men, some pirates were female. One of the most notorious female pirates was Anne Bonny, the daughter of a well-to-do lawyer who amassed a fortune in North Carolina. Bonny was disowned by her father when she married a pirate. Bonny grew tired of her husband and eventually slipped away with a more notorious man nicknamed Calico Jack. In 1720, Bonny was caught and imprisoned and after being sentenced to hang, pleaded for her life based on the fact that she was pregnant. She disappeared before her hanging date, and some people believe that her father forgave her and paid handsomely for her release.

Living in Victorian London

Stevenson wrote *Treasure Island* while living in London. Queen Victoria (1819–1901), for which the age is named, deeply affected the people and culture of this world city with her sense of duty, her belief in moral righteousness, and her patriotism—traits that are mirrored in some of Stevenson's characters. Because Victorian England was involved in the internal affairs of many other countries with its vast empire and the largest navy in the world, the population of London was made up of people from all over the world, and, in the 1880s, London had one of the largest international shipping ports in the world, receiving million of tons of goods each year.

The Houses of Parliament were built between 1840 and 1860, and Big Ben first rang in 1859. Compulsory universal education became law with the passage of the Education Act in 1870 (a secondary school education act passed in 1902). The first underground railway system in London began operation in 1863. However, illness and poverty were rampant. A significant proportion of the population died of tuberculosis each year. (Many people believe that this was the lung disease that Stevenson suffered from.) Child labor was prevalent—a condition that inspired Charles Dickens to write his novel *Oliver Twist* (1837).

Critical Overview

The publication of *Treasure Island* marked the beginning of Stevenson's reputation as a writer worth reading. By the end of the nineteenth century, Stevenson enjoyed what William B. Jones Jr. refers to in the preface to *Robert Louis Stevenson Reconsidered* as the "heights of near idolatry." However,

the public fervor and appreciation of Stevenson's life's work would both rise and fall. His contemporaries and fellow British authors, such as Virginia Woolf, often belittled his work, accusing Stevenson of not challenging himself with serious topics. Despite this, Jones writes, "Stevenson actually never lost his popularity with readers, as the countless editions and numerous film versions of *Treasure Island* and *Dr. Jekyll and Mr. Hyde* attest."

Despite many critical statements about the lack of depth of Stevenson's material, Ian Bell, writing in the preface to his book *Dreams of Exile: Robert Louis Stevenson*, states that nonetheless, Stevenson was able to connect with "public taste" at a "deep level" and marvels at the continued popularity of Stevenson's work. "What was it," Bell asks, "he [Stevenson] did in his 'children's stories,' his 'adventure tales,' his 'romances,' that others failed—fail—to do?" Bell continues, "We can admit that there have been better writers than Stevenson, writers more subtle and ambitious, more tenacious, certainly more profound. Then it is necessary to remind ourselves that many of the names offered have long since faded from the public's memory. Whatever Stevenson had they lacked. The durability and ubiquity of his tales suggest a man touching something basic." As if to bolster Bell's commentary, in a review of a recent edition of Stevenson's novel, Laura Moore, writing in *Urbana*, concludes that *Treasure Island* "is perhaps the best adventure story ever written."

Criticism

Joyce Hart

Hart has degrees in English and creative writing and is the author of several books. In this essay, Hart studies the concept of money, how it applies to the story, and how it affects the characters.

When Robert Louis Stevenson wrote *Treasure Island*, he was still financially dependent on his father. So the pressure of writing a good story, one that had public appeal, was not the only concern on his mind as he progressed through this romantic tale of high adventure. Stevenson was out to prove that he could write well that he could support himself through his own publications. He was thirty-one years old, married, and the stepfather of two children. It was time that he earned his title as head of household. Therefore, whether it was a conscious or subconscious act, it is no wonder that the

Lon Chaney as Pew in the 1921 film rendition of Treasure Island

subject of money is woven through this work. This might be a story of adventure and a tale of a young boy coming of age, but neither of those two elements pushes the story forward. If readers looked closely, they will come to see that the real power that drives this novel is not adventure but money.

No more than five lines into the story, young Jim Hawkins makes reference to money. He has been asked by Squire Trelawney and Dr. Livesey to write from memory the things that occurred on their treasure-hunt adventure. Hawkins is to give all the particular details of their trip except for the "bearings of the island," because "there is still treasure not yet lifted." With this comment, Stevenson sets up his readers to focus on the money. Readers immediately become alert to the idea that there is still treasure to be found. Like the pirates who have buried their loot on some deserted island, Stevenson has buried the idea of money in his readers' minds. And like the characters themselves who push their way across the ocean, readers plod their way through the story, hoping they too discover in the pages of this story some clue regarding the island's location. If they can uncover that secret, maybe they too can set out on their own adventure and claim the remaining treasure. Having set this tone, Stevenson next introduces his characters, each with his own claims and desires for money.

The first to arrive on the scene is the pirate Billy Bones. One of the interesting and mysterious features of this old seaman is the large chest he drags behind him. Since the title of this novel is *Treasure Island* and since, according to old myths, it is said that treasures are often buried in old chests, readers, as well as the characters in this story cannot help but wonder what Bones is hiding in that chest. Bones throws a few coins around, promising to pay Hawkins to keep a lookout for a one-legged man and prepaying Hawkins' father for his keep. Readers as well as the affected characters wonder where those coins come from and if there are more to be found at their source. But Bones' payments soon become a point of contention when he often forgets to give young Hawkins his wages. Bones also forgets, or refuses, to pay Hawkins' father for his extended keep. And these omissions come into play later, after Bones has died. That is when young Hawkins and his mother rationalize their rifling through Bones' mysterious chest in search of what they consider is rightfully owed to them. They find what they want or rather what they have justified is theirs. And they discover even more. Hawkins comes upon the map that will take the story into its further development— the search for more money. It is interesting to note, before moving on with the rest of the story, that Hawkins' relationships with Bones and with their fellow villagers, as far as Stevenson portrays it, are all based on money. There is little mention of any emotional involvement either when Bones dies or when Hawkins father dies. The emphasis of the story is on the survival of those left behind, and that survival is based on money. Debts must be paid. The Admiral Benbow Inn must reopen as soon as possible so the flow of money is not interrupted.

The story progresses with Dr. Livesey comprehending the significance of the map that Hawkins shows him. When he concludes that it is a treasure map, plans are immediately made to find the island. Here a medical doctor, upon whom a whole countryside depends, leaves his patients, as does young Hawkins leave his widowed mother, all in the name of gold. It is also in the name of money that the doctor warns his comrades they must be silent. No one must know that the true motivation of their sea journey (like the motivation for writing this story) is money. However, Stevenson knows that the thought of money inspires every man, so he cannot keep it a secret. Money is the driving force; therefore, every character in this story must be energized by it. Thus he must have

> It is the thought of riches in the crew's minds, more than the wind that fills the ship's sails, that drives the *Hispaniola* across the ocean."

a character who cannot keep a secret. That character is Squire Trelawney, who spreads the word so far that every man involved in the trip, even before the *Hispaniola* leaves the dock, knows that the purpose behind the journey is the search for gold. It is the thought of riches in the crew's minds, more than the wind that fills the ship's sails, that drives the *Hispaniola* across the ocean.

In the midst of the trip, Stevenson does a curious thing. He has Long John Silver, the most respected of pirates, hold a discussion with his men on economics. As Hawkins sits hidden in the depths of an apple barrel, the young boy listens as Silver discusses not only the act of mutiny with the other pirates but also the best ways to make one's money work for oneself. It is not wise to take money one finds (or steals) and squander it on rum or on women, but rather, Silver tells the men, one should invest it. That is just what Silver has done, he explains. He has bought the Spyglass Inn, which he runs (when he is not off on an ocean voyage) with his woman. What Silver has not invested in real estate and small business, he has stashed in several banks. "I laid by nine hundred safe, from England, and two thousand after Flint. That ain't bad for a man before the mast—all safe in the bank." Then he adds: "It's saving does it, you may lay to that." He continues his lecture by warning the men that most pirates throw their money away and then end up begging for food. His men, misunderstanding Silver's lessons, state that money then "ain't such use, after all." But Silver is already one step ahead of his men, as usual. "'T ain't much use for fools," he tells them. Then Silver begins a long monologue on what makes the typical "gentlemen of fortune," pirates who win big but lose it completely. "But that's not the course I lay. I puts it all away, some here, some there, and none too much anywheres, by reason of suspicion." He is not only, Silver assures them, a gentleman of fortune. He is also a "gentleman in earnest." So in the midst of mutiny and adventure, Stevenson sneaks

What Do I Read Next?

- Stevenson's 1886 novel, *The Strange Case of Dr. Jekyll and Mr. Hyde* studies conflicting emotions associated with what society considers good and evil. Stevenson's other 1886 novel, *Kidnapped*, follows the ordeals of protagonist David Balfour who is left with no money to live on after the death of his father. Like *Treasure Island*, *Kidnapped* is a coming-of-age novel.

- Louis Sachar's *Holes* (2000) is also a coming-of-age novel about a young boy who claims he has been cursed. He always seems to be in the wrong place at the wrong time and ends up in a juvenile detention hall somewhere in the middle of a desert. His task is to dig holes each day of his sentence. His journey, however, is to find out why he is digging these holes, and his discovery frees him from his curse.

- Daniel Defoe's *Robinson Crusoe* (1719) inspired Stevenson (especially the marooned Ben Gunn). Defoe's story centers on the life of Crusoe as he is marooned on an island off the coast of South America after suffering conflicts with pirates.

- *The Swiss Family Robinson* (1812), by Johann David Wyss, tells the story of a Swiss family that is shipwrecked on a deserted island on their way to Australia. The family learns to live by their wits, far from the civilized world that they know.

in a lesson on how to find money and how to keep it and invest it so it will grow. As proof that this lesson has been learned, at least in the mind of one of the pirates, Stevenson has a young pirate tell Silver, "Well, I tell you now . . . I didn't half a quarter like the job till I had this talk with you, John; but there's my hand on it now." This youngster has been set straight. One has only to work hard and think of riches to alleviate the pain of the hard labor, and all is set well with the world.

But there is one foolish fellow in this adventure, and that is Ben Gunn. Gunn has been on Treasure Island for three years with more gold than he ever imagined. And yet the one thing he craves even more than money is some English food. Only on Treasure Island is money not worth anything. Gunn could not eat the gold, nor would the treasure help him sail off the island. The true worth of money is as currency, the passing of the gold from one hand to another in exchange for some material that either satisfies one's hunger and thirst or promotes an easier style of living. The cave filled with gold provides none of these for Gunn. His survival depends solely on his own hands and his wit. This man, although his loneliness has made him a bit eccentric, is the only character in the story who is truly independent. For three years, he figures out a way to stay alive without money—the same thing that drives all the other characters nearly crazy. The other men in the story are willing to leave their families, their homes, their patients, their colleagues and risk their lives for the buried treasure. They are willing to maim and kill for it—but not Gunn. For this difference, Stevenson makes Gunn look like a fool.

As the novel comes to a close, Stevenson paints the portrait of Gunn in ridiculous colors. First Gunn helps Silver escape from the *Hispaniola*, then he allows Silver to take one of the sacks of gold. Thus Silver, the old economics professor, once again finishes in the black—in profit. Then Stevenson writes about how Captain Smollet, because of the found treasure, is able to retire. Another man uses his money to further his education and invest in a ship and then lives happily ever after with a wife and family. But not poor Ben Gunn. The money he is given ("a thousand pounds"), readers find out, Gunn, foolish man that he is, "spent or lost in three weeks." Gunn is reduced to a beggar. Although Stevenson does not dwell on it or praise it, he does write that once again Gunn manages to do fairly well for himself without money. He is given a place to live and becomes "a great favourite, though something of a butt" with the local country people.

In the very last paragraph of the book, young Hawkins reminds the reader that although they brought much treasure back with them, there still lay, somewhere on that Treasure Island, bars of silver, thus enticing the dreams, once again, of all those who believe money will solve their problems and make their lives better. And then, with the final words of the story, Hawkins imagines Captain Flint singing out: "Pieces of eight! pieces of eight!" Or in other words: Money, money, money!

Source: Joyce Hart, Critical Essay on *Treasure Island*, in *Novels for Students*, Thomson Gale, 2005.

Catherine Dybiec Holm

Holm is a freelance writer as well as a genre novel and short story author. In this essay, Holm discusses tools of the writing craft that Stevenson uses to make this story engaging and suspenseful.

Stevenson's *Treasure Island* has the characteristics of a successful suspense novel and an entertaining story. There is a lot in this book that serves as a good example of the craft of fine storytelling. Stevenson's adept use of the tools of good storytelling make this story a good read for adults as well as younger audiences.

Immediately apparent in *Treasure Island* is Stevenson's economical use of language. The economy, however, does not sacrifice description, observation, or suspense. Sentences are generally short and peppered with sensory description and keen observations about the human psyche and the characters' motivations. Close to the beginning of the book, Stevenson's protagonist describes the mysterious, somewhat frightening pirate who has become a fixture at Jim's family inn.

> He was a very silent man by custom. All day he hung round the cove, or upon the cliffs, with a brass telescope; all evening he sat in a corner of the parlor next to the fire, and drank rum and water very strong. Mostly he would not speak when spoken to; only look up sudden and fierce, and blow through his nose like a foghorn; and we . . . learned to let him be.

In a few short sentences, the reader has learned quite a bit about Billy Bones, including that everyone else is at least slightly leery of the drunken pirate. Blowing a nose "like a foghorn" is a wonderful sensory detail that the reader can easily imagine and will not soon forget. Stevenson's prose is richly loaded with detail—the warmth of a fire, strong rum and water, a brass telescope, cliffs. None of it bogs the reader down, nor interferes with the tight and rapid pace of the story because the details are worked so economically into the narrative.

> "
>
> Deft (and not overdone) foreshadowing prepares the observant reader for complications and gives the added mystery of a superstitious hunch."

Throughout the book, there are countless examples of description that do double or triple duty. These descriptions also move the story forward and emphasize a particular clue for the reader, which prepares him for future story twists and turns. Jim describes his dreams of the "seafaring man with one leg," and the reader hears the surf roaring, feels the house shaking, and sees the one-legged man leaping over hedges to pursue the protagonist. The reader hears the drunken pirate singing "yo-ho-ho, and a bottle of rum" and feels the unease of the boy and the inn patrons. The doctor on the *Hispaniola* discovers Jim missing and captures the moment with a number of sensory details that also hint at danger on Treasure Island and prepare the reader for foreboding.

> We ran on deck. The pitch was bubbling in the seams; the nasty stench of the place turned me sick; if ever a man smelled fever and dysentery, it was in that abominable anchorage.

Not only does this give the reader a clear moment of description and foreboding, it also allows the doctor to share knowledge of possible risk for disease—knowledge that another character would not have.

Stevenson uses foreshadowing throughout Treasure Island as hints to readers to look for certain key characters or situations. Flint's fear of a "seafaring man with one leg" is emphasized by his effort to bribe the boy to watch for such a person. Long John Silver does become quite important in the story later on, and the reader has been prepared. In another example of foreshadowing, Captain Smollett seems to have a superstitious reservation about the voyage for treasure ("all I say is we're not home again, and I don't like this cruise") even though he has taken a "downright fancy" to the ship. Of course, the reader knows that something is going to happen and that it will probably involve struggle or danger otherwise there would not be much of a story. Deft (and not overdone) foreshadowing prepares the observant reader for complications and gives the added mystery of a superstitious hunch. More foreshadowing is used when the characters on the ship first view Treasure Island. Jim says

> Perhaps it was this—perhaps it was the look of the island, with its gray, melancholy woods, and wild stone spires, and the surf that we could both see and hear foaming and thundering on the steep beach—at least, although the sun shone bring and hot, and the shore birds were fishing and crying all around us . . . my heart sank . . . into my boots; and from that first look onward, I hated the very thought of Treasure Island.

In a paragraph, the reader feels the danger on Treasure Island and again is given rich sensory detail to experience the first view of the island through the eyes of Jim.

Another method of sustaining suspense in an adventure story is to end a chapter at a crucial moment, which is generally known as a cliffhanger. Stevenson uses a number of these in *Treasure Island*. The point of such endings is to make the reader want to read further, at any cost. When Jim climbs into the ship's apple barrel and inadvertently hears Long John Silver's first dozen words, he understands "that the lives of all the honest men aboard depended upon me alone." Suddenly the stakes have been raised tremendously. Jim is hiding, is in possible danger of discovery, and most of all, is just becoming aware of a huge personal responsibility for the "honest men" on the ship.

There are many cliffhangers in *Treasure Island* and they all incorporate good storytelling techniques. At the end of Chapter 32, Silver (with Jim in tow as prisoner) and his band of pirates finally locate the site of the treasure, only to discover that the cache is already missing and all that is left is a hole that has been empty for some time. Up until that point, the reader had no clue about the outcome; no foreshadowing had been provided about the location of the treasure. But that is almost secondary; the reader assumes that the treasure will eventually be found. What is more important is that the missing treasure will create an explosive situation among the band of pirates. The reader has been prepared for this possibility through the protagonist's keen observations of Long John Silver's mercurial and untrustworthy nature. Stevenson does not let the reader down. The face-off between the men gets going right away in the next chapter.

Not every chapter in *Treasure Island* ends with a cliffhanger, but the ending of chapters can also serve as a powerful place to emphasize a particular character nuance, or important story information. Such is the case when Jim reboards the *Hispaniola* and takes command. At the end of this chapter, Jim notices the "odd smile" on Hands's face, a "haggard, old man's smile; but there was, besides that, a grain of derision, a shadow of treachery in his expression as he craftily watched, and watched, and watched me at my work." Again, the reader is being prepared for possible danger from Hands, and the point is given particular emphasis because the author places it at the end of a chapter.

Stevenson also times the revelation of information to the reader, and to the characters, to help create suspense in *Treasure Island*. This is similar to foreshadowing, but foreshadowing may rely more on implied symbolism or the ambiguous, seemingly illogical statement of a character (a gray island, or the unease of a superstitious captain). The timing of how information is revealed in storytelling is an important consideration in a suspense story. A good example of this in *Treasure Island* takes place when Hands and Jim are alone on the ship, and Hands asks Jim to go fetch a bottle of wine. There is something strange about the way Hands words his request that clues the reader into feeling that something is not quite right.

> I'll take it kind if you'd step down into that there cabin and get me a—well, a—shiver my timbers! I can't hit the name on't; well, you get me a bottle of wine, Jim—this here brandy's too strong for my head.

An astute reader might immediately notice that something seems slightly unnatural about Hands's manner of speaking. Suddenly, he seems to be hesitating too much, or trying a little too hard. This is confirmed in the next paragraph when Jim has the same suspicions. However, the reader figured this out first and is then free to enjoy watching Jim come to the same realization. It is a well-timed revelation because the reader is prepared for what's coming.

Although *Treasure Island* is a suspenseful adventure story, it contains wonderful observations about various aspects of the human psyche. These are presented economically and enhance the story rather than bogging it down. Often, these observations give the reader insight into the protagonist. A reader might, for example, be impressed with Jim's ability to notice that Black Dog tries to sound "bold and big." Jim has a number of observations about the lack of help he and his mother get when they seek assistance in defending their inn. "Cowardice is infectious," remarks Jim, noting that none of the neighbors would return to the inn and would only promise ready horses or loaded pistols. This is realistic, which adds to the believability of the story, but it also advances the plot because it raises the stakes for the main characters. If neighbors had gladly come to defend the inn, a real opportunity for excitement and danger would have been lost, and Jim may never have ended up on the voyage to Treasure Island.

Jim gets more chances to comment on human nature when he describes the band of pirates that return to ransack the inn. They have "half an eye to their own danger all the time, while the rest stood irresolute on the road." It is a good observation by the protagonist, and it also sets the reader's expectation about the pirates' actions later in the story.

By the time the pirates discover that the treasure is missing, Jim already has a good understanding of Silver's unethical, changeable character. Still, this does not diminish the power of Jim's observation of Silver at that moment. Stevenson also uses the moment as an opportunity to slip in a little dialogue: "His looks were now quite friendly; and I was so revolted at these constant changes that I could not forbear whispering, 'So you've changed sides again.'"

There are other techniques that Stevenson uses to make this story enjoyable, suspenseful, and tightly plotted. The author makes extensive use of lively dialogue, which brings the reader close to the characters and gives the reader the experience of "hearing" pirates and other characters. Stevenson also disposes of characters when they are no longer needed. Billy Bones is killed because he has served his purpose—he has brought his trunk and treasure map to the inn where it will fall into Jim's hands. Pew is killed off after Jim has heard enough to learn what type of danger he may be heading into. Long John Silver lives through the entire book because he is a critical character and is crucial to the plot until the treasure is located. Stevenson uses a number of methods, including rich description, foreshadowing and timing, tight plotting, and economical prose to make *Treasure Island* an enjoyable adventure story for all ages.

Source: Catherine Dybiec Holm, Critical Essay on *Treasure Island*, in *Novels for Students*, Thomson Gale, 2005.

Margot Livesey

In the following essay, the author discusses the influence Stevenson's personal life had on his novels.

My principal qualification for writing about Robert Louis Stevenson is affection. He is the only author of whom I can say that I have been reading him all my life. *Kidnapped* was the first book I read

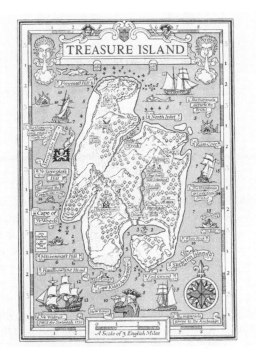

Map of Treasure Island

that had chapters, and I can still recall the maroon binding and the weight of the book in my hand. At that time I lived with my parents in the valley of Glenalmond, at the edge of the Scottish Highlands. Perhaps Stevenson knew of that place, for Lord Glenalmond plays a role in his last work, *Weir of Hermiston*. I had only to look out the windows of our house to see the stark hills, the heather, and the bracken, the landscape so bare of hiding places, over which David Balfour and Alan Breck made their way. And in those years of genderless reading it never occurred to me that I could not go with them.

Besides being the first full-length book I read, *Kidnapped* was the first book whose author's name I knew. Indeed, I hadn't previously known there was such a thing as an author. Books had fallen from the bookshelves like leaves from the trees. I did not question their origins; they were absolute in themselves. But in the case of the maroon book the music of Stevenson's name impressed me. I also owned a copy of *A Child's Garden of Verses*. "My Shadow," with its mixture of observation and mystery, was one of my favorite poems.

Such early recognition might seem like a good thing for an author's reputation, but it is in fact part of the long process by which Stevenson's work has been devalued. That I and so many others came to his work so young has made us consider him a

> I would argue that in his best work . . . Stevenson, perhaps in spite of himself, failed to emasculate his art."

children's author from whom we have little to learn as adults. This opinion is one that his contemporaries would not have shared, either in his particular case or as a general rule. Victorian adults felt free to embrace so-called children's books without apology. Stevenson's father often reread *The Parent's Assistant,* a volume of children's stories, and Virginia Woolf records being taken to *Peter Pan* on her twenty-third birthday with no signs that this was a childish treat.

Like the shadow in his poem, Stevenson's reputation has waxed and waned at an alarming rate. The blaze of hagiography in which he died seems to have incited critics to special fury. F. R. Leavis, in *The Great Tradition*, dismissed Stevenson as a romantic writer guilty of fine writing, and the critical community in general has designated him a minor author not worthy of the serious admiration that we accord his friend Henry James. People comment with amazement that Borges and Nabokov liked his work. This year marks the centenary of Stevenson's death, and I am not alone in believing that it is time to reconsider his reputation.

Two obvious factors in Stevenson's fall from grace are quantity and fashion. The list of his publications is much longer than most people realize, but the few works by which we remember him do not constitute a recognizable oeuvre. And literary taste has swung in a direction that Stevenson disliked and did his best to avoid—namely, pessimism. While admiring the early Hardy, for instance, he hated *Tess of the D'Urbervilles,* and he took James to task for *The Portrait of a Lady.* John Galsworthy commented memorably on this when he said that the superiority of Stevenson over Hardy was that Stevenson was all life, while Hardy was all death.

There are, of course, more-crucial reasons why Stevenson's shadow has dwindled. He often falls short of our expectations of a serious novelist; his plots tend to be too simple in psychological terms and too fantastic in terms of events. The former problem stemmed partly from his theory of fiction;

the latter he knew to be a fault and blamed on the tales of his childhood. Typically he worked on several projects at once, a sign of his natural prolixity but also of the difficulty he had in reaching conclusions. History, which gave him so many of his plots, was not so generous with endings, and in trying to invent them, Stevenson often either overreached the bounds of credibility, as in *The Master of Ballantrae,* or fell into flatness, as in *Kidnapped.*

The most complete account we have of his theory of fiction is contained in "A Humble Remonstrance," the essay he wrote in reply to James's "The Art of Fiction." Here we see him rebutting James's view that art should compete with life:

Man's one method, whether he reasons or creates, is to half-shut his eyes against the dazzle and confusion of reality. . . . Life is monstrous, infinite, illogical, abrupt and poignant; a work of art, in comparison, is neat, finite, self-contained, rational, flowing, and emasculate. . . . The novel, which is a work of art, exists, not by its resemblances to life, which are forced and material . . . but by its immeasurable difference from life, which is designed and significant.

In fact many of his critics have brought just this charge against Stevenson: that in the pursuit of significance he departed too far from life.

I would argue that in his best work—most notably *Kidnapped*, *The Strange Case of Dr. Jekyll and Mr. Hyde,* and *Weir of Hermiston*—Stevenson, perhaps in spite of himself, failed to emasculate his art. He opens his eyes, and ours, to the confusion of reality, and what he shows us is something that the modern reader is vitally concerned with: the inescapable duality of our existence.

Shortly before his death Stevenson wrote,

I cannot get used to this world, to procreation, to heredity, to sight, to hearing; the commonest things are a burthen. The prim obliterated police face of life, and the broad, bawdy, and orgiastic—or maenadic—foundations, form a spectacle to which no habit reconciles me.

He dramatized this spectacle with lyrical specificity and, as his work matured, increasing subtlety. And no one has ever described better what I saw from the window of my first bedroom.

How Stevenson grew to be preoccupied with duality can be seen in even a brief examination of his life. He was born on November 13, 1850, in Edinburgh. His father, Thomas, came from a line of lighthouse engineers. His mother, Margaret, was the youngest of the thirteen children of the Reverend Lewis Balfour. Louis, as the boy was called, had a formidable Scottish nanny, Cummy, who he later claimed was a major influence. By the time he was seven, the family had moved to 17 Heriot Row in the New Town of Edinburgh, a highly respectable address from which Stevenson later ventured forth to explore the more salacious neighborhoods of the city.

He began writing at an early age, dictating "A History of Moses" to his mother when he was six. Unlike me, he knew about authors and referred to himself as one. He read widely, not least history, and grew up vividly aware that Scotland was divided by both politics and temperament. The natural enmity between the cold, proper Lowland Scots and the fiery Highlanders informs much of his work.

His parents were proud of his precocious literary endeavors, but it never occurred to them that their son would be a writer; he was destined to be a lighthouse engineer. To this end Louis studied engineering at Edinburgh University—very lackadaisically, by all accounts—and accompanied his father to remote lighthouses, trips he later made use of in his work, especially *Kidnapped*. His parents seem to have tolerated his lack of studiousness, but in 1873 there was a terrible crisis when they discovered that Louis had lost his faith. Fortunately, they do not seem to have been aware that he also was involved with prostitutes. Partly as a result of these quarrels Louis collapsed and was sent to recuperate in the south of France. There, in a determined effort to improve his writing, he continued to play "the sedulous ape," as he described it, imitating Wordsworth, Defoe, Hawthorne, and Baudelaire, among others.

Over the next few years he wrote a number of essays, including a highly controversial one in which he took Robert Burns to task for philandering, and reached a modus vivendi with his parents. They gave him an allowance of about £80 a year, and he gave up engineering in favor of law. In 1875 he was admitted to the Scottish bar; his total earnings as a solicitor are recorded as four guineas.

The rapprochement between parents and son weathered even the scandal of Louis's marriage. In 1876, while visiting a cousin in Grez, France, Stevenson met Fanny Osbourne. She was an American, ten years older than he, and estranged from her husband. She had come to Grez with her two children, Lloyd and Belle, to recover from the death of her third child. Later Osbourne claimed that Stevenson fell in love with her at first sight. This seems to have been pure fabrication, but not long after this he visited her in Paris. Osbourne gave an odd picture of her volatile suitor: "I do wish Louis wouldn't burst into tears in such an unexpected way," she wrote. He also suffered from cataracts

of laughter the only cure for which, he claimed, was to have someone bend back his fingers. Osbourne and Stevenson almost certainly became lovers around this time.

In 1878 Osbourne returned to America and Stevenson, briefly, to Scotland. That autumn he was back in France, where he bought a donkey for sixty-five francs. He named her Modestine, and during their twelve-day journey in the Cévennes he reduced her value by nearly half. Later he immortalized her in *Travels With a Donkey*. We do not know on exactly what terms he and Osbourne had parted, but in July of 1879 she sent him a telegram. In the most romantic gesture of his life he set sail secretly for America. His account of the voyage and the subsequent train journey to San Francisco was so grim that his father persuaded him not to publish *The Amateur Emigrant*. By the time he reached Osbourne, in Monterey, Stevenson needed a nurse more than a wife. Their marriage, the following year, was described by both parties as taking place in extremis.

Fanny is a major battleground for Stevenson biographers, as two recent books—*Robert Louis Stevenson*, by Frank McLynn, and *Dreams of Exile*, by Ian Bell—demonstrate. Whatever came later, it seems clear that the unlikely couple were initially in love. For Stevenson, Fanny was the apogee of several significant relationships with older women. As for her, surely love was the only argument for marrying a sickly, impoverished writer. Later Fanny advertised herself as Stevenson's muse, collaborator, and nursemaid, claims that are vigorously, and often convincingly, challenged by Frank McLynn. Still, I find myself reluctant to apportion blame. Who can say who are the criminals in love? Stevenson lived with Fanny for fourteen years, and during that time wrote the works by which we know him.

For the first few years of their marriage the Stevensons shuttled back and forth between Scotland and the Continent, finally settling in 1884 in the English seaside town of Bournemouth. Louis spent much of the next three years in bed, and later described himself as having lived there "like a weevil in a biscuit." During this time he became better acquainted with Henry James, who came to Bournemouth to visit another invalid: his sister, Alice. The two passed from admiration into a friendship that survived a number of aesthetic disagreements. Why not write about women? James suggested, What about action? Stevenson urged. How different the work of each might have been if he had heeded the other.

In spite of ill health Stevenson was wonderfully productive. In rapid succession he published *A*

Child's Garden of Verses, Jekyll and Hyde, and *Kidnapped.* By the time he and Fanny left Britain, in 1887, he was a well-known writer. Thomas Stevenson had died in May of that year, and with his death Louis felt free to go abroad. In August he and Fanny sailed to America, and for a time they led an extreme version of the itinerant life that used to be common for writers. Eventually they made their way to the South Seas and Samoa, where in 1889 they bought an estate called Vailima. To the public this was the realization of the myth: the author of *Treasure Island* was now living on his own island.

Life at Vailima, however, was far from idyllic. Fanny, who had long suffered from nervous illnesses, became increasingly difficult, and Stevenson, though he was earning more than ever before, was worried about money. These anxieties go some way toward explaining why, in spite of his better health, so little of the work by which we remember him comes from this period. Not that he was idle—he wrote constantly, but mostly travel books and a history of Samoa, all of which provoked James to urge him not to squander his gifts.

Perhaps James was prescient. On December 3, 1894, Stevenson wrote fiction in the morning, wrote letters in the afternoon, and died in the evening. He was helping Fanny to make mayonnaise dressing, adding the oil drop by drop, when he collapsed. By dawn the following day the Samoans were at work cutting a road up the slopes of Mount Vaea with knives and axes. That afternoon his coffin was carried in relays to the summit.

To map Stevenson's life is to produce a complex diagram in which we can see, I think, why dualism was such a central concern for him. As the bohemian child of conventional parents, as a Lowland Scot, as an invalid, as an exile, he was always living a double life, trying to be in two places, or two postures, at the same time, and nowhere more so than in his difficult relationship with his father. This relationship was for Stevenson the central dualism: his father was the prim face, he was the orgiastic foundations, and the resulting quarrel between them was simultaneously a great force and a great barrier in his work. In *Treasure Island* and *Kidnapped* he offered a preliminary solution to the quarrel by killing off the narrator's father—in the opening chapters of the former, before the novel begins in the latter. Until after Thomas's death Stevenson had trouble keeping fictional fathers alive.

Like many great writers, Stevenson was slow to discover his true subjects. "I . . . sit for a long while silent on my eggs," he wrote. He was thirty when he began what would be his first success, *Treasure Island.* The genesis of the novel is revealing. The family was staying in the small Scottish town of Braemar. One rainy afternoon Stevenson drew a map of an island and began to make up a story to go with it to entertain his stepson, Lloyd. Thomas Stevenson was visiting at the time and enthusiastically contributed suggestions to his son's project. Early chapters were read aloud to the appreciative family. The novel went on to be serialized in a boys' magazine and was published as a book in 1883. It is surely no accident that Stevenson found narrative luck on the first occasion for which we have any record of his father's approval.

Stevenson's avowed aim in *Treasure Island* was to write a story for boys—"No need of psychology or fine writing," he said. Many readers, including James, praised the novel. Probably no one at the time, including Stevenson himself, recognized his most significant accomplishment. With the tap of Pew's cane and a few choruses of yo-ho-ho, he liberated children's writing from the heavy chains of Victorian didacticism.

One of the great pleasures of reconsidering Stevenson was rereading *Kidnapped.* I came back to it hesitantly, nervously, expecting to take my seven-year-old self to task, and found from the beautiful, stately opening pages, wherein David Balfour leaves his home for the last time, that I was captivated. Alan Breck remains a wonderfully jaunty character, and I was struck afresh by Stevenson's gift for describing landscapes that both shape and reveal the actions of the characters.

Only after I closed the book did it occur to me that the story was set almost a century before Stevenson's birth. I attribute this oversight not to my obtuseness but to his genius. As he liberated children's literature from didacticism, so he liberated the historical novel from creaking obeisance toward the past. He presented the characters in a prose that is lively and lucid and, best of all, unstrained by nostalgia.

Jekyll and Hyde, the quintessential novel of a double life, was written "in a white heat" around the same time as *Kidnapped*, and had a long hatching period—Stevenson had known about Deacon Brodie, the eighteenth-century Edinburgh cabinetmaker on whom he based Jekyll and Hyde, since childhood. The novel, published in 1886, achieved something even better than good reviews; it became the subject of numerous sermons. Forty thousand copies were sold within the first six months, and since then the phrase "Jekyll and Hyde" has entered the culture.

To go back and read what Stevenson actually wrote is disorienting for several reasons. The novel is firmly in the romantic tradition wherein amazing events are reported by a dry-as-dust narrator. We tend to overlook the cold, silent lawyer Utterson who guides us through the story and who, precisely because of his reserve, is the best possible witness to the horror of Hyde. Part of our disorientation is not merely forgetfulness but the result of Stevenson's cunning design. The labyrinthine streets through which we pursue Hyde increasingly depart from the map of the known city. Slowly but inexorably we are being led into a strange country, where the relationship between Jekyll's prim white hand and Hyde's orgiastic hairy paw will be revealed. The two are not merely opposites, or alter egos. In Nabokov's helpful analogy Hyde is a precipitate of Jekyll. We might also think of him as Jekyll's son.

Critics have speculated that both Jekyll and Hyde are guilty of sexual misdemeanors. But I read the novel as essentially Scottish; the sins I attribute to Jekyll are the Edinburgh ones of secrecy and puritanism that governed Stevenson's youth and my own. Whatever the author had in mind, vagueness has served the novel well. Sin dates, and modern readers, although frustrated, are left free to imagine their own version of horror.

Between *Jekyll and Hyde* and *Weir,* Stevenson wrote several more novels, among them *The Master of Ballantrae* and *David Balfour.* The former is commonly regarded as his greatest full-length work, although the plot, about a life-long duel between two brothers, one of whom turns out to be an incubus, defeated even as staunch an admirer as André Gide. What is notable in terms of Stevenson's development as a writer is that the father remains alive through the first half of the novel and that the characters include a strong-minded, intelligent woman.

Both these promises are fulfilled in the unfinished *Weir of Hermiston.* Here Stevenson at last explored the quarrel between father and son and created two superb female characters. Lord Braxfield, the notorious Scots hanging judge, was, like Deacon Brodie, a famous Edinburgh character. Stevenson became convinced that Braxfield was his great subject, the one that would allow him to achieve the epic qualities his work to that point had lacked.

The plot combines the dazzle of reality with the significance of art. Archie, the only son of ill-matched parents, is raised at Hermiston by his religious mother, who unthinkingly teaches him to criticize his father. After her death he moves to Edinburgh to live with his father, the judge. The crisis between them comes when Archie, now a law student, watches his father sentence a man to death.

Archie denounces the hanging as murder, and his father banishes him to Hermiston. There the older Kirstie, his housekeeper, falls in love with him, while he falls in love with her niece, the younger Kirstie. The idyllic pursuit of the latter, secret relationship is interrupted by the arrival of Frank, an Iago-like figure. Frank discovers the relationship and, with the worst intentions, warns Archie against it. His advice is seconded by the older Kirstie, for very different reasons. In chapter nine we see Archie attempting to act on it.

From letters and notes we have an idea of how Stevenson imagined the remainder of the book. Frank was going to seduce the younger Kirstie. Archie would shoot Frank and be arrested. He would come to trial, and in some way—Stevenson was desperate to make this work—he would be tried by his father and condemned to death.

All this, whatever its credibility, does have the resonance of an epic. It is also Stevenson's profoundest exploration of duality. Finally he laid aside the subterfuges of the supernatural and created characters who are both in opposition to each other and at war within themselves. In his single person the judge upholds the polite face of society while remaining firmly rooted in the orgiastic foundations, and it is crucial to the tragedy that Archie is his father's son as well as his mother's. Here we see him describing his tangled feelings:

> I will be baldly frank. I do not love my father, I wonder sometimes if I do not hate him. There's my shame; perhaps my sin; at least, and in the sight of God, not my fault. How was I to love him? . . . You know the way he talks? . . . My soul is sick when he begins with it; I could smite him in the mouth.

And yet, Archie goes on, he has asked his father's pardon and placed himself wholly in his hands. The two Kirsties also show us terrific vitality and subtlety of motivation.

That Stevenson died in the midst of this story is tragic; that he lived to write it at all is a marvel. The canon has taught us to value a body of work over a single work, but at this late date in the twentieth century, drowning in books, surely we can afford to esteem quality even when it comes without quantity. If Stevenson deserves a place in our adult lives, his reputation must, like a number of authors', rest on only a few works. As we love Shelley for *Frankenstein,* Di Lampedusa for *The Leopard,* Fournier for *The Lost Domain,* so we can love Stevenson for his vaulted ambition and because in those last days of his life, at least, he wrote pages worthy of that ambition and of our admiration. He worked on *Weir of Hermiston* intermittently from 1892 onward. The last words were dictated the morning of his death.

Source: Margot Livesey, "The Double Life of Robert Louis Stevenson," in the *Atlantic Monthly*, Vol. 274, No. 5, November 1994, pp. 140–46.

Sources

Bell, Ian, "Preface," in *Dreams of Exile: Robert Louis Stevenson: A Biography*, Mainstream Publishing, 1992.

Jones, William B., Jr., ed. "Preface," in *Robert Louis Stevenson Reconsidered*, McFarland, 2003.

Moore, Laura, "Voices from the Middle," in *Urbana*, Vol. 8, No. 2, December 2000, p. 75.

Stevenson, Robert Louis, "Essay: *Treasure Island*," in *Treasure Island*, Courage Books, 1995, pp. 202–07.

Further Reading

Cordingly, David, *The Black Flag*, reprint, Harvest Books, 1997.

Cordingly looks pirates in the eye and discovers the truth of their lives, which is far from the romanticized versions in literature. The author also ponders the myths of pirates in an attempt to figure out where and how those myths were born.

Lapierre, Alexandra, *Fanny Stevenson: A Romance of Destiny*, Carroll & Graf, 1995.

Stevenson met Fanny, an American woman, in France and supposedly fell immediately in love with her, and she later became his wife. In the biography of Stevenson's wife, Lapierre exposes Fanny's emotions and her devotion to her husband, for whom she gave up her own creative endeavors as an artist.

McLynn, Frank, *Robert Louis Stevenson: A Biography*, Random House, 1994.

McLynn believes that Stevenson was much more than a writer of boys' adventure stories. He sets out to demonstrate through this biography that Stevenson was a superb writer and also a great influence on other writers, such as Joseph Conrad, Oscar Wilde, and William Butler Yeats.

Pool, Daniel, *What Jane Austin Ate and Charles Dickens Knew: From Fox Hunting to Whist—The Facts of Daily Life in Nineteenth-Century England*, reprint, Touchstone Books, 1994.

Pool offers a glimpse into Victorian England, with interesting information on grave robbers, debtors' prison, and other curiosities. Other topics include religion, sex, dinner parties, and politics.

The War of the Worlds

H. G. Wells
1898

H. G. Wells's science fiction masterpiece *The War of the Worlds* was originally published in *Pierson's* magazine in 1897 and was issued as a novel the following year. A century later, it has never been out of print. The story has become an integral part of our culture, frequently retold in graphic novels and films. In 1938, it became part of one of the greatest and most horrifying media events of all times. The Mercury Theatre on the Air, headed by twenty-three-year-old Orson Welles, broadcast over the radio an adaptation of the book that was so realistic that it caused widespread public panic, mob violence, and looting. Until the night of that broadcast, few people realized the power of broadcast media to make whole populations feel powerless when faced with breaking events.

Like the radio program, much of the novel takes its power from appearing to be real. Wells, who had an intense interest in science from an early age, created his Martian invaders with a strict sense of the laws of biology and physics. They are not super beings, but bodiless heads, barely able to move because the atmosphere of Earth is so much thicker than that of their own planet. Still, their advanced intelligence gives them the power to create powerful weapons, such as Heat-Ray guns that can level whole towns; tripods with hundred-foot legs, that give them mobility; and even flying machines, which, in 1898, were beyond human technology. Humanity has entered into space exploration since this novel was published, and many of the specific details are no longer of con-

H. G. Wells

cern. But there will always be uneasiness about the unknown and curiosity about what might happen when people of Earth contact lives from other worlds.

Author Biography

Herbert George Wells was born on September 21, 1866, in Bromley, Kent, in England. His father was a shopkeeper and a professional cricket player with the Bromley team; his mother was a part-time housekeeper. When Wells was seven, he was injured while playing with a friend of his father. He broke a bone in his leg and was forced to spend two months in bed. He looked back on this as a lucky turn of events, as it was then that he developed the habit of reading.

Because his family did not have much money, Wells became an apprentice to a draper at age thirteen, working twelve-hour days. He was determined to become educated, and earned a scholarship to Midhurst Grammar School by agreeing to function as a student teacher. He entered the Normal School of Science at South Kensington when he was eighteen and studied under famed biologist T. H. Huxley. After college, he took a position teaching, but a bout with tuberculosis forced him to become bedridden again. It was then, while

reading constantly, that he decided that he did not want to be not a teacher but a writer.

In 1891, while making money by grading lessons for the University Correspondence College at Cambridge, Wells published several short stories in *Science Schools Journal*. These stories were later collected to make his first novel, *The Time Machine* (1895). Next followed a series of science fiction classics that are read to this day and often adapted to films, including *The Island of Dr. Moreau* (1896), *The Invisible Man* (1897), and *The War of the Worlds* (1898). The widespread popularity of these books, all published when the author was barely thirty, gave him an income that would make him financially comfortable for the rest of his life.

As he aged, Wells's books concentrated more and more on scientific and philosophical matters. He became a leading voice in the Fabian society, which was a socialist movement. His first marriage ended in divorce, and his second, to one of his students, was an "open" marriage: his wife knew about his many affairs, including at least one that resulted in a child, and raised no objection, though his lifestyle hurt his public image. After World War I (1914–1918) he wrote books about social order, such as *The Outline of History* (1920) (one of his most famous works) and *The Common Sense of World Peace* (1929). He lived to the age of seventy nine, having spent much of his life as one of the world's most famous authors. Wells died on August 13, 1946 after a prolonged illness.

Plot Summary

Book 1, Chapter 1: The Eve of the War

The narrator of *The War of the Worlds* is never identified by name. He refers to a "great light" seen on the planet Mars in 1894, explaining that this was six years before the time when he is writing. Earth's astronomers were perplexed about what to make of it, he says, but later realized that it was the invading forces, being shot toward Earth as if out of a gun.

Book 1, Chapter 2: The Falling Star

People think that the first Martian ship is a falling star, then a meteor. An astronomer hears something within the metal tube that landed.

Book 1, Chapter 3: On Horsell Common

The narrator goes to investigate the crash site, where a crowd of spectators has gathered. Also there are several astronomers gathered.

Media Adaptations

- An audiocassette version of Wells's *The War of the Worlds* is available from Books in Motion. It was released in 1982.

- The 1938 radio adaptation of *The War of the Worlds*, by Orson Welles's *Mercury Theatre on the Air* company, is of course the most famous and has become an important piece of American history because of the panic that it induced when it went out across the country.

- *The War of the Worlds* was loosely adapted into a movie in 1953 by producer George Pal, and it starred Gene Barry and Ann Robinson. The adaptation won the Academy Award for Best Special Effects. It is available on VHS and DVD from Paramount.

- A stage musical version of the story was produced in London in 1978. *Jeff Wayne's Musical Version of the "War of the Worlds"* starred Richard Burton and had songs by David Essex and musicians from the bands The Moody Blues and Tin Lizzy. The soundtrack album achieved multi-platinum status and is available on CBS Records.

Book 1, Chapter 4: The Cylinder Opens

The top of the cylinder opens, and the crowd scatters. A Martian, with huge eyes and flailing antennae, jumps out, and another looks out the top. One man who slipped into the crater that the cylinder made tries to crawl out of the hole, but the Martian grabs him and pulls him back.

Book 1, Chapter 5: The Heat-Ray

Because the Martians do not seem able to climb out of the pit their ship is in, people crowd around again. A group of men approach the Martians with a white flag, signaling that they come in peace, but they are incinerated by a Heat-Ray that is fired at them.

Book 1, Chapter 6: The Heat-Ray in the Chobham Road

Word of the Heat-Ray spreads to the nearby towns of Cobham, Woking, and Ottershaw. Hundreds of people come to observe what is coming on. When the ray is turned on the crowd, it is unable to kill everyone because it is being fired from down in the pit, but two women and a little boy are trampled in the rush to get away from the Martians.

Book 1, Chapter 7: How I Reached Home

The narrator returns to his home, on the way hearing people talk about the Martian ship. His wife has dinner on the table. She has not heard anything about all of this until he tells her what he saw. The morning newspapers report on the Martians, but they say that they would never be able to threaten the planet because the Earth's gravity, much stronger than the gravity of Mars, would weigh them down.

Book 1, Chapter 8: Friday Night

While they can hear hammering sounds from within the pit where the Martians have landed, the army sends soldiers to surround the cylinder. A second cylinder from Mars arrives on Earth, landing not too far from the first.

Book 1, Chapter 9: The Fighting Begins

The day is like an ordinary Saturday, except that everyone is talking about the Martians. The Martians release the Heat-Ray across the countryside, and it reaches for miles around. The narrator rents a dog cart from his landlord to take his wife away from their home, which is too close to the invaders, to live with his cousin in Leatherhead, twelve miles away.

Book 1, Chapter 10: In the Storm

There is a thunderstorm when he tries to return. On the road, he encounters the Martians, mobilized in a pod that walks on three hundred-foot-tall legs. As he goes toward his house, he encounters the charred remains of people.

Book 1, Chapter 11: At the Window

From the upstairs window of his house, the narrator sees fires across the whole countryside, and several Martian tripods lumbering across the valley. He sees an artilleryman outside of his house and has him come inside; the man tells of how the Martians' Heat-Ray wiped out his army division.

Book 1, Chapter 12: What I Saw of the Destruction of Weybridge and Shepperton

The narrator and the artilleryman leave for London. They come across another army division and tell them of the destruction they have seen. They also come across refugees fleeing their homes. When the Martians arrive, the narrator is able to survive their Heat-Rays by diving under water. One Martian pod is destroyed by artillery fire before the people are wiped out by the Heat-Ray.

Book 1, Chapter 13: How I Fell in with the Curate

The narrator floats downstream in a boat, scorched from the heating of the river water. He meets a curate who is turning crazy with panic and takes him with him toward London.

Book 1, Chapter 14: In London

Chapter 14 is about how the narrator's brother, a medical student in London, learned of the Martians. While battles are being waged against the Martians to the south, little news had reached the city: telegraph lines are down and observers are dead. There are rumors about the one Martian cylinder that has been destroyed, and refugees from the countryside tell stories about what they have seen. Finally, reports reach the city of the Black Smoke, which hovers near the ground and waterways and suffocates anyone whose lungs it seeps into.

Book 1, Chapter 15: What Happened in Surrey

The narrator and the curate watch the human military forces smashed by three Martian tripods using the Heat-Ray and the Black Smoke.

Book 1, Chapter 16: The Exodus from London

This chapter chronicles the attempts of the narrator's brother to escape from London. All trains are overcrowded, and the tracks are crammed with people trying to escape. The Black Smoke is traveling up the river from the south. The narrator's brother helps two women as some men are trying to steal their horse carriage from them, and they invite him to travel with them.

Book 1, Chapter 17: The Thunder Child

The narrator's brother and his companions have their horse taken away from them. They make it to the sea just as the Martians are approaching, but they manage to escape on a boat. A naval ship manages to destroy a Martian tripod before a flying ship that the Martians have made on Earth flies overhead, spreading the Black Smoke.

Book 2, Chapter 1: Under Foot

Book 2 chronicles "The Earth under the Martians." The narrator decides that the curate is too much trouble to stay with him, and decides to part ways. They arrive at London and find it deserted, but a strange red plant is growing everywhere: it is something that came with the Martians from their planet. The house where the curate and the narrator have stopped to look for food is nearly hit by a new cylinder arriving from Mars, and they are then stuck there because the Martians will see them if they leave.

Book 2, Chapter 2: What We Saw from the Ruined House

In the ruined house on the edge of the crater, the men watch the Martians build new machines, which look like themselves but have the mobility to attack the human race.

Book 2, Chapter 3: The Days of Imprisonment

Trapped in the ruined house with food supplies dwindling, the narrator comes to hate the curate, who complains constantly and eats and drinks, which makes him loud, threatening their hiding place. They watch the Martians take human prisoners and suck the blood out of them.

Book 2, Chapter 4: The Death of the Curate

When the curate panics and makes too much noise, the narrator hits him with a cleaver. A Martian reaches into the house with its tentacle: it comes close to the narrator but does not find him, and instead drags the curate's body away.

Book 2, Chapter 5: The Stillness

After fifteen days in the house, the narrator steps outside to find that the pit where the Martians were working is abandoned. Birds and dogs scrounge among the discarded skeletons of humans.

Book 2, Chapter 6: The Work of Fifteen Days

The narrator wanders through London and finds it deserted.

Book 2, Chapter 7: The Man on Putney Hill

The narrator meets the artilleryman from Chapter 12 who has a pragmatic idea for the regeneration of humanity. He plans to start a new society in the sewers, and they will adapt to the new reality of Martian dominance and focus on the disciplined struggle for life. Despite what he says, the man works little and wants to spend his time playing cards, drinking, and smoking.

Book 2, Chapter 8: Dead London

Wandering through the desolate streets of London, the narrator comes to realize that the Martian tripods are not moving. The Martians are dead. He explains that scientists later determined that they had no natural defenses for Earth's bacteria.

Book 2, Chapter 9: Wreckage

The narrator is driven nearly mad with the idea that he is the last man alive. A family looks after him until his delirium breaks. Then he goes home, sorrowful that he will not see his wife ever again, but she shows up there, thinking he is dead, and they are reunited.

Book 2, Chapter 10: The Epilogue

Once news of the Martians' demise spread, countries from all over the world send food and aid, and those who had survived by leaving return. The government believes that the Martians may have colonized Venus and that might satisfy their needs, but the narrator still is uneasy about whether they might try another attack against Earth some time in the future.

Characters

The Artilleryman

The narrator first encounters him outside of the window of his house. He is from a regiment of the army that has been destroyed by the Martians' Heat-Ray, and he is shocked and barely able to speak. They travel together until they come upon a cavalry unit, who tell the artilleryman where he can find a superior officer to whom he can report. The army is in such disarray that he has trouble finding who is in charge. The narrator is separated from him when the Martians attack with their Heat-Ray, and the narrator escapes by diving under the river.

Their paths cross again in Chapter 7 of Book 2, when London is just a ghost town. The artilleryman is protective of his territory and food until he recognizes the narrator as the man who had helped him before. Then he shares his idea about how the human race will repopulate itself. The Martians, he explains, will imprison those who fight them, and fatten them up for food and breed them like cattle, but humans who manage to stay out of their way and who do not prove to be difficult will probably be left alone. He has planned out a new, underground society, living in sewers, led by the strongest. They will keep learning until they acquire knowledge of how to beat the Martians.

The narrator is impressed with the artilleryman's plan until he notices that, for all of his talk, the man is not really willing to work hard at all. The man has dug a small hole, and then he wanders outside to look at the sky; instead of working through the night, he wants to smoke, drink champagne, and play cards. The narrator soon leaves him, disillusioned.

The Curate

In Chapter 13 of Book 1, the narrator finds the curate looking over him after he has fallen asleep on a river bed, and they travel together. He quickly finds that the holy man's fears are unnerving to him, a position that angers him all the more because he feels that there is no point to being a religious man if religion cannot at least give the curate the courage to face his situation. When a cylinder from Mars lands next to a house that they are ransacking together, the narrator and the curate find themselves trapped, afraid of going outside because the Martians who have just arrived might find them and feast upon them. Food becomes scarce, but the curate continues to eat wastefully and to cry out in fear. Finally, when he becomes mentally unstable and makes enough noise to attract the nearby Martians, the narrator hits him in the head with an ax (although, he points out, he has mercy and hits him with the blunt end). The Martian who investigates the sound takes the curate's body with him, presumably to drink his blood.

Mrs. Elphinstone

Mrs. Elphinstone is a woman who is escaping from London with her sister. Thieves are trying to steal their horse carriage from them when the narrator's brother intervenes. Mrs. Elphinstone is pale in complexion and dressed in white. She is nervous, screaming for her husband George. Her sister-in-law, on the other hand, is dark, slim, and cool; it is she who draws a gun and fires at the attackers.

Lord Garrick

Lord Garrick is the Chief Justice. When the narrator's brother is trying to escape London, Lord Garrick is brought through the crowd on a stretcher. despite his high place in society, he receives no special treatment in all of the turmoil.

Henderson

Henderson is a journalist from London, who lives near where the first Martian cylinder arrives. He dispatches an early report of the situation, but he is one of the first people killed by the Martians when they emerge from the cylinder and fire their Heat-Rays.

The Narrator

The name of the first-person narrator of this novel is never given to the reader. He is a philosopher, working on series of papers that are to discuss the development of moral ideas, when the invasion begins. He lives southeast of London, not far from where the Martian invasion begins. Because of his connection to the world of academia, he is invited to look at Mars through the telescope of Ogilvy, a prominent astronomer, and is given updates on the knowledge of the canister that lands on Earth as Ogilvy receives them. He borrows a wagon to take his wife away to live with relatives, but returns to his home as the tide of refugees starts arriving.

The stress of the situation takes its toll on the narrator. Trapped in a house just outside of a Martian encampment, his irritation with the curate that he has been traveling with turns to panic when the man will not be quiet. Fearful of being discovered, the narrator murders the other man and hides while Martian tentacles drag the body away.

His calm philosophical attitude is also broken when he listens to the artilleryman's plans to restore the human population. Having earlier hoped for a victory over the Martians, he comes to realize that the best that can be hoped for would be for some humans to escape from them, like insects that manage to survive by staying out of sight. In the course of a few weeks his understanding of the world has gone from assuming that humans dominate to viewing humans as relatively insignificant.

At the end of the book, his mind snaps briefly. Finding the Martians dead, he thinks that he is the only human who has survived. He is later told about his ravings on this subject by people who care for

him, who he does not notice. Having survived this episode, his despair reaches its depth when he returns to his house with the thought that he will never see his wife again. After her return, he settles into a domestic pattern somewhat like the life he once led, but he can never really be comfortable again.

The Narrator's Brother

Chapters 14, 16 and 17 of Book 1 relate the experiences of the narrator's brother, who is a medical student in London. At the same time that the narrator is fleeing from the Martians' Heat-Rays, his brother is unaware of anything that is happening. It is through his eyes that readers experience the invasion's effect on the large city. He sees the gossip and the panicked exodus of thousands of people once they become convinced that the rumors of an alien invasion are true. He reads the news of the release of the Black Smoke that the Martians use to exterminate masses of people.

When he does join all the people fleeing the city with whatever belongings they can carry, the narrator's brother joins up with a woman, Mrs. Elphinstone, and her sister-in-law, after saving them from bandits who are trying to steal their carriage and horse. The sister-in-law fires a pistol at the thieves, and then gives it to the narrator's brother, trusting him with their security. He travels with them along the Thames River to the sea, where they pay their way onto a boat. As the boat is going out to sea, they see a flying ship that the Martians have evidently made since arriving on Earth, spraying the Black Smoke on the people on shore. Readers must assume, from the fact that the narrator knows these stories, that the brother survived the Martian attack.

The Narrator's Wife

The narrator's wife plays a minor role in this novel. When he first comes home from examining the unidentified metal canister that has arrived from Mars, she has dinner on the table, providing a contrast between the strange adventure that is beginning and the normal life he is used to. When the Martian advance is predicted, he borrows a dog cart and takes her to Leatherhead to live with his cousin. Later in the book, he hears that Leatherhead has been destroyed and all of its inhabitants killed. He despairs that he will never see his wife again, but she shows up at their house after the invasion is all over.

Ogilvy

An astronomer friend of the narrator's, he invites the narrator to look at Mars through his telescope after the first cylinder is fired from Mars at the Earth. Later, he joins Stent and some other astronomers to investigate the cylinder where it has landed at Horsell Common. He is with the party that approaches the cylinder with a white flag of peace, and the Martians that emerge from the cylinder obliterate the members of the peace party with their Heat-Ray.

Stent

The Astronomer Royal, he leads the expedition team that includes Ogilvy in investigating the first Martian cylinder when it arrives. He is one of the first people killed by the Martians.

Themes

Ambiguity

One reason that the invasion against the Earth is so successful is that the humans do not know what to make of it. The first Martian craft to arrive lies in the crater made by its arrival, seeming to be powerless. There is a noise from within, but that stops, leading astronomers to believe that the creatures inside have perished. When the Martians emerge from the cylinder, they are weak, gelatinous organisms, and their inability to move very freely in Earth's thick atmosphere leads scientists to believe that they do not pose much of a threat. These assumptions are based on what little information can be gleaned from the spacecraft's behavior. The Martians seem to pose no threat, until they swiftly begin their destructive attacks.

Even after the Martians prove hostile, the people of London do not see the danger facing them because the news is so sketchy. While people are being cut down by Heat-Rays just twenty miles away, Londoners go about their daily business. The novel seems to be making the point that, given an ambiguous situation, people will prefer to believe that all things are going to remain as they were. The view of the Martians that the narrator gets from his secluded house on the end of a Martian crater, where he watches them drain the blood from humans and throw away their bodies, is vastly different from the early assumption that they were disabled. Action is forestalled for crucial days by uncertainty about what these very strange visitors want or are capable of.

Victory and Defeat

Once the humans in this novel realize that the Martians can and will destroy them, they see the entire adventure in terms of victory and defeat. Early

on, a party of scientists approaches the Martian cylinder with a white flag, to signify a willingness to live in peace, but that peace party is incinerated by the Martians. After that, the reports about the invasion are all sweetened with false hope because an artillery shell manages to destroy one of the Martian pods. The fact that they can be destroyed indicates to the hopeful that they will be, although no similar victories occur. By Book 2, there is no longer any pretense that humanity might be victorious. The narrator finds great appeal in the plan that the artilleryman puts forth: he cedes inevitable victory to the Martians, but says that, if it is able to survive and reproduce, the human race might find a way to be victorious at some distant time in the future.

Man versus Machine

One reason that the Martians do not seem all that threatening is that they are small and weak. They lack mobility, being made of large heads that slither slowly around on tentacles. Their power makes itself manifest when they climb into the tall tripod machines that can carry them high above the ground and shoot Heat-Rays. In Chapter 10 of Book 1, when the narrator first encounters one of the Martian tripods up close, he constantly refers to it as a machine but is also amazed at how responsive it is to the controls of the Martian inside:

> . . . it was no mere insensate machine driving on its way. Machine it was, with a ringing metallic pace, and long, flexible, glittering tentacles (one of which gripped a young pine tree) swinging and rattling about its strange body. It picked its road as it went striding along, and the brazen hood that surmounted it moved to and fro with the inevitable suggestion of a head looking about.

The suggestion here is that neither the Martians nor their machines would independently be able to vanquish humanity but that the combination of living creature and metal machine would prevail.

Persistence

Persistence is at the heart of Herbert Spencer's social Darwinian concept of "survival of the fittest." In this book, it shows itself on levels grand and miniscule. At the level of world dominance, there is the theory that, although greatly overpowered, the human race could survive and eventually win out over the Martians over the course of generations, but only if some humans are willing to adapt to the new reality of being conquered. These people would have to live underground and train themselves: "We can't have any weak or silly," the artilleryman explains. "Life is real again, and the weak and the cumbersome and mischievous have

Topics For Further Study

- This novel is specific about what sorts of physical characteristics the Martians would have developed, due to the kind of atmosphere Wells believed Mars to have. Using current information about Mars, describe what types of creatures would live there if there were any Martians at all.

- Examine the information that has been printed by people who suspect that aliens have already come to Earth, especially the theories around Roswell, New Mexico, and the government facility at Area 51 in Nevada. After reading the information, explain why you do or do not believe that the government is keeping the presence of aliens a secret.

- Listen to a recording of the Mercury Theatre's 1938 broadcast of their adaptation of *The War of the Worlds*, and then read about the panic that broadcast caused. Compare the public's response to that fictional account with the reaction to the real-life destruction of the World Trade Center, which was broadcast live throughout the world. Explain whether you think people in the 1930s acted rationally or irrationally.

- The invasion of London in this novel can be compared to the attack against New York City in 2001. Write a report about the ways people behaved at that time, comparing and contrasting them to the behaviors that Wells describes.

---

to die. They ought to be willing to die. It's sort of a disloyalty, after all, to live and taint the race." His theory that the race can live on, with modifications, makes sense, but then he proves unwilling to make those necessary modifications.

The ultimate defeat of the Martians comes, not from the persistence of human willpower, but from the persistence of the human biological organism. The human bodies that have survived over the course of millions of years are the ones that have been able to survive exposure to bacteria: the ones that have not have died off. The Martians, with no history of exposure to these bacteria, die quickly. The Martians' swift invasion is terrifying and effective, but it is the bacteria that have persisted that make the survival of humanity possible.

Style

Narrative

In order to present this story as a first person narrative, told by an "I" speaker who is a character in the book, Wells has to resort to some clever tricks. For one thing, the narrator is a scientist and a friend of an astronomer, Ogilvy: this gives him access to

the world of astronomy when most of the news about the first projectile from Mars is not commonly talked about. Another method used is to have the narrator speaking from six years after the action has taken place, so that information that would not have been available during the Martian invasion, such as the details of their physiognomy, can be introduced into the book at appropriate times.

The most obvious narrative device, though, is in switching the action's point of view for several chapters into that of the narrator's brother. This is not a character whom readers come to know with any depth. The details of his experience are known without much insight into his personality. The function of these chapters is to show what the general reaction to the invasion was around London, and perhaps to introduce a dashing, romantic figure aiding damsels in distress without breaking away from the reality of the narrator's perspective.

Foreshadowing

Once readers reach the end of *The War of the Worlds*, many realize that they should have seen the Martians' defeat clearly prepared in the course of the story. When an action in the story prepares readers for what is going to be done, it is called foreshadowing. Done well, readers will not even

Compare & Contrast

- **1898:** One of the most frightening aspects of the Martian invasion is when they master the concept of flight, giving them the ability to spread their dominance across the globe.

  Today: Humans have been able to fly since the Wright Brothers were able to attain lift-off at Kitty Hawk, North Carolina, in 1903.

- **1898:** Wells presents interplanetary travel as being a matter of a canister projected from Mars to Earth like a bullet from a gun.

  Today: Humanity understands the principles of rocket propulsion well enough to explore the far reaches of our solar system.

- **1898:** In the novel, Wells describes lakes of water on Mars, visible through telescopes.

  Today: For a long time, theories about Martian water have been discredited as a misinterpretation of the visible data; however, in recent years, probes on the surface of Mars have determined that there is in fact significant water.

- **1898:** The only means of communication are telegraphs. When the Martians are a few miles away from London, people in the city go about their ordinary business, unaware.

  Today: Wireless phones with video capabilities make it possible for an average citizen to send sound and images from any remote corner of the world.

---

notice foreshadowing until after they have seen the event foreshadowed.

As early as Chapter 2 of Book 2, the narrator explains that

> Micro-organisms, which cause so much disease and pain on earth, have either never appeared upon Mars or Martian sanitary science eliminated them ages ago. A hundred diseases, all the fevers and contagions of human life, consumption, cancers, tumours and such morbidities, never enter the scheme of their life.

Readers who do not see this as a clue to the Martians' eventual inability to survive on Earth are given further evidence when the narrator goes on to introduce the red weed that came with them from Mars, which grew prodigiously but was unable to survive local bacteria. The end is foreshadowed early on, but readers who are engrossed in the story might miss it.

Historical Context

Fear of Invasion

At the end of the nineteenth century, the nations of Europe were divided into strategic alliances that pitted them against each other in the event of a war. From 1882 onward, these military associations resulted in a greater military buildup than the world had ever known before. The proof that this trend created a dangerous political situation can be seen in the fact that it ended in the largest and bloodiest confrontation that had ever happened up to that time, the Great War.

The roots of this division of Europe came in 1871, when Prussia conquered France. Prussia, the kingdom state that included Germany, sought to prevent France from coming back at some future time to take back the land that had been taken from it by forming alliances with first Austria-Hungary and, later, Russia. By the 1880s, Germany had signed on to a Triple Alliance with Italy and Austria-Hungary. Britain, France, and Russia, in turn, signed on to a Triple Entente, promising to defend each other in case of attack. By the time Wells wrote *The War of the Worlds* in the late 1890s, all of the nations of Europe were aligned with one of these organizations. The balance of military power was strictly monitored and maintained: for instance, the German naval build-up in the 1890s spurred Great Britain to pour resources into their own navy, which caused Italy, France, the United States, and Japan to follow suit. The political scene in which Wells wrote about the Martian invasion was a stable one, then, but one that was expected to explode.

The military melee that was expected throughout Europe did not actually occur until nearly twenty years later. When it did, though, it followed a course that by then seemed inevitable. When Archduke Ferdinand of Austria-Hungary was assassinated by Serbians in 1914, Austria-Hungary declared war on Serbia. Within a week, Germany, France, and Russia were involved, and days later Belgium, Great Britain, and Japan were drawn in. By the time of the war's end four years later, ten million had died, and twenty million were wounded.

Darwinism

One of the greatest influences on scientific thought at the end of the nineteenth century was the theory of biological evolution that had been put forward by the British naturalist Charles Darwin. Darwin's theory of natural selection, which posits that organisms evolve over the course of generations, is prominent in *The War of the Worlds*, particularly in the way that the Martians are said to have lost any need for bodies or sexual reproduction, and in the way that the bleak fate of humanity is viewed as perhaps regrettable but nonetheless unavoidable.

In 1859, Darwin outlined his theories in his book *On the Origin of the Species*. Based on observations made in previously unexplored regions of the South Pacific, he concluded that similar species were actually related to each other, and that those that had grown up under different circumstances had evolved in ways that best suited their individual environments. The book was a sensation after its publication, and the theory of evolution was applied to other fields as well, leading to such concepts as Herbert Spencer's competitive "social darwinism" to explain the survival of some social traits over others. One of Wells's teachers, T. H. Huxley, has been recognized as perhaps the single most influential writer to popularize Darwinism.

Critical Overview

The War of the Worlds was published early in Wells's career, at the tail of a string of successful novels that are still considered classics today: *The Time Machine* (1895), *The Island of Dr. Moreau*

(1896), and *The Invisible Man* (1897). Critics of the time were split between finding the book a marked improvement on his earlier works and a repeat of the same old formula. For instance, John St. Loe Strachey, in a review in the English magazine *The Spectator*, notes that "One reads and reads with an interest so unflagging that it is positively exhausting. *The War of the Worlds* stands, in fact, the final test of fiction. When one has taken it up, one cannot bear to put it down without a pang." In addition, an unsigned review in the American publication *The Critic* concludes that "The author has written an ingenious and original work.... The book has the tone of intense modernity, with notes of convincing realism and morbid horror." *Academy* starts its review with "Mr. Wells has done good work before, but nothing quite so fine as this." Basil Williams, writing in *Athenaeum*, finds the prose to be too flat to make the story exciting: "There is too much of the young man from Clapham attitude about the book; the narrator sees and hears exciting things, but he has not the gift of making them exciting to other people."

In the decades that have passed, *The War of the Worlds* has come to be considered one of Wells's best books, if not his best one. One problem that modern readers might have in appreciating the story is that it has been retold frequently in many different forms so that it seems all too familiar. As Richard Hauer Costa puts it in his 1967 study of Wells's career,

> *The War of the Worlds* is the archetype of all B-Grade films which present giant creatures from another world who invade the earth armed with death-ray guns. The imagery of the novel is so vivid that it is no wonder film scenarists have always thought of outer-space invasions in Wellsian terms.

Criticism

David Kelly

Kelly is an instructor of literature and creative writing at two schools in Illinois. In this essay, Kelly examines the role that is played in the novel by the two women that the narrator's brother meets while fleeing London.

The early novels that H. G. Wells wrote are remembered for infusing a groundbreaking sense of realism into unlikely situations, all the while holding fast to the principles of science. *The War of the Worlds*, in particular, is considered as "realistic" as a book can be when there are slimy

1953 film portrayal of H. G. Well's The War of the Worlds

tentacled creatures cutting down whole countrysides with ray guns. The book is apocalyptic, showing a very convincing vision of how the human race could quite conceivably end. It dismisses the most dominant factors of our society, presuming that they would be unable to rise to the kind of challenge presented by a Martian invasion.

The novel follows its vision of mankind's defeat through until the end, when, in the depth of his despair, its unnamed narrator finds out that the invasion has been defeated, mostly by a fluke. From there, things pick up: he returns to his home, he is reunited with his wife, international aid packages

arrive for the displaced and there is hope that such an invasion could not work as well a second time without the element of surprise. In the end, though, the sense of hope is tinged with the kind of fear that any war survivor would harbor, having once seen how easily the life he knows can collapse in on itself.

Even with the final reconciliations, this is an almost unrelentingly bleak story. Wells seems to be saying, as he was to throughout his writings, that humanity is nothing but a cog in the greater machine of science. This message comes across in the narrator's tone, in the losses that the world

> " While there might seem no reason to dwell upon one hysterical person during the evacuation of a city of millions, Mrs. Elphinstone does serve to provide a clean contrast to her sister-in-law, who provides the book's romantic center."

encounters, and even in the unexpected way in which the Martians die.

There is, though, in the middle of this dark story, a small episode that reflects the romantic ideals of courage, love, and mystery. As the world faces the destruction of London—possibly the worst imaginable catastrophe for an Englishman—the story's focal character at that point, the narrator's brother, becomes involved with two interesting women. Their story is not by any means adequately examined, but the fact that they appear in this novel at all opens a window to a worldview that the rest of the book labors hard to shut out.

That this ray of hope should come to the narrator's brother should be no surprise. The narrator's story has no place for romance. He is presented as a moral pragmatist, a philosopher who sees the doom and destruction and, like the true philosopher that he is, considers its place in his understanding of the world. The fact that the book gives readers a happy ending when he is reunited with his wife does nothing to negate the fact that that he does not think of her while he is out on the road, struggling for survival. His rationalism is what makes him turn the others whom he encounters into symbols for society's doomed framework. The curate, for example, stands for religion, and when the narrator sees him crumble psychologically he realizes that faith is not strong enough to offer solace when the pressure is truly on. The artilleryman seems to have a better idea for how to cope with humanity's destruction, an intricate plan that includes long-term and short-term goals and an abandonment of any hope for comfort in the foreseeable future. After mouthing his theories, though, he quits work and digs in to the comfort of cigars, whiskey, and cards. The narrator

simply walks away from him, an act even more disdainful than bashing the curate's head in. These two odd, dead-end relationships fit perfectly into the mood of the rest of the narrator's tale, in which humanity is beaten by the invaders at every turn.

Critics have noted that the section of the book that breaks away from the narrator's story to tell the story of his brother—Chapters 14, 16, and 17—show a weakness in Wells's ability as a novelist. This break does not appear to be the result of any overall narrative strategy but is instead just a matter of convenience: it enables Wells to keep with his narrator from the discovery of the first alien through the invasion's end, while showing what happened in the crowded metropolis at the same time. Certainly, there must be some way to do this that would be more grounded in the story, but most readers seem to feel that it is worth a little cheating in the story telling if that is what it takes to work the destruction of London into the book. Generally, then, the brother's story is considered a small, forgivable misstep, and little is said about it.

And, in fact, this break in the narrative continuity hardly makes any difference at all. The narrator and his brother are barely distinguishable from one another. Neither shows any independent characteristics, other than the roles they have to play in the book: one is a philosopher and the other a medical student, and both are motivated by staying alive. The most important differences between them seem to be those that are implied, rather than stated: the brother is younger, and unmarried. These qualify him to be a romantic hero in a way that the narrator could not.

On the road out of London, the narrator's brother stops to aid two women who are being accosted by some thugs. He is injured in the skirmish, and they take him into the carriage that he helped save for them. This act is, in itself, remarkable: it does come after he has risked his life for them, but it also comes during the exodus, while anyone slowed down is likely to be killed. The fact that they take him in shows two distinct traits. First, there is a sense of indebtedness, which the narrator himself encounters when he meets up with the artilleryman the second time; if he had not helped the man earlier, he may have been shot. Second, there is the need for protection, in a traditional gender-role sense. These women, traveling with a gun, a carriage, and money, know that they will need someone to save them from looters.

The two women are drawn as opposites. The first, Mrs. Elphinstone, is one of the few characters

What Do I Read Next?

- Readers interested in reading more of Wells's work can find this novel and *First Men in the Moon* (1901), *The Invisible Man* (1897), *The Island of Dr. Moreau* (1896), *The Time Machine* (1895) and several science fiction short stories all collected in a box set entitled *Science Fiction Classics of H. G. Wells* (2001) from Dover Thrift Editions.

- Before Wells, French author Jules Verne was considered to be the top science fiction writer of the nineteenth century. Verne's novels have stood the test of time. While *The War of the Worlds* might be looked at as the prototype for all sci-fi stories about alien invasions, Verne's *Journey to the Center of the Earth* (1864) has influenced an entire category of subterranean fiction.

- Ray Bradbury's 1950 novel *The Martian Chronicles* tells the reverse of this story, as humans colonize Mars to escape a destroyed Earth and impose themselves on Martian culture.

- Wells's life, spanning from the Victorian period to World War II, was one of the most interesting in twentieth century literature. One of the best biographies of him is *H. G. Wells: Desperately Mortal* (1986) by David C. Smith.

- *The H. G. Wells Scrapbook*, edited by Peter Haining, is organized, as its title says, as a scrapbook—it collects various bits of material related to Wells's life, including possible sources of inspiration, newspaper clips, and artwork from and inspired by his books. It was published in 1978 by Clarkson N. Potter, Inc.

---

in the book to be given a name, and certainly the only one to be named after the invasion begins. This can be contrasted with the main characters that the narrator meets, who are referred to by their social functions, curate and artilleryman. She, in turn, frequently talks about another named character, George, who is presumably Mr. Elphinstone. Her function in the novel is to become hysterical, unable to keep her wits about her in what are, admittedly, trying circumstances. While there might seem no reason to dwell upon one hysterical person during the evacuation of a city of millions, Mrs. Elphinstone does serve to provide a clean contrast to her sister-in-law, who provides the book's romantic center.

Mrs. Elphinstone is short and dressed in white, and her sister-in-law is slim and dark complexioned; she is nervous, while her sister-in-law is "astonishingly quiet and deliberate"; she speaks out loud to George as if he were there, while her sister-in-law has the present situation well in hand. The sister-in-law, who is never given a name, also has a pistol, which she does not hesitate to use. And she has the courage to tell the narrator's brother, "We have money," at a time when the road is filled with thieves.

Mrs. Elphinstone's sister-in-law, George's sister, is the most unique character in the book. She cuts a dashing figure. She can be vicious, but she can be kind. One has to wonder how she turned up in the middle of a story that has all of the rest of the race bowing down to the inevitable or, like the artilleryman, too lazy to resist.

The story of these two women is woven with romantic imagery. The threatening highwaymen and the out-of-control horses are conventions of Victorian bodice-rippers. That in itself would make their appearance unusual, but one could see it, like the appearance of the curate, as Wells's commentary on a particular social convention. But, within the dashing romance, Wells turns the convention on its head by giving the sister-in-law characteristics that were at that time traditionally left to men. She not only produces the pistol, but she fires it without flinching; she takes the horse's reigns after the narrator's brother enters the carriage; and, besides, she has the smoldering dark looks that one expects of a male character from a Brontë novel. Although the narrator's brother ends up as the leader of their small party, as is evidenced by the fact that he is the one who pays the passage of the three onto a boat, Mrs. Elphinstone's sister-in-law is still an independent spirit.

What this character meant to Wells is unclear. Probably, like the entire shift to the narrator's brother's perspective, she just materialized while he was writing and seemed like the right thing to do. He did not even give her a name, although in this section of the book he was naming characters. He did, however, give her a striking presence, making her the type of woman who is a match for a young medical student like the narrator's brother. The reader knows that the brother survived to tell the tale of his escape to the narrator, but nothing more is said of Mrs. Elphinstone's sister-in-law. She is just a strong-willed woman amongst a mood of general panic, and as such she gives the novel a romantic flair that it shows nowhere else. In that way, the brief interlude with the dark lady changes the book's entire meaning.

Source: David Kelly, Critical Essay on *The War of the Worlds*, in *Novels for Students*, Thomson Gale, 2005.

Anonymous

In the following brief review, an early critic praises Wells's novel.

Following in the wake of the sciences for half a century is a new species of literary work, which may be called the quasi-scientific novel. From M. Verne's prophetic submarine boat to Mr. Waterloo's prehistoric caveman, one could classify a score of romances which try to put into imaginative form the latest results in science and mechanics. Like all literature, too, the new novel is not content with presenting living embodiments of truth, but is fain to make guesses at the future. It is as yet experimental, and is quite too young to have produced an enduring masterpiece. The whole group can claim nothing that will live very far into the next century. It is hopelessly doomed, not more by its lack of artistic breadth of treatment than by its slipshod style, which betrays all the haste of the daily 'leader' to get into type.

Had Mr. Wells not been forestalled by Mr. Du Maurier, he would probably have called the novel before us *The Martians*. It is the story of the invasion of our earth by a company of intelligent beings from Mars. Kepler furnishes an appropriate motto: 'But who shall dwell in these worlds, if they be inhabited? Are we or they Lords of the World? And how are all things made for man?' Having created an atmosphere of reality for his story, the author proceeds in journalistic style to tell of the coming of the first cylinder. 'Flying swiftly and steadily towards me across that incredible distance, came the thing they were sending us.' Though the mysterious projectile fell near London, its arrival did not cause the sensation that an ultimatum to Spain would have done. Ten cylinders, each thirty yards in diameter and containing five Martians, arrived at intervals of twenty-four hours.

The war which ensues is melodramatic and shamefully one-sided. The strangers fight in vast spider-like engines, a hundred feet high, which stride along with the speed of a limited express. In each of these 'boilers on stilts' sat the guiding intelligence of the machine, smothering cities with seas of poisonous black smoke, and wiping out of existence artillery and battleships with his heat-ray, a sort of search-light which burned. As the gunner said, it was soon all up with humanity; we were beaten by superior mechanical genius. After completely subjugating humanity, the Martians are attacked from an unexpected quarter, and fall victims to our invisible allies, the bacteria. This is highly satisfactory and the happiest stroke in the plot.

Mr. Wells's conception of the Martians is not only daring as a piece of imaginative work, but interesting for its deduction from biological laws. He, in common with Mr. Du Maurier and Miss Corelli, is evidently a close student of M. Camille Flammarion. The highest intelligence in Mars, through the processes of evolution, is embodied in what is scarcely more than a huge round head with large protruding eyes, and a mouth surrounded by sixteen whip-like tentacles—a kind of octopus that is all brain. The complex apparatus of digestion is dispensed with, for he injects directly into his veins the blood of living creatures, including man. The interest of Mr. Wells's work is divided between the excitement of the story and speculations on the differentiated forms of life on this and other planets.

The author has written an ingenious and original work. Now and again in the intervals of a colloquial or hysterical style, one comes upon passages of sweetness and virility. The book has the tone of intense modernity, with notes of convincing realism and morbid horror. One misses the simplicity of Gulliver and the epic impressiveness of the stories of Sodom and Mt. Carmel. It is an Associated Press dispatch, describing a universal nightmare.

Source: Anonymous, "18. Unsigned Review, *Critic*," in *H. G. Wells: The Critical Heritage*, edited by Patrick Parrinder, Routledge and Kegan Paul, 1972, pp. 68–69.

Richard Hauer Costa

In the following excerpt, Costa discusses the structure and prose of The War of the Worlds.

The War of the Worlds is the archetype of all B-Grade films which present giant creatures from another world who invade the earth armed with death-ray guns. The imagery of the novel is so vivid that it is no wonder film scenarists have always thought of outer-space invasions in Wellsian terms. Moreover, one grasps from this novel the essential technique of all of Wells's scientific romances, *Dr. Moreau* excepted: the pinning of strange events to an everyday locale. The attraction of *The Invisible Man* lay in placing the astounding dilemma of Griffin within the slow village life of Iping. In *The War of the Worlds*, the narrator sees the effects of the Martian invasion on a village in Woking, a place familiar to Wells because he once retreated there to convalesce from illness. Wells wrote in his autobiography of bicycling about the district and "marking down suitable places and people for destruction by my Martians." However, unless one counts Wells's characteristic chiding of the clergy in the sketch of a curate whose corner on salvation barely tides him over the invasion period, there is no evidence that Wells was writing autobiographically or even thought of his Woking villagers as individuals.

Combined with a faultless adherence to down-to-earth physical details is a sense of time; the chronology of invasion is attributable about equally to a boy's imaginative grasp of war games and to a man's foreboding vision of terrestrial resistance turned to panic:

> About three o'clock there began the thud of a gun at measured intervals from Chertsey to Addlestone. I learnt that the smouldering pine-wood into which the second cylinder had fallen was being shelled in the hope of destroying that object before it opened. It was only about five, however, that a field gun reached Chobham for use against the first body of Martians.

> About six in the evening, as I sat at tea with my wife in the summer-house talking vigorously about the battle that was lowering upon us, I heard a muffled detonation from the common, and immediately after a gust of firing. Close on the heels of that came a violent rattling crash, quite close to us, that shook the ground; and, starting out upon the lawn, I saw the tops of the trees about the Oriental College burst into smoky red flame, and the tower of the little church beside it slide down the ruin. The pinnacle of the mosque had vanished, and the roof-line of the college itself looked as if a hundred-ton gun had been at work upon it. One of our chimneys cracked as if a shot had hit it, flew, and a piece of it came clattering down the tiles and made a heap of broken red fragments upon the flowerbed by my study window.

> I and my wife stood amazed. Then I realized that the crest of Mayberry Hill must be within range of the Martians' Heat-Ray now that the college was cleared out of the way.

❝ This extraordinary grasp of moment-to-moment detail made the novel easy prey for Orson Welles when in 1938 he converted it into the script which panicked a national radio audience."

This extraordinary grasp of moment-to-moment detail made the novel easy prey for Orson Welles when in 1938 he converted it into the script which panicked a national radio audience. Welles changed the setting from a British district to Grover Mill, New Jersey. That he drew from Wells the essential imagery of the invasion can be seen by a comparison of the novel's description of the Martian emerging from the space-cylinder with that of the radio script. In *The War of the Worlds*, Wells writes:

> A big greyish rounded bulk, the size, perhaps, of a bear, was rising slowly and painfully out of the cylinder. As it bulged up and caught the light, it glistened like wet leather.

> Two large dark-coloured eyes were regarding me steadfastly. The mass that framed them, the head of the thing, it was rounded, and had, one might say, a face. There was a mouth under the eyes, the lipless brim of which quivered and panted, and dropped saliva. The whole creature heaved and pulsated convulsively. A lank tentacular appendage gripped the edge of the cylinder, another swayed in the air.

In the scenario, the announcer gasps: "Good heavens, something's wriggling out of the shadow like a grey snake. Now it's another one, and another. They look like tentacles to me. There, I can see the thing's body. It's large as a bear and it glistens like wet leather. . . . The mouth is V-shaped with saliva dripping from its rimless lips that seem to quiver and pulsate. . . ."

Wells, apostle of the possible, registers himself in *The War of the Worlds* as the arch-enemy of the smug heralders of a new-century utopia in which the Union Jack would always prevail. "With infinite complacency," he writes in the opening paragraph of this novel about the routing of civilization, "men went to and fro over the globe about their little affairs, serene in their assurance of their empire over matter." Even as they luxuriate in a mental inertia of "all's well," keener intelligences from Mars covet the earth and lay plans to conquer it.

The same cautionary message, told in fable, is sounded in the previous romances: Man has no right to take control of the cosmic process for granted. Wells warns the reader to look at what happened to Mars—not only more distant from life's beginning but nearer its end. The conditions on Mars became increasingly uncongenial to higher life, Wells speculated, citing dropping temperature, thinning atmosphere, water drying up. Eventually, the planet was forced to search space for some buffer to cosmic annihilation. Once again Wells reinforces his convictions by presenting a picture of the expiring planet of war as a preview of earth's fate: an earth moving in Huxleyan inexorability along the declining parabola of evolution.

Wells, in effect, gives the reader a step-by-step report on how a breakup of metropolitan society would come about. Whereas *The Time Machine* and the yet-to-come *First Men in the Moon* are conceived poetically—that is, the myths of time travel and of moon visitation are rendered in such a way as to suspend the demands of verisimilitude—in *The War of the Worlds* the myth-poeic mood is exchanged for the methods of documentary realism. The Martian invasion is treated as an event of contemporary history.

It is not necessary to review the invasion in detail. Suffice it to say that the Martians are octopus-like creatures who are as far above mankind in intellect and command of machinery as humans are above animals. The Martians stride over the earth in machines of impregnable armor and devastate town and country with searchlights projecting rays more destructive than those of radium. They feed on human blood, and they force humanity, if it is not to perish or become as docile as the Eloi, to seek subterranean refuge. In the robot-like calculations of the Martians, Wells again underscores Huxley: evolution may produce creatures with superior brains, but it will not inevitably lead to a millennium.

In one of Wells's best passages of dramatic sociological speculation, a courageous artilleryman speaks of what life will be like for the survivors: "The tame ones [of us] will go like all tame beasts. . . . The risk is that we who keep well will go savage—degenerate into a sort of big, savage rat. . . . You see, how I mean to live is underground. I've been thinking about the drains. . . . Then there's cellars, vaults, stores, from which bolting passages may be made to the drains. And the railway tunnels and subways. Eh? You begin to see? And we form a band—able-bodied, clean-minded men. We're not going to pick any rubbish that drifts in. Weaklings go out again." The artilleryman's formula is suggestive of the fallout fears of a more modern day which Wells did not quite live to see. In *The War of the Worlds,* the worldlings are relieved of the necessity of putting survival conditions to the test by the intervention of an unexpected ally, the most minute of rescuers: the microbe. The invaders from Mars, lacking immunity to terrestrial diseases, are annihilated by one of them.

The possibility of life on Mars was part of the folklore in Britain at the end of the nineteenth century. The first volume of Camille Flammarion's *La Planète Mars* had appeared in 1892, thus making, as Bernard Bergonzi suggests, "a convenient and plausible superhuman adversary for mankind." Passages in Chapter I of Wells's novel are probably imitations of Flammarion; they describe the physical conditions of Mars and are strikingly similar to descriptions in Flammarion's books. Wells's theories of the superhuman qualities of the Martians were also in line with those of the *American* astronomer Percival Lowell, who in 1896 advanced the idea that the canals on Mars were the work of intelligent beings.

But H. G. Wells's "scientific" knowledge of Mars, impressive as it was, has in the years since the book's publication become secondary to the message that underlies the romance—a message few of Wells's early readers understood. The novel continued his practice of bludgeoning the complacent bourgeois. He who had forced his mean little undernourished and illness-ridden body out of dingy shops was at century's end, by dint of the scientific romances, forcing himself on literary society.

Who can say how many of Wells's dread forebodings in these four novels had their origin in Huxley's laboratory and how many in severe social maladjustment? The H. G. Wells of 1897, barely thirty but soon to be famous, was encountering difficulties in gaining acceptance in the cultivated world with its necessary insincerities and demand for credentials. It may be that the early Wells might have welcomed some such social upheaval concomitant upon invasion or similar catastrophe. As he wrote to his close friend George Gissing that very year, he might see in such an event, "a return to the essential, to honorable struggle as the epic factor in life. . . ."

At any rate, the assertions of the coarse artilleryman, though somewhat discredited later in the novel, mark perhaps a beginning toward a new, sociological Wells—one who, within less than a decade, would project in a landmark utopian book, *A Modern Utopia*, a thoroughgoing blueprint for world revolution in the hands of an intellectual and physical élite, the Samurai. If, as St. John Ervine insists, sociology ruined H. G. Wells, the beginnings of that forty-year penchant may be gleaned even in a masterful scientific romance like *The War of the Worlds*.

Source: Richard Hauer Costa, "The Scientific Romances," in *H. G. Wells*, Twayne, 1967, pp. 42–46.

Sources

Costa, Richard Hauer, *H. G. Wells*, Twayne's English Author Series, No. 43, Twayne Publishers, 1967, p. 42.

Review, in *Academy*, January 29, 1898, pp. 121–22.

Review, in *Critic*, April 23, 1898, p. 282.

St. Loe Strachey, John, Review, in the *Spectator*, Vol. LXXX, January 20, 1898, pp. 168–69.

Wells, H. G., *War of the Worlds*, Harper & Brothers, 1898.

Williams, Basil, Review, in *Athenaeum*, February 3, 1898, p. 178.

Further Reading

Bergonzi, Bernard, *The Early H. G. Wells: A Study of the Scientific Romances*, University of Toronto Press, 1961.
  Wells changed much after the turn of the twentieth century. By focusing on the early novels, Bergonzi is able to give concentrated consideration to the style that was evolving.

Haynes, Roslynn D., *H. G. Wells: Discoverer of the Future*, New York University Press, 1980.
  Haynes focuses on the influence of science on Wells's ideas, giving the history of scientific development in the nineteenth and twentieth centuries in the balance.

Hillegas, Mark R., *The Future as Nightmare: H. G. Wells and the Anti-Utopians*, Southern Illinois University Press, 1967.
  This book is principally about Wells, but it draws connection to the other writers who have raised fears about what the future might bring, including George Orwell (*1984*) and Aldous Huxley (*Brave New World*).

Huntington, John, "The Logical Web," in *The Logic of Fantasy: H. G. Wells and Science Fiction*, Columbia University Press, 1982, pp. 57–84.
  Huntington examines Wells's novels as an expression of thought, using *The War of the Worlds* as an example of his overall thesis.

The Wind in the Willows

Kenneth Grahame

1908

The Wind in the Willows was published near the turn of the century—1908 in England and 1909 in America. It was based on stories that Kenneth Grahame, the author, told to his son Alastair, starting on Alastair's fourth birthday. The principle characters of these stories are talking animals who live in and around a river, though to the animals, it is "*the* River" (author's emphasis). At the time of the work's publication, Grahame had already published four books of fiction. He was most well known for his collections of stories *The Golden Age* and its sequel *Dream Days*. Though the works were written about children, they were not written for children. *The Wind in the Willows* was not initially well received because it deviated from his previous works; however, it eventually became the work that he is most famous for, enjoyed by children and adults alike.

The principle characters in the novel, though they all have their faults, are idealized in many ways. Several virtues are epitomized in Mole, Rat, Badger, and Toad, so much so that they become themes. There are numerous examples of hospitality, forgiveness, compassion, generosity, and humility. Even the arrogant Toad is able to humble himself and put aside his conceited ways in the end, having matured though a succession of trying circumstances with the guidance and help of loyal friends.

Author Biography

Kenneth Grahame was born in Edinburgh, Scotland, on March 8, 1859, the third of four children to James Cunningham and Bessie Ingles Grahame. When Grahame was just five years old, his mother contracted scarlet fever and died. James Grahame "never recovered from the loss of his wife and did virtually nothing to help his children recover from it," as Kuznets says in *Kenneth Grahame*, and the Grahame children moved with their maternal grandmother, Granny Ingles, to Cookham Dene, a town in Berkshire, along the Thames River.

At age nine, Grahame began school at St. Edward's School in Oxford with his older brother Willie. Here, Grahame excelled at both academics and athletics and still had "time to roam the gardens of Oxford and to continue his loving relationship with the river Thames, which runs through Oxford as it does through Cookham Dene, and indeed through most of Grahame's life," as Kuznets states in her biography. Although Grahame was an accomplished scholar, his family refused to further his education, and at age 16, he ended his schooling and applied for a clerkship at the Bank of England in London.

Banker's hours were short in London, and Grahame participated in the London Scottish Regiment drills, volunteered at Toynbee Hall, served as honorary secretary of the Shakespeare Society, and explored the city and the countryside. Shortly after his father's death in 1887, Grahame began to submit his writing for publication, usually anonymously. His description of the Berkshire Downs, "By a Northern Furrow," was published in December of 1888 and is the first published piece definitively attributed to Grahame. The following decade was a productive one for Grahame's writing. He published *Pagan Papers* (1893), *The Golden Age* (1895), *The Headswoman* (1898), and *Dream Days* (1898), as well as many essays and stories.

On July 22, 1899, the forty-year-old Grahame married Elspeth Thomson, despite the disapproval of their family and friends. Their only child, Alastair, was born on May 12, 1900. In 1906, the Grahames moved back to Cookham Dene, and Grahame commuted to work until he resigned in 1908, citing health problems.

The origin of *The Wind in the Willows* dates back to 1904, when Grahame began telling bedtime stories featuring a mole, a giraffe (later replaced by Toad), and a rat to celebrate Alastair's fourth birthday. After some urging by Constance Smedley of the American magazine *Everybody's,* Grahame

Kenneth Grahame

collected the stories into a single manuscript. *The Wind in the Willows* was initially rejected by publishers as "it was apparently written for children, not for adults who wanted to reminisce about childhood," as Kuznets says, but was eventually published in 1908. *The Wind in the Willows* became a classic children's book, and A. A. Milne later used the novel as the basis for the play *Toad of Toad Hall*, produced in 1930.

Grahame wrote little after the publication of *The Wind in the Willows*. His next published work after *The Wind in the Willows* was a 1913 essay, "The Fellow That Goes Alone," about the joys of solitude in country life. Grahame enjoyed country living and non-literary pursuits in his later years, but he was troubled by circulatory problems, the strains of his marriage, and the death of their son in 1920. On July 6, 1932, Grahame died in his home in Pangbourne of a cerebral hemorrhage.

Plot Summary

Chapter 1: The River Bank

The Wind in the Willows begins with Mole who is spring-cleaning his house when he finds that "something up above was calling him imperiously."

Media Adaptations

- In 1930, A. A. Milne wrote a successful musical stage version called *Toad of Toad Hall*, which focuses on the adventures of Toad. A. A. Milne is most well-known for his *Winnie-the-Pooh* books.

- Numerous animated film adaptations have been made of *The Wind in the Willows*. One of the earliest and most interesting is the 1949 Disney version entitled *Ichabod and Mr. Toad*, which also included stories from Washington Irving's *Sketch Book of Geoffrey Crayon*. A recent popular version was produced by HBO Studios in 1996.

- Several audio versions of *The Wind in the Willows* have been recorded, including one produced by Naxos on Audio CD in 2002.

Giving in to curiosity, he quickly digs his way to the world above. Everything is new to him. He has not even seen a river before. The first person he makes an acquaintance with is Water Rat, who invites Mole on a boat ride and an impromptu picnic. Rat explains much to Mole about aspects of the world above ground and the River Bank community. After the picnic, they head back upstream towards Rat's hole in the bank of the river. Mole ends up almost tipping the boat when he excitedly grabs the sculls (or oars) from Rat, which Rat readily forgives.

Chapter 2: The Open Road

Mole and Rat pay a visit to Mr. Toad. Toad is happy to have the company and pleased to meet Mr. Mole, and he convinces them to join him in a cart and horse trip, which is his latest craze. Their first two days on the road are fairly uneventful. On the third day, they come to their first high road, where they are nearly run down by an automobile moving at high speed. The cart is wrecked from veering off the road. Toad is taken by a new craze—automobiles—and becomes useless as Mole and Rat deal with the situation. They walk to the nearest town where they catch a train that takes them home.

Chapter 3: The Wild Wood

Mole decides to journey alone to the Wild Wood so he can meet Mr. Badger when he is unable to convince Rat to take him. At first, Mole is not alarmed upon entering the Wild Wood, but he quickly becomes lost and frightened. He ends up hiding in the hollow of a tree. When Rat becomes aware of Mole's absence, he sets out after him. He finds Mole and allows him to rest awhile before heading home. A sudden snowstorm hits in the meantime, making it difficult for them to find their way, and they become lost. Luckily they stumble upon the home of Mr. Badger.

Chapter 4: Mr. Badger

Mr. Badger promptly takes in the lost travelers. He feeds them, gives them dry clothes, and allows them to warm themselves by his fire. Rat fills in Mr. Badger on Toad's automobile craze, and they decide that once the winter has passed, they will "take Toad seriously in hand." Otter also arrives at Mr. Badger's. He explains how the River Bank community has been worried about Rat and Mole being gone. Mole and Badger get more acquainted while they tour the many passages of his home. Badger eventually takes his visitors to the edge of the Wild Wood in one of his extensive passages so that they can get home without further incident.

Chapter 5: Dulce Domum

Mole has a sudden and almost irresistible urge to see his home again after encountering its smell on a journey. Rat decides that they should go and see it, to Mole's delight. Since he has been away for so long, he doesn't have much for them to eat. A group of field mice stop by to sing carols. Mole is distressed at having nothing to feed them, as he has traditionally done in the past. Rat sends one of the mice off to buy groceries. The mice continue to entertain Mole and Rat until the food arrives, and they have supper. Rat tells Mole that he has a "ripping little house."

Chapter 6: Mr. Toad

Spring arrives, and Rat and Mole are preparing the boat for another season when Badger stops by to tell them that the time has come to intervene with Toad's irresponsible behavior with motorcars. Badger makes an unsuccessful attempt to requite Toad, after which they lock him in his room and guard him "till the poison has worked itself out of his system." Toad manages to escape. He steals a car, smashes it, and ends up in jail.

Chapter 7: The Piper at the Gates of Dawn

Rat, returning from an engagement with the Otters, brings news to Mole of the family's missing child, Portly. They decide to search for the boy by paddling upstream in the boat. Rat starts to hear beautiful music, which Mole is also eventually able to hear. They follow it until they find a mythical creature with horns and hoofed feet, at which lies the lost child, asleep. The creature vanishes, and they take the child to his father. Rat and Mole seem to forget their mythical helper, though they feel a little strange.

Chapter 8: Toad's Adventures

The jailor's daughter takes pity on Toad and devises a plan for his escape that involves disguising him as a washerwoman. Toad is able to attain his freedom but finds that he has rather limited resources since his coat and money, among other things, are still in his jail cell. An engine driver allows Toad aboard his train after being convinced that Toad is "a poor unhappy washerwoman." After riding for several miles, the engine driver realizes that they are being pursued by the police. Toad confesses all to the driver, who still manages to take pity on him. The driver slows down the train at an advantageous point and Toad jumps off. Having evaded his pursuers, he finds himself in an unfamiliar wood.

Chapter 9: Wayfarers All

Rat finds himself restless on a beautiful summer day. He encounters field mice making early preparations for winter as well as swallows who reminisce of their southern winter homes. Rat is thinking about what it would be like to do more traveling when a seafaring rat wanders by. The Sea Rat tells him of his experiences abroad. Upon his departure, the Sea Rat has convinced Rat to come with him. Rat returns home to gather a few things before heading off, but Mole is ultimately able to prevent him from leaving.

Chapter 10: The Further Adventures of Toad

Having spent a night in the unfamiliar wood, Toad is a little cold but happy to be free. He follows a canal and eventually encounters a horse towing a barge with a stout woman aboard. Using his washerwoman outfit to his advantage, he is able to convince the bargewoman to take him aboard. The woman sees through his disguise when Toad is unable to help her with her washing and throws him overboard. Insulted, he steals her horse, which he sells to a gypsy. Still needing a way to get home, he hails a passing motorcar, which turns out to be the car he had stolen earlier. He is not recognized through his disguise. Toad convinces the gentlemen in the car to let him drive for a while. In his excitement at being behind the wheel again, he reveals his identity and ends up smashing the car again. He is once more pursued by the police but escapes when he falls into the swift-moving river and is swept downstream.

Chapter 11: "Like Summer Tempests Came His Tears"

The Water Rat pulls Toad from the water. After telling Rat of his adventures, he gets cleaned up. Rat tells Toad that Toad Hall has been taken over by Stoats and Weasels. Toad, infuriated, attempts to infiltrate his home twice but is repelled by the Stoat guards. Badger arrives at Rat's, having devised a plan that will allow Toad, Rat, Mole, and himself to liberate Toad Hall while the Weasels are enjoying a banquet in celebration of the Chief Weasel's birthday. On the morning they intend to carry out the plan, Mole journeys to Toad Hall alone and, using Toad's washerwomen disguise, beguiles the Stoats into believing that a massive invasion of Badgers, Rats, and Toads would be coming that night.

Chapter 12: The Return of Ulysses

After being outfitted with weapons by Rat, they follow a passage that takes them underneath Toad Hall and into the pantry. The Chief Weasel is in the midst of singing a derisive song about Toad when the four friends spring forth from the pantry, scaring away the Weasels at the banquet and the Stoats outside. The morning after the attack, Badger convinces Toad that he needs to have a banquet to celebrate. Preparations are made and invitations sent out. Shortly before the event, Toad gives a speech and sings a song to an imaginary audience in his room, though he is very humble when the actual guests arrive.

Characters

Badger

Badger, sometimes referred to as Mr. Badger, commands great respect as well as fear among the animals. Rat is the first to mention him: "Dear old Badger! Nobody interferes with *him*. They'd better not." By the end of the novel, he is especially feared by the Weasels, who quiet their infants by telling them that "if they didn't hush them and not fret them, the terrible gray Badger would up and get them." Toad is able to humble himself and apologize for his reckless behavior with automobiles when Badger has him alone in a room. It is only after he is with Rat and Mole again that is able to say "No! . . . I'm *not* sorry!"

Badger is also considered very wise. He is rarely questioned by Rat and Mole and only occasionally by the arrogant Toad. He is also impartial in his shrewdness. When Toad says "I'll learn 'em to steal my house!" in reference to the Stoats and Weasels, Rat corrects him, replacing "learn" with "teach." However, Badger insists that Toad's manner of speaking is more appropriate. Later, however, when Mole recounts how he visited the Stoat guards in disguise and exaggerated their coming attack, Rat and Toad both reprimand him for giving away the element of surprise while Badger commends him for his cleverness at putting the animals on edge.

Although he is wise, respected, and feared, he is not above being compassionate and forgiving. He is always willing to assist those in need, especially friends. He takes in Mole and Rat without hesitation when they are lost in the Wild Wood. He gives them dry clothes and food and allows them to stay the night. He takes great pains in attempting to get Toad to behave responsibly during his motorcar craze and is still selfless towards him when his efforts do not work. He looks after Toad Hall while Toad is in jail and helps Toad retake his home when it is overrun with Weasels and Stoats.

Bargewoman

Toad meets with the bargewoman shortly after his escape from jail when he is lost in the woods. She is a stout and rather rustic woman. She seems quite willing to assist Toad when she thinks he is a washerwoman that might be able to help her with her laundry, but wastes no time in throwing him overboard when it turns out that he has no skill whatsoever at washing.

Engine Driver

The engine driver seems willing to help anyone in a desperate situation. When Toad is disguised as a washerwoman, he gives Toad a ride on his train because Toad, as the washerwoman, can't get home to see her kids because she has lost her money. When they are later pursued by the police, Toad confesses to his crimes and trickery, but the engine driver is still willing to help him evade his pursuers, saying ". . . you are evidently in sore trouble and distress, so I will not desert you."

Gentlemen in the Motorcar

The gentlemen with the motorcar mostly serve to move the plot along. The first time they appear in the text, they merely provide Toad with a car to steal. When they appear later on, they pick Toad up on the side of the road and let him try driving their automobile, intrigued by the idea of a washerwoman driving. Toad becomes so elated at being behind the wheel again, after spending so many days in jail, that he gives himself away and also ends up smashing the car. One of the gentlemen, after finding a policeman, pursues Toad across a field until Toad falls into the river, which sweeps him back to the River Bank community.

Gypsy

Toad encounters the gypsy after riding a few miles on the horse he stole from the bargewoman. Finding himself famished, he moves toward a caravan, or covered wagon, beside which are the gypsy and a pot over a fire radiating delicious smells. He goes over to see if he can find a way to get something to eat. The gypsy quickly asks if he can buy Toad's horse. Toad bargains with him and eventually gets six shillings and six pence for it, plus as much of the gypsy's stew as he can eat.

Jailor's Daughter

The jailer, knowing how fond his daughter is of taking care of animals, allows her to take care of Toad upon her request. She brings his meals, which are likely better than what the other inmates get, and she keeps him company. They grow to like each other more and more, so much so that the jailer's daughter can no longer stand seeing Toad locked up. She devises a successful plan for him to escape in which Toad is disguised in the clothes of her aunt, who is the washerwoman for the jail.

Mole

Mole is arguably the most passionate of all of *The Wind in the Willows* characters. He is always willing to help another animal in need. Even when Rat, a rather compassionate character himself, is not able to muster the initiative to go looking for the

Otter family's lost child, Portly, Mole insists they do something, saying "I simply can't go and turn in, and go to sleep, and *do* nothing, even though there doesn't seem to be anything to be done." Mole is generally very excited about people, whether meeting them for the first time, or seeing them after a long absence. When Toad returns home from his "adventures," Badger is somewhat sympathetic in his greeting, but a little too reserved for Toad's liking, while Mole is ecstatic at seeing him and gives Toad exactly the type of greeting he wants, telling him that he is a "clever, ingenious, intelligent Toad!" Mole's emotions are stirred by more than just people. When seeing Rat's boat for the first time, his "whole heart went out to it at once. . . ."

Mole is new to the River Bank community and to the entire world above ground. In the beginning of the novel, he is much like a child, seeing everything for the first time, as demonstrated when he says to Rat, "all this is so new to me. So—this—is—a—River!" He is very eager to do and experience new things, as when he grabs the oars from Rat in order to try rowing. He is quite astute, quickly picking up skills and subtle intuitions, as demonstrated in the following lines:

> He learnt to swim and to row, and entered into the joy of running water; and with his ear to the reed stems he caught, at intervals, something of what the wind went whispering so constantly among them.

Mole is also rather independent for someone so new to the area, which gets him into trouble at the beginning of the novel. In his usual manner, he is very anxious to meet Mr. Badger, whom he's heard much about from Rat. Rat, who is content to wait for Badger to call on them, is too passive for him. Mole decides he will venture into the Wild Wood alone in order to meet Badger, which leads to him getting lost and stuck in a snowstorm. But he does get to meet Badger before his journey is over. Toward the end of the novel, Mole again ventures out alone in disguise and convinces the Stoats that a massive attack is coming to Toad Hall. This makes their small ambush more effective and also shows how much wiser he has become in the ways of the above ground world.

Otter

Otter is a good friend of the novel's four main characters, Rat, Mole, Badger, and Toad, and comes into the story several times in person and by name. He often serves as a link to the River Bank community at large. Upon his first appearance in the text, he says, "All the world seems out on the river today. I came up this backwater to try to get a moment's peace, and then stumble upon you fellows!" There are several more occurrences of Otter bringing information from the larger community into the reader's scope, another important one being when he arrives at Badger's house and describes how the community was alarmed that Rat and Mole were missing.

Otter is also distinct in that he has the closest thing to a representation of a family in the book. The four main characters are all bachelors. Otter not only has a son, Portly, but seems to have a family, which is referred to as "the Otters." The Otters are never specifically called a family, but it is clearly implied by the fact that they entertain Rat at their house as a unit and inquire about Portly as a unit.

Portly

While Portly does not affect the overall events in *The Wind in the Willows*, he is central to chapter 7, "The Piper at the Gates of Dawn." Portly is Otter's son and is so young that he is referred to as a baby at one point. Portly has a tendency to wonder off alone, which is usually not a worrisome event since everyone in the River Bank knows and looks after him. In this chapter, however, he is gone for multiple days, which causes the Otters a certain amount of anxiety. Rat and Mole find him at the feet of a mythological creature, presumably the "piper" mentioned in the chapter title, by following his music. Portly is not mentioned elsewhere in the book, which is in keeping with this anomalous chapter that also presents the one-time development of magic as well as the strongest development of a character's family, i.e., the Otters.

Rat

Rat, also known as River Rat, is one of the four central figures in the novel. One of the first noticeable characteristics about Rat is his generosity. He is the first person that Mole meets above ground, and Rat welcomes him to the River Bank by taking him on a boat ride and bringing along a picnic for them to share, which includes "coldtonguecoldhamcoldbeefpickledgherkinssal adfrenchrollscresssandwichespottedmeatginger beerlemonadesodawater —." Coming home after the picnic, Rat invites Mole to stay at his house for the night. The novel spans roughly a year, and Mole lives in Rat's house for almost that entire time. One of the few exceptions is when they stay at Mole's house for a night, and even then, Rat demonstrates his generosity by giving one of the field mice money to buy groceries for a nice supper, allowing Mole to be a good host to his visitors.

Rat is also a compassionate character, though he seems to be more inclined to help others when it is a matter of proper appearance or behavior. When he finds Mole after he wandered off alone in the Wild Wood, the first thing Rat says to him is, "You shouldn't really have gone and done it.... We river-bankers, we hardly ever come here by ourselves." When he pulls Toad from the river after he has escaped the police, he immediately tells him to "go off upstairs at once ... and put on some of my clothes and try and come down looking like a gentleman." This may explain why he is at first inclined to do nothing when young Portly goes missing. He may feel helpless since solving the problem has nothing to do with instilling proper animal behavior.

Sea Rat

The Sea Rat is another character that is central to one chapter, "Wayfarers All," but appears no where else in the text. Rat encounters the Sea Rat one day when he is feeling restless, and he doesn't know why. The Sea Rat tells Rat of his adventures abroad. Rat is swept away in his stories and intends to go with the Sea Rat to his next destination, but he is stopped by Mole. The encounter with the Sea Rat enhances one of themes of the novel—the struggle between a desire to indulge in the familiarity of home and the desire to experience new things away from home.

Stoats and Weasels

The Stoats and Weasels take over Toad Hall while Toad is in jail, to the surprise of Badger and Mole who are looking after it. Rat tells Toad how "they took and beat them severely with sticks . . . and turned them out into the cold...." They are the antagonists for the last two chapters of *The Wind in the Willows*, "'Like Summer Tempests Came His Tears,'" and "The Return of Ulysses." However, they are more complex than that, as Rat explains: "They're all right in a way—I'm very good friends with them ... but they break out sometimes ... and then—well, you can't really trust them...." In keeping with Rat's description, one of the Weasels, shortly after being expelled, comes back to Toad Hall to see if he can be of service in any way.

Toad

Toad is the driving force for the plot twists of a large portion of the book. His automobile craze leads to him stealing a car and getting sentenced to twenty years in prison. He escapes from prison and returns home, being periodically pursued by the police on the way. As he journeys home, he meets several interesting people, including the engine driver, the bargewoman, and the gypsy. He eventually finds himself at Rat's house, who tells him that the Stoats and Weasels have taken over his house. Thus the four principle characters must join together to recapture Toad Hall.

Rat gives a fairly accurate description of Toad's personality, though he is probably being a little too kind:

> So simple, so good-natured, and so affectionate. Perhaps he's not very clever—we can't all be geniuses; and it may be that he is both boastful and conceited. But he has got some great qualities, has Toady.

Toad does enjoy a simple life. Having inherited a great amount of wealth, he does not have to work to provide for himself. Instead he is constantly looking to fill his life with whatever hobby most captures his attention at the time. He also enjoys entertaining and will often try to combine entertaining his friends with his hobbies, which leads to the cart trip with Mole and Rat. Toad is also indeed arrogant and enjoys being the center of attention. He often dreams of delivering speeches and singing songs describing his exploits to a captivated audience, as he pretends to do just before the party celebrating the recapture of Toad Hall. In the very end, Toad seems to have mended his ways, no longer acting so arrogant and self-centered. As the text indicates, "He was indeed an altered Toad!"

Themes

Hospitality

Hospitality comes naturally to many of the characters in *The Wind in the Willows*. The text is filled with occurrences of one animal offering food and/or shelter to another. At times it is merely a casual exchange among friends, like Rat's long standing engagement of going to the Otters' for dinner, or Rat paying a call on Toad and introducing his friend Mole. At other times, there is a specific need, as when Badger brings Rat and Mole out of the cold of a snowstorm, followed by a pair of lost hedgehogs the next morning. The novel's most impressive example of hospitality is that of Rat taking Mole into his home, which ends up lasting at least a year, having only met Mole that day. There is neither discussion of payment nor any sort of anticipation that Mole will return the favor. It is simply accepted. Shortly after Mole is invited to stay at Rat's, the text reads, "When they got home, the Rat made a bright fire in the parlor...." It does not

Topics For Further Study

- Grahame focuses on the mammals, and one amphibian, that live in and around a river. What else can be found in a riverbank ecosystem? Write a 500-word essay considering Grahame's depiction of a riverbank as it compares with actual river ecology.

- Read *Animal Farm*, by George Orwell. How does his use of anthropomorphized animals differ from that of Grahame's? How are they similar? What sort of literary devices does each take advantage of through the use of animals?

- Read or attend a performance of A. A. Milne's *Toad of Toad Hall*. Milne did not cover the events of all the chapters in *The Wind in the Willows*. Identify a chapter that was omitted by Milne. Write a stage version of that chapter and direct a performance of it.

- What literary work is Grahame referring to when he titles the final chapter of *The Wind in the Willows* The Return of Ulysses? What parallels can be made between Toad and the protagonist of this literary work?

---

say "when they got to Rat's home" because it is now home to them both.

Forgiveness

Forgiveness comes quickly and easily in *The Wind in the Willows*, regardless of the size the offense. When Mole apologizes to Rat for taking the sculls away from him in the boat, which leads to Mole and the luncheon basket going overboard, Rat immediately responds with "That's all right, bless you!" He then goes on to invite Mole to stay with him awhile so that he can learn to row and swim.

Toad is forgiven several times throughout the book for much more serious misconduct. Even four Weasels, taken prisoner during the recapture of Toad Hall, are treated kindly when they demonstrate contrition: "They were very penitent, and said they were extremely sorry. . . . So I [Mole] gave them a roll apiece, and let them out at the back, and off they ran." Toad is also able to let bygones be bygones when one of the Weasels returns to Toad Hall looking to be of service. It is only with the slightest condescension that he pats the Weasel on the head and gives him an errand to run.

Humility

While there are not obvious examples of humility throughout the text, it is a major theme because it is a virtue that one of the principle characters, Toad, clearly does not possess but clearly needs to learn. His friends are very patient with him as he, time and time again, embarrasses them by making a fool of himself. As Rat says, "Do you suppose it is any pleasure for me . . . to hear animals saying . . . that I'm the chap that keeps company with jailbirds?"

In the end, after a series of trying circumstances that Toad manages to fare only through the kindness of strangers and the loyalty of his friends, he is finally able to humble himself. Even when Otter encourages him during the celebration of the recapture of Toad Hall, Toad responds with "I merely served in the ranks and did little or nothing."

Compassion

The events of *The Wind in the Willows* are often shaped by characters helping other characters. Toad is most frequently the person in need of assistance. His friends Badger, Mole, and Rat are always there for him, whether they are locking him in a room in order to cure him of his automobile craze or putting together a plan to drive the Stoats and Weasels out of Toad Hall. Toad's escape from prison would have been impossible if it wasn't for the kindness of complete strangers. The jailor's daughter takes pity on Toad merely because she hates to see animals suffer. The engine driver helps Toad upon their first meeting, both when he thinks Toad is a washerwoman and when he is aware that he is a Toad on the run from the law. The gentlemen that

Toad steals the car from are a little too angry to help Toad as Toad, but they do not hesitate to help him when he is disguised as the washerwoman.

Toad is not the only one who gets himself into trouble. As soon as Rat realizes that Mole has gotten himself lost in the Wild Wood, he starts out after him. When Rat and Mole both end up lost in the snowstorm, Badger keeps them from freezing by taking them into his home. Otter, also worried about Rat and Mole, comes to find them at Badger's and offers to guide them home. Rat and Mole are able to return the favor when they find Otter's son Portly when he goes missing.

Home

A tension exists in *The Wind in the Willows* between the desire to stay near the comforts of home and the urge to see and explore new places. In the very beginning, Mole, tired of spring-cleaning, decides to leave his home. "Something up above was calling him imperiously." For nearly all of the rest of the novel, Mole lives away from his underground dwelling, returning only once, again, at the beckon of an overwhelming urge: "the wafts from his old home pleaded, whispered, conjured, and finally claimed him imperiously." The same word is used to describe both urges—"imperiously"—possibly to indicate the parallel strength of their call.

Rat also struggles within this dichotomy. He is generally a person that enjoys being home; both on the cart trip with Toad and when visiting Badger's house, his desire to return to his hole in the riverbank is explicitly indicated. Nonetheless, in the chapter entitled "Wayfarers All," he is determined to partake of the adventures described by the Sea Rat. It is only by force that he is he prevented from leaving.

As demonstrated by the recapture of Toad Hall, home is something worth fighting for. Yet Toad, probably more than any of the principle characters, is afflicted by a powerful wanderlust, which is apparent when he coaxes Rat before the cart trip:

> You surely don't mean to stick to your dull fusty old river all your life, and just live in a hole in a bank, and *boat*? I want to show you the world! I'm going to make an *animal* of you, my boy!

By the end of the book, there is no reason to believe that Rat, Toad, and Badger have not returned to their homes. As for Mole, it is not specified whether he continues to live with Rat or goes back to his own quaint lodgings. The "joy and contentment" they all find is not contingent on whether they live near or far away from their home. *The*

Wind in the Willows shows the appeal of either possibility but not which one to choose.

Style

Golden Age of Children's Literature

The Golden Age of children's literature has been defined as lasting from the publication of Lewis Carroll's *Alice's Adventures in Wonderland* in 1865 until World War I. Before that time, literature written for children was primarily considered a didactic tool, leaving little room for the imagination. During the Golden Age, the imaginative aspect of children's literature blossomed. The works within the genre were more readily enjoyed by children.

Scholars consider *The Wind in the Willows* to be a contributor to the Golden Age, published near the period's end. Though it may be valued for the examples the animals provide to children with their loyal friendships and displays of hospitality and compassion, its primary purpose is to entertain, in true Golden Age form.

Animal Novel

The tradition of using anthropomorphized animals in both oral and written storytelling is quite old and worldwide spread. Up until the Golden Age, its usual form was the animal fable: short tales in which anthropomorphized animals are used to parody or otherwise criticize human failings. These were often archetypal characters with one or two dominant attributes. One of the most common archetypes is the trickster, an example of which is the Big Bad Wolf from the story of Little Red Riding Hood. The characters in *The Wind in the Willows* are not archetypes, nor is the novel allegorical like fables. As Kuznets points out in her biography of Grahame:

> *The Wind in the Willows* is a book of fair length, with well-developed animal protagonists, who participate in a similarly well-developed plot, built on conflict, both internal and external, to some resolution of those conflicts.

This defies the form of the fable, and, in fact, shares more characteristics with the novel, which is intended for entertainment rather than moral instruction. It was in fact, one of the first animal novels, which paved the way for others to come, such as *Charlotte's Web*, published in 1952, or more recently, *Redwall*, published in 1986.

Compare & Contrast

- **1908:** The speed limit for automobiles is 20 miles per hour (mph) in England. Automobiles are found mostly in Western Europe and North America.

  Today: The speed limit for automobiles in England is as high 70 mph, though it is not uncommon for the flow of traffic to move at 80 mph. Automobiles are found in virtually every country in the world.

- **1908:** The population of the Great Britain is approximately 40,000,000.

  Today: The population of Great Britain is approximately 60,000,000. While this is a 50 percent growth, roads and urban development have increased at a drastically higher rate, countered by a sharp decrease in cultivated and undeveloped land.

- **1908:** Women in Great Britain do not have the right to vote and have little political power in general, especially with the death of Queen Victoria in 1901 and the ascension of King Edward VII to the throne.

  Today: Women over the age of thirty have had the right to vote since 1918, with women over the age of twenty-one gaining the right in 1928. Women occupy many high level political positions, including seats in the parliament. Margaret Thatcher was elected prime minister in 1979. The monarchy is again occupied by a woman, Queen Elizabeth II.

Historical Context

Grahame was born during the Victorian Era, when the British Empire was at its peak. Its financial institutions were strong and stable. Their manufacturing industries were ever-growing. However, right about the time the first major tragedies were occurring in Grahame's life—the death of his mother at age five and his father's desertion of his family when Grahame was eight—Britain found that its stable roots were being shaken. The Crimean war with Russia from 1854 to 1856 had already cast doubt on England's military strength. Threats of war with Germany, France, Russia, and even the United States compromised overall confidence in the Empire.

British society was also stressed by unrest and fluctuation. In 1870, educational reform brought literacy to the working classes, allowing them to expand their awareness within the political, intellectual, and literary arenas, shifting focus and power away from the old land-owning families. The Trade Union Amendment Act of 1876 gave legal sanction to trade unions, leading to dissatisfaction among industries and major strikes in the 1880s and 1890s. In the beginning of the twentieth century, laborers found a major political voice with the formation of the Labour Party, which is still one of the two main political parties in England to this day. Education reform continued with the founding of the Worker's Education Association in 1903. The roots of the Irish independence movement were also established around this time.

The women's movement contributed to this period of social upheaval. Britain's male-dominated society, though oppressive to half of the population, had maintained a certain amount of stability in the early part of the Victorian age. When liberation organizations established themselves, like the National Union of Women's Suffrage Societies in 1897, the Woman's Social and Political Union in 1903, and the Women's Freedom League in 1908, the male-dominated status quo began to break down.

Changes were occurring throughout England, not just in the cities and industrial areas, but also in the countryside. The rural life was diminishing as urbanization spread. According to Peter Hunt in *The Wind in the Willows: A Fragmented Arcadia*, the last three decades of the nineteenth century saw Britain's cultivated land reduce by half. Railroad lines crisscrossed England as well as roadways, with the automobile becoming more and more

1996 film portrayal of Kenneth Grahame's The Wind in the Willows, *with (from left) Terry Jones as Toad, Steve Coogan as Mole, and Eric Idle as Rat*

popular. Not only was the countryside disappearing, but it was becoming less pristine and much more easily accessible.

Hunt suggests that all these changes gave rise to a nostalgic attitude toward the Victorian life-style that was reflected in some of the literature of the times: "the post-Romantic fashions of the Victorian age became more and more 'precious' and, by Victorian standards, corrupt." He goes on to explain that these writers "would look 'inward' but they also looked out to the countryside, to an arcadian past...."

Grahame was among these writers. As Kuznets quotes in her article "Kenneth Grahame and Father Nature, or Whither Blows *The Wind in the Willows*?" Grahame once said to his Scribner's editor that he wanted to write a book that was "free of problems, clear of the clash of sex." Grahame certainly had his share of problems in his lifetime, not only during his childhood, but also later with an unhappy marriage, and a nearly blind son. *The Wind in the Willows* was a window to a simpler place and a simpler life: a life "clear of the clash of sex," and thus no unhappy marriages and no women's movements disrupting a male-dominated society: a life "free of problems," where children don't have disabilities, and where a child may sometimes get lost but is found again

through the help of a magical piper: a place where there are no wars, but only the occasional skirmishes with Stoats and Weasels, who are repentant enough the next morning to get pats on the head: most importantly, a place where a small riverbank community is still intact, pristine, and buffered from the world at large by an untamed wood.

Critical Overview

Grahame at first had trouble placing *The Wind in the Willows* with a publisher. His English editor, John Lane, rejected the manuscript, as did *Everybody's*, the American periodical that initially solicited it. It was finally picked up in 1908 by Methuen in England. Methuen was still skeptical; so much so that he would not pay an advance on it, though Curtis Brow, Grahame's literary agent, was able to get him to agree to rising royalties. In 1909, Scribner published the book in America, but only after receiving a letter from President Theodore Roosevelt in its praise.

Critics did not receive Grahame's new work favorably. After publishing *The Golden Age* in

1895 and its sequel, *Dream Days*, in 1898, both to wide acclaim, his readers were in anticipation of another book involving the Gold Age children. As Peter Hunt puts it in *The Wind in the Willows: A Fragmented Arcadia*: "Kenneth Grahame had been a famous and much-admired writer *about* children, and here, it seemed, was a book *for* children. . . ." It was flouted as an "animal fable," as Lois Kuznets points out in *Kenneth Grahame*. As Grahame's audience adapted and began to appreciate the novel for what it was, its success slowly came to fruition. By 1959, Peter Green reports, in his well-known biography of Grahame, that "*The Wind in the Willows* has achieved over a hundred editions, and an average sale of about 80,000 copies." Its success has continued to grow since. It is now, without a doubt, considered a classic of children's literature.

Criticism

Daniel Toronto

Toronto has a bachelor's degree in creative writing and literature and currently works as an editor. In the following essay, Toronto considers why Grahame chose to write a story about animals that behave like humans.

Grahame's *The Wind in the Willows* is one of the first English examples of a novel using animals as protagonists. Using animals that talk and behave like humans in storytelling is by no means unique to Grahame; the tradition of using anthropomorphized animals dates back thousands of years, appearing in the mythology and tales of many ancient cultures. In Lewis Carroll's *Alice's Adventures in Wonderland*, published more that forty years earlier, Carroll had a talking rabbit and a talking cat, among others. However, Grahame's novel is distinct from Carroll's in that the animals are the protagonists, with well-developed, complex personalities. They are the ones who move the plot along.

The lack of predecessors to rely on or imitate begs the question of why he chose to write such a book. What tools or advantages does he gain when it comes to the reader's perception of the text? Kuznets, in her article, "Kenneth Grahame and Father Nature," quotes Grahame as once saying that he wanted to write a novel "free of problems, clear of the clash of sex." Many scholars argue that Grahame did not succeed in this regard, saying that there are still underlying class conflicts, age conflicts, as well as sex conflicts, despite the fact that there are very few characters specified as female

> Again, Grahame is drawing on the anthropomorphic tradition. Readers willing to accept talking animals are also willing to accept that they are about the same size as humans, regardless of what kind of animal it is."

and no major female characters. Bonnie Gaarden describes her initial reaction to this scholarship in "The Inner Family of *The Wind in the Willows*":

> The small but emphatic voice of my childhood reading insisted that these characters were like nothing so pedestrian as adult human males; they were the Rat, the Mole, the Toad, and the Badger—ageless, timeless, genderless.

Indeed, it is difficult for most readers to deny a certain light-hearted feel to *The Wind in the Willows*, even when Mole is lost in the woods, Toad is sentenced to jail, or the four main characters fight to liberate Toad Hall. The prose is free of many of the burdensome issues that come with having human protagonists. Kuznets, in her biography, *Kenneth Grahame*, writes, "Grahame derives from the [anthropomorphic] tradition a . . . sense of the possibilities of eluding both internal and external censors in using animals rather than humans." The use of animal protagonists suppresses a reader's tendency to question the credulity or quality of the work when certain inconsistencies and improbabilities occur, such as those relating to sex, age, and size. Grahame, however, does more than just fool our censors; he uses the advantages that these characters have as animals as well.

It would be scholastically irresponsible to say that the dearth of female characters in *The Wind in the Willows* is not noticeable. A substantial amount of criticism has been written addressing that very issue (and no doubt casual readers have also noticed this). I would venture, however, that it is less noticeable because the large majority of the characters are animals. Gaarden, writing in "The Inner Family of *The Wind in the Willows*," proffers the following reason:

> Grahame's refusal to so much as name any female animal until the very last page of the book does not

What Do I Read Next?

- Grahame's *The Golden Age* (1895) is a collection of stories about five imaginative children retreating from their repressive families and into their own fantasies. This work made Grahame famous.

- *Dream Days* (1898) is another collection of stories by Grahame. It is the sequel to *The Golden Age*, involving the same five children. It furthered Grahame's success as a writer.

- *Charlotte's Web* (1952) by E. B. White, like *The Wind in the Willows*, is a novel featuring animal protagonists. In it a pig is saved from being slaughtered through the efforts of a spider who writes words in her web.

- *Redwall* (1986) by Brian Jacques is an animal novel that tells a magical and adventuresome story in which a civilization of rats plays out the age-old conflict of good versus evil. This is the beginning of an entire series of books.

- Several abridged versions of *The Wind in the Willows* have appeared over the years. Joan Collins adapted it into a fifty-two-page "retold for easy reading" version, which was published in Britain in 1983 by Ladybird Books. Bob Blaisdell adapted it into a slightly longer version, which was published in 1995 by Dover publications.

- Several sequels were written by William Horwood, which are entitled *The Willows in the Winter* (1993), *Toad Triumphant* (1995), and *The Willows and Beyond* (1996).

---

obliterate the feminine. Rather, it circumvents the reader's habit of classifying individuals primarily by sex, and leads us to differentiate, instead, by species.

The casual observer generally cannot identify the sex of most animals. With some it is more obvious, but certainly not with Rats, Moles, Badgers, and Toads, especially if they are solitary, i.e., without the opposite sex with which to compare. This can lead to an impression that animals are sexless as well as a tendency to give animals a default gender. It the case of *The Wind in the Willows*, it is male.

There are a number of inconsistencies having to do with age throughout the text. Rat, for example, is usually portrayed as an adult, but not always, as when Toad remarks, "My! won't he catch it when the Badger gets back!" This puts Badger in the role of the father figure, and reduces Rat to a child who has done something wrong. Mole, on the other hand, usually takes on the role of the child, or the "good child" as Gaarden describes him in her article "The Inner Family of *The Wind in the Willows*. He is dependant on Rat for rescue and emotional support, he overestimates his capacities, he has fits of impatience, and he is full of wonder. However, with the very first page of the novel, Mole is "spring-cleaning his little home." Children do not own their own homes, and they generally refrain from cleaning their own rooms, much less an entire house, without being asked. This flexibility in age, like sex, may go unnoticed by readers because of an ageless quality animals seem to possess. Even more than sex, age is very difficult to determine in animals. On the other hand, humans are quite aware of their own life cycle and what each of its stages entails. A human child that owns a home would be much more perplexing to readers.

The sizes of the animals are not so much inconsistent, but rather, incorrect. No toad in the world is large enough to drive a car. No mole is tall enough to walk with its head "beside a horse's head." A badger is vastly larger than a toad. Again, Grahame is drawing on the anthropomorphic tradition. Readers willing to accept talking animals are also willing to accept that they are about the same size as humans, regardless of what kind of animal it is. However, Grahame does more than give animals human qualities. He also takes advantage of their animal abilities, as Cynthia Marshall explains in "Bodies and Pleasures in *The Wind in the Willows*:

Indeed, so successfully does Grahame effect the bond between readers and characters on the basis of shared pleasures that on those rare occasions when the beastly status of a character does receive explicit mention, we feel our own senses expanding to encompass the experience.

One of the more poignant examples of "our own senses expanding" is when Mole encounters the smells of home:

> We others, who have long lost the more subtle of the physical senses, have not even proper terms to express an animal's intercommunications with his surroundings, living or otherwise, and have only the word "smell," for instance, to include the whole range of delicate thrills which murmur in the nose of the animal night and day, summoning, warning, inciting, repelling. It was one of these mysterious fairy calls from out the void that suddenly reached Mole in the darkness, making him tingle through and through with its very familiar appeal. . . .

Not only do the readers get to perceive the world though animal sensitivities, they are also allowed to enjoy closeness to nature without the burdens that go along with it. There is a strong sense of home, and the comforts of home, throughout the story. Yet the characters spend most of the time outside or in holes or along riverbanks or in a wood. It would be difficult to write such a story about humans without the connotation of effort. At best, the characters might enjoy the comforts of a nice, long camp out. Since animals always live in the wild, and since people are not always aware of what they must do for survival, it is easier to believe that they live effortlessly in their holes along the river and in the woods.

In "Bodies and Pleasures in *The Wind in the Willows*," Marshall writes:

> At once beast and human, small and large, the characters move easily between radically discontinuous positions, partaking of the delights available to all and the troubles germane to none. The animal characters are undifferentiated, unrestrained. . . .

Many scholars argue that Grahame did not achieve a story either clear of problems or free of the clash of sex. Their reasoning is often quite sound, and I agree with some of it. *The Wind in the Willows* is certainly not rid of all the cares of the world. Subtextual layers of the cultural context in which it was written can be unearthed. Signs of Grahame's own personal troubles and his family's dysfunction may be detectable. Still, he is able to draw on the anthropomorphic tradition as well as his own imagination in order to find a space for a story that is somewhat uncluttered by the rules of sex, size, and age. He constructed a sort of imperfect umbrella under which he could shelter his captivating novel from many of the burdens of the world. He did this so that he might entertain his

disabled son Alastair with stories at the age of four. He has done it for countless other children.

Source: Daniel Toronto, Critical Essay on *The Wind in the Willows*, in *Novels for Students*, Thomson Gale, 2005.

Kathryn V. Graham

In the following essay, Grahame discusses the intended readership of The Wind in the Willows, *asserting that the novel's form and structure were meant to prepare Grahame's son for what to expect when attending school.*

The Wind in the Willows is most innocently appreciated as nostalgic animal fantasy: a pastoral celebration of animal life along the riverbank, where the four primary "animal gentlemen" Mole, Rat, Badger, and Toad enjoy a series of picaresque adventures that often involve "messing about in boats" but always end with a return to their snug and comfortable homes. The novel's episodes promote friendship, courtesy, competence, courage, and generosity in an idyllic world where sex, work, violence, and death are beyond the horizon. Experienced readers contextualize the story in various ways. For Humphrey Carpenter the riverbank constitutes an Arcadia, one of the secret gardens characterizing the Golden Age of children's literature. Kenneth Grahame's biographer Peter Green sees the novel as a psychological escape for its author, Grahame's refuge from his disastrous marriage and his mundane, if well-compensated, job in the Bank of England. Lois Kuznets points out the mock-epic Odyssean theme and structure. Peter Hunt sees the novel as animal idyll, *Bildungsroman,* sociological document on class warfare, anarchist comedy, burlesque, nostalgia, sexist conservative tract—"by fits and starts, all of these" (97).

The novel richly repays all such readings, but here, I would like to head back to the text's origins, curiously neglected by most interpreters of the book and warranting examination of the sort Marilyn Butler calls for when she observes, "The writings of the past ask for an educated reading, as far as possible from within their own discourse or code or cultural system" (43). It is particularly worth remembering that the narrative involves not only a specific author but also a specific addressee. *The Wind in the Willows* began as a series of bedtime stories that Grahame told his son Alastair in 1904, evolved into story letters when the two were apart in 1907, and finally took published form in 1908. In this essay, I contend that what Grahame wanted to pass down to Alastair, from father to son, from public-school old boy to future new boy, is material designed to

> Though *The Winds in the Willows* serves admirably as a general guidebook to the ways of that interesting young animal the English schoolboy, its fictive and rhetorical strategies specifically reflect the particular anxieties and circumstances of its author and its addressee."

inform the child about his future education, presented in a form meant to be palatable and accessible to the four-year-old audience of the oral stories and the seven-year-old on holiday with his governess. The story of the neophyte Mole, who makes friends, acquires knowledge and skills, and widens his world, is specifically applicable to the situation Alastair was shortly to face. Though *The Winds in the Willows* serves admirably as a general guidebook to the ways of that interesting young animal the English schoolboy, its fictive and rhetorical strategies specifically reflect the particular anxieties and circumstances of its author and its addressee. In that sense, this obliquely cautionary and educational tale written by an initiate of the system is schoolboy lore customized to meet the needs of a one-boy audience.

* * * * * *

Interestingly, the one piece of schoolboy fiction we are sure Grahame read, *Tom Brown's Schooldays* (1857), resulted from the identical impulse: Thomas Hughes wrote the novel as he pondered what to tell his eight-year-old son Maurice about entry into the world of school. But if Alastair—eccentric, overemotional, physically handicapped, precocious, maternally dependent—were to meet and recognize himself in late-Victorian realistic schoolboy fiction, he would see his prototype mocked, bullied, and tagged with a derisive effeminate nickname, such as "Molly" or "Fluff." Such misfits, in fiction, faced the torment of being tossed in a blanket or held over a fire—or in the real-life case of Lewis Carroll at Rugby, might have books defaced with such a taunt as "C. L. Dodgson is a

muff." *The Wind in the Willows*'s covert resemblances to classic school stories suggest that rather than frighten Alastair by modeling his work on the available realistic novels and periodicals (*The Captain, The Boy's Own Paper*), Grahame chose a more oblique and palatable form for dispensing schoolboy survival tips.

The choice to present material through animal fantasy rather than school story would have been heartily endorsed by C. S. Lewis, a near contemporary of Alastair Grahame's, had he read *The Wind in the Willows* in childhood rather than first encountering it in his twenties. In "On Three Ways of Writing for Children," Lewis articulates his dislike of the realistic schoolboy fiction he had read as a child. Lewis's hostility centers on the disappointing illusions of realism: "I never expected the real world to be like the fairy tales. I think that I did expect school to be like the school stories. The fantasies did not deceive me; the school stories did" (1078). Such stories gripped him with the longing to be a popular, athletic, and successful schoolboy; they returned him to his own world "undivinely discontented" (1078). This discontentment, perhaps the natural lot of the ordinary many, would be a still greater risk for a boy carrying Alastair Grahame's extraordinary burdens.

In his excellent biography of Kenneth Grahame, Green reports that "Alastair Grahame was born, prematurely, on 12th May 1900; and to his parents' intense distress, proved to have congenital cataract of the right eye, which was completely blind, together with a pronounced squint in the left—which was also 'over-sighted'" (227). The delicate child of unhappily married parents, Alastair "became the recipient of both his parents' thwarted emotions" (227). To say that he was spoiled would be an understatement. Carpenter comments on Alastair's "precocious, cheeky manner which nauseated Grahame's friends" (152). Green deplores Elspeth Grahame's refusal to recognize her son's physical handicaps and mental instability and argues that she created a fantasy of his physical prowess and mental brilliance: "The boy's whole life became a struggle to live up to the impossible ideal she set him; and in the end the strain proved too great" (228). Kenneth Grahame did not share his wife's illusions about Alastair. As a former public-school boy himself, Grahame knew from experience what his overindulged and overpraised son would face. As he was writing the story-letters to the seven-year-old Alastair in 1907, he must have been agonizing over the ordeal that according to upper-middle-class convention lay ahead: departure from the cocoon of mother's adoration and nanny's cosseting to the harsh male world of the English public school.

Grahame himself had enjoyed success in this overwhelmingly masculine world, where boys slept five or six to a room, the teachers were all men, and there was only the rarest contact with woman in the form of Matron, who helped the smaller boys and sometimes dispensed treats in the kitchen to the homesick and dispirited. After early experiences with the arbitrary and bizarre ways of the schoolmasters at St. Edward's School, Oxford, he learned to conceal or indirectly present his own ideas while winning prizes for Divinity and Latin prose in 1874 and the Sixth Form Class Prize in 1875. He earned the respect of his fellow students through gaining First Fifteen colors for Rugby, making the second eleven in cricket, and serving as Senior Prefect (head of school). He wrote essays for the school paper and spoke in the Debating Society. But despite his successes, Grahame clearly remembered the pain of his own entry into the world of the public school. In an essay called "The Fairy Wicket," published in *The National Observer* in 1892, he sketches the vivid image of "a small school-boy, new kicked out of his nest into the draughty, uncomfortable outer world, his unfledged skin still craving the feathers where into he was wont to nestle." Green reports Grahame's belief that "the ordeal of school is unavoidable; henceforth one must live in the enemy's camp, wear his colors, and mouth his public shibboleths. What is more insidious is the possibility that one may come to believe in them" (32).

Most written records of school days, autobiographical and fictional alike, fall into one of several categories, depending on the writer's attitude. Royston Lambert identifies five distinct types of schoolboy, three of whose attitudes are likeliest to result in written accounts: the conformist, who believes in both the ends and the means of his particular school's system; the innovator, who seeks reform and improvement; and the rebel, who rejects the institution outright (358). The attitude Grahame expresses comes closest to fitting into the category Lambert calls "ritualist," that of a boy who follows school rules without accepting them. As a ritualist and as a parent who seems to have understood his son's particular circumstances, Grahame apparently found none of the usual direct methods of instruction appropriate for Alastair but instead encoded the lore necessary for schoolboy survival in the anthropomorphic animal story that became *The Wind in the Willows*. It may be, then, that one reason Grahame did not directly offer advice about

schoolboy life was an ambivalent reluctance to either ally himself with the "enemy camp"—the world of arbitrary, dogmatic adults—or directly attack the system propounded in that camp, a system under which he himself had done well. Another reason might be his understanding that Alastair would never excel at sports requiring hand-eye coordination and stamina and his tactful reluctance to draw attention to his own successes in such schoolboy endeavors.

Whatever his reasons, Grahame's strategy involved doing what is implicit above in such previously quoted phrases as "kicked out of the nest" and "unfledged skin." He transmuted school into the Riverbank, schoolboys in general into animals, Alastair in particular into Mole, who, involved in explicitly domestic doings as chapter one of *Wind in the Willows* begins, says "Hang spring-cleaning," leaves his dark hole, and scratches his way upward into the sunlit meadow. The choice of a mole as the story's new boy is particularly well calculated given its immediate audience, the partially blind Alastair. But any new boy at school might, to a lesser extent, be a mole of sorts—obliged to leave the dark, womblike confines of home and nursery for enlightenment. Like the mole (if we are to take his animal nature with any seriousness), the new boy ejected from his nest cannot at first see the spring charms of his new environment. He must learn the ways of the Riverbank (or school); get along with the other animals (or boys); find a particular ally to protect, instruct, and befriend him; and win the respect of his comrades through athletic endeavor.

In making the place of learning a river and its environs, Grahame appropriates an accessible and popular metaphor. As land-dwelling humans find, water is an alien element but one to which they can, with practice and instruction, grow accustomed. Horace Annesley Vachell's *The Hill*, a 1905 novel about contemporary Harrow, begins with a didactic passage based on this likeness: "You're about to take a header into a big river. In it are rocks and rapids, but you know how to swim, and after the first plunge, you'll enjoy it." Besides being alien, "not-home," a river is dynamic. Like school, it is not simply a place but a means of taking those who embark away from home or back again, a motif Christopher Clausen delineates in "Home and Away," his comparison of *The Wind in the Willows* and *Huckleberry Finn*. Finally, the river is a distinctively congenial choice for Grahame's immediate audience. The Grahame family lived on the Thames, at Cookham Dene in Alastair's childhood, later at Pangbourne. Interestingly, the primary sport in *Wind in the Willows*, boating, was Kenneth

Grahame's favorite recreation; and Alastair, despite his visual impairment, was a competent boater and swimmer.

Having found his way to the riverbank and met one of its habitués, the Water Rat, Mole candidly admits that he has never been in a boat or lived the jolly river life. Rat takes the neophyte under his wing, as an older boy might a younger, and shares the lore of the world that is, in his words, "brother and sister to me . . . and company, and food and drink. . . . It is my world, and I don't want any other. What it hasn't got is not worth having, and what it doesn't know is not worth knowing." Rat smooths Mole's way with introductions to other members of his set. He warns Mole away from undesirables, notably the animals of the Wild Wood: "weasels—and stoats—and foxes and so on. They're all right in a way—I'm very good friends with them—pass the time of day when we meet and all that—but they break out sometimes, there's no denying it, and then—well, you can't really trust them, and that's a fact." Some critics read the Wild Wooders as projections of Grahame's bourgeois social fears (proletarians, socialists, radicals); but in the context of life at school they are equally apt representations of the bounders, blighters, and cads a keen schoolboy loathes, those who are not "our sort" once the process of indoctrination has taken hold. Such indoctrination is a staple of realistic schoolboy fiction, where, for instance, it takes the form of feuds between classical and modern students ("our sort" and "cads" respectively) in Talbot Baines Reed's *The Cock House of Fellsgarth* (1891) and Compton Mackenzie's *Sinister Street* (1913).

The Wind in the Willows begins this process by offering a series of object lesson for Alastair, or any other new-boy-to-be. In one such instance, Mole

> began to feel more and more jealous of Rat, sculling so strongly and easily along, and his pride began to whisper that he could do it every bit as well. He jumped up and seized the sculls so suddenly that Rat . . . was taken by surprise and fell backwards off his seat. . . . "Stop it you *silly* ass!" cried the Rat, from the bottom of the boat. "You can't do it! You'll have us over!" The Mole flung his sculls back with a flourish, and made a great dig at the water. He missed the surface altogether, his legs flew up above his head, and he found himself lying on top of the prostrate Rat.

The immediate result may be humiliation for the rash and untutored new boy—Mole has to "brush away a tear or two with the back of his paw" while Rat "kindly looked in another direction"—but the more enduring result is Rat's transmitting to Mole the lore of river life, and "very thrilling stories they were, too, to an earth-dwelling animal like Mole."

Having met the friend who will be David to his Jonathan, Mole makes the acquaintance of authority as it exists for the Riverbank animals—Badger, who resembles nothing so much as a gruff but kindly headmaster of the Arnoldian type. As Grahame's text describes Badger, "He seemed, by all accounts, to be such an important personage and, though rarely visible, to make his unseen influence felt by everybody about the place." Literally the *eminence grise* of the story, Badger embodies moral authority; his purpose is to encourage, exhort, and, if necessary, reform those under his protection. Mole's first sustained encounter with Badger begins as he and Rat, frightened and exhausted, knock at Badger's door. Badger's initially sharp and suspicious response turns quickly to fatherly concern: "He looked kindly down on them and patted both their heads. 'This is not the sort of night for small animals to be out,' he said paternally. 'I'm afraid you've been up to some of your pranks again, Ratty.'" after taking care of their physical comforts—a fire, dry clothes, supper— Badger assumes the place of adult authority "in his armchair at the head of the table" and evokes Rat and Mole's explanation of the suspected "pranks." He "nodded gravely at intervals as the animals told their story, and he did not seem surprised or shocked at anything, and he never said, 'I told you so,' or 'Just what I always said,' or remarked that they ought to have done so-and-so, or ought not to have done something else" (the last two things Badger left unvoiced are clear echoes of the Anglican prayerbook's General Confession). Avoiding heavy-handed didacticism, Badger allows the two animals to examine their own behavior and mistakes and to draw conclusions for themselves—rather like Mr. Rastle's gentle guidance of Stephen Greenfield in Reed's *The Fifth Form at St. Dominic's* (1871). This lighter approach that trusts to Rat's and Mole's essential good instincts, however, will not be Badger's way with the fascinating bad boy of the River, Toad of Toad Hall. Hearing of Toad's latest outrageous behavior, Badger announces, "Well, we'll take Toad seriously in hand. We'll stand no nonsense whatever. . . . We'll *make* him be a sensible Toad." When Rat and Mole inquire about Badger the next morning, the two young hedgehogs (who from their deferential behavior might be seen as representatives of lower school or a lower class) inform them, "The master's gone into his study, Sir . . . and on no account wants to be disturbed." Remote or nurturing, gruff or sympathetic as circumstances demand, patiently attentive, decisive but not judgmental, morally upright but not censorious, Badger is the ideal headmaster for the Riverbank "school."

The attempted reform of Toad is perhaps Badger's greatest pedagogical challenge, variously referred to as "taking in hand," "rescue," "conversion," and "mission of mercy." Because of his particular status, Toad must change for his own good and for the good of Riverbank society. Arguably the most memorable character in the novel, Toad is rich, self-centered, charming, and driven by the impulse of the moment. No discreet and dutiful member of the middle class, he never delays gratification, pursues fad after fad to comically catastrophic conclusions, and brags about his home, wealth, wit, and good looks. Along with Mole and Rat, Toad can be seen as a recognizable type of schoolboy: like Flashman of *Tom Brown's Schooldays* or "Demon" Scaife of *The Hill,* Toad is a flamboyant narcissist, a sort likely to run into trouble at school. Indeed, when Carpenter speculates humorously on the animals' educational backgrounds, he says, "One could imagine Toad enjoying a brief period at Eton or Harrow before being expelled."

Toad's determination not only to break ranks but to go out-of-bounds into the Wide World of society—and women—sets him apart from the school community. Claudia Nelson points out that "of all the animals, Toad has the greatest affinity with the human (adult and—worse—female) world" (167). His passion for motor cars has an undoubted sexual quality and brings him into contact with nurses, jailer's daughters, washerwomen, and the dreaded bargewoman. As *The Wind in the Willows* demonstrates, to follow the errant path of a character like Toad invites disaster. His unfettered individualism is personally harmful; but worse, in the eyes of Rat and Badger, it lets the side down. Toad "has been corrupted by modern gadgets; he has made a public fool of himself; he is conceited and irresponsible and a spendthrift; he has disgraced his friends" (Green 245). It is worth noting how this catalogue of sins blends the personal and the collective. Toad's self-indulgence not only hurts him but also rends the fabric of riverbank society. His downfall enables the disreputable stoats and weasels to invade Toad Hall and, ensconced there, to mock the respectable animals of Toad's set. In the cautionary case of Toad, Grahame lays down for a son encouraged to think too much of himself the foundation of public school spirit: loyalty to the group. Observing the perils of Toad, Mole and Alastair learn the importance of team spirit: never, never let the side down. Or in the words of the Eton Boating Song (performed *in situ suo* just a few miles down the Thames from the Grahames' house or the riverside prototype of Toad Hall, Mapledurham House),

"Yes we'll still swing together / And swear by the best of schools."

In Mackenzie's *Sinister Street,* an experienced older boy, Rodber, gives the young protagonist, Michael Fane, some good advice about school life: " 'Look here,' said Rodber, 'I don't mind telling you, as you'll be a new kid, one or two tips about school. Look here, don't tell anybody your Christian name and don't be cocky' " (87). Shortly thereafter, *Sinister Street*'s narrator wryly characterizes the practical schoolboy virtue of anonymity: "Michael congratulated himself that generally his dress and appearance conformed with the fashion of the younger boys' dress at Randall's. It would be terrible to excite notice. In fact, Michael supposed that to excite notice was the worst sin anybody could possibly commit" (92).

Adults may come to learn that several sins are worse than notoriety, but the schoolboy lore that Grahame passes down through *The Wind in the Willows* concurs with that offered in *Sinister Street.* As we have seen, the cockiness of Toad never goes unpunished. We never learn what Rat, Mole, or Toad may have been christened, for the characters never address one another except by surname or the generic "old chap"—only the younger of the hedgehogs, Billy, and Portly, Otter's young son, have the juvenile feature of Christian names, which signal that they are still at home with mother. Conversation in the novel is stylized to the point of impoverishment, in Kuznets's phrase "full of colloquial expressions, some of them juvenile taunts and insults, rather hackneyed in its use of descriptive adjectives like 'jolly' and 'stupid' " (113). (For proof that such adolescent reductiveness transcends cultures, classes, and decades, one need only cite the contemporary equivalent to Mole and Rat's "jolly" and "stupid": Beavis and Butthead's division of all things into what is "cool" and what "sucks.")

As all these conventions would suggest, *The Wind in the Willows,* like other schoolboy fiction, stresses giving up eccentricity and individuality in order to become part of a community. Much of Mole's essential "moleness" is left behind as the novel proceeds. He gives up his underground hole, though, like a schoolboy on holiday, he is allowed a return for Christmas before leaving, presumably forever. Becoming a Riverbanker, he puts aside childish ways. After chapter five we hear no more of his tears; by chapter nine he feels confident enough to persuade Rat against becoming a Wayfarer; and at the conclusion he joins Badger, Rat, and Toad in the mock-epic battle to regain Toad Hall from the stoats and weasels. With Mole's "insider" status solidified, the novel's last image is of the four animals linked together as heroes of their generation, much like Stalky, Beetle, and M'Turk at the end of Kipling's *Stalky & Co.* (1899).

As many nineteenth- and twentieth-century British novels and memoirs testify, schooldays were, or at least were considered, the crucially formative time of a ruling-class man's life. In the Duke of Wellington's memorable pronouncement, "The Battle of Waterloo was won on the playing fields of Eton." Cyril Connolly, an Eton contemporary of Alastair Grahame's, wrote more negatively of the school's potent influence in *Enemies of Promise:*

> In fact were I to deduce any system from my feelings on leaving Eton, it might be called *The Theory of Permanent Adolescence.* It is the theory that the experiences undergone by boys at the great public schools, their glories and disappointments, are so intense as to dominate their lives and to arrest their development. From these it results that the great part of the ruling class remains adolescent, schoolminded.... Early laurels weigh like lead and of many of the boys whom I knew at Eton, I can say that their lives are over. (251–52)

A feminist reader might see indoctrination of the sort Connolly describes and *Wind in the Willows* enacts as the cultural weaning of ruling-class males. Trained to detach themselves from and subsequently to idealize, corrupt, or mystify the influence of mothers, aunts, sisters, and (female) lovers-to-be, Connolly's Etonians and Grahame's Riverbankers remain, like Bertie Wooster and the other Drones of P. G. Wodehouse's fiction, perpetual schoolboys and bachelors at heart. Literary descriptions of their state generally have more charm than do its actual consequences.

* * * * * *

Idyllic though its story may be for many readers, whether children, permanent adolescents, or adults, *The Wind in the Willows* held some dark ironies for its immediate audience of one and its author. When it proved enormously successful, Grahame resigned from the Bank of England to devote himself to writing, but he never produced another book. And if he wrote *The Wind in the Willows* with the primary goal of advising Alastair on the attitudes, behavior, and language that would lead to success in one of England's famous public schools, his narrative failed to achieve its desired effect. Rather than send Alastair away at the customary age of eight (Grahame's own age when he started at St. Edward's), the family kept the child at home with a governess until he was ten. Then, with

trepidation, they sent him to prep at the Old Malthouse School in Dorset. Luckily, it was a cheerful and permissive place. Alastair was not so fortunate when in 1914 he went from his prep school to Rugby, one of the "great schools" and his mother's unrealistic choice. "Rugby," writes Alison Prince, "was a tough school, ruthless in its dealings with any boy who put on airs or who seemed in any way odd or less than a 'good sport.' Alastair, full of airs and debarred by his poor sight from all sports except swimming, had been thrown into a life which was, by his standards, little short of hell" (285). He was desperately unhappy and resigned within months. In January 1915 the Grahames got him into Eton, where he managed to stay a little more than a year. Alastair completed his education under private tutors at home and eventually entered Christ Church College, Oxford. His contemporaries at university recalled that he always seemed miserable. Struck by a train, Alastair died, a probable suicide, at the age of twenty. He seems never to have adjusted to the schoolboy world whose lore is so memorably encoded in *The Wind in the Willows.*

Source: Kathryn V. Graham, "Of School and the River: *The Wind in the Willows* and Its Immediate Audience," in *Children's Literature Review Association Quarterly,* Vol. 23, No. 4, 1998–1999, pp. 181–86.

Michael Mendelson

In the following essay, Mendelson examines the contrary states of "individualistic hedonism and communal affection" in The Wind in the Willows.

All readers or listeners know that there are really two stories in *The Wind in the Willows:* that of the madcap, adventurous Toad the Gaol-breaker; and that of friendship, home life, the simple joys of "messing about in boats," the story of Mole, Rat, and Badger. The story of Toad-of-the-Highways is centrifugal, an outgoing, Odyssean song of the open road; the other is centripetal, a riverbank idyll of domestic, pastoral pleasure. And because the values of the dusty road and the riverbank seem so opposed, readers naturally tend to align themselves with one of these stories at the expense of the other.

Roger Sale, for example, has a distinct predilection for the homely adventures of the River Bank; for him, the book as a whole is "'about' coziness," while Toad belongs "over to one side" (174, 185). William W. Robson also finds the finest insights in the friendship of Rat and Mole, with the Toad chapters playing "a scherzo in the symphony" of quiet domestic life (98). And Humphrey Carpenter, though he grants that Toad "has a certain energy," maintains that the idiom of adventure was not the author's forte and that Toad lies outside the "heart of Grahame's Arcadian dream" (*Gardens* 154, 161). Such priorities were not, of course, shared by the work's first audience, Alistair Grahame, who responded enthusiastically to his father's original stories in which "Toad played the principal part" (Carpenter and Prichard, *Oxford Companion* 573). Most other child readers remain devoted to the Toad, as we may deduce from adaptations of Grahame's story: A. A. Milne's unifocal dramatization of the story in "Toad of Toad Hall"; the 1949 Disney film, which claims that for children Toad is "the most fabulous character in English literature"; and more recently, the Nederlander Theater's production, promoted with buttons that read "I Toad You So."

This split between child and adult sensibility, between what Geraldine Poss calls the mock-heroic and arcadian impulses within the text, has itself been the focus of considerable criticism. Peter Green was perhaps the first to refer to the "double theme" of the book (*Grahame* 202), while Carpenter asserts that "there are really two separate books" (*Gardens* 229n). Peter Hunt has taken this position to its logical end, arguing that "if there are two texts in *The Wind in the Willows,*" they are structurally autonomous: "Mole's serious story once resolved, we can go on to Toad's more farcical one" (116). Criticism, then, has tended to separate the two stories, as if the contrasting impulses that motivate the narrative action operated independently. I will argue, however, that the clash between two such natural instincts as domesticity and romantic enthusiasm generates the special richness of the text as a whole. Instead of separating the two stories and devaluing one, I examine how Grahame not only juxtaposes but interlaces his two different plots and values.

The question of narrative structure becomes all the more provocative when we remember that the oscillation between the two stories resulted from careful engineering. Peter Green has argued plausibly that Grahame composed the Toad sequence first, the episodes of the River Bank and the Wild Wood second, and the two set pieces, "The Piper at the Gates of Dawn" and "Wayfarers all" last (*Beyond the Wild Wood,* chap. 11). In the final . . . 1908 copy, however, Grahame steadily alternated between the stories of the open road and those of the woodlands, an alternation that I will argue functions as a narrative dialectic between the "contrary states" of individualistic hedonism and communal affection. As the plot progresses, Grahame advances ever

> In the end, it is the 'bijou riverside residence' that breeds the heroes of legend, and the life this side of the 'well-metalled road' that 'holds adventure enough.'"

more subtle variations of this dialectical argument. It is my intention, then, to explore Grahame's dialectic by paying close attention to the plotting of the work (the narrative order in which the simple chronology of the two stories is rearranged) and especially to the relation between adjoining chapters and groups of chapters. This method should clarify embedded contrasts and parallels that require the reader to activate their meaning by filling in lines of connection only suggested by the text. Ultimately, this formal, comparative effort will clarify the structural subtlety and interdependence of the two contrasting stories and states.

The first two chapters of the book can be read as companion pieces that illustrate Grahame's comparative method of plotting. In both we find what myth critics refer to as "the call to adventure" (Campbell 49–58). In the first chapter, Mole is busy with spring cleaning at Mole End, deep in the earth, when the call of "something up above" overpowers his commitment to routine and regularity and draws him up into a pastoral world filled with "the joy of living and the delight of spring without cleaning." In this mock-heroic episode of rebirth or "emancipation," the humble hero, "bewitched" by the "imperious" call of nature, happily subordinates mundane responsibility to the pleasure principle. The Mole, then, is the first character to express the romantic, centrifugal pole of Grahame's dialectic. Once emancipated, however, Mole is quickly "absorbed" by the aimless, epicurean life of the River Bank, enjoying the domestic bounty of the Water Rat's picnic. But the idyll is threatened by the sense of intoxication that such pleasure engenders. On his way back from the picnic with Ratty, Mole impetuously grabs the oars and overturns the little scull, almost losing the beautiful picnic basket in the bargain. This scene echoes an earlier incident in which the Rat, waxing rhapsodic, steers the boat into a bank, causing "the joyous oarsman" to flip onto his back in the bottom of the boat, "his heels in the air." By such repetitions and parallels Grahame stresses the nature of his contrary states.

Along the River Bank, however, a sense of moderation and community tempers the excesses of individual adventure, so that the Mole quickly recognizes his mistake and apologizes for his "foolishness and ungrateful conduct." In this world, passion is no excuse for incivility. The threat posed by excess finds additional, emblematic expression in a small vignette characteristic of Grahame's technique. Just after the narrator has introduced the Toad as a rower "splashing badly, and rolling a good deal," we glimpse "an errant May-fly [swerving] unsteadily athwart the current in the intoxicated fashion affected by the young bloods of May-flies seeing life." In the next sentence, the fly is eaten and disappears without comment by the narrator, and we are left to contemplate the relation between this event and the activities of our other intoxicated adventurers. The same technique on the macroscopic level juxtaposes chapters and blocks of chapters to dramatize contraries. Once the initial sense of "divine discontent and longing" in chapter 1 is reinforced by the related impulse toward the open road in chapter 2, the note of concern sounded in the mayfly incident will become considerably more significant.

In "The Open Road," Toad expresses the same longing for adventure, for "travel, change, interest, excitement!" that animated Mole in the first chapter. But the impulse that is controllable in the Mole is excessive in the Toad, as indicated by a change in the means of adventure and emancipation. Mole gives himself up to the spirit of the season and "the joy of running water," both of which bring him into closer contact with nature. But for Toad, boating has become a "silly, boyish amusement," the river "dull" and "fusty." His boats hung up in a deserted boathouse, he now longs for "the dusty highway" and the chance to see "camps, villages, towns, cities!" The desire for adventure may be the same, but the path that desire takes in Mole and Toad is perilously different. As Mole and Rat arrive at Toad Hall, their host easily convinces them to join him in a gypsy caravan in pursuit of the "Life Adventurous." The trio soon meets disaster "fleet and unforeseen . . . disaster momentous"; once again, impetuosity capsizes its victims. In chapter 1, when Mole grabs the oars of the scull, Rat cries, "Stop it, you silly ass . . . You'll have us over," and the damp, repentant Mole quickly acknowledges, "Indeed I have been a complete ass, and I know it." By contrast, when the Toad sits overturned in the road,

"spellbound," it is the Mole who says, "O stop being an ass, Toad." The "crazed" Toad can only dream of renewed risks "on my reckless way." By changing the initial order of composition and placing Mole's springtime adventure of emancipation first, Grahame establishes a dominant mood of temperate indulgence alongside of which the overheated, midsummer's extravagance of the Toad, while charming, seems nonetheless an aberrant response to the call.

Kenneth Burke writes of the "categorical expectations" with which we approach literary form, and which lead us to expect, for example, Pope's couplets to rhyme and epics to begin with an invocation (126–27; see also Philip Stevick). In extended narrative, our expectations are in part chronological; we ask "What happens next?" And when, in a work as lovingly devoted to natural processes as *The Wind in the Willows,* we skip in chapter 3 from midsummer to the depth of winter, we reasonably ask why. The answer, of course, is that while nature may be sequential, art is patterned and thematic. We skip seasons here in order to develop through the Mole the temperate chord of natural instinct rather than the discord of extravagant impulse. The break in our chronological expectations draws our attention to contrast and helps us distinguish between the Toad's summertime intoxication and the Mole's natural desire to explore. Even more important, the shift from summer to winter announces a transition to the text's second movement, a block of three chapters (3–5) that introduces the other pole of Grahame's dialectic, the homing instinct. Devoting an extended sequence to the River Bank friends at this early point in the action effectively links the reader's angle of vision to the Mole's-eye-view and to the powerful claims of home and community. Toad's subsequent adventures may be diverting, even enthralling, but to the reader alert to the thematic resonance that formal juxtaposition can create, they will also seem exorbitant, even "crazed," the escapades of a charming but "silly ass."

This second movement begins with a shift in attention from the gregarious, exhibitionistic Toad to the reserved yet hospitable Mr. Badger. It also begins with repetitions of formal motifs from the two previous chapters: as in chapter 1, the Mole is seized by the impulse to explore, and as in chapter 2, he is excited by the desire "to make the acquaintance of" a new friend. Unlike his springtime excursion, however, Mole's adventure here is not seasonal; for in winter the dominant animal activities are sleep and story-telling. That Mole breaks this natural pattern may explain his eventual difficulties. In the barren winter landscape, Mole initially believes that "he had never seen so far and so intimately into the heart of things." Here is the crystallizing vision of the romantic adventurer, or so we briefly think; but just as Toad's lark on the open road led to unforeseen danger, Mole's excursion soon leads him to "the Terror of the Wild Wood." And just as he and Rat had to rescue the crazed Toad in chapter 2, the Rat must rescue Mole here. This third parallel narrative reinforces a pattern of impulse/adventure/calamity/rescue. Cumulatively such repetitions force our recognition of what we might call the wages of adventure: its tendency toward calamity and the absolute dependence of the impulsive upon the aid of their friends. The Mole's excursion into the Wild Wood is distinct in that it is solitary and thus more intense than its predecessors. A winter's tale in darkening tones, it makes the contrary state, the snug hospitality of the Badger's den, all the more satisfying and meaningful. At this moment, when the two storm-driven friends find safe anchorage with Badger, Grahame's dialectical narrative swings decisively from the call of adventure to the lure of home.

At the Badger's (and later at Mole End), the movement "up and outward" reverses to a centripetal drive: the lure of the burrow. The seasonal changes of the River Bank and the dust of the highway yield to the permanence and warmth of the underground haven. Generically, ironic romance turns to low-mimetic comedy. In a counterpoint to the adventurous values of the first two chapters, Mr. Badger's home offers the very security and tranquility that adventure undermines—a place "to eat and talk and smoke in comfort and contentment." In a characteristic parallel, Grahame introduces two young hedgehogs who, like Rat and Mole, have also been lost in the snow and who also happen across Mr. Badger's back door. The repetition emphasizes the never-ending need for domestic security, and the enduring shelter of home.

For the Mole, the "domestic architecture" of the Badger's home has special psychological significance. Like Badger, "an underground animal by birth and breeding," the Mole immediately responds to the Badger's domain: "once you're underground, you know exactly where you are.... You're entirely your own master." The self-containment and domestic virtues glorified here look forward to the pleasures of the Hobbit-hole; for just as the quiet stability of domestic life nourishes the mild heroism of Tolkien's epic, so does the insulated, centered existence in the burrows of the Wild Wood allow Mole and Badger, like Bilbo and Frodo, to develop the reserves necessary to redeem their

world from threat. Returning home, the Mole clearly recognizes that he is by nature an animal of confined spaces: "For others the asperities, the stubborn endurance, or the clash of actual conflict. . . . He must be wise, must keep to the pleasant places in which his lines were laid and which held adventure enough, in their way, to last for a lifetime." In light of the battle for Toad Hall, this is not, of course, the last word on Mole's abilities; but we realize the appropriateness of Mole's recognition at this point because the new ethic has been juxtaposed so dramatically against its counterpart.

Whereas the relation between preceding chapters has been one of contrast, the winter journey of chapter 5 intensifies the ideas of chapters 3 and 4. Although there is a temporal break between "Mr. Badger" and "Dulce Domum," the same animals reenact a snowbound journey that again climaxes with the unexpected discovery of safety. In this parallel narrative, Grahame corroborates the power of the homing instinct and the satisfactions of the "magic circle." Moreover, since the journey is one of return, not departure (as in "The Wild Wood"), and since the place the travelers return to is not just a friendly haven (like the Badger's) but Mole's own home, the instincts on display are all the stronger. The chapter begins with the two friends, Rat and Mole, coming across a village. Unlike the Toad, Rat and Mole "did not hold with villages, and their own highways . . . took an independent course." Still, they happen to pass a cottage, and in a well-known vignette, Grahame shows us the two looking in on "the little curtained world" of a bird cage from which "the sense of home" pulsates. This episode forms a counterpoint to Ratty's earlier rescue of an overturned bird cage and "its hysterical occupant" from the demolished caravan. Through this reference to an earlier image, Grahame fills out the differences between the homing instinct and its opposite. However, repetition rather than contrast is the dominant note here, as once again the Mole stumbles across a safe haven; once inside all is warmth, dryness, full larders, and merry friendship; instead of hedgehogs, there is a choir of field mice; and instead of Badger, the Rat now plays the gracious "general." The effect of this parallelism is to enhance the potency of the countertheme, a theme repeated because the lure of home is less dramatic than the call of the Life Adventurous. Through such formal emphases, Grahame shifts the weight of his argument from "fresh and captivating experiences" toward "that small inquiring something which all animals carry inside them" and which inevitably leads home. Formal arrangement thereby continues to orient our allegiances.

T. S. Eliot writes that "home is where one starts from," and with "Dulce Domum" we return to Mole's home, the starting point of these adventures and the close of the narrative's second movement. To recapitulate the progress so far: the first movement shows the up-and-down curve of the Life Adventurous (chaps. 1 and 2). The outward drive of these chapters is natural, but it can also be unpredictable and even disastrous. When the drive recurs in chapter 3, a new theme is added: beyond the calamity and exhaustion of adventure lies the contrasting attraction of home. Chapter 3, therefore, functions as a narrative link between the two sets of chapters (1 and 2, 3 through 5) as it begins with adventure but ends with the exhausted friends on the doorstep of "the contrary state." Instead of the up-and-down swing of the first movement, the second set of chapters moves out and back, as the Mole sets out from one home, rests at another, and returns in the end to his own. The initial sense of adventure is decisively offset by a repeated emphasis on the appeal of home. Having introduced the theme and countertheme in these first two movements, Grahame next refines and expands that dialectic through a series of ever more distinct juxtapositions. In the next four chapters, from "Mr. Toad" through "Wayfarers All," he explores the conflict that the romantic impulse to explore and the instinctual need for the magic circle can create within his characters, most of whom quite naturally long for both. Here again, the formal juxtaposition of individual chapters articulates a complex debate. By alternating allegiances Grahame allows his contrary states to interact and reverberate without destroying either the gentle humor of his book or the balance of his argument.

We return to Grahame's formal strategy of contrast in the adventure of "Mr. Toad" (chap. 6), which deals not with the discovery but with the escape from home. It is summer again (the season of the Toad), and Badger arrives to take Toad "in hand." Mole chimes in that "we'll teach him to be a sensible Toad," indicating that as a result of his own experience, Mole is a thorough convert to common sense and domestic practicality. Badger's position is that "independence is all very well, but we animals never allow our friends to make fools of themselves beyond a certain limit," a limit the Toad has reached. However well-intentioned, this point of view is restrictive, even despotic; it casts Toad in the role of the recalcitrant adolescent and invites us to contemplate the potential tyranny of parental, communal strictures. The Mole goes so far as to assert that his friend will be "the most converted Toad

that ever was before we're done with him." As a result, we are partly in sympathy with the Toad's resistance when the friends set themselves up as a tribunal to defend the norm in opposition to individual expression. Ignoring his friends' concern, escaping by a rope of knotted sheets, and "marching off light-heartedly," Toad is at this point the champion of freedom and the willingness to venture forth.

Within moments, however, the narrator establishes the dangers of Toad's rebelliousness. Unlike Mole in "Dulce Domum," who struggles to subordinate his own longing for home to his loyalty to Rat, when Toad sees the motorcar, he immediately surrenders to "the old passion." As a result, he is transformed into "Toad the terror, the traffic queller, the lord of the lone trail, before whom all must give way or be smitten into nothingness and everlasting night." The hedonistic egocentrism of this role represents the dialectical extreme of adventurism: Toad is "fulfilling his instincts, living his hour, reckless of what may come," which turns out to be a sentence of twenty years in jail. Our recognition of Grahame's indictment of the Toad's excess is in part obscured by all the fun along the way and by the inevitability of his escape. Yet as the entire chapter swings back and forth between exuberance and despair, we realize that Toad's irrepressibility has become a form of enslavement, not an expression of freedom.

The transition from chapter 6 to "The Piper" could hardly be more jarring: we go directly from Toad's confinement in the "grimmest dungeon" in the "innermost keep" of the "stoutest castle" in England to the Mole languorously stretched out on the riverbank in the "blessed coolness" of midsummer's eve. Even more important, we shift from the Toad's isolation to an all-encompassing network of mutual aid. Such implicit contrasts require the reader as intermediary to bring the two stories into meaningful interplay. "The Piper" also provides the first significant indication that the domestic and romantic impulses can be resolved. This act of accommodation begins as Rat and Mole go out in search of Portly, the son of Otter, who is always getting lost because "he's so adventurous." Again a desertion from the magic circle leads to a rescue. In the process, however, an ordinary event becomes an extraordinary one: the two rescuers become entranced and transported, emotions that chapters 1 and 2 connected with the excitement of adventure. Yet adventure here is of a different kind, for Pan, the source of their excitement, has revealed himself to them "in their helping."

The desire to help may not seem a spectacular virtue, but for Grahame its power resides in its ability to harmonize the contraries: to put adventure (the willingness to "'do' something," as the Mole has it) at the service of friends and family. This blend of opposite instincts produces what Ratty calls "this new divine thing," powerful yet affectionate, ordinary yet awesome. Indeed the whole chapter provides supporting analogies to this fusion of contraries: the epiphany takes place on a small island, which mingles the important images of river and earth; it happens in the "imminent dawn," which brings together night and day; it is presided over by Pan, the satyr, who is both man and beast; it engenders a state between dreaming and intense wakefulness; and the experience itself, says Ratty, is "something very exciting ... yet nothing in particular has happened." Only when individual power and friendly helping coincide does such fusion take place; and yet, as we now begin to realize, such moments occupy central positions in this narrative, as when the well-armed Rat rescues Mole from the snowdrift or when the friends join together for the siege of Toad Hall. This episode, when the Rat and Mole are vouchsafed their vision of "'power at the helping hour,'" marks the essential moment in Grahame's narrative argument when friendship, home, and helping take on some of the allure of romantic individualism, and when we as readers become alert to the middle ground in Grahame's dialectic.

When we turn from Pan to "Toad's Adventures," we again switch "stories" and move back from the pastoral idyll to the sirens' song of adventure. Grahame, however, continues to explore the middle ground; for if in "The Piper" helping becomes heroic, in chapter 8 heroism needs and elicits a good deal of friendly help. Throughout these adventures, the Toad entertains by his machinations, but he is not quite the Toad of "surpassing cleverness" he takes himself to be. By contrast with the reverence of "The Piper," the playful irony deflates and amuses. Most thoroughly deflated is the "handsome, popular, successful Toad," who on closer inspection betrays the "horrid, proud, ungrateful animal" the gaoler's daughter accuses him of being. Yet Toad, despite his mock-heroic escapades, is constantly in need of help—first from the gaoler's daughter, then from the washerwoman, and finally from the train engineer, who says to Toad, "you are evidently in sore trouble and distress, so I will not desert you." In this narrative world, adventure most often leads to "trouble and distress" and adventurers like Toad or Portly invariably depend on the quiet, domestic types to rescue them. This chapter, then, is an ironic complement to its predecessor, and

it expands our notion of "helping" as a bridge between the contraries.

And yet, in the dialectical progress of Grahame's argument, no synthesis is permanent. Our emotions and instincts are seasonal, subject to "the other call" that in its own time is as "imperious" as the community of friends. No chapter expresses this emotional mutability more poignantly than "Wayfarers All." Once again, a total break shifts the action from the Toad alone, cold, and hungry to the Rat strolling through "late-summer's pomp" among his many friends preparing to migrate. Though he protests that he cannot understand how the swallows can leave "your friends who will miss you and your snug homes that you have just settled into," he too begins to feel "that chord hitherto dormant and unsuspected ... this wild new sensation." He is musing on "the wondrous world . . . and the fortunes and adventures . . . out there beyond" when he encounters his cousin, the seafaring rat. This jaunty mariner praises the domestic bliss of the woodland life; but, like Tennyson's Ulysses, he is now leaving it because he has had his own call, heard his own "wind in the willows" and is heading out on the road to "his heart's desire." His stories make the Water Rat feel the "somewhat narrow and circumscribed" nature of the riverbank; they ask us to reconsider our estimation of "the best life." Despite all the trouble upon the open road, the call to adventure still intoxicates. Like the Mole before him, Rat can feel that impulse so contradictory to his essential nature, and he almost capitulates—until, that is, Mole wrestles him to the ground, talks to him of the "hearty joys" of home life, and the spell is broken. Our comparative method suggests that this episode is especially significant because it happens to the Rat. For shortly before, the Rat heard most clearly the "glad pipings" of Pan and concluded that this melody and its inscrutable message was "the real, the unmistakable thing." On this later day and in this different season, Rat decides that, like his friends the swallows, his own blood now dances to different music. Pan's gift of forgetfulness may explain the Rat's present temptation; nonetheless, after the break of only a single chapter, we find the Rat not only "restless" but actually distressed with the boundaries of his own life. This polarity of supreme satisfaction on the one hand and querulous discontent on the other suggests that despite the hint of accommodation in chapter 7, the contraries continue to make their antithetical claims on our allegiance. And indeed, Grahame argues through the dialectical structure of his plot that both calls must be recognized in their "due season."

Ratty's temptation and the migration of the swallows appear just at a time when the Toad's profligacy might incline us to see the call to adventure as vain and injurious; their instincts lead us to recognize just how imperious that call can be. Similar impulses call the Mole, lure the baby otter, and claim the helpless Toad. Repetition again deepens and universalizes our understanding. Nevertheless, the allure of this drive is affected substantially by the fact that its most attractive presentation (in "Wayfarers All") is bracketed by the excesses of Toad's own adventures. This compromise results from a deliberate artistic choice on Grahame's part: not only is "Wayfarers All" interjected into the chronological order of Toad's adventures, but its late-summer setting, as opposed to the early-summer date of Toad's travels, also breaks the seasonal rhythm and specifically directs our attention to the shift in narrative focus. We are led once again by form to reflect upon the synchronic relationships of the plot as opposed to the linearity of the simple story; we are led, that is, to recognize the interplay between the "two stories" and the need for compromise.

The return to Toad's adventures in chapter 10 marks a transition to the fourth and last cycle of the tale, which focuses primarily on the Toad, making this section (chaps. 10–12) the companion piece to the earlier focus on the Mole (chaps. 3–5). In spite of the title "Further Adventures," the narrative motive here is no longer the expansive, explorative impulse of Toad's earlier forays; instead, the centripetal motive to return home dominates. Narrative juxtaposition suggests a comparison between Rat's spell, which is severe but temporary and which he effectively sublimates, and the manic oscillations of the Toad, who exhibits a hysterical instability totally alien to the seasonal, temperate impulses that affect the swallows, the Sea Rat, and the Mole. One moment Toad is fearless, confident, Odyssean in his resourcefulness; the next he is "sinking down in a shabby, miserable heap." This careening back and forth between vanity ("the cleverest animal in the world") and self-deprecation ("what a conceited ass I am! What a conceited, heedless ass!") exhibits more than just the comic fluctuations of a flimflammer on the loose. Unlike Rat's response to the universality of the call to adventure, which is essentially in tune with the seasonal change around him, Toad's mercurial oscillations show the romantic iconoclast reaping the harvest of his lack of orientation. The vehicles of adventure in chapter 10 (a boat, a caravan, and a motorcar) repeat those of chapters 1 and 2, a parallel suggesting that Toad is still caught up in the same round of excesses. The schizophrenic adventurer can only hope that (like Mole, or Portly, or Rat before him) he will be rescued from himself. It is Grahame's ultimate irony (and insight) that this rescue and the Toad's redemption are the heroic work of those who have chosen to remain at home.

With Toad's rescue by Rat (at the opening of chapter 11) the two stories finally dovetail. Indeed, Grahame connects the stories of Toad and Mole through an explicit repetition of wording: when Mole meets Ratty in chapter 1, he notices first "a dark hole" with a "twinkle" in its depths, then a "brown little face," "grave" and "round," with "neat ears and thick silky hair"; "it was the Water Rat!" Toad's rescue by Rat in chapter 11 recapitulates every detail of the original scene, in the original order and almost in the original languages. Grahame in this way insists upon the parallel: Toad is welcomed back into the family of friends in the same way that Mole was introduced to the "splendid spaces" of the River Bank by the Rat; only Mole was coming out, while the Toad is going back. After this introductory allusion to the text's own opening, the two stories continue to coalesce, as the reunited friends resolve to retake Toad Hall from the weasels and stoats, a consolidating motive that will call up heroic adventurism in the service of the pastoral home.

But before this final, unifying siege, a polite though significant skirmish between Rat and Toad contrasts the two world views they represent. In authority throughout the beginning of "Summer Tempests," the Rat adheres to his position with much greater constancy than he did in chapter 2, when Toad proposed the adventure of the gypsy cart. The returning Toad repeatedly tries to inflate himself by narrating his exploits, while Rat answers him first with "gravity and firmness" and then with a detailed indictment of his foolishness. In response, Toad continues to wax and wane between the extremes of "puffing and swelling" and disingenuous apology. Still unable to control his impetuosity, he runs off to see Toad Hall for himself and narrowly misses being shot. Moments later, in another ill-conceived plan, he succeeds in sinking Ratty's favorite boat. This time the Rat strictly censures him, most specifically for the anticommunal sin of ingratitude. This episode finally brings the two contrary states into direct and extended debate; what before had been presented as a series of alternations between chapters and subtle variations in the dialectical presentation of the contrary states is now a gentlemanly but direct confrontation. Toad's utter inability to recognize his own behavior as disastrous suggests that for Grahame romance and impetuosity make an unending series of claims on common sense, and that impulse always whispers "mutinously" in one's inner ear. The chapter resolves the debate by making Toad the subordinate member of the cast of heroes, a role that indicates the ultimate place of volatile impulse in Grahame's scheme of values.

Toad's contribution to this scheme should not, however, be totally dismissed. For when the ever-sympathetic Mole finally allows Toad to boast of his adventures and relate much that belonged "more properly to the category of what-might-have-happened," the narrator adds, "and why should [such stories] not be truly ours, as much as the somewhat inadequate things that really come off." As a purely imaginative mode, the longing for adventure and the vision of what-might-be can be both compensatory (as is the case with Rat the poet and, we suspect, with Grahame the banker) and inspiring. Certainly Toad's adventures have their effect on the Mole; for this most domestic of animals proves capable now of the highly imaginative scheme of dressing himself in the washerwoman's outfit and reconnoitering among the stoats on sentry at Toad Hall. Whereas Toad chafed in egotistical shame at having to wear such a costume, Mole assumes the disguise effectively because his motives are not self-serving. Naturally, the success of Mole's exploit drives the Toad "wild with jealousy"; but we may plausibly assume that Toad is the model for Mole's adventure. Imagination and derring-do in fact have a place in the life of the River Bank as long as they do not threaten the communal order of things. Once again, then, in the dialectical interplay of the contrary states there are really no absolutes; Toad can be "the best of animals" and the Rat possessed by wanderlust. The fact, however, that the Mole could prove both clever and courageous goes an especially long way toward correcting our conventional view of the domestic, pastoral life by suggesting that there is more at home than we might have guessed, and less to be gained on the open road alone.

It has been argued that the final episode—"The Return of Ulysses"—is not much more than an adventurous tag, a grand finale that forgets the more subtle themes of the River and the Woodland chapters. Close attention to the dialectics of the text, however, would indicate that the climactic episode enlists the adventurous impulse in the recapture of the magic circle and so provides an appropriate knitting together of the novel's contrary states. Certainly, the problem that the friends face is intimately connected with the homing instinct, for the Wild Wooders have usurped the Toad's ancestral home and extended his own bad habits to the point of profligacy. But the problem is not simply Toad's exile from home but also whether or not the magic circle is to be cut off from all approach. For "in their helping," Mole and Badger, those quintessential homebodies, have moved into Toad Hall, been evicted, and are now being forced "to camp out in the open . . . living very rough by day and lying very hard by night." The critical question, then, is whether the Wild Wooders, who are prone "to break out sometimes" and who represent that impulse antithetical to the spirit of "dulce domum," should inherit Toad Hall. It is a question that Grahame shared with contemporaries like John Galsworthy, Arnold Bennett, and E. M. Forster. Grahame responds, however, in the manner of Robert Louis Stevenson. For in the midst of this "civil war," the day is won by a desperate display of heroism and valor: "the mighty Badger" brandishes a great cudgel, Mole terrifies his enemies with "an awful war-cry," Rat brings an entire arsenal to bear upon his foes, and Toad, "swollen to twice his ordinary size" by excitement, takes out after the Chief Weasel. All this is very comic and is over in a page; nonetheless, in taking back the home ground, the domestic corps exhibits the courage and power we conventionally associate with romantic, adventurous heroes who—like Ulysses—spend most of their time on the open road. In the siege of Toad Hall, we are invited again to reject as extreme the view that the love of one's home and the capacity for heroic achievement are irreconcilable, and to contemplate the successful accommodation of contrary states of feeling.

The distinction between these events and the epiphany of "The Piper" is important. In their rescue of Little Portly, Rat and Mole were essentially witnesses to the "'power at the helping hour'" and were overwhelmed by it. In the retaking of Toad Hall, the friends become warriors rather than bystanders, exemplars of that special power. Such a heroic victory does not, of course, belie the fact that theirs is essentially a triumph for domesticity, for good food, clean sheets, and hand-written dinner invitations; nor does the victory mean that Toad is now a convert and that the seasonal impulse to break out has been tamed. Once again, the Toad must be taken into "the small smoking room" and talked to, and once again he protests. And yet, in what may be his own middling reversal, Toad begins to see how modesty, not bombast, can make him "the subject of absorbing interest." What is clear is that our original view of this snugly domestic world has been corrected and that by the close of Grahame's narrative argument "messing about in boats" and feeling the call of "home" do not seem quite so pedestrian. For we are shown something heroic in defending one's own ground, in fighting for domestic values, and in achieving the balance and consistency that only come by recognizing the omnipresence of temptation and the siren call of adventure. In the end, it is the "bijou riverside residence" that breeds the heroes of legend, and the life this side of the "well-metalled road" that "holds adventure enough."

Source: Michael Mendelson, "*The Wind in the Willows* and the Plotting of Contrast," in *Children's Literature*, Vol. 16, 1988, pp. 127–44.

Sources

Gaarden, Bonnie, "The Inner Family of *The Wind in the Willows*," in *Children's Literature: Annual of The Modern Division of Children's Literature and The Children's Literature Association*, Vol. 22, 1994, pp. 43–44, 46.

Grahame, Kenneth, *The Wind in the Willows*, Grosset & Dunlap, 1966, p. 11-221.

Green, Peter, *Kenneth Grahame: A Biography*, World Publishing, 1959, p. 1.

Hunt, Peter, *"The Wind in the Willows": A Fragmented Arcadia*, Twayne Publishers, 1994, pp. 5, 6, 13.

Kuznets, Lois R., *Kenneth Grahame*, Twayne Publishers, 1987, pp. 2, 4, 15, 97, 124, 126.

———, "Kenneth Grahame and Father Nature, or Whither Blows *The Wind in the Willows*?" in *Children's Literature: Annual of The Modern Division of Children's Literature and The Children's Literature Association*, Vol. 16, 1988, p. 175.

Marshall, Cynthia, "Bodies and Pleasures in *The Wind in the Willows*," in *Children's Literature: Annual of The Modern Division of Children's Literature and The Children's Literature Association*, Vol. 22, 1994, p. 60.

Further Reading

Bate, Roger, and Keith Hartley, *Saving Our Streams: The Role of the Anglers' Conservation Association in Protecting English & Welsh Rivers*, Institute of Economic Affairs, 2001.
   Bate and Hartley consider the Anglers' Conservation Association's fight to clean up and preserve English and Welsh rivers that have been damaged through urban development and pollution. The legislation affecting the conservation of river-based ecosystems, also know as riparian systems, is also examined.

Carpenter, Humphrey, *Secret Gardens: A Study of the Golden Age of Children's Literature*, Pubs Overstock, 1991.
   The book examines works from the golden age of children's literature and their authors, including the sources of their inspiration and the cultural circumstances that led these authors to direct their writing towards children.

Eckermann, Erik, and Peter L. Albrecht, *World History of Automobiles*, Society of Automotive Engineers, 2001.
   Eckermann and Albrecht describe the development of the automobile, from what lead to its invention to the most recent technological advances. Photographs and diagrams complement the text.

Green, Peter, *Kenneth Grahame: A Biography*, World Publishing, 1959.
   The earliest comprehensive biography of Grahame, Green's biography is the one most commonly referenced by literary scholars. The book is accompanied by twenty-two pictures and illustrations.

Glossary of Literary Terms

A

Abstract: As an adjective applied to writing or literary works, abstract refers to words or phrases that name things not knowable through the five senses.

Aestheticism: A literary and artistic movement of the nineteenth century. Followers of the movement believed that art should not be mixed with social, political, or moral teaching. The statement "art for art's sake" is a good summary of aestheticism. The movement had its roots in France, but it gained widespread importance in England in the last half of the nineteenth century, where it helped change the Victorian practice of including moral lessons in literature.

Allegory: A narrative technique in which characters representing things or abstract ideas are used to convey a message or teach a lesson. Allegory is typically used to teach moral, ethical, or religious lessons but is sometimes used for satiric or political purposes.

Allusion: A reference to a familiar literary or historical person or event, used to make an idea more easily understood.

Analogy: A comparison of two things made to explain something unfamiliar through its similarities to something familiar, or to prove one point based on the acceptedness of another. Similes and metaphors are types of analogies.

Antagonist: The major character in a narrative or drama who works against the hero or protagonist.

Anthropomorphism: The presentation of animals or objects in human shape or with human characteristics. The term is derived from the Greek word for "human form."

Antihero: A central character in a work of literature who lacks traditional heroic qualities such as courage, physical prowess, and fortitude. Antiheroes typically distrust conventional values and are unable to commit themselves to any ideals. They generally feel helpless in a world over which they have no control. Antiheroes usually accept, and often celebrate, their positions as social outcasts.

Apprenticeship Novel: See *Bildungsroman*

Archetype: The word archetype is commonly used to describe an original pattern or model from which all other things of the same kind are made. This term was introduced to literary criticism from the psychology of Carl Jung. It expresses Jung's theory that behind every person's "unconscious," or repressed memories of the past, lies the "collective unconscious" of the human race: memories of the countless typical experiences of our ancestors. These memories are said to prompt illogical associations that trigger powerful emotions in the reader. Often, the emotional process is primitive, even primordial. Archetypes are the literary images that grow out of the "collective unconscious." They appear in literature as incidents and plots that repeat basic patterns of life. They may also appear as stereotyped characters.

Avant-garde: French term meaning "vanguard." It is used in literary criticism to describe new writing that rejects traditional approaches to literature in favor of innovations in style or content.

B

Beat Movement: A period featuring a group of American poets and novelists of the 1950s and 1960s—including Jack Kerouac, Allen Ginsberg, Gregory Corso, William S. Burroughs, and Lawrence Ferlinghetti—who rejected established social and literary values. Using such techniques as stream of consciousness writing and jazz-influenced free verse and focusing on unusual or abnormal states of mind—generated by religious ecstasy or the use of drugs—the Beat writers aimed to create works that were unconventional in both form and subject matter.

Bildungsroman: A German word meaning "novel of development." The *bildungsroman* is a study of the maturation of a youthful character, typically brought about through a series of social or sexual encounters that lead to self-awareness. *Bildungsroman* is used interchangeably with *erziehungsroman*, a novel of initiation and education. When a *bildungsroman* is concerned with the development of an artist (as in James Joyce's *A Portrait of the Artist as a Young Man*), it is often termed a *kunstlerroman*. Also known as Apprenticeship Novel, Coming of Age Novel, *Erziehungsroman*, or *Kunstlerroman*.

Black Aesthetic Movement: A period of artistic and literary development among African Americans in the 1960s and early 1970s. This was the first major African-American artistic movement since the Harlem Renaissance and was closely paralleled by the civil rights and black power movements. The black aesthetic writers attempted to produce works of art that would be meaningful to the black masses. Key figures in black aesthetics included one of its founders, poet and playwright Amiri Baraka, formerly known as LeRoi Jones; poet and essayist Haki R. Madhubuti, formerly Don L. Lee; poet and playwright Sonia Sanchez; and dramatist Ed Bullins. Also known as Black Arts Movement.

Black Humor: Writing that places grotesque elements side by side with humorous ones in an attempt to shock the reader, forcing him or her to laugh at the horrifying reality of a disordered world. Also known as Black Comedy.

Burlesque: Any literary work that uses exaggeration to make its subject appear ridiculous, either by treating a trivial subject with profound seriousness or by treating a dignified subject frivolously. The word "burlesque" may also be used as an adjective, as in "burlesque show," to mean "striptease act."

C

Character: Broadly speaking, a person in a literary work. The actions of characters are what constitute the plot of a story, novel, or poem. There are numerous types of characters, ranging from simple, stereotypical figures to intricate, multifaceted ones. In the techniques of anthropomorphism and personification, animals—and even places or things—can assume aspects of character. "Characterization" is the process by which an author creates vivid, believable characters in a work of art. This may be done in a variety of ways, including (1) direct description of the character by the narrator; (2) the direct presentation of the speech, thoughts, or actions of the character; and (3) the responses of other characters to the character. The term "character" also refers to a form originated by the ancient Greek writer Theophrastus that later became popular in the seventeenth and eighteenth centuries. It is a short essay or sketch of a person who prominently displays a specific attribute or quality, such as miserliness or ambition.

Climax: The turning point in a narrative, the moment when the conflict is at its most intense. Typically, the structure of stories, novels, and plays is one of rising action, in which tension builds to the climax, followed by falling action, in which tension lessens as the story moves to its conclusion.

Colloquialism: A word, phrase, or form of pronunciation that is acceptable in casual conversation but not in formal, written communication. It is considered more acceptable than slang.

Coming of Age Novel: See *Bildungsroman*

Concrete: Concrete is the opposite of abstract, and refers to a thing that actually exists or a description that allows the reader to experience an object or concept with the senses.

Connotation: The impression that a word gives beyond its defined meaning. Connotations may be universally understood or may be significant only to a certain group.

Convention: Any widely accepted literary device, style, or form.

D

Denotation: The definition of a word, apart from the impressions or feelings it creates (connotations) in the reader.

Denouement: A French word meaning "the unknotting." In literary criticism, it denotes the resolution of conflict in fiction or drama. The *denouement* follows the climax and provides an outcome to the primary plot situation as well as an explanation of secondary plot complications. The *denouement* often involves a character's recognition of his or her state of mind or moral condition. Also known as Falling Action.

Description: Descriptive writing is intended to allow a reader to picture the scene or setting in which the action of a story takes place. The form this description takes often evokes an intended emotional response—a dark, spooky graveyard will evoke fear, and a peaceful, sunny meadow will evoke calmness.

Dialogue: In its widest sense, dialogue is simply conversation between people in a literary work; in its most restricted sense, it refers specifically to the speech of characters in a drama. As a specific literary genre, a "dialogue" is a composition in which characters debate an issue or idea.

Diction: The selection and arrangement of words in a literary work. Either or both may vary depending on the desired effect. There are four general types of diction: "formal," used in scholarly or lofty writing; "informal," used in relaxed but educated conversation; "colloquial," used in everyday speech; and "slang," containing newly coined words and other terms not accepted in formal usage.

Didactic: A term used to describe works of literature that aim to teach some moral, religious, political, or practical lesson. Although didactic elements are often found in artistically pleasing works, the term "didactic" usually refers to literature in which the message is more important than the form. The term may also be used to criticize a work that the critic finds "overly didactic," that is, heavy-handed in its delivery of a lesson.

Doppelganger: A literary technique by which a character is duplicated (usually in the form of an alter ego, though sometimes as a ghostly counterpart) or divided into two distinct, usually opposite personalities. The use of this character device is widespread in nineteenth- and twentieth-century literature, and indicates a growing awareness among authors that the "self" is really a composite of many "selves." Also known as The Double.

Double Entendre: A corruption of a French phrase meaning "double meaning." The term is used to indicate a word or phrase that is deliberately ambiguous, especially when one of the meanings is risqué or improper.

Dramatic Irony: Occurs when the audience of a play or the reader of a work of literature knows something that a character in the work itself does not know. The irony is in the contrast between the intended meaning of the statements or actions of a character and the additional information understood by the audience.

Dystopia: An imaginary place in a work of fiction where the characters lead dehumanized, fearful lives.

E

Edwardian: Describes cultural conventions identified with the period of the reign of Edward VII of England (1901-1910). Writers of the Edwardian Age typically displayed a strong reaction against the propriety and conservatism of the Victorian Age. Their work often exhibits distrust of authority in religion, politics, and art and expresses strong doubts about the soundness of conventional values.

Empathy: A sense of shared experience, including emotional and physical feelings, with someone or something other than oneself. Empathy is often used to describe the response of a reader to a literary character.

Enlightenment, The: An eighteenth-century philosophical movement. It began in France but had a wide impact throughout Europe and America. Thinkers of the Enlightenment valued reason and believed that both the individual and society could achieve a state of perfection. Corresponding to this essentially humanist vision was a resistance to religious authority.

Epigram: A saying that makes the speaker's point quickly and concisely. Often used to preface a novel.

Epilogue: A concluding statement or section of a literary work. In dramas, particularly those of the seventeenth and eighteenth centuries, the epilogue is a closing speech, often in verse, delivered by an actor at the end of a play and spoken directly to the audience.

Epiphany: A sudden revelation of truth inspired by a seemingly trivial incident.

Episode: An incident that forms part of a story and is significantly related to it. Episodes may be either self-contained narratives or events that depend on a larger context for their sense and importance.

Epistolary Novel: A novel in the form of letters. The form was particularly popular in the eighteenth century.

Epithet: A word or phrase, often disparaging or abusive, that expresses a character trait of someone or something.

Existentialism: A predominantly twentieth-century philosophy concerned with the nature and perception of human existence. There are two major strains of existentialist thought: atheistic and Christian. Followers of atheistic existentialism believe that the individual is alone in a godless universe and that the basic human condition is one of suffering and loneliness. Nevertheless, because there are no fixed values, individuals can create their own characters—indeed, they can shape themselves—through the exercise of free will. The atheistic strain culminates in and is popularly associated with the works of Jean-Paul Sartre. The Christian existentialists, on the other hand, believe that only in God may people find freedom from life's anguish. The two strains hold certain beliefs in common: that existence cannot be fully understood or described through empirical effort; that anguish is a universal element of life; that individuals must bear responsibility for their actions; and that there is no common standard of behavior or perception for religious and ethical matters.

Expatriates: See *Expatriatism*

Expatriatism: The practice of leaving one's country to live for an extended period in another country.

Exposition: Writing intended to explain the nature of an idea, thing, or theme. Expository writing is often combined with description, narration, or argument. In dramatic writing, the exposition is the introductory material which presents the characters, setting, and tone of the play.

Expressionism: An indistinct literary term, originally used to describe an early twentieth-century school of German painting. The term applies to almost any mode of unconventional, highly subjective writing that distorts reality in some way.

F

Fable: A prose or verse narrative intended to convey a moral. Animals or inanimate objects with human characteristics often serve as characters in fables.

Falling Action: See *Denouement*

Fantasy: A literary form related to mythology and folklore. Fantasy literature is typically set in non-existent realms and features supernatural beings.

Farce: A type of comedy characterized by broad humor, outlandish incidents, and often vulgar subject matter.

***Femme fatale*:** A French phrase with the literal translation "fatal woman." A *femme fatale* is a sensuous, alluring woman who often leads men into danger or trouble.

Fiction: Any story that is the product of imagination rather than a documentation of fact. Characters and events in such narratives may be based in real life but their ultimate form and configuration is a creation of the author.

Figurative Language: A technique in writing in which the author temporarily interrupts the order, construction, or meaning of the writing for a particular effect. This interruption takes the form of one or more figures of speech such as hyperbole, irony, or simile. Figurative language is the opposite of literal language, in which every word is truthful, accurate, and free of exaggeration or embellishment.

Figures of Speech: Writing that differs from customary conventions for construction, meaning, order, or significance for the purpose of a special meaning or effect. There are two major types of figures of speech: rhetorical figures, which do not make changes in the meaning of the words, and tropes, which do.

***Fin de siecle*:** A French term meaning "end of the century." The term is used to denote the last decade of the nineteenth century, a transition period when writers and other artists abandoned old conventions and looked for new techniques and objectives.

First Person: See *Point of View*

Flashback: A device used in literature to present action that occurred before the beginning of the story. Flashbacks are often introduced as the dreams or recollections of one or more characters.

Foil: A character in a work of literature whose physical or psychological qualities contrast strongly with, and therefore highlight, the corresponding qualities of another character.

Folklore: Traditions and myths preserved in a culture or group of people. Typically, these are passed on by word of mouth in various forms—such as legends, songs, and proverbs—or preserved in customs and ceremonies. This term was first used by W. J. Thoms in 1846.

Folktale: A story originating in oral tradition. Folktales fall into a variety of categories, including legends, ghost stories, fairy tales, fables, and anecdotes based on historical figures and events.

Foreshadowing: A device used in literature to create expectation or to set up an explanation of later developments.

Form: The pattern or construction of a work which identifies its genre and distinguishes it from other genres.

G

Genre: A category of literary work. In critical theory, genre may refer to both the content of a given work—tragedy, comedy, pastoral—and to its form, such as poetry, novel, or drama.

Gilded Age: A period in American history during the 1870s characterized by political corruption and materialism. A number of important novels of social and political criticism were written during this time.

Gothicism: In literary criticism, works characterized by a taste for the medieval or morbidly attractive. A gothic novel prominently features elements of horror, the supernatural, gloom, and violence: clanking chains, terror, charnel houses, ghosts, medieval castles, and mysteriously slamming doors. The term "gothic novel" is also applied to novels that lack elements of the traditional Gothic setting but that create a similar atmosphere of terror or dread.

Grotesque: In literary criticism, the subject matter of a work or a style of expression characterized by exaggeration, deformity, freakishness, and disorder. The grotesque often includes an element of comic absurdity.

H

Harlem Renaissance: The Harlem Renaissance of the 1920s is generally considered the first significant movement of black writers and artists in the United States. During this period, new and established black writers published more fiction and poetry than ever before, the first influential black literary journals were established, and black authors and artists received their first widespread recognition and serious critical appraisal. Among the major writers associated with this period are Claude McKay, Jean Toomer, Countee Cullen, Langston Hughes, Arna Bontemps, Nella Larsen, and Zora Neale Hurston. Also known as Negro Renaissance and New Negro Movement.

Hero/Heroine: The principal sympathetic character (male or female) in a literary work. Heroes and heroines typically exhibit admirable traits: idealism, courage, and integrity, for example.

Holocaust Literature: Literature influenced by or written about the Holocaust of World War II. Such literature includes true stories of survival in concentration camps, escape, and life after the war, as well as fictional works and poetry.

Humanism: A philosophy that places faith in the dignity of humankind and rejects the medieval perception of the individual as a weak, fallen creature. "Humanists" typically believe in the perfectibility of human nature and view reason and education as the means to that end.

Hyperbole: In literary criticism, deliberate exaggeration used to achieve an effect.

I

Idiom: A word construction or verbal expression closely associated with a given language.

Image: A concrete representation of an object or sensory experience. Typically, such a representation helps evoke the feelings associated with the object or experience itself. Images are either "literal" or "figurative." Literal images are especially concrete and involve little or no extension of the obvious meaning of the words used to express them. Figurative images do not follow the literal meaning of the words exactly. Images in literature are usually visual, but the term "image" can also refer to the representation of any sensory experience.

Imagery: The array of images in a literary work. Also, figurative language.

In medias res: A Latin term meaning "in the middle of things." It refers to the technique of beginning a story at its midpoint and then using various flashback devices to reveal previous action.

Interior Monologue: A narrative technique in which characters' thoughts are revealed in a way that appears to be uncontrolled by the author. The interior monologue typically aims to reveal the inner self of a character. It portrays emotional experiences as they occur at both a conscious and unconscious level. Images are often used to represent sensations or emotions.

Irony: In literary criticism, the effect of language in which the intended meaning is the opposite of what is stated.

J

Jargon: Language that is used or understood only by a select group of people. Jargon may refer to terminology used in a certain profession, such as computer jargon, or it may refer to any nonsensical language that is not understood by most people.

L

Leitmotiv: See *Motif*

Literal Language: An author uses literal language when he or she writes without exaggerating or embellishing the subject matter and without any tools of figurative language.

Lost Generation: A term first used by Gertrude Stein to describe the post-World War I generation of American writers: men and women haunted by a sense of betrayal and emptiness brought about by the destructiveness of the war.

M

Mannerism: Exaggerated, artificial adherence to a literary manner or style. Also, a popular style of the visual arts of late sixteenth-century Europe that was marked by elongation of the human form and by intentional spatial distortion. Literary works that are self-consciously high-toned and artistic are often said to be "mannered."

Metaphor: A figure of speech that expresses an idea through the image of another object. Metaphors suggest the essence of the first object by identifying it with certain qualities of the second object.

Modernism: Modern literary practices. Also, the principles of a literary school that lasted from roughly the beginning of the twentieth century until the end of World War II. Modernism is defined by its rejection of the literary conventions of the nineteenth century and by its opposition to conventional morality, taste, traditions, and economic values.

Mood: The prevailing emotions of a work or of the author in his or her creation of the work. The mood of a work is not always what might be expected based on its subject matter.

Motif: A theme, character type, image, metaphor, or other verbal element that recurs throughout a single work of literature or occurs in a number of different works over a period of time. Also known as *Motiv* or *Leitmotiv.*

Myth: An anonymous tale emerging from the traditional beliefs of a culture or social unit. Myths use supernatural explanations for natural phenomena. They may also explain cosmic issues like creation and death. Collections of myths, known as mythologies, are common to all cultures and nations, but the best-known myths belong to the Norse, Roman, and Greek mythologies.

N

Narration: The telling of a series of events, real or invented. A narration may be either a simple narrative, in which the events are recounted chronologically, or a narrative with a plot, in which the account is given in a style reflecting the author's artistic concept of the story. Narration is sometimes used as a synonym for "storyline."

Narrative: A verse or prose accounting of an event or sequence of events, real or invented. The term is also used as an adjective in the sense "method of narration." For example, in literary criticism, the expression "narrative technique" usually refers to the way the author structures and presents his or her story.

Narrator: The teller of a story. The narrator may be the author or a character in the story through whom the author speaks.

Naturalism: A literary movement of the late nineteenth and early twentieth centuries. The movement's major theorist, French novelist Emile Zola, envisioned a type of fiction that would examine human life with the objectivity of scientific inquiry. The Naturalists typically viewed human beings as either the products of "biological determinism," ruled by hereditary instincts and engaged in an endless struggle for survival, or as the products of "socioeconomic determinism," ruled by social and economic forces beyond their control. In their works, the Naturalists generally ignored the highest levels of society and focused on degradation: poverty, alcoholism, prostitution, insanity, and disease.

Noble Savage: The idea that primitive man is noble and good but becomes evil and corrupted as he becomes civilized. The concept of the noble savage originated in the Renaissance period but is more closely identified with such later writers as

Jean-Jacques Rousseau and Aphra Behn. See also Primitivism.

Novel of Ideas: A novel in which the examination of intellectual issues and concepts takes precedence over characterization or a traditional storyline.

Novel of Manners: A novel that examines the customs and mores of a cultural group.

Novel: A long fictional narrative written in prose, which developed from the novella and other early forms of narrative. A novel is usually organized under a plot or theme with a focus on character development and action.

Novella: An Italian term meaning "story." This term has been especially used to describe fourteenth-century Italian tales, but it also refers to modern short novels.

O

Objective Correlative: An outward set of objects, a situation, or a chain of events corresponding to an inward experience and evoking this experience in the reader. The term frequently appears in modern criticism in discussions of authors' intended effects on the emotional responses of readers.

Objectivity: A quality in writing characterized by the absence of the author's opinion or feeling about the subject matter. Objectivity is an important factor in criticism.

Oedipus Complex: A son's amorous obsession with his mother. The phrase is derived from the story of the ancient Theban hero Oedipus, who unknowingly killed his father and married his mother.

Omniscience: See *Point of View*

Onomatopoeia: The use of words whose sounds express or suggest their meaning. In its simplest sense, onomatopoeia may be represented by words that mimic the sounds they denote such as "hiss" or "meow." At a more subtle level, the pattern and rhythm of sounds and rhymes of a line or poem may be onomatopoeic.

Oxymoron: A phrase combining two contradictory terms. Oxymorons may be intentional or unintentional.

P

Parable: A story intended to teach a moral lesson or answer an ethical question.

Paradox: A statement that appears illogical or contradictory at first, but may actually point to an underlying truth.

Parallelism: A method of comparison of two ideas in which each is developed in the same grammatical structure.

Parody: In literary criticism, this term refers to an imitation of a serious literary work or the signature style of a particular author in a ridiculous manner. A typical parody adopts the style of the original and applies it to an inappropriate subject for humorous effect. Parody is a form of satire and could be considered the literary equivalent of a caricature or cartoon.

Pastoral: A term derived from the Latin word "pastor," meaning shepherd. A pastoral is a literary composition on a rural theme. The conventions of the pastoral were originated by the third-century Greek poet Theocritus, who wrote about the experiences, love affairs, and pastimes of Sicilian shepherds. In a pastoral, characters and language of a courtly nature are often placed in a simple setting. The term pastoral is also used to classify dramas, elegies, and lyrics that exhibit the use of country settings and shepherd characters.

Pen Name: See *Pseudonym*

Persona: A Latin term meaning "mask." *Personae* are the characters in a fictional work of literature. The *persona* generally functions as a mask through which the author tells a story in a voice other than his or her own. A *persona* is usually either a character in a story who acts as a narrator or an "implied author," a voice created by the author to act as the narrator for himself or herself.

Personification: A figure of speech that gives human qualities to abstract ideas, animals, and inanimate objects. Also known as *Prosopopoeia*.

Picaresque Novel: Episodic fiction depicting the adventures of a roguish central character ("picaro" is Spanish for "rogue"). The picaresque hero is commonly a low-born but clever individual who wanders into and out of various affairs of love, danger, and farcical intrigue. These involvements may take place at all social levels and typically present a humorous and wide-ranging satire of a given society.

Plagiarism: Claiming another person's written material as one's own. Plagiarism can take the form of direct, word-for-word copying or the theft of the substance or idea of the work.

Plot: In literary criticism, this term refers to the pattern of events in a narrative or drama. In its simplest sense, the plot guides the author in composing the work and helps the reader follow the work. Typically, plots exhibit causality and unity and have a beginning, a middle, and an end. Sometimes, however, a plot may consist of a series of disconnected events, in which case it is known as an "episodic plot."

Poetic Justice: An outcome in a literary work, not necessarily a poem, in which the good are rewarded and the evil are punished, especially in ways that particularly fit their virtues or crimes.

Poetic License: Distortions of fact and literary convention made by a writer—not always a poet—for the sake of the effect gained. Poetic license is closely related to the concept of "artistic freedom."

Poetics: This term has two closely related meanings. It denotes (1) an aesthetic theory in literary criticism about the essence of poetry or (2) rules prescribing the proper methods, content, style, or diction of poetry. The term poetics may also refer to theories about literature in general, not just poetry.

Point of View: The narrative perspective from which a literary work is presented to the reader. There are four traditional points of view. The "third person omniscient" gives the reader a "godlike" perspective, unrestricted by time or place, from which to see actions and look into the minds of characters. This allows the author to comment openly on characters and events in the work. The "third person" point of view presents the events of the story from outside of any single character's perception, much like the omniscient point of view, but the reader must understand the action as it takes place and without any special insight into characters' minds or motivations. The "first person" or "personal" point of view relates events as they are perceived by a single character. The main character "tells" the story and may offer opinions about the action and characters which differ from those of the author. Much less common than omniscient, third person, and first person is the "second person" point of view, wherein the author tells the story as if it is happening to the reader.

Polemic: A work in which the author takes a stand on a controversial subject, such as abortion or religion. Such works are often extremely argumentative or provocative.

Pornography: Writing intended to provoke feelings of lust in the reader. Such works are often condemned by critics and teachers, but those which can be shown to have literary value are viewed less harshly.

Post-Aesthetic Movement: An artistic response made by African Americans to the black aesthetic movement of the 1960s and early '70s. Writers since that time have adopted a somewhat different tone in their work, with less emphasis placed on the disparity between black and white in the United States. In the words of post-aesthetic authors such as Toni Morrison, John Edgar Wideman, and Kristin Hunter, African Americans are portrayed as looking inward for answers to their own questions, rather than always looking to the outside world.

Postmodernism: Writing from the 1960s forward characterized by experimentation and continuing to apply some of the fundamentals of modernism, which included existentialism and alienation. Postmodernists have gone a step further in the rejection of tradition begun with the modernists by also rejecting traditional forms, preferring the anti-novel over the novel and the antihero over the hero.

Primitivism: The belief that primitive peoples were nobler and less flawed than civilized peoples because they had not been subjected to the tainting influence of society. See also Noble Savage.

Prologue: An introductory section of a literary work. It often contains information establishing the situation of the characters or presents information about the setting, time period, or action. In drama, the prologue is spoken by a chorus or by one of the principal characters.

Prose: A literary medium that attempts to mirror the language of everyday speech. It is distinguished from poetry by its use of unmetered, unrhymed language consisting of logically related sentences. Prose is usually grouped into paragraphs that form a cohesive whole such as an essay or a novel.

Prosopopoeia: See *Personification*

Protagonist: The central character of a story who serves as a focus for its themes and incidents and as the principal rationale for its development. The protagonist is sometimes referred to in discussions of modern literature as the hero or antihero.

Protest Fiction: Protest fiction has as its primary purpose the protesting of some social injustice, such as racism or discrimination.

Proverb: A brief, sage saying that expresses a truth about life in a striking manner.

Pseudonym: A name assumed by a writer, most often intended to prevent his or her identification as the author of a work. Two or more authors may work together under one pseudonym, or an author may use a different name for each genre he or she publishes in. Some publishing companies maintain "house pseudonyms," under which any number of authors may write installations in a series. Some authors also choose a pseudonym over their real names the way an actor may use a stage name.

Pun: A play on words that have similar sounds but different meanings.

R

Realism: A nineteenth-century European literary movement that sought to portray familiar characters, situations, and settings in a realistic manner. This was done primarily by using an objective narrative point of view and through the buildup of accurate detail. The standard for success of any realistic work depends on how faithfully it transfers common experience into fictional forms. The realistic method may be altered or extended, as in stream of consciousness writing, to record highly subjective experience.

Repartee: Conversation featuring snappy retorts and witticisms.

Resolution: The portion of a story following the climax, in which the conflict is resolved. See also *Denouement*.

Rhetoric: In literary criticism, this term denotes the art of ethical persuasion. In its strictest sense, rhetoric adheres to various principles developed since classical times for arranging facts and ideas in a clear, persuasive, appealing manner. The term is also used to refer to effective prose in general and theories of or methods for composing effective prose.

Rhetorical Question: A question intended to provoke thought, but not an expressed answer, in the reader. It is most commonly used in oratory and other persuasive genres.

Rising Action: The part of a drama where the plot becomes increasingly complicated. Rising action leads up to the climax, or turning point, of a drama.

Roman a clef: A French phrase meaning "novel with a key." It refers to a narrative in which real persons are portrayed under fictitious names.

Romance: A broad term, usually denoting a narrative with exotic, exaggerated, often idealized characters, scenes, and themes.

Romanticism: This term has two widely accepted meanings. In historical criticism, it refers to a European intellectual and artistic movement of the late eighteenth and early nineteenth centuries that sought greater freedom of personal expression than that allowed by the strict rules of literary form and logic of the eighteenth-century neoclassicists. The Romantics preferred emotional and imaginative expression to rational analysis. They considered the individual to be at the center of all experience and so placed him or her at the center of their art. The Romantics believed that the creative imagination reveals nobler truths—unique feelings and attitudes—than those that could be discovered by logic or by scientific examination. Both the natural world and the state of childhood were important sources for revelations of "eternal truths." "Romanticism" is also used as a general term to refer to a type of sensibility found in all periods of literary history and usually considered to be in opposition to the principles of classicism. In this sense, Romanticism signifies any work or philosophy in which the exotic or dreamlike figure strongly, or that is devoted to individualistic expression, self-analysis, or a pursuit of a higher realm of knowledge than can be discovered by human reason.

Romantics: See *Romanticism*

S

Satire: A work that uses ridicule, humor, and wit to criticize and provoke change in human nature and institutions. There are two major types of satire: "formal" or "direct" satire speaks directly to the reader or to a character in the work; "indirect" satire relies upon the ridiculous behavior of its characters to make its point. Formal satire is further divided into two manners: the "Horatian," which ridicules gently, and the "Juvenalian," which derides its subjects harshly and bitterly.

Science Fiction: A type of narrative about or based upon real or imagined scientific theories and technology. Science fiction is often peopled with alien creatures and set on other planets or in different dimensions.

Second Person: See *Point of View*

Setting: The time, place, and culture in which the action of a narrative takes place. The elements of setting may include geographic location, characters' physical and mental environments, prevailing cultural attitudes, or the historical time in which the action takes place.

Simile: A comparison, usually using "like" or "as", of two essentially dissimilar things, as in "coffee as cold as ice" or "He sounded like a broken record."

Slang: A type of informal verbal communication that is generally unacceptable for formal writing. Slang words and phrases are often colorful exaggerations used to emphasize the speaker's point; they may also be shortened versions of an often-used word or phrase.

Slave Narrative: Autobiographical accounts of American slave life as told by escaped slaves. These works first appeared during the abolition movement of the 1830s through the 1850s.

Socialist Realism: The Socialist Realism school of literary theory was proposed by Maxim Gorky and established as a dogma by the first Soviet Congress of Writers. It demanded adherence to a communist worldview in works of literature. Its doctrines required an objective viewpoint comprehensible to the working classes and themes of social struggle featuring strong proletarian heroes. Also known as Social Realism.

Stereotype: A stereotype was originally the name for a duplication made during the printing process; this led to its modern definition as a person or thing that is (or is assumed to be) the same as all others of its type.

Stream of Consciousness: A narrative technique for rendering the inward experience of a character. This technique is designed to give the impression of an ever-changing series of thoughts, emotions, images, and memories in the spontaneous and seemingly illogical order that they occur in life.

Structure: The form taken by a piece of literature. The structure may be made obvious for ease of understanding, as in nonfiction works, or may be obscured for artistic purposes, as in some poetry or seemingly "unstructured" prose.

Sturm und Drang: A German term meaning "storm and stress." It refers to a German literary movement of the 1770s and 1780s that reacted against the order and rationalism of the enlightenment, focusing instead on the intense experience of extraordinary individuals.

Style: A writer's distinctive manner of arranging words to suit his or her ideas and purpose in writing. The unique imprint of the author's personality upon his or her writing, style is the product of an author's way of arranging ideas and his or her use of diction, different sentence structures, rhythm, figures of speech, rhetorical principles, and other elements of composition.

Subjectivity: Writing that expresses the author's personal feelings about his subject, and which may or may not include factual information about the subject.

Subplot: A secondary story in a narrative. A subplot may serve as a motivating or complicating force for the main plot of the work, or it may provide emphasis for, or relief from, the main plot.

Surrealism: A term introduced to criticism by Guillaume Apollinaire and later adopted by Andre Breton. It refers to a French literary and artistic movement founded in the 1920s. The Surrealists sought to express unconscious thoughts and feelings in their works. The best-known technique used for achieving this aim was automatic writing—transcriptions of spontaneous outpourings from the unconscious. The Surrealists proposed to unify the contrary levels of conscious and unconscious, dream and reality, objectivity and subjectivity into a new level of "super-realism."

Suspense: A literary device in which the author maintains the audience's attention through the buildup of events, the outcome of which will soon be revealed.

Symbol: Something that suggests or stands for something else without losing its original identity. In literature, symbols combine their literal meaning with the suggestion of an abstract concept. Literary symbols are of two types: those that carry complex associations of meaning no matter what their contexts, and those that derive their suggestive meaning from their functions in specific literary works.

Symbolism: This term has two widely accepted meanings. In historical criticism, it denotes an early modernist literary movement initiated in France during the nineteenth century that reacted against the prevailing standards of realism. Writers in this movement aimed to evoke, indirectly and symbolically, an order of being beyond the material world of the five senses. Poetic expression of personal emotion figured strongly in the movement, typically by means of a private set of symbols uniquely identifiable with the individual poet. The principal aim of the Symbolists was to express in words the highly complex feelings that grew out of everyday contact with the world. In a broader sense, the term "symbolism" refers to the use of one object to represent another.

T

Tall Tale: A humorous tale told in a straightforward, credible tone but relating absolutely impossible events or feats of the characters. Such tales were commonly told of frontier adventures during the settlement of the west in the United States.

Theme: The main point of a work of literature. The term is used interchangeably with thesis.

Thesis: A thesis is both an essay and the point argued in the essay. Thesis novels and thesis plays share the quality of containing a thesis which is supported through the action of the story.

Third Person: See *Point of View*

Tone: The author's attitude toward his or her audience may be deduced from the tone of the work. A formal tone may create distance or convey politeness, while an informal tone may encourage a friendly, intimate, or intrusive feeling in the reader. The author's attitude toward his or her subject matter may also be deduced from the tone of the words he or she uses in discussing it.

Transcendentalism: An American philosophical and religious movement, based in New England from around 1835 until the Civil War. Transcendentalism was a form of American romanticism that had its roots abroad in the works of Thomas Carlyle, Samuel Coleridge, and Johann Wolfgang von Goethe. The Transcendentalists stressed the importance of intuition and subjective experience in communication with God. They rejected religious dogma and texts in favor of mysticism and scientific naturalism. They pursued truths that lie beyond the "colorless" realms perceived by reason and the senses and were active social reformers in public education, women's rights, and the abolition of slavery.

U

Urban Realism: A branch of realist writing that attempts to accurately reflect the often harsh facts of modern urban existence.

Utopia: A fictional perfect place, such as "paradise" or "heaven."

V

Verisimilitude: Literally, the appearance of truth. In literary criticism, the term refers to aspects of a work of literature that seem true to the reader.

Victorian: Refers broadly to the reign of Queen Victoria of England (1837-1901) and to anything with qualities typical of that era. For example, the qualities of smug narrowmindedness, bourgeois materialism, faith in social progress, and priggish morality are often considered Victorian. This stereotype is contradicted by such dramatic intellectual developments as the theories of Charles Darwin, Karl Marx, and Sigmund Freud (which stirred strong debates in England) and the critical attitudes of serious Victorian writers like Charles Dickens and George Eliot. In literature, the Victorian Period was the great age of the English novel, and the latter part of the era saw the rise of movements such as decadence and symbolism. Also known as Victorian Age and Victorian Period.

W

Weltanschauung: A German term referring to a person's worldview or philosophy.

Weltschmerz: A German term meaning "world pain." It describes a sense of anguish about the nature of existence, usually associated with a melancholy, pessimistic attitude.

Z

Zeitgeist: A German term meaning "spirit of the time." It refers to the moral and intellectual trends of a given era.

Cumulative Author/Title Index

Cumulative
Nationality/Ethnicity Index

African American

Angelou, Maya
  *I Know Why the Caged Bird
    Sings:* V2
Baldwin, James
  Go Tell It on the Mountain: V4
Cleage, Pearl
  *What Looks Like Crazy on an
    Ordinary Day:* V17
Ellison, Ralph
  Invisible Man: V2
Gaines, Ernest J.
  *The Autobiography of Miss Jane
    Pittman:* V5
  A Gathering of Old Men: V16
  A Lesson before Dying: V7
Haley, Alex
  *Roots: The Story of an American
    Family:* V9
Hurston, Zora Neale
  Their Eyes Were Watching God: V3
Kincaid, Jamaica
  Annie John: V3
Morrison, Toni
  Beloved: V6
  The Bluest Eye: V1
  Song of Solomom: V8
  Sula: V14
Naylor, Gloria
  Mama Day: V7
  The Women of Brewster Place: V4
Shange, Ntozake
  Betsey Brown: V11
Toomer, Jean
  Cane: V11
Walker, Alice
  The Color Purple: V5

Wright, Richard
  Black Boy: V1

Algerian

Camus, Albert
  The Plague: V16
  The Stranger: V6

American

Alcott, Louisa May
  Little Women: V12
Alexic, Sherman
  *The Lone Ranger and Tonto
    Fistfight in Heaven:* V17
Allison, Dorothy
  Bastard Out of Carolina: V11
Alvarez, Julia
  *How the García Girls Lost Their
    Accents:* V5
Anaya, Rudolfo
  Bless Me, Ultima: V12
Anderson, Sherwood
  Winesburg, Ohio: V4
Angelou, Maya
  *I Know Why the Caged Bird
    Sings:* V2
Auel, Jean
  The Clan of the Cave Bear: V11
Banks, Russell
  The Sweet Hereafter: V13
Baum, L. Frank
  The Wonderful Wizard of Oz: V13
Bellamy, Edward
  Looking Backward: 2000–1887:
    V15

Bellow, Saul
  Herzog: V14
Borland, Hal
  When the Legends Die: V18
Bradbury, Ray
  Fahrenheit 451: V1
Bridal, Tessa
  The Tree of Red Stars: V17
Brown, Rita Mae
  Rubyfruit Jungle: V9
Butler, Octavia
  Kindred: V8
Card, Orson Scott
  Ender's Game: V5
Cather, Willa
  Death Comes for the Archbishop:
    V19
  My Ántonia: V2
Chandler, Raymond
  The Big Sleep: V17
Chopin, Kate
  The Awakening: V3
Cisneros, Sandra
  The House on Mango Street: V2
Clavell, James du Maresq
  Shogun: A Novel of Japan: V10
Cleage, Pearl
  *What Looks Like Crazy on an
    Ordinary Day:* V17
Clemens, Samuel
  *The Adventures of Huckleberry
    Finn:* V1
  The Adventures of Tom Sawyer: V6
Conroy, Frank
  Body and Soul: V11
Cooper, James Fenimore
  The Last of the Mohicans: V9

Subject/Theme Index